The FIRST 100 CHINESE CHARACTERS

The quick and easy way to learn the basic Chinese characters

SIMPLIFIED CHARACTER EDITION

Introduction by
Alison and Laurence Matthews

TUTTLE PUBLISHING
Tokyo • Rutland, Vermont • Singapore

Published by Tuttle Publishing, an imprint of Periplus Editions (HK) Ltd, with editorial offices at 364 Innovation Drive, North Clarendon, Vermont 05759 and 61 Tai Seng Avenue, #02-12 Singapore 534167.

ISBN 978-0-8048-3830-6

Distributed by:

Japan
Tuttle Publishing
Yaekari Building 3F
5-4-12 Osaki, Shinagawa-ku
Tokyo 141-0032, Japan
Tel: (81) 3 5437 0171
Fax: (81) 3 5437 0755
Email: tuttle-sales@gol.com

North America, Latin America & Europe
Tuttle Publishing
364 Innovation Drive
North Clarendon, VT 05759-9436
Tel: 1 (802) 773 8930
Fax: 1 (802) 773 6993
Email: info@tuttlepublishing.com
www.tuttlepublishing.com

Asia-Pacific
Berkeley Books Pte Ltd
61 Tai Seng Avenue #02-12
Singapore 534167
Tel: (65) 6280-1330
Fax: (65) 6280-6290
inquiries@periplus.com.sg
www.periplus.com

Indonesia
PT Java Books Indonesia
Kawasan Industri Pulogadung
Jl. Rawa Gelam IV No. 9
Jakarta 13930, Indonesia
Tel: (62) 21 4682 1088
Fax: (62) 21 461 0206
Email: cs@javabooks.co.id

11 10 09   10 9 8 7 6 5 4

Printed in Singapore

Contents

Introduction

Learning the characters is one of the most fascinating and fun parts of learning Chinese, and people are often surprised by how much they enjoy being able to recognize them and to write them. Added to that, *writing* the characters is also the best way of *learning* them. This book shows you how to write the second 100 most common characters and gives you plenty of space to practice writing them. When you do this, you'll be learning a writing system which is one of the oldest in the world and is now used by more than a billion people around the globe every day.

In this introduction we'll talk about:

- how the characters developed;
- the difference between traditional and simplified forms of the characters;
- what the "radicals" are and why they're useful;
- how to count the writing strokes used to form each character;
- how to look up the characters in a dictionary;
- how words are created by joining two characters together; and, most importantly;
- how to write the characters!

Also, in case you're using this book on your own without a teacher, we'll tell you how to get the most out of using it.

Chinese characters are not nearly as strange and complicated as people seem to think. They're actually no more mysterious than musical notation, which most people can master in only a few months. So there's really nothing to be scared of or worried about: everyone can learn them—it just requires a bit of patience and perseverance. There are also some things which you may have heard about writing Chinese characters that aren't true. In particular, you don't need to use a special brush to write them (a ball-point pen is fine), and you don't need to be good at drawing (in fact you don't even need to have neat handwriting, although it helps!).

How many characters are there?

Thousands! You would probably need to know something like two thousand to be able to read Chinese newspapers and books, but you don't need anything like that number to read a menu, go shopping or read simple street signs and instructions. Just as you can get by in most countries knowing about a hundred words of the local language, so too you can get by in China quite well knowing a hundred common Chinese characters. And this would also be an excellent basis for learning to read and write Chinese.

How did the characters originally develop?

Chinese characters started out as pictures representing simple objects, and the first characters originally resembled the things they represented. For example:

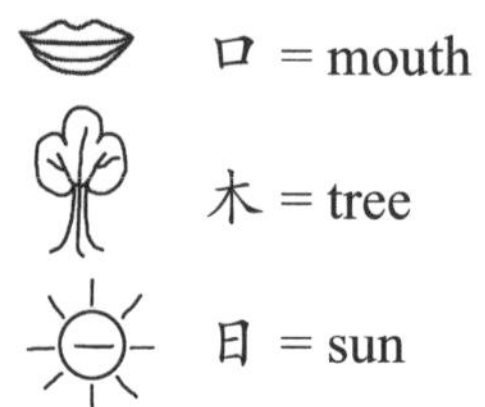

口 = mouth

木 = tree

日 = sun

Some other simple characters were pictures of "ideas":

一 one　　二 two　　三 three

Some of these characters kept this "pictographic" or "ideographic" quality about them, but others were gradually modified or abbreviated until many of them now look nothing like the original objects or ideas.

Then, as words were needed for things which weren't easy to draw, existing characters were "combined" to create new characters. For example, 女 (meaning "woman") combined with 子 (meaning "child") gives a new character 好 (which means "good" or "to be fond of").

Notice that when two characters are joined together like this to form a new character, they get squashed together and deformed slightly. This is so that the new, combined character will fit into the same size square or "box" as each of the original two characters. For example the character 日 "sun" becomes thinner when it is the left-hand part of the character 时 "time"; and it becomes shorter when it is the upper part of the character 星 "star". Some components got distorted and deformed even more than this in the combining process: for example when the character 人 "man" appears on the left-hand side of a complex character it gets compressed into 亻, like in the character 他 "he".

So you can see that some of the simpler characters often act as basic "building blocks" from which more complex characters are formed. This means that if you learn how to write these simple characters you'll also be learning how to write some complex ones too.

How are characters read and pronounced?

The pronunciations in this workbook refer to modern standard Chinese. This is the official language of China and is also known as "Mandarin" or "**putonghua**".

The pronunciation of Chinese characters is written out with letters of the alphabet using a romanization system called "Hanyu Pinyin"—or "**pinyin**" for short. This is the modern system used in China. In pinyin some of the letters have a different sound than in English—but if you are learning Chinese you'll already know this. We could give a description here of how to pronounce each sound, but it would take up a lot of space—and this workbook is about writing the characters, not pronouncing them! In any case, you really need to hear a teacher (or recording) pronounce the sounds out loud to get an accurate idea of what they sound like.

Each Chinese character is pronounced using only one syllable. However, in addition to the syllable, each character also has a particular *tone*, which refers to how the pitch of the voice is used. In standard Chinese there are four different tones, and in pinyin the tone is marked by placing an accent mark over the vowel as follows:

1st tone (high, flat) **mā**
2nd tone (rising) **má**
3rd tone (down-up) **mǎ**
4th tone (falling) **mà**

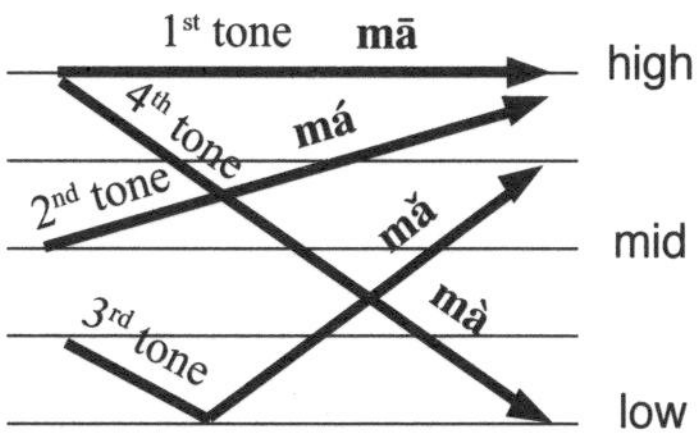

1st tone **mā** — high
4th tone — **má** — 2nd tone — **mǎ** — mid
3rd tone — **mà** — low

The pronunciation of each character is therefore a combination of a syllable and a tone. There are only a small number of available syllables in Chinese, and many characters therefore share the same syllable—in fact many characters share the same sound plus tone combination. They are like the English words "here" and "hear"—when they are spoken, you can only tell which is which from the context or by seeing the word in written form.

Apart from **putonghua** (modern standard Chinese), another well-known type of Chinese is Cantonese, which is spoken in southern China and in many Chinese communities around the world. In fact there are several dozen different Chinese languages, and the pronunciations of Chinese characters in these languages are all very different from each other. But the important thing to realize is that the characters themselves do *not* change. So two Chinese people who can't understand each other when they're talking together, can write to one another without any problem at all!

Simplified and traditional characters

As more and more characters were introduced over the years by combining existing characters, some of them became quite complicated. Writing them required many strokes which was time-consuming, and it became difficult to distinguish some of them, especially when the writing was small. So when writing the characters quickly in hand-written form, many people developed short-cuts and wrote them in a more simplified form. In the middle of the 20th century, the Chinese decided to create a standardised set of simplified characters to be used by everyone in China. This resulted in many of the more complicated characters being given simplified forms, making them much easier to learn and to write. Today in China, and also in Singapore, these simplified characters are used almost exclusively, and many Chinese no longer learn the old traditional forms. However the full traditional forms continue to be used in Taiwan and in overseas Chinese communities around the world.

Here are some examples of how some characters were simplified:

Traditional		Simplified
見	→	见
飯	→	饭
號	→	号
幾	→	几

Modern standard Chinese uses only simplified characters. But it is useful to be able to recognize the traditional forms as they are still used in many places outside China, and of course older books and inscriptions were also written using the traditional forms. This workbook teaches the full simplified forms. If there is a traditional form, then it is shown in a separate box on the right-hand side of the page so that you can see what it looks like. Where there is no traditional form, the character was considered simple enough already and was left unchanged.

How is Chinese written?

Chinese was traditionally written from top to bottom in columns beginning on the right-hand side of the page and working towards the left, like this:

幸福一点儿也不难拥有。只要你常为人着想，带来欢乐，你会发觉到那也是一种幸福呀！

This means that for a book printed in this way, you start by opening it at (what Westerners would think of as) the back cover. While writing in columns is sometimes considered archaic, you will still find many books, especially novels and more serious works of history, printed in this way.

Nowadays, though, most Chinese people write from left to right in horizontal lines working from the top of a page to the bottom, just as we do in English.

Are Chinese characters the same as English words?
Although each character has a meaning, it's not really true that an individual character is equivalent to an English "word". Each character is actually only a single *syllable*. In Chinese (like in English) some words are just one syllable, but most words are made up of two or more syllables joined together. The vast majority of words in Chinese actually consist of two separate characters placed together in a pair. These multi-syllable words are often referred to as "compounds", and this workbook provides a list of common compounds for each character.

Some Chinese characters are one-syllable words on their own (like the English words "if" and "you"), while other characters are only ever used as one half of a word (like the English syllables "sen" and "tence"). Some characters do both: they're like the English "light" which is happy as a word on its own, but which also links up to form words like "headlight" or "lighthouse".

The Chinese write sentences by stringing characters together in a long line from left to right (or in a column from top to bottom), with equal-sized spaces between each character. If English were written this way—as individual syllables rather than as words that are joined together—it would mean all the syllables would be written separately with spaces in between them, something like this:

If you can un der stand this sen tence you can read Chi nese too.

So in theory, you can't see which characters are paired together to form words, but in practice, once you know a bit of Chinese, you can!

Punctuation was not traditionally used when writing Chinese, but today commas, periods (full stops), quotation marks, and exclamation points are all used along with other types of punctuation which have been borrowed from English.

Two ways of putting characters together
We have looked at *combining characters* together to make new *characters*, and *pairing characters* together to make *words*. So what's the difference?

Well, when two *simple characters* are combined to form a new *complex character*, they are squashed or distorted so that the new character fits into the same size square as the original characters. The meaning of the new character *may* be related to the meaning of its components, but it frequently appears to have no connection with them at all! The new complex character also has a new single-syllable pronunciation, which may or may not be related to the pronunciation of one of its parts. For example:

女 **nǚ** woman	+	也 **yě** also	=	她 **tā** she
日 **rì** sun	+	月 **yuè** moon/month	=	明 **míng** bright

On the other hand, when characters are *paired together* to create *words*, the characters are simply written one after the other, normal sized, with a normal space in between (and there are no hyphens or anything to show that these characters are working together as a pair). The resulting word has a pronunciation which is *two* syllables—it is simply the pronunciations of the two individual characters one after the other. Also, you're much more likely to be able to guess the meaning of the word from the meanings of the individual characters that make it up. For example:

大 **dà** big	+	人 **rén** person	=	大人 **dà rén** adult
姐 **jiě** older sister	+	妹 **mèi** younger sister	=	姐妹 **jiě mèi** sisters
四 **sì** four	+	月 **yuè** moon/month	=	四月 **sì yuè** April
再 **zài** again	+	见 **jiàn** see; meet	=	再见 **zài jiàn** Goodbye!

Is it necessary to learn words as well as characters?
As we've said, the meaning of a compound word is often related to the meanings of the individual characters. But this is not always the case, and sometimes the word takes on a new and very specific meaning. So to be able to read Chinese sentences and understand what they mean, it isn't enough just to learn individual character—you'll also need to learn words. (In fact, many individual characters have very little meaning at all by themselves, and only take on meanings when paired with other characters).

Here are some examples of common Chinese words where the meaning of the overall word is not what you might expect from the meanings of the individual characters:

明 **míng** bright	+	天 **tiān** day/sky	=	明天 **míng tiān** tomorrow
好 **hǎo** good	+	在 **zài** be present at/ live at	=	好在 **hǎo zài** fortunately

If you think about it, the same thing happens in English. If you know what "battle" and "ship" mean, you can probably guess what a "battleship" might be. But this wouldn't work with "championship"! Similarly, you'd be unlikely to guess the meaning of "honeymoon" if you only knew the words "honey" and "moon".

The good news is that learning compound words can help you to learn the characters. For example, you may know (from your Chinese lessons) that **xīng qī** means "week". So when you see that this word is written 星期, you will know that 星 is pronounced **xīng**, and 期 is pronounced **qī**—even when these characters are forming part of *other* words. In fact, you will find that you remember many characters as half of some familiar word.

When you see a word written in characters, you can also often see how the word came to mean what it does. For example, **xīng qī** is 星期 which literally means "star period". This will help you to remember both the word *and* the two individual characters.

What is a stroke count?
Each Chinese character is made up of a number of pen or brush strokes. Each individual stroke is the mark made by a pen or brush before lifting it off the paper to write the next stroke. Strokes come in various shapes and sizes—a stroke can be a straight line, a curve, a bent line, a line with a hook, or a dot. There is a traditional and very specific way that every character should be written. The order and direction of the strokes are both important if the character is to have the correct appearance.

What counts as a stroke is determined by tradition and is not always obvious. For example, the small box that often appears as part of a character (like the one on page 32, in the character 名) counts as three strokes, not four! (This is because a single stroke is traditionally used to write the top and right-hand sides of the box).

All this may sound rather pedantic but it is well worth learning how to write the characters correctly and with the correct number of strokes. One reason is that knowing how to count the strokes correctly is useful for looking up characters in dictionaries, as you'll see later.

This book shows you how to write characters stroke by stroke, and once you get the feel of it you'll very quickly learn how to work out the stroke count of a character you haven't met before, and get it right!

What are radicals?
Although the earliest characters were simple drawings, most characters are complex with two or more parts. And you'll find that some simple characters appear over and over again as parts of many complex characters. Have a look at these five characters:

她 she
妈 mother
姐 older sister
好 good
姓 surname

All five of these characters have the same component on the left-hand side: 女, which means "woman". This component gives a clue to the meaning of the character, and is called the "radical". As you can see, most of these five characters have something to do with the idea of "woman", but as you can also see, it's not a totally reliable way of guessing the meaning of a character. (Meanings of characters are something you just have to learn, without much help from their component parts).

Unfortunately the radical isn't always on the left-hand side of a character. Sometimes it's on the right, or on the top, or on the bottom. Here are some examples:

Character	Radical	Position of radical
都	阝	right
星	日	top
您	心	bottom
这	辶	left and bottom

Because it's not always easy to tell what the radical is for a particular character, it's given explicitly in a separate box for each of the characters in this book. However, as you learn more and more characters, you'll find that you can often guess the radical just by looking at a character.

Why bother with radicals? Well, for hundreds of years Chinese dictionaries have used the radical component of each character as a way of indexing them. All characters, even the really simple ones, are assigned to one radical or another so that they can be placed within the index of a Chinese dictionary (see the next section).

Incidentally, when you take away the radical, what's left is often a clue to the *pronunciation* of the character (this remainder is called the "phonetic component"). For example, 吗 and 妈 are formed by adding different radicals to the character 马 "horse" which is pronounced **mǎ**. Now 吗 is pronounced **ma** and 妈 is pronounced **ma**, so you can see that these two characters have inherited their pronunciations from the phonetic component 马. Unfortunately these "phonetic components" aren't very dependable: for example 也 on its own is pronounced **yě** but 他 and 她 are both pronounced **tā**.

How do I find a character in an index or a dictionary?
This is a question lots of people ask, and the answer varies according to the type of dictionary you are using. Many dictionaries today are organized alphabetically by pronunciation. So if you want to look up a character in a dictionary and you know its pronunciation, then it's easy. It's when you don't know the pronunciation of a character that there's a problem, since there is no alphabetical order for characters like there is for English words.

If you don't know the pronunciation of a character, then you will need to use a radical index (which is why radicals are useful). To use this you have to know which part of the character is the radical, and you will also need to be able to count the number of strokes that make up the character. To look up 姓, for example, 女 is the radical (which has 3 strokes) and the remaining part 生 has 5 strokes. So first you find the radical 女 amongst the 3-stroke radicals in the radical index. Then, since there are lots of characters under 女, look for 姓 in the section which lists all the 女 characters which have 5-stroke remainders.

This workbook has both a Hanyu Pinyin index and a radical index. Why not get used to how these indexes work by picking a character in the book and seeing if you can find it in both of the indexes?

Many dictionaries also have a pure stroke count index (i.e. ignoring the radical). This is useful if you cannot figure out what the radical of the character is. To use this you must count up all the strokes in the character as a whole and then look the character up under that number (so you would look up 姓 under 8 strokes). As you can imagine, this type of index can leave you with long columns of characters to scan through before you find the one you're looking for, so it's usually a last resort!

All these methods have their pitfalls and complications, so recently a completely new way of looking up characters has been devised. The *Chinese Character Fast Finder* (see the inside back cover) organizes characters purely by their shapes so that you can look up any one of 3,000 characters very quickly without knowing its meaning, radical, pronunciation or stroke count!

How should I use this workbook?
One good way to learn characters is to practice writing them, especially if you think about what each character means as you write it. This will fix the characters in your memory better than if you just look at them without writing them.

If you're working on your own without a teacher, work on a few characters at a time. Go at a pace that suits you; it's much better to do small but regular amounts of writing than to do large chunks at irregular intervals. You might start with just one or two characters each day and increase this as you get better at it. Frequent repetition is the key! Try to get into a daily routine of learning a few new characters and also reviewing the ones you learned on previous days. It's also a good idea to keep a list of which characters you've learned each day, and then to "test yourself" on the characters you learned the previous day, three days ago, a week ago and a month ago. Each time you test yourself they will stay in your memory for a longer period.

But *don't* worry if you can't remember a character you wrote out ten times only yesterday! This is quite normal to begin with. Just keep going—it will all be sinking in without you realizing it.

Once you've learned a few characters you can use flash cards to test yourself on them in a random order. You can make your own set of cards, or use a ready-made set like *Chinese in a Flash* (see the inside back cover).

How do I write the characters?
Finally, let's get down to business and talk about actually writing the characters! Under each character in this book, the first few boxes show how the character is written,

stroke by stroke. There is a correct way to draw each character, and the diagrams in the boxes show you both the order to draw the strokes in, and also the direction for each stroke.

Use the three gray examples to trace over and then carry on by yourself, drawing the characters using the correct stroke order and directions. The varying thicknesses of the lines show you what the characters would look like if they were drawn with a brush, but if you're using a pencil or ball-point pen don't worry about this. Just trace down the middle of the lines and you will produce good hand-written characters.

Pay attention to the length of each of the strokes so that your finished character has the correct proportions. Use the gray dotted lines inside each box as a guide to help you start and end each stroke in the right place.

You may think that it doesn't really matter how the strokes are written as long as the end result looks the same. To some extent this is true, but there are some good reasons for knowing the "proper" way to write the characters. Firstly, it helps you to count strokes, and secondly it will make your finished character "look right", and also help you to read other people's hand-written characters later on. It's better in the long run to learn the correct method of writing the characters from the beginning because, as with so many other things, once you get into "bad" habits it can be very hard to break them!

If you are left-handed, just use your left hand as normal, but still make sure you use the correct stroke order and directions when writing the strokes. For example, draw your horizontal strokes left to right, even if it feels more natural to draw them right to left.

For each Chinese character there is a fixed, correct order in which to write the strokes. But these "stroke orders" do follow some fairly general rules. The main thing to remember is:

- Generally work left to right and top to bottom.

Some other useful guidelines are:

- Horizontal lines are written before vertical ones (see 十, page 19);
- Lines that slope down and to the left are written before those that slope down and to the right (see 文, page 41);
- A central part or vertical line is written before symmetrical or smaller lines at the sides (see 小, page 47);
- The top and sides of an outer box are written first, then whatever is inside the box, then the bottom is written last to "close" it (see 国, page 56).

As you work through the book you'll see these rules in action and get a feel for them, and you'll know how to draw virtually any Chinese character without having to be shown.

Practice, practice, practice!

Your first attempts at writing will be awkward, but as with most things you'll get better with practice. That's why there are lots of squares for you to use. And don't be too hard on yourself (we all draw clumsy-looking characters when we start); just give yourself plenty of time and practice. After a while, you'll be able to look back at your early attempts and compare them with your most recent ones, and see just how much you've improved.

After writing the same character a number of times (a row or two at most), move on to another one. Don't fill up the whole page at one sitting! Then, after writing several other characters, come back later and do a few more of the first one. Can you remember the stroke order without having to look at the diagram?

Finally, try writing out sentences, or lines of different characters, on ordinary paper. To begin with you can mark out squares to write in if you want to, but after that simply imagine the squares and try to keep your characters all equally sized and equally spaced.

Have fun, and remember—the more you practice writing the characters the easier it gets!

一

yī one; single; a(n)

common words

一个 **yí ge** a(n); one (of something)
一次 **yí cì** once
一同/一起 **yī tóng/yī qǐ** together
一月 **yí yuè** January
十一 **shí yī** eleven
第一 **dì yī** first
星期一 **xīng qī yī** Monday

1 stroke

radical

一

1

二

èr two (number)

common words

二十 **èr shí** twenty
二妹 **èr mèi** second younger sister
二月 **èr yuè** February
二手 **èr shǒu** second hand
十二 **shí èr** twelve
第二 **dì èr** second
星期二 **xīng qī èr** Tuesday

2 strokes

radical
一

二 1	二 2	二	二	二			
二							
二							

三

sān three

common words

三十 **sān shí** thirty
三月 **sān yuè** March
三个月 **sān ge yuè** three months
三明治 **sān míng zhì** sandwich
十三 **shí sān** thirteen
第三 **dì sān** third
星期三 **xīng qī sān** Wednesday

3 strokes

radical
一

1 2 3

四

sì four

common words

四十 **sì shí** fourty
四百 **sì bǎi** four hundred
四月 **sì yuè** April
四处 **sì chù** everywhere
十四 **shí sì** fourteen
第四 **dì sì** fourth
星期四 **xīng qī sì** Thursday

5 strokes

radical
口

五

wǔ five

common words

五十 **wǔ shí** fifty
五月 **wǔ yuè** May
五年 **wǔ nián** five years
五本 **wǔ běn** five (books)
十五 **shí wǔ** fifteen
第五 **dì wǔ** fifth
星期五 **xīng qī wǔ** Friday

4 strokes

radical
一

一 1 丅 2 五 3 五 4 五 五 五

五

六 **liù** six	common words 六十三 **liù shí sān** sixty-three 六月 **liù yuè** June 六个月 **liù ge yuè** six months 六天 **liù tiān** six days 十六 **shí liù** sixteen 第六 **dì liù** sixth 星期六 **xīng qī liù** Saturday	4 strokes radical 亠

七 **qī** seven	**common words** 七十七 **qī shí qī** seventy-seven 七百 **qī bǎi** seven hundred 七月 **qī yuè** July 十七 **shí qī** seventeen 七七八八 **qī qī bā bā** almost complete 七上八下 **qī shàng bā xià** worry; anxious 第七 **dì qī** seventh	**2 strokes** **radical** 一

八

bā eight

common words

八十二 **bā shí èr** eighty-two
八百零五 **bā bǎi líng wǔ** eight-hundred and five
八月 **bā yuè** August
八成 **bā chéng** 80 per cent
八折 **bā zhé** 20 per cent discount
十八 **shí bā** eighteen
第八 **dì bā** eighth

2 strokes

radical
八

1
2

九

jiǔ nine

common words

九十八 **jiǔ shí bā** ninety-eight
九百一十 **jiǔ bǎi yí shí** nine-hundred and ten
九月 **jiǔ yuè** September
九号 **jiǔ hào** number/size nine; ninth (of a month)
九分 **jiǔ fēn** nine points
十九 **shí jiǔ** nineteen
第九 **dì jiǔ** ninth

2 strokes

radical
丿

丿 1 九 2 九 九 九

九

十

shí ten

common words

十千/一万 **shí qiān/yí wàn** ten thousand
十月 **shí yuè** October
十一月 **shí yī yuè** November
十二月 **shí èr yuè** December
十分 **shí fēn** 1. ten points 2. very
十全十美 **shí quán shí měi** perfect; ideal
第十 **dì shí** tenth

2 strokes

radical
十

1 2

你

nǐ you

common words

你好 **nǐ hǎo** How do you do?
你的 **nǐ de** your; yours
你们 **nǐ men** you (plural)
你们的 **nǐ men de** your; yours (plural)

7 strokes

radical
人（亻）

nín you (polite)

common words

您好 **nín hǎo** How do you do? (polite)
您早 **nín zǎo** Good morning!
您贵姓？**nín guì xìng** your family name?

11 strokes

radical
心

好

hǎo/hào 1. good 2. alright 3. like

common words

好啊! **hǎo a** Good!; OK!
好看 **hǎo kàn** 1. good show 2. good looking
好久 **hǎo jiǔ** a long time
很好 **hěn hǎo** very good
还好 **hái hǎo** still alright
那好 **nà hǎo** alright then ... (agreeing to a suggestion)

6 strokes

radical
女

请

qǐng 1. please
2. to invite

common words

请问 **qǐng wèn** May I ask ...?
请坐 **qǐng zuò** Please sit down.
请进 **qǐng jìn** Please come in.
请客 **qǐng kè** play host; treat
请教 **qǐng jiào** seek advice
请假 **qǐng jià** take leave

10 strokes

radical
讠

traditional form
請

问 **wèn** ask	common words 问好 **wèn hǎo** say hello to... 问题 **wèn tí** question; problem 问答 **wèn dá** question and answer 学问 **xué wèn** knowledge 访问 **fǎng wèn** 1. visit 2. interview	6 strokes radical 门 traditional form 問

贵 **guì** 1. honorable 2. expensive; valuable	**common words** 贵姓 **guì xìng** your honorable surname? 贵人 **guì rén** respected person 贵客/贵宾 **guì kè/guì bīn** distinguished guest; VIP 太贵了 **tài guì le** too expensive 名贵 **míng guì** valuable	**9 strokes** **radical** 贝 **traditional form** 貴

1 2 3 4 5 6 7 8 9

贵 贵 贵 贵

姓

xìng surname

common words

姓名 **xìng míng** full name
同姓 **tóng xìng** having the same surname
老百姓 **lǎo bǎi xìng** common people

8 strokes

radical

女

他 **tā** he	**common words** 他的 **tā de** his 他们 **tā men** they; them (male) 他们的 **tā men de** their; theirs (male) 他人/其他人 **tā rén/qí tā rén** other people 其他 **qí tā** other	**5 strokes** **radical** 人（亻）

1 2 3 4 5

他 他 他

她

tā she

common words

她的 **tā de** hers
她们 **tā men** they; them (female)
她们的 **tā men de** their; theirs (female)

6 strokes

radical
女

叫 **jiào** 1. call; be called 2. shout 3. order	**common words** 叫门 **jiào mén** call at the door 叫好 **jiào hǎo** cheer 叫喊 **jiào hǎn** shout; yell 叫做 **jiào zuò** be called 叫车 **jiào chē** order a cab 大叫 **dà jiào** call out loudly	**5 strokes** **radical** 口

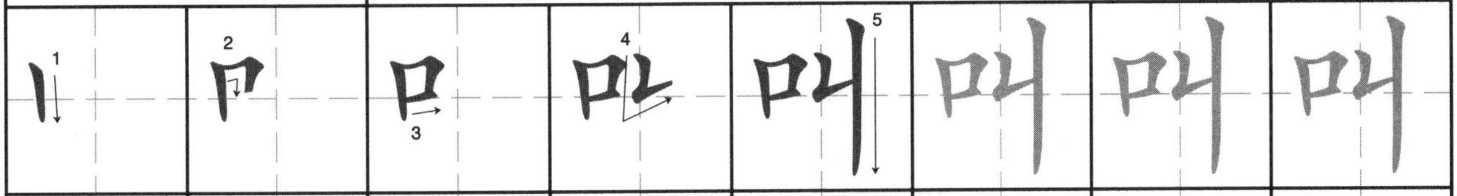

什

shén/shí 1. mixed
2. tenth (mathematics)

common words

什么 **shé me** what
什么的 **shé me de** etc; so on...
什至 **shén zhì** even to the point that

4 strokes

radical
人（亻）

丿 1	亻 2	亻 3	什 4	什	什	什	

么 **me** interrogative particle	**common words** 什么 **shén me** what 怎么 **zěn me** how 那么 **nà me** in that way; so... 多么 **duō me** no matter how 为什么？**wèi shèn me** why?	**3 strokes** **radical** 厶 **traditional form** 麼

1 2 3

名

míng 1. name
2. fame

common words

名字 **míng zi** name
名叫 **míng jiào** named
名人 **míng rén** celebrity; famous person
同名 **tóng míng** having the same name
出名 **chū míng** become famous; well-known
第一名 **dì yī míng** first in position

6 strokes

radical
夕

字

zì written character

common words

字母 **zì mǔ** letter (alphabet)
字典 **zì diǎn** dictionary
十字 **shí zì** cross
汉字 **hàn zì** Chinese (Han) character
写字 **xiě zì** write word
生字 **shēng zì** new word

6 strokes

radical
宀

我

wǒ I; me

common words

我的 **wǒ de** my; mine
我们/咱们 **wǒ men/zán men** we; us
我国 **wǒ guó** our country
我家 **wǒ jiā** my family; my home
自我 **zì wǒ** self

7 strokes

radical
戈

是

shì to be; yes

common words

是的 **shì de** yes
是啊 **shì a** yes; yeah
是不是 **shì bu shì** to be or not to be
不是 **bú shi** 1. not to be; no 2. fault
还是 **hái shì** or
老是 **lǎo shì** always

9 strokes

radical
日

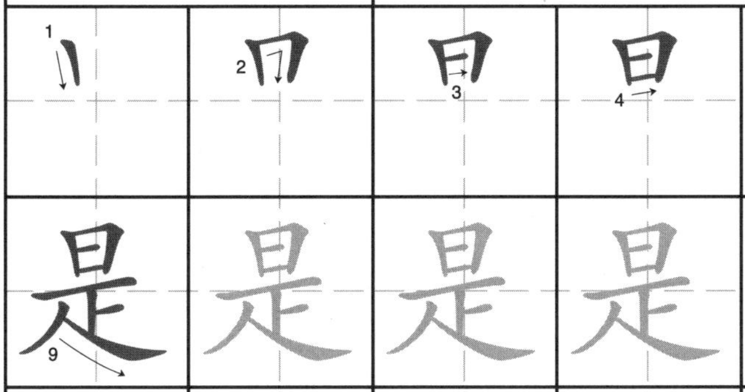

大 **dà** big; great	**common words** 大声点 **dà shēng diǎn** louder 大家 **dà jiā** everybody 大不了 **dà bu liǎo** at the worst 大多/大都/大半 **dà duō/dà dū/dà bàn** mostly 大便 **dà biàn** shit 大概 **dà gài** probably 自大 **zì dà** proud; arrogant	**3 strokes** **radical** 大

1 2 3

学

xué learn

common words

学会 **xué huì** learned; mastered
学习 **xué xí** study
上学 **shàng xué** go to school
放学 **fàng xué** finish school for the day
开学 **kāi xué** school reopens
小学 **xiǎo xué** primary school
中学 **zhōng xué** middle/secondary school

8 strokes

radical
子

traditional form
學

1 2 3 4 5 6 7 8

学 学 学

生

shēng 1. give birth; born 2. raw

common words

生日 **shēng rì** birthday
生气 **shēng qì** angry
生病 **shēng bìng** fall sick; not well
生吃 **shēng chī** eat raw food
学生 **xué sheng** student
先生 **xiān sheng** 1. Mr 2. husband
医生 **yī shēng** doctor

5 strokes

radical

丿

1 2 3 4 5

生 生 生

中

zhōng/zhòng 1. among 2. (in the) course 3. hit by

common words

中国 **zhōng guó** China
中文 **zhōng wén** Chinese language (written)
中间 **zhōng jiān** between; in the middle
中年 **zhōng nián** middle-aged
中奖 **zhòng jiǎng** win a prize
心中 **xīn zhōng** in one's heart
手中 **shǒu zhōng** on hand

4 strokes

radical
丨

1 2 3 4

英

yīng 1. related to England 2. hero

common words

英国 **yīng guó** England
英文 **yīng wén** English language (written)
英语 **yīng yǔ** English language
英俊 **yīng jùn** handsome
英明 **yīng míng** wise
英雄 **yīng xióng** hero

8 strokes

radical
艹

1 2 3 4 5 6 7 8

英 英 英

文

wén written language; writing

common words

文字 **wén zì** script; writing
文具 **wén jù** stationery
文学 **wén xué** literature
语文 **yǔ wén** language (spoken and written)
法文 **fǎ wén** French (written)
日文 **rì wén** Japanese (written)

4 strokes

radical
文

课

kè lesson; class

common words

课本 **kè běn** textbook
课题 **kè tí** topic (of lessons)
课文 **kè wén** text
上课 **shàng kè** attend class
下课 **xià kè** finish class
功课 **gōng kè** homework
第一课 **dì yī kè** first lesson; lesson one

10 strokes

radical
讠

traditional form
課

1 2 3 4 5 6 7 8 9 10

老 **lǎo** old	common words 老师 **lǎo shī** teacher 老大 **lǎo dà** 1. eldest sibling 2. gang leader 老婆 **lǎo po** wife (informal) 老公 **lǎo gōng** husband (informal) 老婆婆 **lǎo pó po** old woman 老外 **lǎo wài** foreigner 古老 **gǔ lǎo** ancient	6 strokes radical 老（耂）

1	2	3	4	5	6	老	老
老							

师 **shī** teacher; master	**common words** 师生 **shī shēng** teacher and student 师父 **shī fu** master 老师/教师 **lǎo shī/jiào shī** teacher 律师 **lǜ shī** lawyer 厨师 **chú shī** chef	**6 strokes** **radical** 巾 **traditional form** 師

1 2 3 4 5 6

师 师 师

同

tóng the same; together

common words

同学 **tóng xué** classmate
同班 **tóng bān** same class
同时 **tóng shí** same time
同样 **tóng yàng** the same; alike
同事 **tóng shì** colleague
一同/一起 **yī tóng/yī qǐ** together

6 strokes

radical
冂

校

xiào school

common words

校长 **xiào zhǎng** principal
校服 **xiào fú** school uniform
校友 **xiào yǒu** schoolmate; alum
学校 **xué xiào** school
同校 **tóng xiào** same school
上校 **shàng xiào** colonel

10 strokes

radical
木

1 2 3 4 5 6 7 8 9 10

小

xiǎo small; little

common words

小姐 **xiǎo jiě** Miss; lady
小时 **xiǎo shí** hour
小时候 **xiǎo shí hou** childhood
小心 **xiǎo xīn** (be) careful
小看 **xiǎo kàn** belittle; underestimate
小便 **xiǎo biàn** urine; urinate

3 strokes

radical
小 (⺌)

朋

péng friend

common words

朋友 **péng you** friend
好朋友 **hǎo péng you** good friend
男朋友 **nán péng you** boyfriend
女朋友 **nǚ péng you** girlfriend
老朋友 **lǎo péng you** old friend
小朋友 **xiǎo péng you** kid; child

8 strokes

radical
月

友

yǒu friend

common words

友人 **yǒu rén** friend
友谊/友情 **yǒu yì/yǒu qíng** friendship
好友 **hǎo yǒu** good friend
男友 **nán yǒu** boyfriend
女友 **nǚ yǒu** girlfriend
工友 **gōng yǒu** fellow worker; caretaker

4 strokes

radical
又

1 2 3 4

们	common words	5 strokes
men plural suffix (for persons)	你们 **nǐ men** you (plural) 我们/咱们 **wǒ men/zán men** we; us 女士们 **nǚ shì men** ladies 男士们 **nán shì men** gentlemen 同学们 **tóng xué men** classmates 人们 **rén men** people	radical 人 (亻) traditional form 們

呢

ne question particle

common words

你呢？ **nǐ ne** How about you?
他（她）呢？ **tā ne** How about him (her)?
我们呢？ **wǒ men ne** How about us?
人呢？ **rén ne** Where's the person?

8 strokes

radical
口

谢

xiè thank

common words

谢谢 **xiè xie** thank you
谢词 **xiè cí** thank you speech
多谢 **duō xiè** many thanks
不谢 **bú xiè** don't mention it
答谢 **dá xiè** express appreciation

12 strokes

radical
讠

traditional form
謝

再

zài again

common words

再见/再会 **zài jiàn/zài huì** Goodbye!
再三 **zài sān** again and again; repeatedly
再次 **zài cì** once more
再不 **zài bu** or; or else
一再 **yí zài** again and again; repeatedly
不再 **bú zài** no longer; never again

6 strokes

radical
一

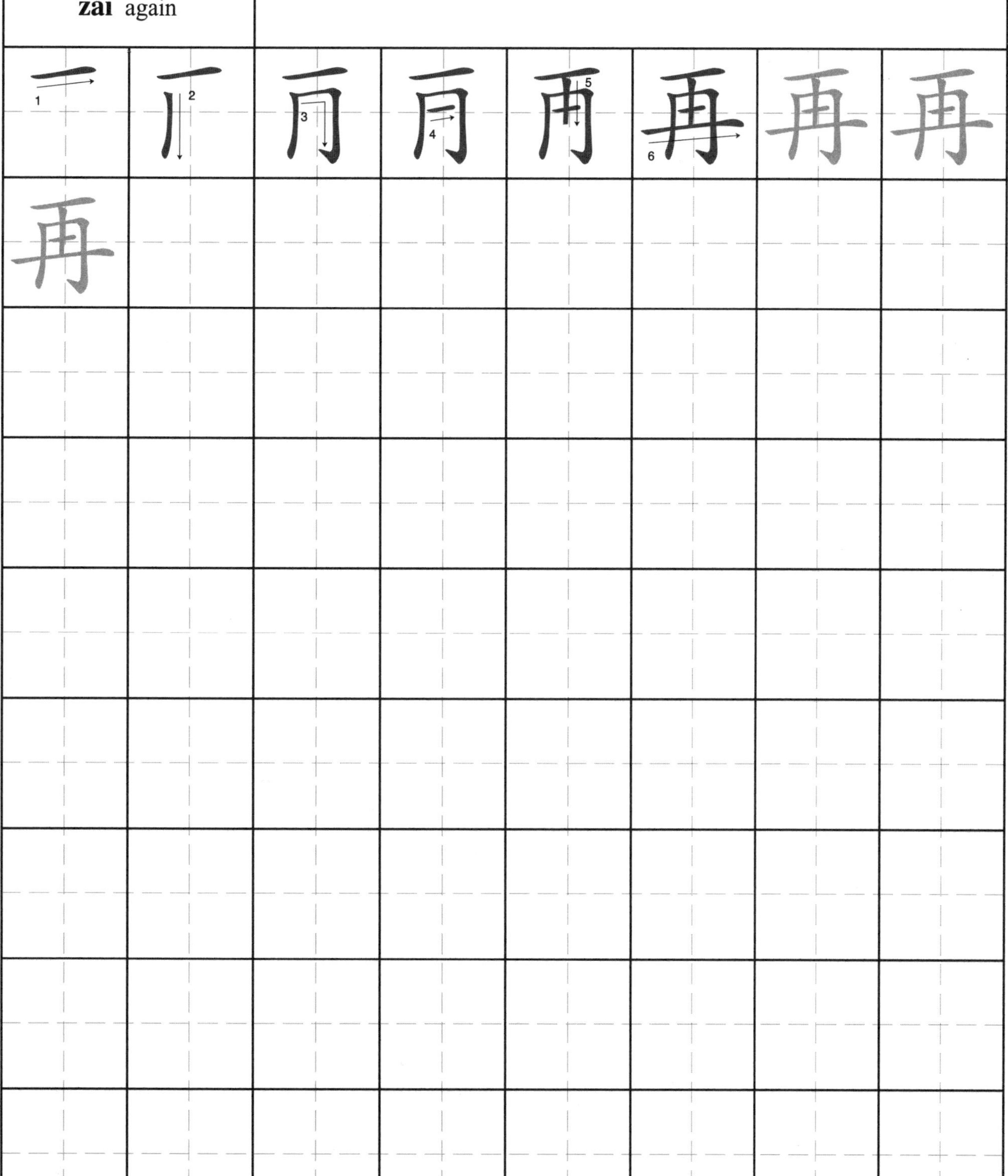

见

jiàn see; meet

common words

见好 **jiàn hǎo** get better (from an illness)
见面 **jiàn miàn** meet
不见了 **bú jiàn le** missing; can't be found
不见得 **bú jiàn de** not necessarily
看见 **kàn jiàn** see
少见 **shǎo jiàn** rare
听见 **tīng jiàn** hear

4 strokes

radical
见

traditional form
見

美

měi beautiful

common words

美丽 **měi lì** beautiful; pretty
美好 **měi hǎo** wonderful
美食 **měi shí** delicacy
美女/美人 **měi nǚ/měi rén** beautiful girl/woman
美国 **měi guó** the Unites States of America
很美/太美了 **hěn měi/tài měi le** very beautiful

9 strokes

radical
羊 (⺶)

1 2 3 4 5 6 7 8 9

国

guó country; national

common words

国家 **guó jiā** country
国人 **guó rén** the people in a country
国王 **guó wáng** king
出国 **chū guó** go abroad
外国 **wài guó** foreign country
外国人 **wài guó rén** people from other country

8 strokes

radical
口

traditional form
國

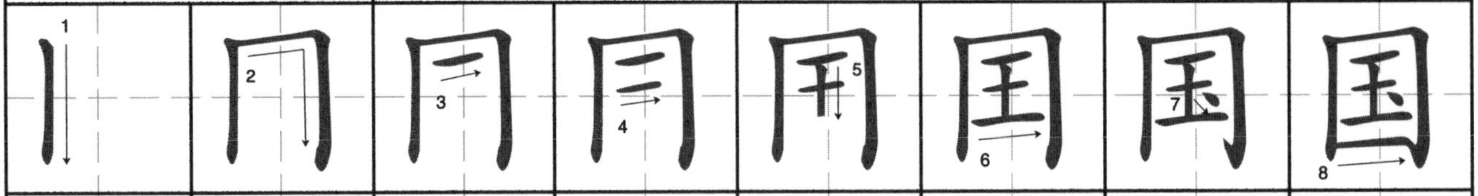

人 rén person; people	common words 人人/每人 **rén rén/měi rén** everyone 人口 **rén kǒu** population 工人 **gōng rén** worker 大人/成人 **dà rén/chéng rén** adult 本人 **běn rén** oneself 客人 **kè rén** guest	2 strokes radical 人

丿 人 人 人 人

吗

ma question particle

common words

是吗？ **shì ma** Is that so?; Is it?
好吗？ **hǎo ma** good?; alright?
忙吗？ **máng ma** busy?
行吗？ **xíng ma** Is it okay?
可以吗？ **kě yǐ ma** May I?
有事吗？ **yǒu shì ma** what's up?

6 strokes

radical

口

traditional form

嗎

也 **yě** also; too	**common words** 也是 **yě shì** is also ... 也好 **yě hǎo** may as well 也许 **yě xǔ** perhaps	**3 strokes** **radical** 乙

不 **bù** not; no	common words 不对 **bú duì** 1. incorrect 2. something is wrong 不要 **bú yào** don't want 不会 **bú huì** don't know 不同/不一样 **bù tóng/bù yí yàng** it's different 不客气 **bú kè qi** not at all; don't mention it 不好意思 **bù hǎo yì si** 1. embarrassed 2. excuse me 对不起 **duì bu qǐ** sorry	**4 strokes** **radical** 一

1 2 3 4

谁

shéi/shuí who

common words

谁的 **shéi de/shuí de** whose
谁知道 **shéi zhī dào/shuí zhī dào** no one knows

10 strokes

radical
讠

traditional form
誰

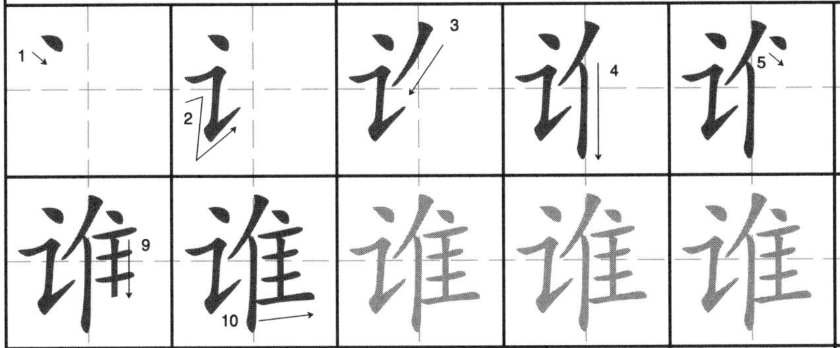

的

de particle

common words

我的 **wǒ de** my; mine
你的 **nǐ de** your; yours
他的/她的 **tā de** his/hers
谁的 **shéi de/shuí de** whose
有的 **yǒu de** some
挺好的 **tǐng hǎo de** quite good

8 strokes

radical
白

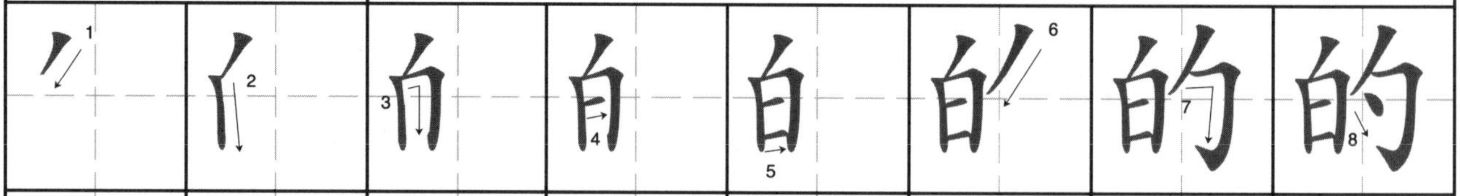

家

jiā family; home

common words

家庭 **jiā tíng** family
家人 **jiā rén** family member
人家 **rén jiā** other people
回家 **huí jiā** return home
每家/家家 **měi jiā/jiā jiā** every family; every household
一家大小 **yī jiā dà xiǎo** everyone in a family

10 strokes

radical
宀

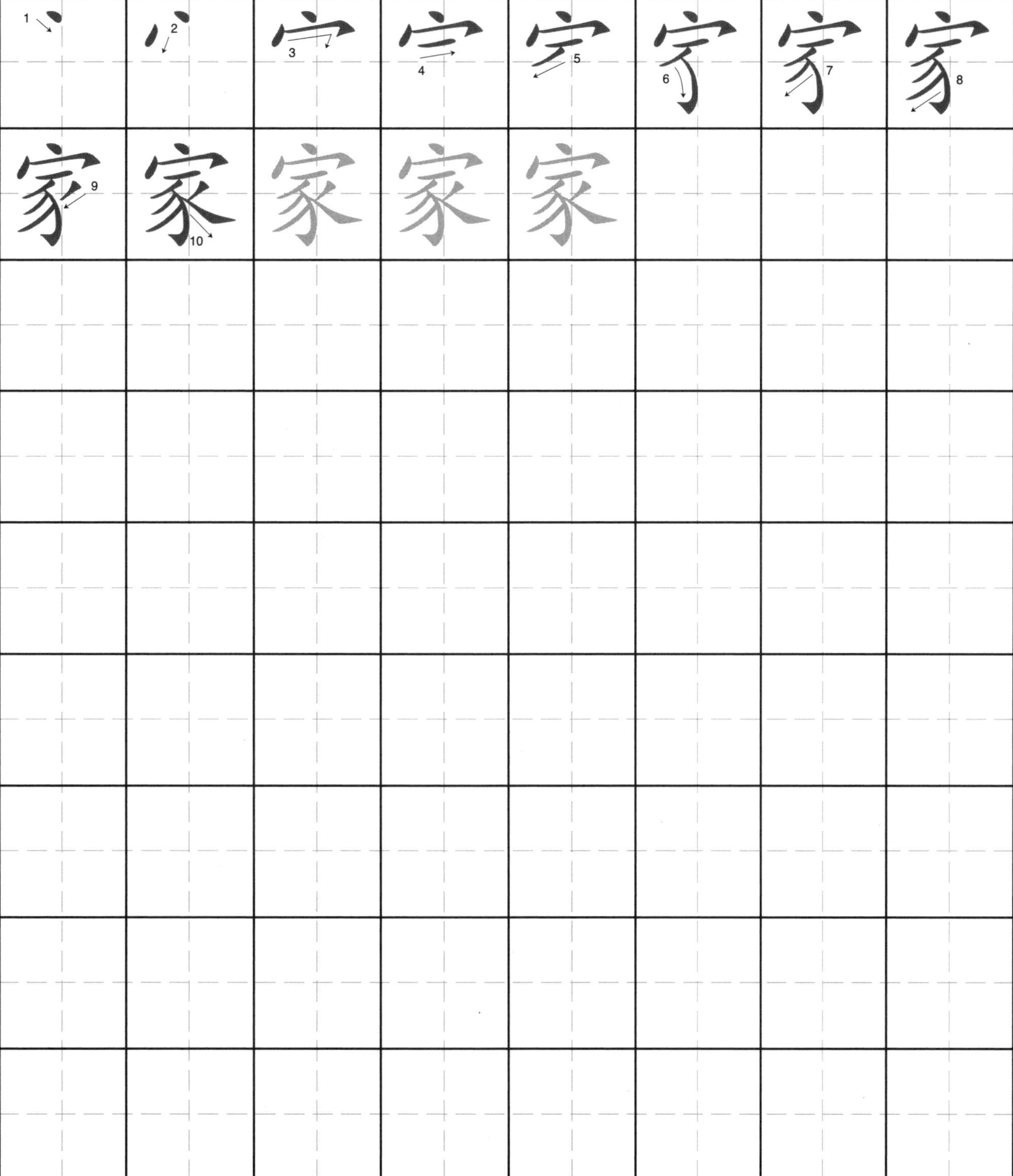

爸

bà father

common words

爸爸 **bà ba** father
爸爸妈妈 **bà ba mā ma** parents
老爸 **lǎo bà** father (informal)

8 strokes

radical
父

1 2 3 4 5 6 7 8

和

hé 1. ...and...
2. harmony

common words

和好 **hé hǎo** reconcile
和气 **hé qì** amiable; friendly
和平 **hé píng** peace
和事老 **hé shì lǎo** mediator

8 strokes

radical
禾

妈

mā mother

common words

妈妈 **mā ma** mother
姨妈 **yí mā** aunt (mother's married sister)
姑妈 **gū mā** aunt (father's married sister)

6 strokes

radical
女

traditional form
媽

1 2 3 4 5 6

哥 **gē** older brother	**common words** 哥哥 **gē ge** older brother 大哥 **dà gē** eldest brother 二哥 **èr gē** second elder brother 哥儿们 **gēr men** 1. brothers 2. buddies 帅哥 **shuài gē** handsome man	**10 strokes** **radical** 一

1 2 3 4 5 6 7 8 9 10

姐

jiě older sister

common words

姐姐 **jiě jie** older sister
姐妹 **jiě mèi** sisters
大姐 **dà jiě** 1. eldest sister 2. older woman
二姐 **èr jiě** second elder sister
小姐 **xiǎo jiě** Miss; lady
空姐 **kōng jiě** air stewardess

8 strokes

radical
女

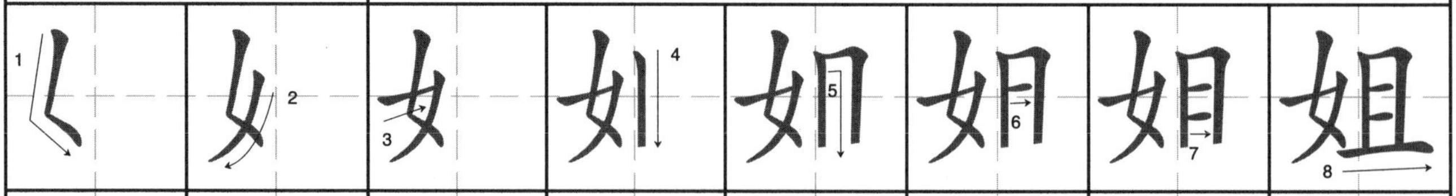

弟

dì younger brother

common words

弟弟 **dì di** younger brother
弟妹 **dì mèi** younger brother and sister
兄弟 **xiōng dì** brothers
姐弟 **jiě dì** older sister and younger brother
徒弟 **tú dì** disciple; follower

7 strokes

radical

八 (丷)

1 2 3 4 5 6 7

妹

mèi younger sister

common words

妹妹 **mèi mei** younger sister
大妹 **dà mèi** first younger sister
三妹 **sān mèi** third younger sister
小妹 **xiǎo mèi** youngest sister
姐妹 **jiě mèi** sisters
兄弟姐妹 **xiōng dì jiě mèi** brothers and sisters

8 strokes

radical
女

1 2 3 4 5 6 7 8

住

zhù 1. live; stay
2. stop

common words

住家 **zhù jiā** residence
住址 **zhù zhǐ** address
住口 **zhù kǒu** shut up
住手 **zhù shǒu** Hands off!
站住 **zhàn zhù** Halt!
记住 **jì zhù** remember

7 strokes

radical
人（亻）

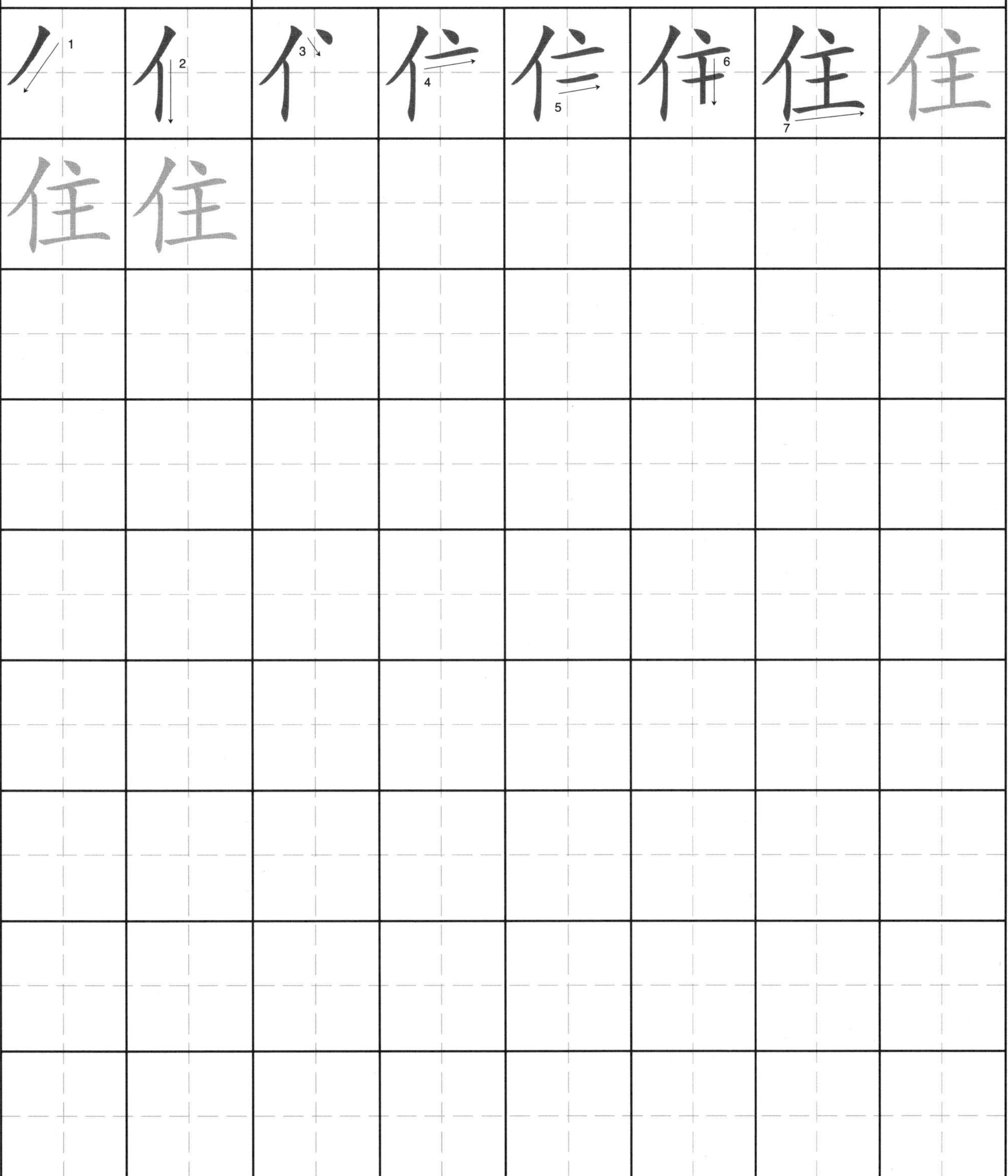

在

zài 1. be; at 2. live

common words

在吗？ **zài ma** in?
在家里 **zài jiā lǐ** at home
不在 **bú zài** not in
现在 **xiàn zài** now; currently
还在 **hái zài** still there
好在 **hǎo zài** fortunately

6 strokes

radical
土

这

zhè this

common words

这个 **zhè ge** 1. this one 2. in this case; in this matter
这儿/这里/这边 **zhèr/zhè lǐ/zhè biān** here
这些 **zhè xiē** these
这样 **zhè yàng** this way; like this
这么 **zhè me** such, so
这次 **zhè cì** this time
到儿这来 **dào zhèr lái** Come here!

7 strokes

radical

辶

traditional form

這

1 2 3 4 5 6 7

女

nǚ female

common words

女儿 **nǚ ér** daughter
女生 **nǚ shēng** female student; school girl
女性 **nǚ xìng** female gender
女士 **nǚ shì** Madam
女人 **nǚ rén** 1. wife 2. mistress
妇女 **fù nǚ** woman

3 strokes

radical
女

1 2 3

儿

ér/r 1. child 2. suffix

common words

儿子 **ér zi** son
儿童 **ér tóng** child
大儿子 **dà ér zi** eldest son
小儿子 **xiǎo ér zi** youngest son
一会儿 **yí huìr** a moment; a short while
一点儿 **yī diǎnr** a little

2 strokes

radical
儿

traditional form
兒

丿 1 儿 2 儿 儿 儿

那

nà/nèi 1. that
2. in that case

common words

那个 **nà ge** that
那里/那儿/那边 **nà li/nàr/nà biān** there
那些 **nà xiē** those
那样 **nà yàng** 1. same as 2. that type
那么 **nà me** 1. in that case; then 2. same way
那么点儿 **nà me diǎnr** such small amount ...

6 strokes

radical
阝

男

nán male

common words

男孩/男孩子 **nán hái/nán hái zi** boy
男生 **nán shēng** male student; school boy
男人 **nán rén** man
男性 **nán xìng** male gender
男男女女 **nán nán nǚ nǚ** boys and girls
男厕/男厕所 **nán cè/nán cè suǒ** man's toilet

7 strokes

radical
田

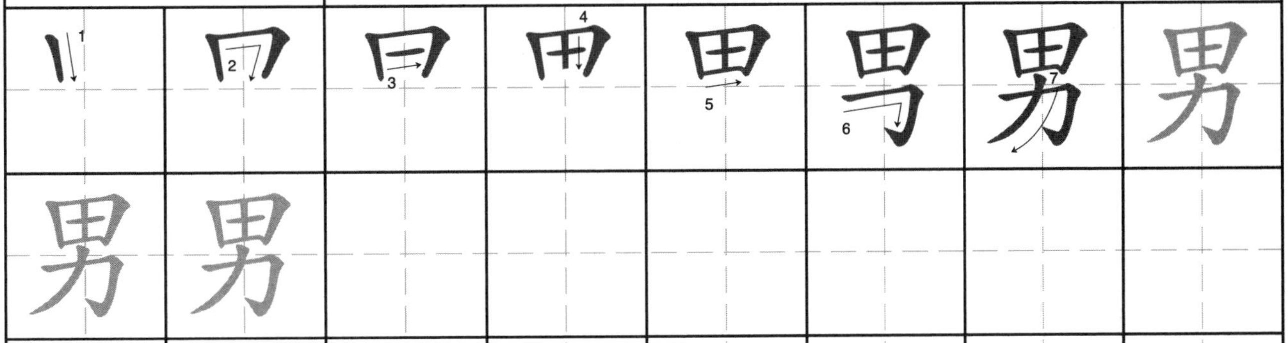

孩

hái child

common words

孩子/小孩 **hái zi/xiǎo hái** child
孩子气 **hái zi qì** childish
孩子话 **hái zi huà** childish words
男孩/男孩子 **nán hái/nán hái zi** boy
女孩/女孩子 **nǚ hái/nǚ hái zi** girl

9 strokes

radical
子

子	common words	3 strokes
zi/zǐ 1. son 2. seed 3. suffix (noun)	子女/儿女 **zǐ nǚ/ér nǚ** son and daughter; children 儿子 **ér zi** son 妻子 **qī zi** wife 桌子 **zhuō zi** table; desk 车子 **chē zi** 1. vehicle (small scale) 2. bicycle 一下子 **yí xià zi** 1. all of a sudden 2. all at once	radical 子

1 2 3

都

dōu/dū 1. all; even
2. big city

common words

都有 **dōu yǒu** all have
都是 **dōu shì** all are
都会 **dōu huì** all know how to do
都市/都会 **dū shì/dū huì** big city
首都 **shǒu dū** capital city

10 strokes

radical
阝

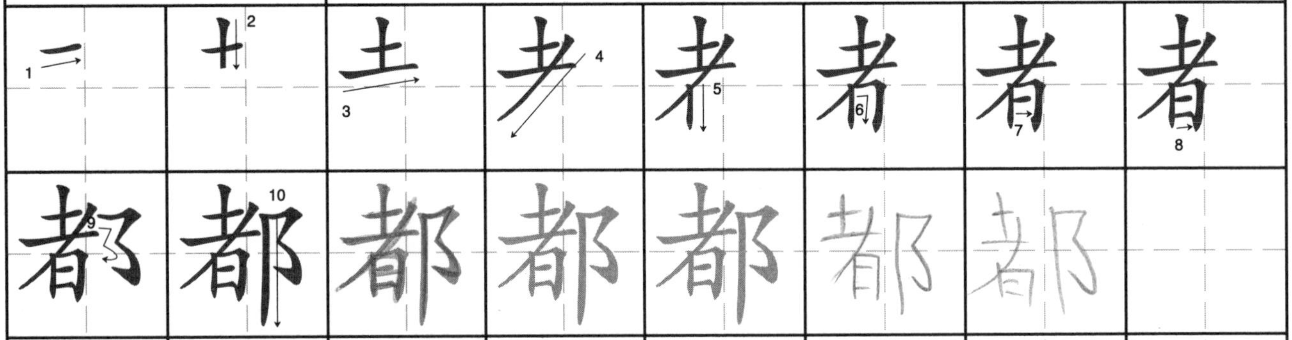

1 2 3 4 5 6 7 8 9 10

没

méi haven't; without

common words

没有 **méi yǒu** don't have; haven't
没错 **méi cuò** correct
没问题 **méi wèn tí** no question; no problem
没事 **méi shì** 1. free 2. no problem; alright
没关系/没什么 **méi guān xi/méi shén me** it doesn't matter
还没 **hái méi** not yet

7 strokes

radical

氵

traditional form

沒

有

yǒu has; have

common words

有的/有些 **yǒu de/yǒu xiē** some
有学问 **yǒu xué wèn** knowledgeable
有点儿 **yǒu diǎnr** a little; somewhat
有没有(?) **yǒu méi yǒu** 1. did you? 2. whether or not
只有 **zhǐ yǒu** there's only ...
还有 **hái yǒu** moreover; furthermore

6 strokes

radical
月

做 **zuò** do; make	**common words** 做好/做完 **zuò hǎo/zuò wán** finish; complete 做错 **zuò cuò** do wrongly 做人 **zuò rén** be an upright person 做饭 **zuò fàn** cook a meal 做作业 **zuò zuò yè** do assignment 做工 **zuò gōng** work	**11 strokes** **radical** 人（亻）

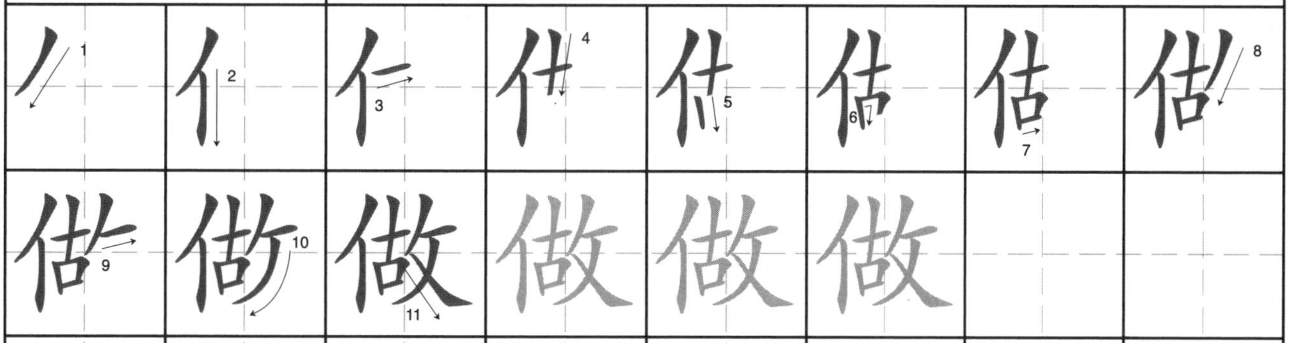

事

shì matter

common words

事事/每事 **shì shì/měi shì** every matter
事前 **shì qián** in advance; beforehand
事后 **shì hòu** afterwards; after the event
小事 **xiǎo shì** trivial matter
故事 **gù shì** story
做事 **zuò shì** 1. work 2. deal with matters

8 strokes

radical
一

1 2 3 4 5 6 7 8

两

liǎng two

common words

两个月 **liǎng ge yuè** two months
两百 **liǎng bǎi** two hundred
两次 **liǎng cì** twice
两样 **liǎng yàng** two types; different
两口子 **liǎng kǒu zi** a couple; husband and wife
没两样 **méi liǎng yàng** the same

7 strokes

radical
一

traditional form
兩

1 2 3 4 5 6 7

两 两 两

个

gè most common measure word

common words

个个/每个 **gè gè/měi ge** each one (of something)
个人 **gè rén** individual
个子 **gè zi** body size
两个门 **liǎng ge mén** two doors
那个 **nà ge** that
这个 **zhè ge** 1. this one 2. in this case; in this matter

3 strokes

radical
人

traditional form
個

1 2 3

多	common words	6 strokes
duō 1. many, much 2. far more	多少(?) **duō shǎo** 1. how many/much? 2. tend to 多大(?) **duō dà** 1. how old(?) 2. how big(?) 多半 **duō bàn** more often than not 多么 **duō me** no matter how 差不多 **chà bu duō** about; more or less	radical 夕

1 2 3 4 5 6

多 多 多

少

shǎo/shào 1. few; little 2. young

common words

少女 **shào nǚ** teenage girl
少不了 **shǎo bu liǎo** can't do without
青少年 **qīng shào nián** teenager
很少 **hěn shǎo** very little; very few
不少 **bù shǎo** quite a lot
男女老少 **nán nǚ lǎo shào** young and old

4 strokes

radical
小

时

shí time

common words

时间 **shí jiān** time
时期 **shí qī** period of time
时时/不时 **shí shí/bù shí** often
一时 **yī shí** temporarily; momentarily
有时/有时候 **yǒu shí/yǒu shí hou** sometimes
到时 **dào shí** when the time comes

7 strokes

radical
日

traditional form
時

1 2 3 4 5 6 7

间

jiān 1. between 2. room 3. measure word

common words	
时间 **shí jiān** time	
中间 **zhōng jiān** between; in the middle	
房间 **fáng jiān** room	
夜间 **yè jiān** at night; night time	
洗手间 **xǐ shǒu jiān** washroom	
一间客房 **yī jiān kè fáng** a guest room	

7 strokes

radical

门

traditional form

間

今

jīn now; at present

common words

今天/今日 **jīn tiān/jīn rì** today
今早 **jīn zǎo** this morning
今晚 **jīn wǎn** tonight; this evening
今年 **jīn nián** this year
今后 **jīn hòu** from now on
至今 **zhì jīn** up to now; so far
如今 **rú jīn** now; nowadays

4 strokes

radical
人

天

tiān 1. day 2. sky

common words

天天/每天 **tiān tiān/měi tiān** every day
天上/天空中 **tiān shàng/tiān kōng zhōng** in the sky
天气 **tiān qì** weather
明天 **míng tiān** tomorrow
昨天 **zuó tiān** yesterday
白天 **bái tiān** daytime

4 strokes

radical
大

几

jǐ/jī 1. how many 2. several 3. almost

common words

几个(?) **jǐ ge** 1. how many? 2. several (of something)
几次(?) **jǐ cì** 1. how many times? 2. several times
几时(?) **jǐ shí** 1. when? 2. anytime
几天(?) **jǐ tiān** 1. how many days? 2. several days
几分(?) **jǐ fēn** 1. how many points? 2. somewhat
几点(?) **jǐ diǎn** 1. what time? 2. several dots

2 strokes

radical
几

traditional form
幾

1 2

几 几 几 几 几

号

hào 1. date 2. size 3. sequence 4. signal

common words

号码 **hào mǎ** number
几号? **jǐ hào** which number?; what size?; what date?
十号 **shí hào** number ten; size ten; tenth (of a month)
句号 **jù hào** full-stop
逗号 **dòu hào** comma
问号 **wèn hào** question mark

5 strokes

radical
口

traditional form
號

明

míng bright

common words

明明 **míng míng** obviously
明白 **míng bai** understand
明天/明日 **míng tiān/míng rì** tomorrow
明亮 **míng liàng** bright
文明 **wén míng** civilized; civilization
发明 **fā míng** invent

8 strokes

radical
日

1 2 3 4 5 6 7 8

年

nián year

common words

年年/每年 **nián nián/měi nián** every year
年纪 **nián ji** age
明年 **míng nián** next year
后年 **hòu nián** year after next year
去年 **qù nián** last year
前年 **qián nián** year before last year

6 strokes

radical
丿

1 2 3 4 5 6

年 年 年

月 **yuè** 1. month 2. moon	**common words** 月亮/月球 **yuè liang/yuè qiú** moon 月光 **yuè guāng** moonlight 这个月 **zhè ge yuè** this month 上个月 **shàng ge yuè** last month 下个月 **xià ge yuè** next month	**4 strokes** **radical** 月

丿 1 月 2 月 3 月 4 月 月 月

日

rì day

common words

日本 **rì běn** Japan
日期 **rì qī** date
日子 **rì zi** 1. date; day 2. time 3. life
今日 **jīn rì** today
明日 **míng rì** tomorrow
昨日 **zuó rì** yesterday
每日 **měi rì** every day

4 strokes

radical
日

星

xīng star

common words

星星 **xīng xing** star
星期 **xīng qī** week
星座 **xīng zuó** 1. constellation 2. sign of zodiac
星球 **xīng qiú** heavenly body; planet
歌星 **gē xīng** singer
明星 **míng xīng** star (celebrity)

9 strokes

radical
日

1 2 3 4 5 6 7 8 9

期

qī period

common words

期间/时期 **qī jiān/shí qī** period of time
学期 **xué qī** school term; semester
假期 **jià qī** holiday
到期 **dào qī** expire
早期 **zǎo qī** earlier time; early stage
上星期 **shàng xīng qī** last week
下星期 **xià xīng qī** next week

12 strokes

radical
月

1 2 3 4 5 6 7 8 9 10 11 12

早

zǎo early; morning; Good morning!

common words

早安 **zǎo ān** Good morning!
早上 **zǎo shang** morning
早日 **zǎo rì** (at an) early date; soon
早晚 **zǎo wǎn** 1. day and night 2. sooner or later
早饭/早点/早餐 **zǎo fàn/zǎo diǎn/zǎo cān** breakfast
一早 **yī zǎo** early in the morning
明早 **míng zǎo** tomorrow morning

6 strokes

radical
日

1 2 3 4 5 6

上

shàng 1. above; go up 2. attend 3. previous

common words
上面 **shàng mian** above; top
上来 **shàng lái** come up
上去 **shàng qù** go up
上班 **shàng bān** go to work
上厕所 **shàng cè suǒ** go to the toilet
上次 **shàng cì** last time
马上 **mǎ shàng** immediately

3 strokes

radical
⺊

1 2 3

上 上 上

下

xià 1. under; go down 2. finish 3. next

common words

下面 **xià mian** underneath; below
下来 **xià lái** come down
下去 **xià qù** go down
下班 **xià bān** finish work
下雨 **xià yǔ** rain
下次 **xià cì** next time
一下 **yí xià** 1. one time 2. a short while

3 strokes

radical
一

1 2 3

午

wǔ noon

common words

午饭/午餐 **wǔ fàn/wǔ cān** lunch
午觉/午睡 **wǔ jiào/wǔ shuì** afternoon nap
午夜 **wǔ yè** midnight
上午/午前 **shàng wǔ/wǔ qián** morning (a.m.)
中午 **zhōng wǔ** noon
下午/午后 **xià wǔ/wǔ hòu** afternoon (p.m.)

4 strokes

radical
十

1 2 3 4

吃

chī eat

common words

吃饭 **chī fàn** have a meal
吃饱了 **chī bǎo le** eaten; eaten enough
吃不饱 **chī bu bǎo** not full; not enough to eat
吃不下 **chī bu xià** not able to eat; have no appetite
小吃 **xiǎo chī** snack
好吃 **hǎo chī** tasty; delicious

6 strokes

radical
口

1 2 3 4 5 6

吃 吃 吃

晚

wǎn night; late

common words

晚上 **wǎn shang** evening; night
晚安 **wǎn ān** Good night!
晚饭/晚餐 **wǎn fàn/wǎn cān** dinner
晚班 **wǎn bān** evening shift; night shift
晚点 **wǎn diǎn** be late
起晚了 **qǐ wǎn le** got up late

11 strokes

radical
日

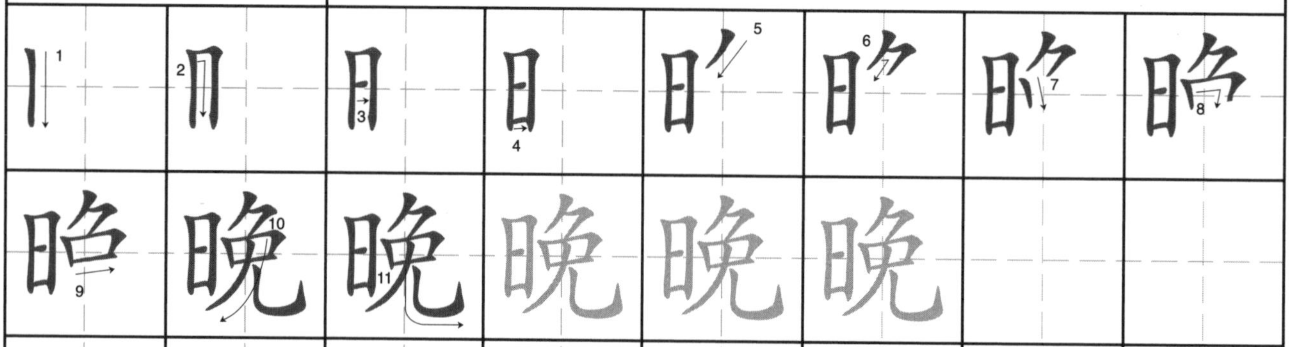

饭

fàn meal; cooked rice

common words

饭前 **fàn qián** before a meal
饭后 **fàn hòu** after a meal
饭菜 **fàn cài** rice and dishes
饭店 **fàn diàn** 1. restaurant 2. hotel
白饭 **bái fàn** cooked white rice
开饭 **kāi fàn** start serving a meal

7 strokes

radical

饣

traditional form

飯

了

le/liǎo particle

common words

了不起 **liǎo bu qǐ** fantastic; amazing
对了 **duì le** That's right!
算了 **suàn le** forget it
都上学了 **dōu shàng xué le** all have gone to school
受不了 **shòu bu liǎo** unbearable
吃了 **chī le** had eaten

2 strokes

radical

乛

1 2

了 了 了

哪 nǎ/něi which; any	common words 哪个(?) **nǎ ge** 1. which? 2. any; anyone 哪里(?) **nǎ li** 1. where? 2. not at all 哪样(?) **nǎ yàng** 1. what kind? 2. whatever 哪天(?) **nǎ tiān** 1. which day? 2. anyday; someday 哪些(?) **nǎ xiē** 1. which of those? 2. any of those 哪怕 **nǎ pà** no matter	9 strokes radical 口

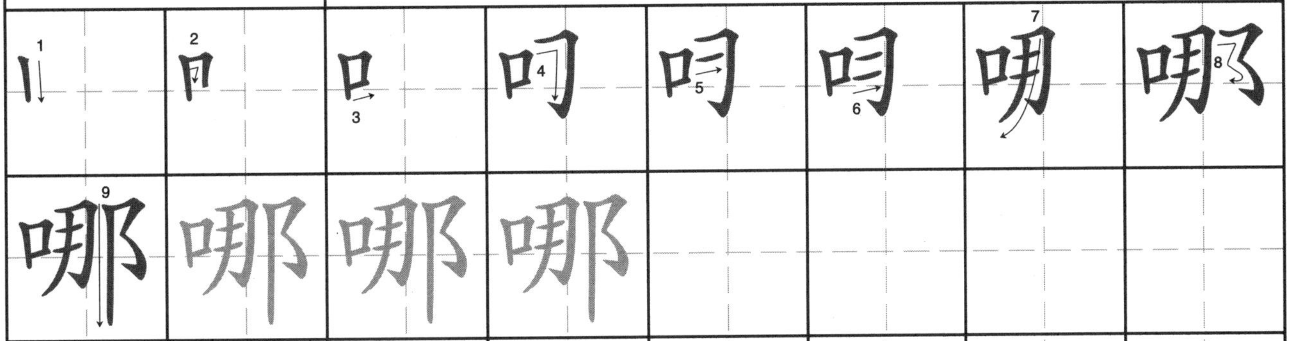

Hanyu Pinyin Index

B

bā 八 17
bà 爸 64
bà ba 爸爸 64
bà ba mā ma 爸爸妈妈 64
bā bǎi líng wǔ 八百零五 17
bā chéng 八成 17
bā shí èr 八十二 17
bā yuè 八月 17
bā zhé 八折 17
bái fàn 白饭 107
bái tiān 白天 92
běn rén 本人 57
bù 不 60
bú duì 不对 60
bù hǎo yì si 不好意思 60
bú huì 不会 60
bú jiàn de 不见得 54
bú jiàn le 不见了 54
bú kè qi 不客气 60
bù shǎo 不少 88
bú shi 不是 35
bù shí 不时 89
bù tóng 不同 60
bú xiè 不谢 52
bú yào 不要 60
bù yí yàng 不一样 60
bú zài 不再 53
bú zài 不在 72

C

chà bu duō 差不多 87
chē zi 车子 79
chéng rén 成人 57
chī 吃 105
chī bǎo le 吃饱了 105
chī bu bǎo 吃不饱 105
chī bu xià 吃不下 105
chī fàn 吃饭 105
chī le 吃了 108
chū guó 出国 56
chū míng 出名 32
chú shī 厨师 44

D

dà 大 36
dà bàn 大半 36
dà biàn 大便 36
dà bu liǎo 大不了 36
dà dū 大都 36
dà duō 大多 36
dà ér zi 大儿子 75
dà gài 大概 36
dà gē 大哥 67
dà jiā 大家 36
dà jiào 大叫 29
dà jiě 大姐 68
dà mèi 大妹 70
dà rén 大人 57
dà shēng diǎn 大声点 36
dá xiè 答谢 52
dào qī 到期 100
dào shí 到时 89
dào zhèr lái 到这儿来 73
de 的 62
dì 弟 69
dì bā 第八 17
dì di 弟弟 69
dì èr 第二 11
dì jiǔ 第九 18
dì liù 第六 15
dì mèi 弟妹 69
dì qī 第七 16
dì sān 第三 12
dì shí 第十 19
dì sì 第四 13
dì wǔ 第五 14
dì yī 第一 10
dì yī kè 第一课 42
dì yī míng 第一名 32
dōu/dū 都 80
dòu hào 逗号 94
dōu huì 都会 80
dōu shàng xué le 都上学了 108
dōu shì 都是 80
dōu yǒu 都有 80
dū huì 都会 80
dū shì 都市 80
duì bu qǐ 对不起 60
duì le 对了 108
duō 多 87
duō bàn 多半 87
duō dà 多大(?) 87
duō me 多么 31, 87
duō shǎo 多少(?) 87
duō xiè 多谢 52

E

èr 二 11
ér/r 儿 75
èr gē 二哥 67
èr jiě 二姐 68
èr mèi 二妹 11
ér nǚ 儿女 79
èr shí 二十 11
èr shǒu 二手 11
ér tóng 儿童 75
èr yuè 二月 11
ér zi 儿子 75, 79

F

fā míng 发明 95
fǎ wén 法文 41
fàn 饭 107
fàn cài 饭菜 107
fàn diàn 饭店 107
fàn hòu 饭后 107
fàn qián 饭前 107

fáng jiān	房间	90
făng wèn	访问	24
fàng xué	放学	37
fù nǚ	妇女	74

G

gē	哥	67
gè	个	86
gē ge	哥哥	67
gè gè	个个	86
gè rén	个人	86
gē xīng	歌星	99
gè zi	个子	86
gēr men	哥儿们	67
gōng kè	功课	42
gōng rén	工人	57
gōng yǒu	工友	49
gǔ lǎo	古老	43
gū mā	姑妈	66
gù shì	故事	84
guì	贵	25
guì bīn	贵宾	25
guì kè	贵客	25
guì rén	贵人	25
guì xìng	贵姓	25
guó	国	56
guó jiā	国家	56
guó rén	国人	56
guó wáng	国王	56

H

hái	孩	78
hái hǎo	还好	22
hái méi	还没	81
hái shì	还是	35
hái yǒu	还有	82
hái zài	还在	72
hái zi	孩子	78
hái zi huà	孩子话	78
hái zi qì	孩子气	78
hàn zì	汉字	33
hǎo/hào	好	22
hào	号	94
hǎo a	好啊	22
hǎo chī	好吃	105
hǎo jiǔ	好久	22
hǎo kàn	好看	22
hǎo ma	好吗?	58
hào mǎ	号码	94
hǎo péng you	好朋友	48
hǎo yǒu	好友	49
hǎo zài	好在	72
hé	和	65
hé hǎo	和好	65
hé píng	和平	65
hé qì	和气	65
hé shì lǎo	和事老	65
hěn hǎo	很好	22
hěn měi	很美	55
hěn shǎo	很少	88
hòu nián	后年	96
huí jiā	回家	63

J

jǐ/jī	几	93
jǐ cì	几次(?)	93
jǐ diǎn	几点(?)	93
jǐ fēn	几分(?)	93
jǐ ge	几个(?)	93
jǐ hào	几号?	94
jǐ shí	几时(?)	93
jǐ tiān	几天(?)	93
jì zhù	记住	71
jiā	家	63
jiā jiā	家家	63
jià qī	假期	100
jiā rén	家人	63
jiā tíng	家庭	63
jiàn	见	54
jiān	间	90
jiàn hǎo	见好	54
jiàn miàn	见面	54
jiào	叫	29
jiào chē	叫车	29
jiào hǎn	叫喊	29
jiào hǎo	叫好	29
jiào mén	叫门	29
jiào shī	教师	44
jiào zuò	叫做	29
jiě	姐	68
jiě dì	姐弟	69
jiě jie	姐姐	68
jiě mèi	姐妹	68, 70
jīn	今	91
jīn hòu	今后	91
jīn nián	今年	91
jīn rì	今日	91, 98
jīn tiān	今天	91
jīn wǎn	今晚	91
jīn zǎo	今早	91
jiǔ	九	18
jiǔ bǎi yī shí	九百一十	18
jiǔ fēn	九分	18
jiǔ hào	九号	18
jiǔ shí bā	九十八	18
jiǔ yuè	九月	18
jù hào	句号	94

K

kāi fàn	开饭	107
kāi xué	开学	37
kàn jiàn	看见	54
kè	课	42
kè běn	课本	42
kè rén	客人	57
kè tí	课题	42
kè wén	课文	42
kě yǐ ma	可以吗?	58
kōng jiě	空姐	68

L

lǎo	老	43
lǎo bà	老爸	64
lǎo bǎi xìng	老百姓	26

xiōng dì jiě mèi	兄弟姐妹	70
xué	学	37
xué huì	学会	37
xué qī	学期	100
xué sheng	学生	38
xué wèn	学问	24
xué xiào	学校	46
xué xí	学习	37

Y

yě	也	59
yě hǎo	也好	59
yè jiān	夜间	90
yě shì	也是	59
yě xǔ	也许	59
yī	一	10
yí cì	一次	10
yī diǎnr	一点儿	75
yí ge	一个	10
yí huìr	一会儿	75
yī jiā dà xiǎo	一家大小	63
yī jiān kè fáng	一间客房	90
yí mā	姨妈	66
yī qǐ	一起	10, 45
yī shēng	医生	38
yī shí	一时	89
yī tóng	一同	10, 45
yí wàn	一万	19
yí xià	一下	103
yí xià zi	一下子	79
yí yuè	一月	10
yí zài	一再	53
yī zǎo	一早	101
yīng	英	40
yīng guó	英国	40
yīng jùn	英俊	40
yīng míng	英明	40
yīng wén	英文	40
yīng xióng	英雄	40
yīng yǔ	英语	40
yǒu	友	49
yǒu	有	82
yǒu de	有的	62, 82
yǒu diǎnr	有点儿	82
yǒu méi yǒu	有没有	82
yǒu qíng	友情	49
yǒu rén	友人	49
yǒu shí	有时	89
yǒu shí hou	有时候	89
yǒu shì ma	有事吗？	58
yǒu xiē	有些	82
yǒu xué wèn	有学问	82
yǒu yì	友谊	49
yǔ wén	语文	41
yuè	月	97
yuè guāng	月光	97
yuè liang	月亮	97
yuè qiú	月球	97

Z

zài	再	53
zài	在	72
zài bu	再不	53
zài cì	再次	53
zài huì	再会	53
zài jiā lǐ	在家里	72
zài jiàn	再见	53
zài ma	在吗？	72
zài sān	再三	53
zán men	咱们	34, 50
zǎo	早	101
zǎo ān	早安	101
zǎo cān	早餐	101
zǎo diǎn	早点	101
zǎo fàn	早饭	101
zǎo qī	早期	100
zǎo rì	早日	101
zǎo shang	早上	101
zǎo wǎn	早晚	101
zěn me	怎么	31
zhàn zhù	站住	71
zhè	这	73
zhè biān	这边	73
zhè cì	这次	73
zhè ge	这个	73, 86
zhè ge yuè	这个月	97
zhè lǐ	这里	73
zhè me	这么	73
zhè xiē	这些	73
zhè yàng	这样	73
zhèr	这儿	73
zhì jīn	至今	91
zhǐ yǒu	只有	82
zhōng/zhòng	中	39
zhōng guó	中国	39
zhōng jiān	中间	39, 90
zhòng jiǎng	中奖	39
zhōng nián	中年	39
zhōng wén	中文	39
zhōng wǔ	中午	104
zhōng xué	中学	37
zhù	住	71
zhù jiā	住家	71
zhù kǒu	住口	71
zhù shǒu	住手	71
zhù zhǐ	住址	71
zhuō zi	桌子	79
zì	字	33
zi/zǐ	子	79
zì dà	自大	36
zì diǎn	字典	33
zì mǔ	字母	33
zǐ nǚ	子女	79
zì wǒ	自我	34
zuò	做	83
zuò cuò	做错	83
zuò fàn	做饭	83
zuò gōng	做工	83
zuò hǎo	做好	83
zuò rén	做人	83
zuó rì	昨日	98
zuò shì	做事	84
zuó tiān	昨天	92
zuó wán	做完	83
zuò zuò yè	做作业	83

Radical Index

1 stroke

[一]
一 yī 10
二 èr 11
七 qī 16
三 sān 12
下 xià 103
五 wǔ 14
不 bù 60
再 zài 53
两 liǎng 85
哥 gē 67
事 shì 84

[丨]
中 zhōng/zhòng 39

[丿]
九 jiǔ 18
生 shēng 38
年 nián 96

[乛]
了 le/liǎo 108
也 yě 59

2 strokes

[⺊]
上 shàng 102

[十]
十 shí 19
午 wǔ 104

[冂]
同 tóng 45

八 [丷]
八 bā 17
弟 dì 69

人 [亻]
人 rén 57
个 gè 86
今 jīn 91
什 shén/shí 30
他 tā 27
们 men 50
你 nǐ 20
住 zhù 71
做 zuò 83

[儿]
儿 ér/r 75

[几]
几 jǐ/jī 93

[亠]
六 liù 15

[讠]
谁 shéi/shuí 61
请 qǐng 23
课 kè 42
谢 xiè 52

[阝]
那 nà/nèi 76
都 dōu/dū 80

[厶]
么 me 31

[又]
友 yǒu 49

3 strokes

[土]
在 zài 72

[艹]
英 yīng 40

[小]
小 xiǎo 47
少 shǎo/shào 88

[大]
大 dà 36
天 tiān 92

[口]
叫 jiào 29
号 hào 94
吃 chī 105
吗 ma 58
呢 ne 51
哪 nǎ/něi 109

[囗]
四 sì 13
国 guó 56

[巾]
师 shī 44

[夕]
名 míng 32
多 duō 87

[饣]
饭 fàn 107

[门]
问 wèn 24
间 jiān 90

[氵]
没 méi 81

English–Chinese Index

A

a(n) 一 yī *10*
a(n) (of something) 一个 yī ge *10*
a couple 两口子 liǎng kǒu zi *85*
a guest room 一间客房 yī jiān kè fáng *90*
a little 一点儿 yī diǎnr *75*; 有点儿 yǒu diǎnr *82*
a long time 好久 hǎo jiǔ *22*
a moment 一会儿 yí huìr *75*
a short while 一会儿 yí huìr *75*; 一下 yí xià *103*
about 差不多 chà bu duō *87*
above 上/上面 shàng/shàng mian *102*
address 住址 zhù zhǐ *71*
adult 大人/成人 dà rén/chéng rén *57*
after a meal 饭后 fàn hòu *107*
afternoon (p.m.) 下午/午后 xià wǔ/wǔ hòu *104*
afternoon nap 午觉/午睡 wǔ jiào/wǔ shuì *104*
afterwards/after the event 事后 shì hòu *84*
again 再 zài *53*
again and again 再三/一再 zài sān/yí zài *53*
age 年纪 nián ji *96*
air stewardess 空姐 kōng jiě *68*
alike 同样 tóng yàng *45*
all 都 dōu *80*
all are 都是 dōu shì *80*
all at once 一下子 yí xià zi *79*
all have 都有 dōu yǒu *80*
all have gone to school 都上学了 dōu shàng xué le *108*
all know how to do 都会 dōu huì *80*
all of a sudden 一下子 yí xià zi *79*
almost 几 jī *93*
almost complete 七七八八 qī qī bā bā *16*
alright 好 hǎo *22;* 没事 méi shì *81*
alright? 好吗? hǎo ma *58*
alright then ... 那好 nà hǎo *22*
also 也 yě *59*
alum 校友 xiào yǒu *46*
always 老是 lǎo shì *35*
...and... 和 hé *65*
amazing 了不起 liǎo bu qǐ *108*
amiable 和气 hé qì *65*
among 中 zhōng *39*
ancient 古老 gǔ lǎo *43*
angry 生气 shēng qì *38*
anxious 七上八下 qī shàng bā xià *16*
any 哪/哪个 nǎ/nǎ ge *109*
any of those 哪些 nǎ xiē *109*
anyday 哪天 nǎ tiān *109*
anyone 哪个 nǎ ge *109*
anytime 几时 jǐ shí *93*
April 四月 sì yuè *13*
arrogant 自大 zì dà *36*
ask 问 wèn *24*
at 在 zài *72*
at home 在家里 zài jiā lǐ *72*
at night 夜间 yè jiān *90*
at present 今 jīn *91*
at the worst 大不了 dà bu liǎo *36*
attend 上 shàng *102*
attend class 上课 shàng kè *42*
August 八月 bā yuè *17*
aunt (father's married sister) 姑妈 gū mā *66*
aunt (mother's married sister) 姨妈 yí mā *66*

B

be 在 zài *72*
be an upright person 做人 zuò rén *83*
be called 叫/叫做 jiào/jiào zuò *29*
be late 晚点 wǎn diǎn *106*
beautiful 美/美丽 měi/měi lì *55*
beautiful girl 美女 měi nǚ *55*
beautiful woman 美人 měi rén *55*
become famous 出名 chū míng *32*
before a meal 饭前 fàn qián *107*
beforehand 事前 shì qián *84*
belittle 小看 xiǎo kàn *47*
below 下面 xià mian *103*
between 间/中间 jiān/zhōng jiān *39, 90*
bicycle 车子 chē zi *79*
big 大 dà *36*
big city 都市/都会 dū shì/dū huì *80*

E

F

matter 事 shì *84*
May 五月 wǔ yuè *14*
may as well 也好 yě hǎo *59*
May I? 可以吗? kě yǐ ma *58*
May I ask ...? 请问 qǐng wèn *23*
me 我 wǒ *34*
meal 饭 fàn *107*
measure word (most common) 个 gè *86*
measure word (for room) 间 jiān *90*
mediator 和事老 hé shì lǎo *65*
meet 见/见面 jiàn/jiàn miàn *54*
middle 中 zhōng *39*
middle school 中学 zhōng xué *37*
middle-aged 中年 zhōng nián *39*
midnight 午夜 wǔ yè *104*
mine 我的 wǒ de *34, 62*
Miss 小姐 xiǎo jiě *47, 68*
missing 不见了 bú jiàn le *54*
mistress 女人 nǚ rén *74*
mixed 什 shí *30*
momentarily 一时 yī shí *89*
Monday 星期一 xīng qī yī *10*
month 月 yuè *97*
moon 月/月亮/月球 yuè/yuè liang/yuè qiú *97*
moonlight 月光 yuè guāng *97*
more often than not 多半 duō bàn *87*
more or less 差不多 chà bu duō *87*
moreover 还有 hái yǒu *82*
morning (a.m.) 早/早上 zǎo/zǎo shang *101*; 上午/午前 shàng wǔ/wǔ qián *104*
mostly 大多/大都/大半 dà duō/dà dū/dà bàn *36*
mother 妈/妈妈 mā/mā ma *66*
Mr 先生 xiān sheng *38*
my 我的 wǒ de *34, 62*
my family 我家 wǒ jiā *34*
my home 我家 wǒ jiā *34*

N

name 名/名字 míng/míng zi *32*
named 名叫 míng jiào *32*
national 国 guó *56*
never again 不再 bú zài *53*
new word 生字 shēng zì *33*
next 下 xià *103*
next month 下个月 xià ge yuè *97*
next time 下次 xià cì *103*
next week 下星期 xià xīng qī *100*
next year 明年 míng nián *96*
night shift 晚班 wǎn bān *106*
night 晚/晚上 wǎn/wǎn shang *106*
night time 夜间 yè jiān *90*
nine 九 jiǔ *18*
nine points 九分 jiǔ fēn *18*
nine-hundred and ten 九百一十 jiǔ bǎi yī shí *18*
nineteen 十九 shí jiǔ *18*
ninety-eight 九十八 jiǔ shí bā *18*
ninth 第九 dì jiǔ *18*
ninth (of a month) 九号 jiǔ hào *18*
no 不是 bú shì *35*; 不 bù *60*
no longer 不再 bú zài *53*
no matter 哪怕 nǎ pà *109*
no matter how 多么 duō me *31, 87*
no one knows 谁知道 shéi zhī dào *61*
no problem 没问题/没事 méi wèn tí/méi shì *81*
no question 没问题 méi wèn tí *81*
noon 午/中午 wǔ/zhōng wǔ *104*
not 不 bù *60*
not able to eat 吃不下 chī bu xià *105*
not at all 不客气 bú kè qi *60*; 哪里 nǎ li *109*
not full/not enough to eat 吃不饱 chī bu bǎo *105*
not in 不在 bú zài *72*
not necessarily 不见得 bú jiàn de *54*
not to be 不是 bú shì *35*
not well 生病 shēng bìng *38*
not yet 还没 hái méi *81*
November 十一月 shí yī yuè *19*
now 现在 xiàn zài *72*; 今 jīn *91*
nowadays 如今 rú jīn *91*
number 号码 hào mǎ *94*
number nine 九号 jiǔ hào *18*
number ten 十号 shí hào *94*

O
obviously 明明 míng míng *95*
October 十月 shí yuè *19*
often 时时/不时 shí shí/bù shí *89*
OK! 好啊! hǎo a *22*
old 老 lǎo *43*
old friend 老朋友 lǎo péng you *48*
old woman 老婆婆 lǎo pó po *43*
older brother 哥/哥哥 gē/gē ge *67*
older sister 姐/姐姐 jiě/jiě jie *68*
older sister and younger brother 姐弟 jiě dì *69*
older woman 大姐 dà jiě *68*
on hand 手中 shǒu zhōng *39*
once 一次 yí cì *10*
once more 再次 zài cì *53*
one 一 yī *10*
one (of something) 一个 yí ge *10*
one time 一下 yí xià *103*
oneself 本人 běn rén *57*
or 还是 hái shì *35*
or/or else 再不 zài bu *53*
order 叫 jiào *29*
order a cab 叫车 jiào chī *29*
other 其他 qí tā *27*
other people 他人/其他人 tā rén/qí tā rén *27*
other people 人家 rén jiā *63*
our country 我国 wǒ guó *34*

P
parents 爸爸妈妈 bà ba mā ma *64*
particle 的 de *62*; 了 le/liǎo *108*
peace 和平 hé píng *65*
people 人们 rén men *50*
people from other country 外国人 wài guó rén *56*
people in a country 国人 guó rén *56*
perfect 十全十美 shí quán shí měi *19*
perhaps 也许 yě xǔ *59*
period of time 时期 shí qī *89, 100*; 期间 qī jiān *100*
person/people 人 rén *57*
planet 星球 xīng qiú *99*
play host 请客 qǐng kè *23*
please 请 qǐng *23*
Please come in. 请进 qǐng jìn *23*
Please sit down. 请坐 qǐng zuò *23*
plural suffix (for persons) 们 men *50*
population 人口 rén kǒu *57*
pretty 美丽 měi lì *55*
previous 上 shàng *102*
primary school 小学 xiǎo xué *37*
principal 校长 xiào zhǎng *46*
probably 大概 dà gài *36*
problem 问题 wèn tí *24*
proud 自大 zì dà *36*

Q
question 问题 wèn tí *24*
question and answer 问答 wèn dá *24*
question mark 问号 wèn hào *94*
question particle 呢 ne *51*; 吗 ma *58*
quite a lot 不少 bù shǎo *88*
quite good 挺好的 tǐng hǎo de *62*

R
rain 下雨 xià yǔ *103*
rare 少见 shǎo jiàn *54*
raw 生 shēng *38*
reconcile 和好 hé hǎo *65*
related to England 英 yīng *40*
remember 记住 jì zhù *71*
repeatedly 再三/一再 zài sān/yí zài *53*
residence 住家 zhù jiā *71*
respected person 贵人 guì rén *25*
restaurant 饭店 fàn diàn *107*
return home 回家 huí jiā *63*
rice and dishes 饭菜 fàn cài *107*
room 间/房间 jiān/fáng jiān *90*

S
same as 那样 nà yàng *76*
same class 同班 tóng bān *45*

T

U

underestimate 小看 xiǎo kàn *47*
underneath 下面 xià mian *103*
understand 明白 míng bai *95*
United States of America 美国 měi guó *55*
up to now 至今 zhì jīn *91*
urine/urinate 小便 xiǎo biàn *47*
us 我们/咱们 wǒ men/zán men *34, 50*

V
valuable 贵/名贵 guì/míng guì *25*
vehicle (small scale) 车子 chē zi *79*
very 十分 shí fēn *19*
very beautiful 很美/太美了 hěn měi/tài měi le *55*
very few/little 很少 hěn shǎo *88*
very good 很好 hěn hǎo *22*
VIP 贵客/贵宾 guì kè/guì bīn *25*
visit 访问 fǎng wèn *24*

W
washroom 洗手间 xǐ shǒu jiān *90*
we 我们/咱们 wǒ men/zán men *34, 50*
weather 天气 tiān qì *92*
Wednesday 星期三 xīng qī sān *12*
week 星期 xīng qī *99*
well-known 出名 chū míng *32*
what 什么 shén me *30, 31*
what's up? 有事吗? yǒu shì ma *58*
what date? 几号? jǐ hào *94*
what kind? 哪样? nǎ yàng *109*
what size? 几号? jǐ hào *94*
what time? 几点? jǐ diǎn *93*
whatever 哪样 nǎ yàng *109*
when? 几时? jǐ shí *93*
when the time comes 到时 dào shí *89*
where? 哪里? nǎ li *109*
Where's the person? 人呢? rén ne *51*
whether or not 有没有? yǒu méi yǒu *82*
which? 哪?/哪个? nǎ/nǎ ge *109*
which day? 哪天? nǎ tiān *109*
which number? 几号? jǐ hào *94*
which of those? 哪些? nǎ xiē *109*
who 谁 shéi/shuí *61*
whose 谁的 shéi de *61, 62*
why? 为什么? wèi shèn me *31*
wife 女人 nǚ rén *74*; 妻子 qī zi *79*
wife (informal) 老婆 lǎo po *43*
win a prize 中奖 zhòng jiǎng *39*
wise 英明 yīng míng *40*
without 没 méi *81*
woman 妇女 fù nǚ *74*
wonderful 美好 měi hǎo *55*
work 做工 zuò gōng *83*; 做事 zuò shì *84*
worker 工人 gōng rén *57*
worry 七上八下 qī shàng bā xià *16*
write word 写字 xiě zì *33*
written character 字 zì *33*
written language 文 wén *41*
writing 文/文字 wén/wén zì *41*

Y
yeah 是啊 shì a *35*
year 年 nián *96*
year after next year 后年 hòu nián *96*
year before last year 前年 qián nián *96*
yell 叫喊 jiào hǎn *29*
yes 是/是的/是啊 shì/shì de/shì a *35*
yesterday 昨天 zuó tiān *92*; 昨日 zuó rì *98*
you 你 nǐ *20*
you (plural) 你们 nǐ men *20, 50*
you (polite) 您 nín *21*
young 少 shào *88*
young and old 男女老少 nán nǚ lǎo shào *88*
younger brother 弟/弟弟 dì/dì di *69*
younger brother and sister 弟妹 dì mèi *69*
younger sister 妹/妹妹 mèi/mèi mei *70*
youngest sister 小妹 xiǎo mèi *70*
youngest son 小儿子 xiǎo ér zi *75*
your family name? 您贵姓 nín guì xìng *21*
your honorable surname? 贵姓 guì xìng *25*
your/yours 你的 nǐ de *20, 62*
your/yours (plural) 你们的 nǐ men de *20*

List of Radicals

— 1 stroke —
1 丶 dot
2 一 one
3 丨 down
4 丿 left
5 乛 "back-turned stroke"
6 𠃌 "top of 刁"
7 乙 twist

— 2 strokes —
8 冫 ice
9 亠 lid
10 讠 (side-) words
11 二 two
12 十 ten
13 厂 slope
14 𠂇 "top of 左"
15 匚 basket
16 卜 (⺊) divine
17 刂 (side) knife
18 冖 crown
19 冂 borders
20 𠂉 "top of 每"
21 亻 (side-)man
22 ⺁ "top of 后"
23 人 (入) person (enter)
24 八 (丷) eight
25 乂 "bottom of 义"
26 勹 wrap
27 刀 (⺈) knife
28 力 strength
29 儿 son
30 几 (⺇) table
31 龴 "top of 予"
32 卩 seal
33 阝 (on the left) mound
34 阝 (on the right) city
35 又 right hand
36 廴 march
37 厶 cocoon
38 凵 bowl
39 匕 ladle

— 3 strokes —
40 氵 "three-dots water"
41 忄 (side-) heart
42 丬 bed
43 亡 to flee
44 广 lean-to
45 宀 roof
46 门 gate
47 辶 halt
48 工 work
49 土 (士) earth (knight)
50 艹 grass
51 廾 clasp
52 大 big
53 尢 lame
54 寸 thumb
55 扌 (side-) hand
56 弋 dart
57 巾 cloth
58 口 mouth
59 囗 surround
60 山 mountain
61 屮 sprout
62 彳 step
63 彡 streaks
64 夕 dusk
65 夂 follow, slow
66 丸 bullet
67 尸 corpse
68 饣 (side-) food
69 犭 (side-) dog
70 彐 (⺕,彑) pig's head
71 弓 bow
72 己 (巳) self
73 女 woman
74 子 (孑) child
75 马 horse
76 幺 coil
77 纟 (糸) silk
78 巛 river
79 小 (⺌) small

— 4 strokes —
80 灬 "fire-dots"
81 心 heart
82 斗 peck
83 火 fire
84 文 pattern
85 方 square
86 户 door
87 礻 (side-) sign
88 王 king
89 龶 "top of 青"
90 天 (夭) heaven (tender)
91 韦 walk off
92 耂 "top of 老"
93 廿 twenty
94 木 tree
95 不 not
96 犬 dog
97 歹 chip
98 瓦 tile
99 牙 tooth
100 车 car
101 戈 lance
102 止 toe
103 日 sun
104 曰 say
105 中 middle
106 贝 cowrie
107 见 see
108 父 father
109 气 breath
110 牛 cow
111 手 hand
112 毛 fur
113 攵 knock
114 片 slice
115 斤 ax
116 爪 (⺥) claws
117 尺 foot (length)
118 月 moon/meat
119 殳 club
120 欠 yawn
121 风 wind
122 氏 clan
123 比 compare
124 肀 "top of 聿"
125 水 water

— 5 strokes —
126 立 stand
127 疒 sick
128 穴 cave
129 衤 (side-) gown
130 𡗗 "top of 春"
131 玉 jade
132 示 sign
133 去 go
134 龷 "top of 劳"
135 甘 sweet
136 石 rock
137 龙 dragon
138 戊 halberd
139 龸 "top of 常"
140 业 business
141 目 eye
142 田 field
143 由 from
144 申 stretch
145 罒 net
146 皿 dish
147 钅 (side-) gold
148 矢 arrow
149 禾 grain
150 白 white
151 瓜 melon
152 鸟 bird
153 皮 skin
154 癶 back
155 矛 spear
156 疋 bolt

— 6 strokes —
157 羊 (⺶, ⺷) sheep
158 龹 roll
159 米 rice
160 齐 line-up
161 衣 gown
162 亦 (亦) also
163 耳 ear
164 臣 bureaucrat
165 𢦏 "top of 栽"
166 西 (覀) cover (west)
167 朿 thorn
168 亚 inferior
169 而 beard
170 页 head
171 至 reach
172 光 light
173 虍 tiger
174 虫 bug
175 缶 crock
176 耒 plow
177 舌 tongue
178 竹 (⺮) bamboo
179 臼 mortar
180 自 small nose
181 血 blood
182 舟 boat
183 羽 wings
184 艮 (𥃭) stubborn

— 7 strokes —
185 言 words
186 辛 bitter
187 辰 early
188 麦 wheat
189 走 walk
190 赤 red
191 豆 flask
192 束 bundle
193 酉 wine
194 豕 pig
195 里 village
196 足 foot
197 采 cull
198 豸 snake
199 谷 valley
200 身 torso
201 角 horn

— 8 strokes —
202 青 green
203 龺 "side of 朝"
204 雨 rain
205 非 wrong
206 齿 teeth
207 黾 toad
208 隹 dove
209 金 gold
210 鱼 fish

— 9 strokes —
211 音 tone
212 革 hide
213 是 be
214 骨 bone
215 香 scent
216 鬼 ghost
217 食 food

— 10 strokes —
218 高 tall
219 鬲 cauldron
220 髟 hair

— 11 strokes —
221 麻 hemp
222 鹿 deer

— 12 strokes —
223 黑 black

— 13 strokes —
224 鼓 drum
225 鼠 mouse
226 鼻 big nose

Houghton Mifflin

Texas Math

count

HOUGHTON MIFFLIN BOSTON

Printed in the U.S.A.

GRADE 1 STUDENT RESOURCES VOLUME

ISBN-13: 978-0-618-98663-7

ISBN-10: 0-618-98663-4

GRADE 1 STUDENT BOOK

ISBN-13: 978-0-618-82746-6

ISBN-10: 0-618-82746-3

8 9 10 11 12 13 14 15 1678 17 16 15 14 13 12
4500361588

Houghton Mifflin

Texas Math

Authors & Consultants

Authors

Kay Frantz
Math Consultant
Frisco, TX

Mary Alice Hatchett
K-12 Math Consultant
Georgetown, TX

Dr. Matt Larson
Curriculum Specialist for Mathematics
Lincoln Public Schools
Lincoln, NE

Dr. Miriam A. Leiva
Bonnie E. Cone Distinguished Professor Emerita
Professor of Mathematics Emerita
University of North Carolina
Charlotte, NC

Dr. Jean M. Shaw
Professor Emerita of Curriculum and Instruction
University of Mississippi
Oxford, MS

Dr. Lee Stiff
Professor of Mathematics Education
North Carolina State University
Raleigh, NC

Dr. Bruce Vogeli
Clifford Brewster Upton Professor of Mathematics
Teachers College, Columbia University
New York, NY

Consultants

Mental Math Strategies

Greg Tang
Author and Mathematics Consultant
Belmont, MA

English Language Learners

Dr. Joyce F. Fischer
Principle Investigator,
Mathematics for English Language Learners Initiative
Assistant Professor of Mathematics
Texas State University San Marcos
San Marcos, TX

Dr. Russell M. Gersten
Executive Director, Institutional Research Group & Professor Emeritus
College of Education, University of Oregon
Long Beach, CA

Language and Vocabulary

Dr. Shane Templeton
Foundation Professor, Department of Educational Specialties
University of Nevada at Reno
Reno, NV

Special Projects

Catherine Valentino
Author-in-Residence
Houghton Mifflin
West Kingston, Rhode Island

Strategic Consultant

Dr. Liping Ma
Senior Scholar
Carnegie Foundation for the Advancement of Technology
Palo Alto, California

Texas Reviewers

Grade K

Theresa Burke-Garcia
Walnut Creek Elementary School
Austin, TX

Wendi Groves
McWhorter Elementary School
Lubbock, TX

Jana Hughey
McWhorter Elementary School
Lubbock, TX

Elizabeth Maynes
Baskin Academy
San Antonio, TX

Kimberly Smith
Quest Academy
McAllen, TX

Mary Zinno
DeZavala Elementary School
Fort Worth, TX

Grade 1

Juanita Evans
Walzem Elementary School
San Antonio, TX

Lindsay Loucks
Lee Britain Elementary School
Irving, TX

Priscilla O'Connor
Olmos Elementary School
San Antonio, TX

Sara Puente
Castaneda Elementary School
McAllen, TX

Robin Randall
Quest Academy
McAllen, TX

Grade 2

Jessica Martinez
Japhet Elementary School
San Antonio, TX

Jana Underwood
Waverly Park Elementary School
Fort Worth, TX

Grade 3

Ashley Adamson
McWhorter Elementary School
Lubbock, TX

Dinorah Bores
Pecan Springs Elementary School
Austin, TX

Reba Brown
Alief Independent School District
Houston, TX

Kerry Haupert
Martha Mead Elementary School
San Antonio, TX

Idida McCasland
Quest Academy
McAllen, TX

Kelly Miksch
Longs Creek Elementary School
San Antonio, TX

These people helped make this book the best it can be.

Texas Reviewers

Grade 4

Elizabeth Flores-Vidales
Glen Cove Elementary School
El Paso, TX

Kasie Kline
Mittelstädt Elementary School
Spring, TX

Theresa Luera
Castaneda Elementary School
McAllen, TX

Toni Pouttu
Martha Reid Elementary School
Arlington, TX

Grade 5

Rana Boone
School at Post Oak
Houston, TX

Mathilda Griffith
Will Rogers Elementary School
San Antonio, TX

José Márquez
Cedar Grove Elementary School
El Paso, TX

Maria Romero
North Hi Mount Elementary School
Fort Worth, TX

Norma Vogel
McAuliffe Elementary School
McAllen, TX

Across Grades

Nicola Britton
UT Austin
Austin, TX

Diann Dillon
Viking Hills Elementary School
Waco, TX

Maria Jazinski
McAuliffe Elementary School
McAllen, TX

Donna Johnson
Sam Rosen Elementary School
Fort Worth, TX

Matthew Osher
Mary Hull Elementary School
San Antonio, TX

Virginia Robertson-Baker
Carver Academy
Amarillo, TX

Nancy Sipes
Bonham Elementary School
Midland, TX

Bonnie Vangsnes
Quest Academy
McAllen, TX

They really love teaching math, too.

TEKS and TAKS

What are the TEKS and TAKS?

- TEKS means Texas Essential Knowledge and Skills.
- The TEKS are what you will learn this year.
- TAKS means Texas Assessment of Knowledge and Skills.
- The TAKS is a test you will take in Grade 3.
- You can start getting ready now.

How will this book help you succeed?

It's easy as one, two, three.

1. Look for **TEKS** and TAKS in this book.
2. Do your best work. Ask questions.
3. Use the TAKS Success pages on pages TS1–TS12.

Doing well feels terrific!

Education Place
Visit **www.eduplace.com/txmap/** for **Test-Taking Tips** and more **TAKS Practice.**

TAKS Objective 1

Number, Operation, and Quantitative Reasoning

	TEKS You Will Learn	Some Places to Look
(1.1)	The student uses whole numbers to describe and compare quantities. The student is expected to:	
(A)	compare and order whole numbers up to 99 (less than, greater than, or equal to) using sets of concrete objects and pictorial models;	Lessons 2.3, 2.4, 3.3, 3.4, 3.5, 15.1, 15.2, 15.3 Science p. 34; Social Studies p. 294; Math Works pp. 49, 293
(B)	create sets of tens and ones using concrete objects to describe, compare, and order whole numbers;	Lessons 13.1, 13.2, 13.3, 13.4, 14.1, 14.2, 14.3, 14.4, 15.1, 15.2, 15.3, 15.4 Technology p. 257; Unit 6 Game
(C)	identify individual coins by name and value and describe relationships among them; and	Lessons 20.1, 20.2, 20.3, 20.4, 20.5 Social Studies p. 392; Math Music p. 410
(D)	read and write numbers to 99 to describe sets of concrete objects.	Lessons 2.1, 2.2, 2.5, 3.1, 3.2, 13.1, 13.2, 13.3, 13.4, 14.1, 14.2, 14.3, 14.4 Science p. 34; Math Music p. 50; Unit 6 Game
(1.2)	The student uses pairs of whole numbers to describe fractional parts of whole objects or sets of objects. The student is expected to:	
(A)	separate a whole into two, three, or four equal parts and use appropriate language to describe the parts such as three out of four equal parts; and	Lessons 10.1, 10.2, 10.3 Math Music p. 192
(B)	use appropriate language to describe part of a set such as three out of the eight crayons are red.	Lesson 10.4 Math Works p. 191; Teacher Activity p. 189A
(1.3)	The student recognizes and solves problems in addition and subtraction situations. The student is expected to:	
(A)	model and create addition and subtraction problem situations with concrete objects and write corresponding number sentences; and	Lessons 4.1, 4.2, 4.5, 5.1, 5.2, 5.5, 7.6, 18.5, 24.1, 24.5, 25.5 Math Music p. 92 Science pp. 74, 478
(B)	use concrete and pictorial models to apply basic addition and subtraction facts (up to 9 + 9 = 18 and 18 - 9 = 9).	Lessons 4.3, 4.4, 4.5, 5.3, 5.4, 5.5, 6.1, 6.3, 6.4, 6.5, 7.1, 7.4, 7.5, 17.1, 17.2, 17.3, 17.4, 18.1, 18.3, 18.4, 19.1, 19.2, 19.3, 19.4, 24.2, 24.3, 24.4 Math Music p. 496; Science p. 350; Social Studies pp. 116, 334 Units 3, 7, 10 Game

TAKS Objective 2

Patterns, Relationships, and Algebraic Thinking

	TEKS You Will Learn	Some Places to Look
(1.4)	The student uses repeating patterns and additive patterns to make predictions. The student is expected to:	
	identify, describe, and extend concrete and pictorial patterns in order to make predictions and solve problems.	Lessons 1.1, 1.2, 1.3, 1.4, 1.5, 13.5 Technology p. 15 Social Studies p. 16
(1.5)	The student recognizes patterns in numbers and operations. The student is expected to:	
(A)	use patterns to skip count by twos, fives, and tens;	Lessons 16.1, 16.3, 16.4 16.5, 20.2, 20.3 Math Music p. 312; Science p. 276; Unit 8 Game
(B)	find patterns in numbers, including odd and even;	Lesson 16.2 Challenge p. 311; Spiral Review p. 352
(C)	compare and order whole numbers using place value;	Lessons 15.1, 15.2, 15.3, 15.4 Science p. 276; Technology p. 257; Social Studies p. 258
(D)	use patterns to develop strategies to solve basic addition and basic subtraction problems; and	Lessons 6.3, 6.4, 7.1, 17.1, 17.2, 18.2, 24.3 Math Music p. 368; Technology pp. 73, 115
(E)	identify patterns in related addition and subtraction sentences (fact families for sums to 18) such as 2 + 3 = 5, 3 + 2 = 5, 5 - 2 = 3, 5 - 3 = 2).	Lessons 7.4, 7.5, 19.1, 19.2, 19.3, 19.4, 25.3, 25.4, 25.5 Math Music p. 136

TAKS Objective 3

Geometry and Spatial Reasoning

	TEKS You Will Learn	Some Places to Look
(1.6)	The student uses attributes to identify two- and three-dimensional geometric figures. The student compares and contrasts two- and three-dimensional geometric figures or both. The student is expected to:	
(A)	describe and identify two-dimensional geometric figures, including circles, triangles, rectangles, and squares (a special type of rectangle);	Lesson 8.2 Science p. 176 Social Studies p. 160 Technology p. 159
(B)	describe and identify three-dimensional geometric figures, including spheres, rectangular prisms (including cubes), cylinders, and cones;	Lessons 9.2, 9.3, 9.5
(C)	describe and identify two- and three-dimensional geometric figures in order to sort them according to a given attribute using informal and formal language; and	Lessons 8.1, 8.3, 9.1, 9.3, 9.4 Unit 4 Game
(D)	use concrete models to combine two-dimensional geometric figures to make new geometric figures.	Lessons 8.4, 8.5 Social Studies p. 160

TAKS Objective 4
Measurement

TEKS You Will Learn		Some Places to Look
(1.7)	The student directly compares the attributes of length, area, weight/mass, capacity, and temperature. The student uses comparative language to solve problems and answer questions. The student selects and uses nonstandard units to describe length. The student is expected to:	
(A)	estimate and measure length using nonstandard units such as paper clips or sides of color tiles;	Lessons 22.2, 22.5 Challenge pp. 433, 453
(B)	compare and order two or more concrete objects according to length (from longest to shortest);	Lesson 22.1 Science p 434; Unit 9 Game;Unit 9 Take-Home Book
(C)	describe the relationship between the size of the unit and the number of units needed to measure the length of an object;	Lessons 22.2, 22.5 Challenge p. 453
(D)	compare and order the area of two or more two-dimensional surfaces (from covers the most to covers the least);	Lessons 22.3, 22.4 Teacher Activity p. 429A
(E)	compare and order two or more containers according to capacity (from holds the most to holds the least);	Lessons 23.3, 23.4 Math Music p. 454
(F)	compare and order two or more objects according to weight/mass (from heaviest to lightest); and	Lessons 23.1, 23.2 Math Music p. 454
(G)	compare and order two or more objects according to relative temperature (from hottest to coldest).	Lessons 23.5, 23.6 Challenge p. 495
(1.8)	The student understands that time can be measured. The student uses time to describe and compare situations. The student is expected to:	
(A)	order three or more events according to duration; and	Lessons 21.1, 21.2 Teacher Activity p. 401A
(B)	read time to the hour and half-hour using analog and digital clocks.	Lessons 21.3, 21.4, 21.5

TAKS Objective 5

Probability and Statistics

	TEKS You Will Learn	Some Places to Look
(1.9)	The student displays data in an organized form. The student is expected to:	
(A)	collect and sort data; and	Lessons 11.2, 11.5, 12.1, 12.4, 12.5
(B)	use organized data to construct real-object graphs, picture graphs, and bar-type graphs.	Lessons 11.1, 11.3, 11.5 Math Music p. 234
(1.10)	The student uses information from organized data. The student is expected to:	
(A)	draw conclusions and answer questions using information organized in real-object graphs, picture graphs, and bar-type graphs; and	Lessons 11.1, 11.3, 11.4, 11.5, 12.1, 12.2 Technology p. 215
(B)	identify events as certain or impossible such as drawing a red crayon from a bag of green crayons.	Lessons 12.3, 12.4, 12.5

TAKS Objective 6

Underlying Processes and Mathematical Tools

TEKS You Will Learn	Some Places to Look
(1.11) The student applies Grade 1 mathematics to solve problems connected to everyday experiences and activities in and outside of school. The student is expected to:	
(A) identify mathematics in everyday situations;	Lessons and Take-Home Books show math in everyday life. Lessons 5.5, 7.6, 10.5, 11.5, 12.5, 14.5, 15.5, 21.5, 22.5, 23.6, 24.5, 25.5 Science pp. 176, 478; Social Studies pp. 116, 160; Math Works pp. 49, 191, 293, 367
(B) solve problems with guidance that incorporates the processes of understanding the problem, making a plan, carrying out the plan, and evaluating the solution for reasonableness;	Problem Solving Handbook pp. PS1, PS14 Lessons 1.5, 2.5, 4.5, 6.5, 8.5, 12.5, 14.5, 16.5, 17.5, 20.5, 21.5, 22.5, 24.5
(C) select or develop an appropriate problem-solving plan or strategy including drawing a picture, looking for a pattern, systematic guessing and checking, or acting it out in order to solve a problem; and	Problem Solving Handbook pp. PS3, PS5, PS7, PS9, PS11, PS13 Lessons 1.5, 2.5, 4.5, 6.5, 8.5, 12.5, 13.5, 14.5, 15.5, 16.5, 17.5, 19.5, 20.5, 21.5, 22.5, 24.5 Science p. 276; Social Studies pp. 16, 392
(D) use tools such as real objects, manipulatives, and technology to solve problems.	Lessons 4.5, 5.5, 7.6, 8.5, 9.5, 12.5, 14.5, 15.5, 18.5, 20.5, 22.5, 24.5 Technology pp. 15, 73, 115, 477
(1.12) The student communicates about Grade 1 mathematics using informal language. The student is expected to:	
(A) explain and record observations using objects, words, pictures, numbers, and technology; and	Lessons 1.1, 1.2, 1.3, 3.5, 4.1, 4.2, 4.5, 5.1, 5.4, 5.5, 6.5, 7.6, 9.4, 11.5 Technology pp. 15, 73, 115, 257, 333, 391, 477
(B) relate informal language to mathematical language and symbols.	Lessons 4.2, 5.2, 5.3, 9.1, 15.1, 15.3, 15.4, 20.1, 22.1
(1.13) The student uses logical reasoning. The student is expected to:	
justify his or her thinking using objects, words, pictures, numbers, and technology.	In Math Talk and Unit Wrap Ups children can justify their thinking. Lessons 1.1, 1.2, 1.3, 4.5, 5.4, 5.5, 7.6, 15.5, 22.5, 23.6; Technology pp. 73, 115, 257; Social Studies p. 334

Name ______________________________

Unit 1 This page includes skills you learned in Unit 1.

1. Katie plants flowers. Which flower comes next in the pattern?

 ○  ○  ○  ○

TEKS 1.4

2. Justin needs 10 apples. Which basket should he buy?

TAKS TIP
Count the apples in each basket.

 ○ 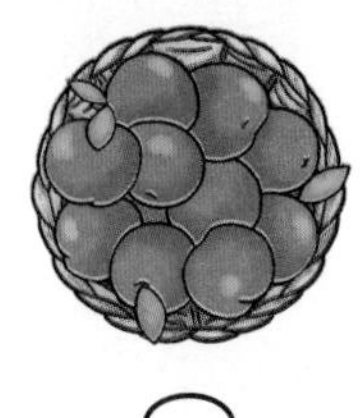 ○  ○  ○

TEKS 1.1A

3. Andy grows beans. Which vine has the fewest beans?

 ○  ○  ○  ○

TEKS K.1A

4. Which shows the numbers in order from greatest to least?

12, 6, 3 ○ 6, 3, 12 ○ 3, 6, 12 ○ 6, 12, 3 ○

TEKS 1.5B

Unit 2 This page includes skills you learned in Units 1–2.

1. 4 children are on the swings.
A greater number of children wait for the swings.
Which shows the number of children waiting?

○ ○ ○ ○

TEKS 1.1A

2. Which number tells how many buildings are in the picture?

8 ○ | 11 ○ | 2 ○ | 12 ○

TEKS 1.1D

3. Joseph and his mom see ducks.
Which shows how many ducks in all?

6 − 5 = 1 ○ | 6 + 5 = 11 ○ | 6 + 6 = 12 ○ | 6 + 5 = 10 ○

TEKS 1.3B

4. Which number comes next in the pattern?

3, 2, 3, 2, 3, 2

TAKS TIP
Look at the pattern made by the numbers.

1 ○ | 2 ○ | 3 ○ | 5 ○

TEKS 1.4

Name ____________________

Unit 3 This page includes skills you learned in Units 1–3.

1. Jill catches 8 fireflies. Max catches the same number of fireflies. Which jar shows the number of fireflies that Jill catches?

TAKS TIP
Same number means equal to.

 ○  ○  ○  ○

TEKS 1.1A

2. A spider has 8 legs. An ant has 6 legs. How many legs are there in all?

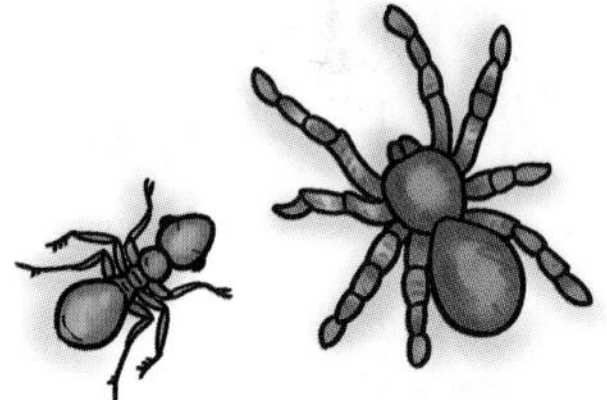

2	10	14	15
○	○	○	○

TEKS 1.3B

3. Maya sees 5 cocoons. Jared sees 9 cocoons. Which shows how many cocoons there are in all?

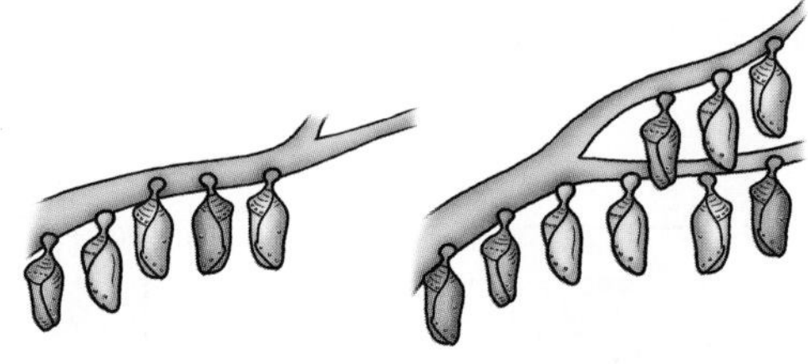

$5 + 9 = 14$	$14 - 5 = 9$	$9 + 5 = 15$	$9 - 5 = 4$
○	○	○	○

TEKS 1.3B

4. Miguel sees 9 butterflies. 3 fly away. How many butterflies are left?

3	6	9	12
○	○	○	○

TEKS 1.3B

Unit 4 This page includes skills you learned in Units 1–4.

1. Marisel draws a house with 10 windows. She erases 4 windows. How many windows are left?

4 ○ 6 ○ 10 ○ 14 ○

TEKS 1.3B

2. Mateo and his dad bake 4 square cookies and 6 round cookies. Which shows the cookies they bake?

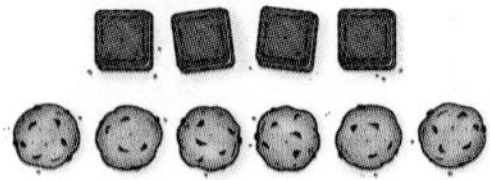 ○

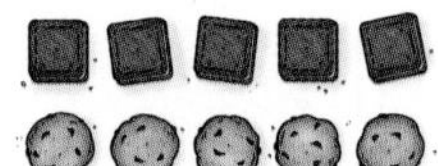
 ○

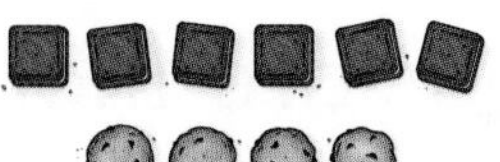
 ○

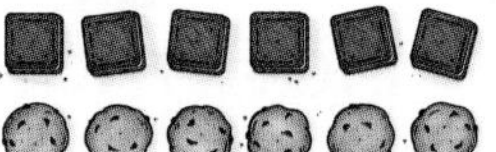
 ○

TEKS 1.3B

3. Which sign is shaped like a triangle?

TAKS TIP
A triangle has 3 sides.

 ○

○

○

○

TEKS 1.6A

4. Anna draws a pattern. Which comes next?

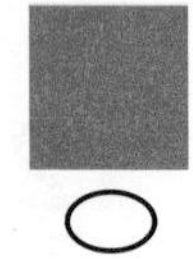 ○

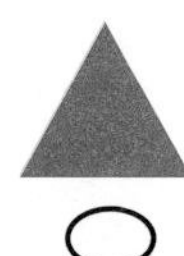 ○

 ○

 ○

TEKS 1.4

Name ______________________________

Unit 5 This page includes skills you learned in Units 1–5.

1. Brendan has 9 computer games. He buys 4 more games. How many games does he have now?

4 ○ 9 ○ 13 ○ 14 ○

TEKS 1.3B

2. Juan eats an ice cream. Which figure looks like the cone?

 ○ 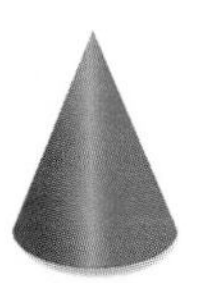 ○  ○  ○

TEKS 1.6B

3. Amanda goes on 10 rides at the park. Betsy rides an amount equal to Amanda. Glenn goes on 6 rides. Who went on the fewest rides?

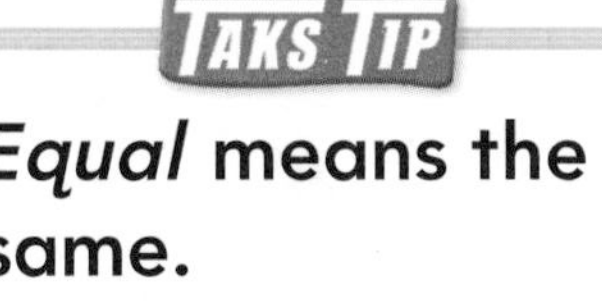

TAKS TIP

Equal **means the same.**

Amanda ○ Betsy ○ Glenn ○ No one ○

TEKS 1.1A

4. Which spinner shows 3 out of 4 equal parts colored blue?

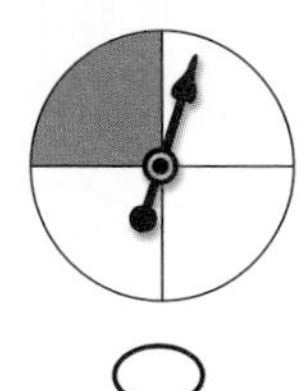 ○ 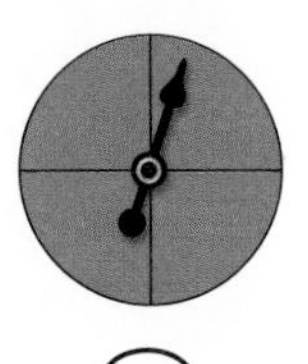 ○ 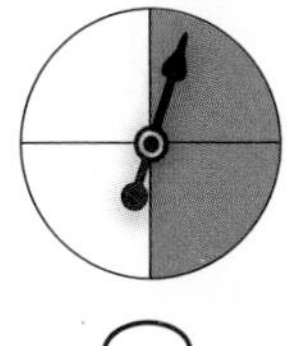 ○ 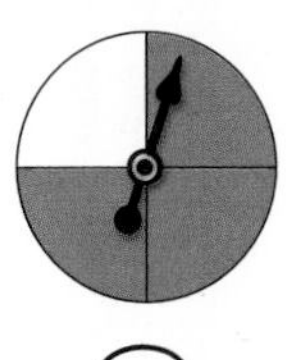 ○

TEKS 1.2A

Unit 6 This page includes skills you learned in Units 1–6.

1. Nadia sells apples, bananas, and oranges. How many apples does she sell?

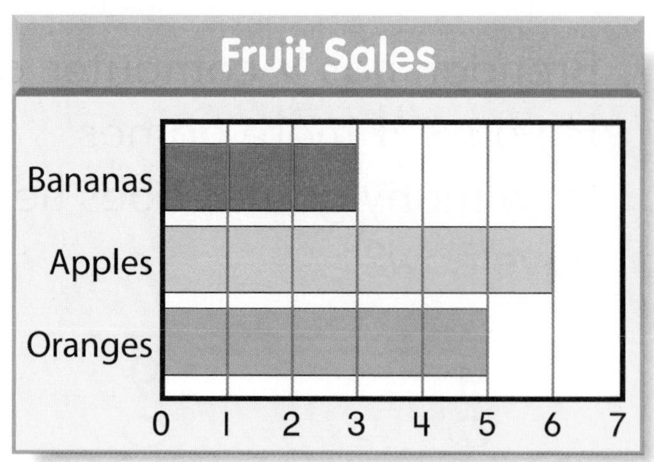

3 ○ 5 ○ 6 ○ 8 ○

TEKS 1.10A

2. Which group shows 2 red balls out of 6 balls?

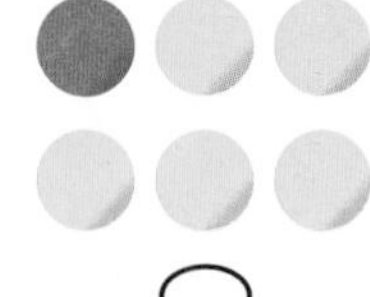 ○ 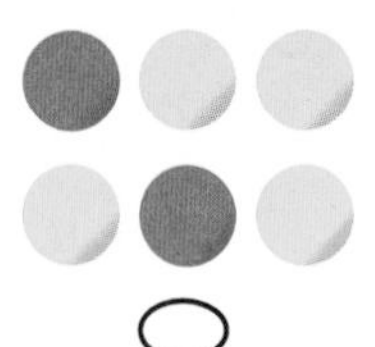 ○ 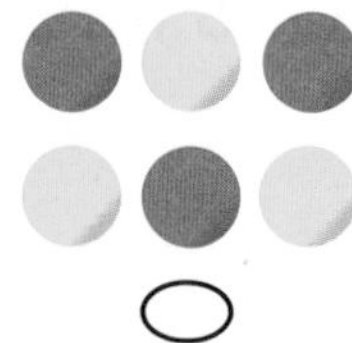 ○ 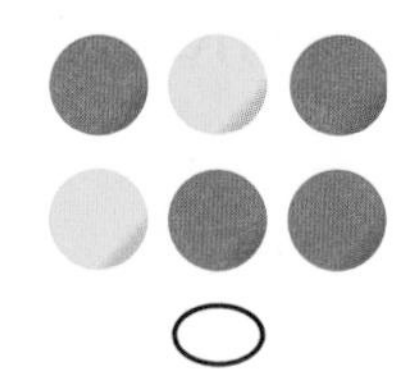 ○

TEKS 1.2B

3. Which is **NOT** in the same fact family as

$7 + 5 = 12$?

$12 - 7 = 5$ ○ $7 + 5 = 12$ ○ $12 - 6 = 6$ ○ $5 + 7 = 12$ ○

TEKS 1.5E

4. Which model shows 49?

TAKS TIP
Remember, count a tens block as 10 ones.

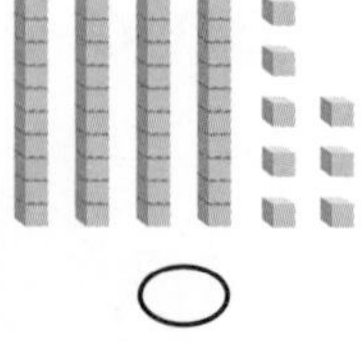 ○ 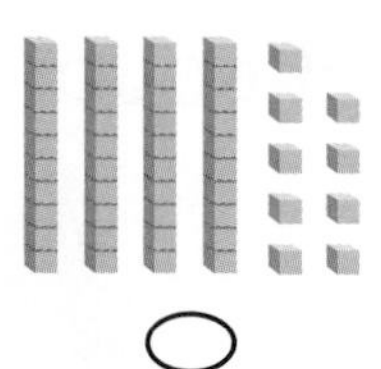 ○ 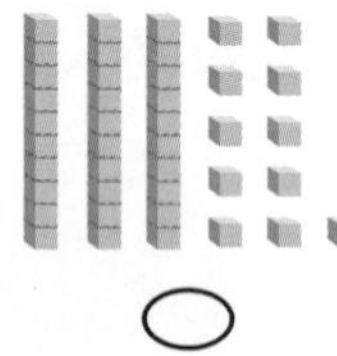 ○ 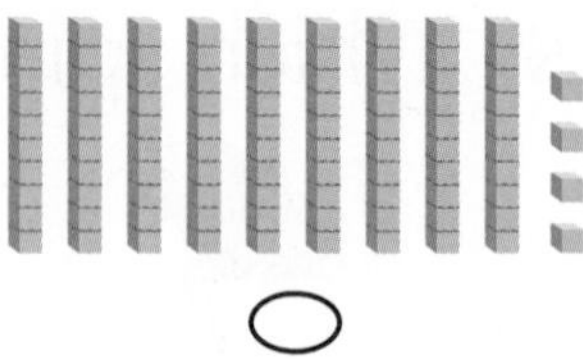 ○

TEKS 1.1A

Name ______________________________

Unit 7 These pages include skills you learned in Units 1–7.

1. Emily has more than 52 shells.
   She has fewer than 54 shells.
   How many shells does Emily have?

51 ○ 53 ○ 55 ○ 56 ○

TEKS 1.5C

2. Which figure has 0 sides and 0 corners?

TAKS TIP
A corner is formed when 2 sides meet.

○ ○ ○ ○

TEKS 1.6A

3. Which figure is made up of square faces?

○ ○ ○ ○

TEKS 1.6C

4. Which number does not belong?

5, 7, 9, 11, 12, 13

TAKS TIP
Think about odd numbers and even numbers.

5 ○ 12 ○ 13 ○ 11 ○

TEKS 1.5B

5. Vincent wants a piece of fruit. Which fruit is it impossible for him to choose?

peach	banana	apple	strawberry
○	○	○	○

TEKS 1.10B

6. Which number comes next?

20, 25, 30, 35, 40, 45, 50, ■

55	52	65	70
○	○	○	○

TEKS 1.5A

7. Mrs. Ebony took a class survey. The graph shows the sports they play. Each 웃 stands for one child. Which sport do most children play?

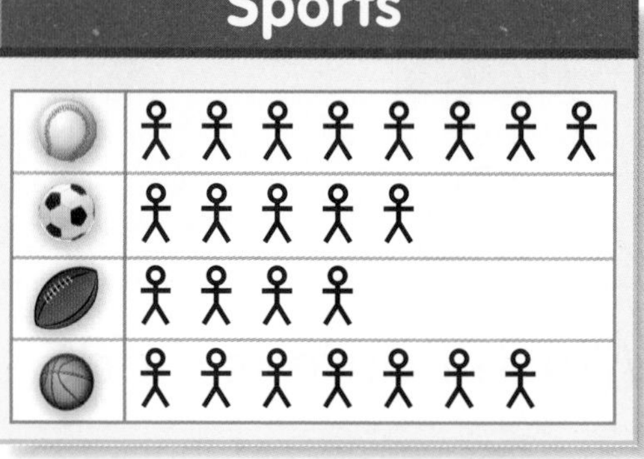

 ○  ○  ○   ○

TEKS 1.10A

8. Mr. Minn took a survey. The graph shows the children's pets. Each 웃 stands for one child. How many children have a dog?

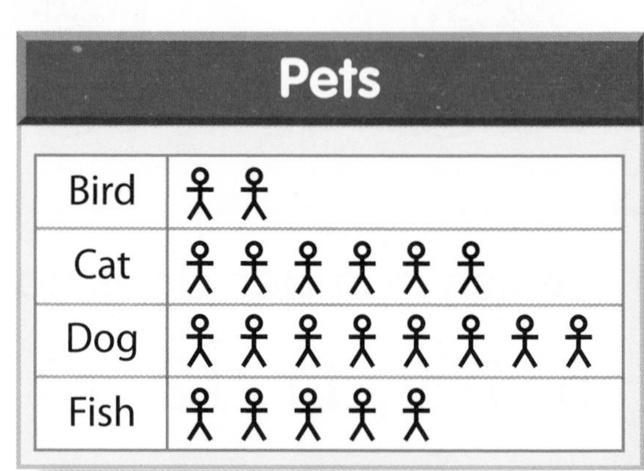

2	5	6	8
○	○	○	○

TEKS 1.10A

Name ______________________________

Unit 8 This page includes skills you learned in Units 1–8.

1. Adam makes a snack. He has 4 crackers. He puts cheese on 2 crackers. Which shows Adam's snack?

TAKS TIP
Look for the picture that shows 2 out of 4 crackers with cheese.

○ ○ ○ ○

TEKS 1.2A

2. Amanda sorts figures. In which group should she put the cone?

All flat surfaces	Curved surfaces and flat surfaces	All curved surfaces	No curved surfaces
○	○	○	○

TEKS 1.6B, 1.6C

3. Brian has more than 56 baseball cards. He has fewer than 58. How many baseball cards does Brian have?

55	56	57	58
○	○	○	○

TEKS 1.5C

4. What figure can be made if two squares are joined together?

cube	triangle	rectangle	circle
○	○	○	○

TEKS 1.6D

Unit 9 This page includes skills you learned in Units 1–9.

1. How many nickels equal one quarter?

TAKS TIP
A nickel is worth 5¢.

1	4	5	25
○	○	○	○

TEKS 1.1C

2. Which pizza shows 3 slices out of 4 slices with pepperoni?

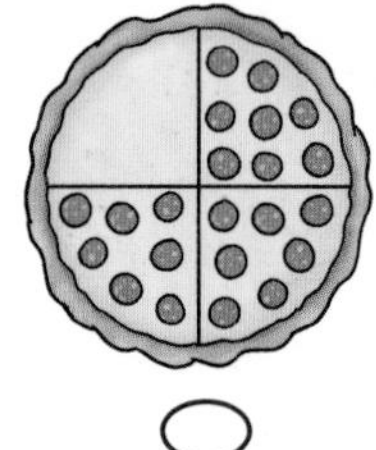 ○
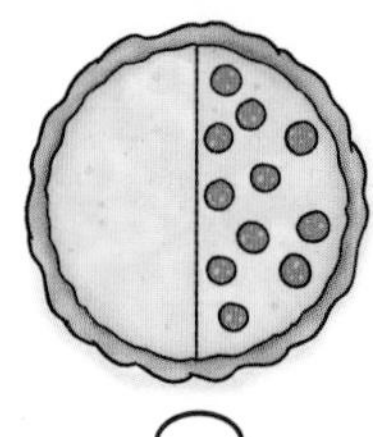 ○
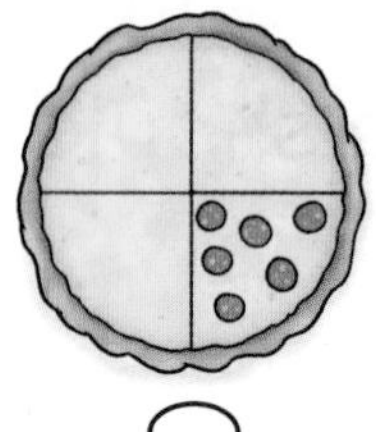 ○
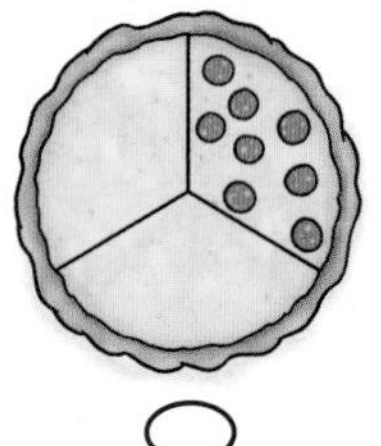 ○

TEKS 1.2B

3. Which is the missing number sentence in the fact family shown below?

$12 + 3 = 15$ $3 + 12 = 15$ $15 - 12 = 3$

$12 - 3 = 9$	$15 - 3 = 12$	$15 + 3 = 18$	$15 + 12 = 27$
○	○	○	○

TEKS 1.5E

4. Matthew has 4 bags of marbles. From which bag is he certain to pull out a red marble?

 ○
 ○
 ○
 ○

TEKS 1.10B

Name ______________________________

Unit 10 These pages include skills you learned in Units 1–10.

TAKS TIP
Half past seven is another way to say 7:30.

1. Michael wakes up at half past seven. Which clock shows the time he wakes up?

○ ○ ○ ○

TEKS 1.7B

2. About how many color tiles would be the same length as this fence?

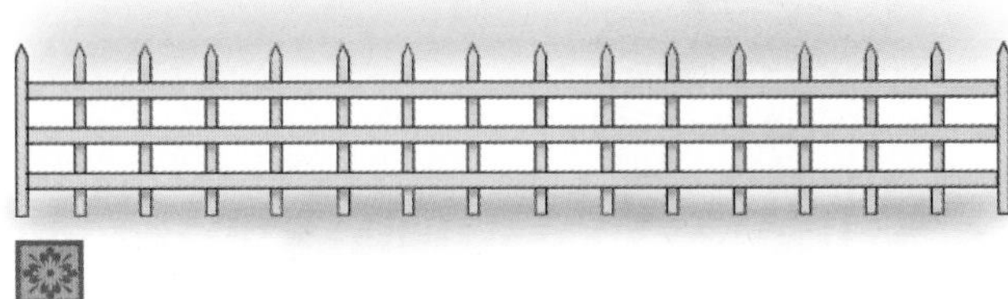

about 8 ○ about 10 ○ about 15 ○ about 20 ○

TEKS 1.7A

3. Pedro has a pencil, a paintbrush, and an eraser. He puts them in order from longest to shortest. Start at the top. Which shows the correct order?

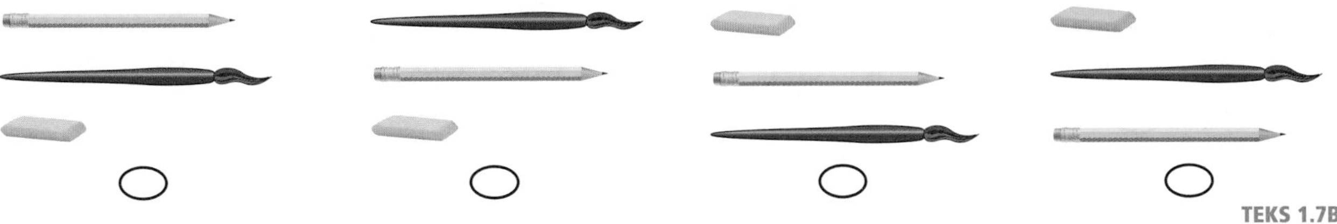

○ ○ ○ ○

TEKS 1.7B

4. Jeremy wants to measure the length of his desk using the fewest number of objects. Which object should he use?

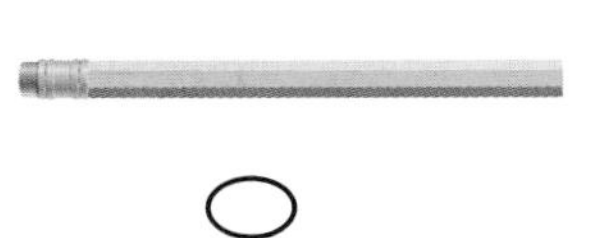 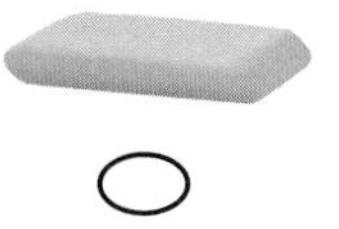 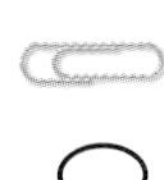 

○ ○ ○ ○

TEKS 1.7C

5. Jimmy's mom bought 4 rugs for his room.
Which color rug will cover the most area of the floor?

red ◯ green ◯ blue ◯ orange ◯

TEKS 1.7D

6. Which of the following containers will hold the least amount of water?

◯

◯

◯

◯

TEKS 1.7E

7. Which shows the objects in order from the heaviest to the lightest?

◯

◯

◯

◯

TEKS 1.7F

8. Anya buys lunch.
She buys the hottest item.
What did Anya buy for lunch?

◯

◯

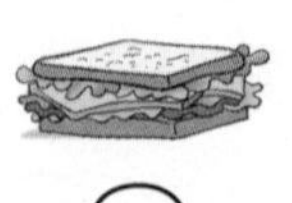
◯

◯

TEKS 1.7G

Using the Table of Contents

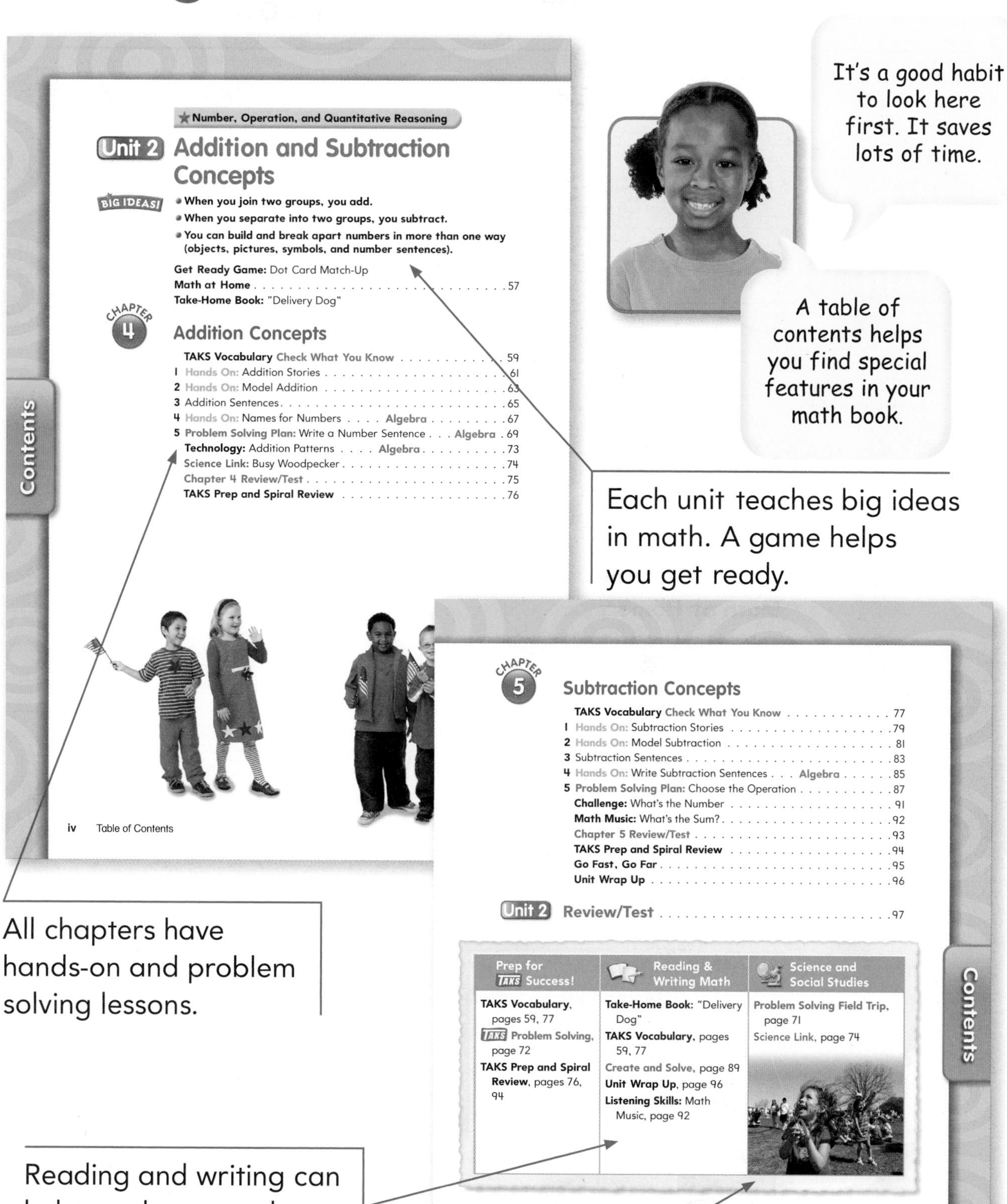

Number, Operation, and Quantitative Reasoning
Unit 2 Addition and Subtraction Concepts
BIG IDEAS!
When you join two groups, you add.
When you separate into two groups, you subtract.
You can build and break apart numbers in more than one way (objects, pictures, symbols, and number sentences).
Get Ready Game: Dot Card Match-Up
Math at Home . . . 57
Take-Home Book: "Delivery Dog"
CHAPTER 4
Addition Concepts
TAKS Vocabulary Check What You Know . . . 59
1 Hands On: Addition Stories . . . 61
2 Hands On: Model Addition . . . 63
3 Addition Sentences . . . 65
4 Hands On: Names for Numbers . . . Algebra . . . 67
5 Problem Solving Plan: Write a Number Sentence . . . Algebra . 69
Technology: Addition Patterns . . . Algebra . . . 73
Science Link: Busy Woodpecker . . . 74
Chapter 4 Review/Test . . . 75
TAKS Prep and Spiral Review . . . 76
iv Table of Contents
Contents
CHAPTER 5
Subtraction Concepts
TAKS Vocabulary Check What You Know . . . 77
1 Hands On: Subtraction Stories . . . 79
2 Hands On: Model Subtraction . . . 81
3 Subtraction Sentences . . . 83
4 Hands On: Write Subtraction Sentences . . . Algebra . . . 85
5 Problem Solving Plan: Choose the Operation . . . 87
Challenge: What's the Number . . . 91
Math Music: What's the Sum? . . . 92
Chapter 5 Review/Test . . . 93
TAKS Prep and Spiral Review . . . 94
Go Fast, Go Far . . . 95
Unit Wrap Up . . . 96
Unit 2 Review/Test . . . 97
Prep for TAKS Success!
TAKS Vocabulary, pages 59, 77
TAKS Problem Solving, page 72
TAKS Prep and Spiral Review, pages 76, 94
Reading & Writing Math
Take-Home Book: "Delivery Dog"
TAKS Vocabulary, pages 59, 77
Create and Solve, page 89
Unit Wrap Up, page 96
Listening Skills: Math Music, page 92
Science and Social Studies
Problem Solving Field Trip, page 71
Science Link, page 74
Contents
Table of Contents v
It's a good habit to look here first. It saves lots of time.
A table of contents helps you find special features in your math book.
Each unit teaches big ideas in math. A game helps you get ready.
All chapters have hands-on and problem solving lessons.
Reading and writing can help you learn math.
Field Trips let you do math in special places in Texas.

Contents

Table of Contents

Contents

Numbers 10 Through 20

Prep for TAKS Success!	 Reading & Writing Math	 Science and Social Studies
TAKS Vocabulary, pages 3, 19, 37 TAKS **Problem Solving**, page 32 **TAKS Prep and Spiral Review**, pages 18, 36, 52	**Take-Home Book:** "Frog's Garden" **TAKS Vocabulary**, pages 3, 19, 37 **Create and Solve**, page 47 **Unit Wrap Up**, page 54 **Listening Skills:** Math Music, page 50	**Problem Solving Field Trip**, page 31 **Science Link**, page 34 **Social Studies Link**, page 16 **Math Works**, page 49 

Contents

★ Number, Operation, and Quantitative Reasoning

Unit 2 Addition and Subtraction Concepts

BIG IDEAS!

- When you join two groups, you add.
- When you separate into two groups, you subtract.
- You can build and break apart numbers in more than one way (objects, pictures, symbols, and number sentences).

CHAPTER 4

Addition Concepts

Contents

Subtraction Concepts

Prep for TAKS Success!	 Reading & Writing Math	 Science and Social Studies
TAKS Vocabulary, pages 59, 77 TAKS **Problem Solving**, page 72 **TAKS Prep and Spiral Review**, pages 76, 94	**Take-Home Book:** "Delivery Dog" **TAKS Vocabulary**, pages 59, 77 **Create and Solve**, page 89 **Unit Wrap Up**, page 96 **Listening Skills:** Math Music, page 92	**Problem Solving Field Trip**, page 71 **Science Link**, page 74 

Contents

★ Number, Operation, and Quantitative Reasoning

Unit 3 Addition and Subtraction Facts Through 10

- You can count objects and use pictures to find how many in all or how many are left.
- You can find patterns in basic addition and subtraction facts.
- You can relate addition and subtraction number sentences (fact families).

Addition Facts Through 10

Graphing and Probability

Prep for  Success!	 Reading & Writing Math	Science and Social Studies
TAKS Vocabulary, pages 201, 219 TAKS **Problem Solving**, page 232 **TAKS Prep and Spiral Review**, pages 218, 236	**Take-Home Book:** "My Nature Walks" **TAKS Vocabulary**, pages 201, 219 **Create and Solve**, page 213 **Unit Wrap Up**, page 238 **Listening Skills:** Math Music, page 234 	**Problem Solving Field Trip**, page 231 **Science Link**, page 216 

Contents

★ Number, Operation, and Quantitative Reasoning
★ Patterns, Relationships, and Algebraic Thinking

Unit 6 Numbers Through 99

BIG IDEAS!

- You can model and name the numbers through 99 in more than one way.
- You can count on, count back, or skip count to make a number pattern.
- You can use pairs of numbers to compare and order numbers.

Place Value Through 50

Place Value Through 99

Contents

Chapter 7 Subtraction Facts Through 10

Prep for  Success!	 Reading & Writing Math	Science and Social Studies
TAKS Vocabulary, pages 101, 119 TAKS Problem Solving, page 114 **TAKS Prep and Spiral Review,** pages 118, 138	**Take-Home Book:** "Bug Jamboree" **TAKS Vocabulary**, pages 101, 119 Create and Solve, page 133 **Unit Wrap Up,** page 140 **Listening Skills:** Math Music, page 136	Problem Solving Field Trip, page 113 Social Studies Link, page 116 

Contents

★ Geometry and Spatial Reasoning
★ Number, Operation, and Quantitative Reasoning

Unit 4 Geometry and Fractions

- You can use attributes to describe and identify geometric figures.
- You can sort geometric figures into groups.
- You can separate a whole or a set into equal parts.

Two-Dimensional Figures

Three-Dimensional Figures

Contents

Fractions

Prep for TAKS Success!	 Reading & Writing Math	 Science and Social Studies
TAKS Vocabulary, pages 145, 163, 179 **TAKS Problem Solving**, page 158 **TAKS Prep and Spiral Review**, pages 162, 178, 194	**Take-Home Book:** "City Figures" **TAKS Vocabulary**, pages 145, 163, 179 **Create and Solve**, page 189 **Unit Wrap Up**, page 196 **Listening Skills:** Math Music, page 192	**Problem Solving Field Trip**, page 157 **Science Link**, page 176 **Social Studies Link**, page 160 **Math Works**, page 191 

Contents

★ Probability and Statistics

Data

BIG IDEAS!

- **You can collect and sort data.**
- **You can use graphs and tallies to record and organize data.**
- **You can use data to answer questions and make predictions.**

Graphs and Tables

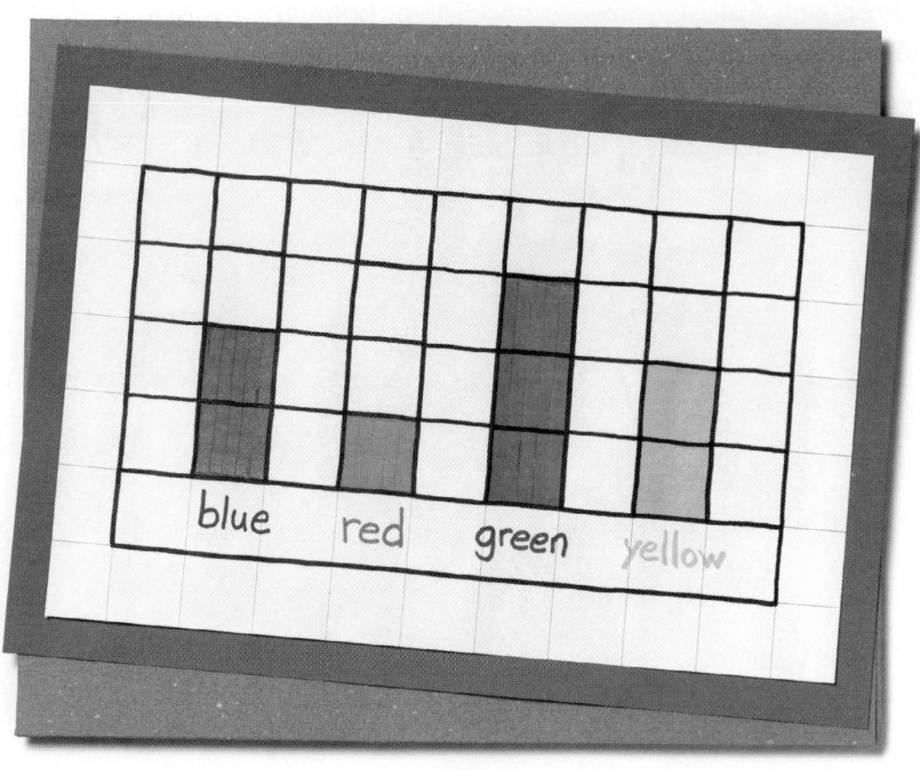

Contents

Compare and Order Numbers

CHAPTER 16

Number Patterns

★ Number, Operation, and Quantitative Reasoning

Unit 7 Addition and Subtraction Facts Through 12

- It doesn't matter in what order you add numbers. The sum is still the same.
- You can relate addition and subtraction number sentences (fact families).
- Making a 10 can help you add greater numbers.

Addition Facts Through 12

Subtraction Facts Through 12

Contents

Relate Addition and Subtraction

Contents

Prep for TAKS Success!

Reading & Writing Math

Science and Social Studies

★ Number, Operation, and Quantitative Reasoning
★ Measurement

Unit 8 Money and Time

BIG IDEAS!

- **Each coin has a different value. You can count to find the value of a group of coins.**
- **You can use a clock to tell time.**
- **You can use time to compare and order events.**

Chapter 20 Money

Time

Prep for TAKS Success!	Reading & Writing Math	Science and Social Studies
TAKS Vocabulary, pages 377, 395 **TAKS Problem Solving**, page 408 **TAKS Prep and Spiral Review**, pages 394, 412	**Take-Home Book:** "Jenny Hen's Penny Bakery" **TAKS Vocabulary**, pages 377, 395 **Create and Solve**, page 389 **Unit Wrap Up**, page 414 **Listening Skills:** Math Music, page 410	**Problem Solving Field Trip**, page 407 **Social Studies Link**, page 392

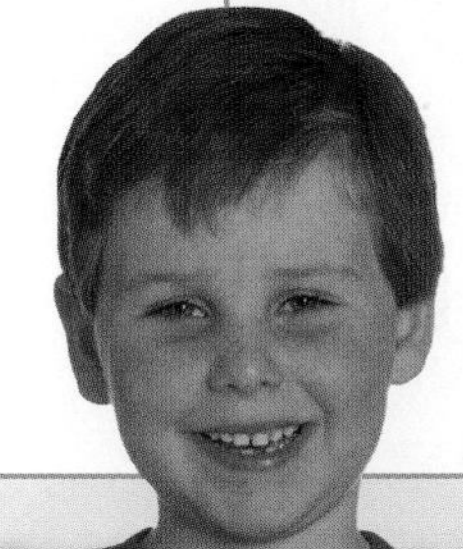

Contents

Unit 9 Measurement

BIG IDEAS!

- You can compare and order length, area, weight, capacity, and temperature.
- You can use units to measure the length of an object.
- The smaller the unit, the greater the measure.

CHAPTER 22

Length and Area

Contents

Weight, Capacity, and Temperature

Prep for  Success!	 Reading & Writing Math	Science and Social Studies
TAKS Vocabulary, pages 419, 437 TAKS **Problem Solving**, page 432 **TAKS Prep and Spiral Review**, pages 436, 456	**Take-Home Book:** Our Classroom **TAKS Vocabulary**, pages 419, 437 **Create and Solve**, page 451 **Unit Wrap Up**, page 458 **Listening Skills:** Math Music, page 454	**Problem Solving Field Trip**, page 431 **Science Link**, page 434 

Contents

★ Number, Operation, and Quantitative Reasoning

Unit 10 Addition and Subtraction Facts Through 18

BIG IDEAS!

- Sums of 10 can help you add greater numbers.
- You can relate addition and subtraction number sentences (fact families).
- You can model and name numbers using addition, subtraction, or both.

Chapter 24 Addition Facts Through 18

Contents

Subtraction Facts Through 18

Unit 10 Review/Test

Contents

Prep for  Success!	 Reading & Writing Math	Science and Social Studies
TAKS Vocabulary, pages 463, 481 TAKS **Problem Solving**, page 476 **TAKS Prep and Spiral Review**, pages 480, 498	**Take-Home Book:** "My Farm" **TAKS Vocabulary**, pages 463, 481 **Create and Solve**, page 493 **Unit Wrap Up**, page 500 **Listening Skills:** Math Music, page 496	**Problem Solving Field Trip**, page 475 **Science Link**, page 478 

I like to solve problems in math.

You have learned different ways to solve problems.

This handbook can help you remember what you learned.

Look here for problem solving help during the year!

This is what problem solving means to me.

I find math all around me.

Where do you see math?

I follow four steps.

Understand
Plan
Solve
Look Back

Do you ask questions?

I use strategies.

Problem Solving Strategies
Act It Out
Draw a Picture
Find a Pattern
Guess and Check

Which strategy do you like?

I use tools to solve problems.

What tools do you use?

Name ______________________

Follow the Four Steps

I follow the four steps. I ask questions.

3 children are playing.
1 more child joins them.
How many children are playing now?

1 Understand

What do I know? What do I need to find out?

- There are 3 children playing.
- 1 more joins.
- How many children are there?

2 Plan

What is one way to find out?

I can count on.

I count 3 and 1 more.

3 Solve

I solve using my plan.

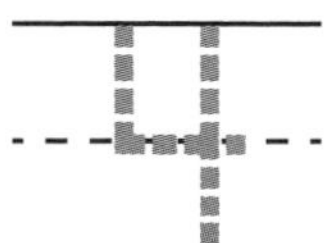

____ children

1
2
3
4

4 Look Back

Does my answer make sense?

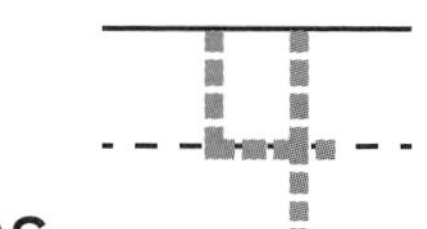

Yes, ____ makes sense.

Let's Try It!

1. Jo has 5 balloons.
   2 balloons pop.
   How many balloons are left?

1 Understand

What do you know?
What do you need to find out?

2 Plan

What is one way to find out?

3 Solve

Solve using your plan.

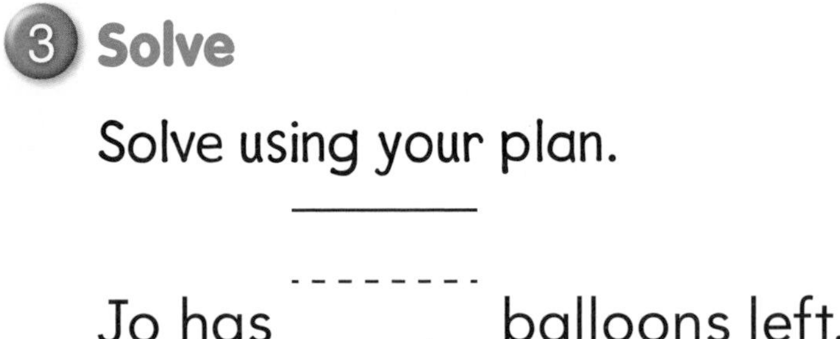

Jo has ______ balloons left.

4 Look Back

Does your answer make sense?

On Your Own

Remember!
Follow the four steps.

Solve.

2. Sue has 4 cars.
   Eric has 2 more than Sue.
   How many cars are there in all?

______ cars

At Home Make up simple story problems for your child to solve while doing chores at home.

En casa Cree problemas sencillos para que su niño los resuelva mientras ayuda con los quehaceres del hogar.

Name ___________________________________

Act It Out

I can act out problems.

Max has 4 red cars.
He has 3 yellow cars.
How many cars does he have in all?

1 Understand

What do I know? What do I need to find out?

- Max has 4 red cars.
- He has 3 yellow cars.
- How many are there in all?

2 Plan

What is one way to find out?

I can act it out.

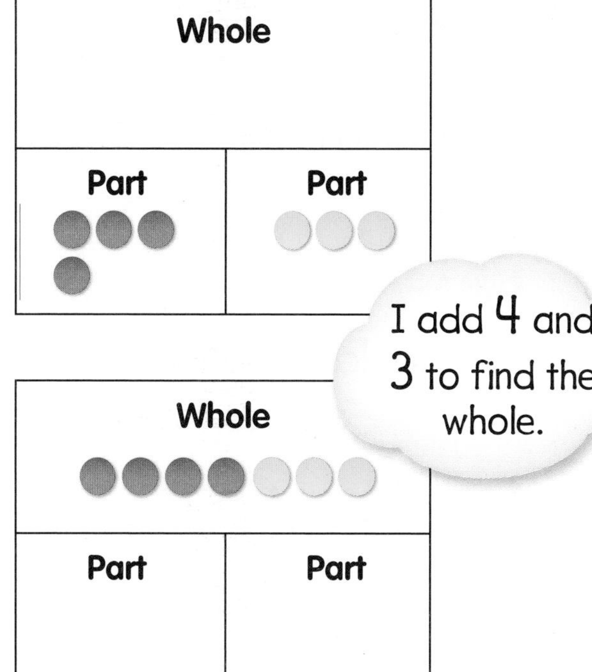

3 Solve

I count red and yellow counters.

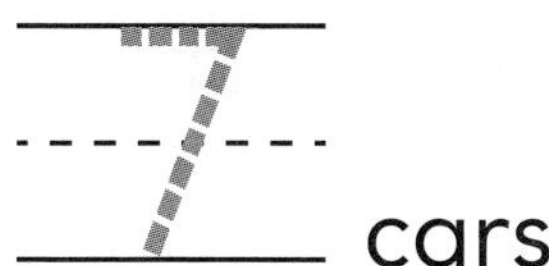

7 cars

4 Look Back

Does my answer make sense?

Yes, 7 makes sense.

Problem Solving Handbook

TAKS Objectives 1, 6
TEKS 1.3A Model and create addition and subtraction problem situations with concrete objects and write corresponding number sentences.

TEKS 1.11C Select or develop an appropriate problem-solving plan or strategy including drawing a picture, looking for a pattern, systematic guessing and checking, or acting it out in order to solve a problem.

Let's Try It!

1. Maria has 6 pears.
   She eats some.
   She has 4 left.
   How many pears does Maria eat?

1 Understand

Think about what you know and need to find out.

I know the whole and one part. I can subtract or add on to find the other part.

2 Plan

What is one way to find out?

Whole	
Part	**Part**

3 Solve

____

- - - - - - - -

Maria eats _______ pears.

4 Look Back

Could the answer be more than 6 pears?

On Your Own

Act it out to solve.

Remember! Follow the four steps.

2. Jill has some crayons.
   She gives 2 to Beth.
   Now she has 7 crayons left.
   How many crayons does Jill start with?

____

- - - - - - - -

_______ crayons

At Home Have your child act out problems you make up using items from their rooms, such as small toys and crayons.

En casa Pida a su niño que, usando objetos de su habitación como juguetes pequeños o crayones, haga una dramatización de problemas que usted invente.

Name ______________________________

Draw a Picture

I can draw pictures to solve problems.

A basket holds 6 red apples.
It also holds 2 yellow apples.
How many apples are there in all?

1 Understand

What do I know? What do I need to find out?

- There are 6 red and 2 yellow apples.
- How many are there in all?

2 Plan

What is one way to find out?

I can draw a picture.

3 Solve

I draw 6 red apples.
Then I draw 2 yellow apples.

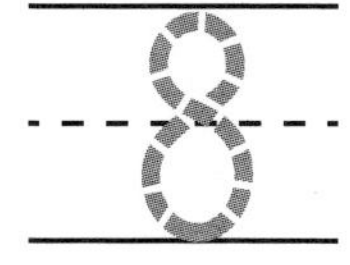

8 apples

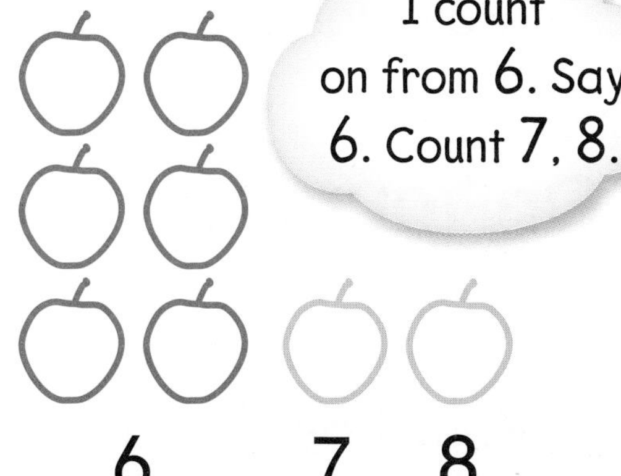

I count on from 6. Say 6. Count 7, 8.

4 Look Back

Does my answer make sense?

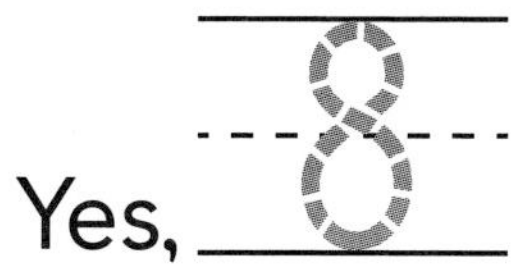

Yes, 8 makes sense.

TAKS Objectives 1, 6
TEKS 1.3A Model and create addition and subtraction problem situations with concrete objects and write corresponding number sentences.

TEKS 1.11C Select or develop an appropriate problem-solving plan or strategy including drawing a picture, looking for a pattern, systematic guessing and checking, or acting it out in order to solve a problem.

Problem Solving Handbook

Let's Try It!

1. There are 2 children. They each want an equal part of the orange.

1 Understand

Think about what you know and need to find out.

A fair share means equal parts.

2 Plan

You can draw a picture to show equal parts.

3 Solve

Draw a picture to solve.

4 Look Back

How does your picture help you solve the problem?

On Your Own

Remember! Follow the four steps.

Solve.

2. Kelly has 7 grapes.
   Zack has 5 grapes.
   How many more grapes does Kelly have?

   ______ grapes

At Home Have your child make up a story problem about a family meal and then draw a picture to solve the problem.

En casa Pida a su niño que invente un problema sobre una comida en familia y que luego haga un dibujo para resolverlo.

Name ______________________________

Find a Pattern

I can find patterns to solve problems.

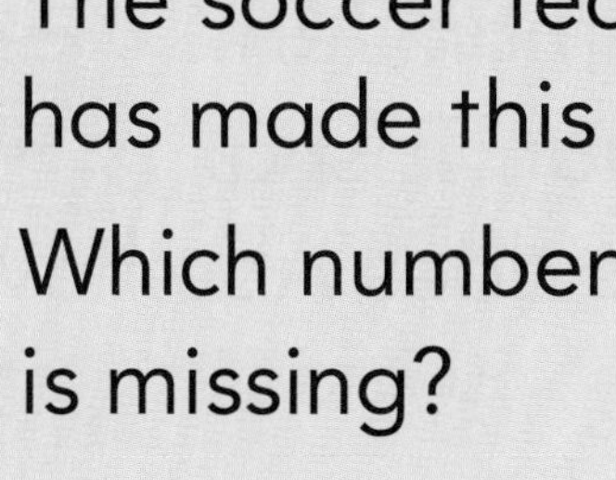

The soccer team has made this sign.

Which number is missing?

1 Understand

What do I know?
What do I need to find out?

- The numbers show skip counting.
- What comes between 4 and 8?

2 Plan

What is one way to find out?

I can skip count to find the pattern.

Think!
I know the answer will be less than 10.

3 Solve

I solve using my plan.

The missing number is 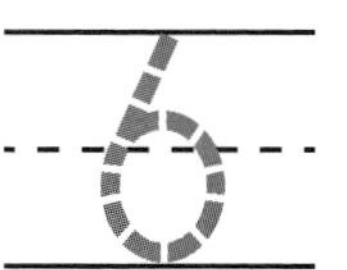 .

I can skip count by twos.
2, 4, 6, 8, 10

4 Look Back

Does my answer make sense?

Yes, my answer is between 4 and 8.

TAKS Objective 1, 6
TEKS 1.4 Identify, describe, and extend concrete and pictorial patterns in order to make predictions and solve problems.

TEKS 1.11C Select or develop an appropriate problem-solving plan or strategy including drawing a picture, looking for a pattern, systematic guessing and checking, or acting it out in order to solve a problem.

Let's Try It!

1. Jeri has 5 cherries.
   Trisha has 1 more than Jeri.
   Abe has 1 more than Trisha.
   How many cherries does Abe have?

1 Understand

Think about what you need to find out.

I know how many Jeri has.

2 Plan

You can look for the pattern.

3 Solve

Write how many cherries for each.

Jeri ______ Trisha ______ Abe ______

4 Look Back

What was the pattern?

On Your Own

Circle what comes next.

2. Anna makes a necklace.
   She uses this pattern.

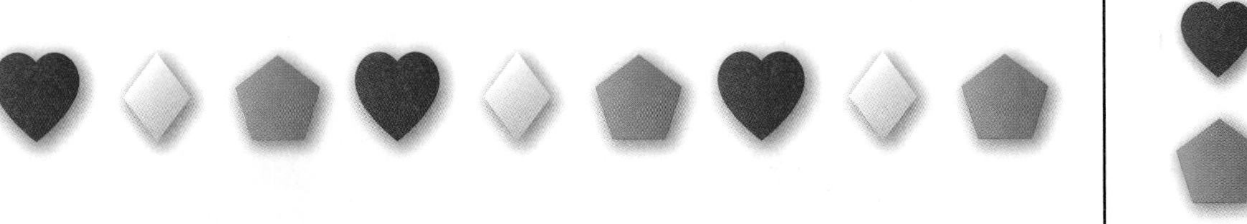

At Home Use buttons or coins to make a pattern that your child can continue.

En casa Use botones o monedas para hacer un patrón que su niño pueda continuar.

Name ___________________________________

Guess and Check

I can make a guess to solve a problem. Then I check my guess.

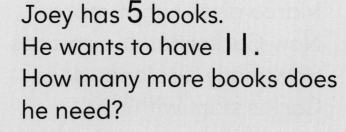

Joey has 5 books.
He wants to have 11.
How many more books does he need?

1 Understand

What do I know? What do I need to find out?

- Joey has 5 books. He wants 11.
- How many more books does he need?

2 Plan

What is one way to find out?

I can make a guess.

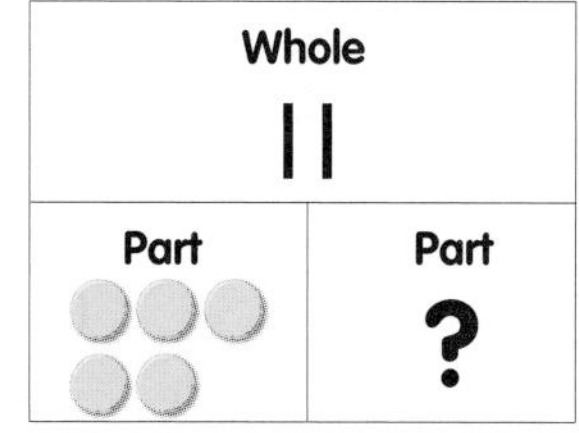

3 Solve

I guess 4 more books. I check.

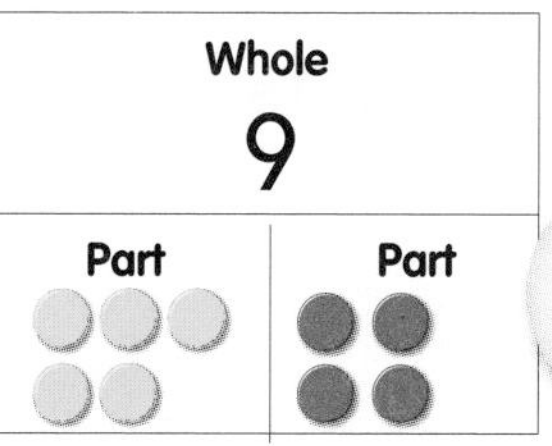

Wrong, so I try again.

I guess 6 more books. I check.

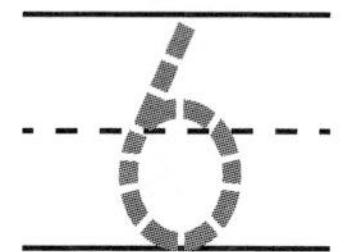 more books

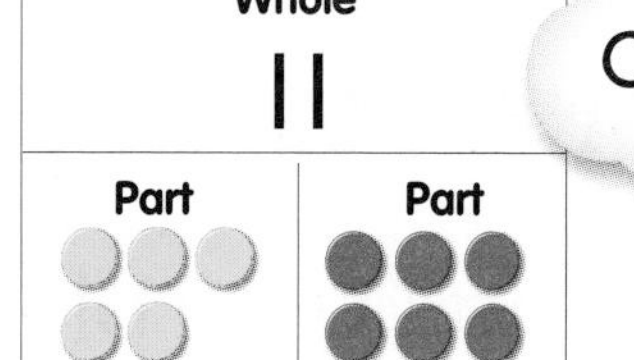

Correct!

4 Look Back

Does my answer make sense?

Yes. My answer adds up to 11.

Let's Try It!

1. Carlos has some airplanes.
Marco gives him 4 more.
Now Carlos has 6 airplanes.
How many airplanes does
Carlos start with?

1 Understand

Think about what you know and what you need to find out.

2 Plan

What is one way to find out?

3 Solve

Guess: ______ Check: ______ + 4 = 6

Is your guess right? If not, try again.

Carlos starts with ______ airplanes.

4 Look Back

Does your answer add up?

On Your Own

Think!
Can you guess and then check?

2. Cindy has 6 airplanes.
She gives some to Will.
Now she has 4 airplanes left.
How many airplanes does she give to Will?

______ airplanes

At Home Ask your child when he or she thinks it is a good idea to guess and when it is not.

En casa Pregunte a su niño cuándo le parece que es buena idea adivinar y cuándo no lo es.

Name ______________________

Choose a Strategy

I can choose how to solve problems.

Jon has 12 grapes in a bag.
He gives some grapes to Jill.
Now they each have the same number.
How many grapes do they each have?

1 Understand

What do I know? What do I need to find out?

- There are 12 grapes. 2 children want the same number of grapes.
- How many do they each have?

2 Plan

I can act it out.

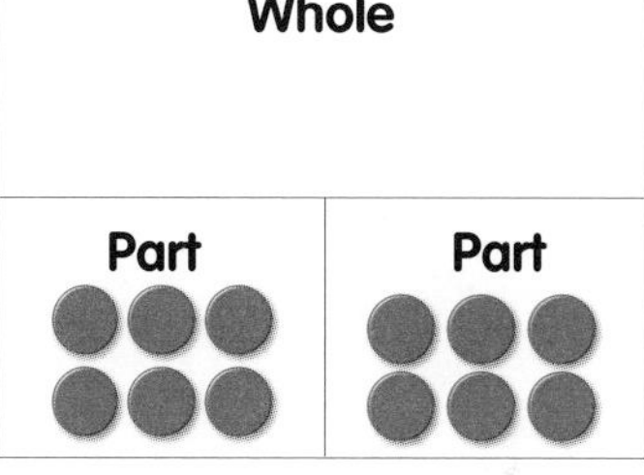

What is one way to find out?

What is another way to find out?

I can draw a picture.

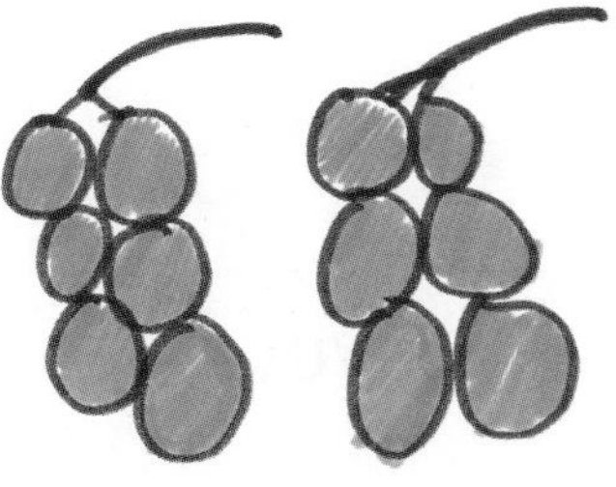

3 Solve

I use my plan to solve.

They each have 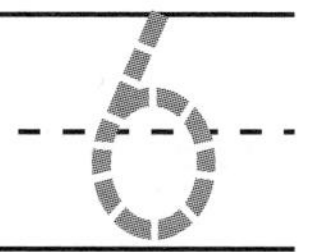 grapes.

4 Look Back

Does my answer make sense?

Yes, because both strategies get the same answer.

Let's Try It!

1. Meg has 8 crayons.
   Alex has 2 more crayons than Meg.
   How many crayons does Alex have?

① Understand

What do you know? What do you need to find out?

② Plan

What is one way to find out?
What is another way to find out?

Problem Solving Strategies
Act It Out
Draw a Picture
Find a Pattern
Guess and Check

③ Solve

______

Alex has ______ crayons.

④ Look Back

Does your answer make sense?

On Your Own

Solve. Draw or write to explain.

2. Emma has some pennies.
   She gives Rachel 8 pennies.
   Now Emma has 4 pennies left.
   How many pennies does Emma start with?

______

______ pennies

Problem Solving Handbook

At Home Discuss the concept of strategy when your child is playing a game such as checkers or hide-and-seek.

En casa Comente el concepto de estrategia cuando su niño esté jugando un juego como damas o las escondidas.

Name ___________________________

Texas Field Trip
Texas Seaport Museum

The Tall Ship *Elissa*

Anna's class visits the *Elissa*.
This ship has 3 masts.
It has 19 sails.
Other ships are there, too.

Use the four steps to solve.

1. One sailboat has 3 sails.
   Another has 5 sails.
   How many sails are there in all?

   ______ sails

sailboat

2. Joey catches 8 shrimp.
   He throws 4 shrimp back.
   How many shrimp are left?

   ______ shrimp

shrimp

3. A chest has 10 gold coins.
   It has 5 silver coins.
   How many more gold coins than silver coins are there?

   ______ more gold coins

coins

Problem Solving Handbook

TAKS Objectives 1, 6
TEKS 1.3B Use concrete and pictorial models to apply basic addition and subtraction facts (up to 9 + 9 = 18 and 18 – 9 = 9).

TEKS 1.11C Select or develop an appropriate problem-solving plan or strategy including drawing a picture, looking for a pattern, systematic guessing and checking, or acting it out in order to solve a problem. Also **1.11A**

TAKS Problem Solving

Listening Skills

Listen to your teacher read the problem. Choose the correct answer.

Think!
Choose a strategy:
Act It Out
Draw a Picture
Find a Pattern
Guess and Check

1. John throws 3 balls in the air.
He catches 2.
How many balls fall to the ground?

0   1   4   5

TEKS 1.3A, 1.11B

---

2. Beth draws a pattern.
Which shape comes next?

TEKS 1.4, 1.11B

---

3. 1   3   4   6

TEKS 1.3A, 1.11B

---

4. 1   3   4   7

TEKS 1.3A, 1.11B

Education Place
Visit www.eduplace.com/txmap/ for Test-Taking Tips and more TAKS Practice.

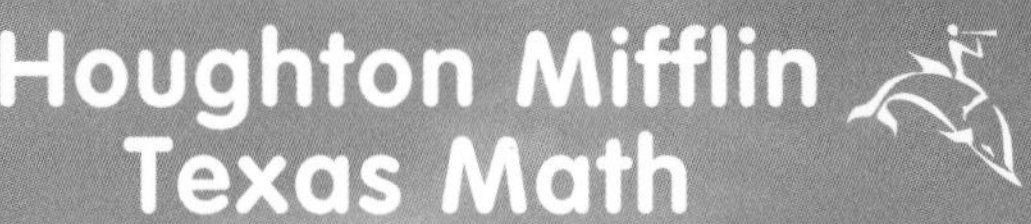

Patterns and Numbers Through 20

BIG IDEAS!

- You can identify and describe a pattern to predict what comes next.
- You can count to tell how many there are in all.
- You can use numbers to describe and compare quantities.
- Numbers have an order.

Songs and Games

Math Music Track 1
Chopping Potatoes

eGames
www.eduplace.com/txmap/

Literature

Literature Big Book

- Teeth, Tails, and Tentacles

Math Readers

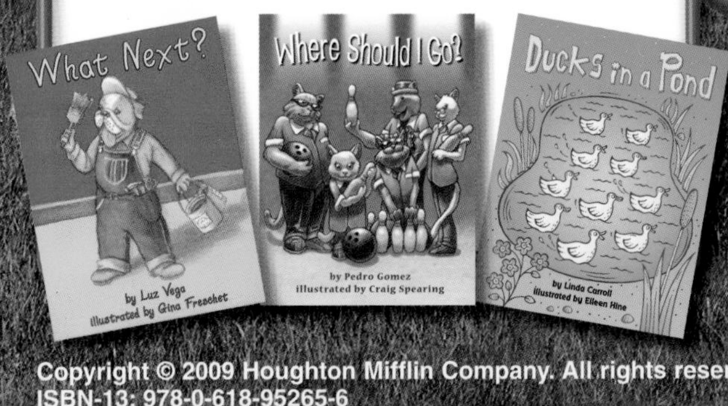

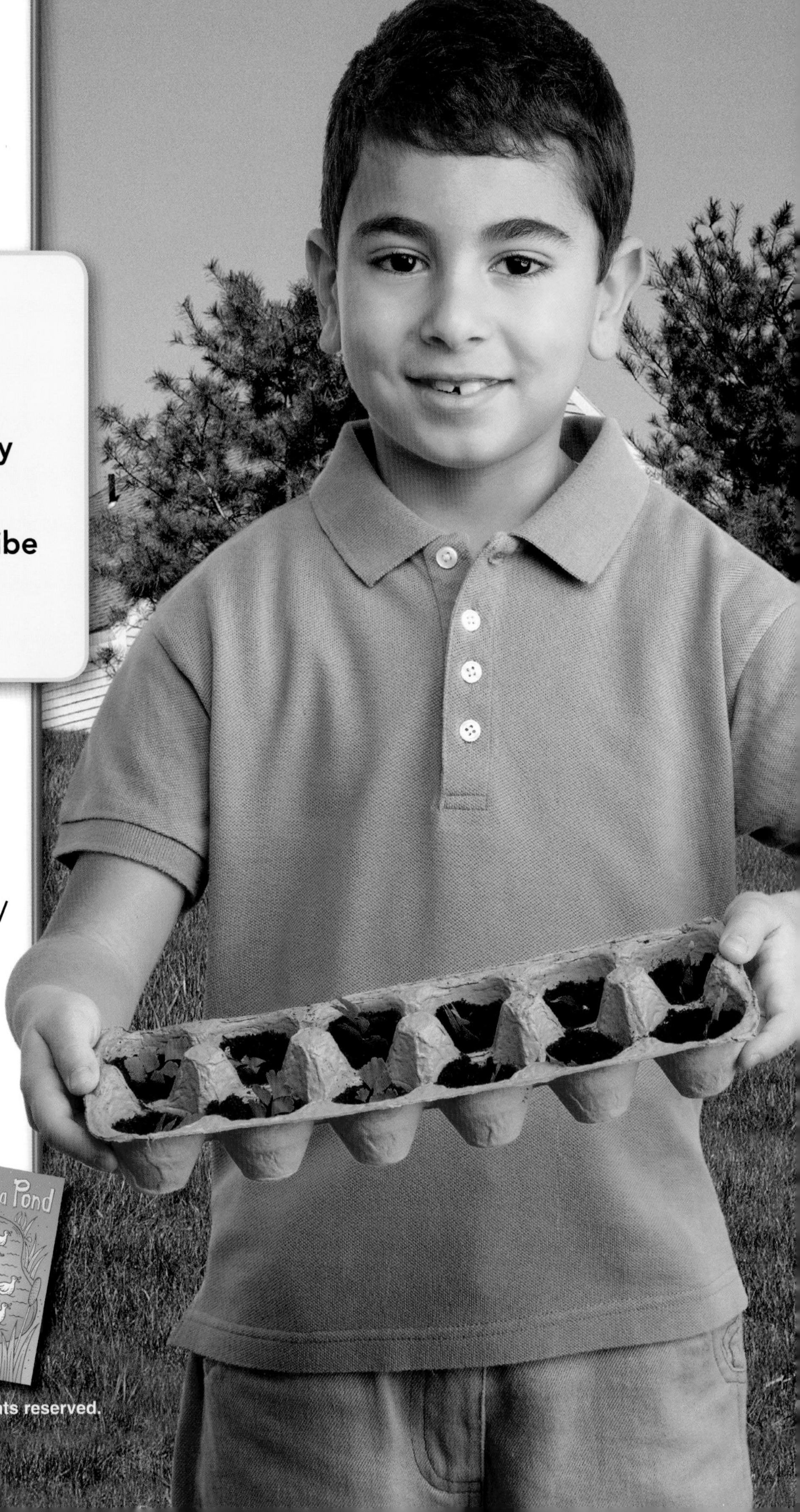

ISBN-13: 978-0-618-95265-6
ISBN-10: 0-618-95265-9
89- WC - 16 15 14 13 12

Get Ready **Game**

What You Need
2 players 
10 ● for each player

Apple Picking

1. Each player picks a basket.
2. Take turns rolling the number cube.
3. Read the number. Put that many ● in your basket.
4. Play until each player has 10 ● .

Math at Home

Dear Family,

My class is starting Unit 1, **Patterns and Numbers Through 20**. I will learn to identify and describe patterns, and count, read, and write numbers through 20. You can help me learn these vocabulary words, and we can do the Math Activity together.

From,

____

Vocabulary

pattern Objects or numbers that repeat according to a rule.

The repeating part of this **pattern** is circle, triangle.

The repeating part of this **pattern** is red, red, yellow.

less than, **greater than**, **equal to** Words used to compare numbers of objects.

6 is **less than** 8.

7 is **greater than** 6.

5 is **equal to** 5.

Education Place
Visit **www.eduplace.com/txmaf/** for
- eGames and Brain Teasers
- Math at Home in other languages

Family Math Activity

Have your child make snack bags filled with crackers or raisins. Write a number on a plastic bag, have your child count that many snacks, and put them into the bag. Save the bags for snacks during the week.

Literature

These books link to the math in this unit. Look for them at the library.

- **Mooove Over!**
  by Karen Magnuson Beil
  (Holiday House, 2004)
- **Counting Is for the Birds**
  by Frank Mazzola, Jr.
- **Math Counts: Patterns**
  by Henry Pluckrose

Matemáticas en casa

Estimada familia:

Mi clase está comenzando la Unidad 1, **Patrones y números hasta el 20**. Voy a aprender a identificar y describir patrones y a contar, leer y escribir números hasta el 20. Me pueden ayudar a aprender estas palabras de vocabulario y podemos hacer juntos la Actividad de matemáticas para la familia.

De:

____

Vocabulario

patrón Objetos o números que se repiten de acuerdo con una regla.

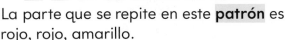

La parte que se repite en este **patrón** es círculo, triángulo.

La parte que se repite en este **patrón** es rojo, rojo, amarillo.

menor que, mayor que, igual que Palabras usadas para comparar números de objetos.

  6 es **menor que** 8

  7 es **mayor que** 6

  5 es **igual que** 5

Education Place

Visite **www.eduplace.com/txmaf/** para

- Juegos en línea y acertijos
- Matemáticas en casa, en otros idiomas

Actividad de matemáticas para la familia

Pida a su niño que llene bolsas de merienda con galletas o pasas. Escriba un número en una bolsa de plástico, pida a su niño que cuente esa cantidad de meriendas y colóquelas en la bolsa. Guarde las bolsas para meriendas durante la semana.

Literatura

Estos libros hablan sobre las matemáticas de esta unidad. Podemos buscarlos en la biblioteca.

- **Veo patrones**
  por Susan Ringer
  (Capstone Press, 2006)
- **El mejor libro para contar de Richard Scarry**
  por Richard Scarry

Frog sells her △, ▭, ○, and □ plants.

Draw what frog sells.

TAKS Objectives 3, 6
TEKS 1.6A, 1.12A

UNIT 1

Frog's Garden

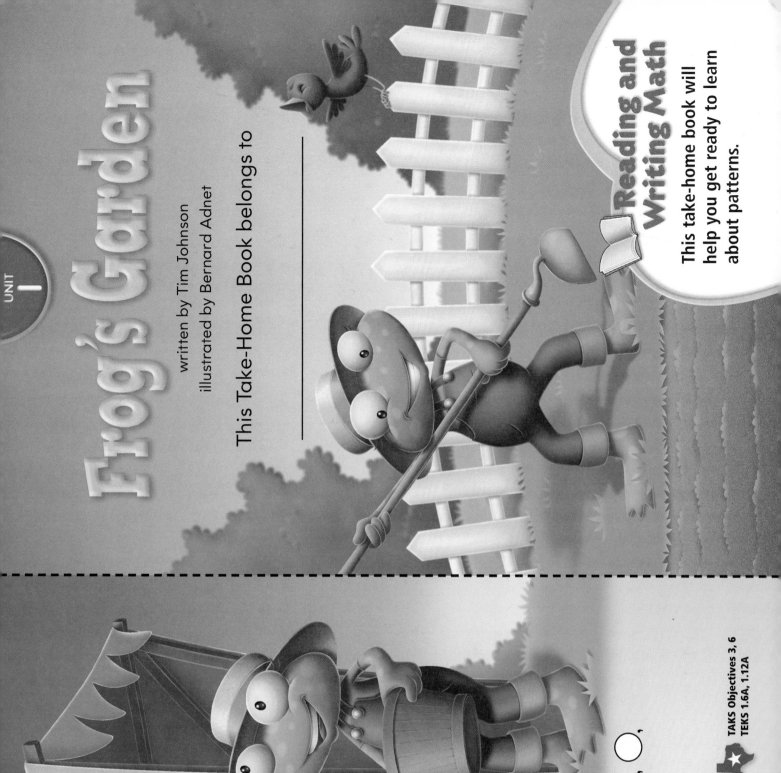

written by Tim Johnson

illustrated by Bernard Adnet

This Take-Home Book belongs to

____

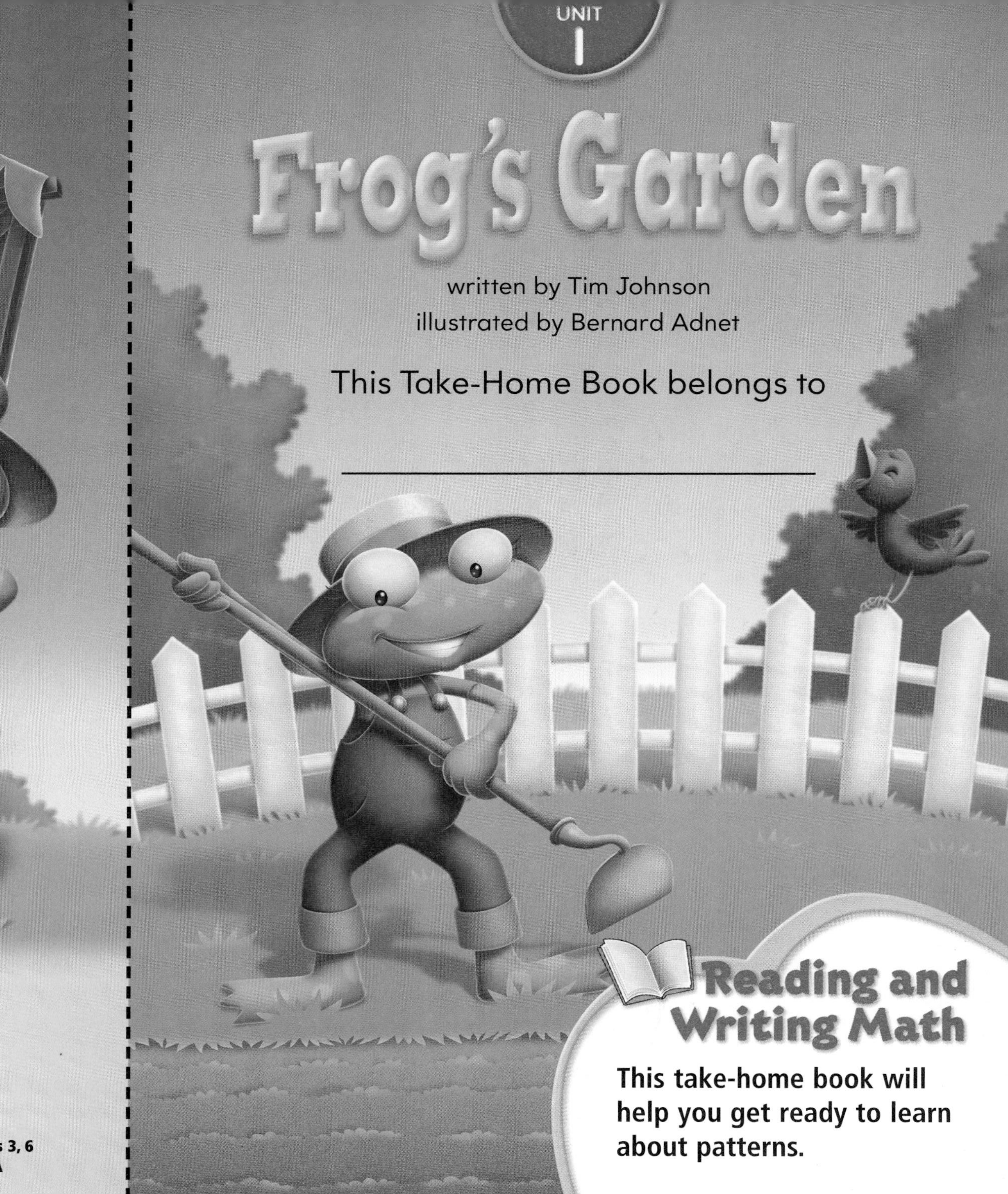

Reading and Writing Math

This take-home book will help you get ready to learn about patterns.

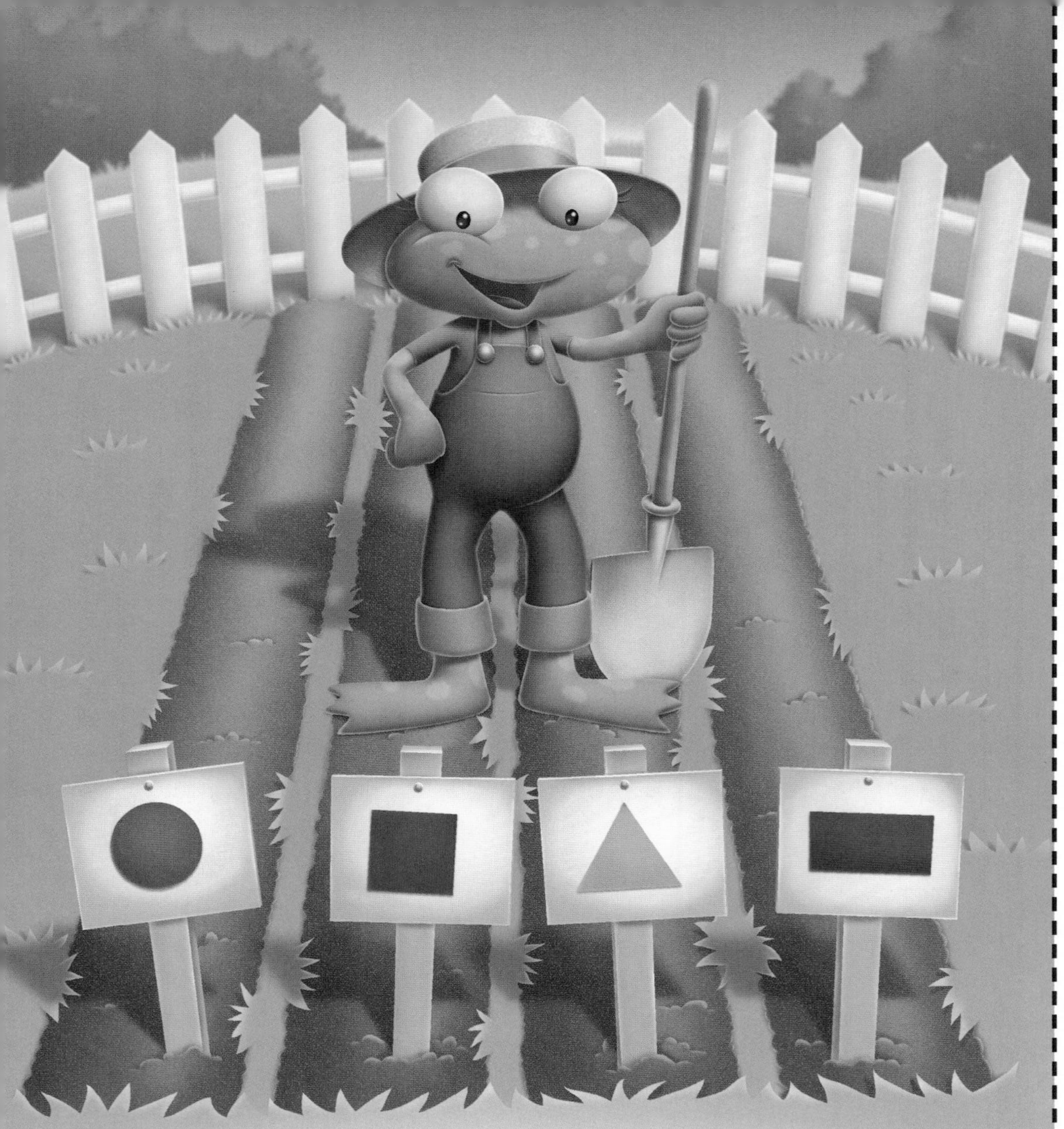

Frog plants a garden.
It is not like most gardens.
What does Frog plant?

How many 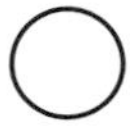 ○ do you see?

How many 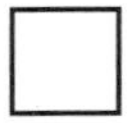 □ do you see?

The plants are big.
How many △ are on this plant?

How many ▭ do you see?

The seeds grow and grow.
How many plants are in each row?

The plants grow and grow.
Bees and butterflies fly around.

Count the bees.
Count the butterflies.

Patterns

TAKS Vocabulary

Here is a vocabulary word you will learn in the chapter.

pattern Objects or numbers that repeat according to a rule

This pattern is made with colors. The part that repeats in the pattern is red, yellow.

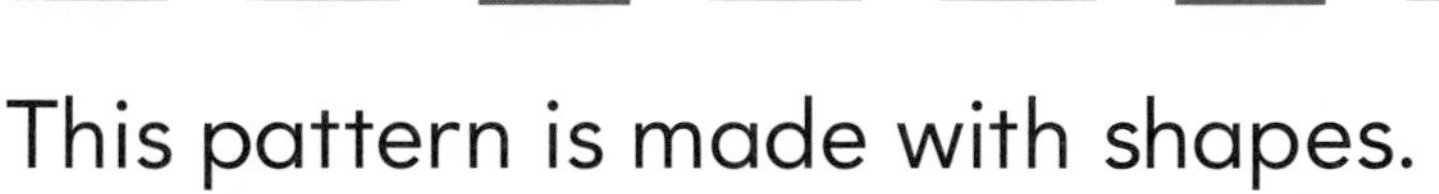

This pattern is made with shapes. The part that repeats in the pattern is triangle, triangle, square.

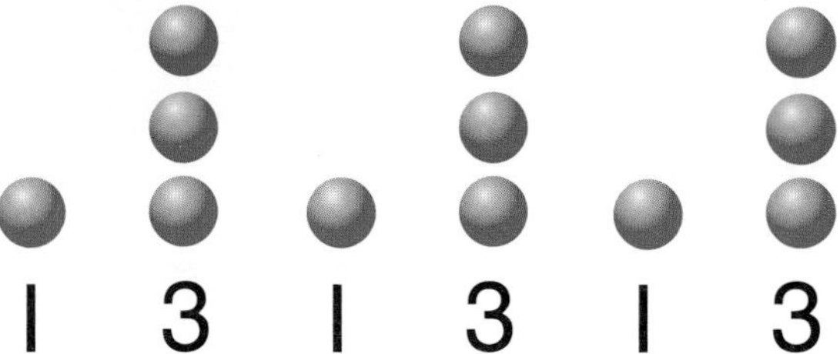

This pattern is made with numbers. The part that repeats in the pattern is 1, 3.

See English-Spanish glossary pages 505–516.

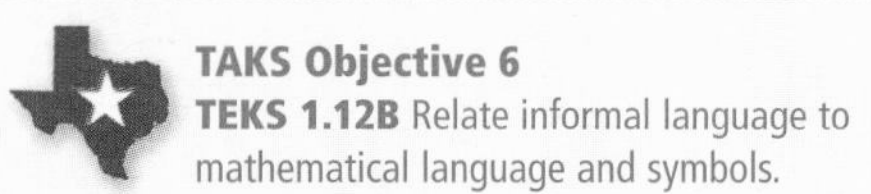

TAKS Objective 6
TEKS 1.12B Relate informal language to mathematical language and symbols.

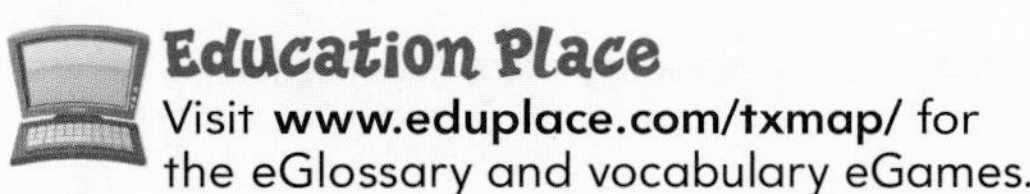

Education Place
Visit **www.eduplace.com/txmap/** for the eGlossary and vocabulary eGames.

Name ______________________________

Circle the figures that are the same shape.

1.    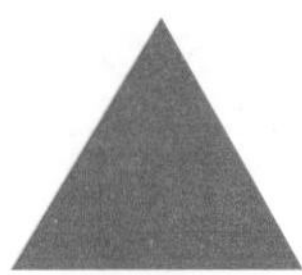

2.    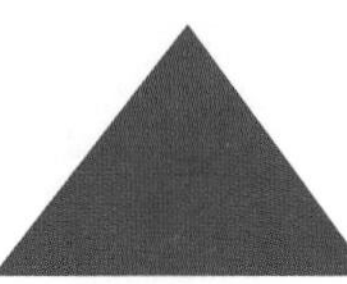

3.    

4.  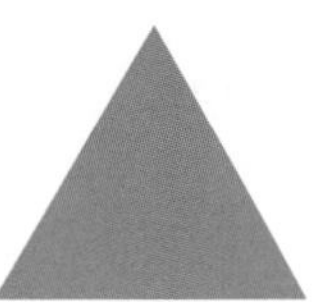  

5.    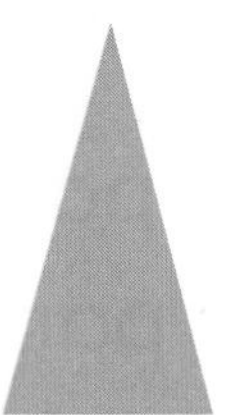

Use this page to review important skills needed for this chapter.

Name ____________________

Chapter 1 Lesson 1

Color Patterns

Hands On

TEKS Objective
Identify, describe, and extend a repeating color pattern.

TAKS Vocabulary
pattern

★ Learn

The colors make a **pattern.** The pattern is red, yellow, red, yellow, red, yellow.

I see two colors.

Red and yellow is the part that repeats.

★ Guided Practice

Show the pattern with cubes.
Color what comes next.

Think!
I see orange, blue, orange, blue...

1.

2.

3.

4. **Math Talk** Look at the pattern in Exercise 3. What can you tell about the pattern?

TAKS Objectives 2, 6
TEKS 1.4 Identify, describe, and extend concrete and pictorial patterns in order to make predictions and solve problems.
TEKS 1.13 Justify thinking using objects, words, pictures, numbers, and technology.
Also **TEKS 1.12A**

★ Practice

Show the pattern with cubes.
Color what comes next.

Remember!
Point to each cube as you say the color.

5.

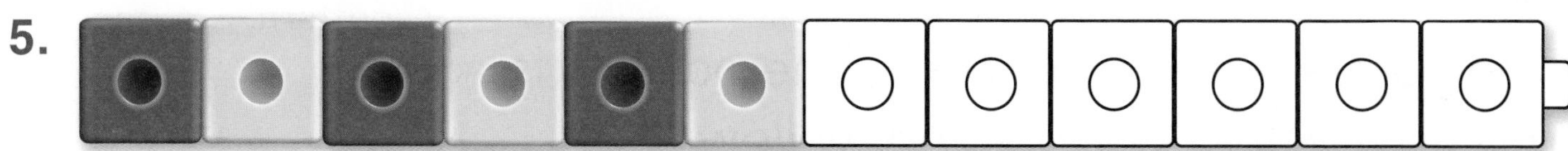

6.

7.

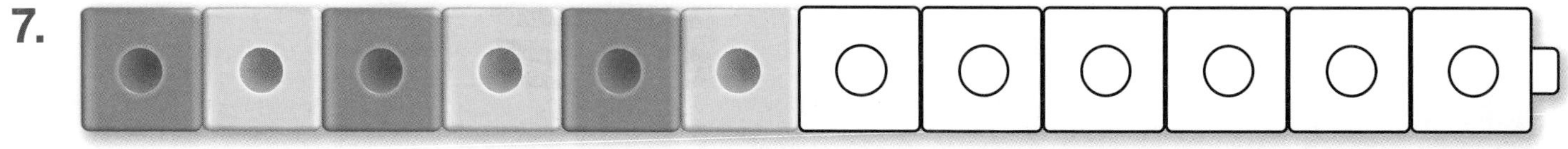

8.

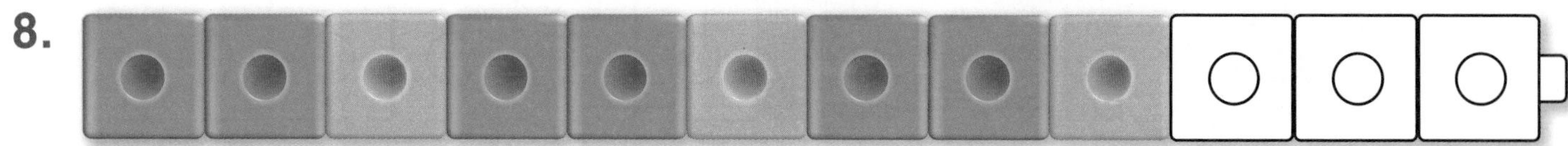

Algebra Readiness: Patterns

Matt made this pattern.

He did not color one cube.

Color that cube.

9.

At Home Have your child describe the repeating part of each pattern on this page.

En casa Pida a su niño que describa la parte que se repite en cada patrón de esta página.

Name ______________________________

Chapter 1 Lesson 2

Shape Patterns

Hands On

TEKS Objective
Identify, describe, and extend a repeating shape pattern.

★ Learn

The shapes make a pattern.

The next shape in the pattern is ▢.

★ Guided Practice

Show the pattern with shapes.
Circle the shape that comes next.

Think!
I can say the pattern out loud.

1.

2.

3. Draw your own pattern.

4. **Math Talk** Look at the patterns in Exercises 1 and 2. How are they the same? How are they different?

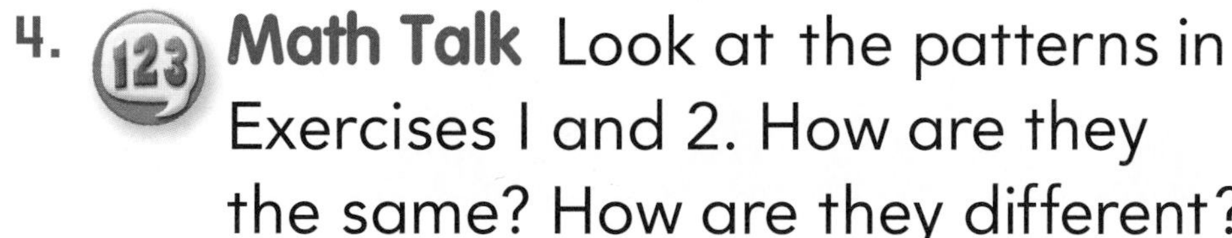

TAKS Objectives 2, 6
TEKS 1.4 Identify, describe, and extend concrete and pictorial patterns in order to make predictions and solve problems.

TEKS 1.12A Explain and record observations using objects, words, pictures, numbers, and technology. Also **TEKS 1.13**

★ Practice

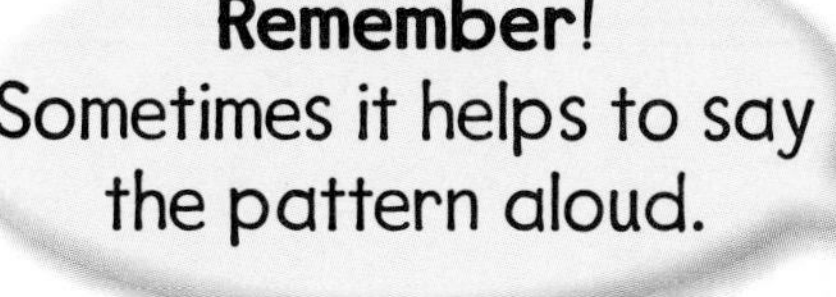

Remember!
Sometimes it helps to say the pattern aloud.

Show the pattern with shapes.
Circle the shape that comes next.

5.     

6. 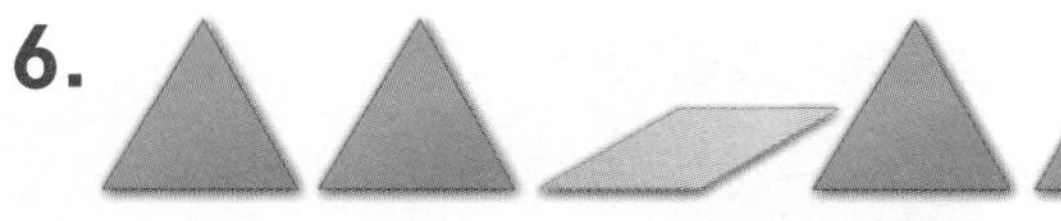  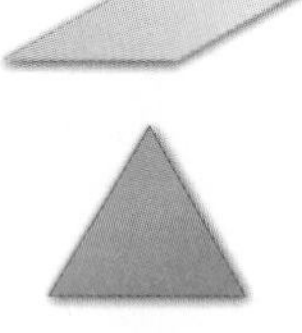

7.  

8. 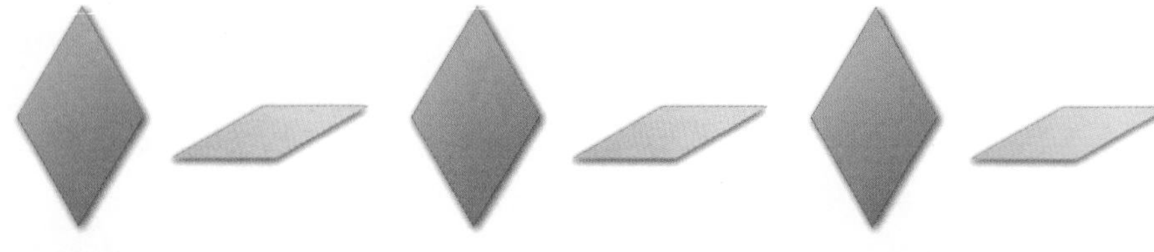 

9. Draw your own pattern.

Algebra Readiness: Patterns

Pam made this pattern.
She left out one shape.
Draw the missing shape.

10.  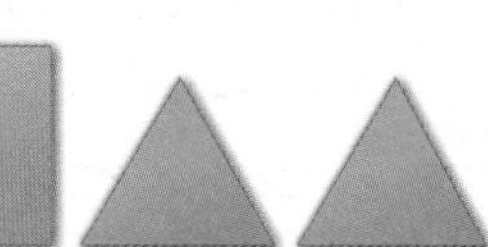   ______ 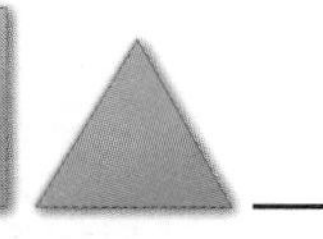 

At Home Arrange two different pasta shapes in a pattern. Have your child identify and extend the pattern.

En casa Use pasta de dos figuras diferentes para hacer un patrón. Pida a su niño que identifique y extienda el patrón.

TEKS Objective
Identify, describe, and extend a repeating number pattern.

Name ______________________________

Chapter 1 Lesson 3

Number Patterns

The dots make a pattern.

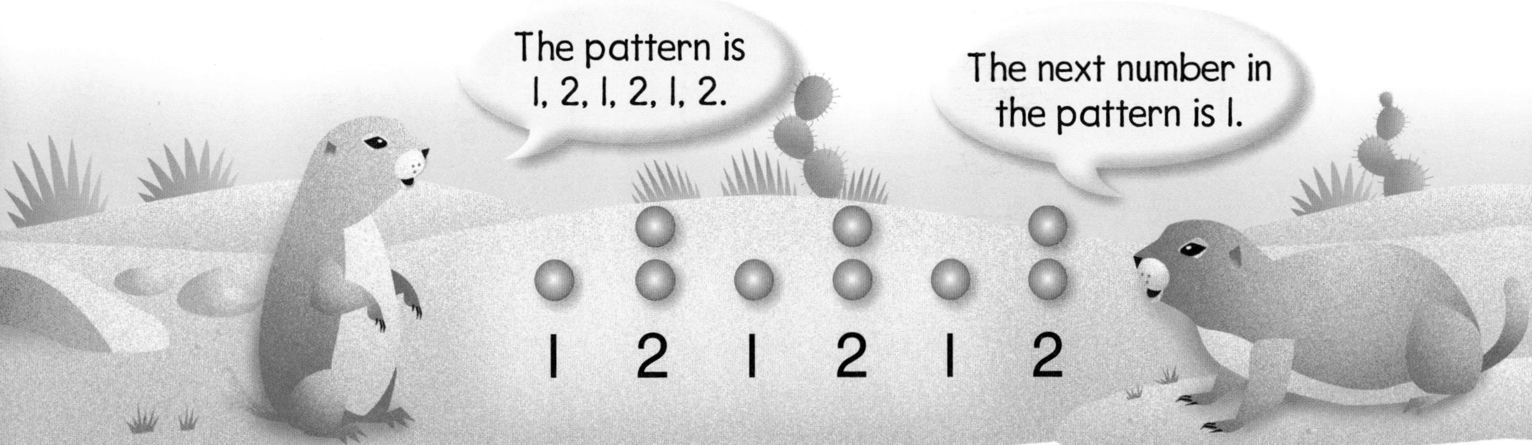

The pattern is 1, 2, 1, 2, 1, 2.
The next number in the pattern is 1.
1 2 1 2 1 2

★ Guided Practice

Show the pattern with counters.
Draw what comes next.

Think!
I see 3, 1, 3, 1...

1.

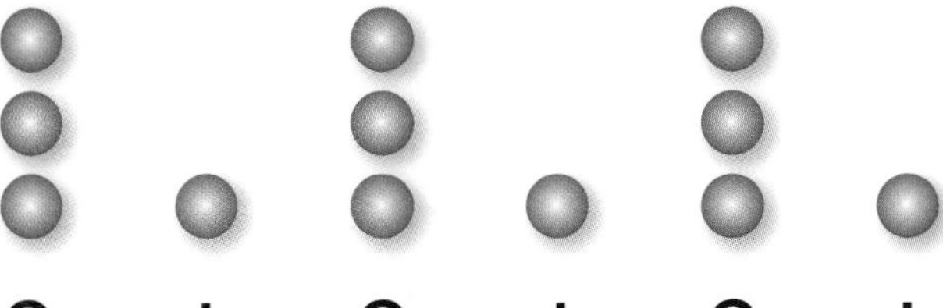

3 1 3 1 3 1 3

2.

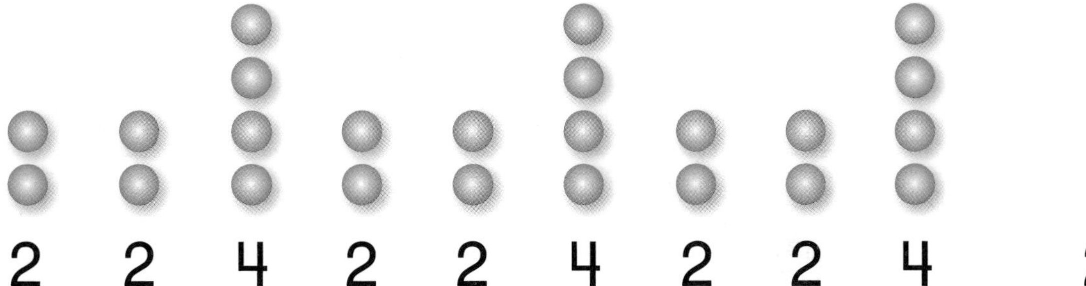

2

3. **Math Talk** Tell about the part that repeats in Exercise 2.

TAKS Objectives 2, 6
TEKS 1.4 Identify, describe, and extend concrete and pictorial patterns in order to make predictions and solve problems.

TEKS 1.12A Explain and record observations using objects, words, pictures, numbers, and technology. Also **TEKS 1.13**

★ Practice

Show the pattern with counters.
Draw what comes next.

Remember!
Think about what repeats.

4.

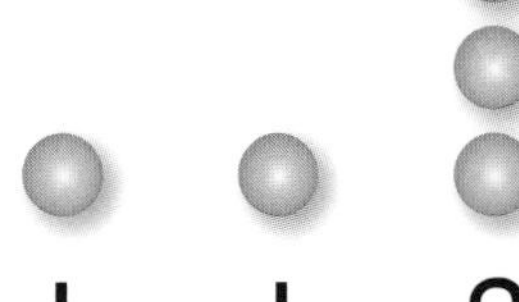

1 1 3 1 1 3 1 1 3 1

5.

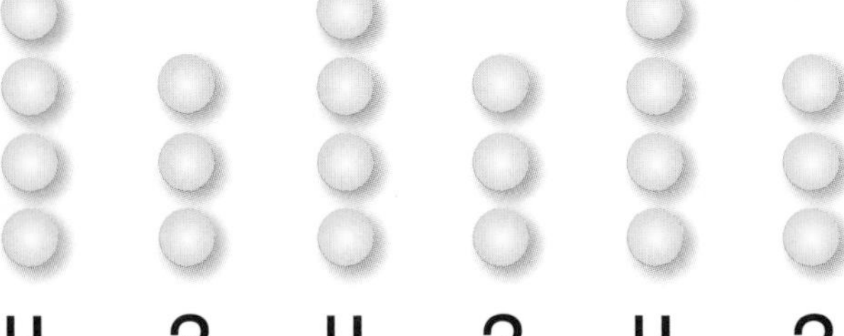

4 3 4 3 4 3 4

6.

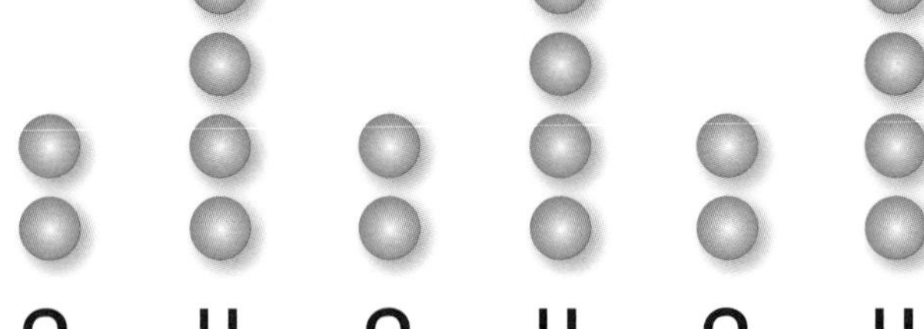

2 4 2 4 2 4 2

7.

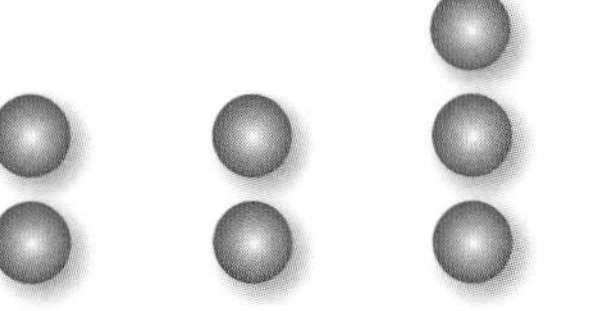

2 2 3 2 2 3 2 2 3 2

Algebra Readiness: Patterns

Write and draw the missing part.

8.

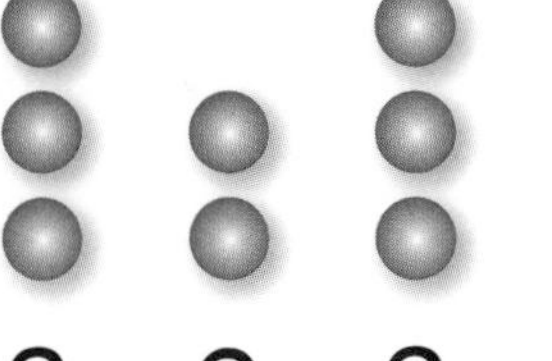

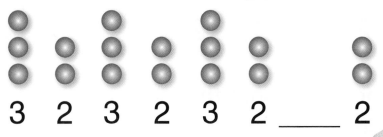

3 2 3 2 3 2 ____ 2

At Home Use small objects to copy a pattern on this page. Ask your child to find and extend the pattern.

En casa Use objetos pequeños para copiar un patrón de esta página. Pida a su niño que busque y extienda el patrón.

Name ______________________________

Chapter 1 Lesson 4

Size Patterns

TEKS **Objective**
Identify, describe, and extend a repeating size pattern.

★ Learn

The blocks make a size pattern. The pattern is big, small, big, small, big, small.

A big block comes next.

★ Guided Practice

Circle the part that repeats.
Color the block that comes next.

Think!
I see small, small, big, small, small, big...

1.

2.

3.

4. **Math Talk** How can you tell what size comes next?

TAKS Objective 2
TEKS 1.4 Identify, describe, and extend concrete and pictorial patterns in order to make predictions and solve problems.

★ Practice

Circle the part that repeats.
Color the block that comes next.

Remember!
Look for the part that repeats.

5.

6.

7.

8.

Algebra Readiness: Patterns

Predict the next two shapes in this pattern.

Draw to solve.

9.

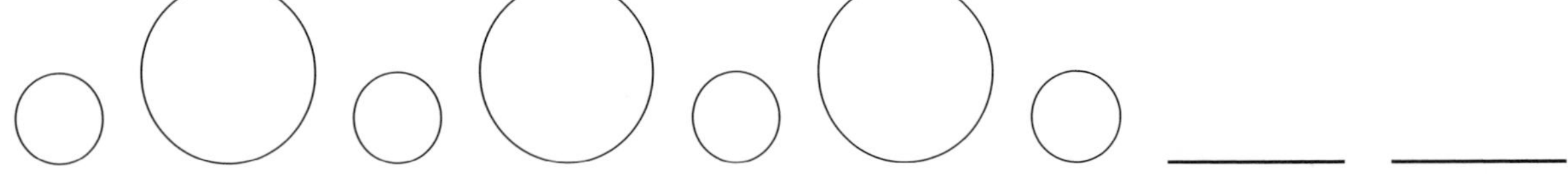

At Home Have your child use big and small objects, such as buttons, to show one of the patterns on this page.

En casa Pida a su niño que use objetos grandes y pequeños, como botones, para mostrar uno de los patrones de esta página.

Name ______________________________

Chapter 1 Lesson 5

Find a Pattern

TEKS Objective
Use repeating patterns to make predictions and solve problems.

★ Learn

Ms. Davis made a pattern.
What comes next in her pattern?

Understand

What do you know?

- The pattern is made with two colors.
- These two colors repeat.

Plan

How does the pattern repeat?

- You can say it:
  red, red, yellow.

Solve

Circle the one that comes next.

Look Back

Say the pattern.
Does the color you picked fit the pattern?

TAKS Objectives 2, 6
TEKS 1.4 Identify, describe, and extend concrete and pictorial patterns in order to make predictions and solve problems.

Also **TEKS 1.11B, 1.11C**

★ Guided Problem Solving

Think!
The part that repeats is small, small, big.

1. Eric puts this pattern on a belt.

Draw a line under the part that repeats.

Circle what comes next.

2. **Math Talk** How does knowing what repeats help you?

★ Problem Solving Practice

Find the part that repeats.
Circle what comes next.

3. Sahil puts this pattern on a hat.

Find the part that repeats.
Draw what comes next.

4. Jen makes a number pattern with stickers.

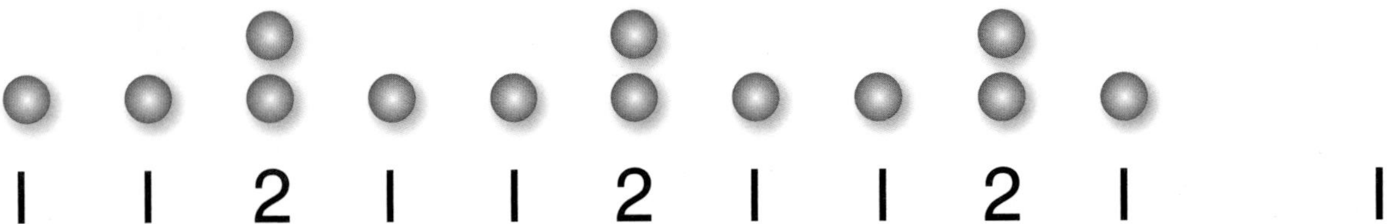

At Home Ask your child to say these patterns and tell how he or she decided what came next.

En casa Pida a su niño que diga estos patrones y que diga cómo decidió lo que venía después.

Name ______________________________

Identify, Describe, and Extend Patterns

Use the cubes found at **www.eduplace.com/txmap/** to make a pattern.

1. Put your pointer over the **stamp** tool.
   - Click the red cube 3 times.
2. Put your pointer over the **stamp** tool.
   - Click the blue cube 3 times.

3. Use the **hand** tool.
   - Move the cubes to make a pattern you might like on a belt.

1. Use cubes to copy the pattern you made. Draw the pattern. Describe your pattern. Draw the next two cubes.

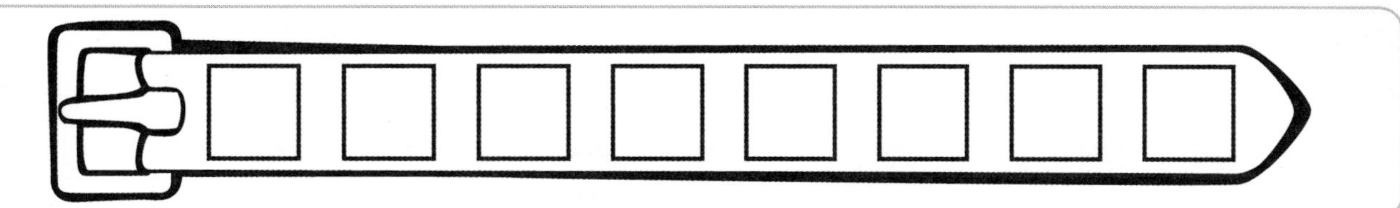

2. Try again. Use different cubes. Make and describe a different pattern.

Social Studies Link

Strawberry Festival

Strawberries grow well where it is warm. At strawberry festivals, farmers sell the strawberries they grow.

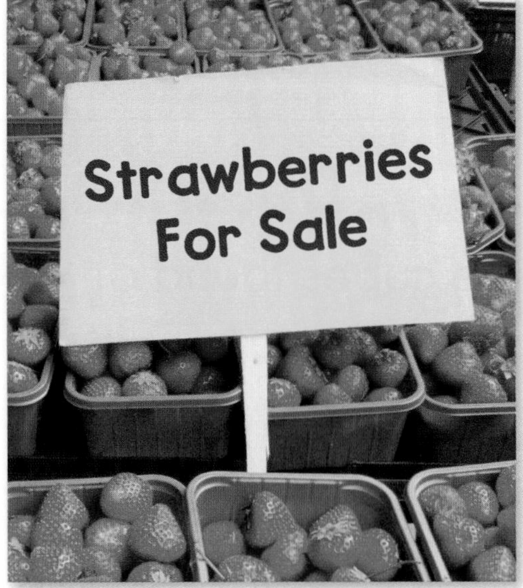

Use counters. Copy the pattern.
Draw what comes next.

1. The farmer made a pattern of strawberries on the table. What comes next in the pattern?

Find the part that repeats.
Circle what comes next.

2. Sylvia made a pattern of strawberry hats at her store. What comes next in the pattern?

TAKS Objectives 2, 6
TEKS 1.4 Identify, describe, and extend concrete and pictorial patterns in order to make predictions and solve problems.

Also **TEKS 1.11C**
TEKS Social Studies 7C

Name ______________________________

Concepts and Skills

Circle the one that comes next. TEKS 1.4

1.

2.

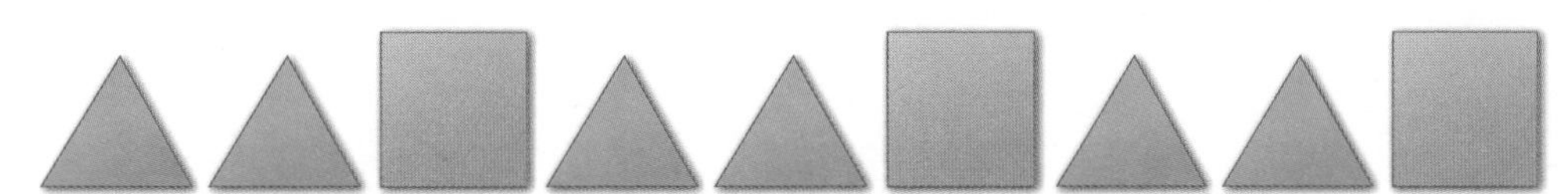

3.

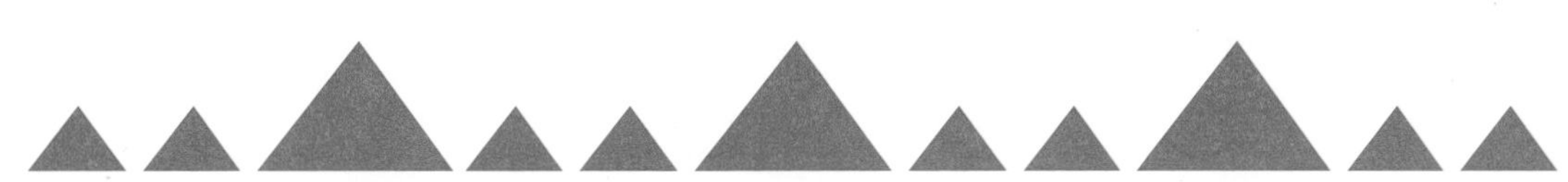

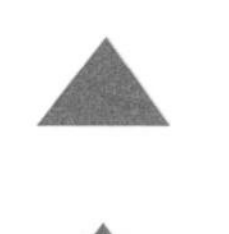

Draw what comes next. TEKS 1.4

4.

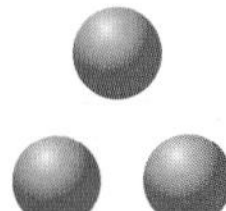

Problem Solving

Find the part that repeats.
Circle what comes next. TEKS 1.4, 1.11B, 1.11C

5. Bess puts this pattern on a belt.

TAKS Prep and Spiral Review

Choose the answer for problems 1–4.

1. Count. Which number tells how many?

6	7	8	9
○	○	○	○

TEKS K.1C (page 151)

2. Kim looks at the garden.
How many flowers does she see?

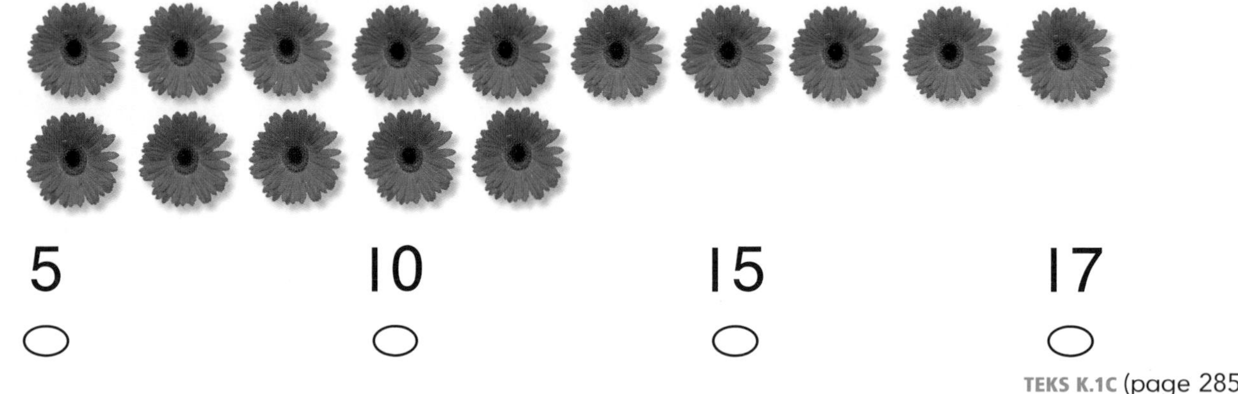

5	10	15	17
○	○	○	○

TEKS K.1C (page 285)

3. What comes next in the pattern?

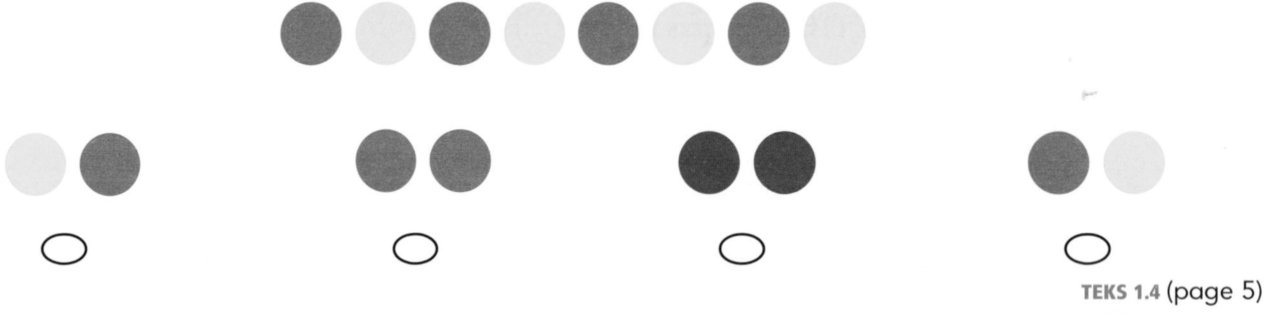

○ ○ ○ ○

TEKS 1.4 (page 5)

4. Juan makes a pattern on his belt.
What comes next in his pattern?

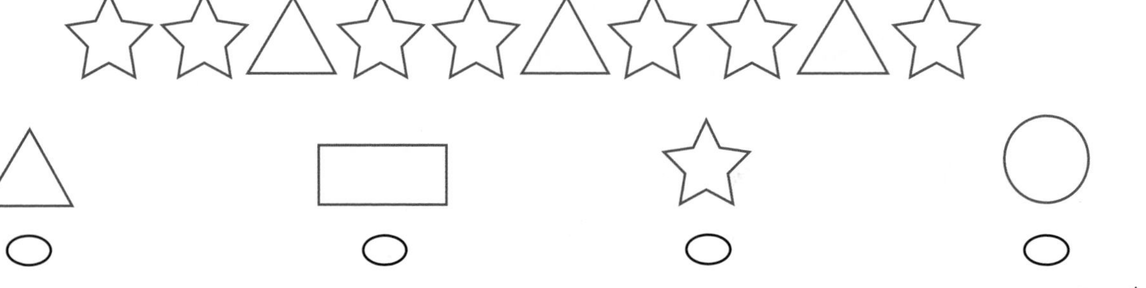

○ ○ ○ ○

TEKS 1.4 (page 7)

Visit **www.eduplace.com/txmap/** for Test-Taking Tips and Extra Practice.

Numbers 0 Through 10

TAKS Vocabulary

Here are some vocabulary words you will learn in the chapter.

less than, greater than, equal to Words used to compare numbers of objects

2 is less than 4

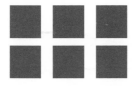

6 is greater than 5

3 is equal to 3

See English-Spanish glossary pages 505–516.

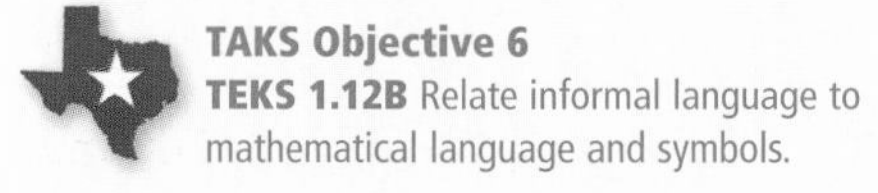

TAKS Objective 6
TEKS 1.12B Relate informal language to mathematical language and symbols.

Education Place
Visit **www.eduplace.com/txmap/** for the eGlossary and vocabulary eGames.

Name ________________________________

Check What You Know

Circle the number that tells how many.

1.

2
3
4

2.

4
5
6

3.

1
2
3

4.

1
2
3

Use this page to review important skills needed for this chapter.

Name ______________________________

Chapter 2 Lesson 1

Build Numbers 0 Through 5

TEKS Objective
Count 0 through 5 objects; read and write the numbers.

TAKS Vocabulary
number words for 0 through 5

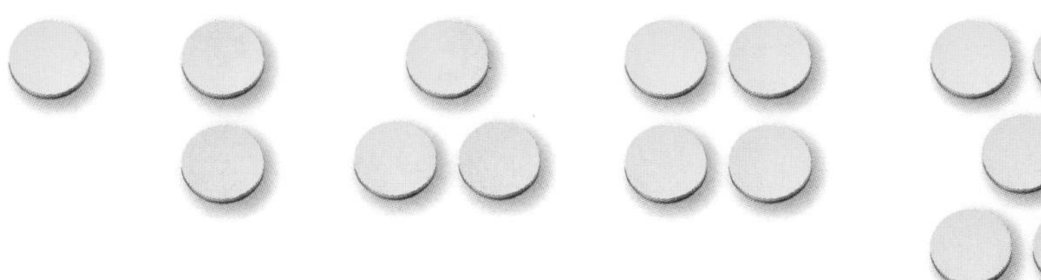

0	1	2	3	4	5
zero	**one**	**two**	**three**	**four**	**five**

Use ◯ to show the number.
Draw to show how many.

1. 3

2. 2

3. 0

4. 5

5. 4

TAKS Objective 1
TEKS 1.1D Read and write numbers to 99 to describe sets of concrete objects.

★ Extend

Count. Write the number.

Remember!

0	zero	3	three
1	one	4	four
2	two	5	five

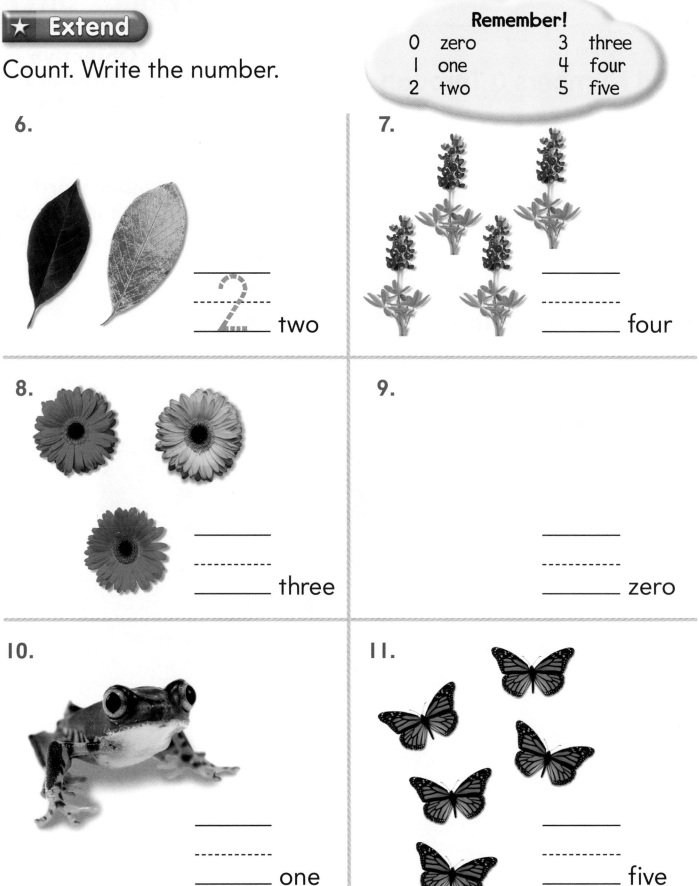

6. 2 two

7. ____ four

8. ____ three

9. ____ zero

10. ____ one

11. ____ five

12. **Math Talk** Which set has more than 4?

At Home Ask your child to count sets of 1 through 5 objects such as cereal or small pasta.

En casa Pida a su niño que cuente conjuntos de 1 a 5 objetos, como cereal o pasta pequeña.

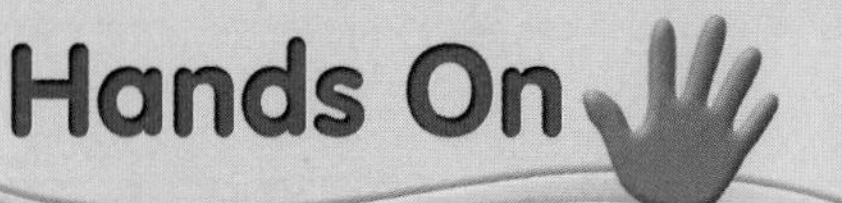

Name ____________________

Chapter 2 Lesson 2

Build Numbers 6 Through 10

TEKS Objective
Count 6 through 10 objects; read and write the numbers.

TAKS Vocabulary
number words for 6 through 10

6	7	8	9	10
six	**seven**	**eight**	**nine**	**ten**

★ Explore

Use ◯ to show the number.
Draw to show how many.

1. 6

2. 9

3. 7

4. 10

5. 8

★ Extend

Count. Write the number.

Remember!

6 six
7 seven
8 eight
9 nine
10 ten

6. 

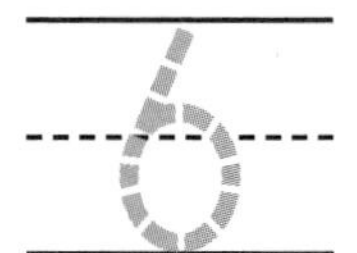

______ six

7. 

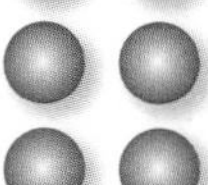

______ ten

8. 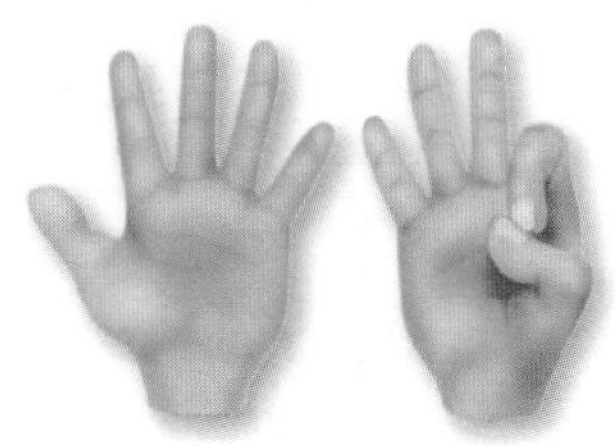

______ eight

9. 

______ six

10. 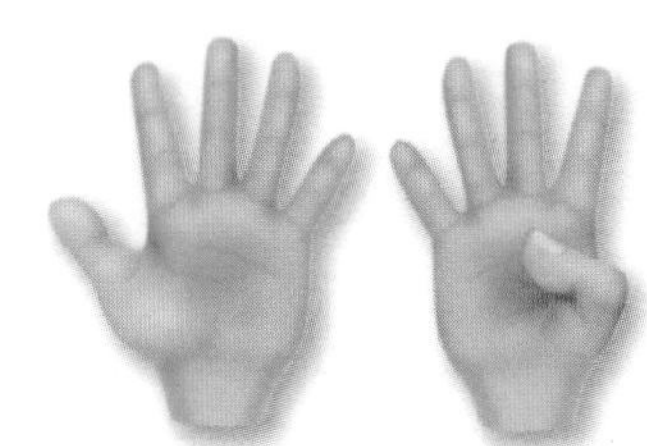

______ nine

11. 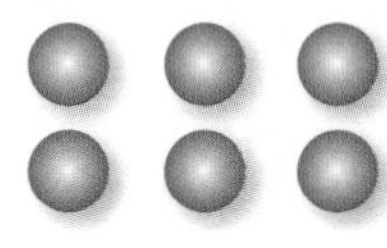

______ eight

12. 

______ seven

13. 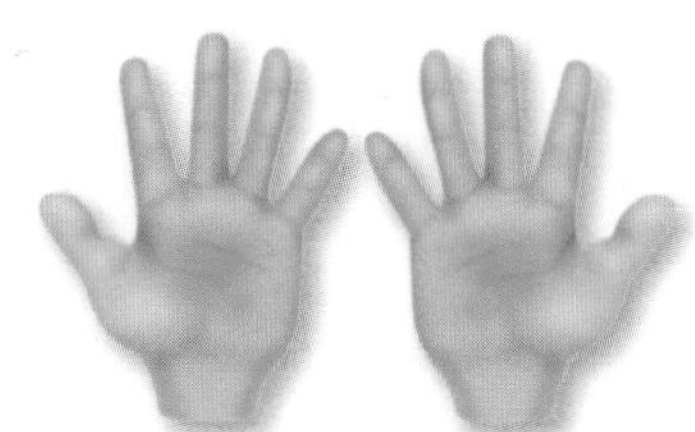

______ ten

14. **Math Talk** Which sets have fewer than 7?

At Home Have your child count sets of 6 through 10 objects such as spoons or cereal.

En casa Pida a su niño que cuente conjuntos de 6 a 10 objetos, como cucharas o cereal.

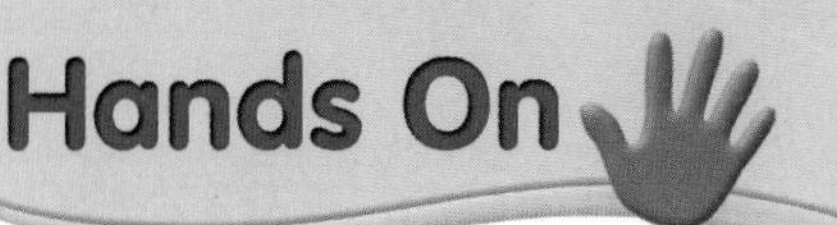

TEKS Objective
Compare numbers through 10 using objects, pictures, and words.

TAKS Vocabulary
less than
greater than
equal to

Name ______________________________

Chapter 2 Lesson 3

Compare Numbers 0 Through 10

7 is **less than** 9

9 is **greater than** 8

7 is **equal to** 7

★ Guided Practice

Think!
5 dots is fewer than 6 dots.
I know which number is less.

Model and draw each set. Circle the words that make the sentence true.

1. 

5 is greater than / is less than 6

2.  

9 is greater than / is equal to 9

3. **Math Talk** Show 2 sets. Compare. Describe them using **greater than**.

★ Practice

Model and draw each set.
Circle the words that make the sentence true.

Remember!
Count the dots to help you compare the numbers.

4.

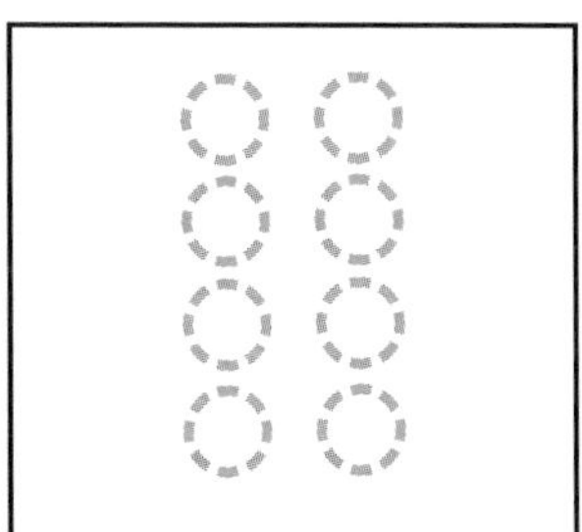

6 is greater than / is less than 8

5.

6 is greater than / is equal to 6

6.

10 is greater than / is equal to 10

7.

8 is greater than / is equal to 7

Problem Solving: Number Sense

Write a number that makes the sentence true.

8. 5 is less than ______.

9. 8 is greater than ______.

At Home Have your child explain how to compare two numbers using greater than, less than, and equal to.

En casa Pida a su niño que explique cómo comparar dos números usando las palabras mayor que, menor que e igual que.

Name ____________________

Chapter 2 Lesson 4

Order Numbers 0 Through 10

7 is the **greatest.**

4

2 is the **least.**

Hands On

TEKS Objective
Order numbers through 10 using objects, pictures, and words.

TAKS Vocabulary
greatest
least

★ Explore

Build cube trains. Put the trains in order.
Color to show your work.
Write the number.

1. Show 3, 1, 10.

greatest ____

____

least ____

2. Show 4, 2, 8.

greatest ____

____

least ____

3. **Math Talk** Read the answer to Exercise 2. How did you know which number was greatest?

TAKS Objective 1
TEKS 1.1A Compare and order whole numbers up to 99 (less than, greater than, or equal to) using sets of concrete objects and pictorial models.

★ Extend

4 is the **least.**

7

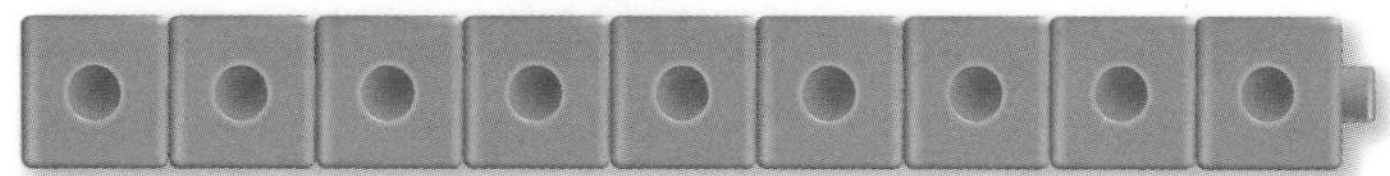

9 is the **greatest.**

Build cube trains. Put the trains in order.
Color to show your work.
Write the number.

4. Show 6, 7, 3.

least ○○○○○○○○○○ 3

○○○○○○○○○○

greatest ○○○○○○○○○○

5. Show 8, 1, 4.

least

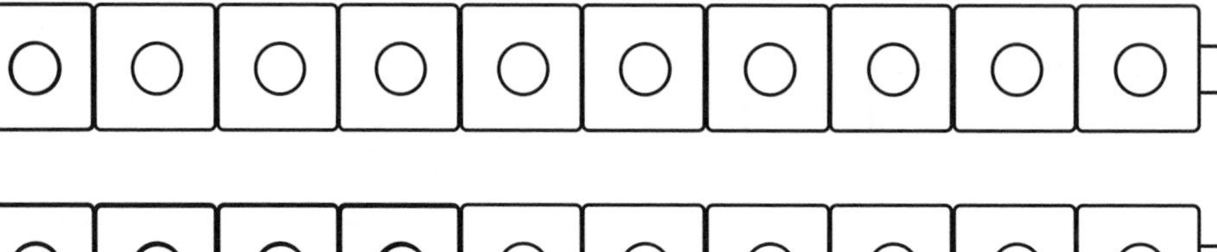

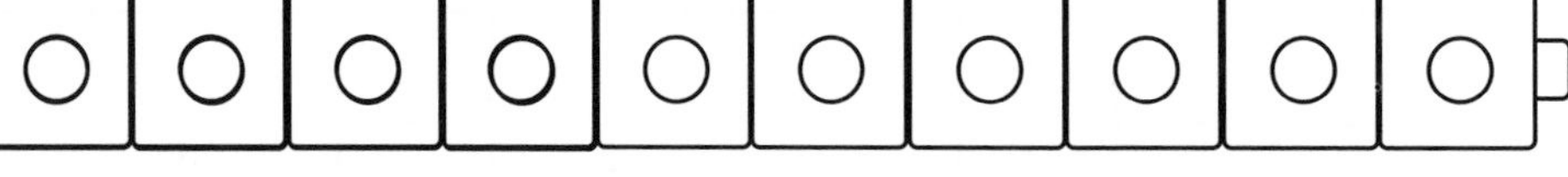

greatest

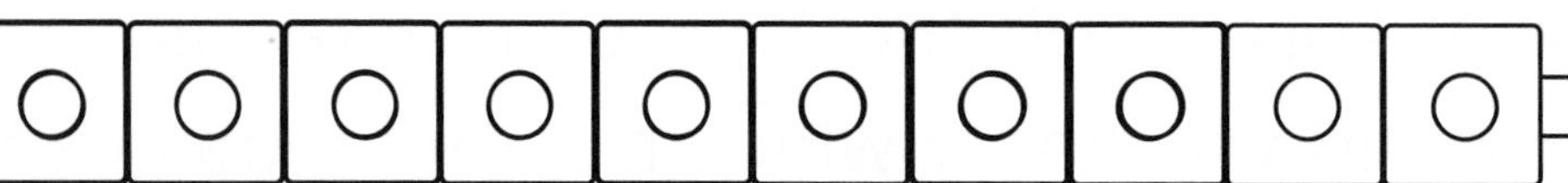

At Home Write 3 numbers from 0 through 10 in any order. Have your child write them in order from least to greatest.

En casa Escriba 3 números del 0 al 10 en cualquier orden. Pida a su niño que los escriba en orden de menor a mayor.

Name ______________________

Chapter 2 Lesson 5

Draw a Picture

Problem Solving Strategy

TEKS Objective
Draw a picture to solve a problem.

★ Learn

Kim has 6 cats.
Han has 1 more cat than Kim.
How many cats does Han have?

Understand

What do you know?

- Kim has 6 cats.
- Han has 1 more cat than Kim.

Plan

Start with Kim's cats.

Kim has __6__ cats.

Solve

Draw a picture.
Draw to show Kim's cats.
Draw 1 more cat.

How many cats does Han have? __7__ cats

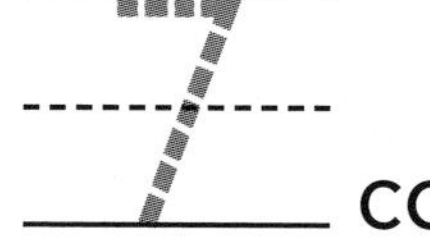

Look Back

Does your answer make sense?

TAKS Objectives 1, 6
TEKS 1.1D Read and write numbers to 99 to describe sets of concrete objects.
TEKS 1.11B Solve problems with guidance that incorporates the processes of understanding the problem, making a plan, carrying out the plan, and evaluating the solution for reasonableness.
Also **TEKS 1.11C**

★ Guided Problem Solving

Think!
Start with Amy's 9 bugs.

1. Amy has 9 bugs. Sam has 1 fewer bug than Amy. How many bugs does Sam have?

   What do you know?
   Draw Amy's bugs. Solve.

   ______ bugs

2. **Math Talk** How did your picture help you solve the problem?

★ Problem Solving Practice

Draw a picture to solve.

3. Lee has 7 flowers. Jan has 1 more flower than Lee. How many flowers does Jan have?

   ______ flowers

4. There are 8 birds. There are the same number of blue birds as yellow birds. How many birds are there of each color?

   ______ blue ______ yellow

At Home Use collections to create problems that your child can solve by drawing a picture.

En casa Use grupos de objetos para crear problemas que su niño pueda resolver haciendo un dibujo.

Name ______________________________

Science

Texas Field Trip

Sunshine Gardens

Sunshine Gardens is a community garden in Austin. Adults and children grow flowers, fruits, and vegetables. They learn about the parts of a plant.

Flower Garden

Draw a picture to solve.

1. Mia waters 6 tomato plants in her garden. Paul waters 1 more than Mia. How many tomato plants does Paul water?

   _____ tomato plants

tomato plant

---

2. Lin picks 9 ears of corn from her garden. Ali picks the same number as Lin. How many ears of corn does Ali pick?

   _____ ears of corn

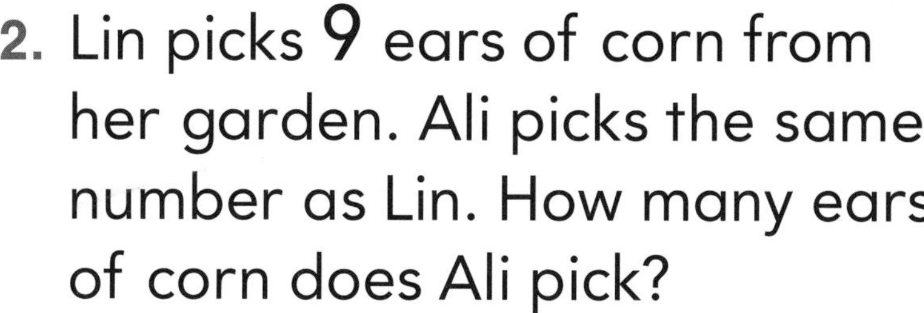

corn

---

3. Jack picks 5 baskets of cherries. Jane picks 1 fewer basket than Jack. How many baskets does Jane pick?

   _____ baskets of cherries

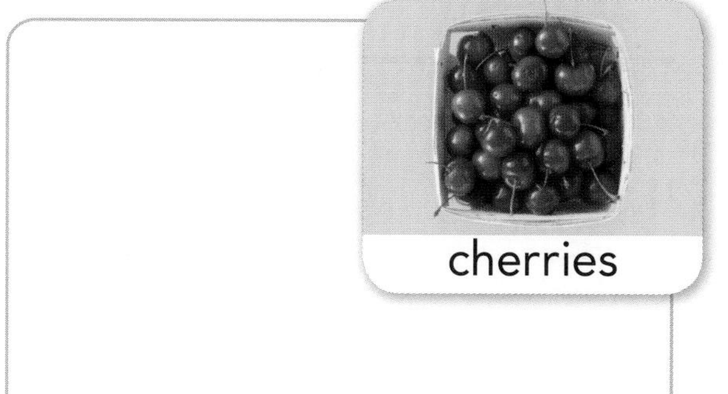

cherries

TAKS Objective 6
TEKS 1.1D Read and write numbers to 99 to describe sets of concrete objects.
1.11C Select or develop an appropriate problem-solving plan or strategy including drawing a picture, looking for a pattern, systematic guessing and checking, or acting it out in order to solve a problem.
TEKS Science 6B

TAKS Problem Solving
Listening Skills

Listen to your teacher read the problem. Choose the correct answer.

Select a Strategy
Act It Out
Draw a Picture

1. Sue picks 8 heads of lettuce. Ty picks 1 more head of lettuce than Sue. How many heads of lettuce does Ty pick?

   6 ○ 7 ○ 8 ○ 9 ○

   TEKS 1.1D

2. There are 6 pepper plants. There is the same number of tomato plants as pepper plants. How many tomato plants are there?

   2 ○ 4 ○ 6 ○ 8 ○

   TEKS 1.1D

3. 3 ○ 4 ○ 5 ○ 6 ○

   TEKS 1.1D

4. 5 ○ 6 ○ 7 ○ 8 ○

   TEKS 1.1D

Education Place
Visit www.eduplace.com/txmap/ for Test-Taking Tips and more TAKS Practice.

Name ______________________

Number Riddles

Read the riddle.
Write the answer.

1. The number of apples Al picked is less than 7. It is greater than 5. How many apples did Al pick? _____ apples

2. The number of apples Bena picked is less than 10. It is greater than 8. How many apples did Bena pick? _____ apples

3. Liz picked 3 apples. Bena picked 4 apples. Sean picked a number of apples equal to the number Liz and Bena picked together. How many apples did Sean pick? _____ apples

4. Otis picked 6 apples. Dora picked 10 apples. Nam picked 9 apples. Who picked the greatest number of apples? __________

Red-eared Sliders

Red-eared sliders live near slow-moving water in eastern Texas. Sliders are cold-blooded. They lie on rocks or logs in the sun. To lay their eggs, female sliders dig holes in the ground.

1. Model the set with counters.
   Write how many in all.

____

2. Write the number of eggs.
   Circle the number that is greater.

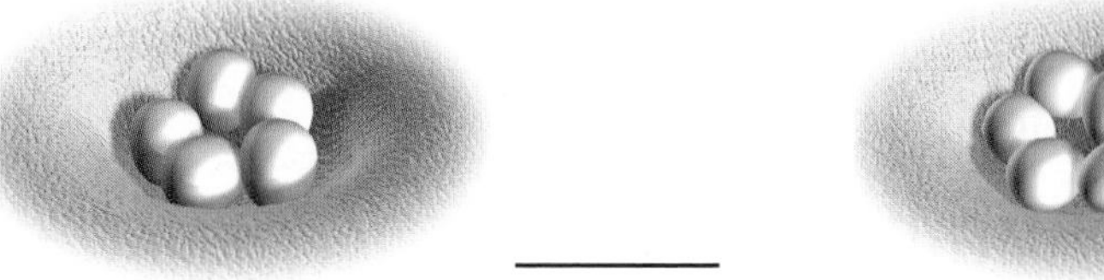

____ ____

3. Draw 10 eggs in a hole.

TAKS Objective 1
TEKS 1.1A Compare and order whole numbers up to 99 (less than, greater than, or equal to) using sets of concrete objects and pictorial models.
TEKS 1.1D Read and write numbers to 99 to describe sets of concrete objects.
TEKS Science 7D

Name ____________________

Concepts and Skills

Count. Write the number. TEKS 1.1D

1. 

____ five

2. 

____ eight

Build cube trains. Put the trains in order.
Color to show your work. Write the numbers. TEKS 1.1A

3. Show 7, 4, 5.

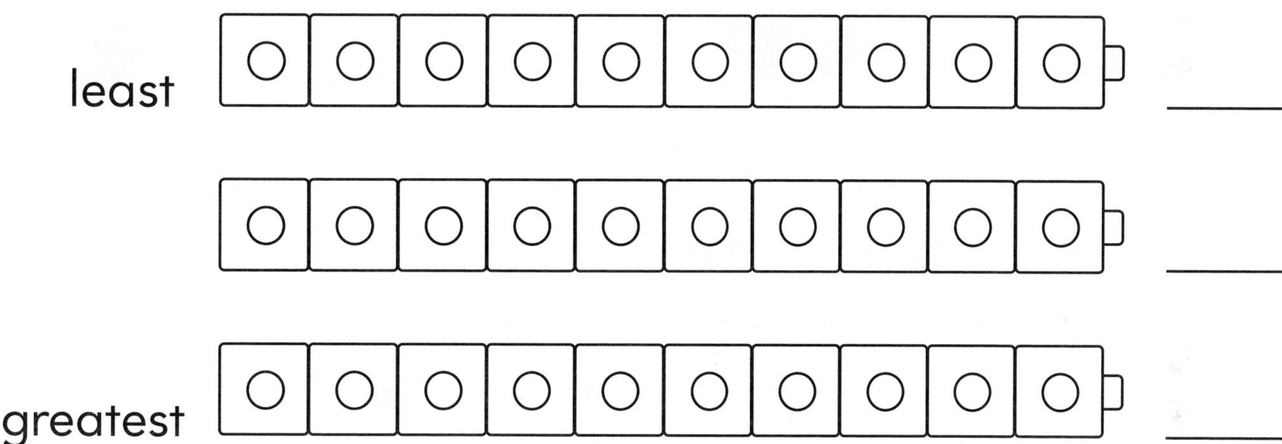

Problem Solving

Draw a picture to solve. TEKS 1.1D, 1.11B, 1.11C

4. Lin has 5 pens. Jack has 1 fewer pen than Lin. How many pens does Jack have?

____ pens

TAKS Prep and Spiral Review

Choose the answer for problems 1–4.

1. How many leaves are on the vine?

2 ◯ 3 ◯ 4 ◯ 5 ◯

TEKS 1.1D (page 21)

2. What comes next in the pattern?

◯ ◯ ◯ ◯

TEKS 1.4 (page 11)

3. Laura saw a dot pattern on a banner. Which number comes next in the pattern?

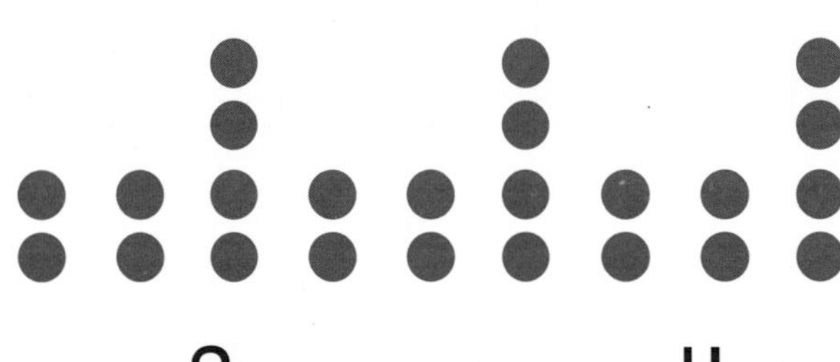

2 ◯ 3 ◯ 4 ◯ 5 ◯

TEKS 1.4 (page 9)

4. Mike picked 9 strawberries. Which plate shows what Mike picked?

◯ ◯ ◯ ◯

TEKS 1.1D (page 23)

Education Place
Visit **www.eduplace.com/txmap/** for Test-Taking Tips and Extra Practice.

Numbers 10 Through 20

TAKS Vocabulary

Here are some vocabulary words you will learn in the chapter.

number words 10 through 20

ten
10

11	12	13
eleven	twelve	thirteen
14	15	16
fourteen	fifteen	sixteen
17	18	19
seventeen	eighteen	nineteen

20
twenty

See English-Spanish glossary pages 505–516.

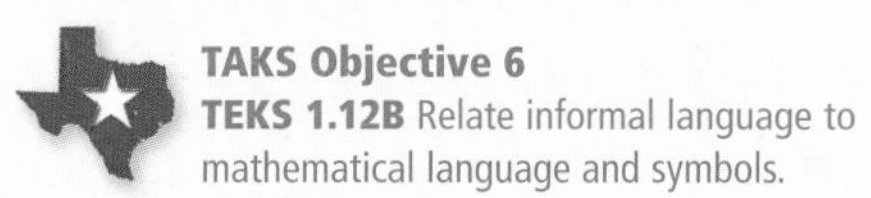

TAKS Objective 6
TEKS 1.12B Relate informal language to mathematical language and symbols.

Education Place
Visit **www.eduplace.com/txmap/** for the eGlossary and vocabulary eGames.

Name ______________________________

Check What You Know

Count.

Draw a line to the number.

1.

2.

3.

4.

5.

6

7

8

9

10

Use this page to review important skills needed for this chapter.

Name ____________________

Chapter 3 Lesson 1

Build Numbers 10 Through 15

Hands On

TEKS Objective
Count 10 through 15 objects; read and write the numbers.

TAKS Vocabulary
number words for 10 through 15

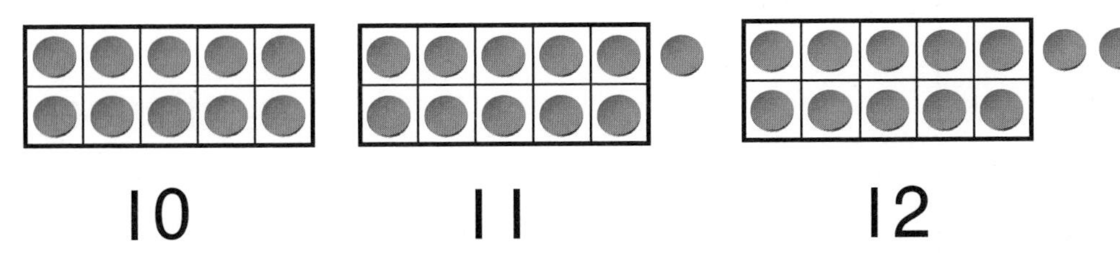

10 **ten**

11 **eleven**

12 **twelve**

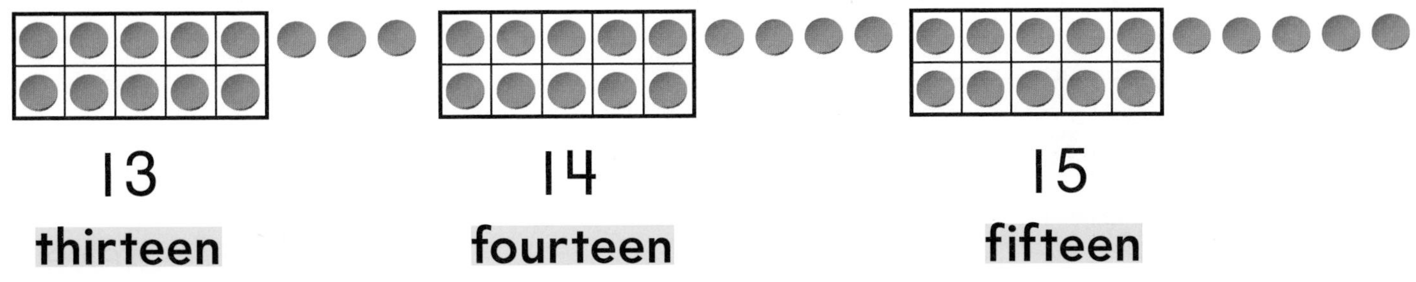

13 **thirteen**

14 **fourteen**

15 **fifteen**

Explore

Use Workmat 1 and ◯ to show the number.
Draw to show how many.

1. 15

2. 12

3. 14

4. 11

TAKS Objective 1
TEKS 1.1D Read and write numbers to 99 to describe sets of concrete objects.

★ Extend

Count. Write the number.

5.    

thirteen

6. 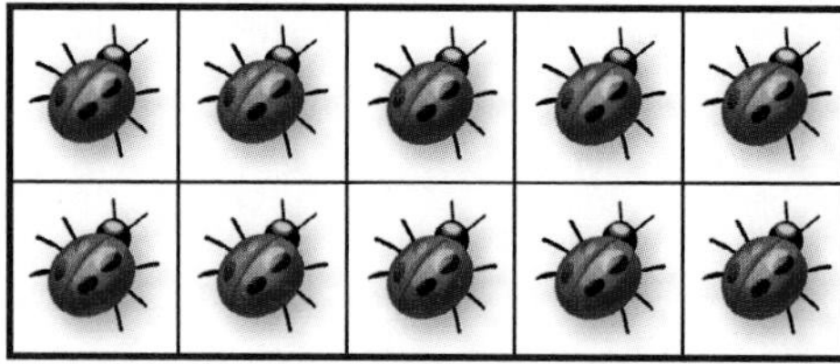

ten

7.  

twelve

8. 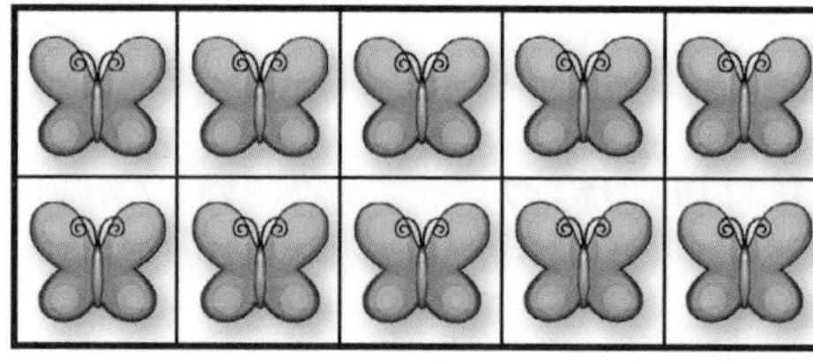 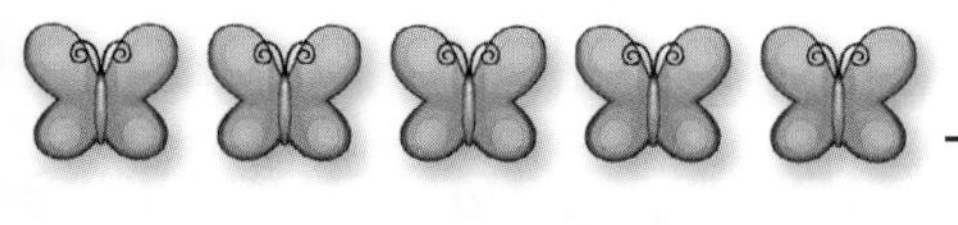

fifteen

9. 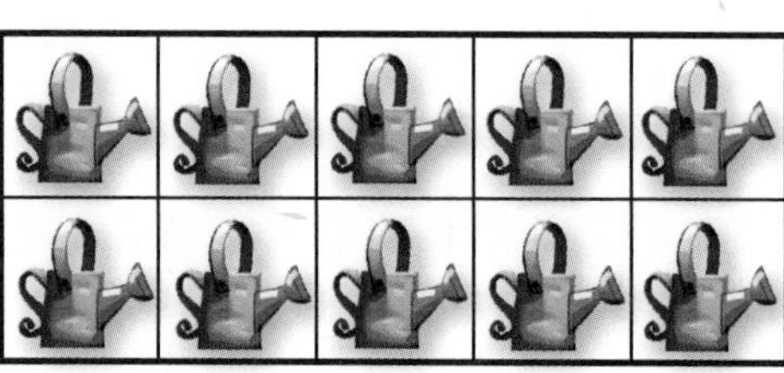 

eleven

10. Draw your own set. Write the number.

11. **Math Talk** Which set has the fewest? How do you know?

At Home Ask your child to count sets of 10 through 15 objects and write the number for each set.

En casa Pida a su niño que cuente conjuntos de 10 a 15 objetos y que escriba el número para cada conjunto.

Hands On

TEKS Objective
Count 16 through 20 objects; read and write the numbers.

TAKS Vocabulary
number words for 16 through 20

Name ______________________________

Chapter 3 Lesson 2

Build Numbers 16 Through 20

16
sixteen

17
seventeen

18
eighteen

19
nineteen

20
twenty

★ Explore

Use Workmat 2 and ◯ to show the number.
Draw to show how many.

1. 17

2. 20

3. 19

4. 18

TAKS Objective 1
TEKS 1.1D Read and write numbers to 99 to describe sets of concrete objects.

★ Extend

Count. Write the number.

Remember!

16 sixteen
17 seventeen
18 eighteen
19 nineteen
20 twenty

5. 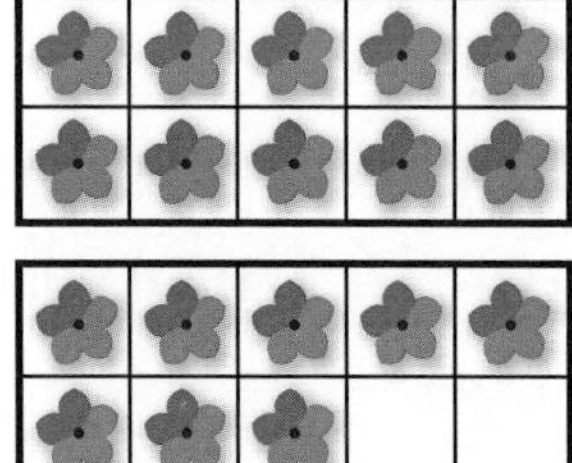

18

eighteen

6. 

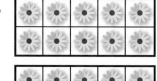

sixteen

7. 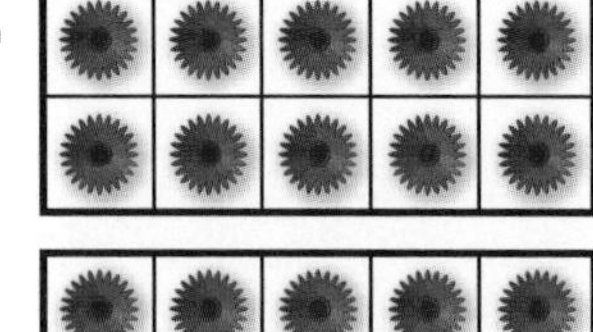

twenty

8. 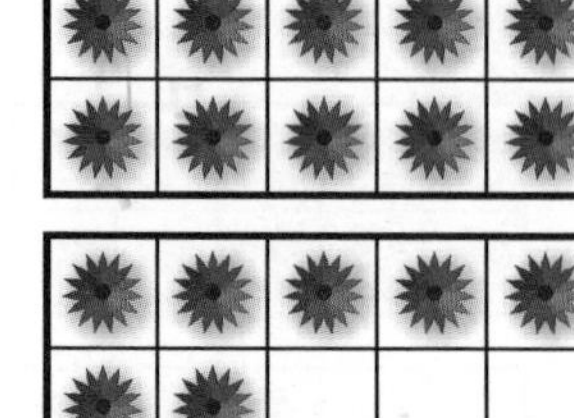

seventeen

9. 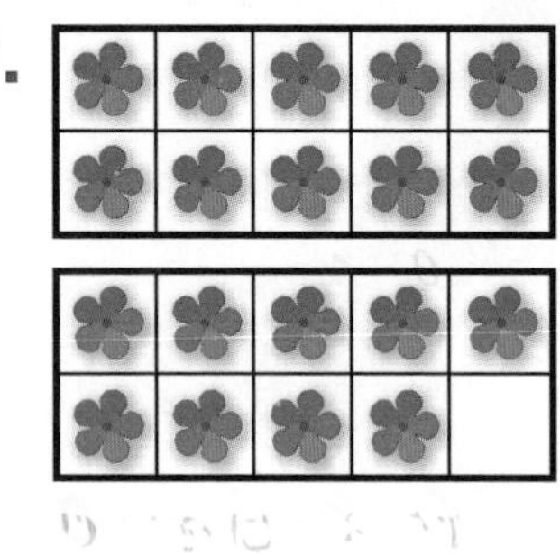

nineteen

10. **Math Talk** Which set has the most? How do you know?

Choose a number from 10 through 20.

11. Write the number.

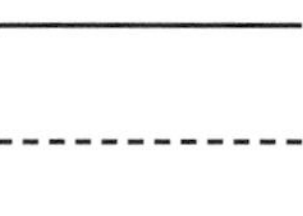

12. Draw that many flowers.

At Home Ask your child to count sets of up to 20 objects and write the number for each set.

En casa Pida a su niño que cuente conjuntos de hasta 20 objetos y que escriba el número para cada conjunto.

Name ______________________

Chapter 3 Lesson 3

Compare Numbers 11 Through 20

Hands On

TEKS Objective
Compare the numbers 11 through 20 using objects, pictures, and words.

★ Learn

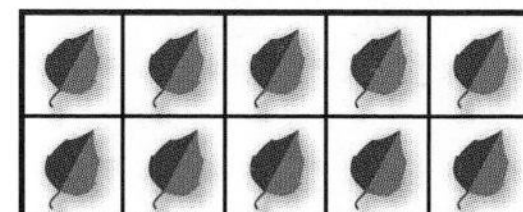
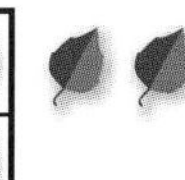
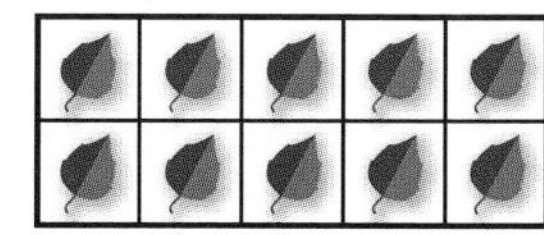

12 is less than 14

14 is greater than 13

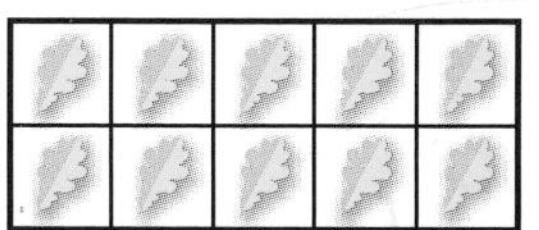

12 is equal to 12

Think!
20 counters is more than 18 counters. I know which number is greater.

★ Guided Practice

Work with a partner. Model and draw each set. Circle the words that make the sentence true.

1. 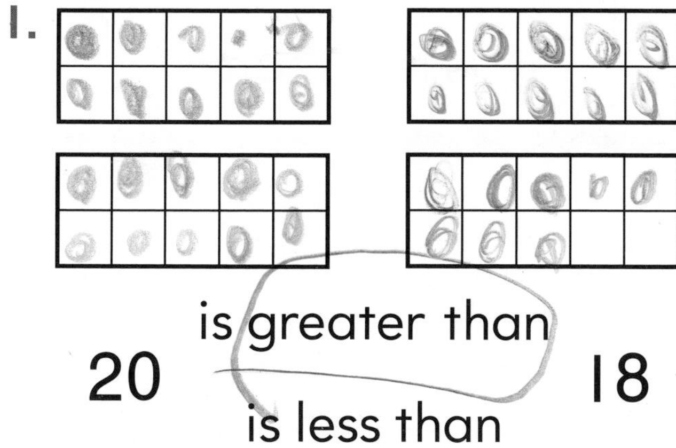

20 is greater than / is less than 18

2. 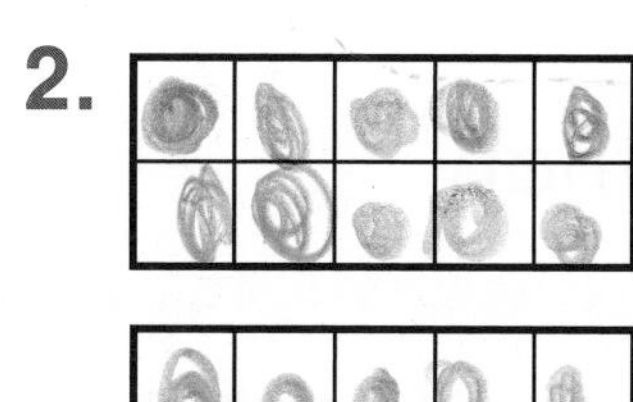 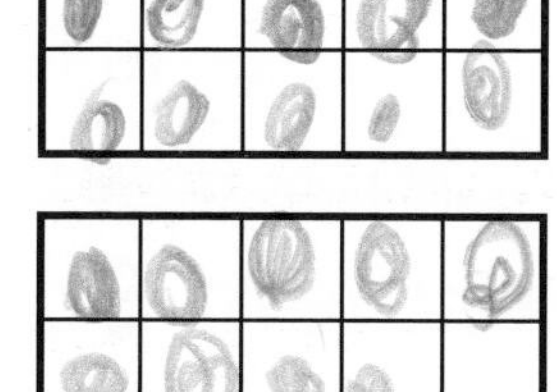

17 is greater than / is equal to 17

3. **Math Talk** Read the answer to Exercise 2. What does it mean?

TAKS Objective 1
TEKS 1.1A Compare and order whole numbers up to 99 (less than, greater than, or equal to) using sets of concrete objects and pictorial models.

★ Practice

Work with a partner.
Model and draw each set.
Circle the words that make the sentence true.

4. 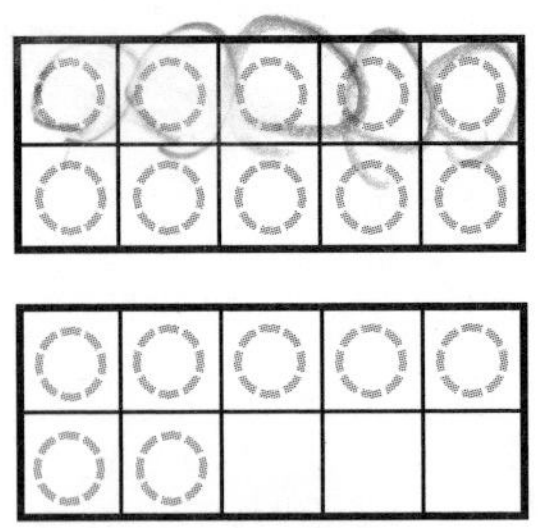

17 is greater than / is less than 20

5. 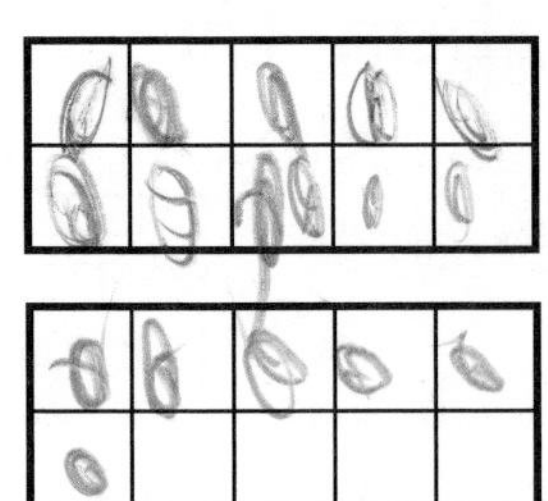

16 is greater than / is equal to 16

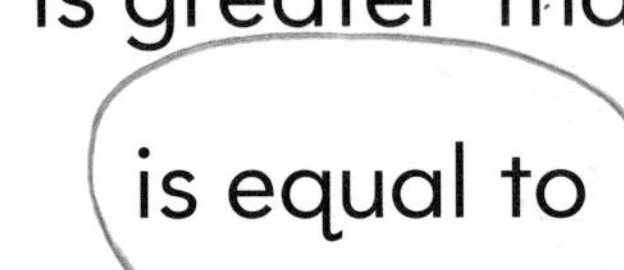

6. 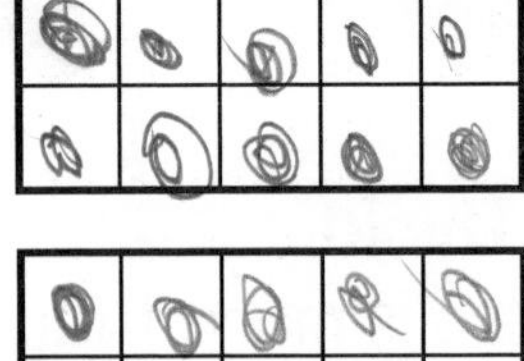

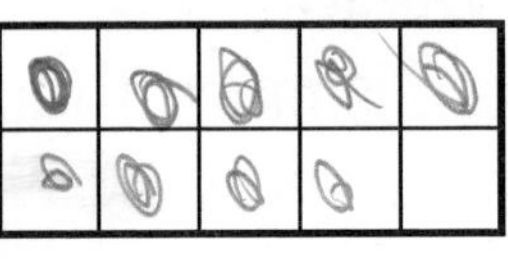

19 is greater than / is less than 17

7. 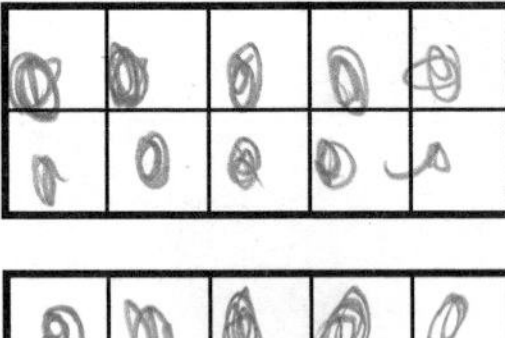

16 is greater than / is less than 18

Problem Solving: Number Sense

8. Write two numbers that are greater than 10 but less than 20.

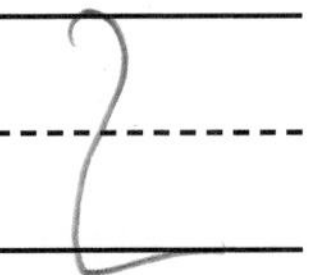

9. Write two numbers that are less than 10.

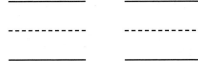

At Home Name two numbers less than 20. Have your child tell which is greater.

En casa Nombre dos números menores que 20. Pida a su niño que diga cuál es mayor.

Name ______________________

Chapter 3 Lesson 4

Order Numbers 11 Through 20

14 is the greatest.

12

11 is the least.

★ Explore

Use cubes and Workmat 2 to show the numbers. Order the workmats. Draw. Write the numbers in order.

Think!
14 is greater than 13 and 11. I know which number is greatest.

1. Show 11, 14, 13.

greatest ______ ______ ______ least

2. Show 15, 18, 16.

greatest ______ ______ ______ least

3. **Math Talk** In Exercise 2 which number is the greatest?

TEKS Objective
Order the numbers 11 through 20 using objects, pictures, and words.

TAKS Objective 1
TEKS 1.1A Compare and order whole numbers up to 99 (less than, greater than, or equal to) using sets of concrete objects and pictorial models.

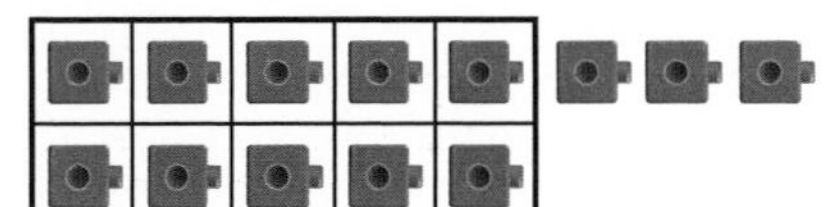
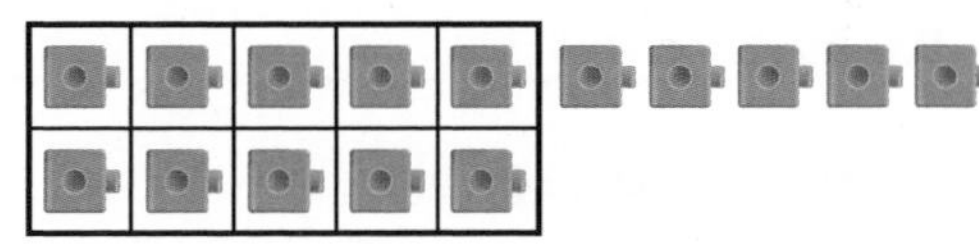

11 is the least. 13 15 is the greatest.

★ Extend

Use cubes and Workmat 2 to show the numbers. Order the workmats. Draw. Write the numbers in order.

4. Show 11, 15, 13.

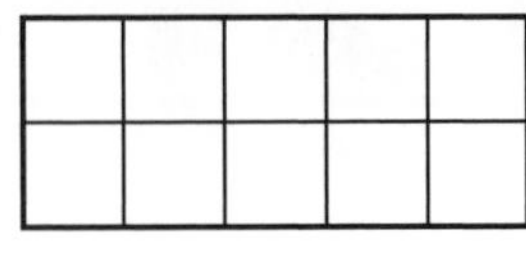
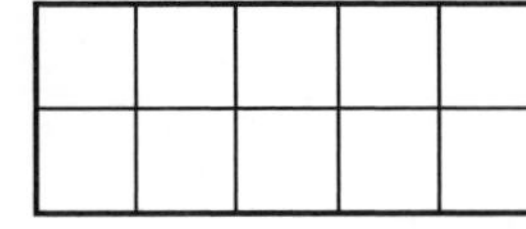
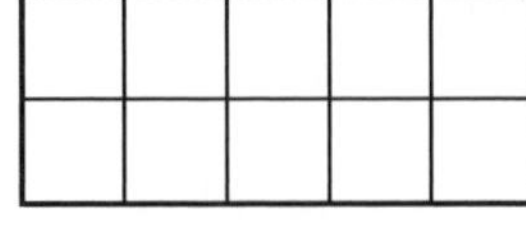

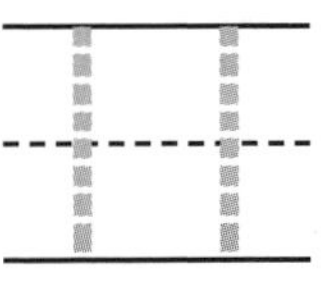

least greatest

5. Show 14, 12, 15.

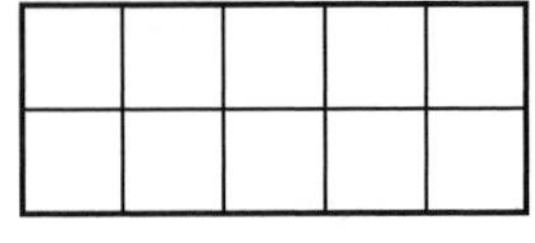
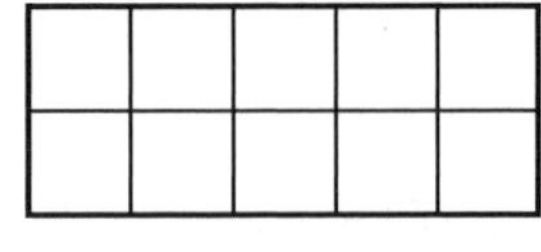

least greatest

6. Show 18, 17, 19.

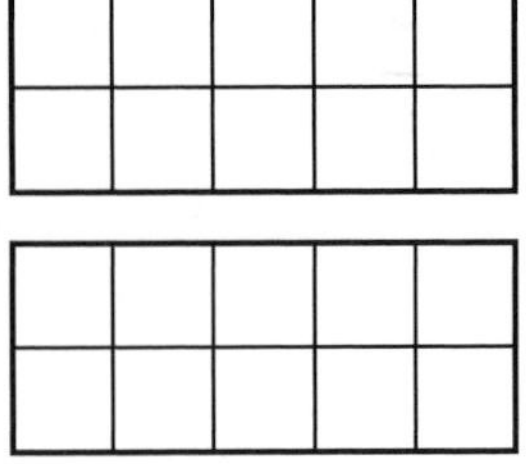
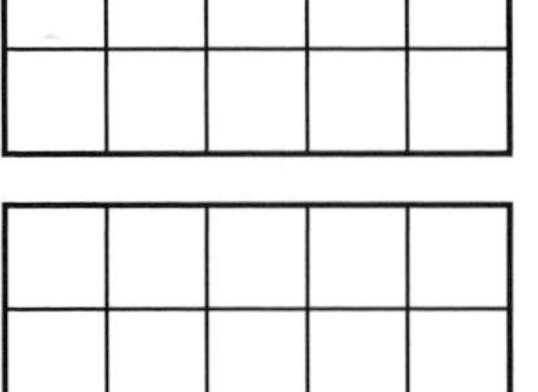
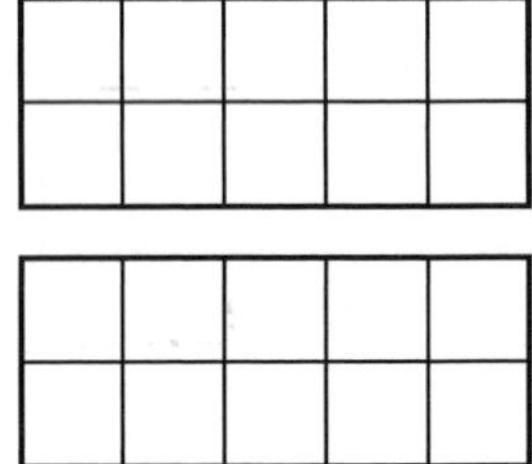

least greatest

At Home Write 3 numbers from 11 through 20 in any order. Have your child write them in order from least to greatest.

En casa Escriba 3 números del 11 al 20 en cualquier orden. Pida a su niño que los escriba en orden de menor a mayor.

TEKS Objective
Create and solve comparison problems.

Name ______________________________

Chapter 3 Lesson 5

Create and Solve

The children went to a park. They saw bluebonnets growing. The chart shows how many they counted.

Bluebonnets We Counted

Kim counted 14.	Kuri counted 11.	Jerome counted 18.

Write a question that compares the numbers.

1. ______________________________

____

Have your partner answer the question.

2. ____________

Write another comparison question.

3. ______________________________

____

Have your partner answer the question.

4. ____________

TAKS Objectives 1, 6
TEKS 1.1A Compare and order whole numbers up to 99 (less than, greater than, or equal to) using sets of concrete objects and or pictorial models.

TEKS 1.12A Explain and record observations using objects, words, pictures, numbers, and technology.

The children went to a park.
They saw sunflowers growing.
The chart shows how many they counted.

Sunflowers We Counted		
Rosa counted 15.	Will counted 17.	Chris counted 12.

Write a question that compares the numbers.

5. ______________________________

____

Have your partner answer the question.

6. __________

Write another comparison question.

7. ______________________________

____

Have your partner answer the question.

8. __________

At Home Help your child create and solve a different problem using the data in the chart.

En casa Ayude a su niño a crear y resolver un problema diferente usando los datos que aparecen en la tabla.

Math Works

Name ______________________

Ride Operator

Luke operates rides at an amusement park. He helps people on and off the rides safely. Luke also collects tickets and counts the people.

Use ⚪ to solve.

1. Luke counts the number of people who ride on the merry-go-round. First he counts 17 people. Next he counts 20 people. Then he counts 14 people. Order the number of people from least to greatest.

   _____, _____, _____

2. Luke counts how many people there are on the red and blue bumper boats. There are 12 people on the red boats. The blue boats have 1 more person than the red boats. How many people are on the blue boats?

   _____ people

3. Luke is holding 19 tickets for go carts. Is 19 greater than or less than 20?

   ____

4. **Math Talk** Tell how you solved Exercise 2.

TAKS Objectives 1, 6
TEKS 1.1A Compare and order whole numbers up to 99 (less than, greater than, or equal to) using sets of concrete objects and pictorial models.
TEKS 1.11A Identify mathematics in everyday situations.

Math Music

Chopping Potatoes

1 potato, 2 potatoes,
What comes next?
It rhymes with key.
The number is 3!

4 potatoes, 5 potatoes,
What comes next?
It rhymes with mix.
The number is 6!

7 potatoes, 8 potatoes,
What comes next?
It rhymes with line.
The number is 9!

10 potatoes, 11 potatoes,
What comes next?
It rhymes with delve.
The number is 12!

1 potato, 2 potatoes,
3 potatoes, 4,
5 potatoes, 6 potatoes,
7 potatoes, more.
8 potatoes, 9 potatoes,
chop, chop, chop,
10 potatoes, 11 potatoes,
12 potatoes stop!

We chopped
12 potatoes and
now we're done.

Chopping
12 potatoes was
lots of fun!

TAKS Objective 1
TEKS 1.1D Read and write numbers to 99 to describe sets of concrete objects.

Name ____________________

Concepts and Skills

Count.
Write the number. TEKS 1.1D

1. 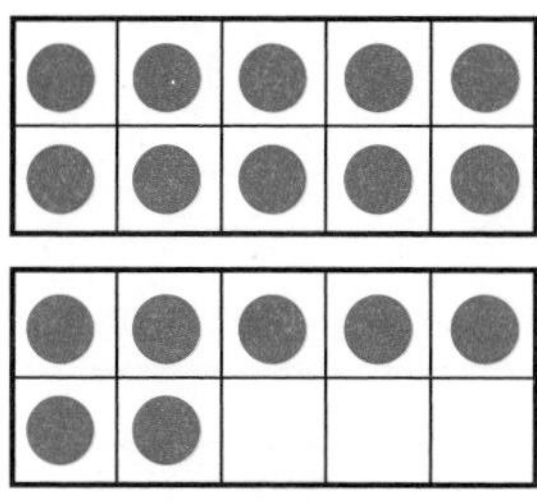

_____ seventeen

Circle the words that make the sentence true. TEKS 1.1A

2. 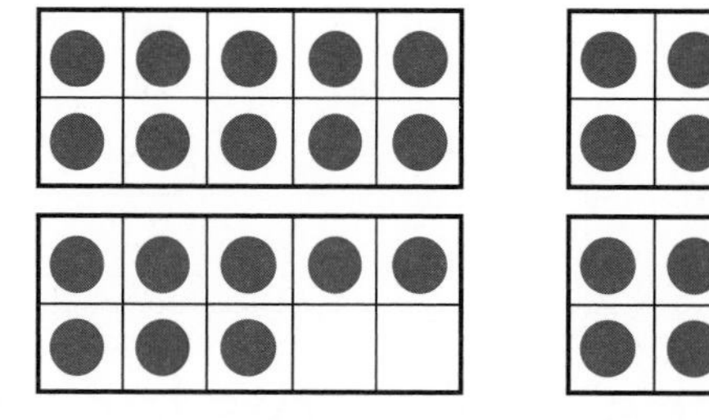

18 is greater than / is less than 19

Use cubes and Workmat 2 to show the numbers. Order the Workmats. Draw. Write the numbers in order. TEKS 1.1A

3. Show 11, 14, 13.

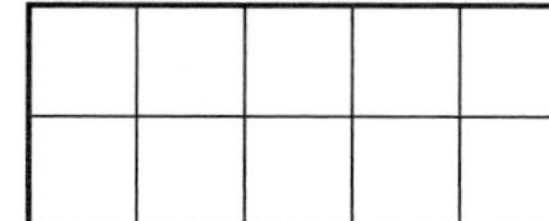 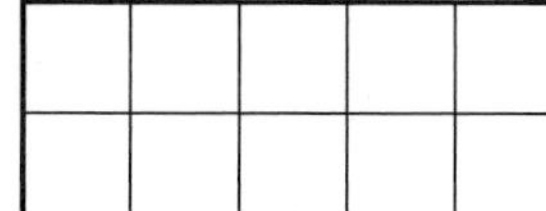 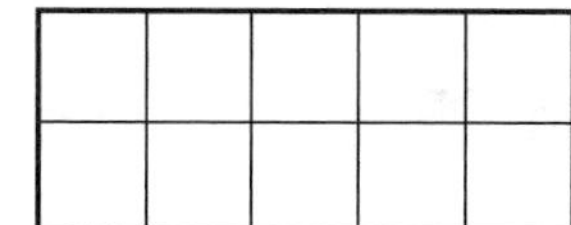

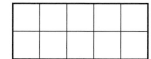

_____ least _____ _____ greatest

Problem Solving TEKS 1.1A, 1.12A

4. Write a question that compares the numbers.

Bluebonnets We Counted

Kim	Kuri	Jerome

____

____

TAKS Prep and Spiral Review

Choose the answer for problems 1–4.

1. Which number tells how many?

5	8	9	10
○	○	○	○

TEKS 1.1D (page 23)

---

2. Greg has some pots for planting. How many pots are there?

12	14	15	16
○	○	○	○

TEKS 1.1D (page 39)

---

3. Which shows the number of seeds in order from least to greatest?

6 seeds  

9, 6, 5	5, 9, 6	5, 6, 9	6, 5, 9
○	○	○	○

TEKS 1.1A (page 27)

---

4. Some children planted flower seeds. Rosa planted 15 seeds. Han planted 20 seeds. Josh planted 18 seeds. Who planted the greatest number of seeds?

Josh	Han	Bess	Rosa
○	○	○	○

TEKS 1.1A (page 45)

Education Place
Visit **www.eduplace.com/txmap/** for Test-Taking Tips and Extra Practice.

Name ______________________________

Greg Tang's **Go Fast, Go Far**

Unit 1 **Mental Math Strategies**

Count All

Have a ball.
Just count all.

1, 2, count more.
3, 4!

1. 4

2. 

3. 

4. 

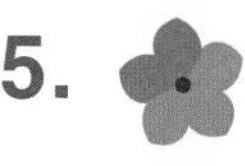

5. 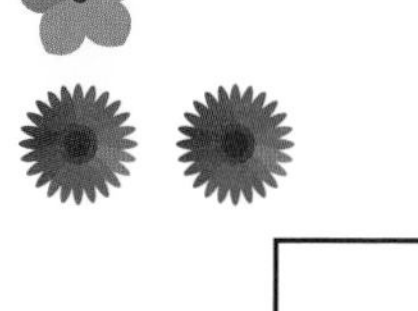

6. 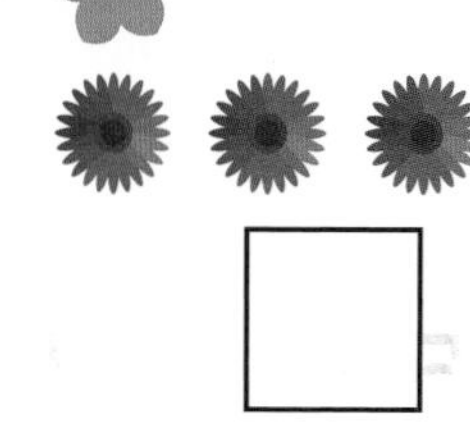

Doing Great!

Take It Further: Count all.

7. 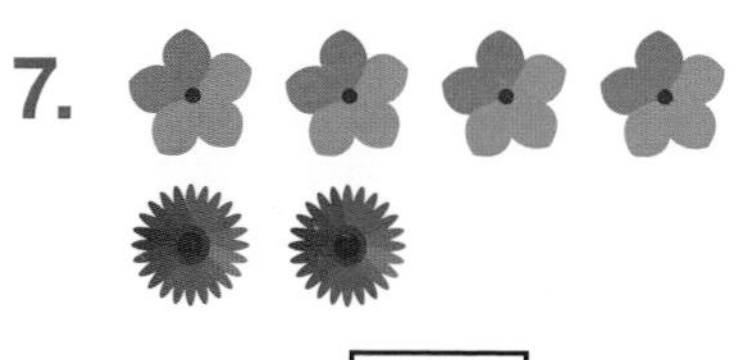

8. 

9. 

Unit 1 Wrap Up

Name ______________________________

Reading and Writing Math

Model and draw each set.
Circle the words that make the sentence true.

1. 

6 is greater than / is less than 5

2.  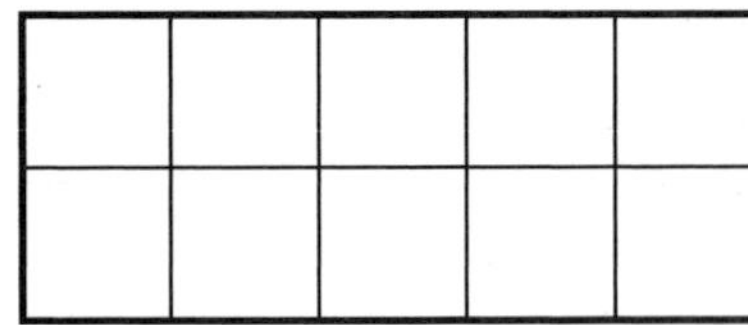

12 is less than / is equal to 14

3. 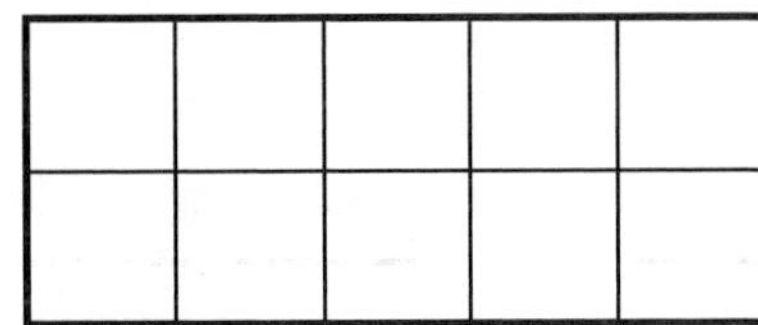 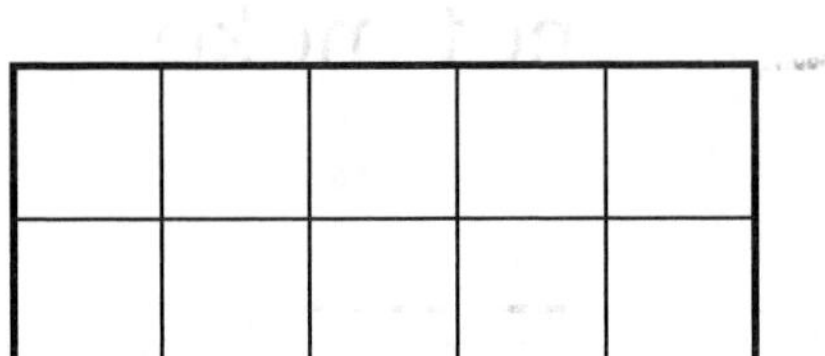

10 is greater than / is equal to 10

4. **Writing Math** Choose three numbers from the exercises. Order the numbers from least to greatest.

____

TEKS 1.12A Explain and record observations using objects, words, pictures, numbers, and technology.

TEKS 1.12B Relate informal language to mathematical language and symbols.

Name ______________________

Concepts and Skills

Find the part that repeats.
Circle what comes next. TEKS 1.4

1.   

2.  

Count. Write the number. TEKS 1.1D

3. 

_______ nine

4. 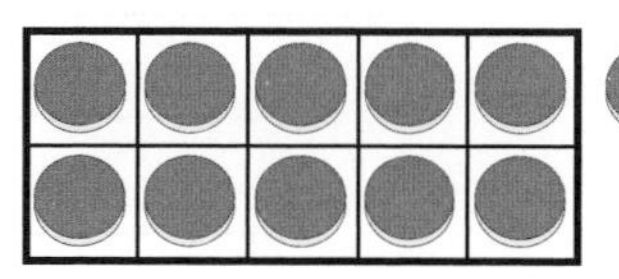

_______ fourteen

Model and draw each set.
Circle the words that make the sentence true. TEKS 1.1A

5. 

8 is greater than / is less than 6

6. 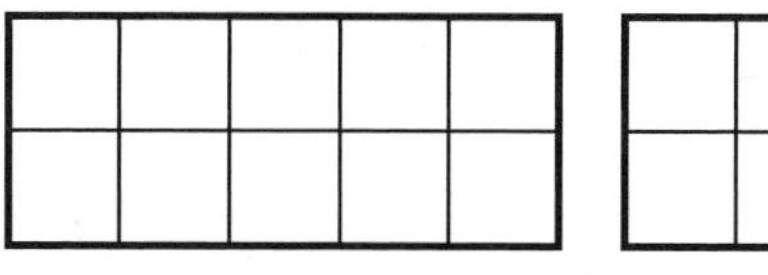 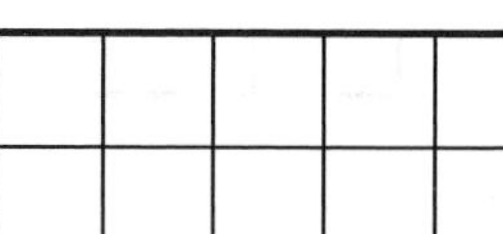 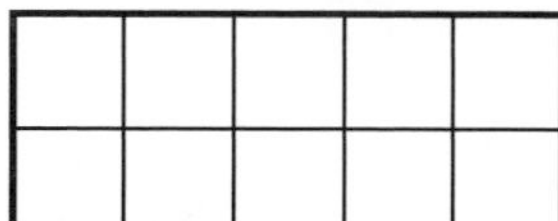 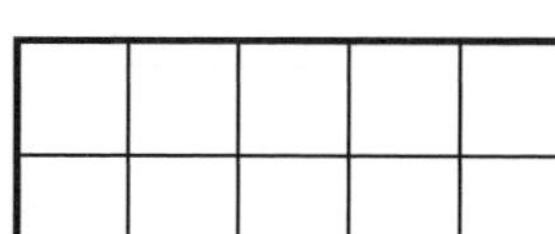

18 is greater than / is less than 16

Use cubes and Workmat 2 to show the numbers. Order the workmats. Draw. Write the numbers in order. TEKS 1.1A

7. Show 11, 15, 13.

least greatest

8. Show 14, 12, 15.

least greatest

Problem Solving

Draw a picture to solve. TEKS 1.1D, TEKS 1.11B, TEKS 1.11C

9. Meg has 8 flowers. Carlos has 1 more flower than Meg. How many flowers does Carlos have?

_____ flowers

10. Jan has 11 seed packets. Li has 1 fewer packet than Jan. How many seed packets does Li have?

_____ seed packets

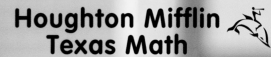

Addition and Subtraction Concepts

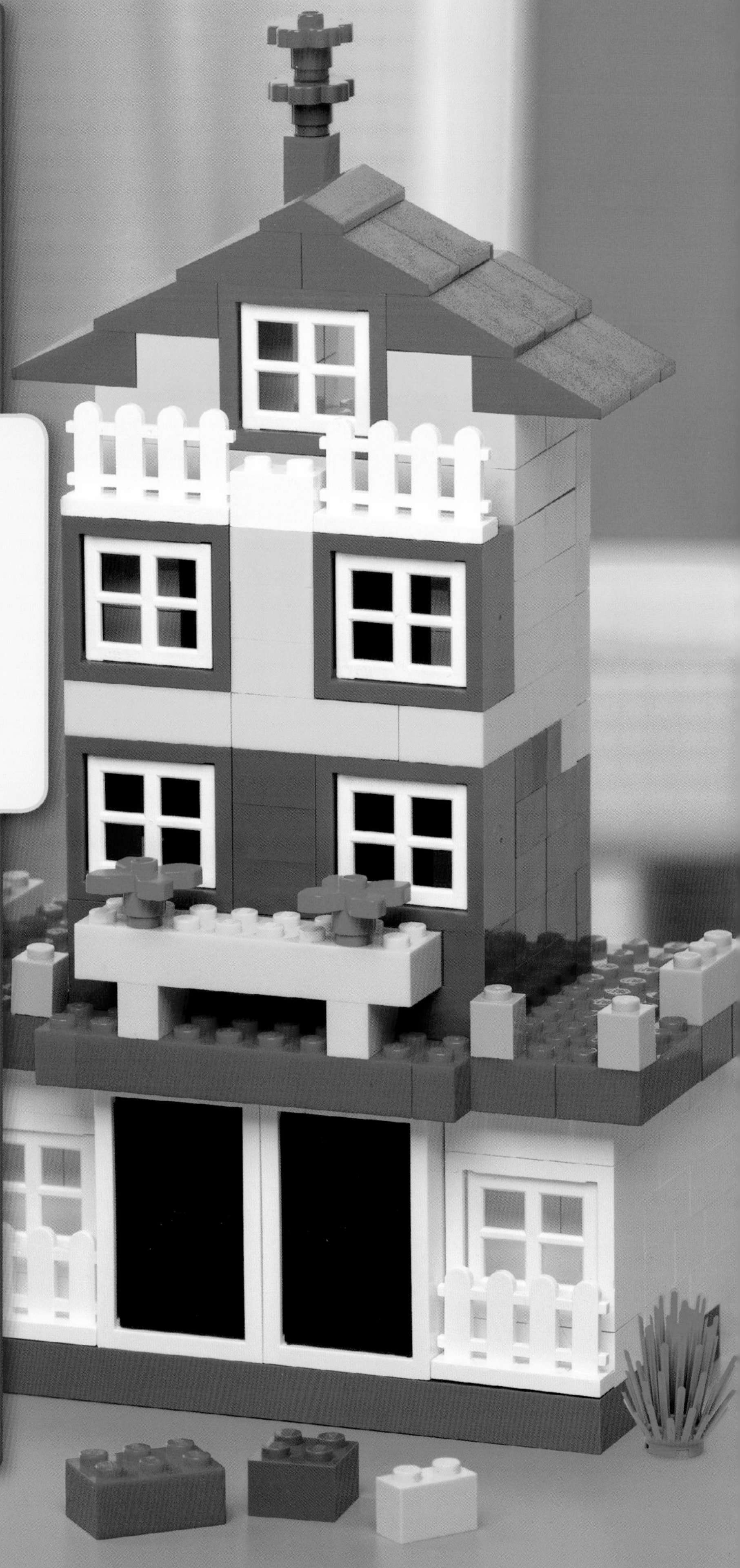

BIG IDEAS!

- When you join two groups, you add.
- When you separate into two groups, you subtract.
- You can build and break apart numbers in more than one way (objects, pictures, symbols, and number sentences).

Songs and Games

Math Music Track 2
What's the Sum?

eGames
www.eduplace.com/txmap/

Literature

Literature Big Book
- Little Quack

Math Readers

ISBN-13: 978-0-618-95269-4
ISBN-10: 0-618-95269-1
89- WC - 16 15 14 13 12

What You Need
2 players 2 sets of dot cards

Dot Card Match-Up

1. Mix the cards. Put them face down.
2. One at a time, turn over 2 cards.
3. If the number of dots on the cards is the same, keep the cards.
4. If the number of dots is not the same, turn the cards back over.
5. Play until all the cards are used.

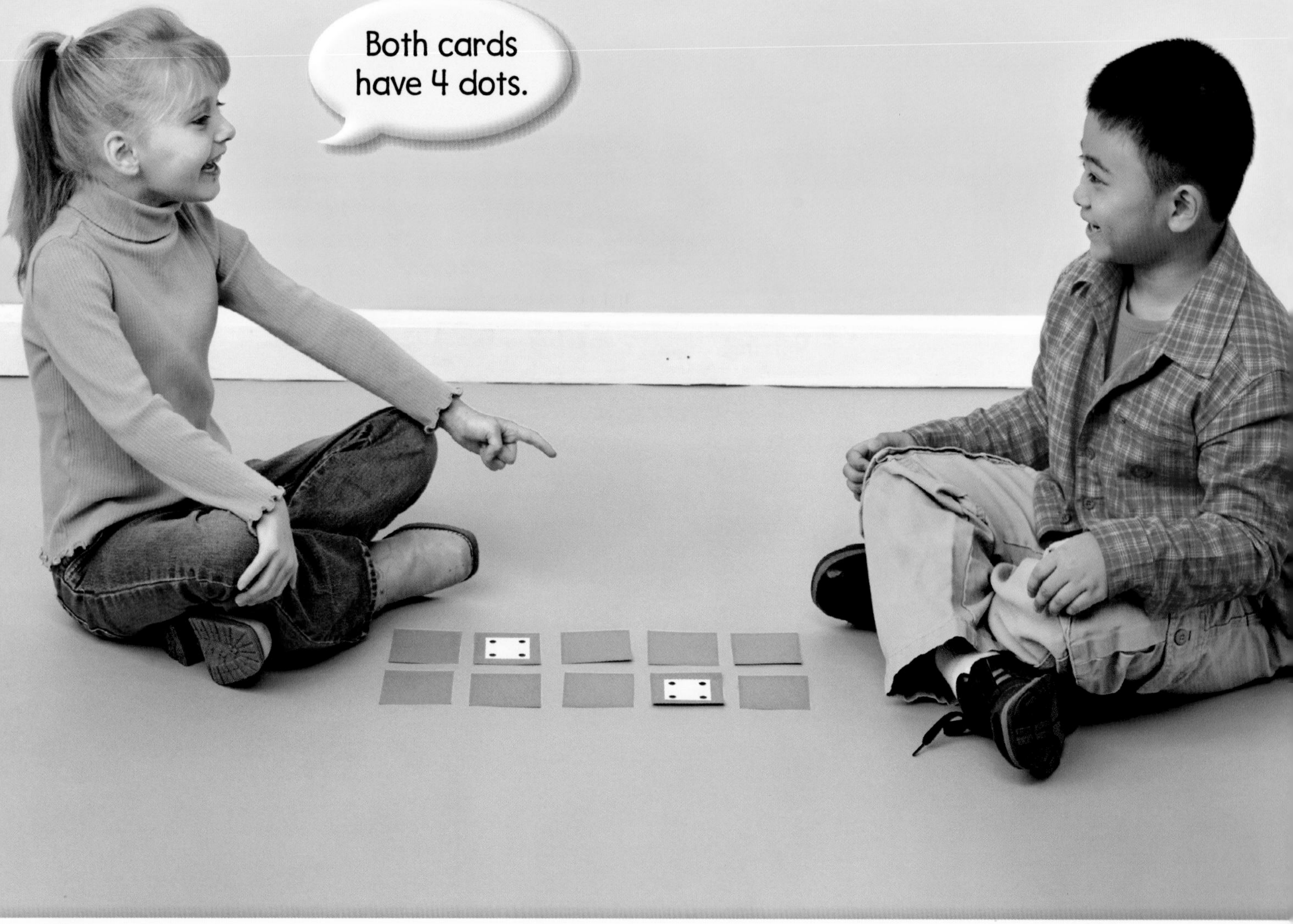

Both cards have 4 dots.

TAKS Objective 1
TEKS 1.1A Compare and order whole numbers up to 99 (less than, greater than, or equal to) using sets of concrete objects and pictorial models.

TEKS 1.1D Read and write numbers to 99 to describe sets of concrete objects.

Education Place
For eGames and Brain Teasers, visit **www.eduplace.com/txmap/**

Math at Home

Dear Family,

My class is starting Unit 2, **Addition and Subtraction Concepts**. I will learn that addition is used to join groups to find how many in all, and subtraction is used when taking away to find how many are left. You can help me learn these vocabulary words, and we can do the Math Activity together.

From,

____

Vocabulary

sum How many in all.

addition sentence A number sentence used to find the sum.

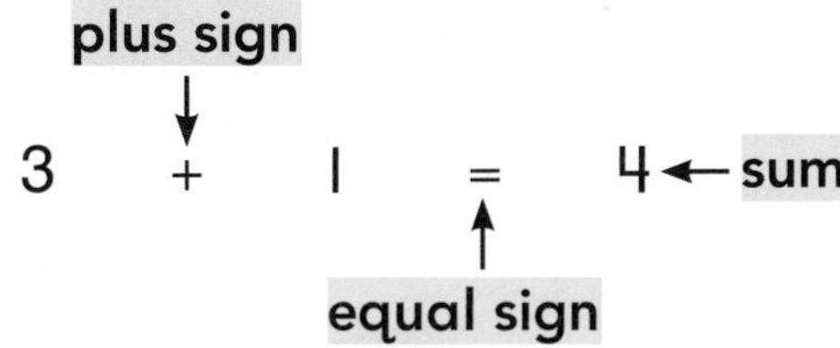

difference How many are left.

subtraction sentence A number sentence used to find the difference.

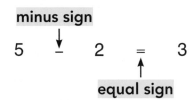

minus sign

5 − 2 = 3

equal sign

Education Place
Visit **www.eduplace.com/txmaf/** for
- eGames and Brain Teasers
- Math at Home in other languages

Family Math Activity

Create addition and subtraction stories up to 8. For example, there are 2 red apples and 2 green apples. How many apples in all? There are 3 bananas. I eat 1. How many bananas are left?

Literature

These books link to the math in this unit. Look for them at the library.

- **Adding Arctic Animals**
  by David Bauer
  (Capstone Press, 2004)
- **Dealing with Addition**
  by Lynette Long, Ph. D.
- **One for Me, One for You**
  by C.C. Cameron

Matemáticas en casa

Estimada familia:

Mi clase está comenzando la Unidad 2, **Conceptos sobre la suma y la resta**. Voy a aprender que la suma se usa para unir grupos y así hallar cuántos hay en total, y que la resta se usa cuando se quita para hallar cuántos quedan. Me pueden ayudar a aprender estas palabras de vocabulario y podemos hacer juntos la Actividad de matemáticas para la familia.

De:

____

Vocabulario

suma Cuántos en total.

oración de suma Oración numérica usada para hallar la suma.

signo de más (+)

3 + 1 = 4 ← **suma**

signo de igual (=)

resta Cuántos quedan.

oración de resta Oración numérica usada para hallar la diferencia.

signo de menos (-)

5 - 2 = 3

signo de igual (=)

Education Place

Visite **www.eduplace.com/txmaf/** para

- Juegos en línea y acertijos
- Matemáticas en casa, en otros idiomas

Actividad de matemáticas para la familia

Cree cuentos de suma y de resta hasta 8. Por ejemplo, hay 2 manzanas rojas y 2 manzanas verdes. ¿Cuántas manzanas hay en total? Hay 3 bananas. Me como 1. ¿Cuántas bananas quedan?

Literatura

Estos libros hablan sobre las matemáticas de esta unidad. Podemos buscarlos en la biblioteca.

- **Restar**
  por Lisa Trumbauer
  (Yellow Umbrella Books, 2005)
- **Un cuento de peces, más o menos**
  por David Wylie y Joanne Wylie
- **Sumar y contar hacia adelante**
  por Richard Leffingwell

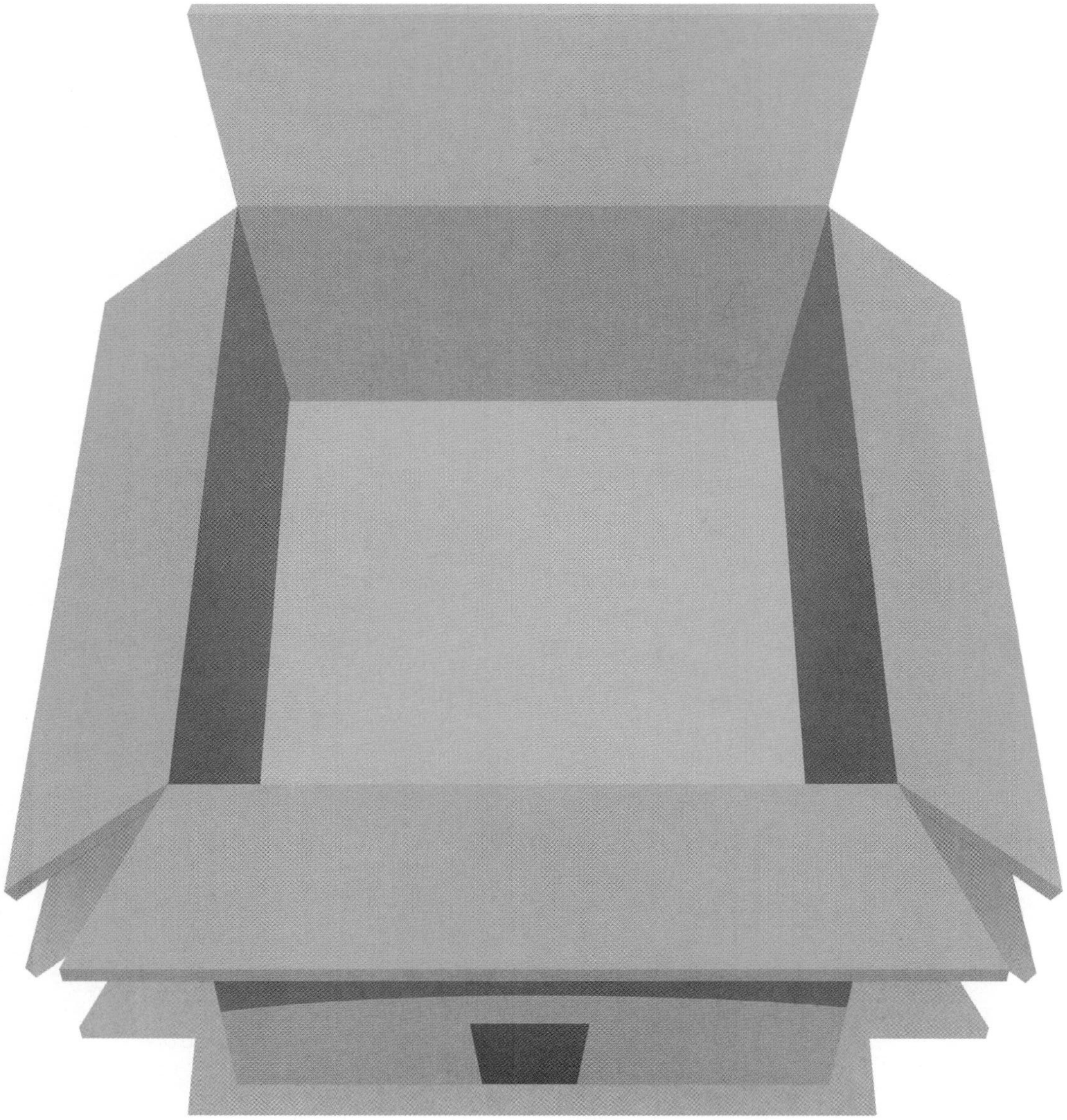

Draw 6 things you wish would arrive in a box addressed to you. Number the things 1, 2, 3, 4, 5, and 6.

TAKS Objectives 1, 6
TEKS 1.3B, 1.11A

UNIT 2

Delivery Dog

written by Tim Johnson
illustrated by Chris Simpson

This Take-Home Book belongs to

____

Reading and Writing Math

This take-home book will help you review counting from 1 to 6.

Delivery Dog delivers mail in our town.
First he delivers 1 big box, and
1 small one, too.
How many boxes are for Officer Lou?

2 boxes are delivered to Firefighter Sue.
That leaves just 1 box
which is addressed to YOU!

4 more boxes to deliver, and
Dog's work is done.
How many boxes are left after
Dog delivers this one?

I letter for Baker Suki,
and 2 for Baker Paul.
How many letters are for
the bakers in all?

Next, boxes of books for the library.
How many boxes do you see?

Billy Bear buys some stamps.
He saves stamps with his gramps.
How many stamps are there in all?

Sari Chipmunk gets 4 cards
and a letter with warm regards.
How many pieces of mail are
there in all?

Mrs. Turner just gets bills.
She smiles and says, "Oh thrills."
How many bills did she get?

3 letters for Dr. Lion,
and 2 for Nurse Cow.

How many letters are delivered
just now?

Addition Concepts

TAKS Vocabulary

Here are some vocabulary words you will learn in the chapter.

add Combine or join to find how many in all

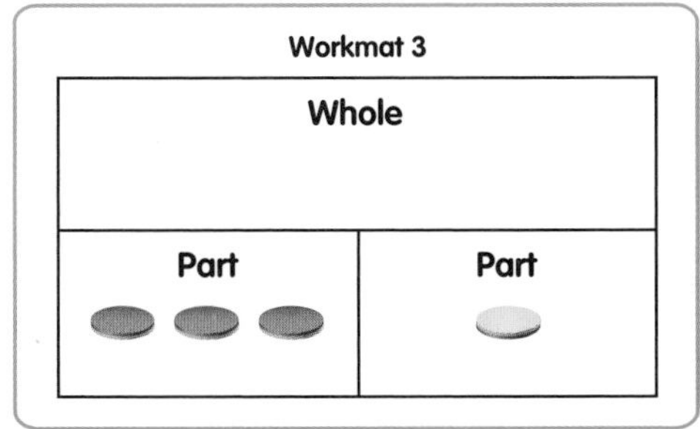

You add the parts to find the whole.

plus sign A symbol that tells you to add

equal sign A symbol that means to be the same as

sum How many in all

addition sentence A number sentence used to find the sum

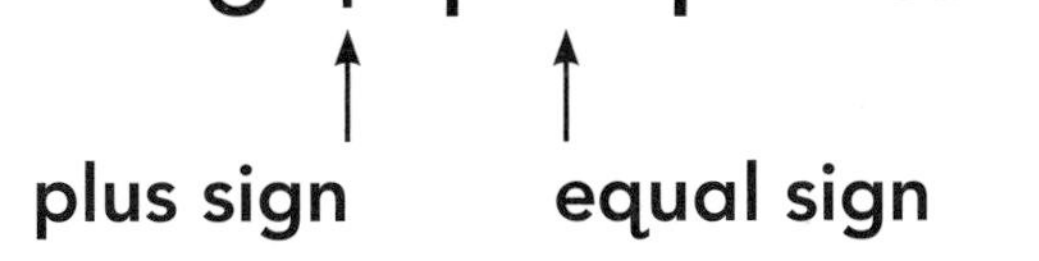

See English-Spanish glossary pages 505–516.

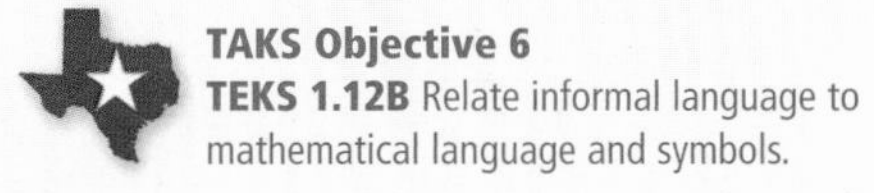
TAKS Objective 6
TEKS 1.12B Relate informal language to mathematical language and symbols.

Education Place
Visit **www.eduplace.com/txmap/** for the eGlossary and vocabulary eGames.

Name ___________________________________

Check What You Know

Count.

Draw a line to the number that matches.

1. 

2.     

3.

4.   

5.    

Use this page to review important skills needed for this chapter.

Name ________________________________

Chapter 4 Lesson 1

Addition Stories

Hands On

TEKS Objective
Model addition situations with concrete objects.

★ Explore

Listen to the story.
Show the story with ◯.

1.

2. Math Talk How do you know if your answer is correct?

TAKS Objectives 1, 6
TEKS 1.3A Model and create addition and subtraction problem situations with concrete objects and write corresponding number sentences.

TEKS 1.12A Explain and record observations using objects, words, pictures, numbers, and technology.

★ Extend

Listen to the story.
Show the story with ◯.
Write the numbers.

Remember!
Listen for the numbers in the story.

3.

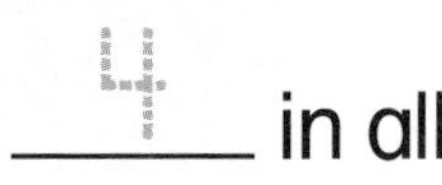

2 girls   2 boys   4 in all

4.

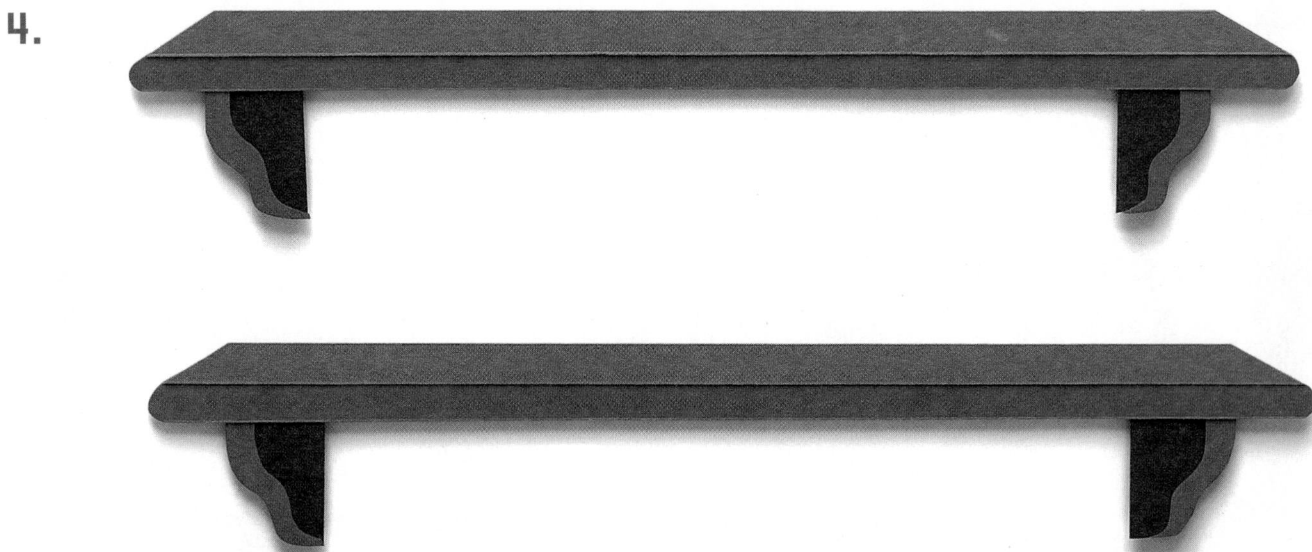

_____ drums   _____ horns   _____ in all

At Home Place a set of 2 objects and a set of 3 objects on a table. Ask your child how many objects there are in all.

En casa Ponga sobre la mesa un conjunto de 2 objetos y otro de 3 objetos. Pregunte a su niño cuántos objetos hay en total.

Name ___________________________

Chapter 4 Lesson 2

Model Addition

Hands On

TEKS Objective
Model addition situations as part-part-whole.

TAKS Vocabulary
add
part
whole

★ Learn

You **add** the **parts** to find the **whole.**
Listen to the story.

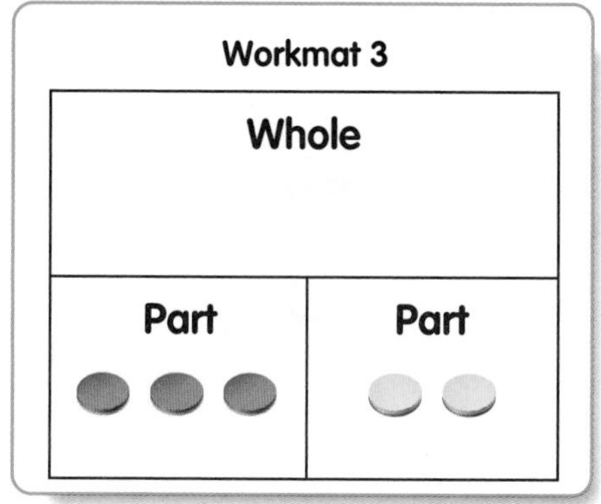

Workmat 3
Whole
Part Part

Whole	
___	
Part	Part
3	2

Whole	
5	
Part	Part
3	2

★ Guided Practice

Use Workmat 3 and ◯.
Show the parts. Find the whole.

1.

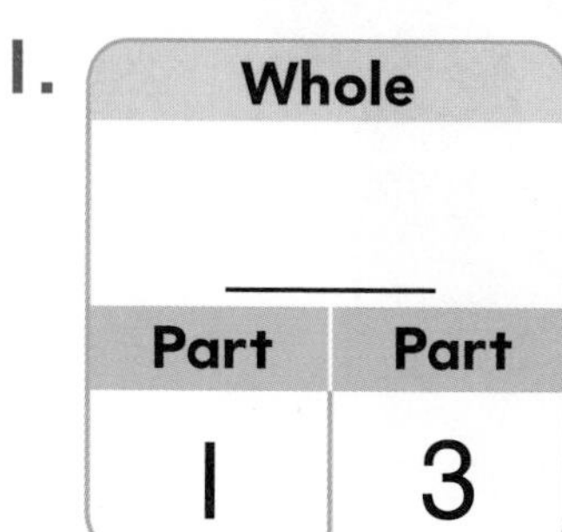

Whole	
___	
Part	Part
1	3

Think!
I add 1 and 3 to find the whole.

2.

Whole	
___	
Part	Part
2	3

3. **Math Talk** What does the word **add** mean?

TAKS Objectives 1, 6
TEKS 1.3A Model and create addition and subtraction problem situations with concrete objects and write corresponding number sentences.

TEKS 1.12A Explain and record observations using objects, words, pictures, numbers, and technology.
TEKS 1.12B Relate informal language to mathematical language and symbols.

★ Practice

Remember!
Add the parts to find how many in all.

Use Workmat 3 and ◯.
Show the parts. Find the whole.

4.

Whole	
3	
Part	**Part**
1	2

5.

Whole	
____	
Part	**Part**
2	3

6.

Whole	
____	
Part	**Part**
3	1

7.

Whole	
____	
Part	**Part**
1	2

8.

Whole	
____	
Part	**Part**
2	2

9.

Whole	
____	
Part	**Part**
1	4

Problem Solving: Number Sense

Write the parts.
Write the whole.

10.

Whole	
____	
Part	**Part**
____	____

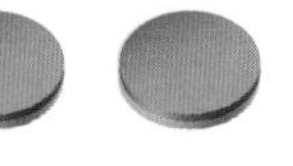

At Home Use dried beans or other objects to help your child model different ways to show 5 in all.

En casa Use frijoles u otros objetos para ayudar a su niño a demostrar diferentes maneras de representar un total de 5.

Name ______________________________

Chapter 4 Lesson 3

Addition Sentences

TEKS Objective
Model and solve addition sentences.

TAKS Vocabulary
plus sign
equal sign
addition sentence
sum

★ Learn

Use the **plus sign** and **equal sign** to write an **addition sentence.**

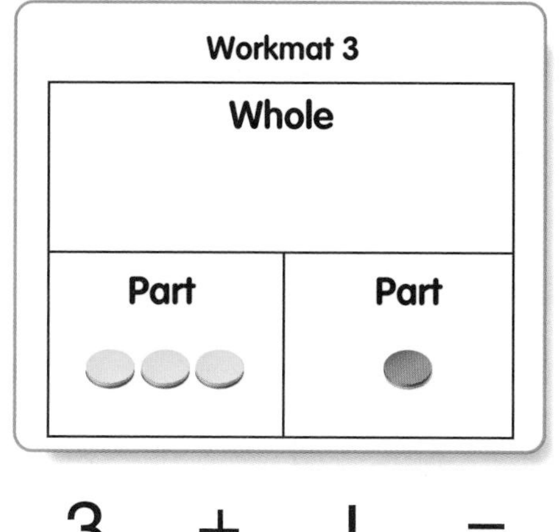

3 + 1 = 4 ← **sum**

↑ plus sign ↑ equal sign

The sum tells how many in all.

★ Guided Practice

Write the sum.

Think! I need to add the parts.

1.

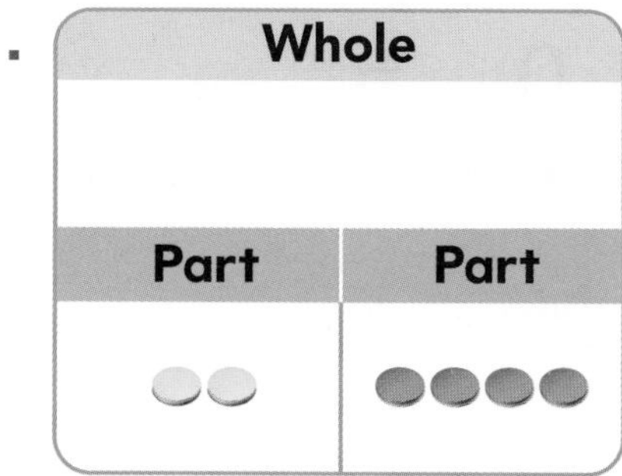

2 + 4 = ____

2.

Whole

Part | Part

3 + 3 = ____

3. **Math Talk** When you find the sum, are you finding the parts or the whole? Tell how you know.

TAKS Objectives 1, 6
TEKS 1.3B Use concrete and pictorial models to apply basic addition and subtraction facts (up to 9 + 9 = 18 and 18 – 9 = 9).

TEKS 1.12B Relate informal language to mathematical language and symbols.

★ Practice

Write the sum.

Remember! Find the sum by putting the parts together.

4.

Whole	
Part	Part
5 counters	1 counter

5 + 1 = 6

5.

Whole	
Part	Part
2 counters	1 counter

2 + 1 = ____

6.

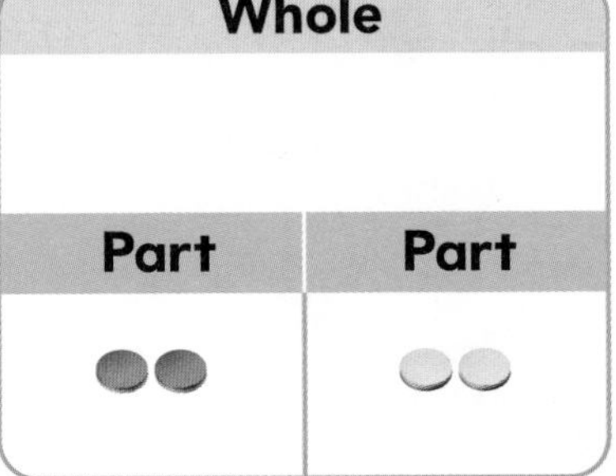

Whole	
Part	Part
2 counters	2 counters

2 + 2 = ____

7.

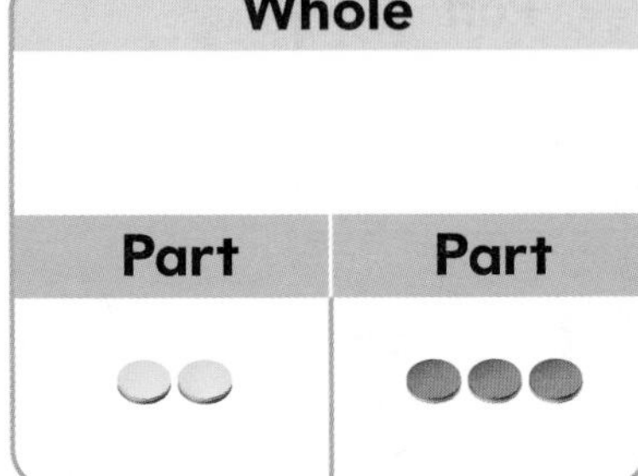

Whole	
Part	Part
2 counters	3 counters

2 + 3 = ____

8.

Whole	
Part	Part
4 counters	2 counters

4 + 2 = ____

9.

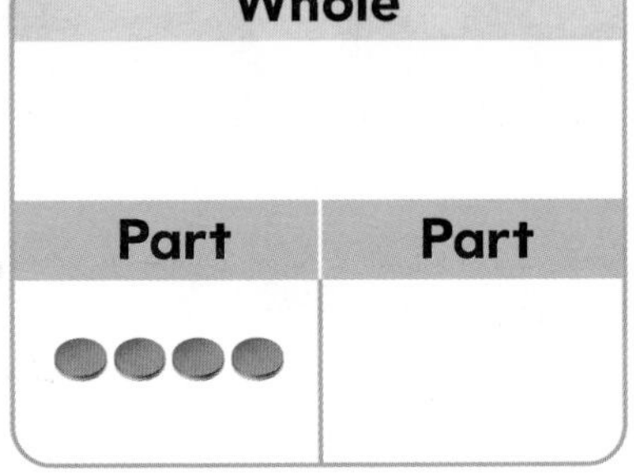

Whole	
Part	Part
4 counters	

4 + 0 = ____

Problem Solving: Visual Thinking

10. Circle the picture that shows 1 + 4 = 5.

Whole	
Part	Part
3 counters	1 counter

Whole	
Part	Part
1 counter	4 counters

Whole	
Part	Part
3 counters	2 counters

At Home Have your child cut out pictures from magazines and paste them onto blank paper to create addition stories with sums of 6 or less.

En casa Pida a su niño que recorte ilustraciones de revistas y que las pegue en una hoja en blanco para crear cuentos de suma con sumas de 6 ó menos.

Name ______________________

Chapter 4 Lesson 4

Names for Numbers

TEKS Objective
Model numbers and complete addition sentences with sums of 6, 7, and 8.

There are different ways to make a number.

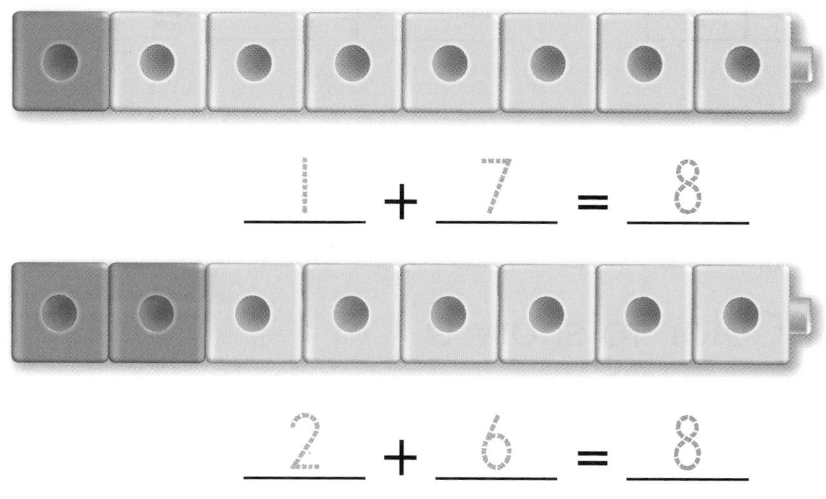

Use [red cube] and [blue cube] to make 7.
Color to show 7.
Complete the addition sentence.

Think!
I can use 5 blue cubes and 2 red cubes.

1. ○ ○ ○ ○ ○ ○ ○   5 + 2 = 7

2. ○ ○ ○ ○ ○ ○ ○   ___ + ___ = ___

3. ○ ○ ○ ○ ○ ○ ○   ___ + ___ = ___

4. **Math Talk** Look at Exercise 1. Why do you get the same sum if you add 2 + 5?

TAKS Objective 1
TEKS 1.3B Use concrete and pictorial models to apply basic addition and subtraction facts (up to 9 + 9 = 18 and 18 – 9 = 9).

★ Practice

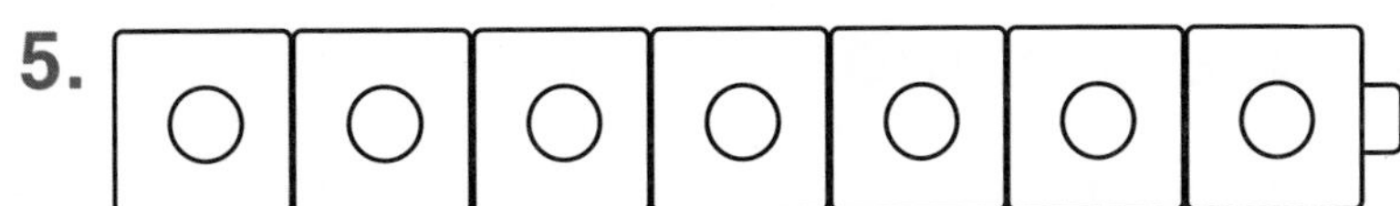

Remember!
There are many ways to make a sum.

Use [cube] and [cube] to make 7.
Color to show 7.
Complete the addition sentence.

5. 3 + 4 = 7

6. ___ + ___ = ___

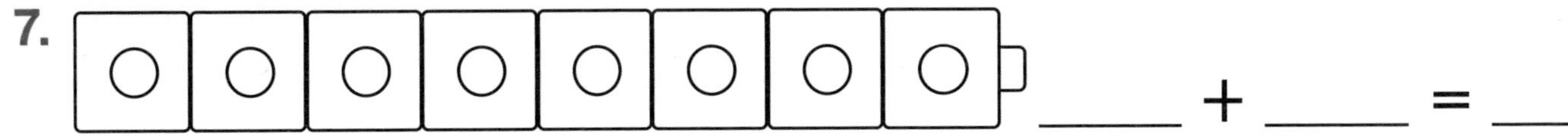

Use [cube] and [cube] to make 8. Color to show 8.
Complete the addition sentence.

7. ___ + ___ = ___

8. ___ + ___ = ___

Use [cube] and [cube] to make 6. Color to show 6.
Complete the addition sentence.

9. ___ + ___ = ___

10. ___ + ___ = ___

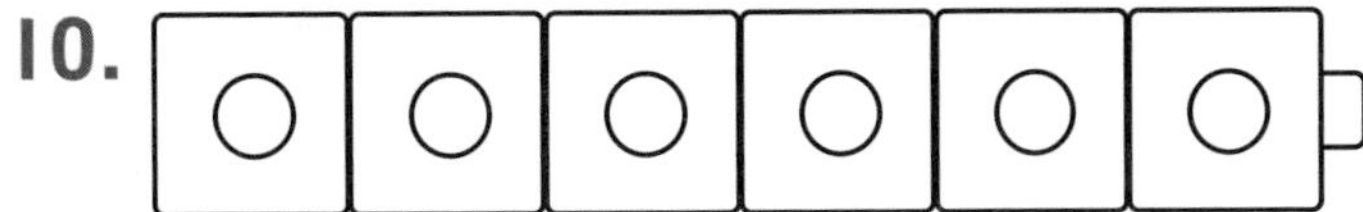

Problem Solving: Number Sense

11. There are 6 cubes in all.
2 cubes are blue. The rest are red.
How many cubes are red? ___

At Home Have your child tell addition stories with sums of 6, 7, or 8.

En casa Pida a su niño que cuente cuentos de suma con sumas de 6, 7 u 8.

Name ______________________________

Chapter 4 Lesson 5

Write a Number Sentence

TEKS Objective
Solve story problems by writing addition sentences.

How many children in all?

Understand

What do you know?

- There are 3 children in a group.
- 2 more children join them.

Plan

Circle how you would solve the problem.

subtract

Solve

Model the story.
Write an addition sentence.

_3_  _2_  _5_

How many children in all? _5_ children

Look Back

Does the addition sentence show the two groups?
Does the sum show how many in all?

TAKS Objectives 1, 6
TEKS 1.3A Model and create addition and subtraction problem situations with concrete objects and write corresponding number sentences.

TEKS 1.3B Use concrete and pictorial models to apply basic addition and subtraction facts (up to 9 + 9 = 18 and 18 − 9 = 9).
Also **TEKS 1.11B, 1.11D, 1.12A, 1.13**

★ Guided Problem Solving

1. There are 6 red flags.
   There are 2 blue flags.
   How many flags are there?

Think!
6 in one group.
2 in the other.

   What do you know?

   Model the story.

   Solve.

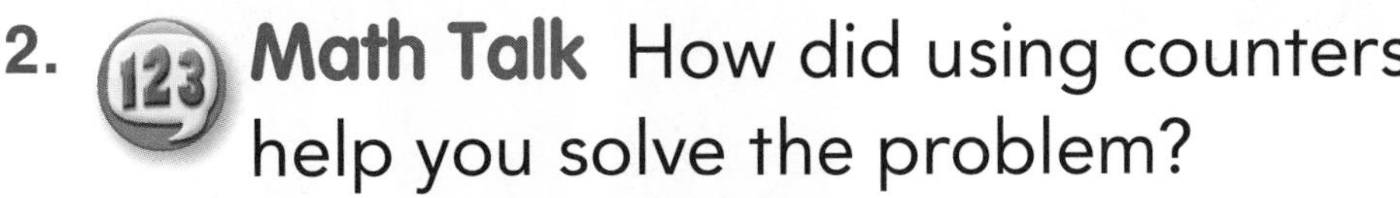

   ____ flags

2. Math Talk How did using counters help you solve the problem?

★ Problem Solving Practice

Model the story with counters.
Write an addition sentence to solve.
Write the answer.

3. There are 4 children
   Then 3 more children come.
   How many children are there now?

   ____ children

4. There are 3 blue drums.
   There are 5 green drums.
   How many drums in all?

   ____ drums

At Home Ask your child to model each problem with beans or other small objects.

En casa Pida a su niño que demuestre cada problema con frijoles u otros objetos pequeños.

Name ______________________

Social Studies

Texas Field Trip

Zilker Park

You can visit Zilker Park in Austin.
Find Austin, Texas on a map.
You can see kites and mockingbirds.
You can take a train ride, too.

Zilker Kite Festival

Model the story. You may use counters. Then write an addition sentence to solve.

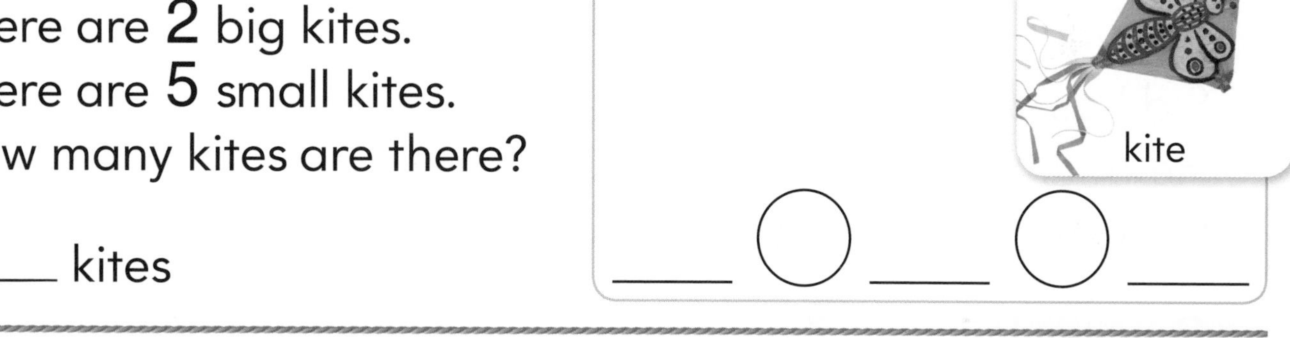

1. There are 2 big kites.
   There are 5 small kites.
   How many kites are there?

   _____ kites

   _____ ◯ _____ ◯ _____

2. There are 5 mockingbirds.
   Then 1 more joins them.
   How many mockingbirds are there now?

   _____ mockingbirds

   _____ ◯ _____ ◯ _____

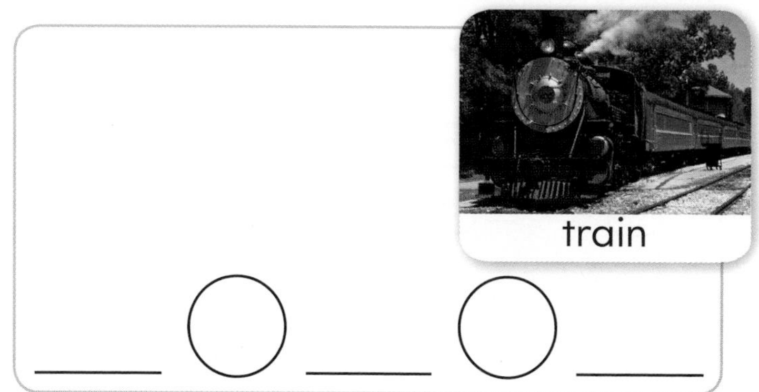

3. 6 children get on the train.
   2 more children come.
   How many children are on the train now?

   _____ children

   _____ ◯ _____ ◯ _____

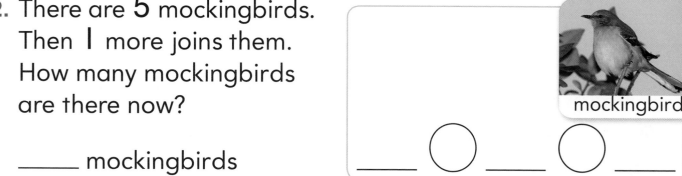

TAKS Objectives 1, 6
TEKS 1.3A Model and create addition and subtraction problem situations with concrete objects and write corresponding number sentences.

Also **TEKS 1.11C, 1.11D**
TEKS Social Studies 5B

TAKS Problem Solving
Listening Skills

Select a Strategy
Draw a Picture
Act It Out

Listen to your teacher read the problem.
Choose the correct answer.

1. There are 4 trucks in the firehouse.
There are 2 trucks outside.
How many trucks are there in all?

2 ○ 4 ○ 5 ○ 6 ○

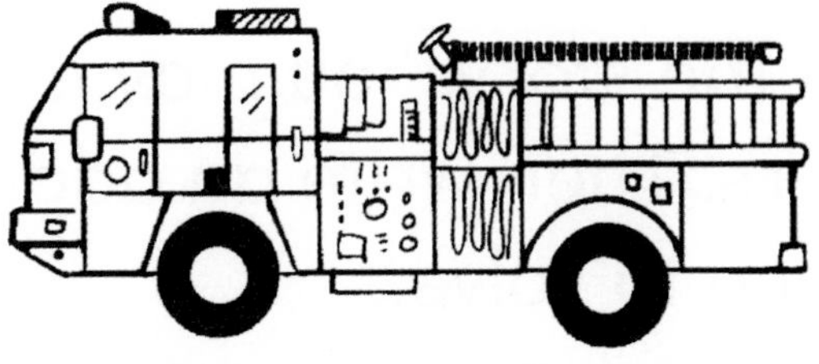

TEKS 1.3B

2. Sid has 3 books.
He gets 4 more books at the library.
How many books does Sid have now?

3 ○ 4 ○ 7 ○ 8 ○

TEKS 1.3B

3. 3 ○ 5 ○ 7 ○ 8 ○

TEKS 1.3B

4. 4 5 6 8

TEKS 1.3B

Education Place
Visit **www.eduplace.com/txmap/** for Test-Taking Tips and more TAKS Practice.

Name ______________________

Addition Patterns

Use a calculator. Press + to add.

5 + 1 = 6

Press = for the sum. Write the sum.

1. 1 + 1 = ______
2. 1 + 2 = ______
3. 2 + 1 = ______
4. 2 + 2 = ______
5. 3 + 1 = ______
6. 3 + 2 = ______
7. 4 + 1 = ______
8. 4 + 2 = ______

9. Write a story about one of the addition sentences.

____

____

____

10. **Math Talk** What patterns do you see?

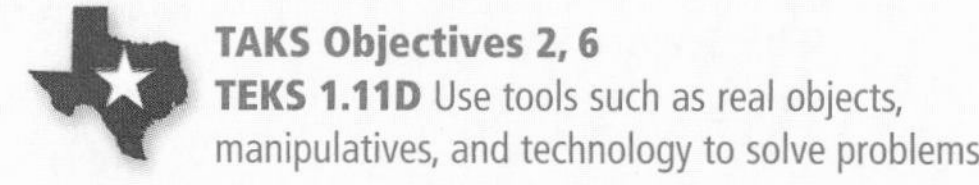
TAKS Objectives 2, 6
TEKS 1.11D Use tools such as real objects, manipulatives, and technology to solve problems.

Also TEKS 1.5D, 1.12A, 1.13

Education Place
Visit www.eduplace.com/txmap/ for more activities.

Busy Woodpecker

Did you know the bill of a woodpecker is a tool? He uses it every day to get insects, nuts, and berries. He uses it to carve a home in a dead tree or telephone pole. He even uses it to make tapping sounds to find another woodpecker!

Model the story with counters.
Write an addition sentence to solve.
Write the answer.

1. Carla puts 3 nuts on top of a bird feeder. Andy puts 2 more nuts on the feeder. How many nuts are on the feeder in all?

   ____ ◯ ____ ◯ ____

   ____ nuts

2. A woodpecker puts 7 red berries in his hole. Another woodpecker puts 2 more in the hole. How many berries are in the hole?

   ____ ◯ ____ ◯ ____

   ____ berries

TAKS Objective 1
TEKS 1.3A Model and create addition and subtraction problem situations with concrete objects and write corresponding number sentences.

TEKS Science 9A

Name ______________________

Concepts and Skills

Use Workmat 3 and ◯.
Show the parts.
Find the whole. TEKS 1.3B

1.

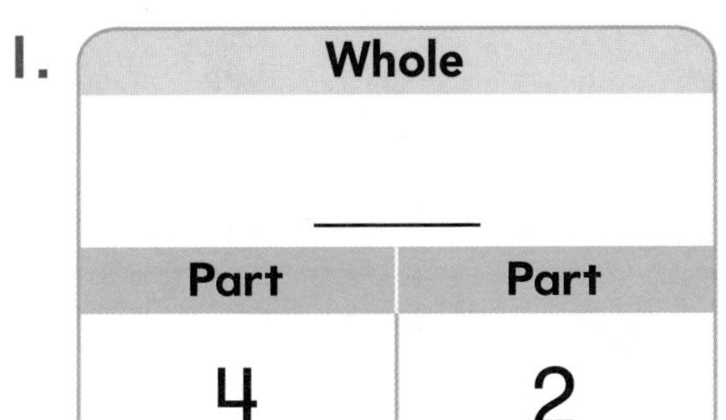

Write the sum. TEKS 1.3B

2.

Whole	
Part	Part
● ●	●

2 + 1 = ____

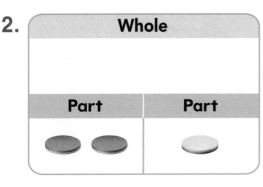

Use ▣ and ▣ to make 8. Color to show 8.
Complete the addition sentence. TEKS 1.3B

3. ◯ ◯ ◯ ◯ ◯ ◯ ◯ ◯

____ + ____ = ____

Problem Solving

Model the story with counters.
Write an addition sentence to solve.
Write the answer. TEKS 1.3A, 1.3B, 1.12A

4. There are 5 dogs.
Then 2 more dogs come.
How many dogs are there now?

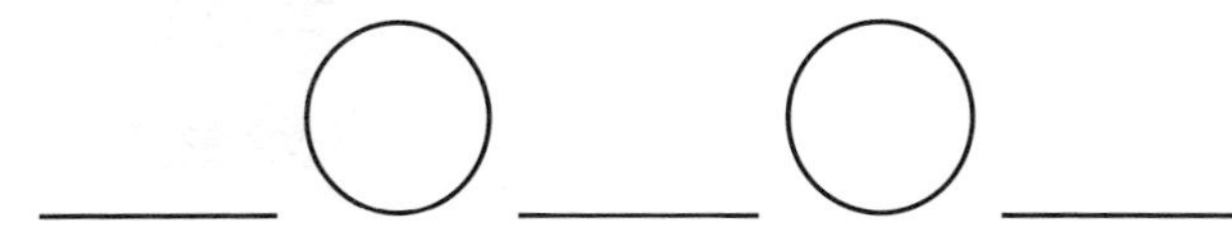

____ dogs

TAKS Prep and Spiral Review

Choose the answer for problems 1–4.

1. Which car comes next in the pattern?

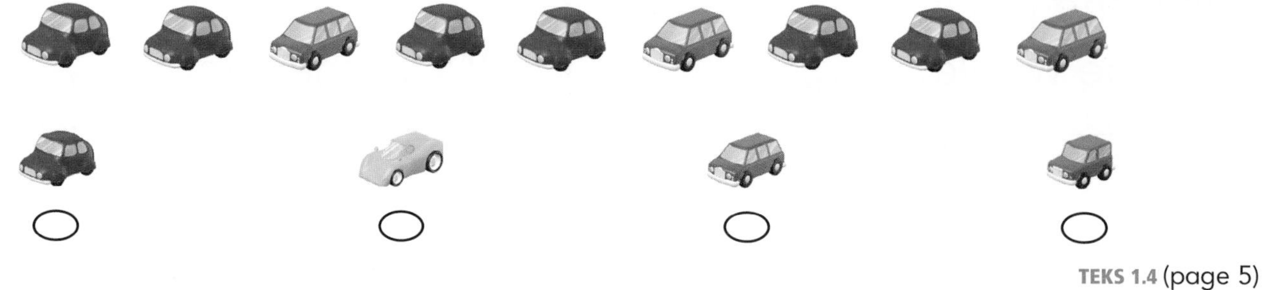

TEKS 1.4 (page 5)

2. Which figures come next in the pattern?

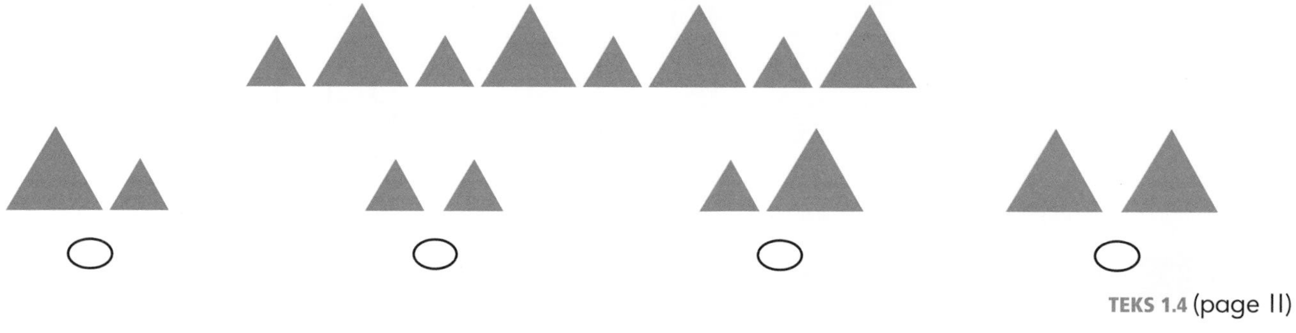

TEKS 1.4 (page 11)

3. Which number tells how many?

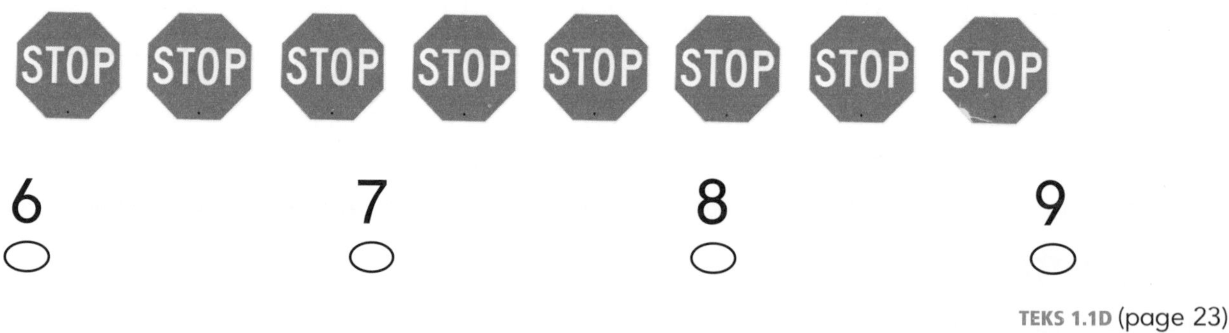

6 ○ 7 ○ 8 ○ 9 ○

TEKS 1.1D (page 23)

4. Tam buys these stamps at the post office.
How many stamps does she buy?

14 ○ 15 ○ 16 ○ 20 ○

TEKS 1.1D (page 41)

Education Place
Visit **www.eduplace.com/txmap/** for Test-Taking Tips and Extra Practice.

Subtraction Concepts

TAKS Vocabulary

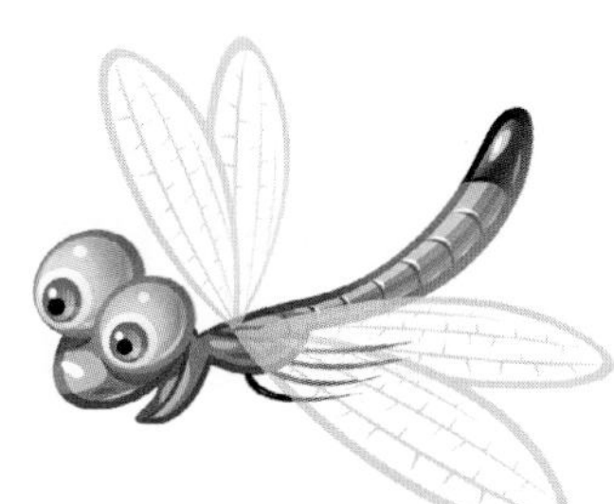

Here are some vocabulary words you will learn in the chapter.

subtract Find how many are left when part is taken away

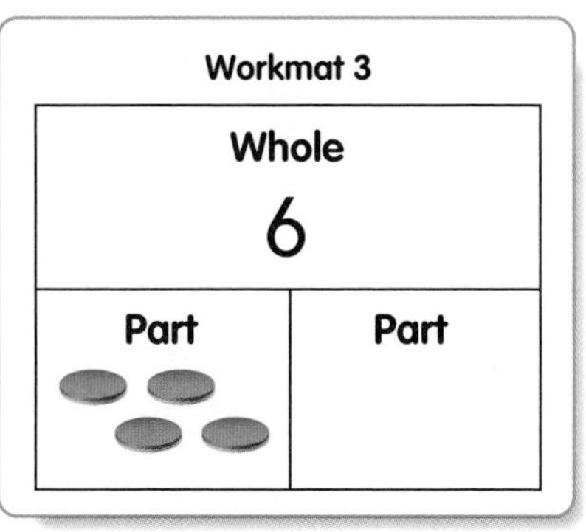

6 − 4 = 2

minus sign A symbol that tells you to subtract

equal sign A symbol that means to be the same as

difference How many are left

subtraction sentence A number sentence used to find the difference

6 − 4 = 2 ←**difference**

↑ **minus sign** ↑ **equal sign**

See English-Spanish glossary pages 505–516.

TAKS Objective 6
TEKS 1.12B Relate informal language to mathematical language and symbols.

Education Place
Visit **www.eduplace.com/txmap/** for the eGlossary and vocabulary eGames.

Name ____________________

Check What You Know

Use the picture.
Count and write the number.

1. How many 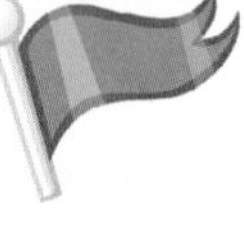 ?  ______

2. How many  ? ______

3. How many  ? ______

4. How many  ? ______

5. How many  ? ______

Use this page to review important skills needed for this chapter.

Name ______________________________

Chapter 5 Lesson 1

Subtraction Stories

Hands On

TEKS Objective
Model subtraction sentences with concrete objects.

★ Explore

Listen to the story.
Show the story with ◯.

1.

2. **Math Talk** Tell how showing subtraction with counters is different from showing addition.

TAKS Objectives 1, 6
TEKS 1.3A Model and create addition and subtraction problem situations with concrete objects and write corresponding number sentences.

TEKS 1.12A Explain and record observations using objects, words, pictures, numbers, and technology.

Listen to the story.
Show the story with ◯.
Write the numbers.

Remember!
Listen for the number that tells how many in all.

3.

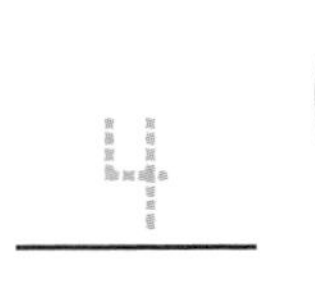

4 ______ 2 ______ picked 2 ______ left

4.

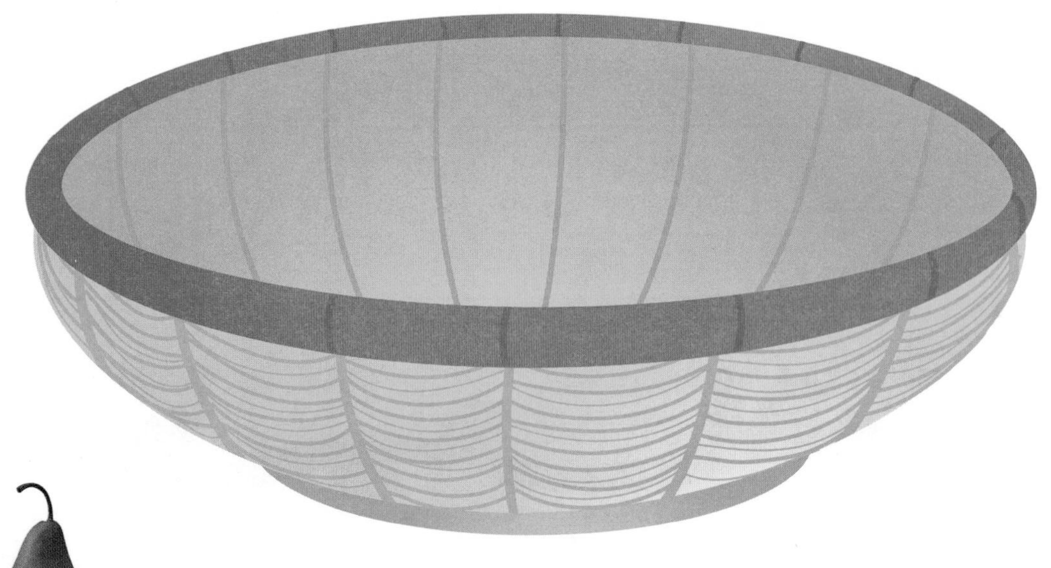

______ ______ eaten ______ left

At Home Ask your child to use objects and create a story about subtracting.

En casa Pida a su niño que use objetos para crear un cuento de resta.

Name ____________________

Chapter 5 Lesson 2

Model Subtraction

Hands On

TEKS Objective
Model subtraction situations as part-part-whole.

TAKS Vocabulary
whole
part
subtract

★ Learn

If you know the **whole** and one of the **parts,** you can **subtract** to find the other part.

There are 4 counters in all.
3 counters are in one part.
How many counters are in the other part?

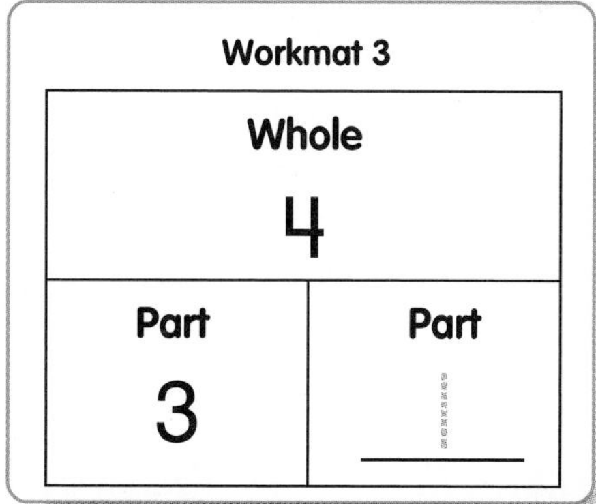

Workmat 3

Whole	
4	
Part	Part
3	1

There is 1 counter in the other part.

★ Guided Practice

Use Workmat 3 and ◯. Show the whole.
Move the counters to one part.
Find the other part.

Think!
There are 3 counters in all. One part has 2 counters.

1\.

Whole	
3	
Part	Part
2	____

2\.

Whole	
4	
Part	Part
2	____

3\.

Whole	
5	
Part	Part
4	____

4\. **Math Talk** If you have 5 in all and 4 is in one part, can you have more than 1 in the other part? Why?

TAKS Objectives 1, 6
TEKS 1.3A Model and create addition and subtraction problem situations with concrete objects and write corresponding number sentences.

TEKS 1.12B Relate informal language to mathematical language and symbols.

Remember!
The parts make the whole.

★ Practice

Use Workmat 3 and ◯.
Show the whole.
Move the counters to one part.
Find the other part.

5.

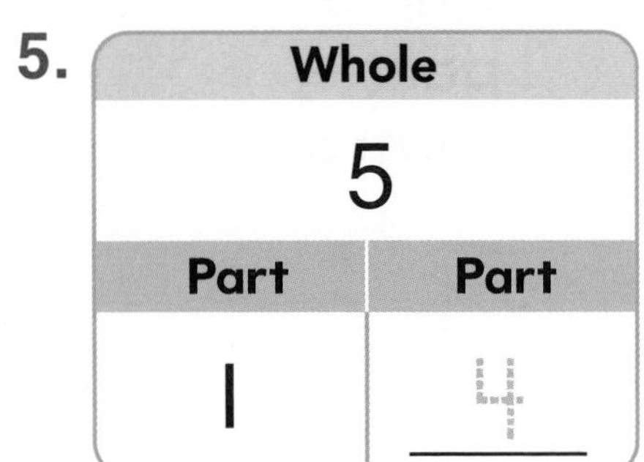

Whole	
5	
Part	**Part**
1	4

6.

Whole	
3	
Part	**Part**
2	____

7.

Whole	
4	
Part	**Part**
3	____

8.

Whole	
5	
Part	**Part**
3	____

9.

Whole	
5	
Part	**Part**
4	____

10.

Whole	
2	
Part	**Part**
1	____

Problem Solving: Number Sense

Draw a set with 1 fewer.

11.    

12.      

13. **Math Talk** How do you know there is 1 fewer object?

At Home Start with a set of 5 objects. Move some to the left to show one part. Have your child tell how many are in the other part.

En casa Comience con un conjunto de 5 objetos. Mueva algunos hacia la izquierda para mostrar una parte. Pida a su niño que diga cuántos hay en la otra parte.

Name ______________________

Chapter 5 Lesson 3

Subtraction Sentences

TEKS **Objective**
Model and solve subtraction sentences.

TAKS **Vocabulary**
minus sign
equal sign

★ Learn

Use the **minus sign** and **equal sign** to write about subtraction.

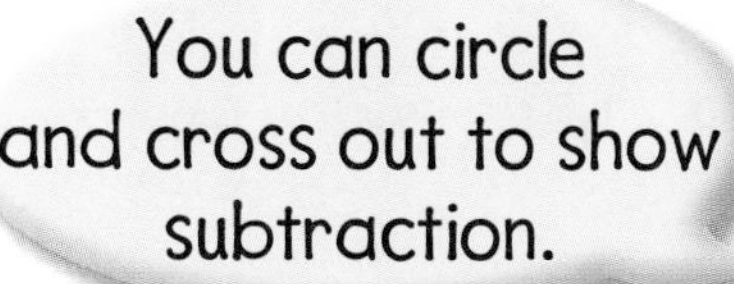

You can circle and cross out to show subtraction.

6 − 2 = 4

★ Guided Practice

Circle and cross out to subtract.
Write how many are left.

1.  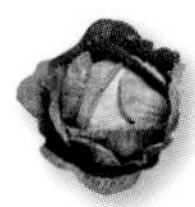    

5 − 3 = ____

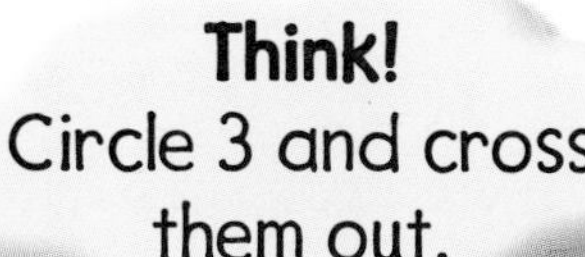

Think!
Circle 3 and cross them out.

2.     

4 − 1 = ____

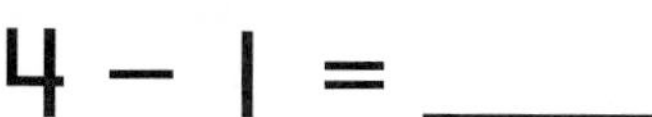

3. 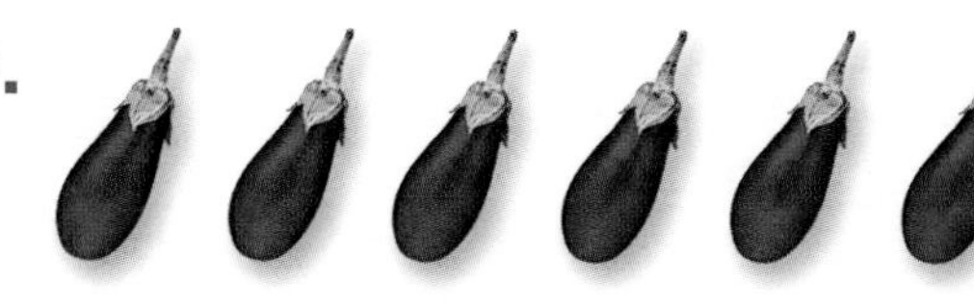

6 − 5 = ____

4.       

6 − 3 = ____

5.     

5 − 2 = ____

6. **Math Talk** In Exercise 5, why do you circle two objects before you subtract?

TAKS Objectives 1, 6
TEKS 1.3B Use concrete and pictorial models to apply basic addition and subtraction facts (up to 9 + 9 = 18 and 18 – 9 = 9).

TEKS 1.12B Relate informal language to mathematical language and symbols.

★ Practice

Circle and cross out to subtract.
Write how many are left.

Remember!
The objects that are not crossed out are the number left.

7.  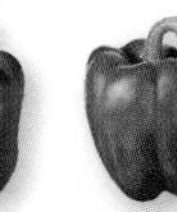   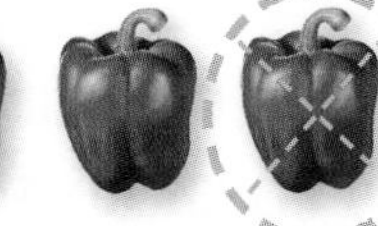

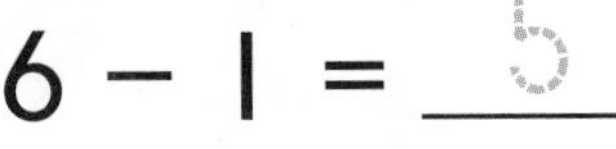

$6 - 1 =$ 5

8. 

$5 - 2 =$ ____

9.     

$4 - 3 =$ ____

10.    

$3 - 1 =$ ____

11.     

$6 - 3 =$ ____

12.    

$4 - 0 =$ ____

13.   

$3 - 2 =$ ____

14. 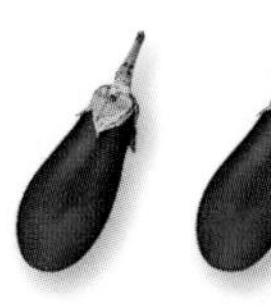 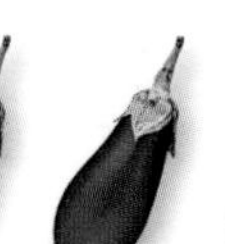  

$6 - 4 =$ ____

Problem Solving: Visual Thinking

15. Circle the picture that shows $5 - 4 = 1$.

At Home Draw 5 or 6 objects. Have your child circle and cross out some and then write how many are left.

En casa Dibuje 5 ó 6 objetos. Pida a su niño que rodee con un círculo y tache algunos objetos, y que luego escriba cuántos quedan.

Name ______________________

Chapter 5 Lesson 4

Write Subtraction Sentences

Write a **subtraction sentence** to find how many are left.

6 – 4 = 2 ← difference

The **difference** tells how many are left.

★ Guided Practice

Use cubes. Snap off some.
Circle and cross out.
Write the subtraction sentence.

Think!
I can snap off 1 cube and find the difference.

Use 7 cubes.

1. 7 ◯ 1 ◯ 6

2. ____ ◯ ____ ◯ ____

Use 8 cubes.

3. ____ ◯ ____ ◯ ____

4. ____ ◯ ____ ◯ ____

5. **Math Talk** What are all the ways to subtract from 7?

Hands On

TEKS Objective
Model and write subtraction sentences to show the difference.

TAKS Vocabulary
subtraction sentence
difference

TAKS Objectives 1, 6
TEKS 1.3B Use concrete and pictorial models to apply basic addition and subtraction facts (up to 9 + 9 = 18 and 18 – 9 = 9).

TEKS 1.12A Explain and record observations using objects, words, pictures, numbers, and technology.
TEKS 1.13 Justify thinking using objects, words, pictures, numbers, and technology.

★ Practice

Use cubes. Snap off some.
Circle and cross out.
Write the subtraction sentence.

Remember!
The number you subtract is the number of cubes you snap off.

Use 7 cubes.

6.  

7 − 4 = 3

7.  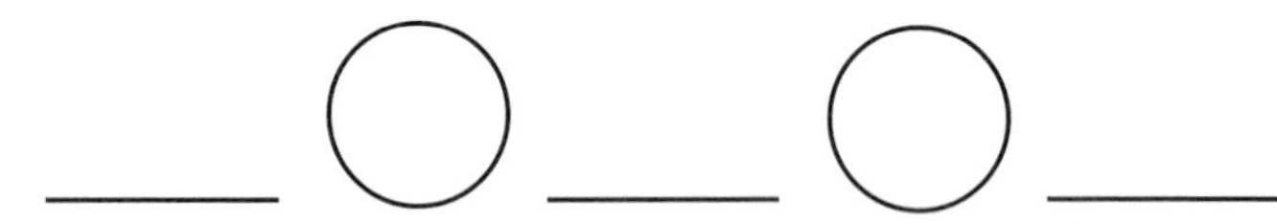

Use 8 cubes.

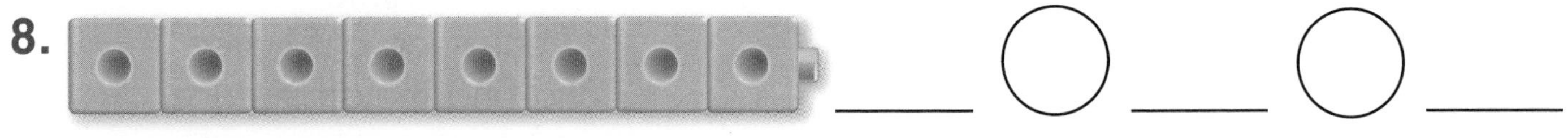

8\.

9\.

Use 6 cubes.

10. 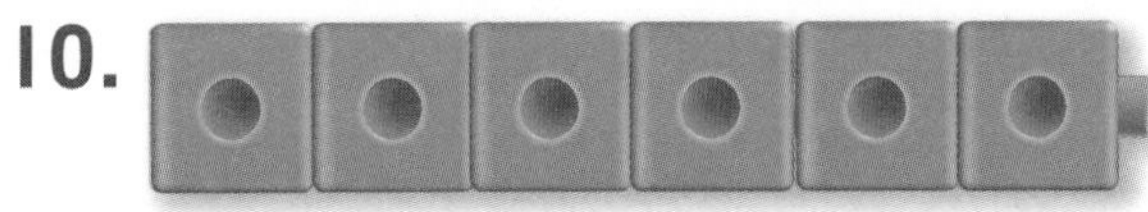 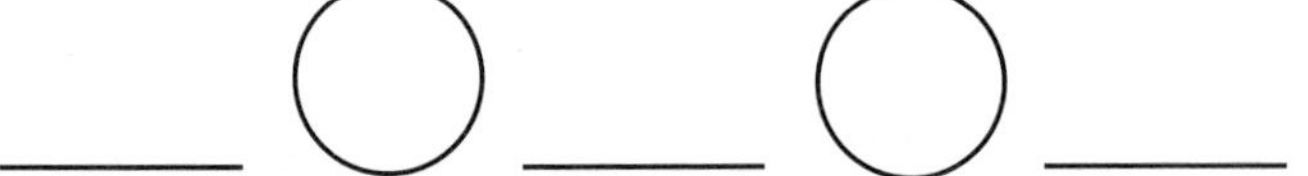

11. 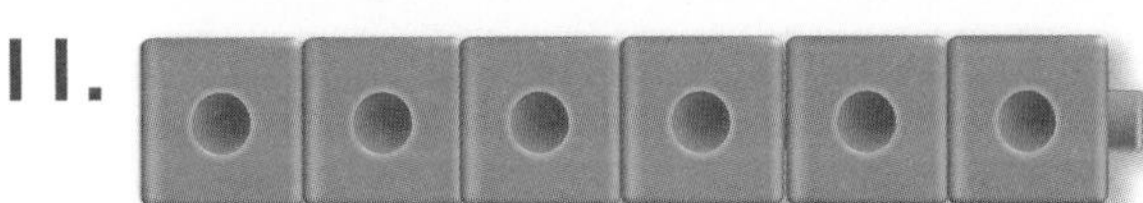 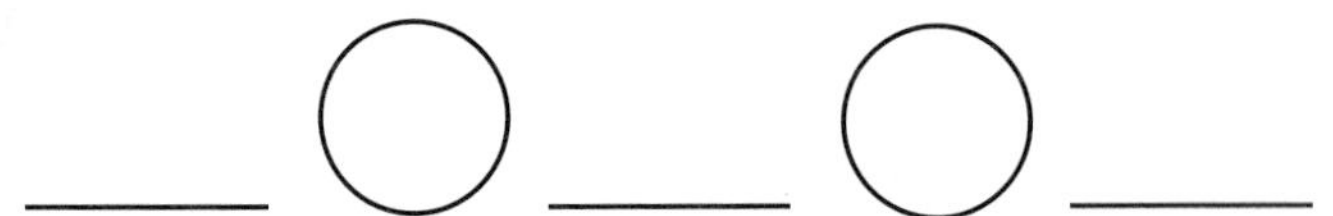

Algebra Readiness: Number Sentences

Write the subtraction sentence.

12. Pat has 7 apples.
He eats 2 of them.
How many apples are left?

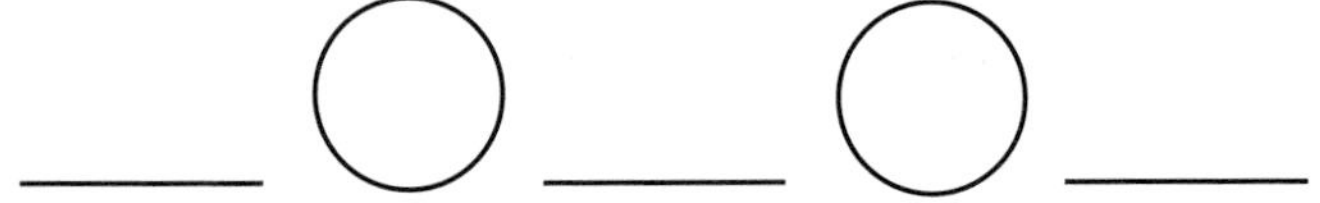

At Home Show 8 or fewer objects. Take some away. Ask your child to write the subtraction sentence.

En casa Muestre 8 objetos o menos. Quite algunos. Pida a su niño que escriba la oración de resta.

Name ______________________

Chapter 5 Lesson 5

Choose the Operation

TEKS Objective
Choose the correct operation and write number sentences; create and solve addition and subtraction problems.

★ Learn

Use subtraction to solve a problem.

7 sheep are eating grass.
1 sheep goes away.
How many sheep are there now?

Think!
I know the whole and one of the parts. I can subtract to find the other part.

sheep eating grass	
7	
sheep that go away	**sheep that are left**
1	

7 sheep − 1 goes away = 6 sheep now

Use addition to solve a problem.

6 ducks are eating seeds.
2 more come to eat.
How many ducks are there in all?

Think!
I know the parts. I can add to find the whole.

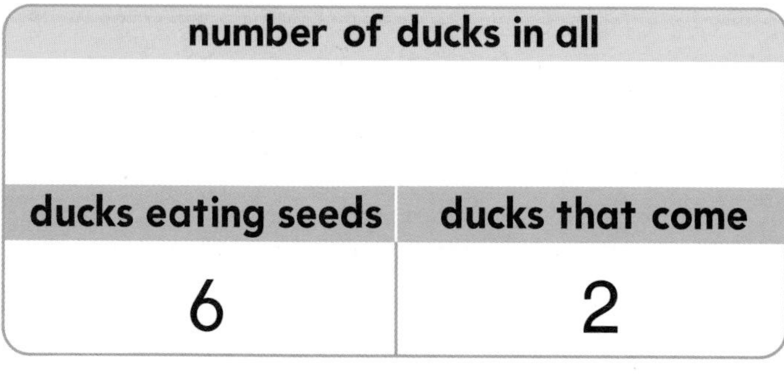

number of ducks in all	
ducks eating seeds	**ducks that come**
6	2

_____ ducks + _____ more = _____ ducks in all

TAKS Objectives 1, 6
TEKS 1.3B Use concrete and pictorial models to apply basic addition and subtraction facts (up to 9 + 9 = 18 and 18 − 9 = 9).

TEKS 1.12A Explain and record observations using objects, words, pictures, numbers, and technology.

★ Guided Problem Solving

1. There are 8 ponies in the barn. 2 ponies leave. How many ponies are in the barn now?

What do you know?

Do you need to add or subtract?

Model the story. Solve.

Think!
If some ponies leave the barn, do I add or subtract?

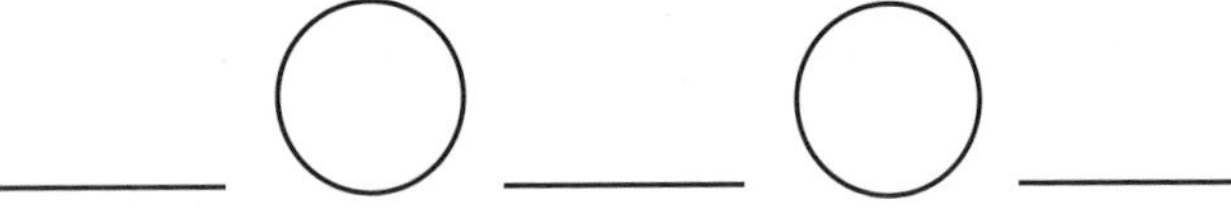

_____ ponies

2. **Math Talk** How did your model help solve the problem?

★ Problem Solving Practice

Choose the operation to solve.
Model. Write the number sentence.

3. 3 cows are eating grass. 4 more join them to eat. How many cows are eating?

_____ ◯ _____ ◯ _____

_____ cows

4. 6 pigs are in the pen. 1 pig goes away. How many pigs are in the pen now?

_____ pigs

At Home Draw a picture that shows 6 or fewer objects. Cross out some. Ask your child to write a subtraction sentence about the picture.

En casa Haga un dibujo que muestre 6 objetos o menos. Tache algunos. Pida a su niño que escriba una oración de resta sobre el dibujo.

Problem Solving

Name ______________________

Create and Solve

Write an addition story about the children.
Write the addition sentence.

1. ______________________________

____

____

2. ____ ◯ ____ ◯ ____

Write a story to match 3 + 3 = 6.
Show the story with ◯.

3. ______________________________

____

____

Draw a picture to show your story.

4.

TAKS Objectives 1, 6
TEKS 1.3A Model and create addition and subtraction problem situations with concrete objects and write corresponding number sentences.

TEKS 1.11A Identify mathematics in everyday situations.
Also **TEKS 1.11D, 1.13**

Write a subtraction story about the bees.
Write the subtraction sentence.

5. ______________________________

____

____

6. ____ ◯ ____ ◯ ____

Write a story to match 4 – 1 = 3.
Show the story with ◯.

7. ______________________________

____

____

Draw a picture to show your story.

8.

Name ______________________

What's the Number?

Use the numbers on the mailboxes to answer the questions.

1. The difference between these two numbers is 4. What are the numbers?

____, ____

2. The difference between these two numbers is 6. What are the numbers?

____, ____

3. The difference between these two numbers is 3. What are the numbers?

____, ____

4. The difference between these two numbers is 2. What are the numbers?

____, ____

TAKS Objective 1
TEKS 1.3B Use concrete and pictorial models to apply basic addition and subtraction facts (up to 9 + 9 = 18 and 18 – 9 = 9).

Education Place
Visit **www.eduplace.com/txmap/** for Brain Teasers.

Math Music

What's the Sum?

Math Music, Track 2

Put together numbers.
Add them up and find the sum.
Figure out the totals,
As the numbers come!

Let's add two numbers.
Find the total with me.
When we add 2 and 1,

The sum is _____ !

Let's add two numbers.
That's what we will do.
When we add 1 and 1,

The sum is _____ !

Let's add two numbers.
It's time to combine.
When we add 7 and 2,

The sum is _____ !

Let's add two numbers.
Sing along some more.
When we add 3 and 1,

The sum is _____ !

Let's add two numbers.
You're doing really great.
When we add 6 and 2,

The sum is _____ !

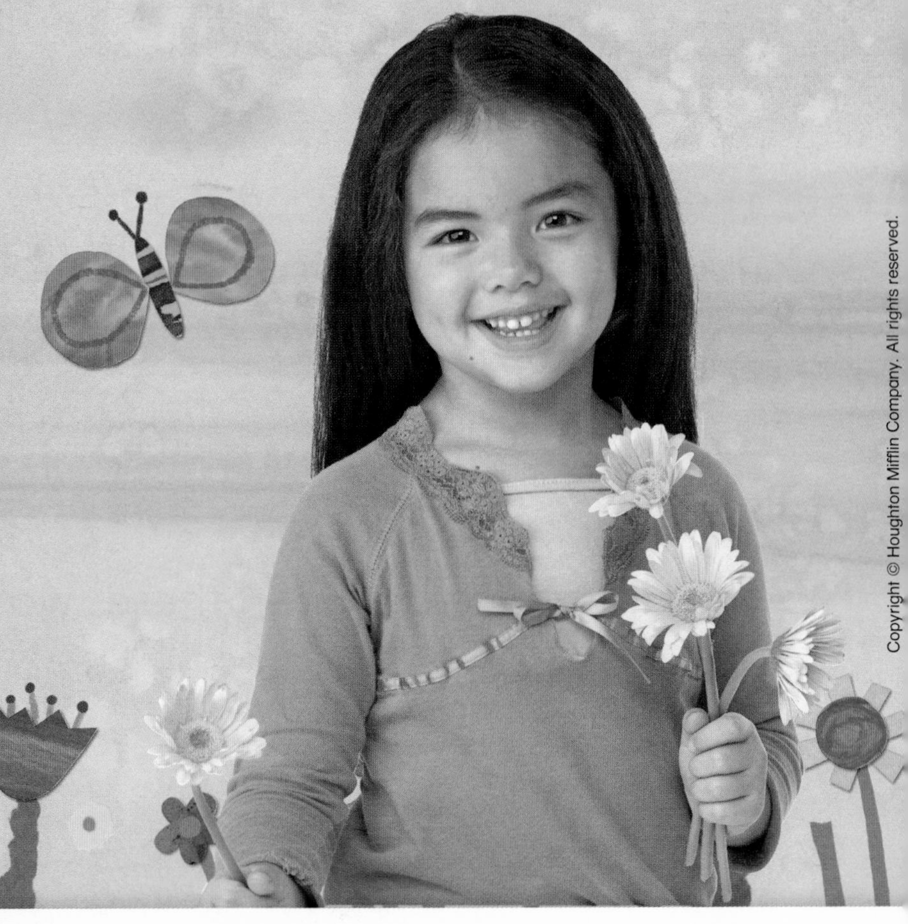

TAKS Objective 1
TEKS 1.3A Model and create addition and subtraction problem situations with concrete objects and write corresponding number sentences.

Name ______________________

Concepts and Skills

Use Workmat 3 and ◯.
Show the whole.
Move counters to one part.
Find the other part. TEKS 1.3B

1.

Whole	
5	
Part	Part
1	____

Circle and cross out to subtract.
Write how many are left. TEKS 1.3B

2.

$6 - 3 =$ ____

Use cubes. Snap some off. Circle and cross out.
Write the subtraction sentence. TEKS 1.3B

3. Use 7 cubes.

____ ◯ ____ ◯ ____

Problem Solving

Model the story. You may use counters. Then write the number sentence to solve. TEKS 1.3B, 1.12A

4. There are 8 birds in a tree. 2 birds fly away. How many birds are in the tree now?

____ ◯ ____ ◯ ____

____ birds

TAKS Prep and Spiral Review

Choose the answer for problems 1–4.

1. 7 buildings are on Paul's street. Bena's street has a greater number of buildings. Which shows the number of buildings on Bena's street?

4 ○

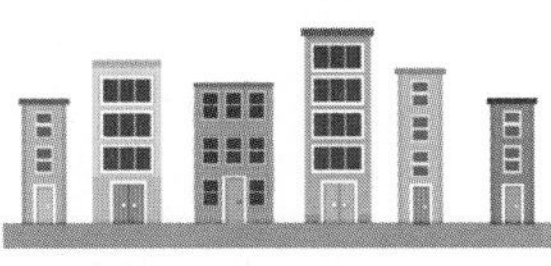
6 ○

7 ○

8 ○

TEKS 1.1A (page 25)

2. Which answer shows the number of cars in order from greatest to least?

14
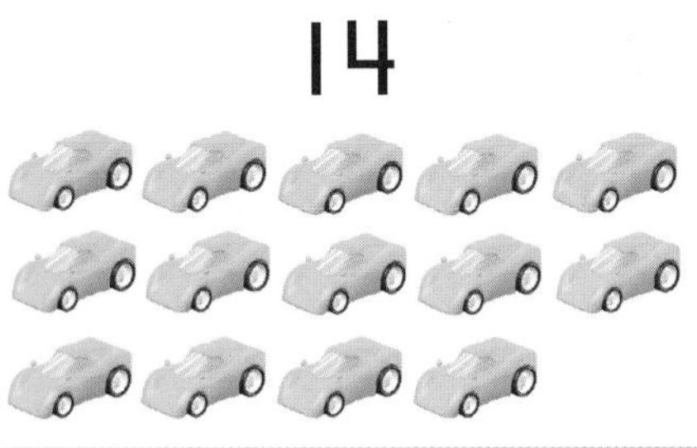

10
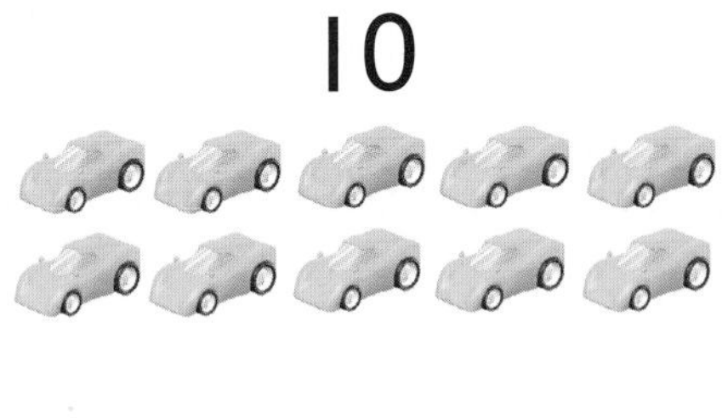

15
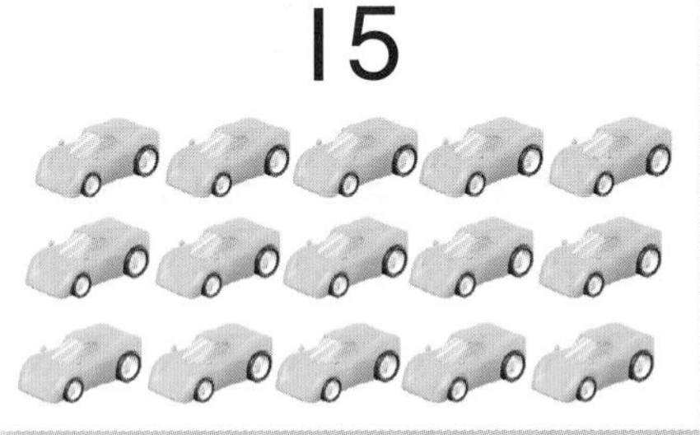

15, 10, 14 ○ 10, 14, 15 ○ 15, 14, 10 ○ 14, 15, 10 ○

TEKS 1.1A (page 45)

3. Which addition sentence matches the cubes?

3 + 1 = 4 ○ 3 + 2 = 5 ○ 3 + 4 = 6 ○ 3 + 5 = 8 ○

TEKS 1.3A (page 65)

4. Which number sentence shows how many apples Noah has left?

6 − 2 = 6 ○ 4 + 2 = 6 ○ 6 − 2 = 4 ○ 6 − 4 = 2 ○

TEKS 1.3A (page 87)

Education Place
Visit **www.eduplace.com/txmap/** for Test-Taking Tips and Extra Practice.

Name ____________________

Greg Tang's **Go Fast, Go Far**

Unit 2 **Mental Math Strategies**

Count All

To add, begin by counting all. Do it fast and have a ball!

I start by counting 2, "one, two." Then I add another 2 by counting, "three, four."

1. 1 2 3 4 ○ ○ ○ ○ ○ ○

$2 + 2 =$ 4

2. 1 2 3 4 5 ○ ○ ○ ○ ○

$2 + 3 =$ ☐

3. 1 2 3 4 5 6 ○ ○ ○ ○

$4 + 2 =$ ☐

Keep It Up!

4. 

$3 + 3 =$ ☐

Take It Further: Now try using your fingers, or better yet, just count in your head!

5. $3 + 1 =$ ☐ 6. $2 + 4 =$ ☐

Name ______________________________

Reading and Writing Math

The words in the box tell about addition and subtraction.
Where does the arrow point?
Write the word that matches.

Word Bank
equal sign
minus sign
plus sign
sum

1. $4 + 2 = 6$ (arrow points to $+$)

   ________ sign

2. $4 + 2 = 6$ (arrow points to 6)

   ____

3. $6 - 2 = 4$ (arrow points to $-$)

   ________ sign

4. $6 - 2 = 4$ (arrow points to $=$)

   ________ sign

5. **Writing Math** Write an addition sentence.
   Then write a subtraction sentence.

   _____ + _____ = _____

   _____ − _____ = _____

TEKS 1.12A Explain and record observations using objects, words, pictures, numbers, and technology.

TEKS 1.12B Relate informal language to mathematical language and symbols.

Name ______________________

Concepts and Skills

Listen to the story.
Show the story with ◯.
Write the numbers. TEKS 1.3A, 1.12A

1. _____ girls _____ boys _____ in all

2. _____ children _____ get off _____ left

Use Workmat 3 and ◯. Show the whole.
Move the counters to one part.
Find the other part. TEKS 1.3A, 1.12B

3.

Whole	
6	
Part	**Part**
4	_____

4.

Whole	
8	
Part	**Part**
4	_____

Write the sum. TEKS 1.3B, 1.12B

5. 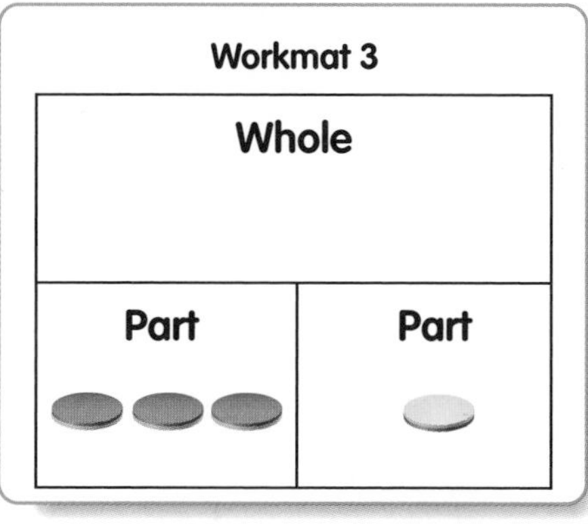

3 + 1 = _____

6. 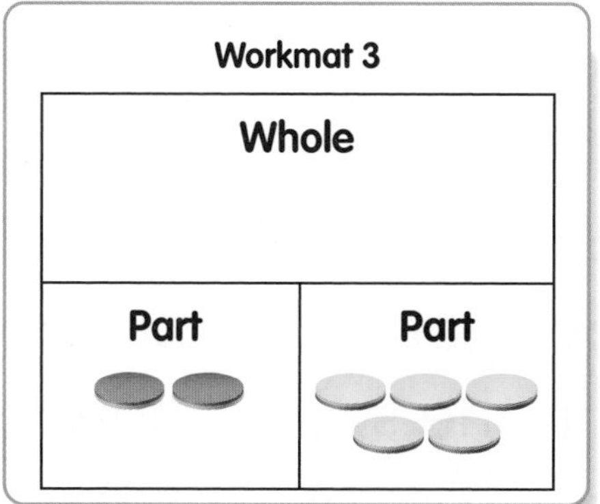

2 + 5 = _____

Circle and cross out.
Use cubes. Snap off some.
Write the subtraction sentence. TEKS 1.3B, 1.12A, 1.13

7. 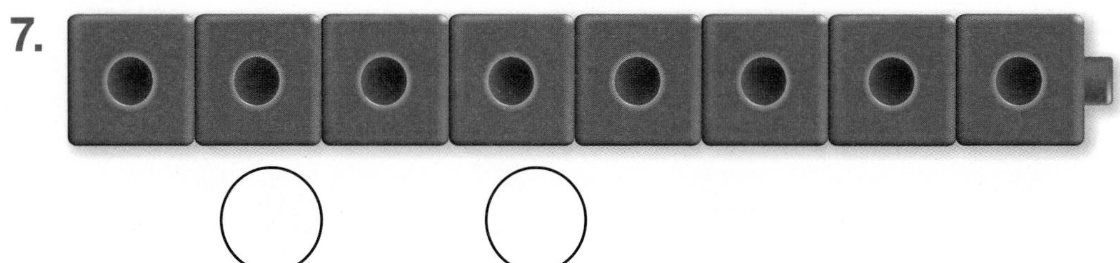

8. 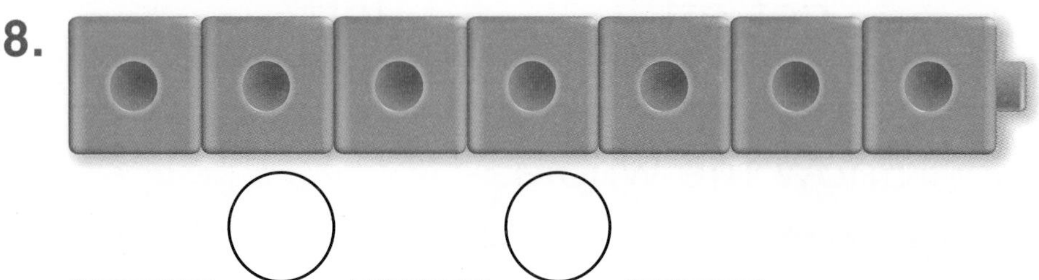

Problem Solving

Choose the operation to solve. TEKS 1.3A, 1.12A
Model. Write the number sentence.

9. 4 children are on the slide.
1 more child comes to play.
How many children are there now?

_____ children

10. 7 boys are on the swings.
3 boys get off. How many boys
are on the swings now?

_____ boys

Houghton Mifflin Texas Math

Unit 3

Addition and Subtraction Facts Through 10

BIG IDEAS!

- You can count objects and use pictures to find how many in all or how many are left.
- You can find patterns in basic addition and subtraction facts.
- You can relate addition and subtraction number sentences (fact families).

Songs and Games

Math Music Track 3
Fact Family Bugs

eGames
www.eduplace.com/txmap/

Literature

Literature Big Book

- Fish Eyes

Math Readers

ISBN-13: 978-0-618-95270-0
ISBN-10: 0-618-95270-5
89- WC - 16 15 14 13 12

Get Ready Game

It Makes a Difference!

What You Need

2 players

2

Start

1. Take turns spinning both spinners.
2. Subtract the number on Spinner 2 from the number on Spinner 1.
3. Move that many spaces.
4. The first player to finish wins!

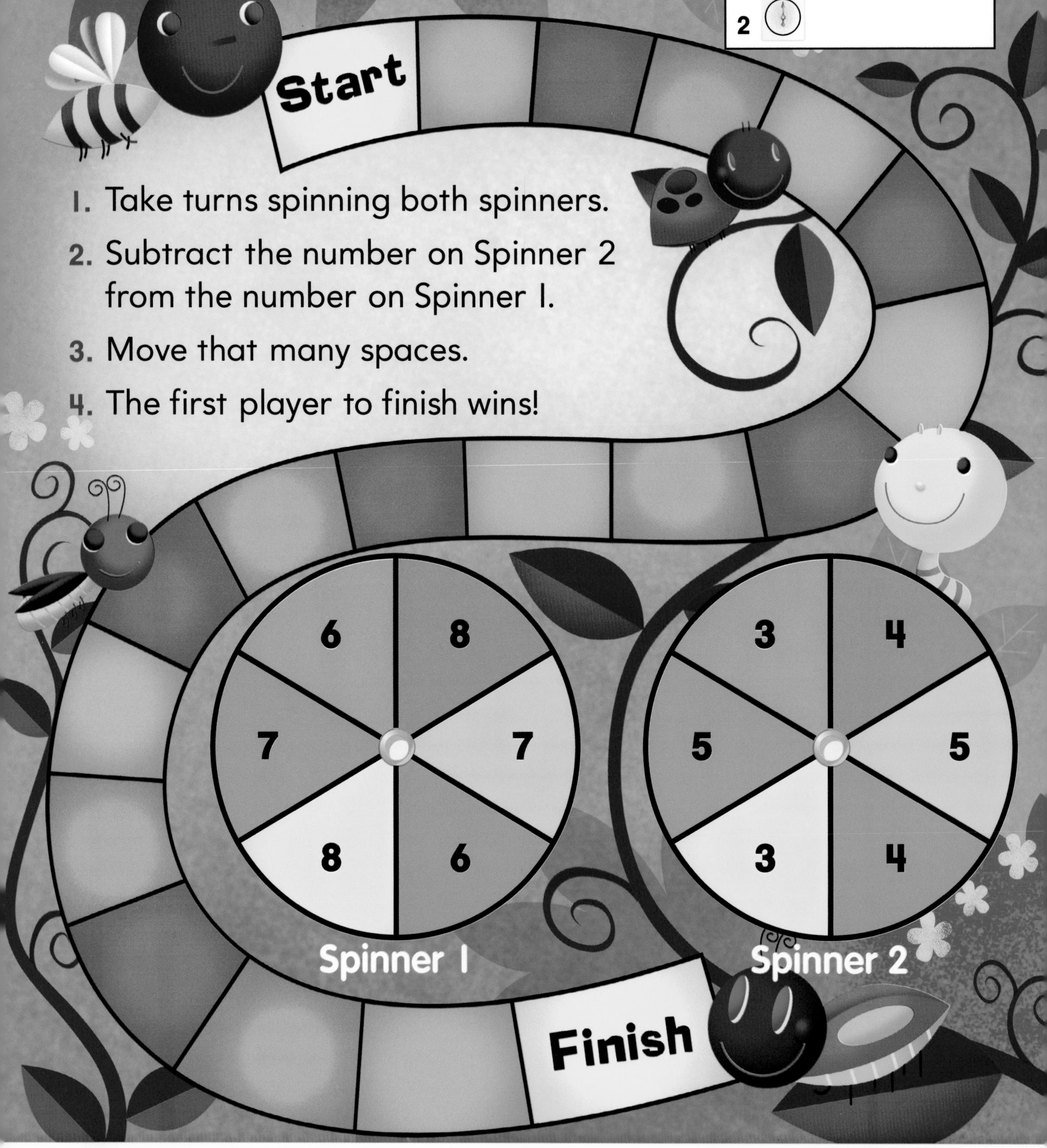

Spinner 1	Spinner 2
6, 8, 7, 7, 8, 6	3, 4, 5, 5, 3, 4

Finish

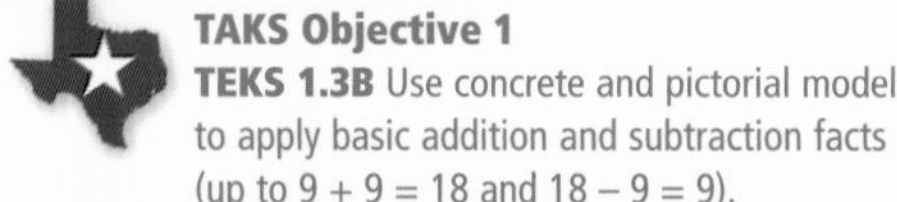
TAKS Objective 1
TEKS 1.3B Use concrete and pictorial models to apply basic addition and subtraction facts (up to 9 + 9 = 18 and 18 – 9 = 9).

For eGames and Brain Teasers, visit **www.eduplace.com/txmap/**

Math at Home

Dear Family,

My class is starting Unit 3, **Addition and Subtraction Facts Through 10.** I will learn strategies to help me add and subtract facts through 10. You can help me learn these vocabulary words, and we can do the Math Activity together.

From,

____

Vocabulary

related facts Addition and subtraction facts that have the same parts and wholes.

2 + 4 = 6 and 6 − 4 = 2 are **related facts.**

fact family All the addition and subtraction facts that use the same numbers.

4 + 2 = 6   6 − 2 = 4
2 + 4 = 6   6 − 4 = 2

This **fact family** uses the numbers 2, 4, and 6.

Education Place
Visit **www.eduplace.com/txmaf/** for
- eGames and Brain Teasers
- Math at Home in other languages

Family Math Activity

Find 4 blue socks and 2 red socks. Have your child tell an addition story. Then tell a related subtraction story together. If your child says all the related facts, then he or she understands the fact family for 4, 2, and 6.

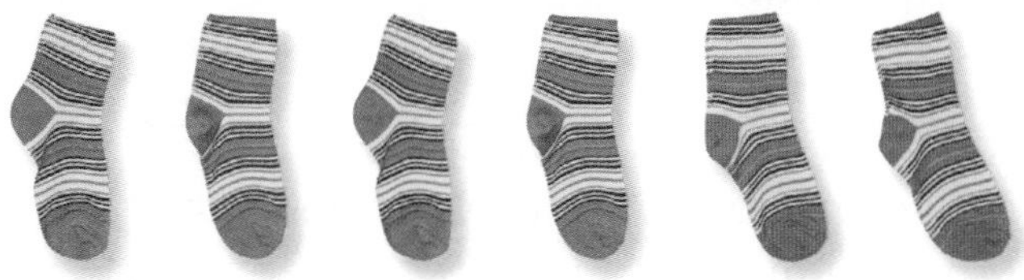

Literature

These books link to the math in this unit. Look for them at the library.

- **Addition Annie**
  by David Gisler
  (Children's Press, 2002)
- **Two of Everything**
  by Lily Toy Hong
- **Subtracting**
  by Rozanne Lanczak Williams

Matemáticas en casa

Estimada familia:

Mi clase está comenzando la Unidad 3, **Operaciones de suma y resta hasta 10**. Voy a aprender estrategias que me ayuden a hacer operaciones de suma y resta hasta 10. Me pueden ayudar a aprender estas palabras de vocabulario y podemos hacer juntos la Actividad de matemáticas para la familia.

De:

____

Vocabulario

operaciones relacionadas Operaciones de suma y de resta que tienen partes y enteros iguales.

2 + 4 = 6 y 6 − 4 = 2 son **operaciones relacionadas.**

familia de operaciones Todas las operaciones de suma y resta que usan los mismos números.

4 + 2 = 6   6 − 2 = 4
2 + 4 = 6   6 − 4 = 2

Esta **familia de operaciones** usa los números 2, 4 y 6.

Education Place
Visite **www.eduplace.com/txmaf/** para
- Juegos en línea y acertijos
- Matemáticas en casa, en otros idiomas

Actividad de matemáticas para la familia

Busque 4 calcetines azules y 2 calcetines rojos. Pida a su niño que diga un cuento de suma. Luego digan juntos un cuento de resta relacionado. Si su niño dice todas las operaciones relacionadas, es que comprende la familia de operaciones para 4, 2 y 6.

Literatura

Estos libros hablan sobre las matemáticas de esta unidad. Podemos buscarlos en la biblioteca.

- **Cuenta ratones**
  por Ellen Stoll Walsh
  (Fondo de Cultura Económica USA, 1996)
- **Diez perros en la tienda**
  por Claire Masurel
- **Una extraña visita**
  por Alma Flor Ada

No one left. They sat and sat.
Won't you draw one more bug act?

TAKS Objectives 1, 6
TEKS 1.3B, 1.11A

UNIT 3

Bug Jamboree

written by Tim Johnson
illustrated by Bill Ledger

This Take-Home Book belongs to

____

Reading and Writing Math

This take-home book will help you review addition and subtraction concepts.

A grasshopper and a bumblebee
Invite you to the jamboree.
The curtain opens and what a hoot.
Bugs play drums wearing striped suits.
How many drums are there in all? ______

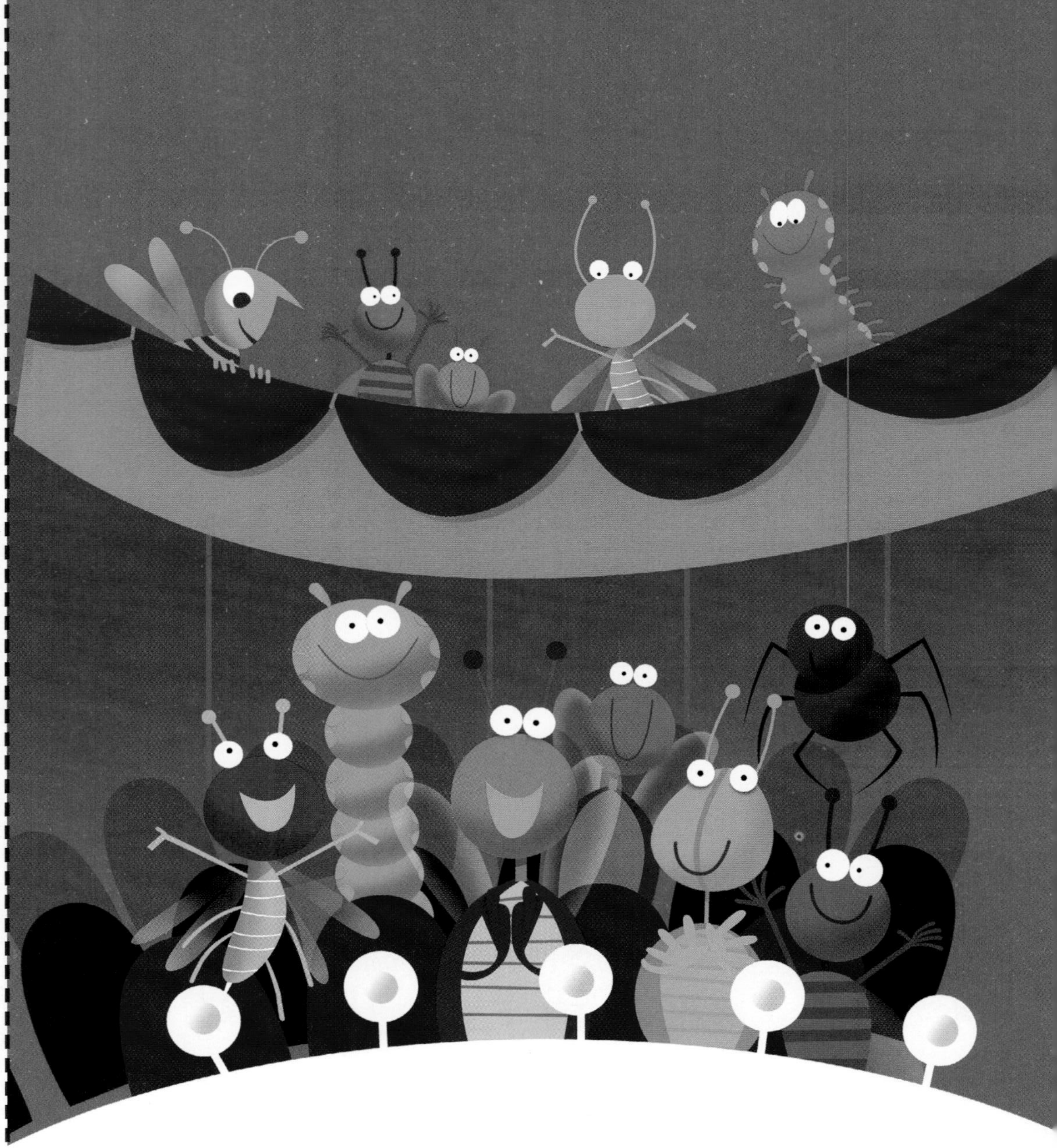

How the bugs all loved the show.
In fact, they did not want to go!

"Our final act," announced the fly,
"4 ants and 1 cricket twice their size."
How many bugs are there in all? _____

3 ladybugs and 1 small flea
Are the next act in this jamboree.
How many fiddles do you see? _____

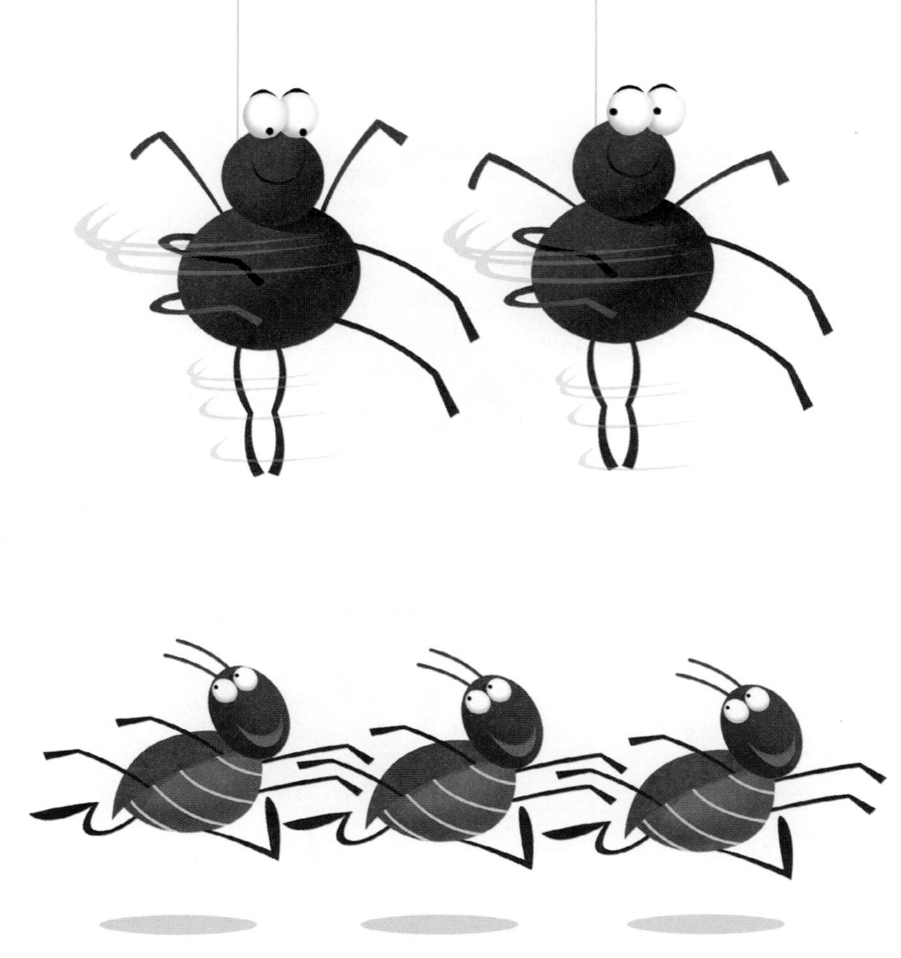

Now it's time for bugs to dance.
Spiders spin and beetles prance.
How many dancers do you see
Dancing in this jamboree? ______

If 2 band members go away,
How many are left to play? ______

Addition Facts Through 10

TAKS Vocabulary

Here are some vocabulary words you will learn in the chapter.

addend A number that is added to another number

5 + 1 = 6

addend ↑ (5) **addend** ↑ (1)

count on A way to add 1, 2, or 3

Start with 4.
Count on 2 by saying 5, 6.

4 + 2 = 6

See English-Spanish glossary pages 505–516.

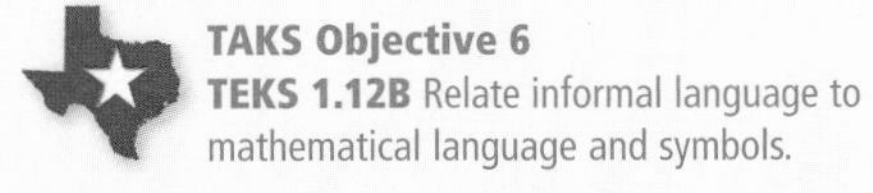

TAKS Objective 6
TEKS 1.12B Relate informal language to mathematical language and symbols.

Education Place
Visit **www.eduplace.com/txmap/** for the eGlossary and vocabulary eGames.

Name ______________________________

Write the number sentence.

1.  

____ + ____ = ____

2.   

____ + ____ = ____

3.  

____ + ____ = ____

4.   

____ + ____ = ____

5.    

____ + ____ = ____

Use this page to review important skills needed for this chapter.

Name ____________________

Chapter 6 Lesson 1

Model Addition

Hands On

TEKS Objective Model the concept of addition as part-part-whole.

★ Learn

You add the parts to find the whole.

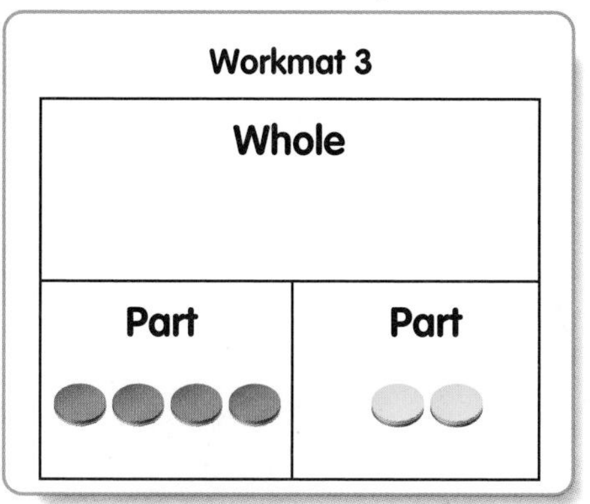

Workmat 3

Whole	
Part	Part

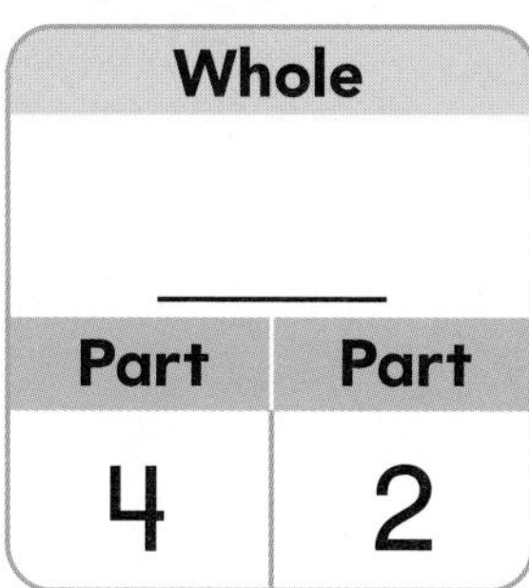

Whole	
6	
Part	Part
4	2

 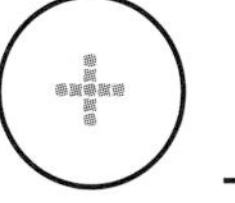  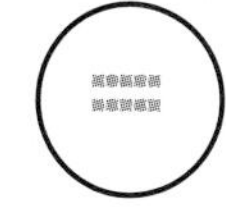 6

★ Guided Practice

Use Workmat 3 and ◯. Show the parts.
Find the whole. Write the number sentence.

1. 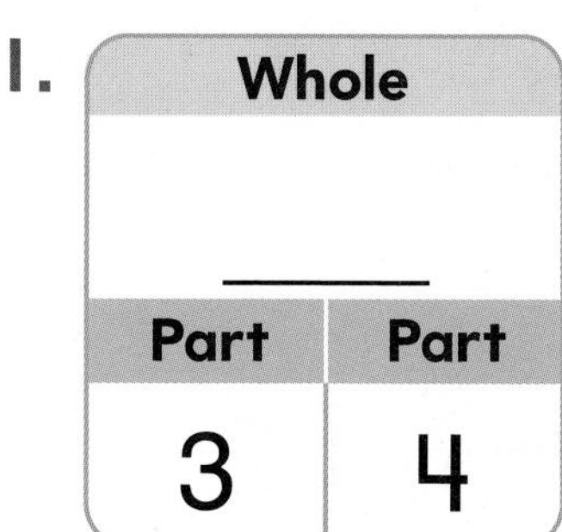

Think! I add 3 and 4 to find the whole.

___ ◯ ___ ◯ ___

2.

Whole	
___	
Part	Part
7	2

___ ◯ ___ ◯ ___

3. **Math Talk** What does the word **whole** mean?

TAKS Objective 1
TEKS 1.3B Use concrete and pictorial models to apply basic addition and subtraction facts (up to 9 + 9 = 18 and 18 − 9 = 9).

★ Practice

Remember!
Add the parts to find how many in all.

Use Workmat 3 and ○.
Show the parts. Find the whole.
Write the number sentence.

4.

Whole	
8	
Part	Part
3	5

3 (+) 5 (=) 8

5.

Whole	
____	
Part	Part
5	5

____ ○ ____ ○ ____

6.

Whole	
____	
Part	Part
6	3

____ ○ ____ ○ ____

7.

Whole	
____	
Part	Part
5	1

____ ○ ____ ○ ____

Algebra Readiness: Number Sentences

Write the sum.

8.   

____ = 6 + 2

At Home Use dried beans or other objects to help your child model different ways to show 10 in all.

En casa Use frijoles u otros objetos para ayudar a su niño a demostrar diferentes maneras de representar un total de 10.

Name ______________________

Chapter 6 Lesson 2

Use Pictures to Add

TEKS Objective
Use pictures to solve addition facts.

★ Learn

You can write an addition fact in two ways.

4 (+) 3 (=) 7

$$\begin{array}{r} 4 \\ +3 \\ \hline 7 \end{array}$$

★ Guided Practice

Write the sum.

Think! There are 3 bugs and 5 more.

1.  

$3 + 5 =$ ____

$$\begin{array}{r} 3 \\ +5 \\ \hline \end{array}$$

2. 

$$\begin{array}{r} 6 \\ +4 \\ \hline \end{array}$$

$6 + 4 =$ ____

3. 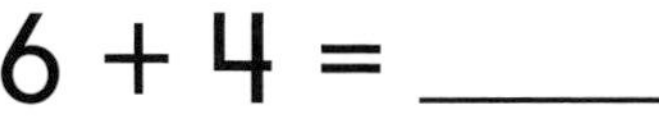

$$\begin{array}{r} 5 \\ +2 \\ \hline \end{array}$$

$5 + 2 =$ ____

4. **Math Talk** Does the sum change when you add in a different way? Why?

TAKS Objective 1
TEKS 1.3B Use concrete and pictorial models to apply basic addition and subtraction facts (up to 9 + 9 = 18 and 18 – 9 = 9).

★ Practice

Remember!
The number of bugs is the same, so the sum is the same.

Write the sum.

5.    

$2 + 3 =$ 5

$$\begin{array}{r} 2 \\ +3 \\ \hline 5 \end{array}$$

6. 

$10 + 0 =$ ____

$$\begin{array}{r} 10 \\ +\ 0 \\ \hline \end{array}$$

7.  

$7 + 1 =$ ____

$$\begin{array}{r} 7 \\ +1 \\ \hline \end{array}$$

8.    

$1 + 8 =$ ____

$$\begin{array}{r} 1 \\ +8 \\ \hline \end{array}$$

Problem Solving: Number Sense

Draw your own picture.
Write the addition fact two ways.

9. ____ + ____ = ____

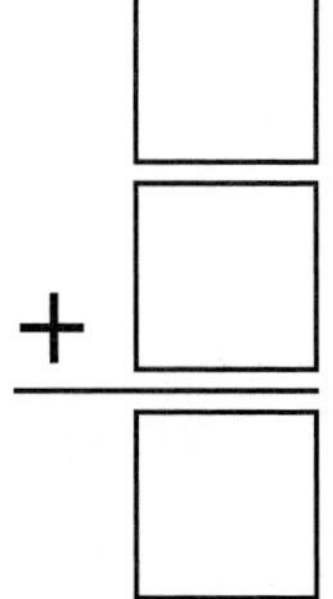

At Home Ask your child to tell an addition story and write the fact for the story both ways.

En casa Pida a su niño que cuente un cuento de suma y escriba la operación para el cuento de ambas maneras.

Name ______________________________

Chapter 6 Lesson 3

Add in Any Order

Hands On

TEKS Objective
Explore order patterns in addition.

TAKS Vocabulary
order
addend

★ Learn

You can change the **order** of the **addends** and get the same sum.

Make a cube train.

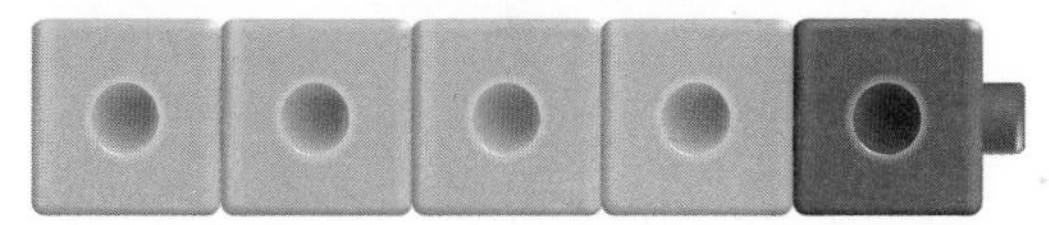

4 + 1 = 5

Turn it around.

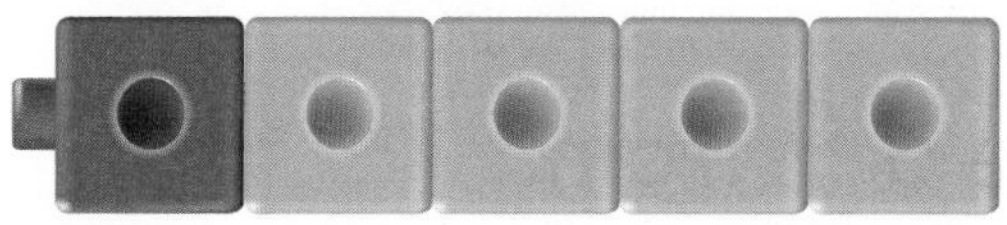

1 + 4 = 5

★ Guided Practice

Use cubes. Make the train. Color and write to show.

Think!
2 plus 5 equals 7.
I change the order of the addends to complete the sentence.

1. Make a 7 train.

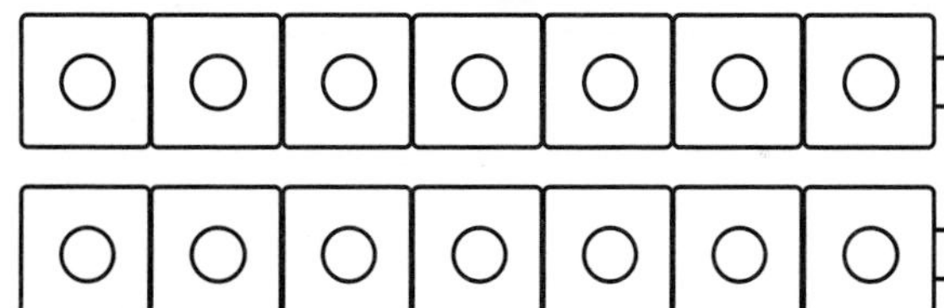

____ + ____ = ____

____ + ____ = ____

2. Make a 6 train.

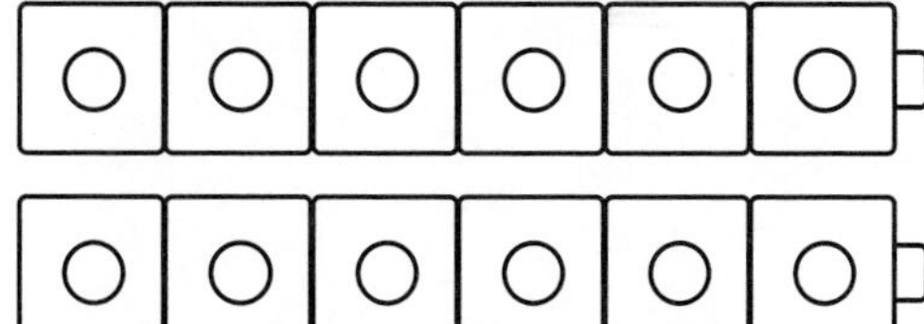

____ + ____ = ____

____ + ____ = ____

3. **Math Talk** Why is the sum of 5 + 1 the same as 1 + 5? What patterns do you see?

TAKS Objectives 1, 2
TEKS 1.3B Use concrete and pictorial models to apply basic addition and subtraction facts (up to 9 + 9 = 18 and 18 – 9 = 9).

TEKS 1.5D Use patterns to develop strategies to solve basic addition and basic subtraction problems.

★ Practice

Use cubes. Make the train.
Color and write to show.

Remember!
Turn your
train around.

4. Make an 8 train.

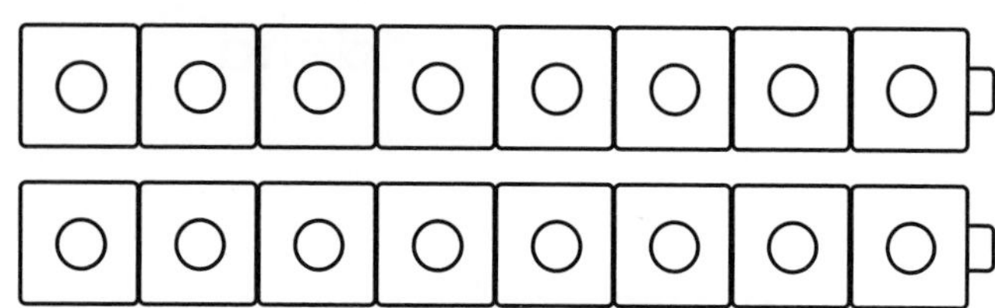

5 + 3 = 8

3 + 5 = 8

5. Make a 9 train.

___ + ___ = ___

___ + ___ = ___

6. Make a 10 train.

___ + ___ = ___

___ + ___ = ___

Algebra Readiness: Patterns

Use the rule. Write the sum.

7.

Rule: Add 1	
2	3
3	4
4	
5	

8.

Rule: Add 2	
2	4
3	5
4	
5	

At Home Write an addition sentence with a sum of 10 or less. Have your child change the order and write a new addition sentence. Repeat.

En casa Escriba una oración de suma con una suma de 10 ó menos. Pida a su niño que cambie el orden y escriba una nueva oración de suma. Repita.

Name ______________________________

Chapter 6 Lesson 4

Count On to Add

TEKS **Objective**
Use a pattern such as count on 1, 2, or 3 to find sums through 10.

TAKS **Vocabulary**
count on

★ Learn

You can **count on** to add.

Find 7 + 1.
Start with 7. Count on 1.

7 8

7 + 1 = 8

Find 7 + 2.
Start with 7. Count on 2.

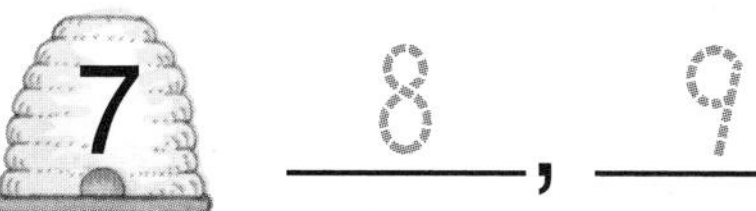
7 8, 9

7 + 2 = 9

★ Guided Practice

Count on to add. Use cubes if you wish.

Think!
I start with 7.
I count on 3.

1.    

7 ____, ____, ____

7 + 3 = ____

2. 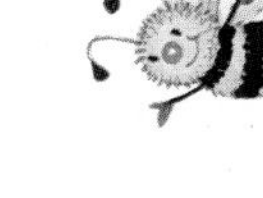

6 ____

6 + 1 = ____

3.  

6 ____, ____

6 + 2 = ____

4.   

6 ____, ____, ____

6 + 3 = ____

5. **Math Talk** What patterns help you find the sum?

TAKS Objectives 1, 2
TEKS 1.3B Use concrete and pictorial models to apply basic addition and subtraction facts (up to 9 + 9 = 18 and 18 − 9 = 9).

TEKS 1.5D Use patterns to develop strategies to solve basic addition and basic subtraction problems.

★ Practice

Remember!
Count on 1, 2, or 3.

Count on to add.
Use cubes if you wish.

6.  

 5  6

$5 + 1 = 6$

7.  

 5 ____, ____

$5 + 2 =$ ____

8.   

 5 ____, ____, ____

$5 + 3 =$ ____

9. 

 4 ____

$4 + 1 =$ ____

10.  

 4 ____, ____

$4 + 2 =$ ____

11.   

 4 ____, ____, ____

$4 + 3 =$ ____

Algebra Readiness: Number Sentences

12. How many and ?

____ $= 4 + 6$

At Home Say a number from 1 through 8. Have your child count on 2 and say the addition fact.

En casa Diga un número del 1 al 8. Pida a su niño que cuente 2 hacia adelante y que diga la operación de suma.

Name ____________________

Chapter 6 Lesson 5

Draw a Picture

TEKS Objective
Draw pictures to solve problems.

★ Learn

Erin looks for ants.
She finds a group of 3 red ants
and a group of 4 black ants.
How many ants does Erin find in all?

Understand

What do you know?

- Erin finds 3 red ants.
- Erin finds 4 black ants.

Plan

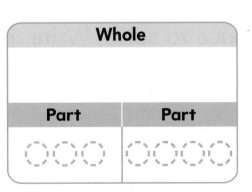

You know the parts.
You need to find the whole.
Draw the parts.

Whole	
Part	**Part**
○○○	○○○○

Solve

Write a number sentence.

3 (+) 4 (=) 7

Erin finds 7 ants in all.

Whole	
7	
Part	**Part**
3	4

Look Back

How do you know your answer makes sense?

TAKS Objectives 1, 6
TEKS 1.3B Use concrete and pictorial models to apply basic addition and subtraction facts (up to 9 + 9 = 18 and 18 – 9 = 9).

TEKS 1.12A Explain and record observations using objects, words, pictures, numbers, and technology. Also **TEKS 1.11B, 1.11C**

I add to find how many.

Guided Problem Solving

1. Bess sees 4 beetles.
   Sam sees 6 beetles.
   How many beetles do both children see?

   Use the numbers in the problem.

   Draw a picture. Solve.

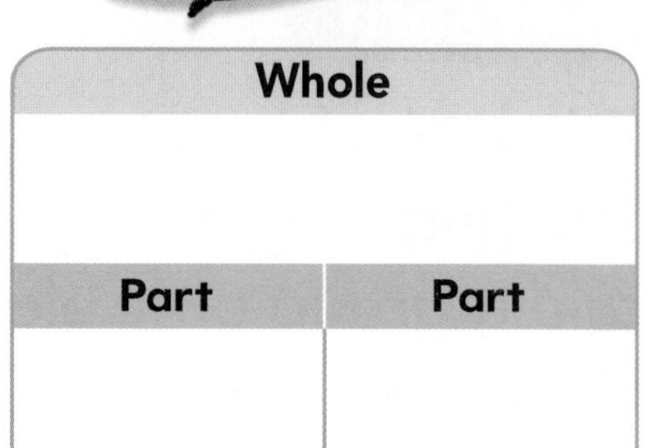

____ beetles

2. **Math Talk** How did drawing a picture help you solve the problem?

Problem Solving Practice

Draw a picture. Write a number sentence to solve. Write the answer.

Whole	
Part	Part

3. There are 6 moths near the light. 3 more moths fly to the light. How many moths are near the light now?

____ ◯ ____ ◯ ____

____ moths

Whole	
Part	Part

4. There are 4 fireflies in the air. 4 fireflies are in the grass. How many fireflies are there altogether?

____ ◯ ____ ◯ ____

____ fireflies

At Home Replace the numbers in the first problem with 2 and 7. Ask your child to draw a picture and write a number sentence to solve.

En casa Sustituya los números en el primer problema con 2 y 7. Pida a su niño que haga un dibujo y escriba una oración numérica para resolver.

Name ______________________________

Science

Texas Field Trip

Houston Museum of Natural Science

Will's class visits the Butterfly Center. Many kinds of butterflies live there. Other insects live there, too.

Butterfly Center

Solve. Show your work.

1. There are 6 butterflies in the air. There are 2 on a flower. How many are there in all?

   ____ ◯ ____ ◯ ____

   ____ butterflies

2. There are 4 beetles on a leaf. 6 more join them. How many are on the leaf now?

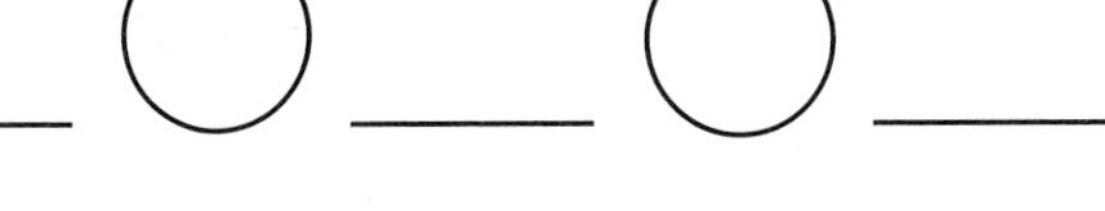

   ____ beetles

3. Rosa sees 5 walking sticks. Nam sees 2 walking sticks. How many do they see in all?

   ____ walking sticks

TAKS Objectives 1, 6
TEKS 1.3B Use concrete and pictorial models to apply basic addition and subtraction facts (up to $9 + 9 = 18$ and $18 - 9 = 9$).

TEKS 1.11A Identify mathematics in everyday situations.
Also **TEKS 1.11C**
TEKS Science 2A

TAKS Problem Solving
Listening Skills

Select a Strategy
Act It Out
Draw a Picture

Listen to your teacher read the problem. Choose the correct answer.

1. The class sees 6 bees on the hive. They see 3 bees on a flower. How many bees do they see altogether?

3	6	9	10
○	○	○	○

TEKS 1.3B

2. There are 2 crickets in the grass. There are 5 crickets on the path. How many crickets are there?

5	7	8	9
○	○	○	○

TEKS 1.3B

3.

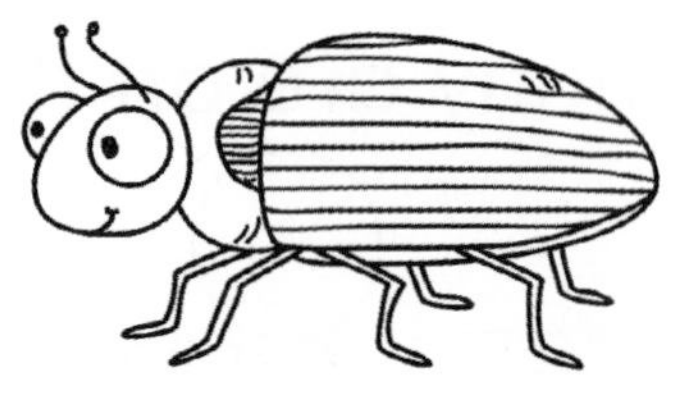

1	6	8	10
○	○	○	○

TEKS 1.3B

4.

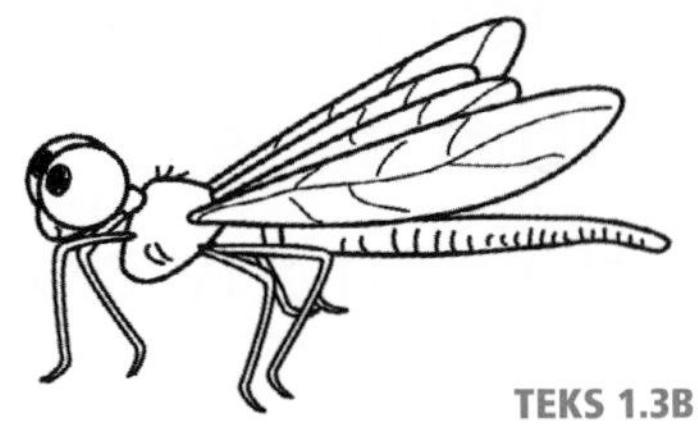

0	6	8	10
○	○	○	○

TEKS 1.3B

Education Place
Visit **www.eduplace.com/txmap/** for Test-Taking Tips and more TAKS Practice.

Name ____________________

More Addition Patterns

Use a calculator. Press + to add.
Press = for the sum. Write the sum.

1. 2 + 3 = [ ]
2. 3 + 2 = [ ]
3. 4 + 1 = [ ]
4. 1 + 4 = [ ]
5. 3 + 4 = [ ]
6. 4 + 3 = [ ]
7. 3 + 5 = [ ]
8. 5 + 3 = [ ]
9. 4 + 5 = [ ]
10. 5 + 4 = [ ]

11. Write a story about one of the addition sentences.

____

____

12. **Math Talk** What patterns do you see?

Social Studies Link

Thomas Edison

Thomas Alva Edison was a famous American inventor. He invented recorded music and motion pictures. After many tries, he also invented the light bulb. People use Thomas Edison's inventions even today.

Read the story. Use counters or draw a picture to solve.

1. One day Lucy went to the store to buy 3 light bulbs. The store was having a sale, so she bought 6 more. How many light bulbs did Lucy buy in all?

   _____ light bulbs

2. On Saturday at the movie theater, 5 movies play on the first screen. 2 movies play on the other screen. How many movies play at the theater in all?

   _____ movies

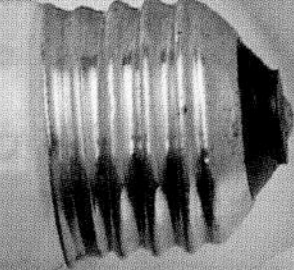

TAKS Objectives 1, 6
TEKS 1.3B Use concrete and pictorial models to apply basic addition and subtraction facts (up to 9 + 9 = 18 and 18 – 9 = 9).

TEKS 1.12A Explain and record observations using objects, words, pictures, numbers, and technology. Also **TEKS 1.11A**
TEKS Social Studies 1B, 9A

Name ______________________________

Concepts and Skills

Write the sum. TEKS 1.3B

1. 

6 + 2 = ____

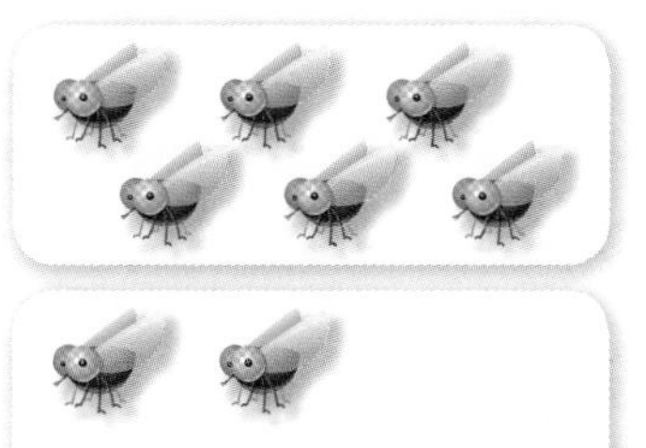

$$\begin{array}{r} 6 \\ +2 \\ \hline \end{array}$$

Use cubes. Make the train.
Color and write to show. TEKS 1.3B, 1.5D

2. Make a 7 train.

____ + ____ = ____

____ + ____ = ____

Count on to add. TEKS 1.3B, 1.5D

3. 5 ____, ____

5 + 2 = ____

Problem Solving

Draw a picture. Write a number sentence to solve. Write the answer. TEKS 1.3B, 1.11C, 1.12A

4. 6 ladybugs are on a leaf.
4 more ladybugs come.
How many ladybugs are there in all?

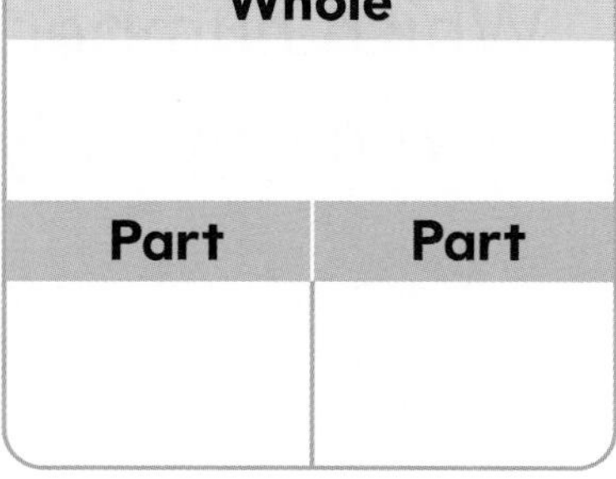

Whole	
Part	Part

____ ◯ ____ ◯ ____

____ ladybugs

TAKS Prep and Spiral Review

Choose the answer for problems 1–4.

1. How many grasshoppers are there?

2	3	4	5
○	○	○	○

TEKS 1.1D (page 21)

2. Hector saw ants crawling on a rock. How many ants did he see?

6	7	8	9
○	○	○	○

TEKS 1.1D (page 23)

3. Which number sentence tells about the picture?

5 + 1 = 6	5 − 4 = 1	5 − 1 = 1	5 − 1 = 4
○	○	○	○

TEKS 1.3A (page 83)

4. There are 2 yellow ladybugs.
There are 5 red ladybugs.
Which number sentence shows how many ladybugs there are in all?

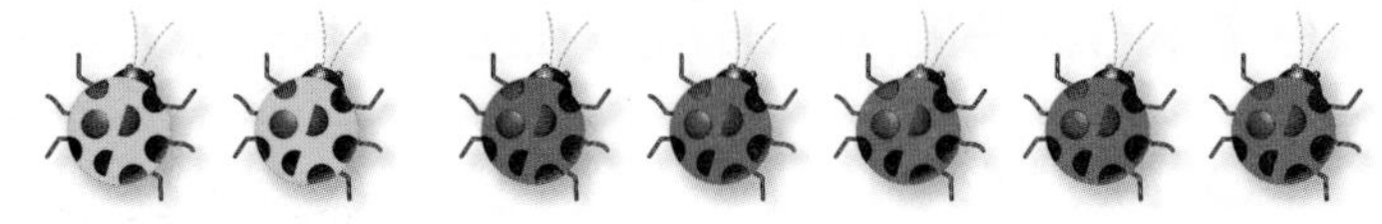

2 + 5 = 7	2 + 4 = 6	2 + 5 = 8	5 − 2 = 3
○	○	○	○

TEKS 1.3A (page 65)

Education Place
Visit www.eduplace.com/txmap/ for Test-Taking Tips and Extra Practice.

Subtraction Facts Through 10

TAKS Vocabulary

Here are some vocabulary words you will learn in the chapter.

count back A way to subtract 1, 2, or 3
Start with 5. Count back 1 by saying 4.

$$5 - 1 = 4$$

related facts Addition and subtraction facts that have the same parts and wholes
$5 + 4 = 9$ and $9 - 4 = 5$ are related facts.

Whole	
9	
Part	Part
5	4

fact family All the addition and subtraction facts that use the same numbers

$5 + 4 = 9$ $9 - 5 = 4$
$4 + 5 = 9$ $9 - 4 = 5$

This fact family uses the numbers 4, 5, and 9.

See English-Spanish glossary pages 505–516.

TAKS Objective 6
TEKS 1.12B Relate informal language to mathematical language and symbols.

Education Place
Visit **www.eduplace.com/txmap/** for the eGlossary and vocabulary eGames.

Name ______________________________

Check What You Know

Use the picture.
Write the number sentence.

1. 

_____ − _____ = _____

2. 

_____ − _____ = _____

3. 

_____ + _____ = _____

4. 

_____ − _____ = _____

Use this page to review important skills needed for this chapter.

Name ______________________

Chapter 7 Lesson 1

Count Back to Subtract

Hands On

TEKS Objective
Use a pattern such as counting back 1, 2, or 3 to find differences through 10.

TAKS Vocabulary
count back

★ Learn

You can **count back** to subtract.

Start with 9.
Count back 1.

8

9 − 1 = 8

Start with 9.
Count back 2.

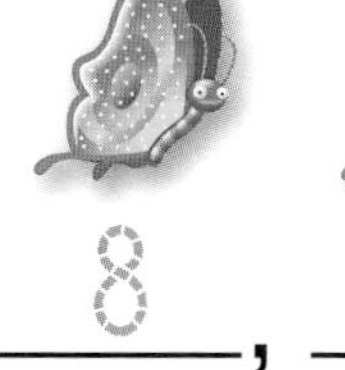

8, 7

9 − 2 = 7

★ Guided Practice

Count back to subtract.
Use cubes if you wish.

Think!
I start with 9.
I count back 3.

1.  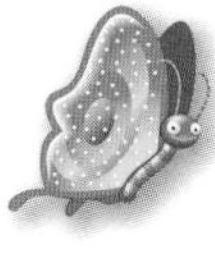  

____, ____, ____

9 − 3 = ____

2. 

____

10 − 1 = ____

3.   

____, ____

10 − 2 = ____

4.    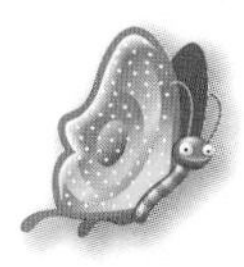

____, ____, ____

10 − 3 = ____

5. **Math Talk** What patterns help you find the difference?

TAKS Objectives 1, 2
TEKS 1.3B Use concrete and pictorial models to apply basic addition and subtraction facts (up to 9 + 9 = 18 and 18 − 9 = 9).

TEKS 1.5D Use patterns to develop strategies to solve basic addition and basic subtraction problems.

★ Practice

Count back to subtract.
Use cubes if you wish.

Remember!
Count back 1, 2, or 3.

6. 

7

8 − 1 = 7

7.   

____, ____

8 − 2 = ____

8.    

____, ____, ____

8 − 3 = ____

9.  

____

7 − 1 = ____

10.   

____, ____

7 − 2 = ____

11.    

____, ____, ____

7 − 3 = ____

Problem Solving: Reasoning

Solve.

12. There are 4 moths.
2 of the moths are black.
How many moths are white?

____ white moths

Draw or write to explain.

At Home Say a number from 4 through 10. Have your child use counting back to subtract 1, 2, or 3.

En casa Diga un número del 4 al 10. Pida a su niño que cuente hacia atrás para restar 1, 2 ó 3.

Name ______________________

Chapter 7 Lesson 2

Use Pictures to Subtract

TEKS Objective
Use pictures to solve subtraction facts.

★ Learn

You can write a subtraction fact in two ways.

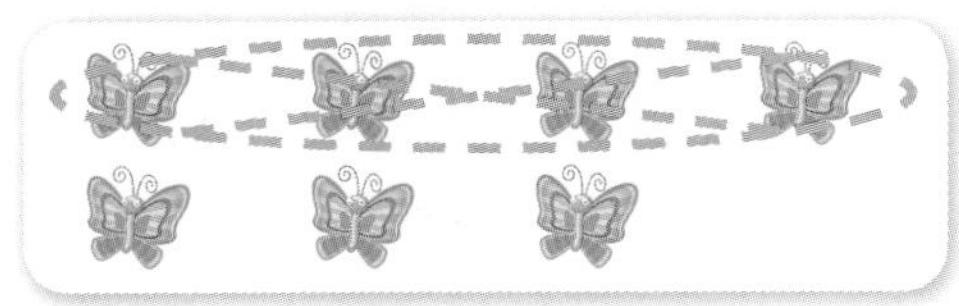

7 − 4 = 3

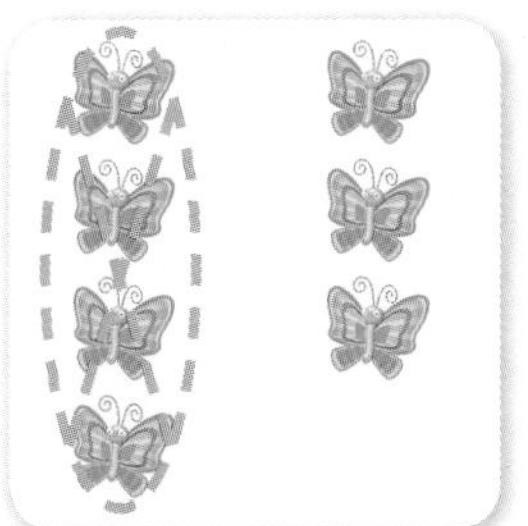

$$\begin{array}{r} 7 \\ -4 \\ \hline 3 \end{array}$$

★ Guided Practice

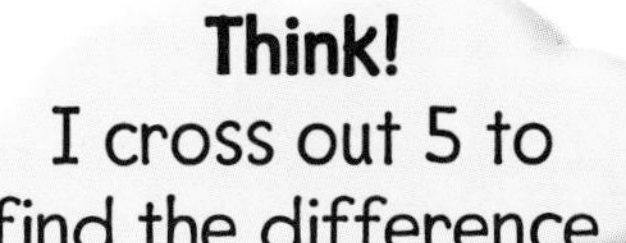

Think!
I cross out 5 to
find the difference.

Circle and cross out to subtract.
Write the difference.

1. 

9 − 5 = ____

$$\begin{array}{r} 9 \\ -5 \\ \hline \end{array}$$

2. 10 − 3 = ____

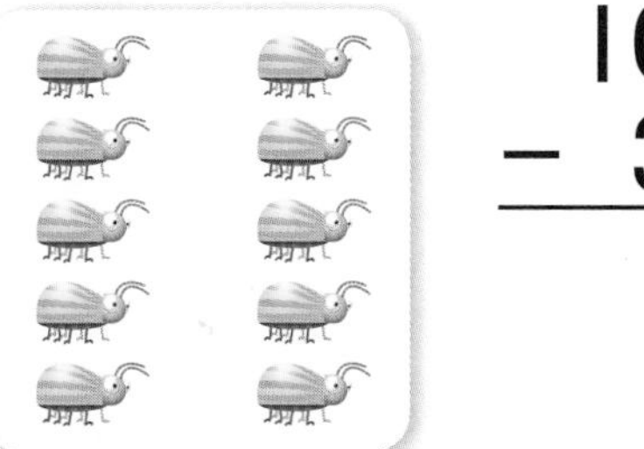

$$\begin{array}{r} 10 \\ -\ 3 \\ \hline \end{array}$$

3. 8 − 0 = ____

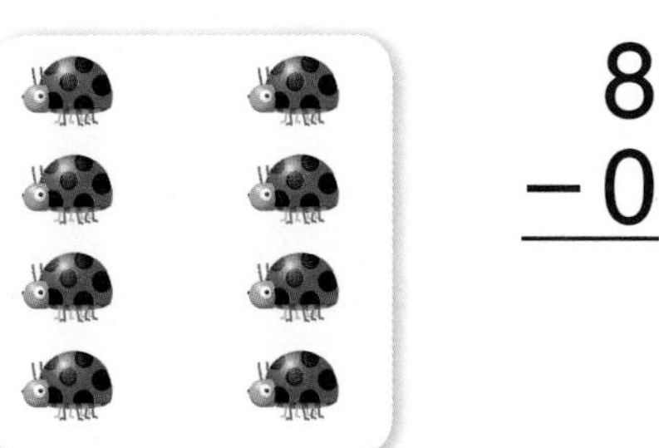

$$\begin{array}{r} 8 \\ -0 \\ \hline \end{array}$$

4. 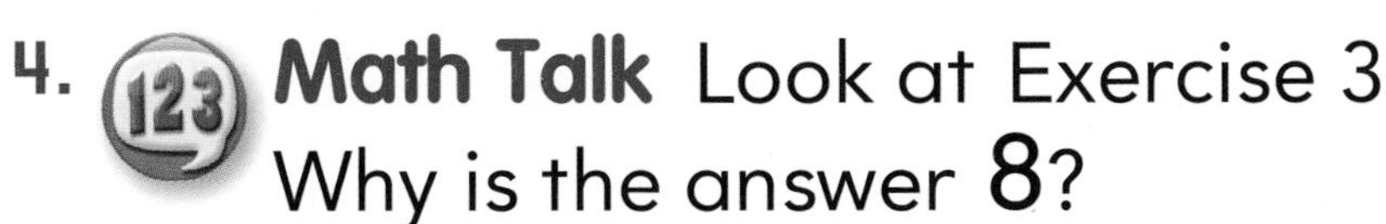
Math Talk Look at Exercise 3.
Why is the answer 8?

TAKS Objective 1
TEKS 1.3B Use concrete and pictorial models to apply basic addition and subtraction facts (up to 9 + 9 = 18 and 18 − 9 = 9).

★ Practice

Circle and cross out to subtract.
Write the difference.

Remember!
The number of objects that are not crossed out is the difference.

5. 

$8 - 4 =$ 4

$$\begin{array}{r} 8 \\ -4 \\ \hline 4 \end{array}$$

6. 

$10 - 9 =$ ____

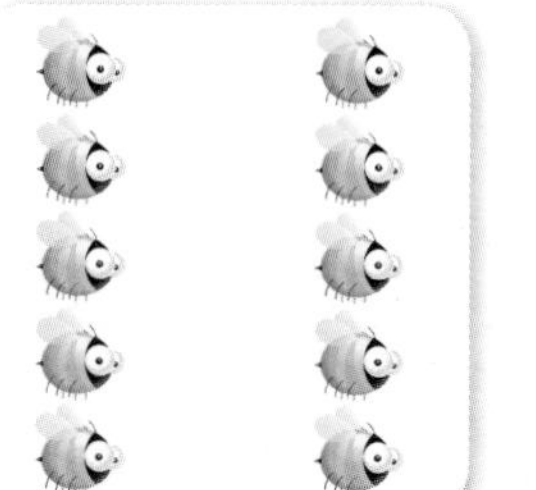

$$\begin{array}{r} 10 \\ -\ 9 \\ \hline \end{array}$$

7. 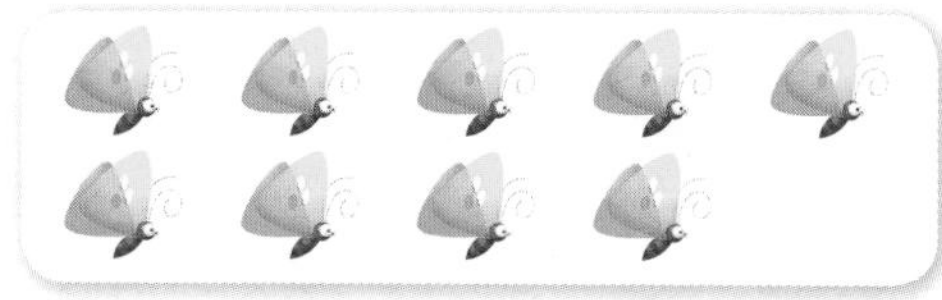

$9 - 2 =$ ____

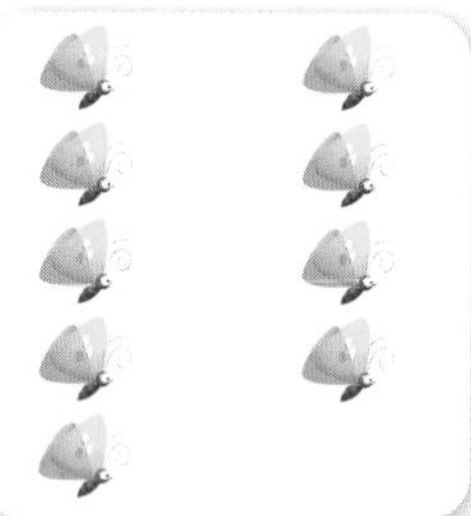

$$\begin{array}{r} 9 \\ -2 \\ \hline \end{array}$$

8. 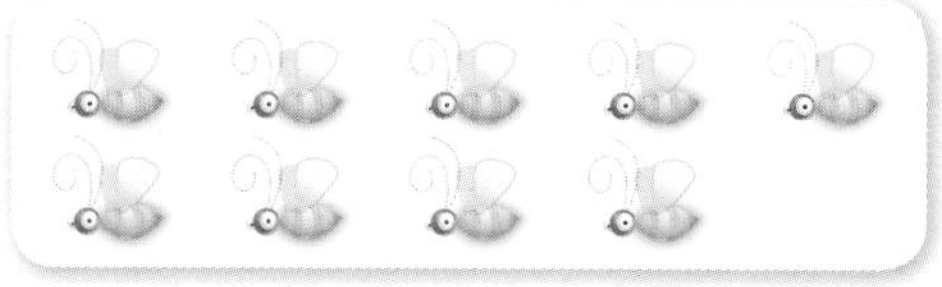

$9 - 7 =$ ____

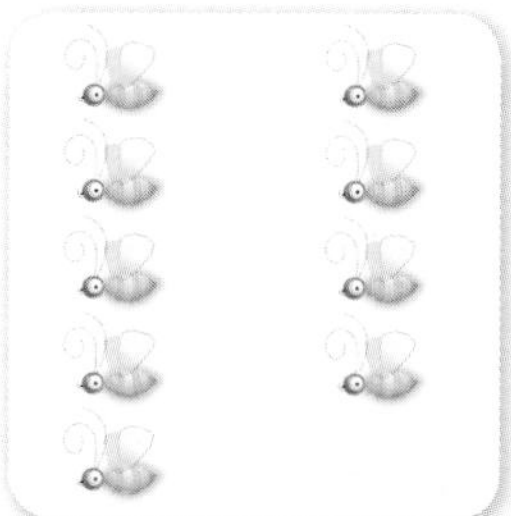

$$\begin{array}{r} 9 \\ -7 \\ \hline \end{array}$$

Problem Solving: Reasoning

Draw your own picture.
Write the subtraction fact two ways.

9.

____ − ____ = ____

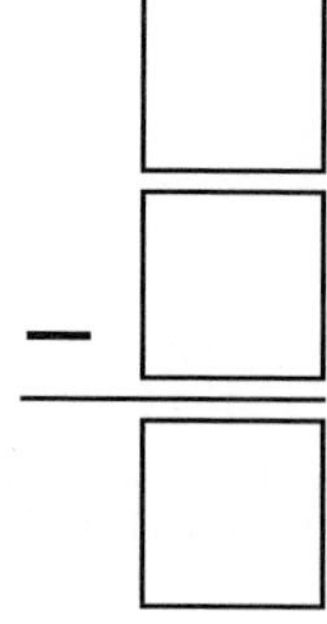

At Home Ask your child to show you how 6 – 6 and 6 – 0 are different.

En casa Pida a su niño que explique la diferencia entre 6 – 6 y 6 – 0.

Name ___________________________

Chapter 7 Lesson 3

Compare More and Fewer

TEKS Objective
Use pictorial models to subtract.

★ Learn

How many more than are there?

Match the to the .

Count how many more than .

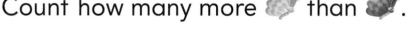

You can subtract to compare sets of objects.

8 − 3 = 5

There are 5 more than .

★ Guided Practice

Think!
I match 4 to 4 .
How many do not have a match?

Match. Then subtract.

1. How many fewer than are there?

9 − 4 = ____

2. **Math Talk** Can you add to compare sets of objects? Why?

TAKS Objective 1
TEKS 1.3B Use concrete and pictorial models to apply basic addition and subtraction facts (up to 9 + 9 = 18 and 18 − 9 = 9).

★ Practice

Match.
Then subtract.

Remember!
Count how many do not have a match.

3. How many more than are there?

8 − 6 = 2

4. How many fewer than are there?

9 − 5 = ____

5. How many more than are there?

10 − 4 = ____

Algebra Readiness: Number Sentences

Compare. Write the difference.

6.

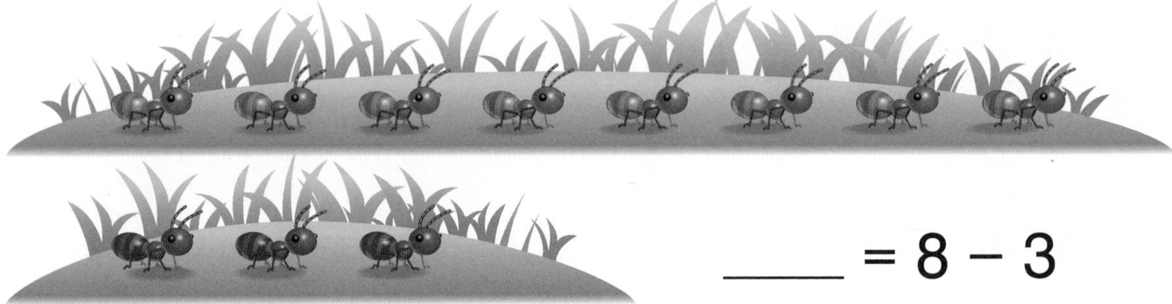

____ = 8 − 3

At Home Make two sets of objects; one with 10 and one with less than 10. Have your child subtract to compare the sets.

En casa Haga dos conjuntos de objetos, uno con 10 y uno con menos de 10. Pida a su niño que reste para comparar los conjuntos.

Name ______________________________

Chapter 7 Lesson 4

Relate Addition and Subtraction

TEKS Objective
Identify patterns in related addition and subtraction facts.

TAKS Vocabulary
related facts

These facts are **related facts.**
They have the same parts and wholes.

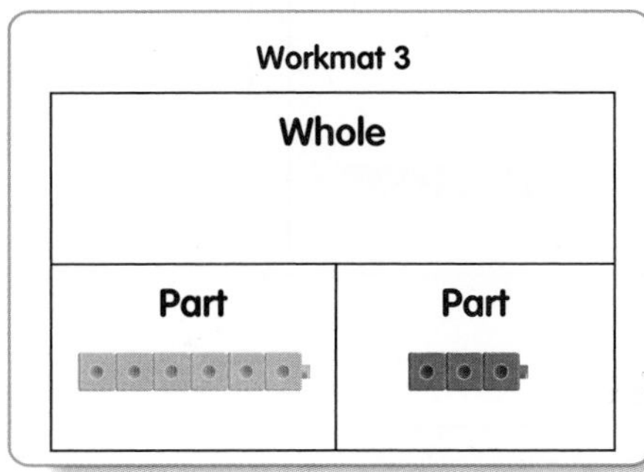

6 orange cubes and 3 blue cubes. How many in all?

6 + 3 = 9

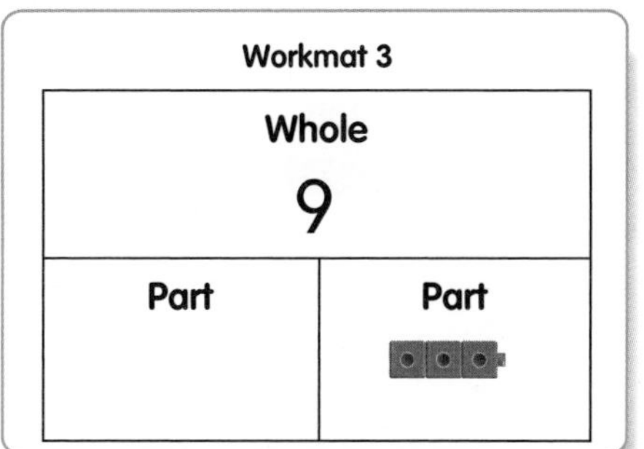

9 cubes. 3 are blue.
How many orange?

9 − 3 = 6

★ Guided Practice

Use orange cube, blue cube, and Workmat 3.
Show the parts. Complete the related facts.

Think!
8 and 1 are the parts. I need to find the whole.

1. 8 and 1	____ + ____ = ____	____ − ____ = ____
2. 5 and 4	____ + ____ = ____	____ − ____ = ____
3. 3 and 3	____ + ____ = ____	____ − ____ = ____

4. **Math Talk** How are the number sentences the same? What patterns do you see?

TAKS Objectives 1, 2
TEKS 1.3B Use concrete and pictorial models to apply basic addition and subtraction facts (up to 9 + 9 = 18 and 18 − 9 = 9).

TEKS 1.5E Identify patterns in related addition and subtraction sentences (fact families for sums to 18) such as 2 + 3 = 5, 3 + 2 = 5, 5 − 2 = 3, and 5 − 3 = 2.

★ Practice

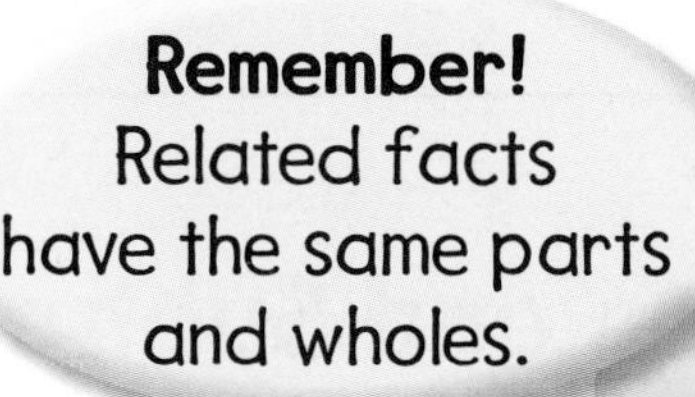

Use [cube], [cube], and Workmat 3.
Show the parts.
Complete the related facts.

5.

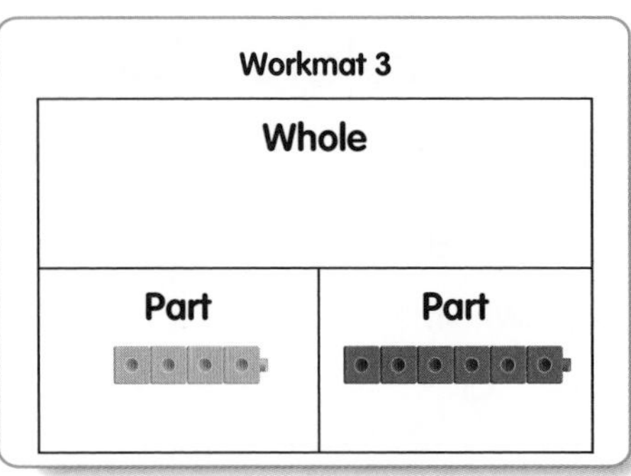

$4 + 6 =$ 10

$10 - 6 =$ 4

6.

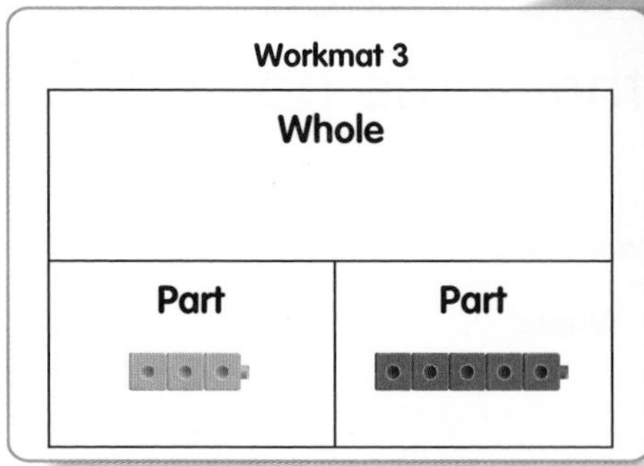

$3 + 5 =$ ____

$8 - 5 =$ ____

7. 7 and 3	____ + ____ = ____	____ − ____ = ____
8. 2 and 7	____ + ____ = ____	____ − ____ = ____
9. 2 and 8	____ + ____ = ____	____ − ____ = ____
10. 4 and 3	____ + ____ = ____	____ − ____ = ____

Algebra Readiness: Number Sentences

Write the difference. Circle the related fact.

11. $\begin{array}{r} 10 \\ -\ 4 \\ \hline \end{array}$

$6 + 4 = 10$
$5 + 4 = 9$

12. $\begin{array}{r} 9 \\ -5 \\ \hline \end{array}$

$5 + 5 = 10$
$4 + 5 = 9$

At Home Ask your child how the two facts in Exercise 11 are related.

En casa Pregunte a su niño cómo están relacionadas las operaciones del Ejercicio 11.

Name ____________________

Chapter 7 Lesson 5

Fact Families

TEKS Objective
Identify patterns in fact families.

TAKS Vocabulary
fact family

★ Learn

Related facts make a **fact family.**
This fact family uses 9, 5, and 4.

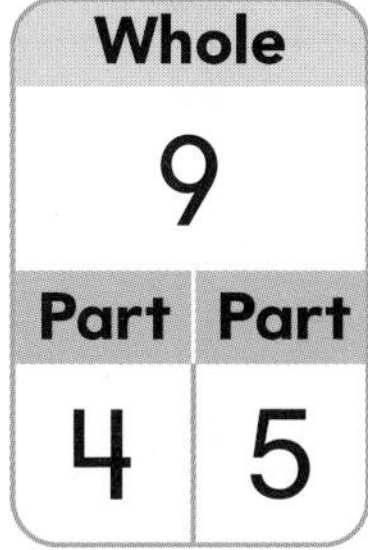

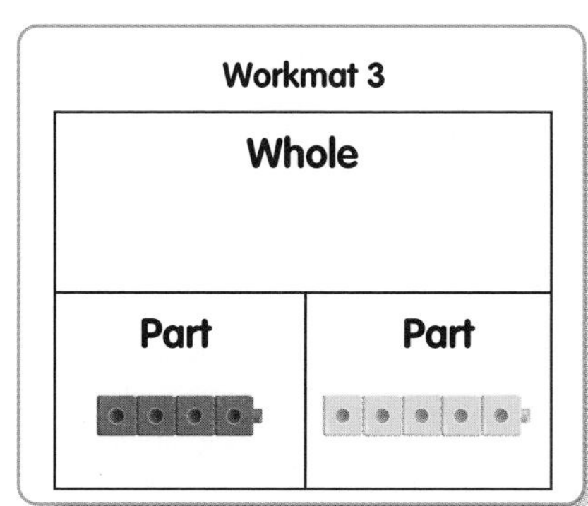

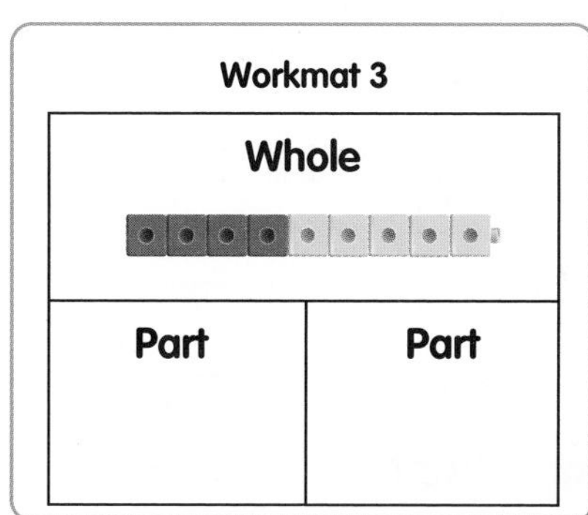

9 is the whole.
4 and 5 are the parts.

4 + 5 = 9　　9 − 5 = 4

5 + 4 = 9　　9 − 4 = 5

★ Guided Practice

Use [red cube], [white cube], and Workmat 3.
Complete the fact family.

Think!
I use 9, 6, and 3 to write the related facts.

1. | Whole | |
|---|---|
| 9 | |
| Part | Part |
| 6 | 3 |

___ + ___ = ___　　___ − ___ = ___

___ + ___ = ___　　___ − ___ = ___

2. **Math Talk** What patterns do you see in the fact families?

TAKS Objectives 1, 2
TEKS 1.3B Use concrete and pictorial models to apply basic addition and subtraction facts (up to 9 + 9 = 18 and 18 − 9 = 9).

TEKS 1.5E Identify patterns in related addition and subtraction sentences (fact families for sums to 18) such as 2 + 3 = 5, 3 + 2 = 5, 5 − 2 = 3, and 5 − 3 = 2.

★ Practice

Use 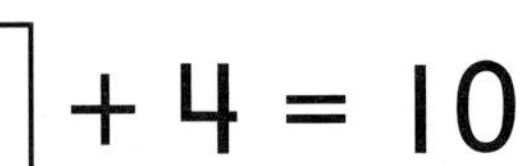, and Workmat 3.
Complete the fact family.

3. | Whole |
|---|
| 10 |
| Part \| Part |
| 7 \| 3 |

7 + 3 = 10   10 − 3 = 7

____ + ____ = ____   ____ − ____ = ____

4. | Whole |
|---|
| 8 |
| Part \| Part |
| 2 \| 6 |

____ + ____ = ____   ____ − ____ = ____

____ + ____ = ____   ____ − ____ = ____

5. | Whole |
|---|
| 10 |
| Part \| Part |
| 2 \| 8 |

____ + ____ = ____   ____ − ____ = ____

____ + ____ = ____   ____ − ____ = ____

6. | Whole |
|---|
| 8 |
| Part \| Part |
| 4 \| 4 |

____ + ____ = ____   ____ − ____ = ____

Algebra Readiness: Missing Addends

Choose a number to complete the number sentence.

7. ☐ + 4 = 10

8. ☐ + 3 = 10

At Home Ask your child to write a fact family using the numbers 3, 4, and 7.

En casa Pida a su niño que escriba una familia de operaciones usando los números 3, 4 y 7.

Name ______________________________

Chapter 7 Lesson 6

Choose the Operation

TEKS Objective
Solve problems by choosing the correct operation; create and solve problems.

Use Workmat 3 and ◯.
Use subtraction to solve the problem.

9 butterflies are on the bush.
1 butterfly flies away.
How many butterflies are there now?

Think!
I know the whole and one of the parts. I can subtract to find the other part.

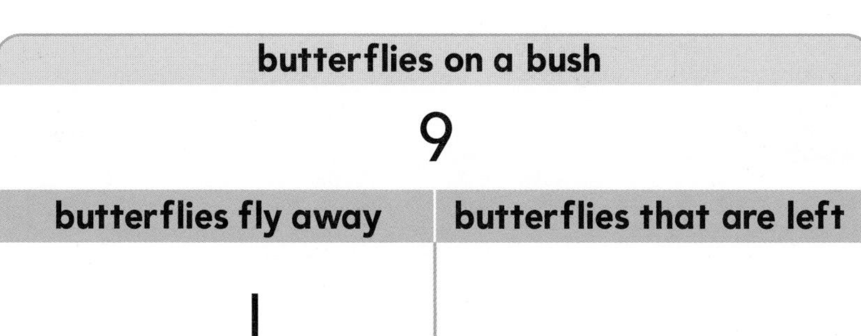

butterflies on a bush	
9	
butterflies fly away	**butterflies that are left**
1	

Use Workmat 3 and ◯.
Use addition to solve the problem.

8 ladybugs are on a log.
2 more come.
How many ladybugs are there in all?

Think!
I know the parts. I can add to find the whole.

ladybugs in all	
ladybugs on a log	**ladybugs that come**
8	2

_____ + _____ = _____

★ Guided Problem Solving

Think!
I need to find how many in all.

1. 5 fleas are on the dog.
4 more land on the dog.
How many fleas are on the dog now?

Draw a line under what you need to find out.

Solve the problem.

_____ fleas

2. **Math Talk** How did you know which operation to use?

★ Problem Solving Practice

Use Workmat 3 and ◯.
Choose the operation to solve.

Draw or write to explain.

3. 9 bees are in the hive.
3 bees fly away. How many bees are in the hive now?

_____ bees

4. 4 moths are near the light.
4 more fly to the light.
How many are near the light now?

_____ moths

At Home Draw a picture of 6 red flowers and 3 yellow flowers. Ask your child to write a subtraction story and a subtraction sentence that compare the flowers.

En casa Dibuje 6 flores rojas y 3 flores amarillas. Pida a su niño que escriba un cuento de resta y una oración de resta que compare las flores.

Problem Solving

Name ______________________

Create and Solve

Write a story about the ants.

1. ______________________

____

____

Tell a friend your story.
Do you add or subtract?
Write the number sentence.

2. ____ ◯ ____ ◯ ____

Tell a different story about the ants.
Model, then draw to show your story.

3.

TAKS Objectives 1, 6
TEKS 1.3A Model and create addition and subtraction problem situations with concrete objects and write corresponding number sentences.
TEKS 1.11A Identify mathematics in everyday situations.
TEKS 1.13 Justify thinking using objects, words, pictures, numbers, and technology.

Write a subtraction story that compares the bugs.

4. ____

____

____

Write the subtraction sentence.

5. ____ ◯ ____ ◯ ____

Tell a story to match 7 − 4 = 3.
Draw a picture to show your story.

6.

Name ______________________________

Subtraction Patterns

Subtract.
Look for a pattern.

1. 8 − 1 = ____
   8 − 2 = ____
   8 − 3 = ____
   8 − 4 = ____
   8 − 5 = ____
   8 − 6 = ____
   8 − 7 = ____
   8 − 8 = ____

2. 8 − 0 = ____
   7 − 0 = ____
   6 − 0 = ____
   5 − 0 = ____
   4 − 0 = ____
   3 − 0 = ____
   2 − 0 = ____
   1 − 0 = ____

3. The pattern I see is ______________________________

____

____

____

TAKS Objectives 2, 6
TEKS 1.5D Use patterns to develop strategies to solve basic addition and basic subtraction problems.

Also **TEKS 1.12A**

Education Place
Visit **www.eduplace.com/txmap/** for Brain Teasers.

Math Music

Fact Family Bugs

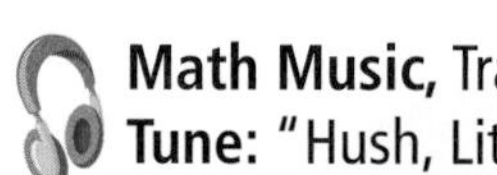

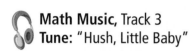

Math Music, Track 3
Tune: "Hush, Little Baby"

Read these numbers: 9, 6, 3.
They are all part of a fact family.

3 little bumblebees start to dine.
6 more join them. Now there are 9.

6 little ants crawl up a vine.
3 more join them. Now there are 9.

9 little spiders spin in a tree.
6 creep away and now there are 3.

9 little butterflies sit on some sticks.
3 fly away and now there are 6.

Write the number sentence for each fact.
Try your best to be exact!

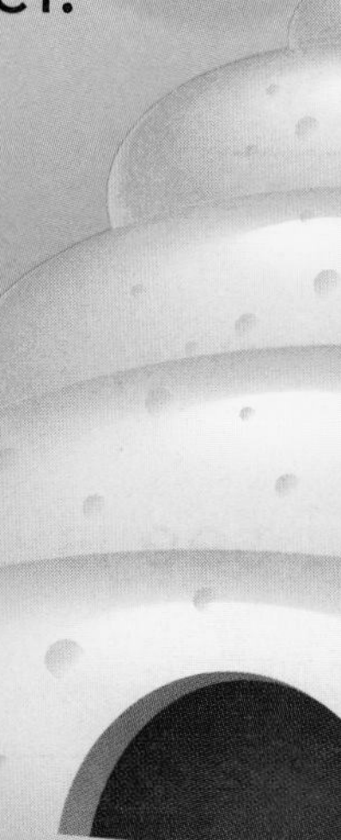

TAKS Objective 2
TEKS 1.5E Identify patterns in related addition and subtraction sentences (fact families for sums to 18) such as 2 + 3 = 5, 3 + 2 = 5, 5 – 2 = 3, and 5 – 3 = 2.

Name ______________________

Concepts and Skills

Circle and cross out to subtract.
Write the difference. TEKS 1.3B

1. 

10 − 6 = ____

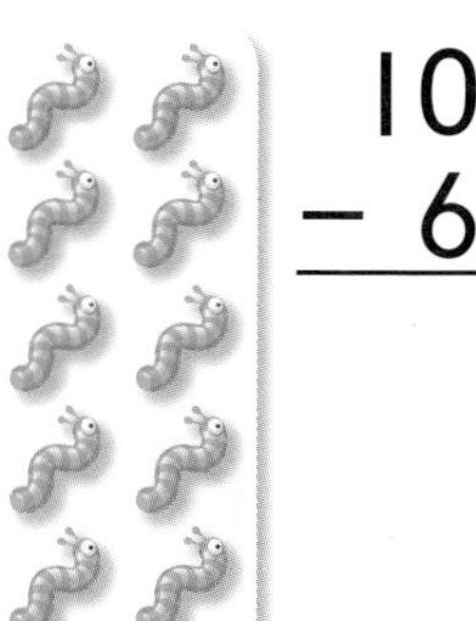

$$\begin{array}{r} 10 \\ -\ 6 \\ \hline \end{array}$$

Match. Then subtract. TEKS 1.3B

2. How many more than are there?

8 − 5 = ____

Use , , and Workmat 3.
Complete the fact family. TEKS 1.3B, 1.5E

3.

Whole	
9	
Part	Part
5	4

____ + ____ = ____ ____ − ____ = ____

____ + ____ = ____ ____ − ____ = ____

Problem Solving

Use Workmat 3 and .
Choose the operation to solve. TEKS 1.3A, 1.12A

4. 8 ants are on a rock.
2 ants go away. How many ants are on the rock now? ____ ants

TAKS Prep and Spiral Review

Choose the answer for problems 1–4.

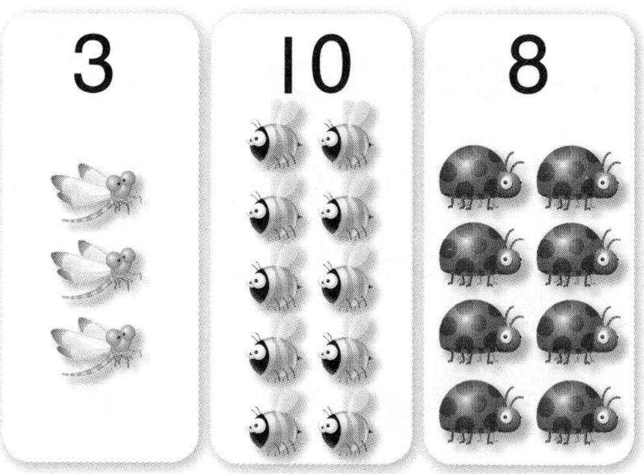

1. Which answer shows the number of stickers in order from greatest to least?

3, 8, 10	10, 3, 8	8, 10, 3	10, 8, 3
○	○	○	○

TEKS 1.1A (page 27)

2. Lindsay saw 14 butterflies.
Matt saw an equal number of beetles.
Which shows the number of beetles Matt saw?

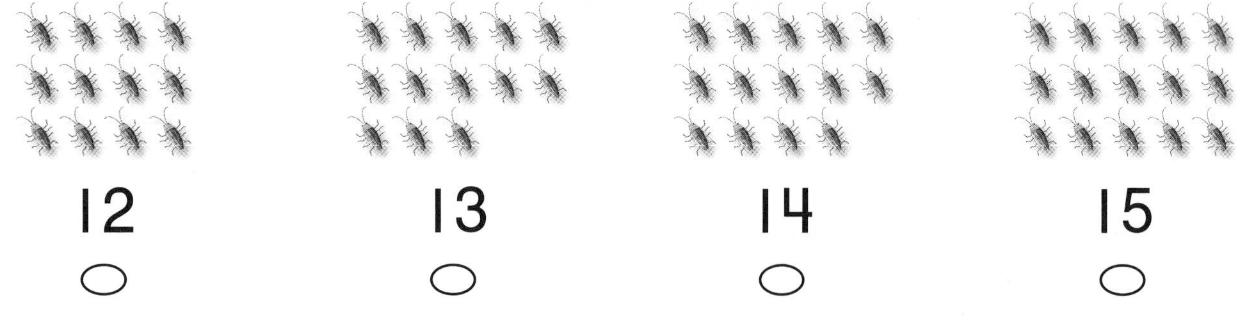

12	13	14	15
○	○	○	○

TEKS 1.1A (page 43)

3. There are 4 ants on a rock.
3 more ants crawl onto the rock.
How many ants are there now?

8	7	4	3
○	○	○	○

TEKS 1.3B (page 105)

4. Jun sees 7 bees.
2 bees fly away.
How many bees are left?

5	7	8	9
○	○	○	○

TEKS 1.3B (page 123)

Education Place
Visit **www.eduplace.com/txmap/** for Test-Taking Tips and Extra Practice.

Name ____________________

Greg Tang's Go Fast, Go Far

Unit 3 Mental Math Strategies

Count On

Counting all is how you start.
Counting ON is really smart!

I start with 3.
Then I count
on 4, 5.

1. 

$3 + 2 = \boxed{5}$

2. $4 + 1 = \square$

3. $5 + 3 = \square$

4. $6 + 2 = \square$

Take It Further: Now just count on in your head!

5. $5 + 2 = \square$

6. $2 + 4 = \square$

Name ______________________________

Reading and Writing Math

7 bees are in the hive.
3 bees are nearby.
How many bees are there in all?

You know the parts. Find the whole.

1. Write the number sentence.

   ____ + ____ = ____

Whole	
?	
Part	Part
7	3

2. Change the order of the addends. Write the number sentence.

   ____ + ____ = ____

3. How many bees are there in all?

   ____ bees

4. Write a related subtraction sentence.

   ____ − ____ = ____

5. **Writing Math** Write the fact family.

Whole	
10	
Part	Part
7	3

____ + ____ = ____ ____ − ____ = ____

____ + ____ = ____ ____ − ____ = ____

TEKS 1.12A Explain and record observations using objects, words, pictures, numbers, and technology.

TEKS 1.12B Relate informal language to mathematical language and symbols.

Name ______________________

Concepts and Skills

Write the sum. TEKS 1.3B

1. 

5 + 3 = ____

$$\begin{array}{r} 5 \\ +3 \\ \hline \end{array}$$

Count on to add. TEKS 1.3B, 1.5D

2.  7  

____, ____

7 + 2 = ____

3.  6   

____, ____, ____

6 + 3 = ____

Count back to subtract. TEKS 1.3B, 1.5D

4.  10   

____, ____, ____

10 − 3 = ____

5.  8  

____, ____

8 − 2 = ____

Circle and cross out to subtract.
Write the difference. TEKS 1.3B

6. 

9 − 5 = ____

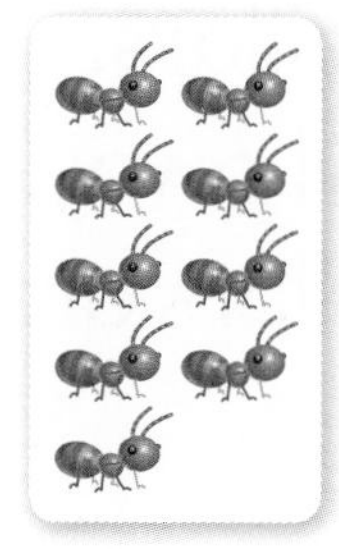

$$\begin{array}{r} 9 \\ -5 \\ \hline \end{array}$$

Use [cube], [cube], and Workmat 3.
Complete the fact family. TEKS 1.3B, 1.5E

7.

Whole	
8	
Part	Part
7	1

____ + ____ = ____   ____ − ____ = ____

____ + ____ = ____   ____ − ____ = ____

8.

Whole	
7	
Part	Part
3	4

____ + ____ = ____   ____ − ____ = ____

____ + ____ = ____   ____ − ____ = ____

Problem Solving

Use Workmat 3 and [counter].
Choose the operation to solve. TEKS 1.3A, 1.12A, 1.13

9. There are 5 black moths.
There are 5 white moths.
How many moths are there in all? ____ moths

10. There are 8 caterpillars.
4 caterpillars crawl away.
How many caterpillars are there now? ____ caterpillars

Houghton Mifflin Texas Math

Unit 4

Geometry and Fractions

BIG IDEAS!

- You can use attributes to describe and identify geometric figures.
- You can sort geometric figures into groups.
- You can separate a whole or a set into equal parts.

Songs and Games

Math Music Track 4
The Equal Parts Game
eGames
www.eduplace.com/txmap/

Literature

Literature Big Book

- Round Is a Mooncake

Math Readers

ISBN-13: 978-0-618-95272-4
ISBN-10: 0-618-95272-1
89- WC - 16 15 14 13 12

Get Ready Game

Fun with Figures!

What You Need
2 players   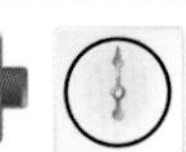

1. Take turns spinning the spinner.
2. Name the figure you land on.
3. Move to the next figure that matches.
4. Play until both players reach the finish.

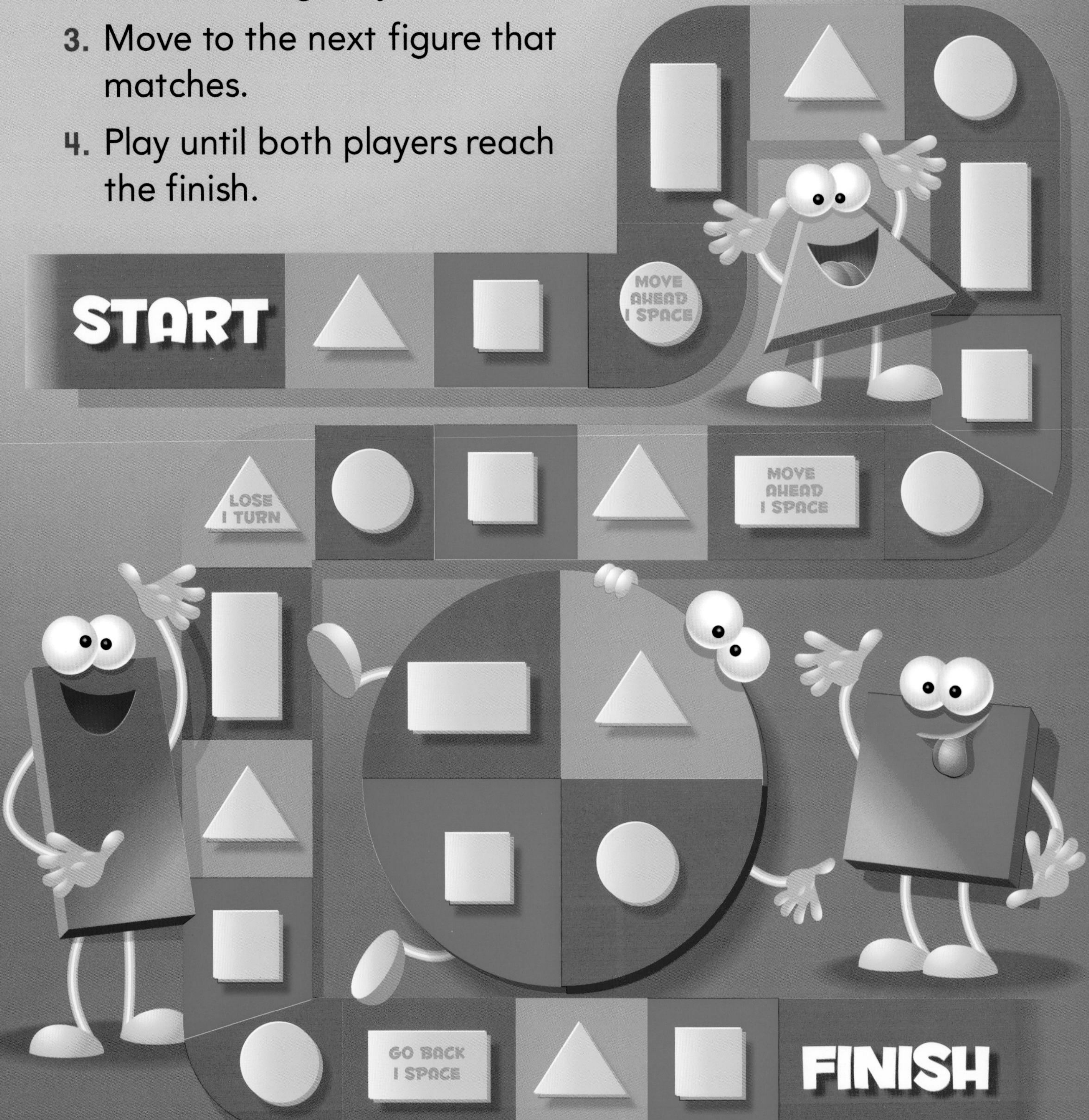

TAKS Objective 3
TEKS 1.6C Describe and identify two- and three-dimensional geometric figures in order to sort them according to a given attribute using informal and formal language.

Education Place
For eGames and Brain Teasers, visit **www.eduplace.com/txmap/**

Math at Home

Dear Family,

My class is starting Unit 4, **Geometry and Fractions**. I will learn how to identify and name two- and three-dimensional geometric figures and recognize equal parts. You can help me learn these vocabulary words, and we can do the Math Activity together.

From,

____

Vocabulary

side The straight part of a figure.

corner The point where the sides meet.

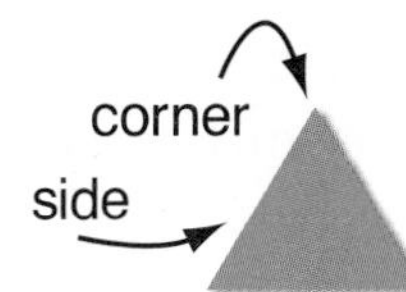

face The part of a three-dimensional figure that is a two-dimensional figure.

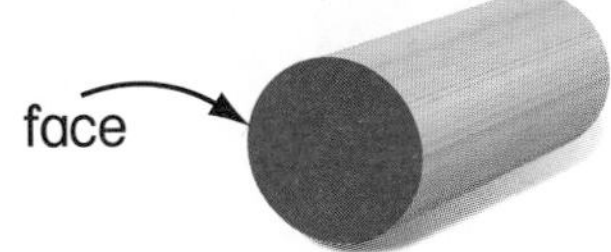

equal parts Parts that are the same size.

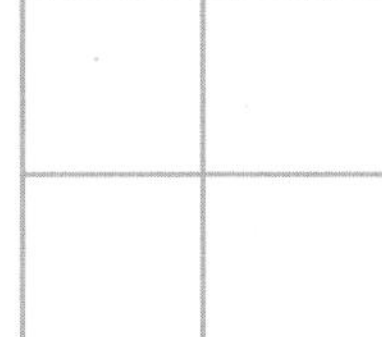

This square has 4 **equal parts**.

Education Place
Visit **www.eduplace.com/txmaf/** for
- eGames and Brain Teasers
- Math at Home in other languages

Family Math Activity

Gather and display objects that have the shape of cones, cylinders, cubes, and other rectangular prisms. Give clues such as, *It rolls and it has no corners*. Have your child name the object and talk about its shape.

Literature

These books link to the math in this unit. Look for them at the library.

- **All Sorts of Shapes**
  by Hannah Reidy
  (Picture Window Books, 2005)
- **Eating Fractions**
  by Bruce McMillan
- **Fraction Fun**
  by David Adler

Matemáticas en casa

Estimada familia:

Mi clase está comenzando la Unidad 4, **Geometría y fracciones**. Voy a aprender a identificar y nombrar figuras de dos y tres dimensiones, y a reconocer partes iguales. Me pueden ayudar a aprender estas palabras de vocabulario y podemos hacer juntos la Actividad de matemáticas para la familia.

De:

____

Vocabulario

lado Parte recta de una figura.

vértice Punto donde los lados se unen.

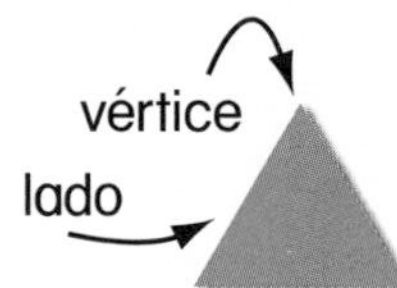

cara Parte de una figura de tres dimensiones que es una figura de dos dimensiones.

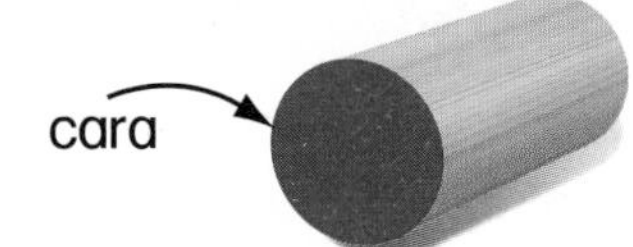

partes iguales Partes del mismo tamaño.

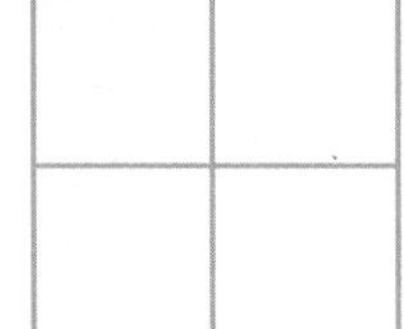

Este cuadrado tiene 4 **partes iguales**

Education Place

Visite **www.eduplace.com/txmaf/** para

- Juegos en línea y acertijos
- Matemáticas en casa, en otros idiomas

Actividad de matemáticas para la familia

Reúna y exhiba objetos con forma de conos, cilindros, cubos y prismas rectangulares. Dé pistas como *Puede rodar y no tiene vértices.* Pida a su niño que nombre el objeto y hable de su figura.

Literatura

Estos libros hablan sobre las matemáticas de esta unidad. Podemos buscarlos en la biblioteca.

- **Llaman a la puerta**
  por Pat Hutchins
  (Sagebrush, 1999)
- **¡A comer fracciones!**
  por Bruce McMillan
- **Mi libro de formas y colores**
  por Silver Dolphin

Our game has ended, but this book is not done.
Draw a city picture. Include all 4 figures just for fun!

TAKS Objectives 3, 6
TEKS 1.6A, 1.11A

UNIT 4

City Figures

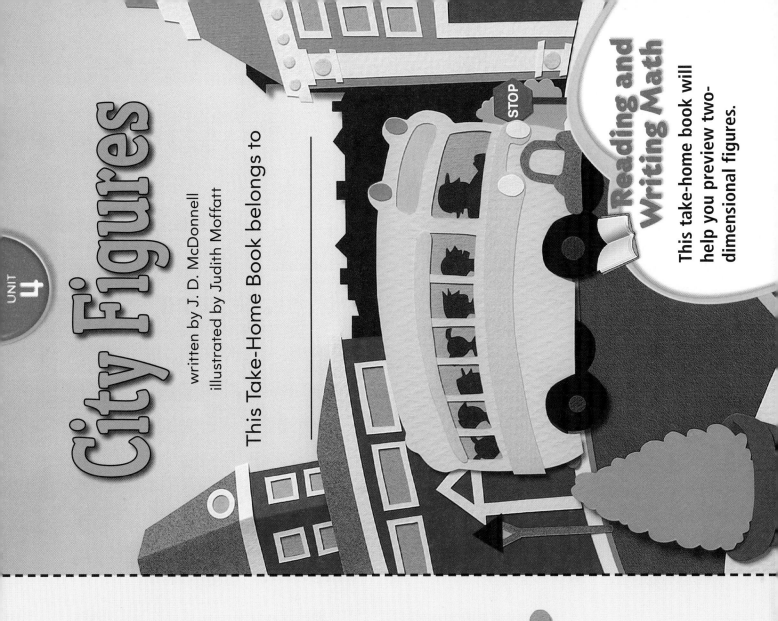

written by J. D. McDonnell
illustrated by Judith Moffatt

This Take-Home Book belongs to

____

Reading and Writing Math

This take-home book will help you preview two-dimensional figures.

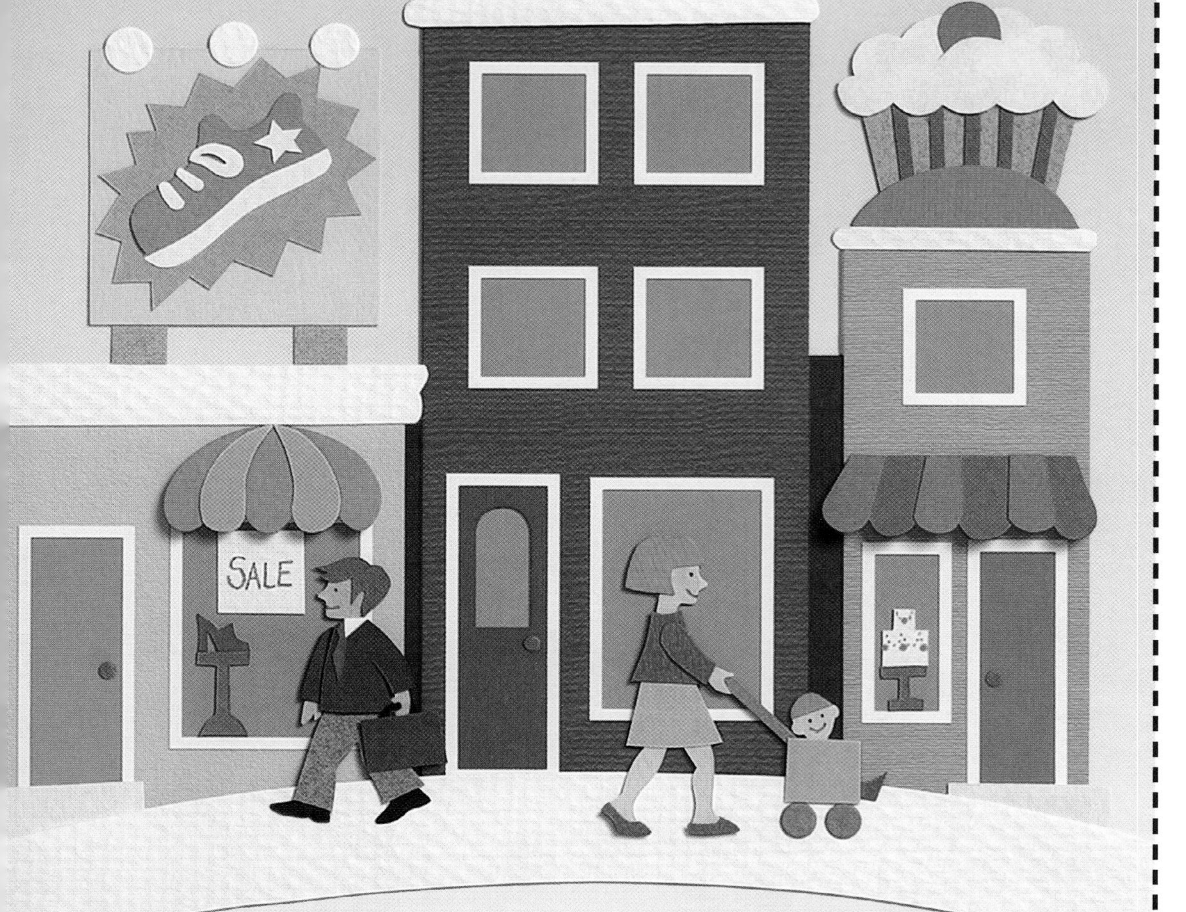

We're on our way to school.
We play a shape hunt. It's so cool!
First find a square with equal sides,
1, 2, 3, 4.
Look! I spy one at the shoe store!

Find other figures shaped like a square.

We're now here in our classroom,
At our desks, and in our chairs.
It was fun finding triangles,
circles, rectangles and squares.

Find and name these figures in
our classroom.

We're almost to our school,
As through the streets we wind.
Wait! We made a simple game rule
4 figures we must find!

Find figures shaped like a rectangle.

The next figure that we look for
Is the circle. It's so round.
Finding them is no chore,
For circles here abound.

Find figures shaped like a circle.

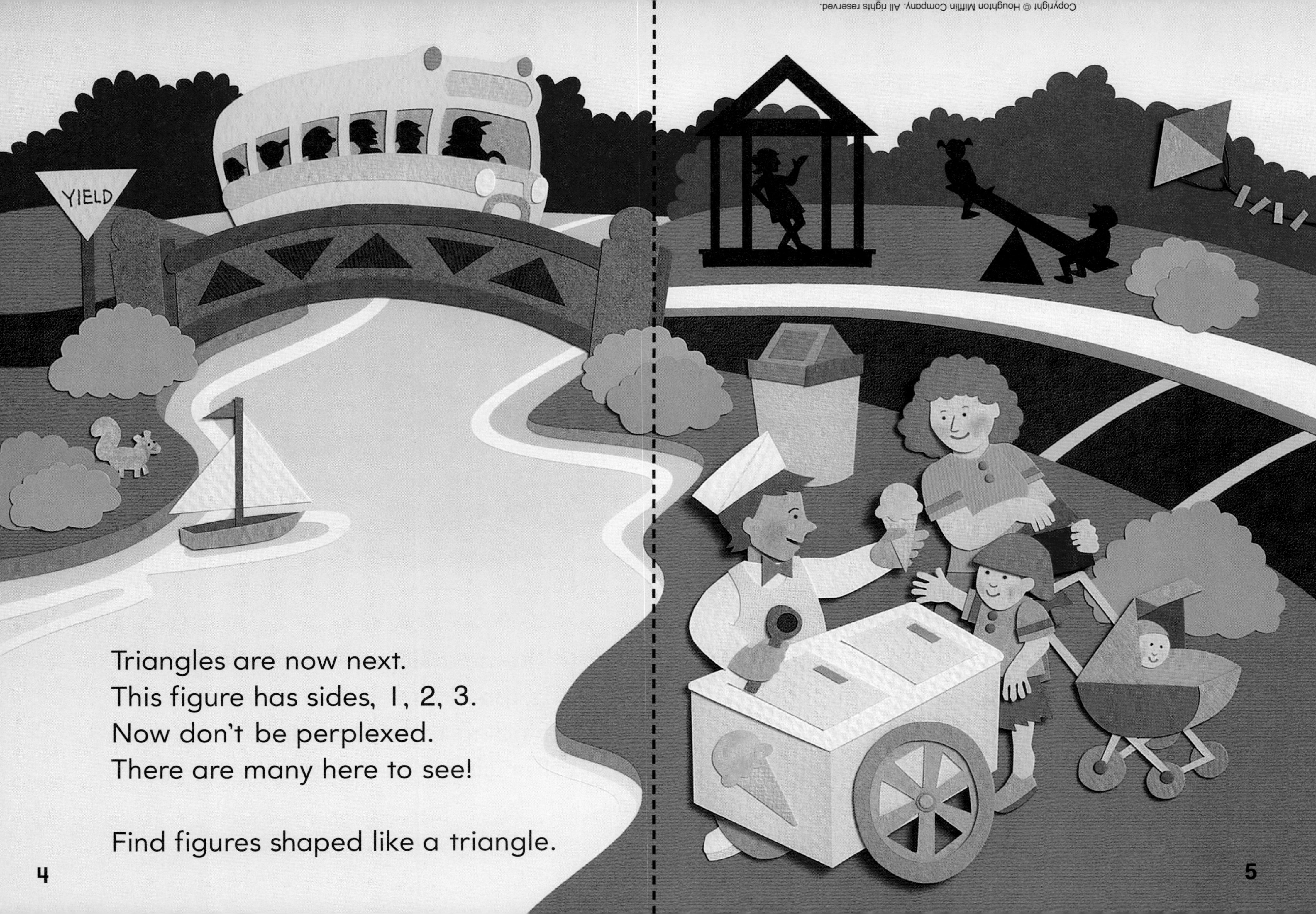

Triangles are now next.
This figure has sides, 1, 2, 3.
Now don't be perplexed.
There are many here to see!

Find figures shaped like a triangle.

Two-Dimensional Figures

TAKS Vocabulary

Here are some vocabulary words you will learn in the chapter.

These are the names of some two-dimensional geometric figures.

circle A figure with no sides and no corners

circle

triangle A figure with 3 sides and 3 corners

triangle

rectangle A figure with 4 sides and 4 corners

rectangle

square A special kind of rectangle

square All 4 sides are the same length.

See English-Spanish glossary pages 505–516.

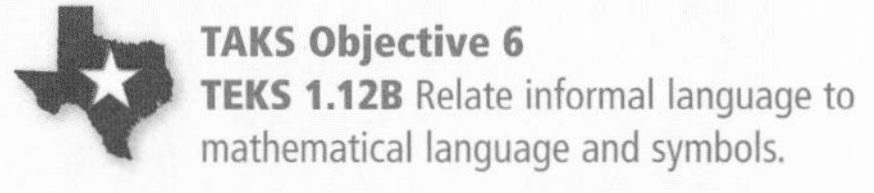

TAKS Objective 6
TEKS 1.12B Relate informal language to mathematical language and symbols.

Education Place
Visit **www.eduplace.com/txmap/** for the eGlossary and vocabulary eGames.

Name ______________________________

Check What You Know

1. Color the ◯ [crayon].

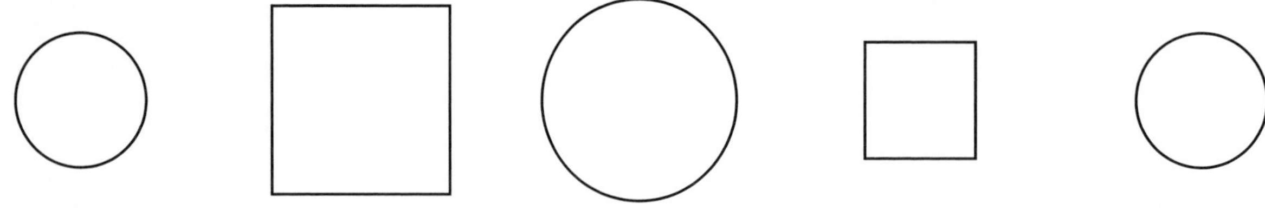

2. Color the □ [crayon].

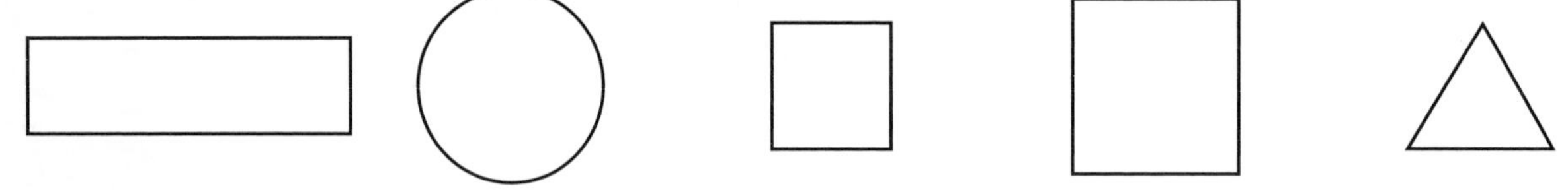

3. Color the ▭ [crayon].

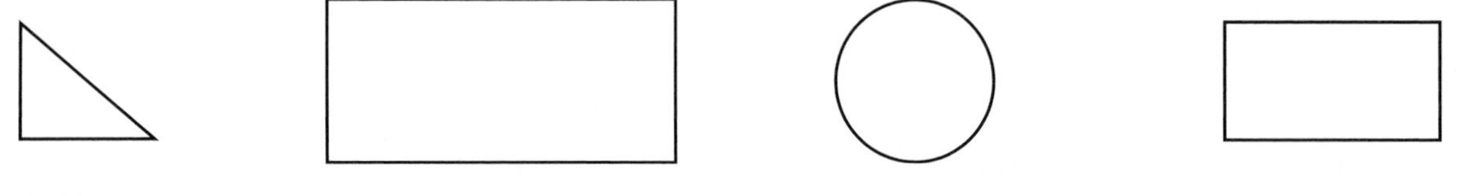

4. Color the △ [crayon].

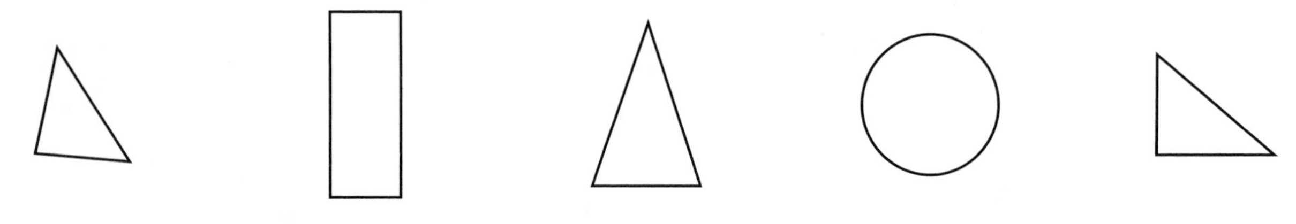

Count the shapes you colored.

5. How many ◯? _____

Use this page to review important skills needed for this chapter.

Name ______________________________

Chapter 8 Lesson 1

Sort Two-Dimensional Figures

Some two-dimensional geometric figures have **sides** and **corners.**

Hands On

TEKS Objective
Sort two-dimensional geometric figures by attributes.

TAKS Vocabulary
sides
corners

Sides are straight.

corner

Corners are where the sides meet.

★ Explore

Sort the figures.
Write Yes or No.

1.

Figure	4 sides	4 corners
circle	No	No
triangle		
rectangle		
square		

2. **Math Talk** Compare the number of sides and corners for each figure. What do you see?

TAKS Objective 3
TEKS 1.6C Describe and identify two- and three-dimensional geometric figures in order to sort them according to a given attribute using informal and formal language.

★ Extend

Remember! Corners are where the sides meet.

3. Draw a figure with 3 corners.

4. Draw a figure with 4 sides.

5. Draw a figure with 0 sides.

6. Draw a figure with 4 corners.

7. Draw a figure with 3 sides.

8. Draw a figure with 0 corners.

9. Draw another figure with 4 sides.

10. Draw another figure with 4 corners.

At Home Point to the top of a table. Ask your child to tell how many sides and corners it has.

En casa Señale la parte de arriba de una mesa. Pregunte a su niño cuántos lados y cuántos vértices tiene.

Name ______________________________

Chapter 8 Lesson 2

Identify Two-Dimensional Figures

TEKS Objective
Describe and identify two-dimensional geometric figures.

TAKS Vocabulary
names for two-dimensional geometric figures

★ Learn

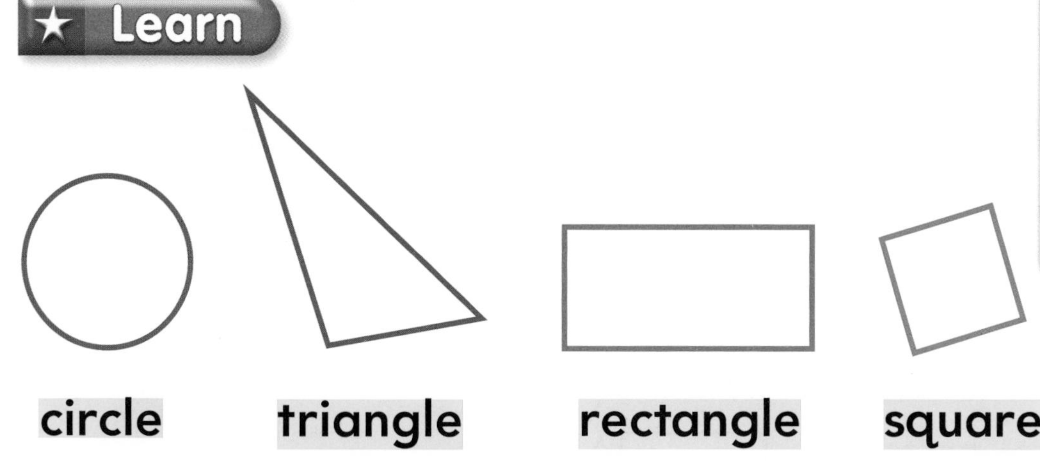

circle triangle rectangle square

★ Guided Practice

Trace the figure.
Write the number of sides and corners.

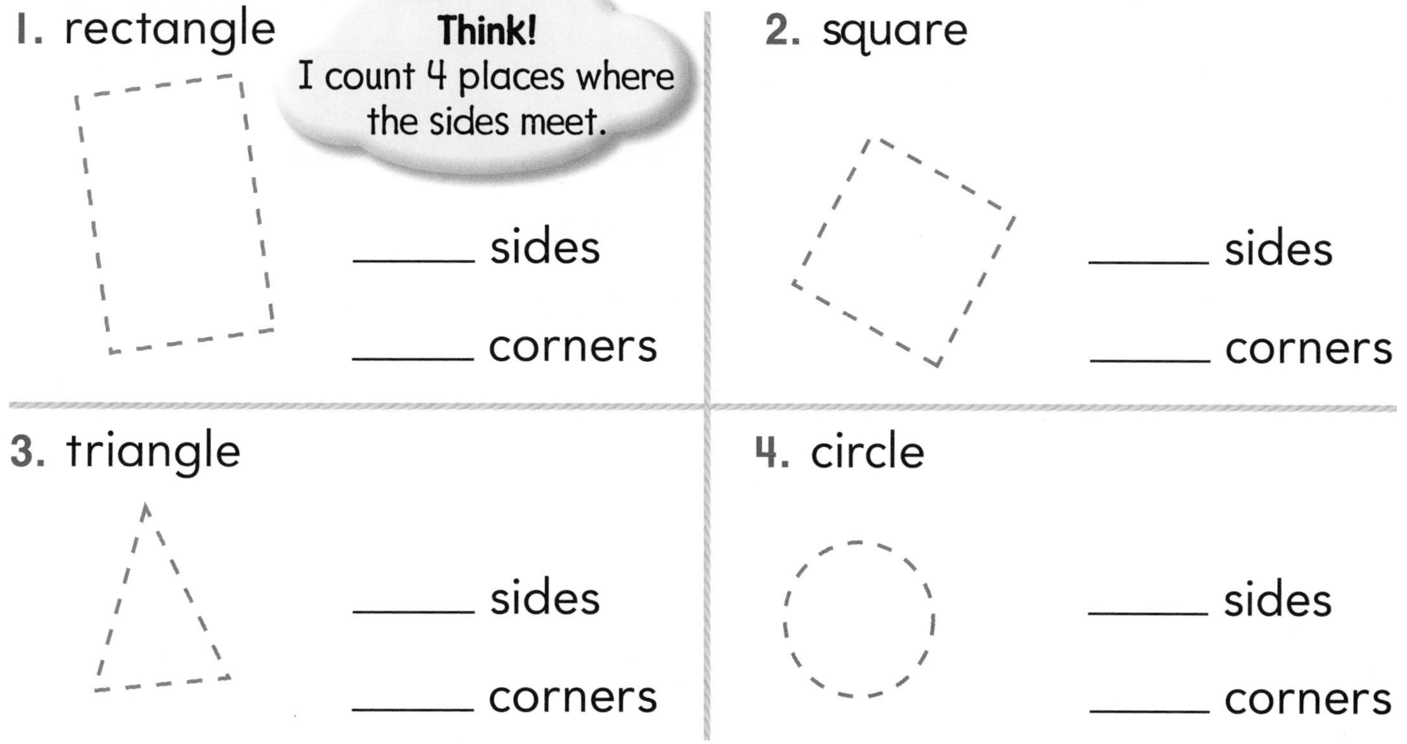

Think!
I count 4 places where the sides meet.

1. rectangle
   ____ sides
   ____ corners

2. square
   ____ sides
   ____ corners

3. triangle
   ____ sides
   ____ corners

4. circle
   ____ sides
   ____ corners

5. **Math Talk** Look at the sides and corners of the square and rectangle. A square is a special kind of rectangle. What makes a square special?

TAKS Objective 3
TEKS 1.6A Describe and identify two-dimensional geometric figures, including circles, triangles, rectangles, and squares (a special type of rectangle).

★ Practice

Remember!

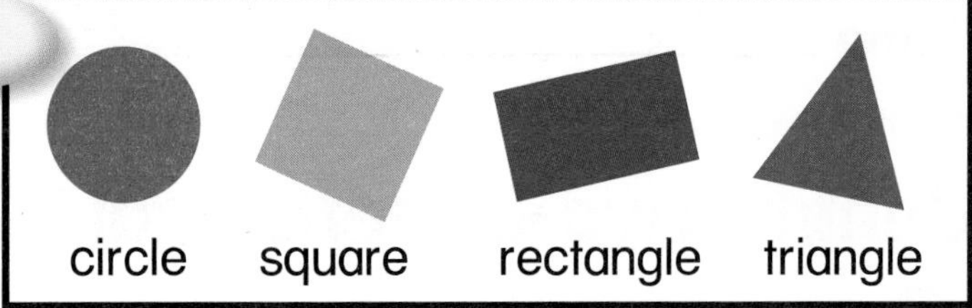

Answer the question.
Color the figures on the bus.

6. How many figures have 0 sides? ______
Color the circles.

7. How many figures have 3 sides? ______
Color the triangles.

8. How many figures have 4 sides the same?

______

Color the squares.

9. What do we call the figures that are not colored?

______

Color them.

Reading Math: Vocabulary

Draw the figure to match the word.

10. circle   square   triangle   rectangle

At Home Ask your child to show you objects in your house that have the same shape as a circle, a triangle, a rectangle, and a square.

En casa Pida a su niño que le muestre objetos en su casa que tengan la misma figura que un círculo, un triángulo, un rectángulo y un cuadrado.

Name ________________________________

Chapter 8 Lesson 3

Classify and Sort Figures

TEKS Objective
Describe, identify, and sort two-dimensional geometric figures.

★ Learn

There are many ways to sort figures.

Figures with corners

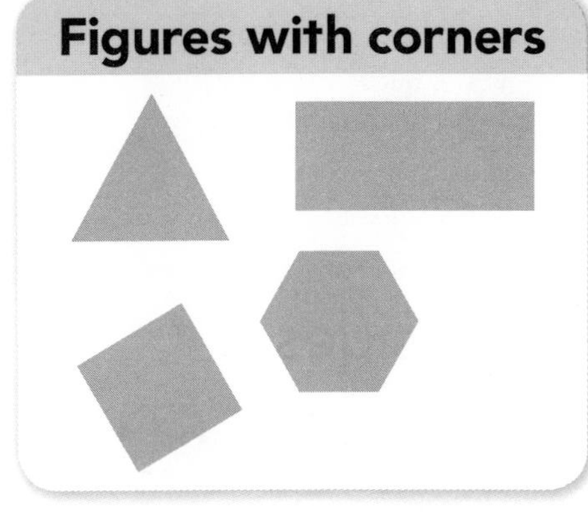

Figures with 3 sides

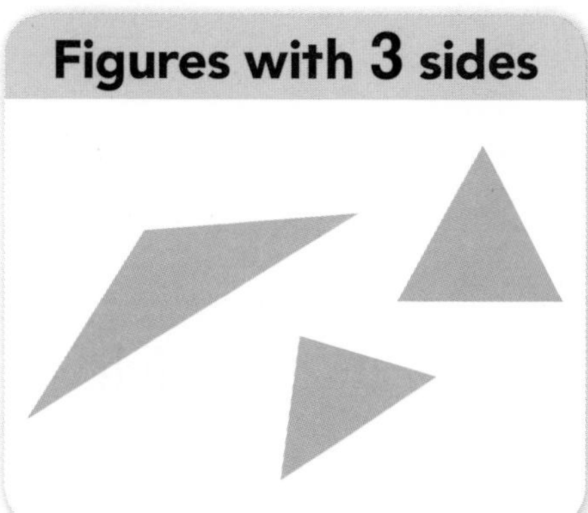

Figures with 4 corners

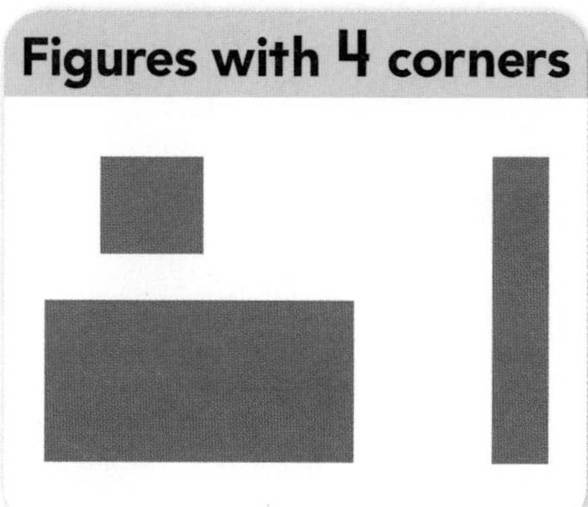

★ Guided Practice

Read the sorting rule.
Circle the figures that follow the rule.

1. 4 corners

Think!
Corners are where the sides meet.

2. 4 sides the same

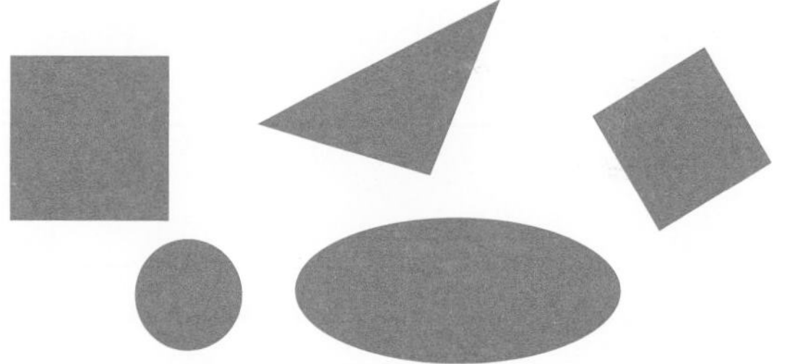

3. More than 3 sides

4. No corners

5. **Math Talk** How could you sort the figures in Exercise 4 another way?

TAKS Objective 3
TEKS 1.6C Describe and identify two- and three-dimensional geometric figures in order to sort them according to a given attribute using informal and formal language.

★ Practice

Read the sorting rule.
Circle the figures that follow the rule.

Remember!
Read the sorting rule first.

6. Small figures

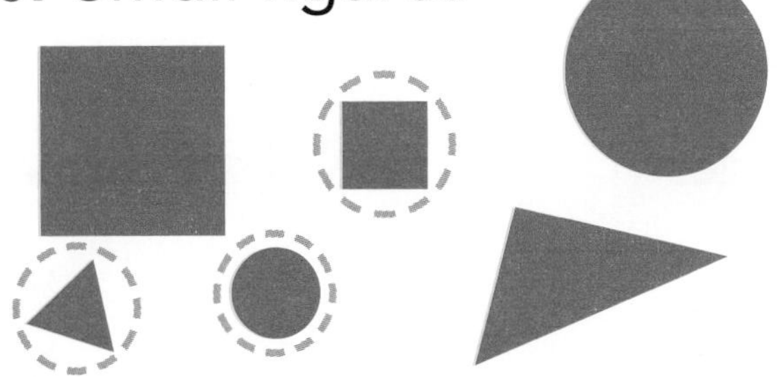

7. No corners

8. 3 corners

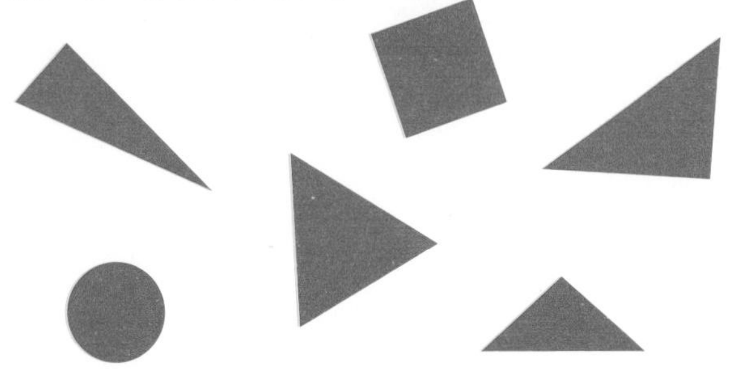

9. More than 2 sides

Write a sorting rule.
Draw 3 figures that follow your rule.

10. ______________________________

____

Problem Solving: Visual Thinking

open figures

closed figures

Circle each open figure.
Color inside each closed figure.

11.

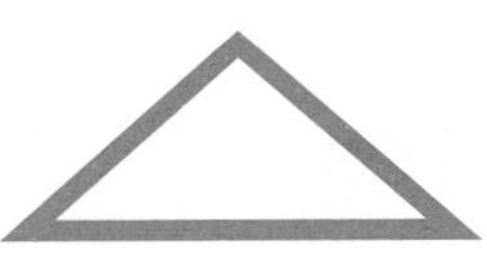

At Home Gather some household objects such as photos, coins, and napkins. Ask your child to sort them by shape or size.

En casa Reúna algunos objetos del hogar como fotos, monedas y servilletas. Pida a su niño que los clasifique según la figura o el tamaño.

Name ______________________

Chapter 8 Lesson 4

Combine Figures

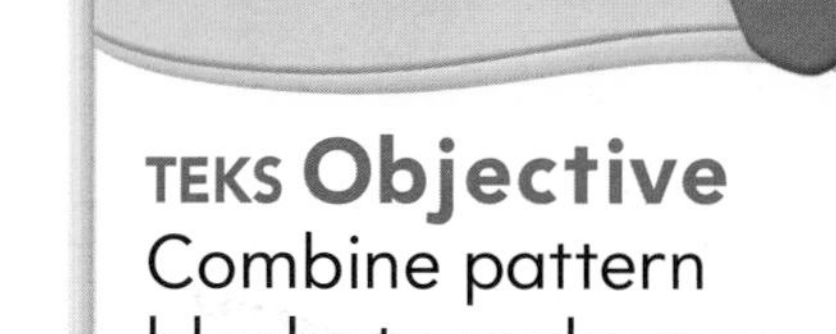

TEKS Objective
Combine pattern blocks to make new geometric figures.

★ Learn

You can use pattern blocks to make new figures.

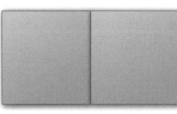

★ Guided Practice

Use the pattern blocks shown.
Make a new figure. Draw your figure.

1. 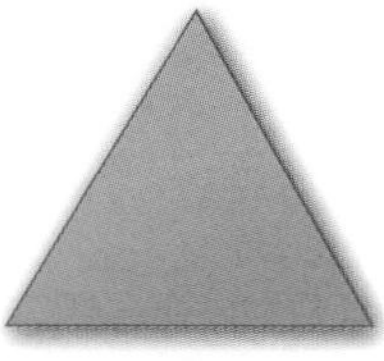

Think!
I can put 2 triangles together.

2. 

3. 

4. **Math Talk** How could you use the pattern blocks in Exercise 3 to make a different figure?

TAKS Objective 3
TEKS 1.6D Use concrete models to combine two-dimensional geometric figures to make new geometric figures.

★ Practice

Use the pattern blocks shown.
Make a new figure. Draw your figure.

Remember!
Use the blocks to make a new figure.

5. 

6. 

7. 

Problem Solving: Visual Thinking

8. Ann has 3 ▲ and 3 ◆.
She used 4 blocks to make this figure. How many of each block did she use?

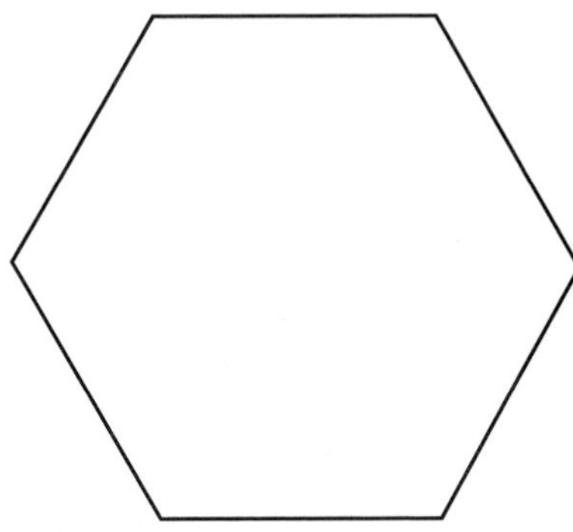

_____ ▲

_____ ◆

At Home Cut out some paper squares and triangles. Have your child put them together in different ways to make new figures.

En casa Recorte algunos cuadrados y triángulos de papel. Pida a su niño que los una de diferentes maneras para hacer figuras nuevas.

Name ______________________________

Chapter 8 Lesson 5

Draw a Picture

TEKS Objective
Draw pictures to solve problems.

Jane is making a picture of a boat.
She uses these figures.
How can she make a boat?

Understand

What do you know?

- Jane is making a boat.
- She uses these figures. 

Plan

You can draw a picture.
Try different ways to use the figures.

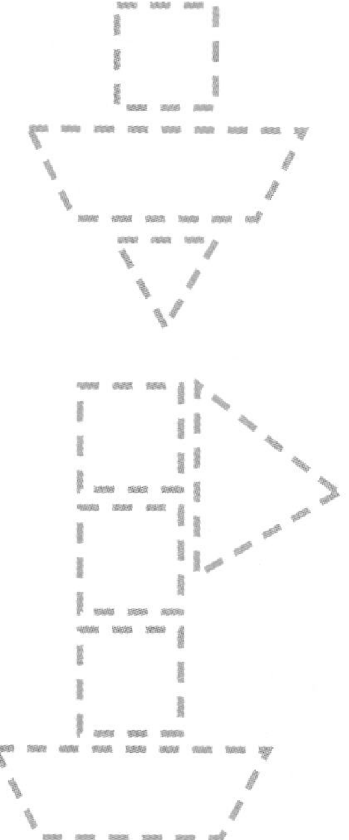

Solve

Draw a picture of a boat.
Use the three figures.

Look Back

Does your answer solve the problem?
What helped you decide how to use the figures?

TAKS Objectives 3, 6
TEKS 1.6D Use concrete models to combine two-dimensional geometric figures to make new geometric figures.

Also **TEKS 1.11B, 1.11C, 1.11D**

Guided Problem Solving

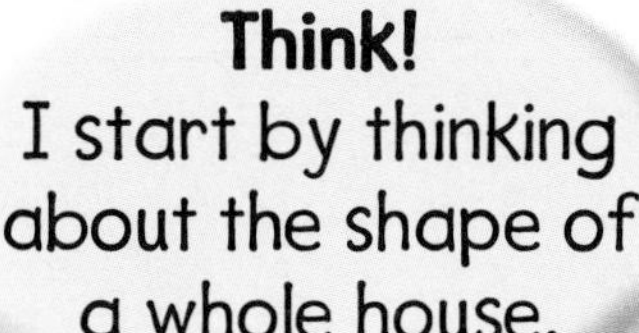

Think!
I start by thinking about the shape of a whole house.

1. Nico wants to make a picture of a house. He uses these figures.

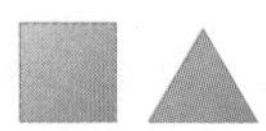

How can he make a house?

What do you need to draw?

Draw to solve.

2. Math Talk How did using the figures help you to solve the problem?

Problem Solving Practice

Draw a picture to solve.

3. Don wants to make a picture of a rocket. He uses these figures.

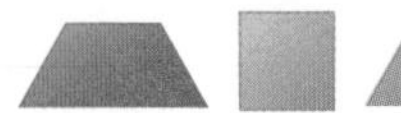

How can he make a rocket?

4. Tarika wants to make a tree. She uses these figures.

How can she make a tree?

At Home Cut out some paper triangles and squares. Ask your child to use them to make pictures.

En casa Recorte algunos triángulos y cuadrados de papel. Pida a su niño que los use para hacer dibujos.

Name ______________________________

Texas Field Trip

Science

Texas Star Ferris Wheel

At Fair Park

Fair Park is in Dallas. You can see the Texas Star Ferris Wheel there. You can learn about science and history, too.

Solve. Show your work.

1. Sergio sees 5 salamanders at the Aquarium. Jill sees 4 more. How many salamanders do they see?

   _____ salamanders

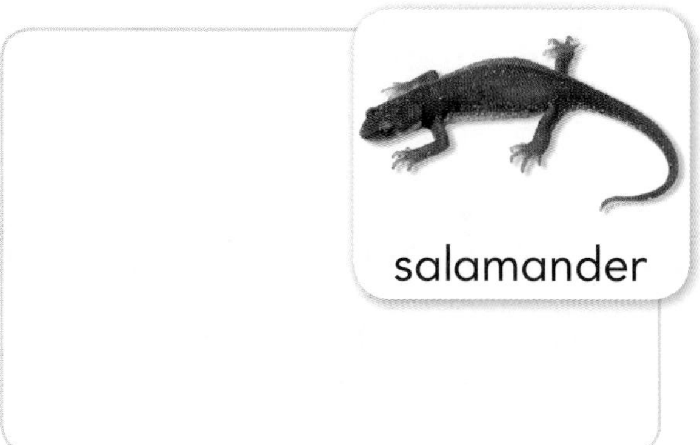

salamander

2. Andy sees 6 turtles by the Lagoon. 2 turtles slide into the Lagoon. How many turtles are left by the Lagoon?

   _____ turtles

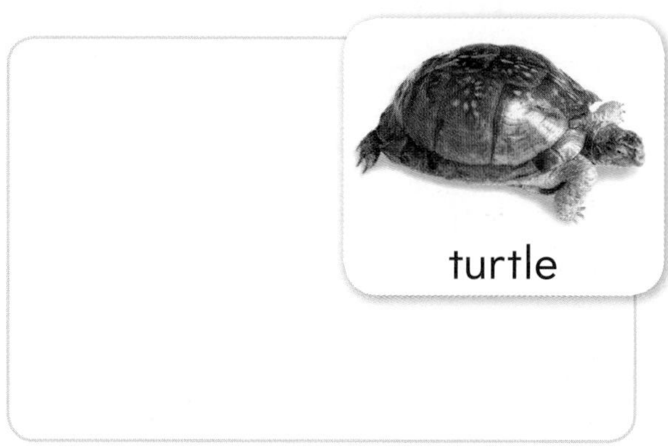

turtle

3. Matt sees 7 statues at the Hall of State. He sees 2 murals. How many pieces of art does he see?

   _____ pieces of art

statue

TAKS Objective 6
TEKS 1.11A Identify mathematics in everyday situations.
TEKS 1.11C Select or develop an appropriate problem-solving plan or strategy including drawing a picture, looking for a pattern, systematic guessing and checking, or acting it out in order to solve a problem.
TEKS Science 2A

TAKS Problem Solving
Listening Skills

Select a Strategy
Draw a Picture
Act It Out

Listen to your teacher read the problem.
Choose the correct answer.

1. Rosa makes this picture of a boat. How many triangles are in the picture?

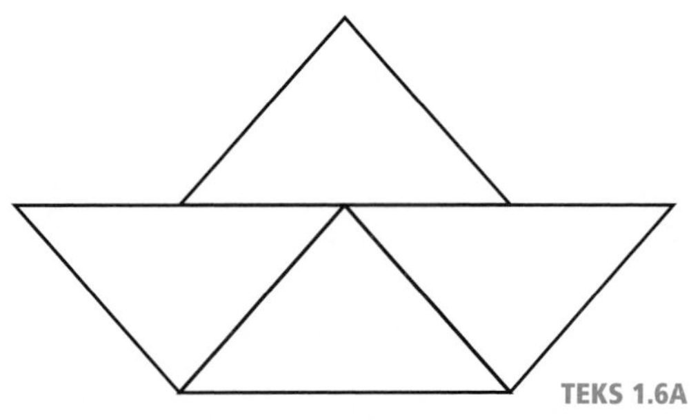

5 ○　　4 ○　　3 ○　　2 ○

TEKS 1.6A

2. Jared makes this picture of a bird. What two figures does he use to make his picture?

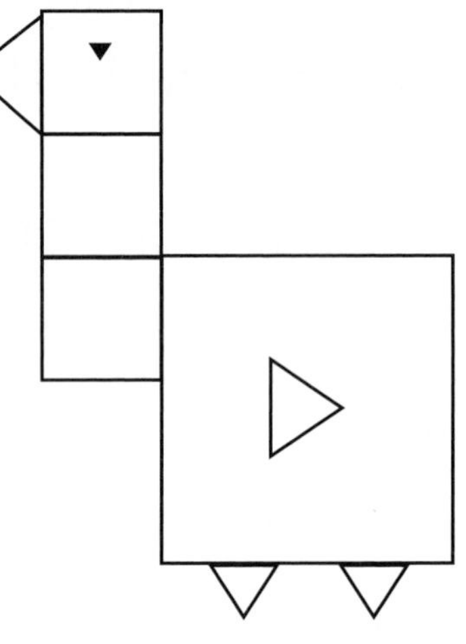

○ rectangles and squares
○ squares and circles
○ squares and triangles
○ triangles and rectangles

TEKS 1.6A

3. 1 ○　　2 ○　　3 ○　　4 ○

TEKS 1.6D

4. 1 ○　　2 ○　　3 ○　　4 ○

TEKS 1.6D

Education Place
Visit **www.eduplace.com/txmap/** for Test-Taking Tips and more TAKS Practice.

Name ______________________________

Figure Pictures

Use the attribute blocks found at **www.eduplace.com/txmap/** to make the figure picture you see here.

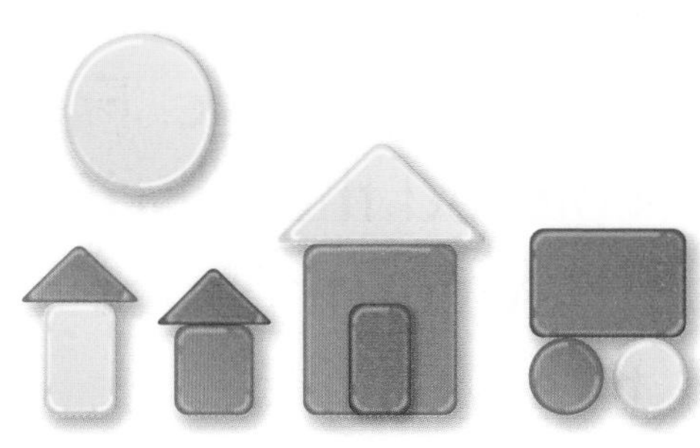

Fill in the chart.
Write the number of sides and corners.

	Figure	Number of sides	Number of corners
1.	rectangle	____	____
2.	circle	____	____
3.	triangle	____	____
4.	square	____	____

5. Make your own figure picture.

6. **Math Talk** Name 2 differences between a triangle and a circle.

TAKS Objective 3
TEKS 1.6A Describe and identify two-dimensional geometric figures, including circles, triangles, rectangles, and squares (a special type of rectangle).

Education Place
Visit **www.eduplace.com/txmap/** for more activities.

Social Studies Link

Quilts

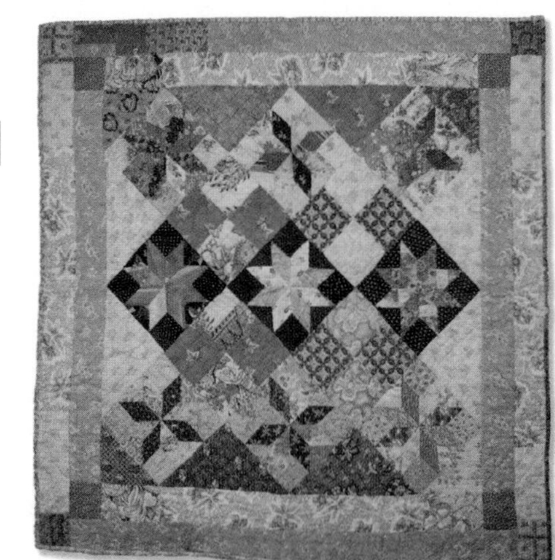

The cotton plant has fibers used to make fabric. Frontier women colored the fabric with dyes. They cut the fabric into figures to sew quilts.

Use pattern blocks.
Draw a picture to solve.

1. Ella makes a quilt. How can she make a quilt square with these figures?

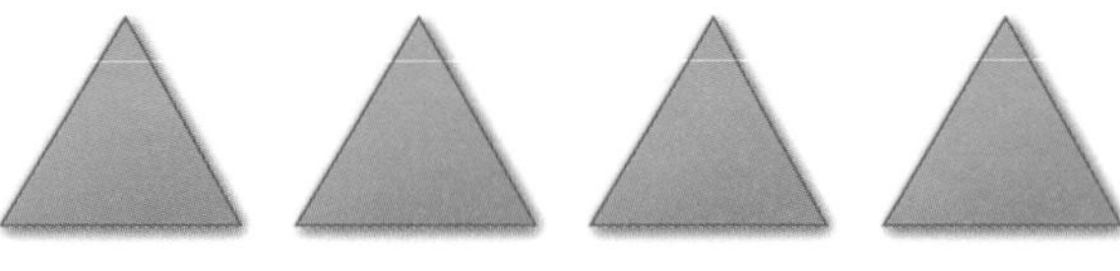

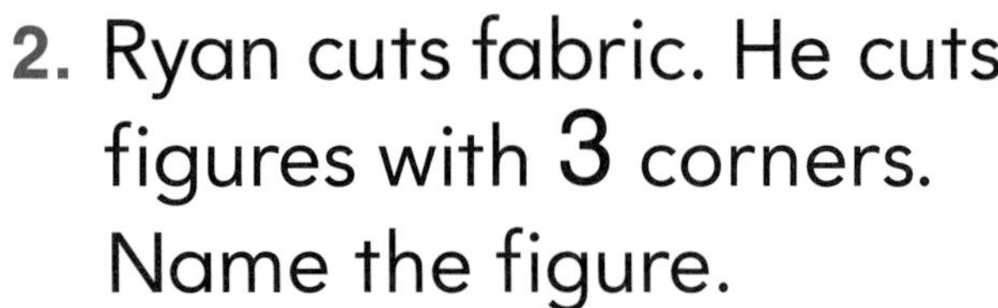

2. Ryan cuts fabric. He cuts figures with 3 corners. Name the figure.

____

3. How can he make a quilt with this figure?

TAKS Objectives 3, 6
TEKS 1.6A Describe and identify two-dimensional geometric figures, including circles, triangles, rectangles, and squares (a special type of rectangle).
TEKS 1.11A Identify mathematics in everyday situations.
Also **TEKS 1.6D**
TEKS Social Studies 6B

Name ______________________

Concepts and Skills

1. How many figures have 0 sides? _____ TEKS 1.6A
   Color the circles.

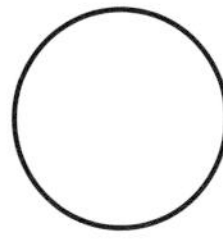

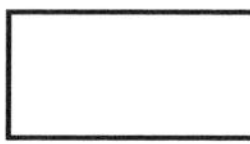
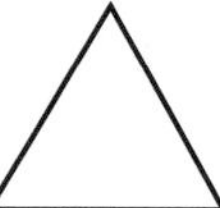
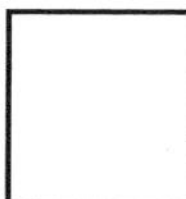

2. Read the sorting rule. Circle the figures that follow the rule. TEKS 1.6C
   3 corners

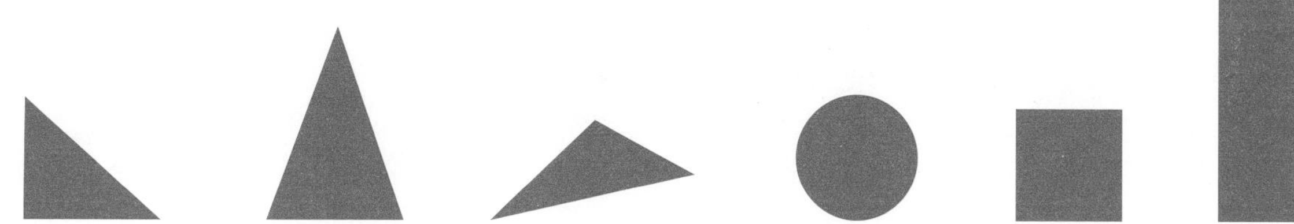

3. Use the pattern block shown. Make a new figure. Draw your figure. TEKS 1.6D

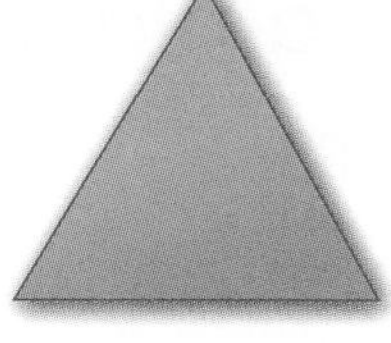

Problem Solving

Draw a picture to solve. TEKS 1.6D, 1.11C, 1.11D

4. Dan wants to make a picture of a boat. He uses these figures.

How can he make a boat?

TAKS Prep and Spiral Review

Choose the answer for problems 1–4.

1. Which group has a greater number of bats than balls?

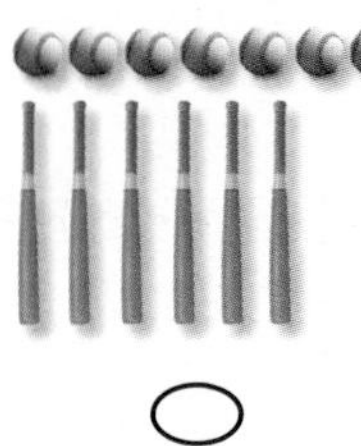 ○  ○  ○ 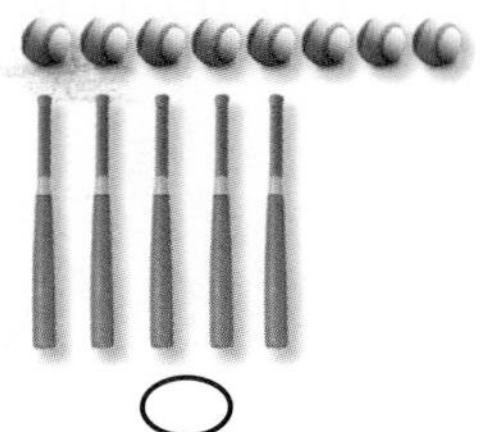 ○

TEKS 1.1A (page 25)

2. Which answer shows the number of cans collected in order from least to greatest?

Lee collected 14 cans.	Anil collected 11 cans.	Ann collected 17 cans.

17, 14, 11 ○ 11, 14, 17 ○ 11, 17, 14 ○ 14, 17, 11 ○

TEKS 1.1A (page 45)

3. Julio has 6 crackers on a plate.
He gets 4 more crackers.
How many crackers does he have now?

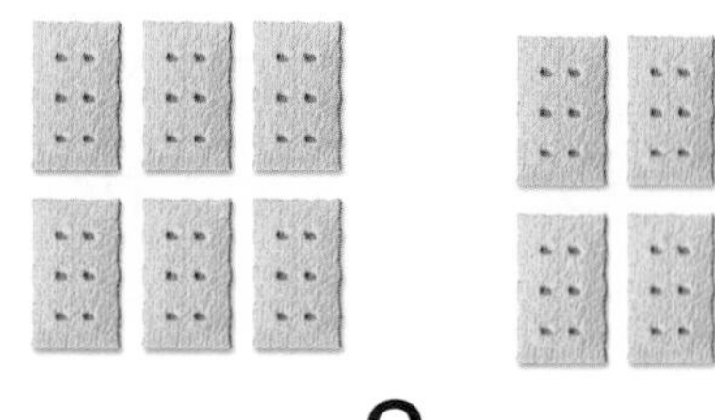

10 ○ 6 ○ 4 ○ 2 ○

TEKS 1.3B (page 105)

4. There are 8 blue trucks. There are 2 green trucks. Which number tells how many more blue trucks than green trucks there are?

2 ○ 6 ○ 8 ○ 10 ○

TEKS 1.3B (page 125)

Education Place
Visit www.eduplace.com/txmap/ for Test-Taking Tips and Extra Practice.

Three-Dimensional Figures

TAKS Vocabulary

Here are some vocabulary words you will learn in the chapter.

These are the names of some three-dimensional figures.

cube

cone

cylinder

sphere

rectangular prism

pyramid

See English-Spanish glossary pages 505–516.

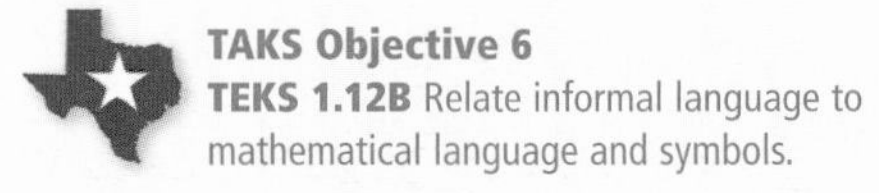

TAKS Objective 6
TEKS 1.12B Relate informal language to mathematical language and symbols.

Education Place
Visit **www.eduplace.com/txmap/** for the eGlossary and vocabulary eGames.

Name ______________________________

Check What You Know

Color the  . Color the  .

Color the  . Color the  .

1. 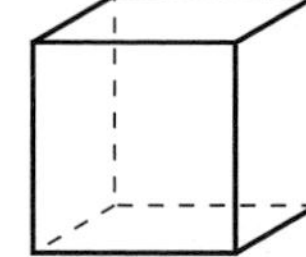 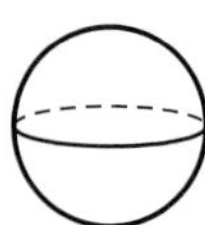 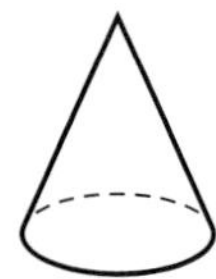 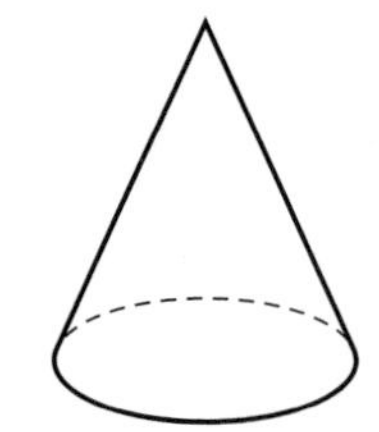 

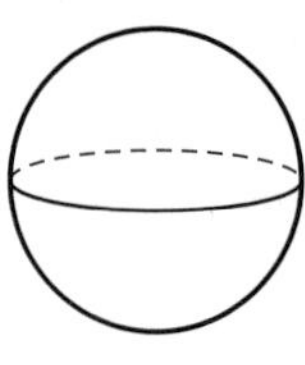 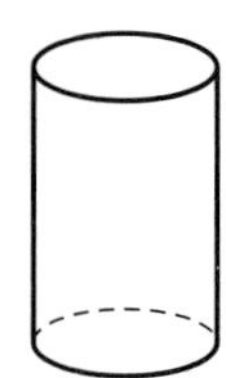 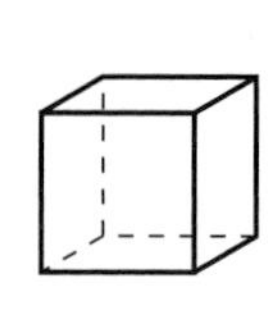 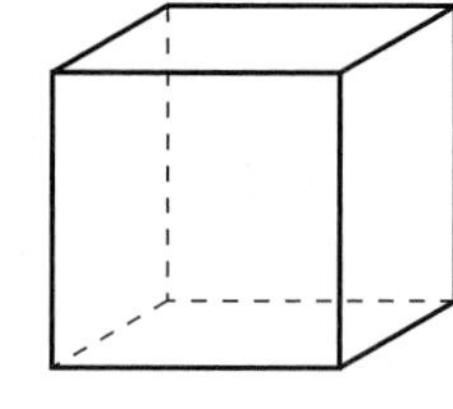 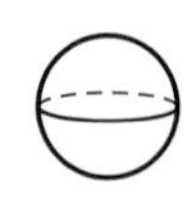

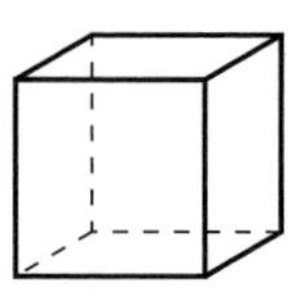 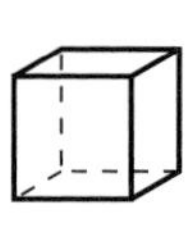 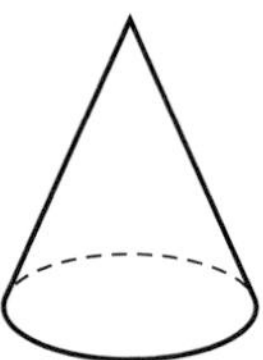  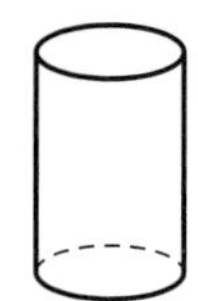 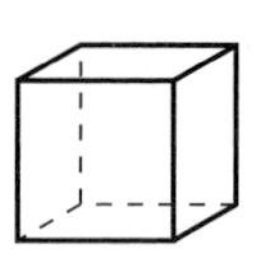

Count.

2. How many  ? _____

3. How many  ? _____

4. How many  ? _____

5. How many ? _____

Use this page to review important skills needed for this chapter.

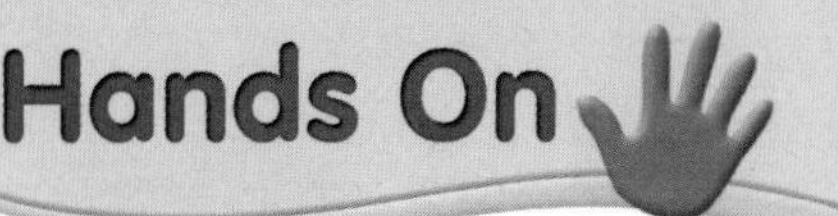

Name ______________________________

Chapter 9 Lesson 1

Sort Three-Dimensional Figures

This three-dimensional figure has a **flat surface** and a **curved surface.**

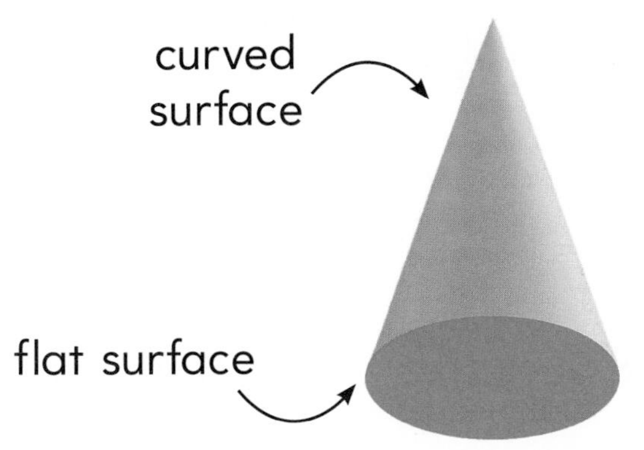

TEKS Objective
Sort three-dimensional figures by attributes.

TAKS Vocabulary
flat surface
curved surface

★ Explore

Find how each figure can move. Complete the table.

		Slide	Stack	Roll
1.		Yes	No	Yes
2.				
3.				
4.				

5. **Math Talk** Use the words **round, flat, curved,** and **straight** to describe the figures you used.

TAKS Objectives 3, 6
TEKS 1.6C Describe and identify two- and three-dimensional geometric figures in order to sort them according to a given attribute using informal and formal language.
Also **TEKS 1.12B**

★ Extend

Use figures.
Complete the table.

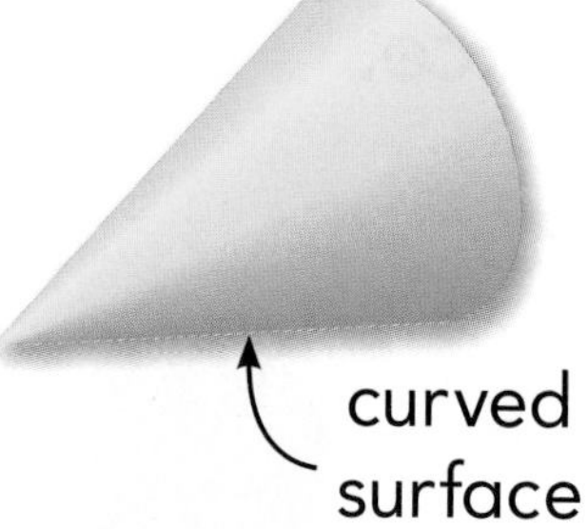

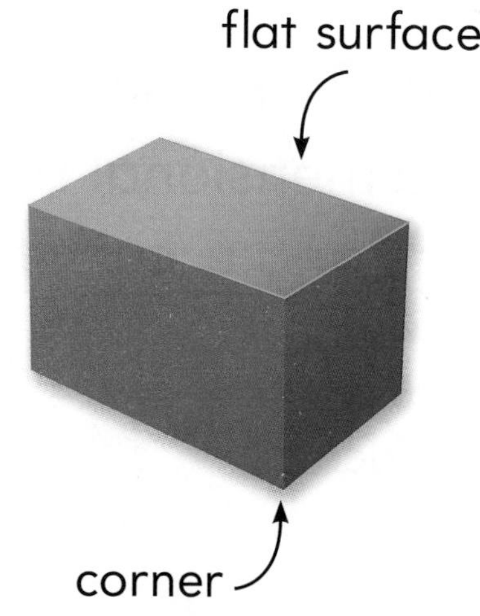

		Flat Surfaces	Curved Surfaces	Corners
6.		Yes		
7.				
8.				
9.				

Circle the figures that match.

10. flat surfaces

11. curved surfaces

At Home Ask your child to find an object in your house that will slide, stack, and roll.

En casa Pida a su niño que busque en la casa un objeto que se traslade, uno que se apile y otro que ruede.

Name ______________________________

Chapter 9 Lesson 2

Identify Three-Dimensional Figures

Hands On

TEKS Objective
Describe and identify three-dimensional figures.

TAKS Vocabulary
names for three-dimensional figures

★ Learn

Three-dimensional figures have special names.

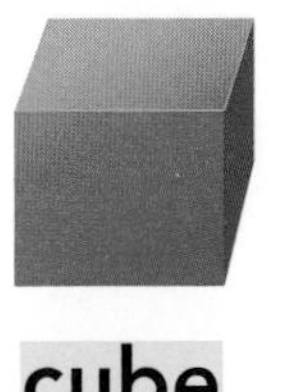
cube

rectangular prism

cone

sphere

cylinder

pyramid

★ Guided Practice

Use and describe the figure.
Circle the objects that match.

Think!
The peanut butter and oatmeal look like cylinders.

1.  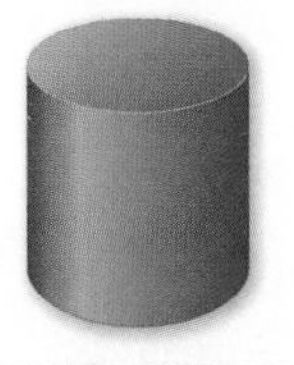  

2.   

3.  

4. 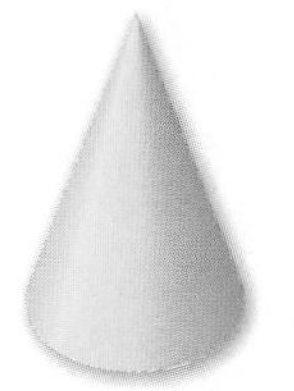   

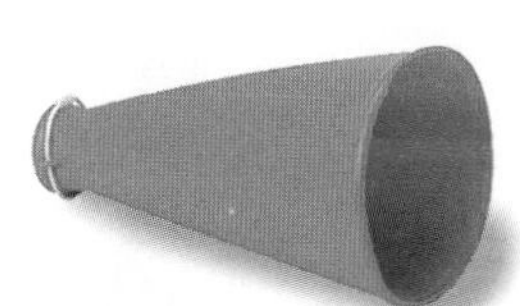

5. **Math Talk** How are a pyramid and a cube alike and different?

TAKS Objective 3
TEKS 1.6B Describe and identify three-dimensional geometric figures, including spheres, rectangular prisms (including cubes), cylinders, and cones.

★ Practice

Color each figure below.

> **Remember!**
> The chart shows you which color to use for each figure.

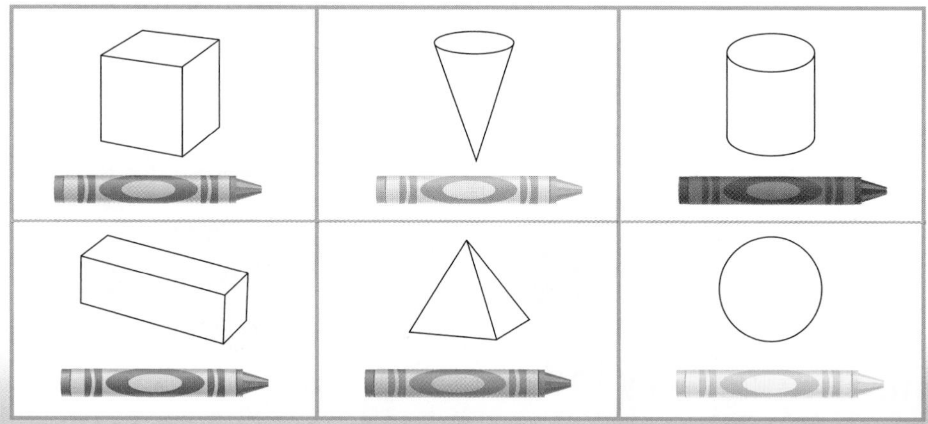

6.

Problem Solving: Visual Thinking

7. Eric made this model.
How many of each figure did he use?

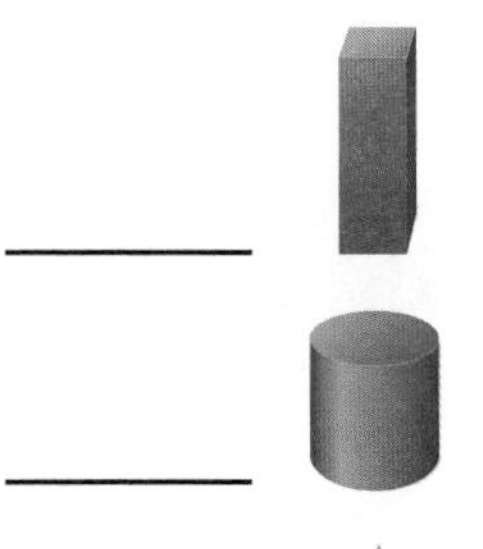

______

______

______

At Home Help your child find objects at home that are shaped like spheres, cubes, rectangular prisms, cylinders, cones, and pyramids.

En casa Ayude a su niño a buscar en su casa objetos con figura de esfera, cubo, prisma rectangular, cilindro, cono y pirámide.

Name ______________________________

Chapter 9 Lesson 3

Classify and Sort Three-Dimensional Figures

TEKS Objective
Describe, identify, and sort three-dimensional geometric figures.

There are many ways to sort three-dimensional figures.

Flat surfaces	Curved surfaces	Corners
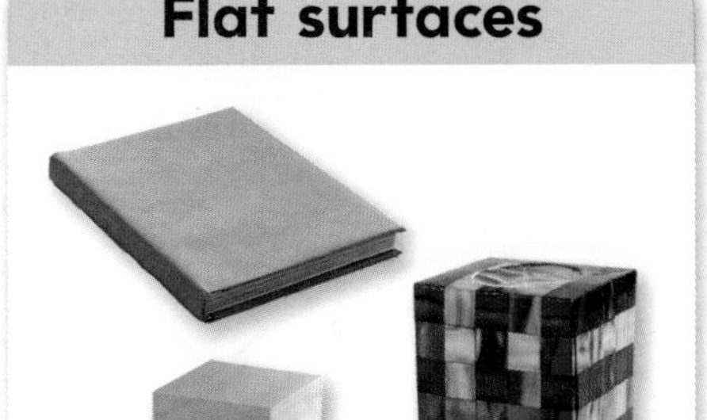		

★ Guided Practice

Think!
The cup and cone have curved parts.

Read the sorting rule.
Circle the figures that follow the rule.

1. All flat surfaces

2. Curved surfaces

3. Corners

4. **Math Talk** Tell how the figures in Exercise 2 are alike and different.

TAKS Objective 3
TEKS 1.6B Describe and identify three-dimensional geometric figures, including spheres, rectangular prisms (including cubes), cylinders, and cones.

TEKS 1.6C Describe and identify two- and three-dimensional geometric figures in order to sort them according to a given attribute using informal and formal language.

★ Practice

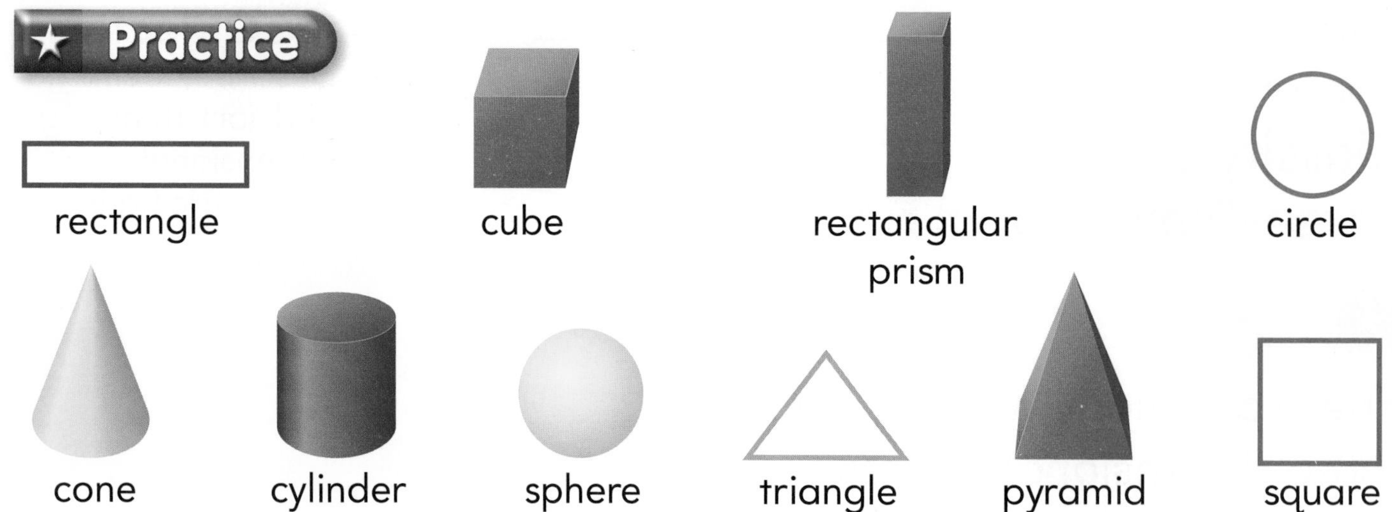

Use the sorting rule to sort the figures.
Draw the figure or write the name.

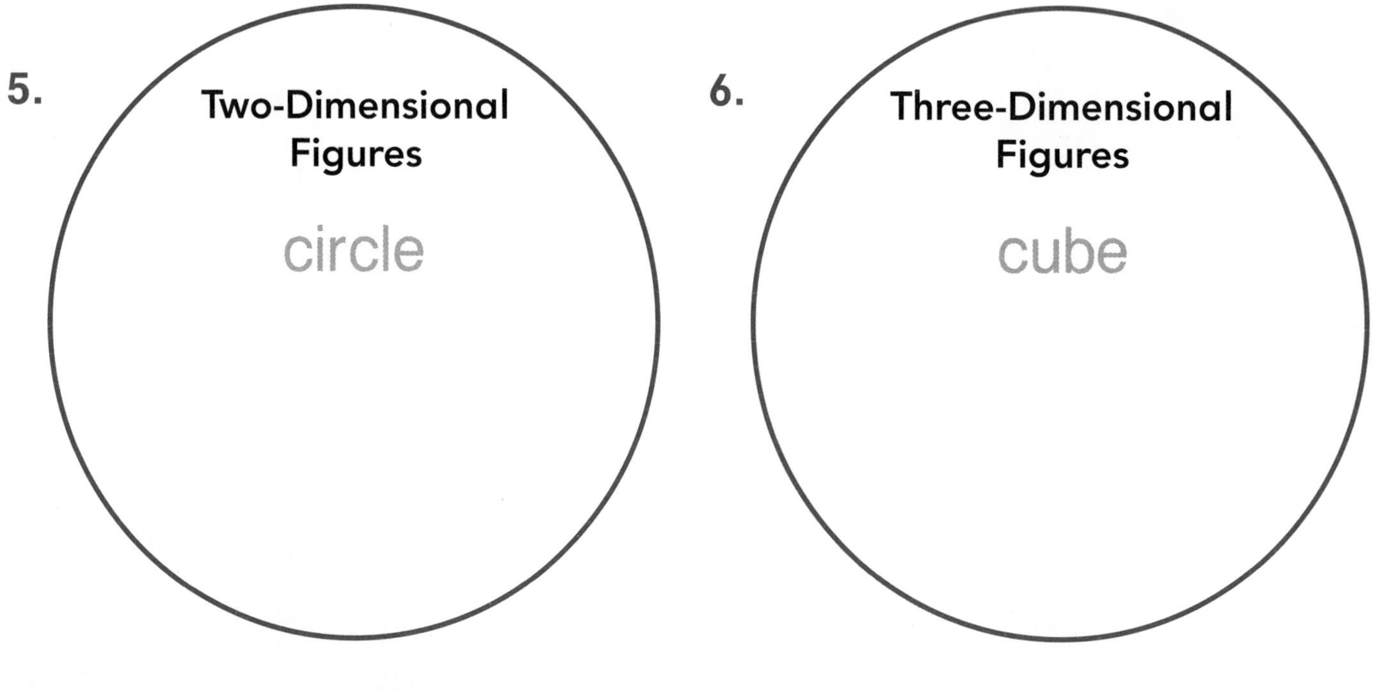

Problem Solving: Reasoning

7. Sort the figures into two groups.
   Color one group .
   Color one group .
   Explain your sorting rule.

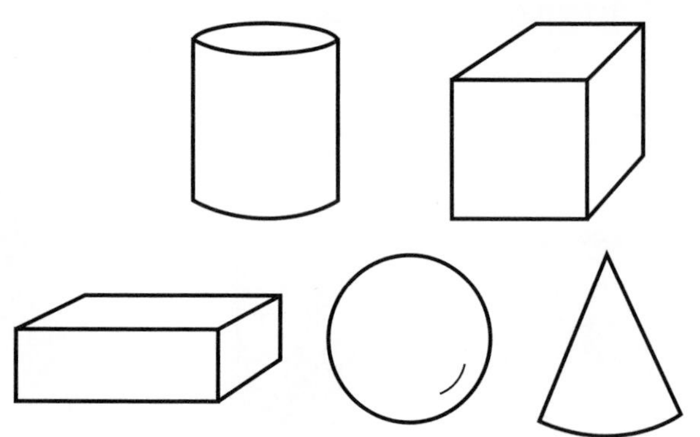

____

____

At Home Have your child choose a figure and find things in your home that are the same shape.

En casa Pida a su niño que escoja una figura y que busque objetos en su casa que tengan la misma figura.

Name ______________________________

Chapter 9 Lesson 4

Identify Faces of a Three-Dimensional Figure

TEKS Objective
Identify the faces of a three-dimensional figure.

TAKS Vocabulary
face

★ Learn

The **face** of a three-dimensional figure is a two-dimensional figure.

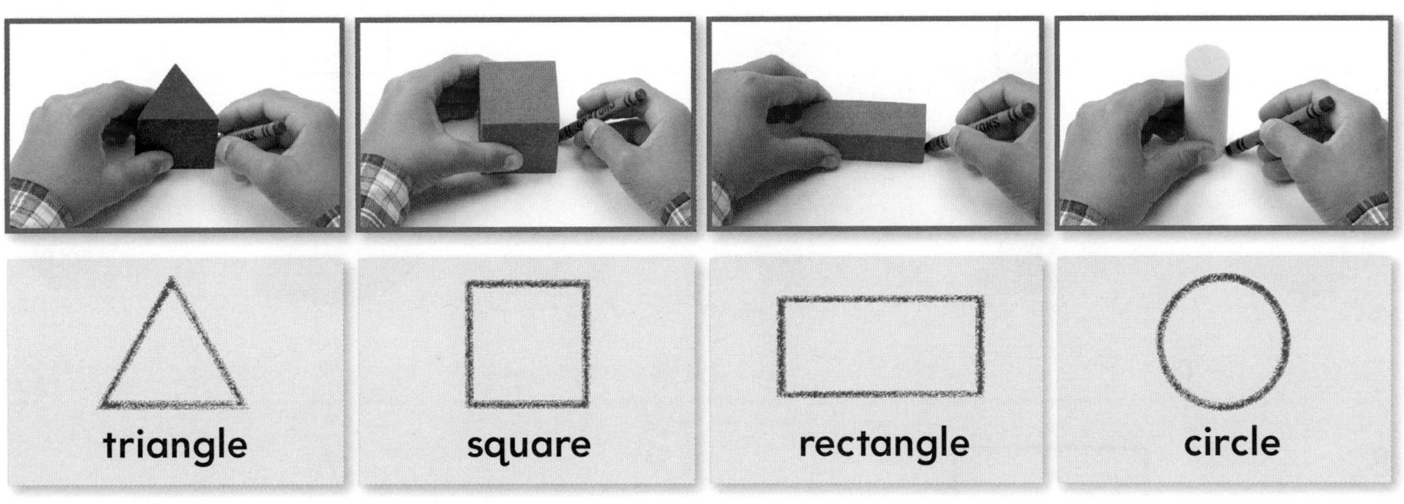

★ Guided Practice

Look at the blue face of the figure. Circle the name of the face.

Think!
I see a figure with 3 sides and 3 corners.

1. 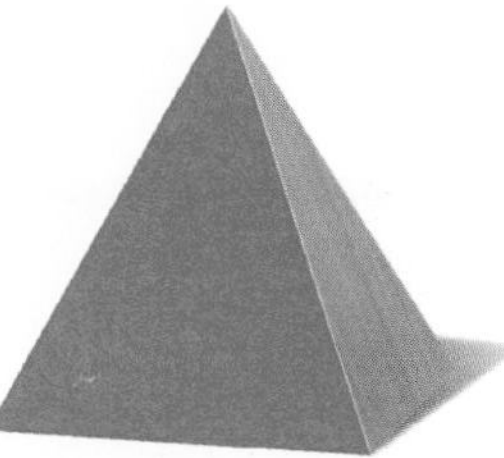 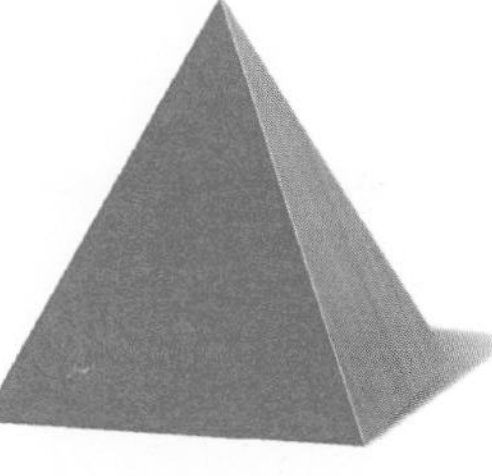
square
circle
triangle

2. 
square
circle
triangle

3. 
rectangle
circle
triangle

4. 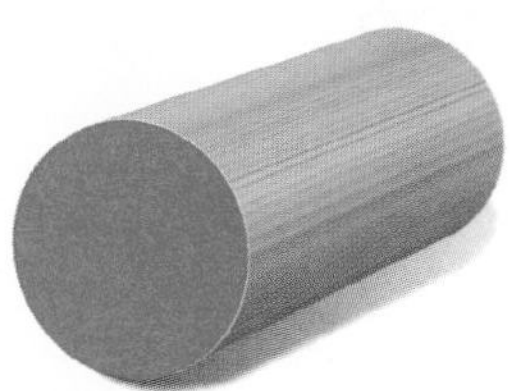
square
circle
triangle

5. **Math Talk** Tell how a cylinder and a cone are alike and different.

TAKS Objectives 3, 6
TEKS 1.6C Describe and identify two- and three-dimensional geometric figures in order to sort them according to a given attribute using informal and formal language.
TEKS 1.12A Explain and record observations using objects, words, pictures, numbers, and technology.

★ Practice

Remember!
Look at all of the faces of the three-dimensional figures.

Look at the two-dimensional figure. Circle the three-dimensional figure with a face like it.

6.

7.

8.

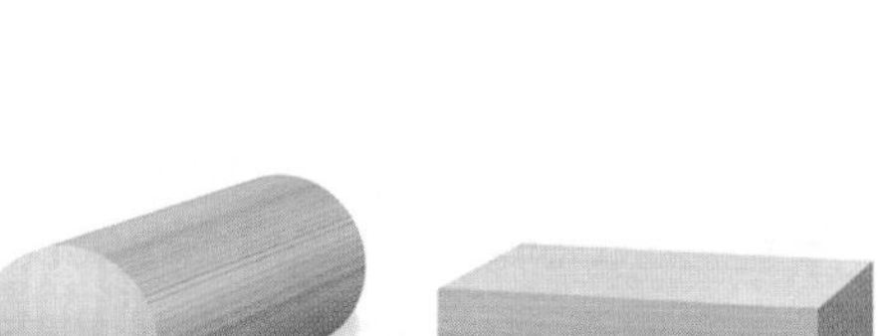

9.

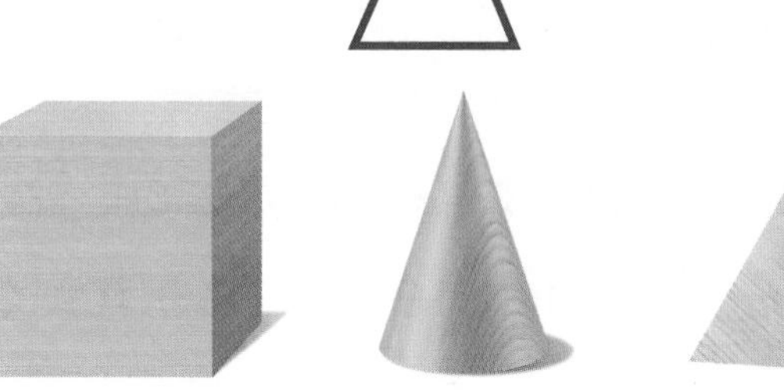

Problem Solving: Reasoning

Circle the three-dimensional figure with a square face.

10.

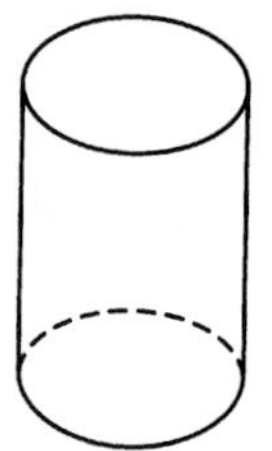

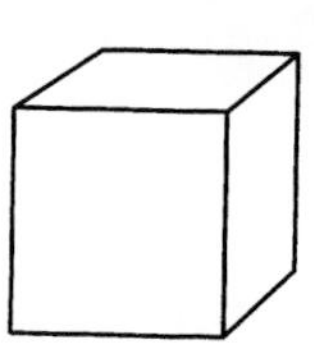

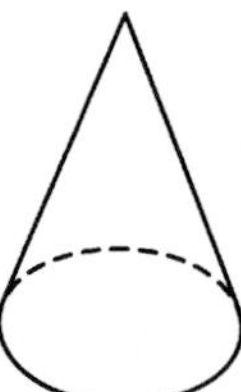

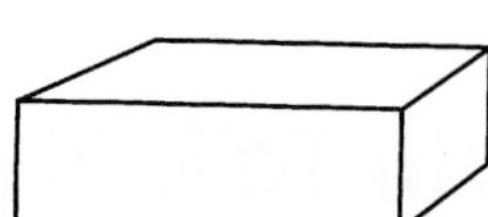

At Home Give your child some boxes. Have your child trace around a face of each and tell you what figure was drawn.

En casa Dele a su niño algunas cajas. Pidale que trace el borde de las caras de cada caja y que le diga qué figura dibujó.

Name ______________________________

Chapter 9 Lesson 5

Use a Picture

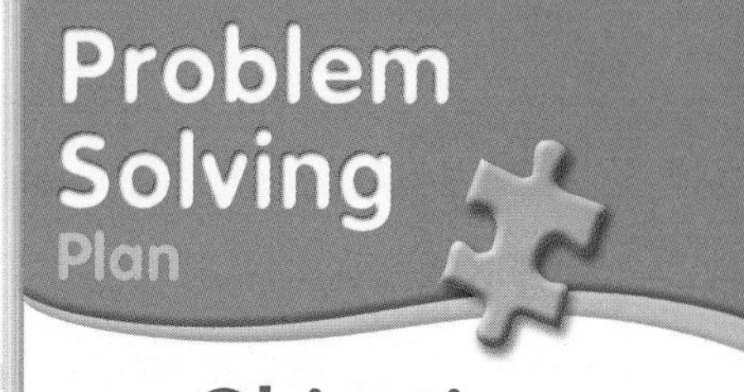

TEKS Objective
Use a picture to solve problems in everyday situations.

You can use a picture to help you solve a problem. Children used three-dimensional figures to make new figures.

Ellis made the barn.
Color the figures to match the ones Ellis used.

Think!
I see a pyramid and a cube.

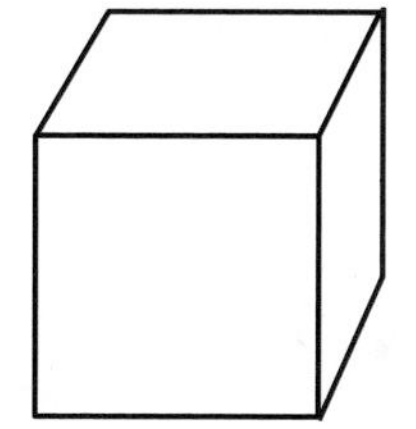
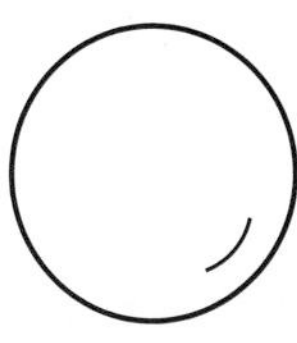
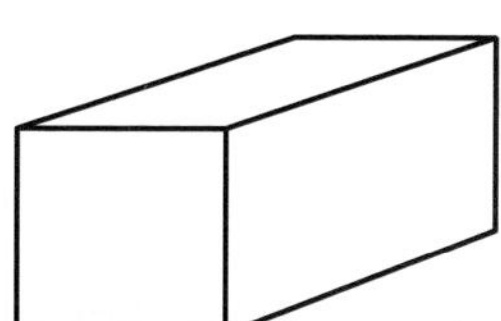

Haley made the silo.
Color the figures to match the ones Haley used.

Think!
I see a yellow cone and a red cylinder.

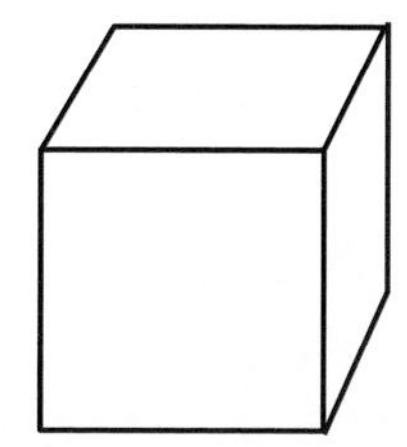

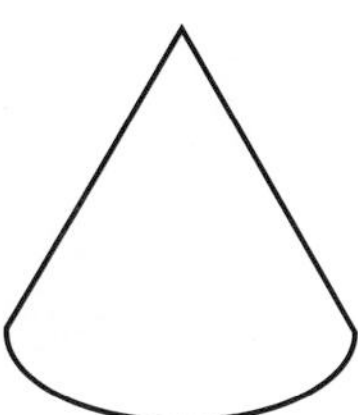

TAKS Objectives 3, 6
TEKS 1.6B Describe and identify three-dimensional geometric figures, including spheres, rectangular prisms (including cubes), cylinders, and cones.
TEKS 1.11A Identify mathematics in everyday situations.
TEKS 1.11D Use tools such as real objects, manipulatives, and technology to solve problems.

★ Guided Problem Solving

Think!
I can look at the picture to see the color of each figure.

1. Tim made this building.
Color the figures to match the ones Tim used.

Cross out each figure as you color.

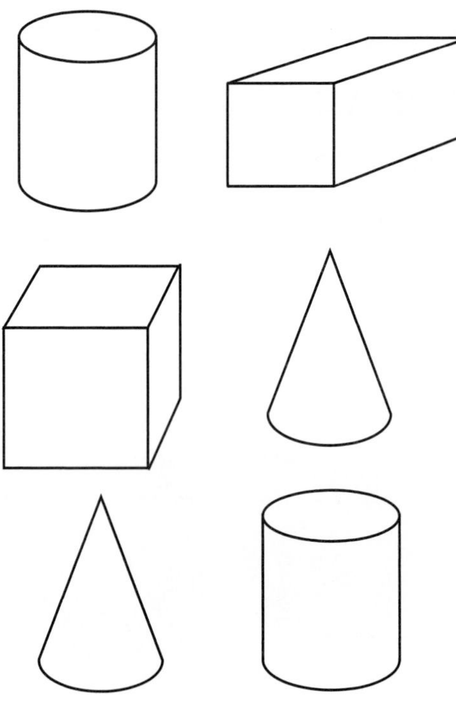

2. Math Talk How does using a picture help you solve the problem?

★ Problem Solving Practice

Use the picture to solve the problem.

3. Max made this wagon.
Color the figures to match the ones Max used.

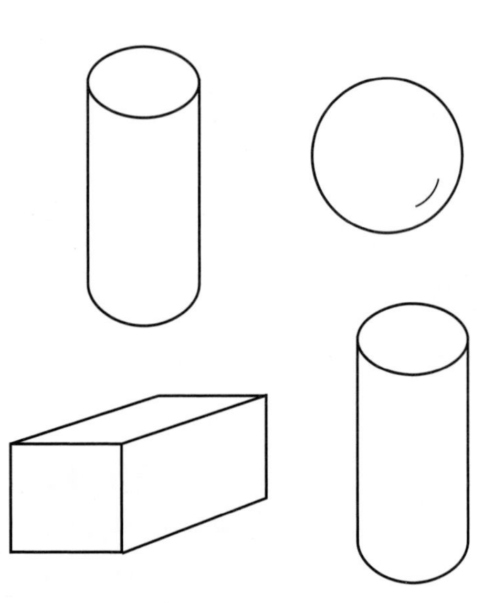

At Home Using pictures in a book or magazine, have your child identify figures in a single object.

En casa Use ilustraciones de un libro o una revista y pida a su niño que identifique figuras en un solo objeto.

Name ______________________

Figure Hunt!

Use the clues. Find the figure.
Write the color and name of the figure.

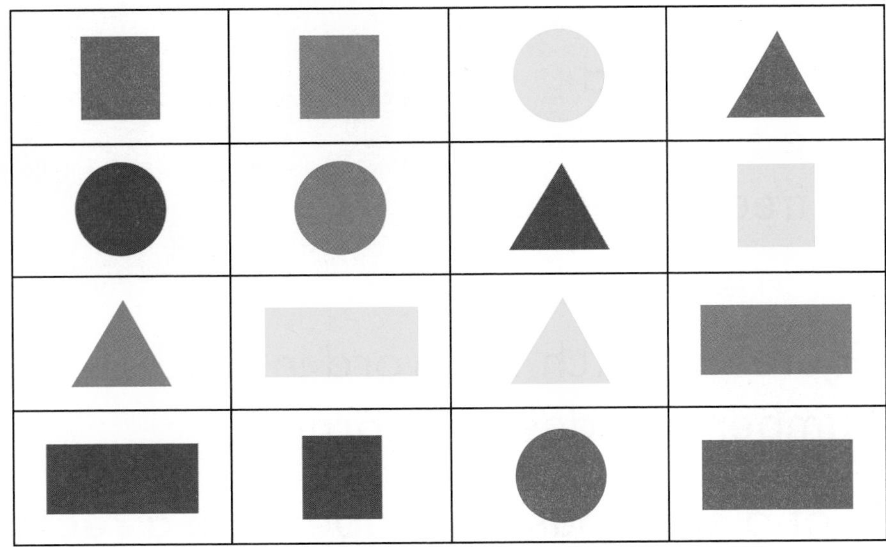

1. It has 3 sides and 3 corners. It is above a square.

   It is a ____________ ____________.

2. It has 4 sides and 4 corners.
   It is to the right of a circle.

   It is a ____________ ____________.

3. It has 0 sides and 0 corners. It is below a square.
   It is to the left of a triangle.

   It is a ____________ ____________.

4. It has 4 sides and 4 corners. All the sides are the same.
   It is to the left of the red circle.

   It is a ____________ ____________.

Early Houses

Early houses were made from natural materials. Native Americans made tepees from animal skins. Settlers used grass and earth to make sod houses. Pioneers cut trees to make log cabins.

Draw the figure to match the word in bold. Write the number of sides and corners.

1. One side of a sod house is shaped like a **rectangle**.

_____ sides

_____ corners

2. One side of a log cabin is shaped like a **square**.

_____ sides

_____ corners

TAKS Objectives 3, 6
TEKS 1.6A Describe and identify two-dimensional geometric figures, including circles, triangles, rectangles, and squares (a special type of rectangle).

TEKS 1.11A Identify mathematics in everyday situations.
TEKS Science 9A

Name ______________________________

Concepts and Skills

Circle the figures that match. TEKS 1.6C

1. curved surfaces

Circle the objects that match. TEKS 1.6B

2.

Look at the two-dimensional figure. Circle the three-dimensional figure with a face like it. TEKS 1.6C

3.

Problem Solving

Use the picture to solve the problem.

4. Jill made this building. Color the figures to match the ones Jill used. TEKS 1.6B, 1.11D

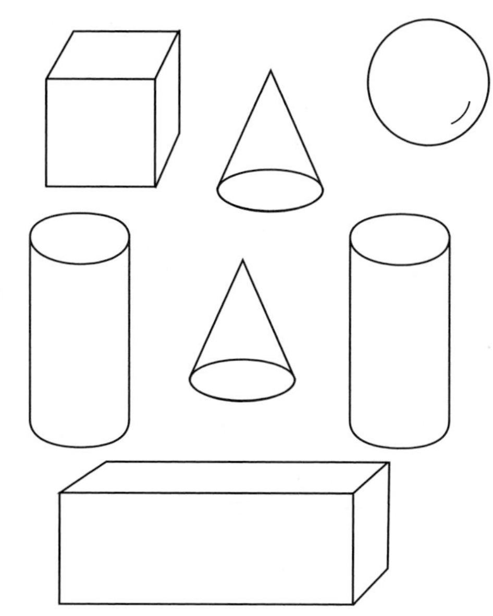

TAKS Prep and Spiral Review

Choose the answer for problems 1–4.

1. Which figure is missing in the pattern?

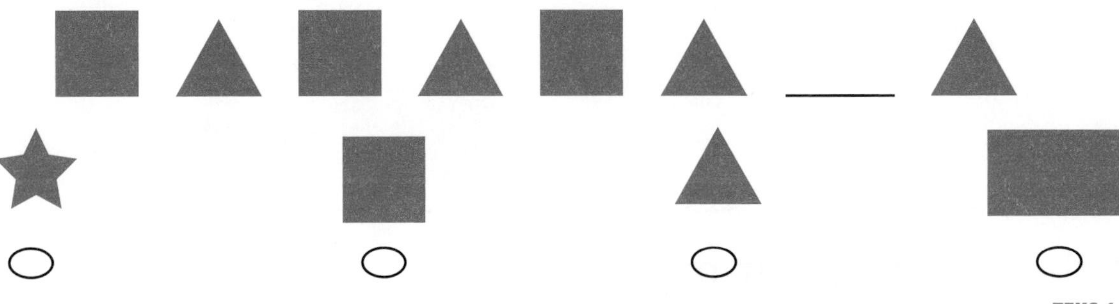

TEKS 1.4 (page 7)

2. Which two shapes come next in the pattern?

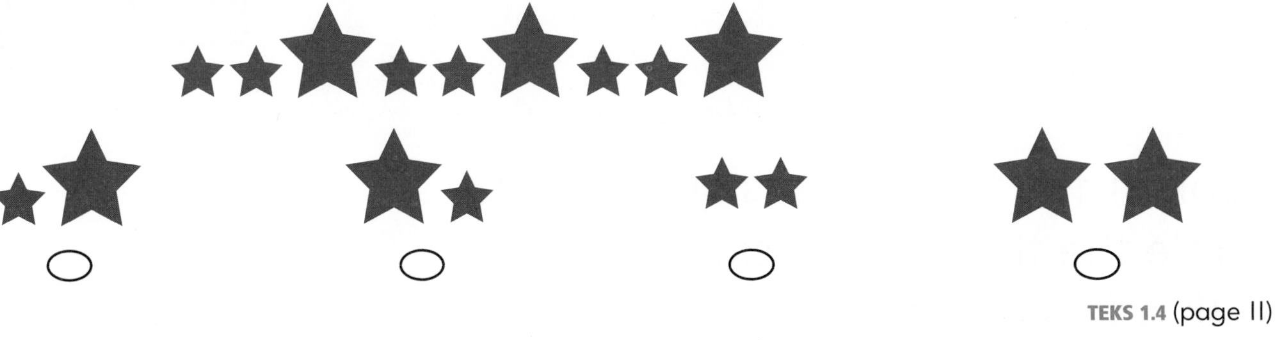

TEKS 1.4 (page 11)

3. Ella read 6 books. Han read 3 books. Which picture shows the total number of books Ella and Han read?

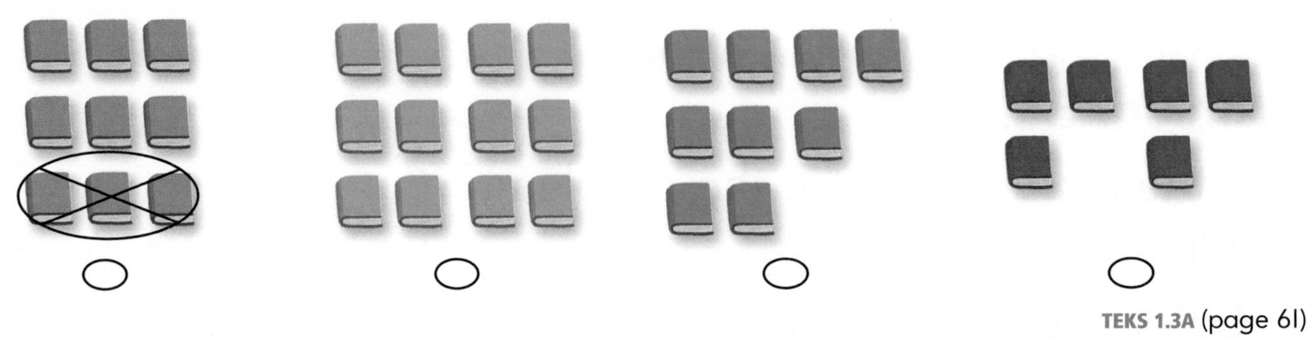

TEKS 1.3A (page 61)

4. Sam has 5 short-sleeved shirts and 3 long-sleeved shirts. Which number sentence shows the total number of Sam's shirts?

$3 + 3 = 6$ ○ $5 - 3 = 2$ ○ $5 + 5 = 10$ ○ $5 + 3 = 8$ ○

TEKS 1.3A (page 87)

Chapter 10 Fractions

TAKS Vocabulary

Here is a vocabulary word you will learn in the chapter.

equal parts Parts that are the same size

Each figure shows equal parts.

2 equal parts

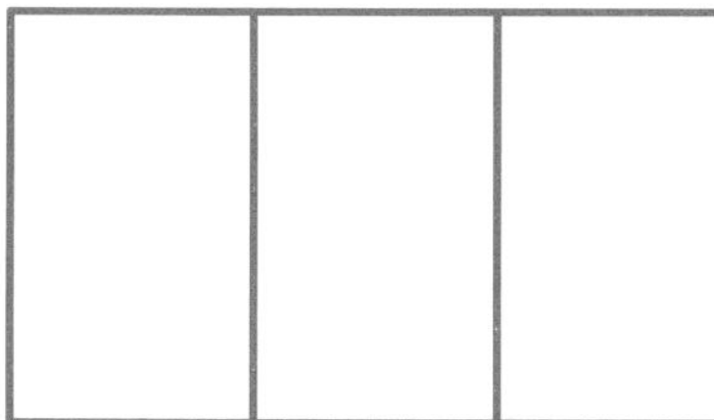

3 equal parts

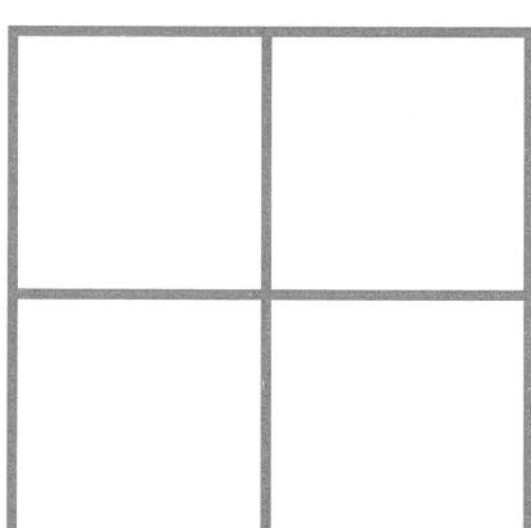

4 equal parts

See English-Spanish glossary pages 505–516.

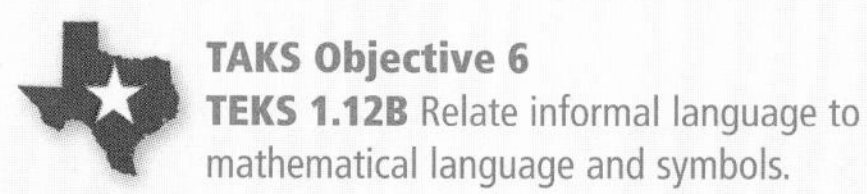

TAKS Objective 6
TEKS 1.12B Relate informal language to mathematical language and symbols.

Education Place
Visit **www.eduplace.com/txmap/** for the eGlossary and vocabulary eGames.

Name ______________________________

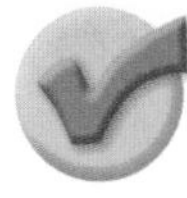

Check What You Know

Circle the figure that shows equal parts.

1.  

2.  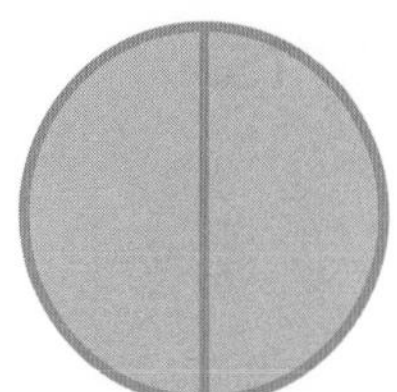 

3.   

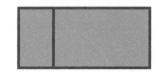

4. 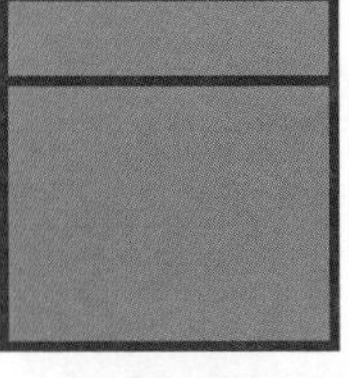  

5. 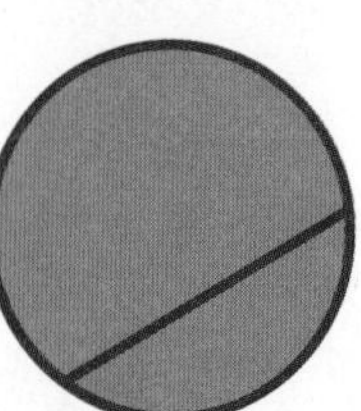 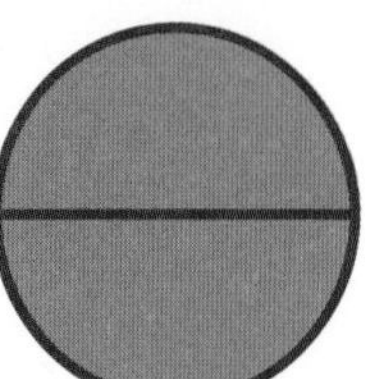 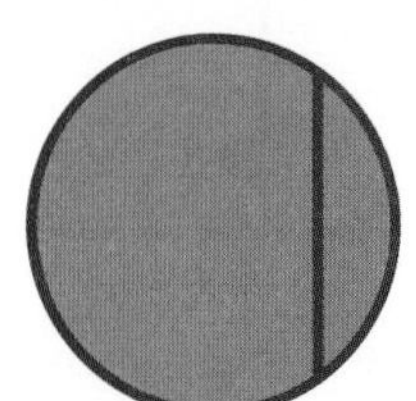

Use this page to review important skills needed for this chapter.

Name ______________________

Chapter 10 Lesson 1

Equal Parts

Hands On

TEKS Objective
Identify and count equal parts.

TAKS Vocabulary
equal parts

★ Explore

Some whole figures can be folded into **equal parts.** Equal parts are the same size.

Fold. Draw each fold line.
Write the number of equal parts.

Start with a whole.

whole

Fold to match sides and corners.

1.

_____ equal parts

Fold one side on top of the other.

2.

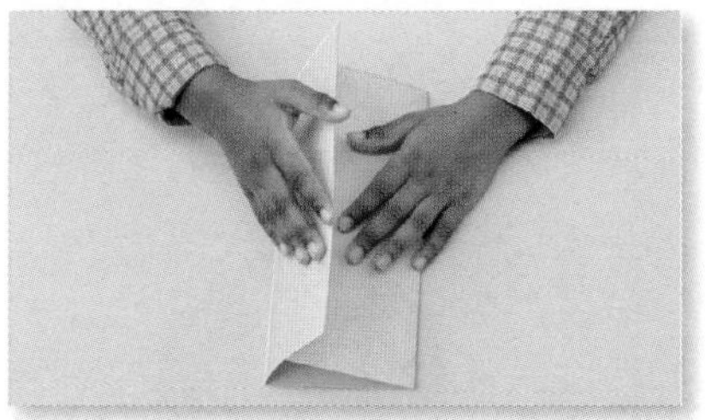

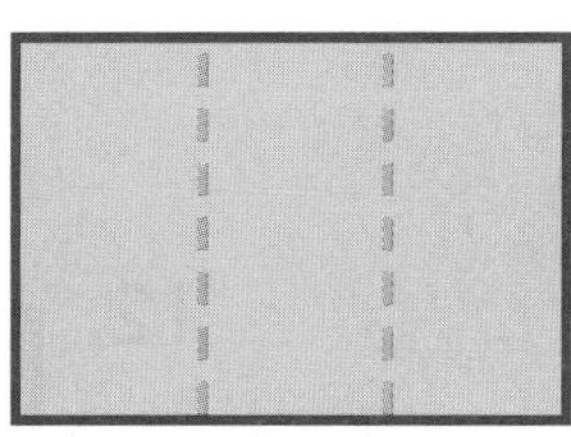

_____ equal parts

Fold to match sides and corners.
Fold again to match sides and corners.

3.

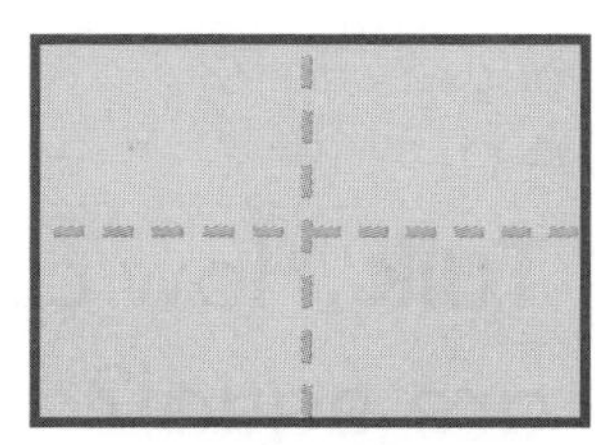

_____ equal parts

TAKS Objective 1
TEKS 1.2A Separate a whole into two, three, or four equal parts and use appropriate language to describe the parts, such as three out of four equal parts.

★ Extend

Remember!
Look for parts that are the same size.

Circle the figure that shows equal parts.

4. 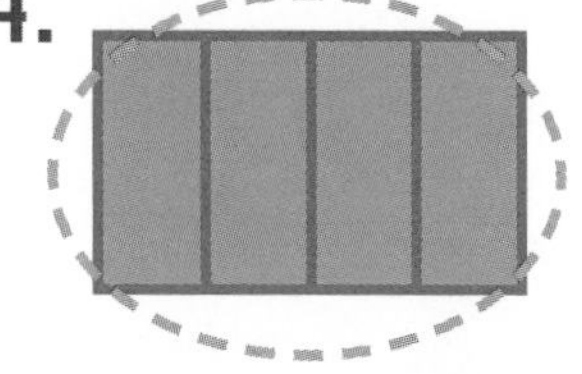 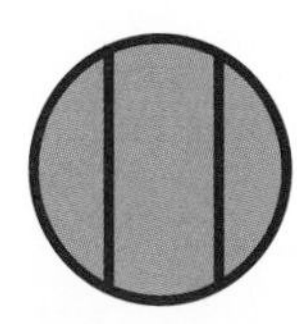

5. 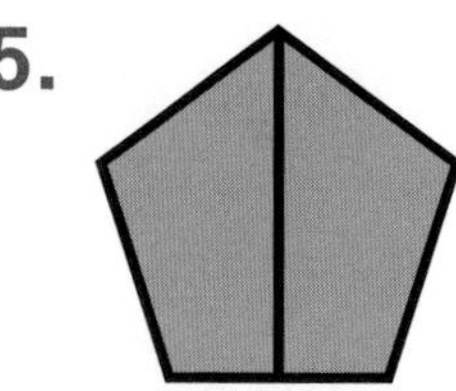 

6.  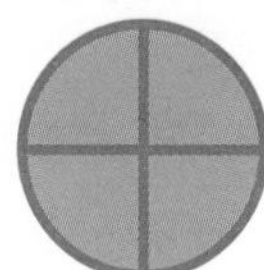

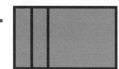

7. 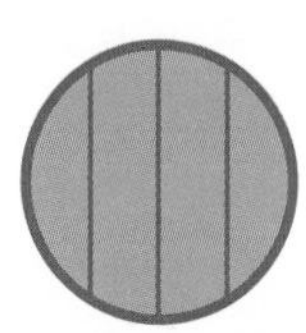 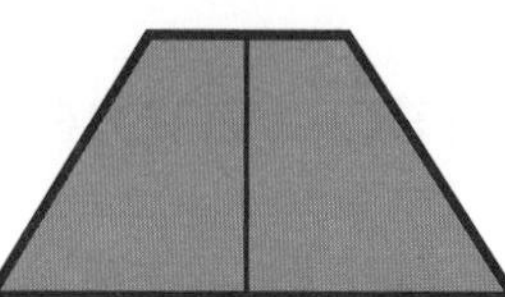

Write the number of equal parts.

8. 

3 equal parts

9. 

_____ equal parts

10. 

_____ equal parts

11. 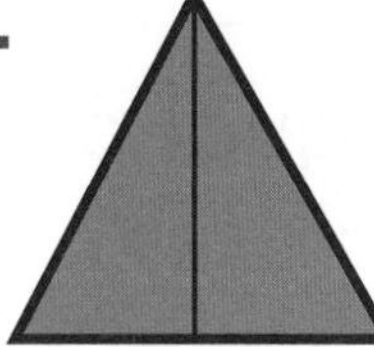

_____ equal parts

12. 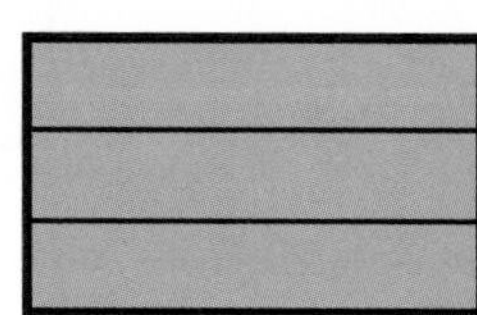

_____ equal parts

13. 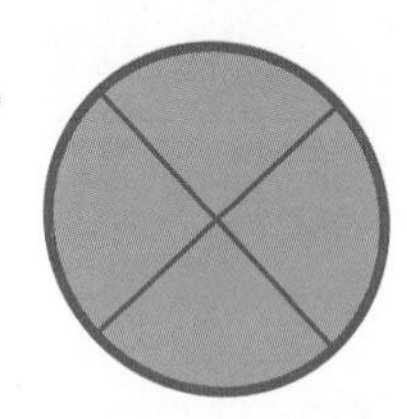

_____ equal parts

14.  **Math Talk** How can you show that two parts are equal?

At Home During a meal, ask your child to name foods that can be cut into equal parts.

En casa Durante la comida, pida a su niño que nombre los alimentos que pueden cortarse en partes iguales.

Name ____________________

Chapter 10 Lesson 2

Two Equal Parts

TEKS **Objective**
Separate a whole into two equal parts; use fractional language to describe the parts.

★ Learn

There are 2 equal parts.

1 out of 2 parts is blue.

★ Guided Practice

Circle the figure that shows 2 equal parts.

Think!
I look for 2 parts that are the same size.

1.

2.

3.

4.

Color 1 out of 2 equal parts.

5.

6.

7.

8. **Math Talk** Does it matter which part of the heart you shaded in Exercise 7? Why?

TAKS Objective 1
TEKS 1.2A Separate a whole into two, three, or four equal parts and use appropriate language to describe the parts, such as three out of four equal parts.

★ Practice

Remember!
Color one part.

Color 1 out of 2 equal parts.

9. 

10. 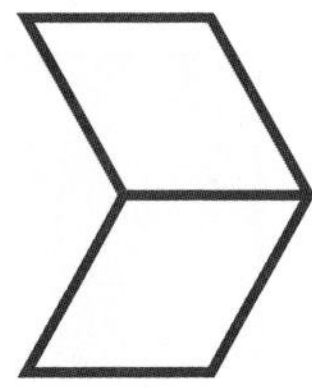

11. 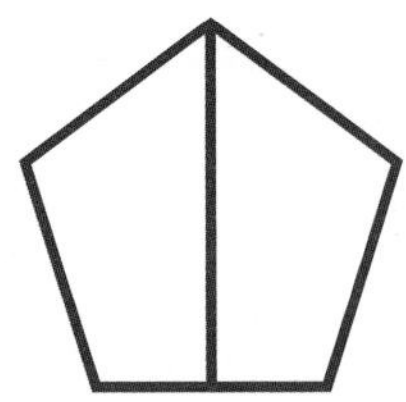

12. 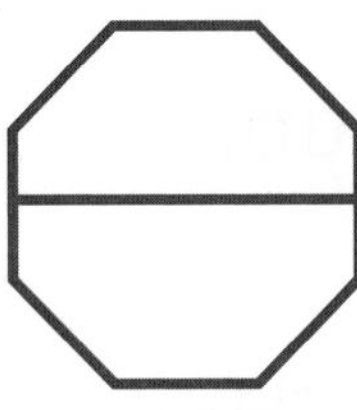

13. 

14. 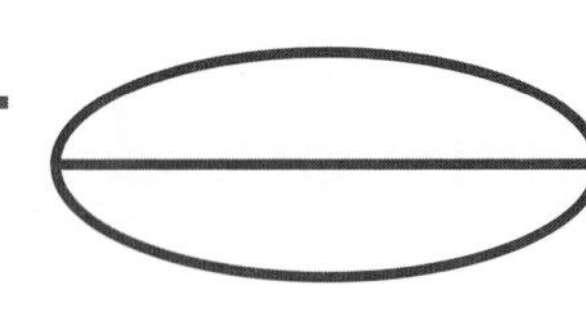

Draw a line to show 2 equal parts.
Color 1 part.

15. 

16. 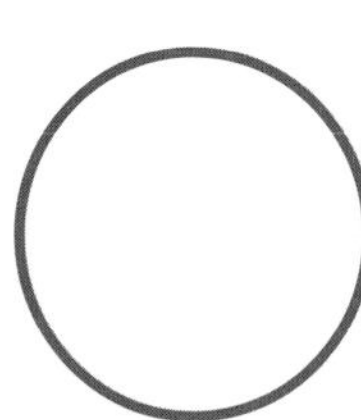

17. 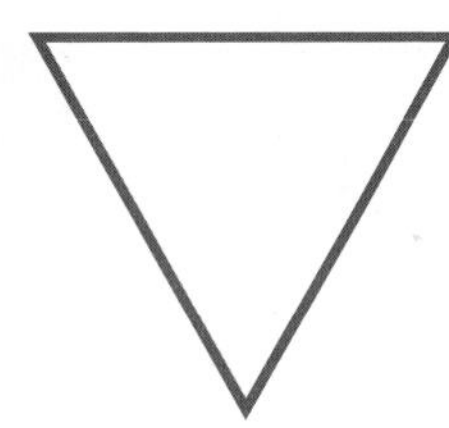

Problem Solving: Visual Thinking

18. Rita and Jerome share this apple.
Draw a line to show 2 equal parts.
Color Rita's part (red crayon).

Complete the sentence with numbers.

19. _____ out of _____ parts is red.

At Home Help your child cut a sandwich into two equal parts. Have your child point to one part.

En casa Ayude a su niño a cortar un sándwich en dos partes iguales. Pida a su niño que señale una parte.

Name ______________________________

Chapter 10 Lesson 3

Three and Four Equal Parts

Hands On

TEKS Objective
Separate a whole into three or four equal parts; use fractional language to describe the parts.

There are 3 equal parts.

1 out of 3 equal parts is red.

2 out of 3 equal parts are yellow.

★ Explore

Make cube trains.
Color and write to show.

1. ____ out of ____ equal parts is green.

2. ____ out of ____ equal parts are blue.

3. ____ out of ____ equal parts are orange.

4. **Math Talk** Use orange and blue cubes to make a 3-cube train. Tell about it.

TAKS Objective 1
TEKS 1.2A Separate a whole into two, three, or four equal parts and use appropriate language to describe the parts, such as three out of four equal parts.

★ Extend

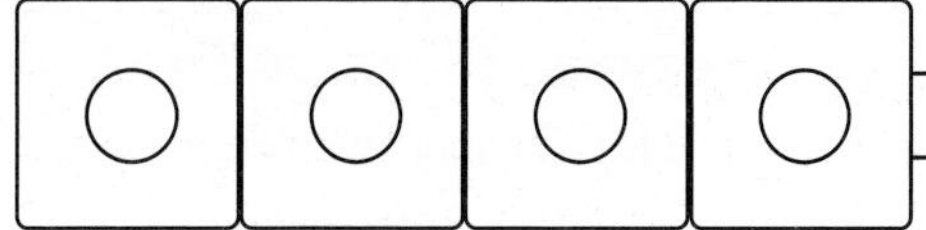

There are 4 equal parts.

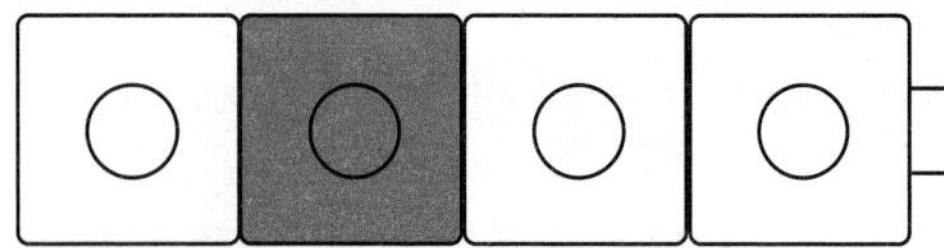

1 out of 4 equal parts is red.

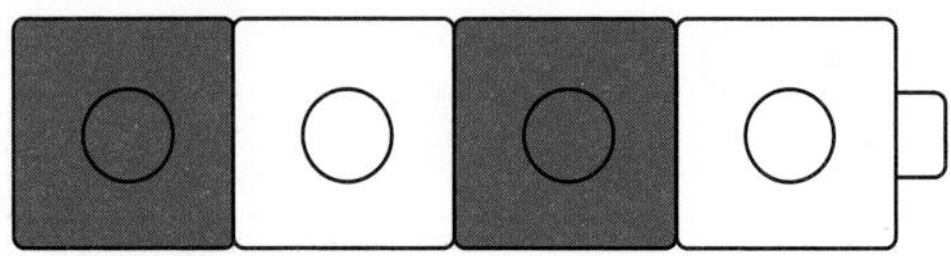

2 out of 4 equal parts are blue.

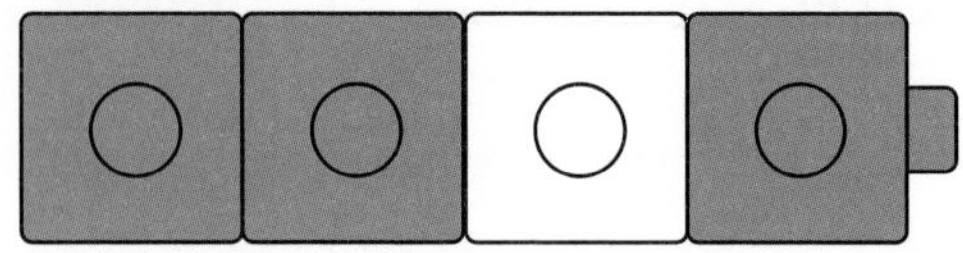

3 out of 4 equal parts are green.

Make cube trains.
Color and write to show.

5.

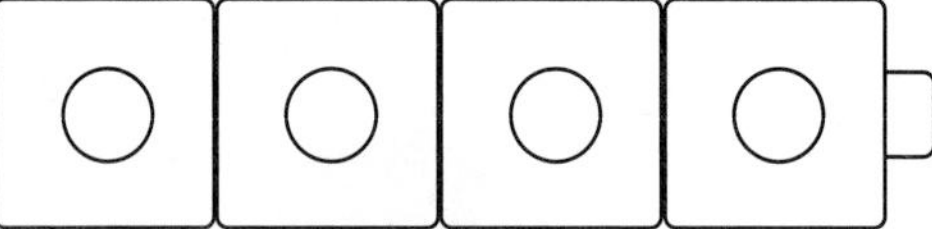

_____ out of _____ equal parts is yellow.

6.

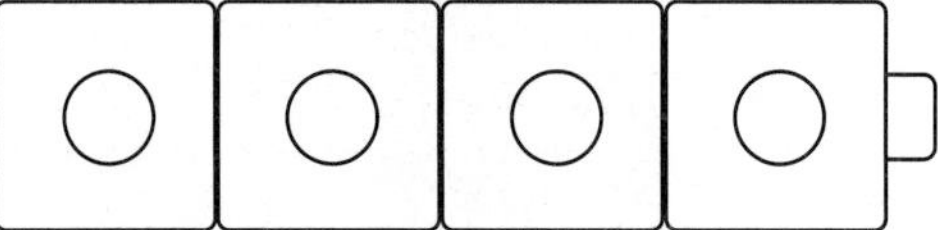

_____ out of _____ equal parts are orange.

Draw lines to make equal parts. Color.

7.

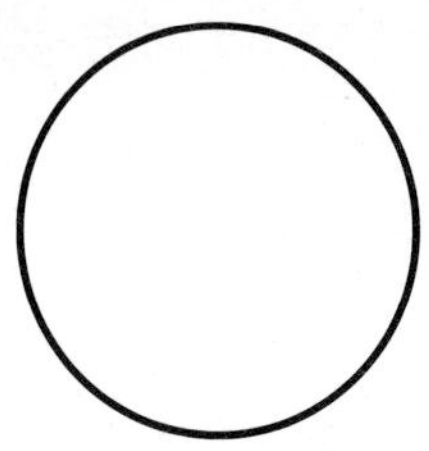

2 out of 4 equal parts

8.

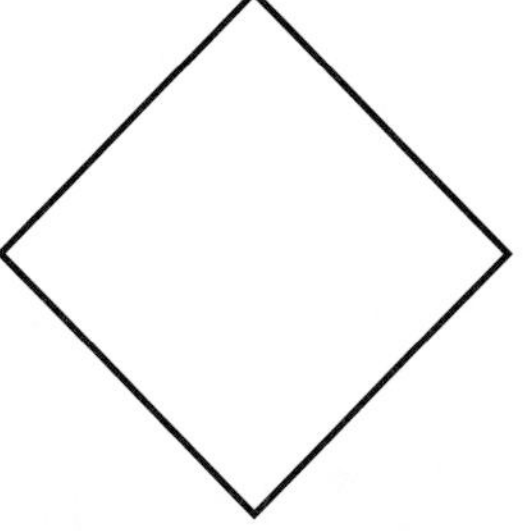

4 out of 4 equal parts

At Home Using food, such as a banana or slice of bread, help your child make 3 or 4 equal parts.

En casa Usando alimentos, como una banana o una rebanada de pan, ayude a su niño a formar 3 ó 4 partes iguales.

Name ______________________________

Chapter 10 Lesson 4

Parts of a Set

Hands On

TEKS Objective
Describe part of a set using fractional language.

★ Learn

You can describe part of a set.

3 out of 5 are red.

Think!
I used 4 counters in all.
I need to count how many are red.

★ Guided Practice

Use counters. Color to show.
Write the answer.

1. ____ out of ____ are red.

2. ____ out of ____ are yellow.

3. ____ out of ____ are red.

4. **Math Talk** Look at Exercise 2. How many parts are in the set? How do you know?

TAKS Objective 1
TEKS 1.2B Use appropriate language to describe part of a set, such as three out of the eight crayons are red.

★ Practice

Use counters. Color to show.
Write the answer.

Remember!
Look to see how many counters you need.

5. 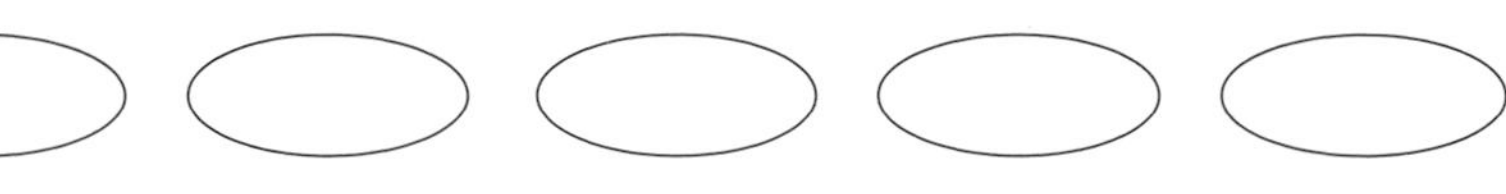

4 out of 5 are red.

6. 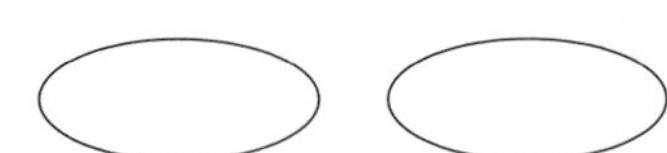

_____ out of _____ are yellow.

7. 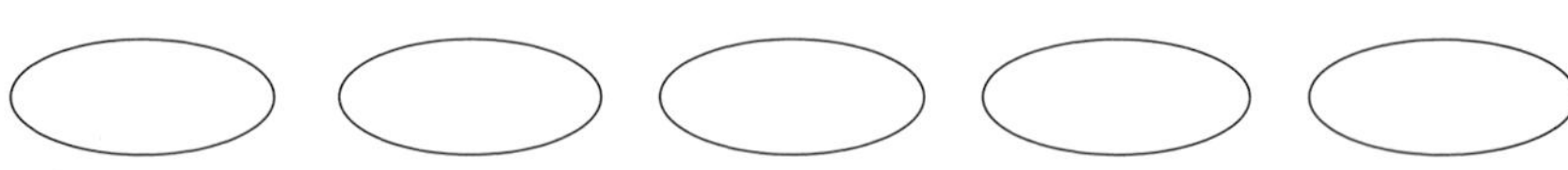

_____ out of _____ are red.

Problem Solving: Reasoning

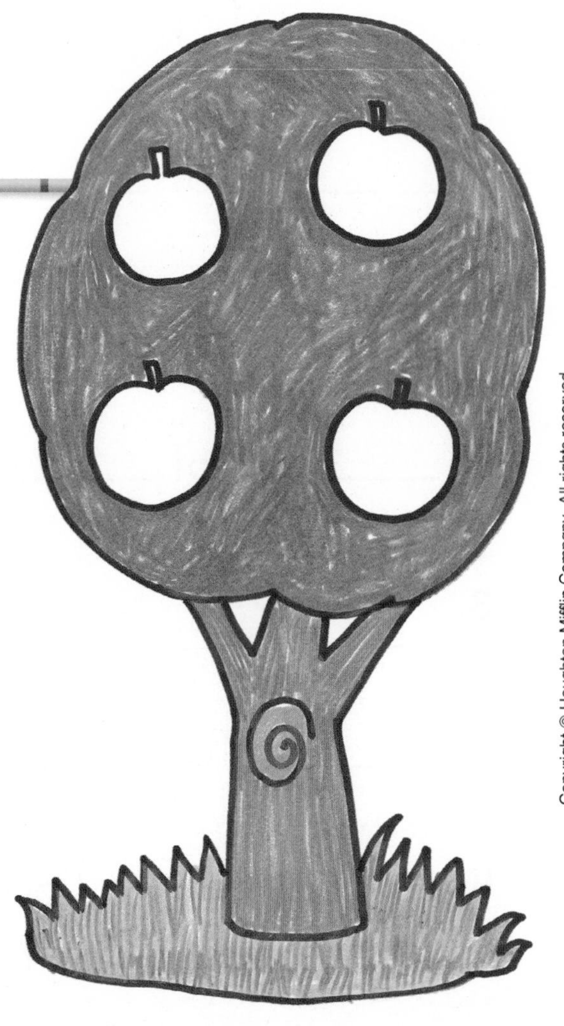

8. Zack draws a tree with 4 apples.
Color 3 of the apples.
Color 1 of the apples.

Complete the sentence.

9. _____ out of _____ apples is green.

10. _____ out of _____ apples are red.

At Home Use a collection of like items to make sets of 2, 3, and 4. Ask your child to use fractional language to describe 1 part of each set.

En casa Use un grupo de objetos iguales para formar conjuntos de 2, 3 y 4. Pida a su niño que use lenguaje de fracciones para describir 1 parte de cada conjunto.

Name ________________________________

Chapter 10 Lesson 5

Create and Solve

TEKS Objective
Create and solve problems about equal parts of a whole.

Look at the picture.
Read the problem. Solve.

1. There are 3 children. They each want an equal part of the pizza. Circle the plate that gives each child an equal part.

Look at the picture.
Write a problem about the children. Solve.

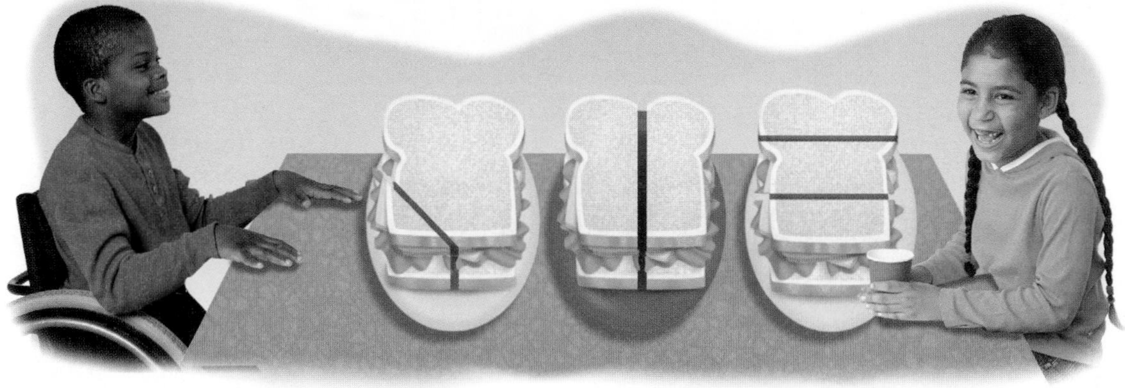

2. ________________________________

____

____

TAKS Objective 6
TEKS 1.11A Identify mathematics in everyday situations.

Look at the picture.
Read the problem. Solve.

3. There are 2 children. They each want an equal part of the apple. Circle the plate that gives each child an equal part.

Look at the picture.
Write a problem about the children. Solve.

4. ______________________________

____

____

At Home Using foods such as crackers or berries, have your child help you distribute fair shares to your family members.

En casa Usando alimentos como galletas o bayas, pida a su niño que lo ayude a distribuir partes iguales a los miembros de su familia.

Math Works

Name ___________________________

Chef

Christine is a chef at a busy restaurant. First she buys the food. Next she measures the amounts. She follows recipes and uses lots of tomatoes. Then she cooks the items on the menu. She makes sure everything tastes good.

1. Christine uses 4 tomatoes to make sauce.
   Color 3 of the tomatoes .
   Color 1 of the tomatoes .
   Complete the sentence.

_____ out of _____ tomatoes are red.

2. Christine chops 3 tomatoes and puts them in a bowl. Color 1 of the tomatoes .
   Color 2 of the tomatoes .
   Complete the sentence.

_____ out of _____ tomatoes are green.

TAKS Objectives 1, 6
TEKS 1.2B Use appropriate language to describe part of a set such as three out of the eight crayons are red.

TEKS 1.11A Identify mathematics in everyday situations.

Math Music

The Equal Parts Game

Math Music, Track 4
Tune: "On Top of Old Smokey"

Can you find the circle,
Rectangle, and square?
You'll find many figures,
Just look everywhere.

This house has some parts now.
Is each part the same?
Can you count the parts shown,
And play the parts game?

This field has some parts now.
Each part is the same.
Can you count the parts shown,
And play the parts game?

This pie has some parts now.
Each part is the same.
Can you count the parts shown,
And play the parts game?

Now look all around you,
At figures you see.
Make parts that are equal,
Then count parts with me.

TAKS Objective 1
TEKS 1.2A Separate a whole into two, three, or four equal parts, and use appropriate language to describe the parts such as three out of four equal parts.

Name ______________________________

Concepts and Skills

Circle the figure that shows equal parts. TEKS 1.2A

1. 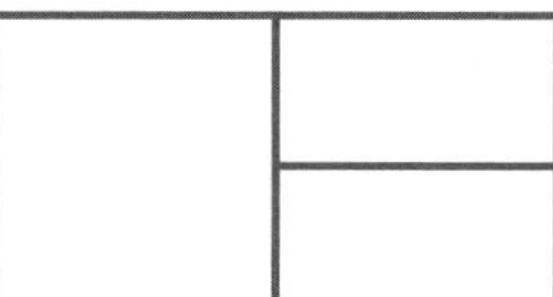 

Write the number of equal parts. TEKS 1.2A

2. 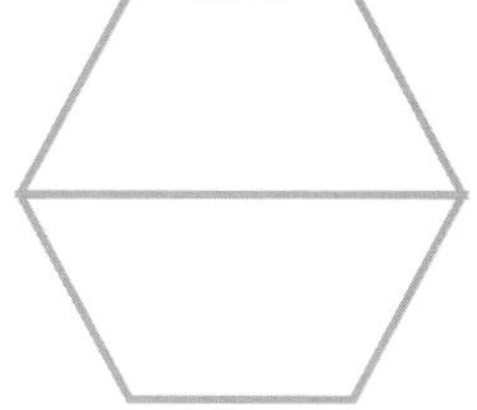

_____ equal parts

3. Color 3 out of 4 equal parts. TEKS 1.2A

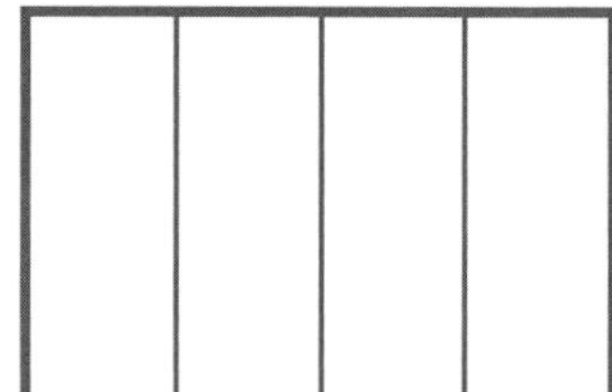

Use counters. Color to show. Write the answer. TEKS 1.2B

4.    

_____ out of _____ are yellow.

Problem Solving

5. There are 3 children. They each want an equal part of the pizza. Circle the plate that gives each child an equal part. TEKS 1.11A

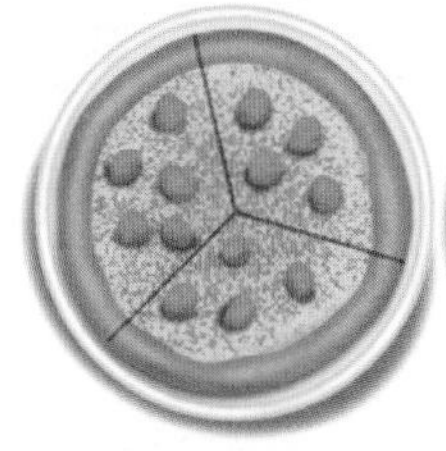 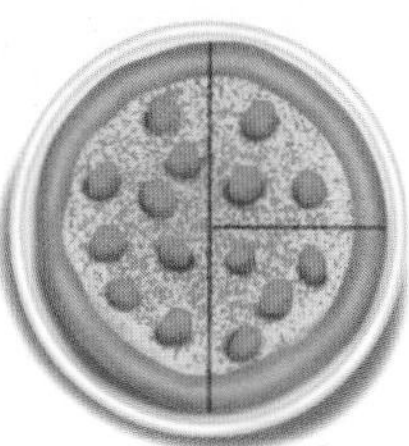 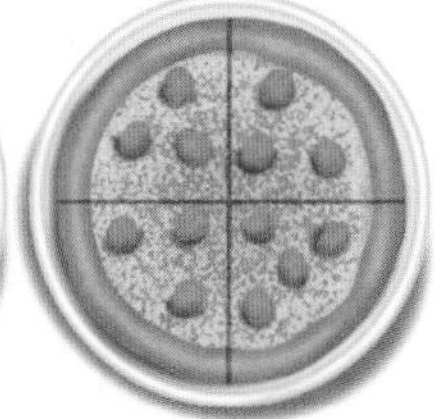

Prep and Spiral Review

Choose the answer for problems 1–4.

1. Which figure is a square?

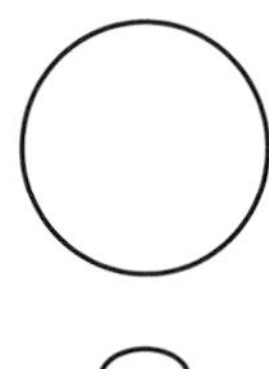 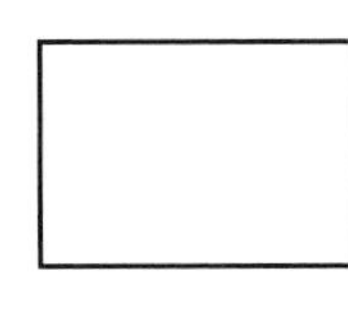 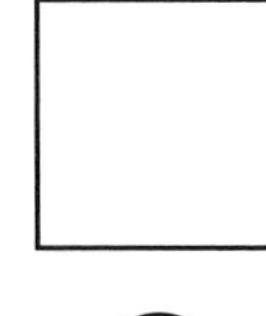 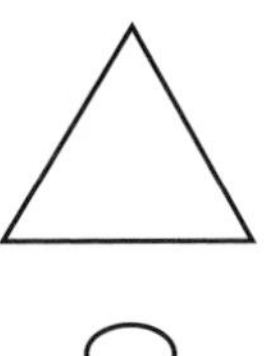

○ ○ ○ ○

TEKS 1.6A (page 149)

2. Which cracker is shaped like a triangle?

TEKS 1.6A (page 149)

3. Which number tells how many?

 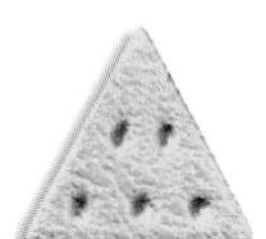  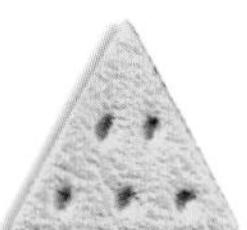 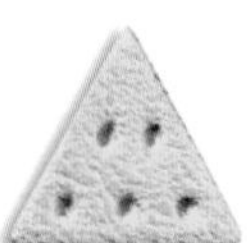 

2 ○ 4 ○ 6 ○ 8 ○

TEKS 1.1D (page 23)

4. Hamid saw juice boxes on a shelf. How many juice boxes did he see?

14 ○ 15 ○ 16 ○ 17 ○

TEKS 1.1D (page 39)

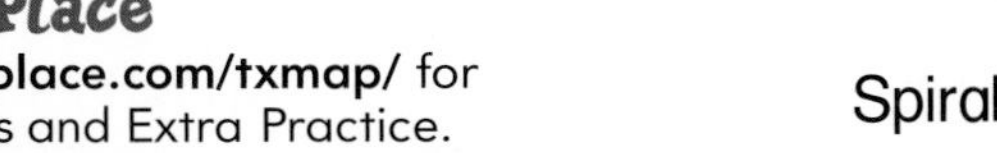
Education Place
Visit **www.eduplace.com/txmap/** for Test-Taking Tips and Extra Practice.

Name ______________________________

Unit 4 **Mental Math Strategies**

Add 2

Adding is easy with a 2.
Skip a number, and you are through!

I start with 2.
Then I skip 3
and go on to 4.

1. 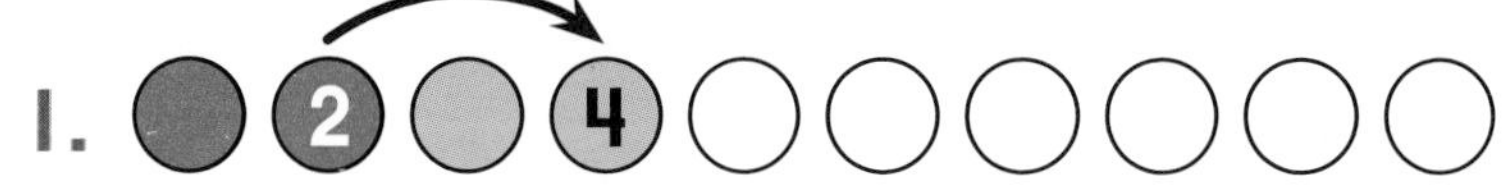

$2 + 2 =$ [4]

2. ● ● ● ④ ○ ⑥ ○ ○ ○ ○

$4 + 2 =$ ☐

3. ① ○ ③ ○ ○ ○ ○ ○ ○ ○

$1 + 2 =$ ☐

4. ● ● ③ ○ ⑤ ○ ○ ○ ○ ○

$3 + 2 =$ ☐

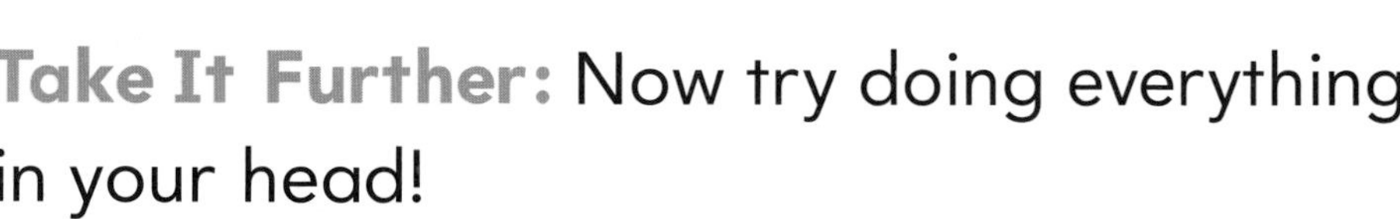

Take It Further: Now try doing everything in your head!

5. $4 + 2 =$ ☐ 6. $6 + 2 =$ ☐

Name ____________________

Reading and Writing Math

Write *yes* or *no* to answer each riddle.

1. I am a two-dimensional figure.
   I have 3 sides.
   I have 3 corners, too.
   I am a triangle.

   ____

2. I am a two-dimensional figure.
   I have 4 sides.
   My sides are the same.
   I am a cube.

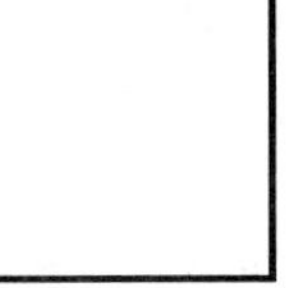

   ____

3. I am a three-dimensional figure.
   I look like a can.
   I can slide, roll, and stack.
   I am a sphere.

   ____

4. I am a three-dimensional figure.
   I look like a box.
   My faces are shaped like rectangles.
   I am a rectangular prism.

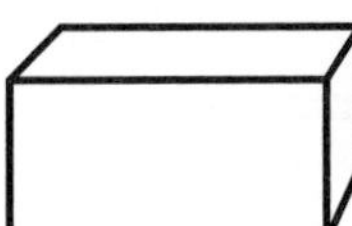

   ____

5. **Writing Math** Draw a two-dimensional figure.
   Show two equal parts.

TEKS 1.12A Explain and record observations using objects, words, pictures, numbers, and technology.

TEKS 1.12B Relate informal language to mathematical language and symbols.

Name ______________________________

Concepts and Skills

Read the sorting rule.
Circle the figures that follow the rule. TEKS 1.6C

1. 4 sides

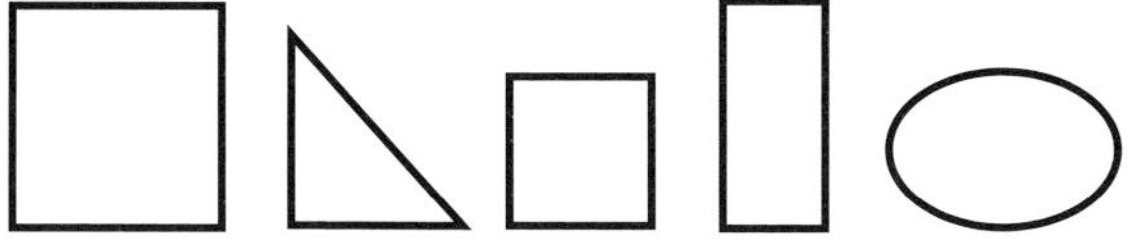

2. 4 corners

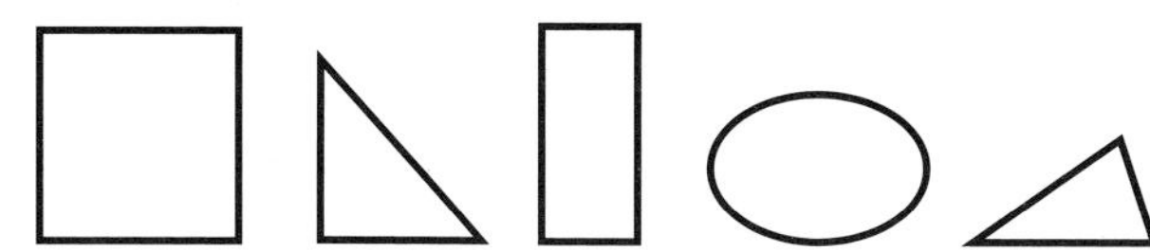

3. No corners

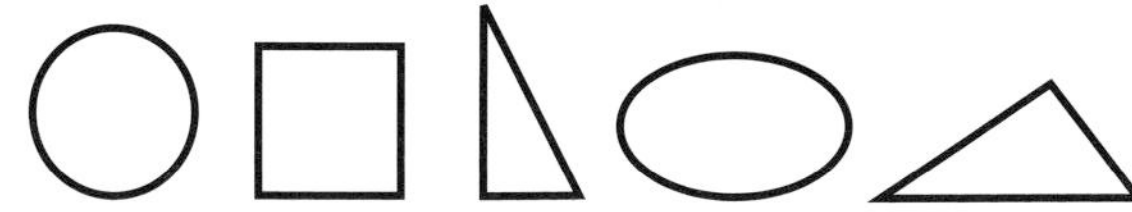

4. More than 3 sides

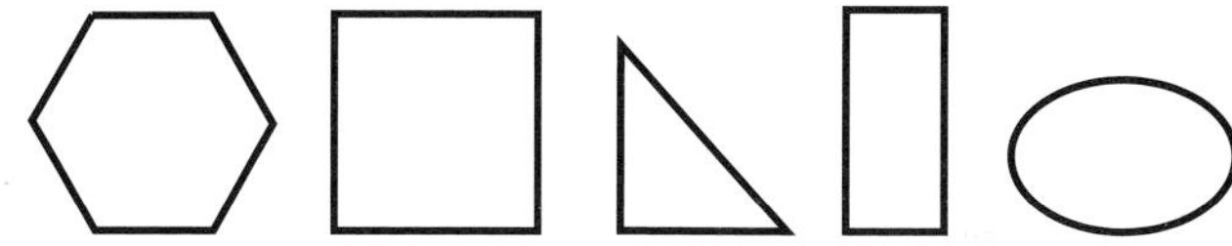

Circle the objects that match. TEKS 1.6B

5.

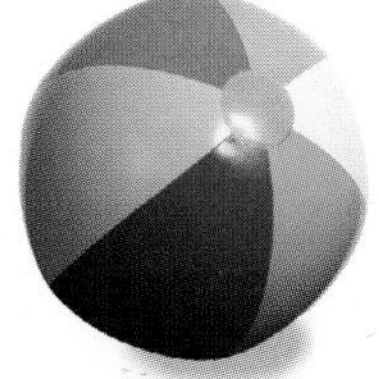

6.

Look at the two-dimensional figure.
Circle the three-dimensional figure with a face like it. TEKS 1.6C

7.

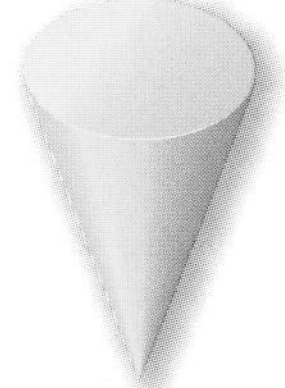

8.

Draw lines to show equal parts.
Color. TEKS 1.2A

9. 1 out of 2 equal parts

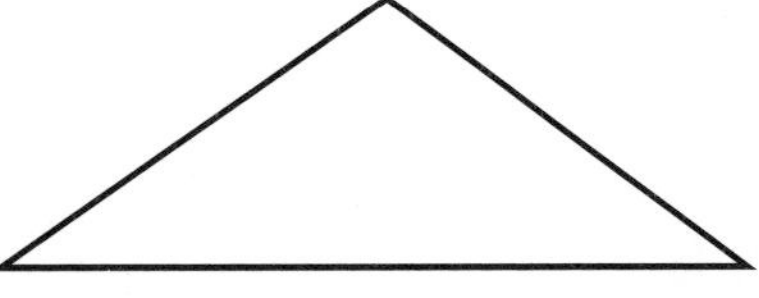

10. 2 out of 3 equal parts

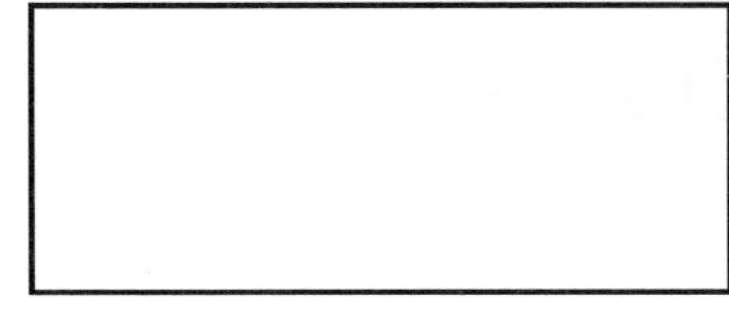

11. 3 out of 4 equal parts

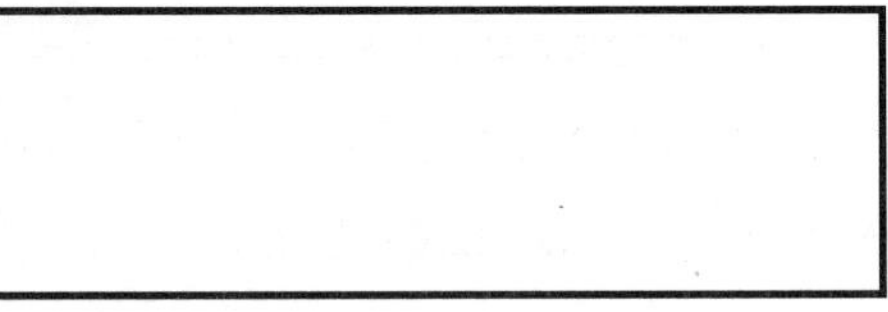

Use counters. Color to show.
Write the answer. TEKS 1.2B

12. 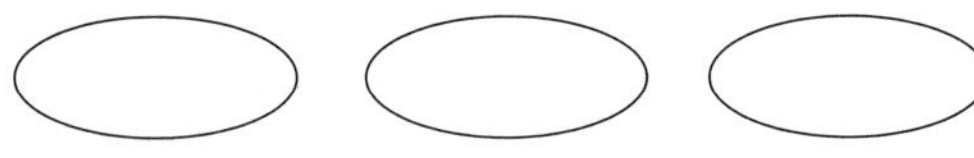

_____ out of _____ are red.

13. 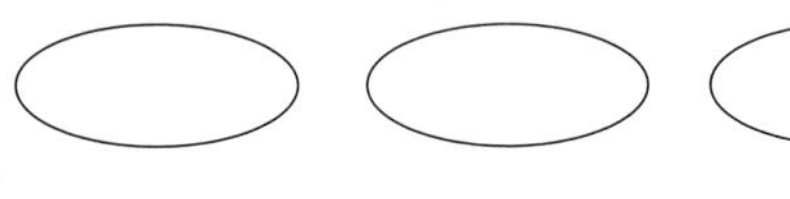 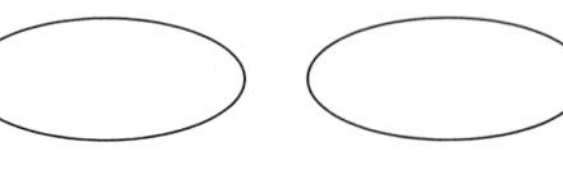

_____ out of _____ are red.

Problem Solving

Draw a picture to solve. TEKS 1.6D, 1.11C, 1.11D

14. Rosa wants to make a picture of a house. She uses these figures.

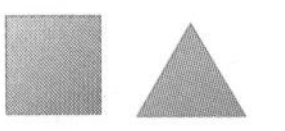

How can she make a house?

15. Cara wants to make a picture of a fish. She uses these figures.

How can she make a fish?

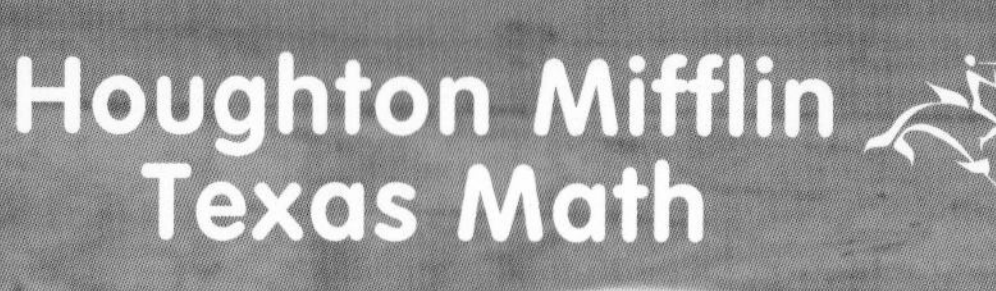

Unit 5

Data

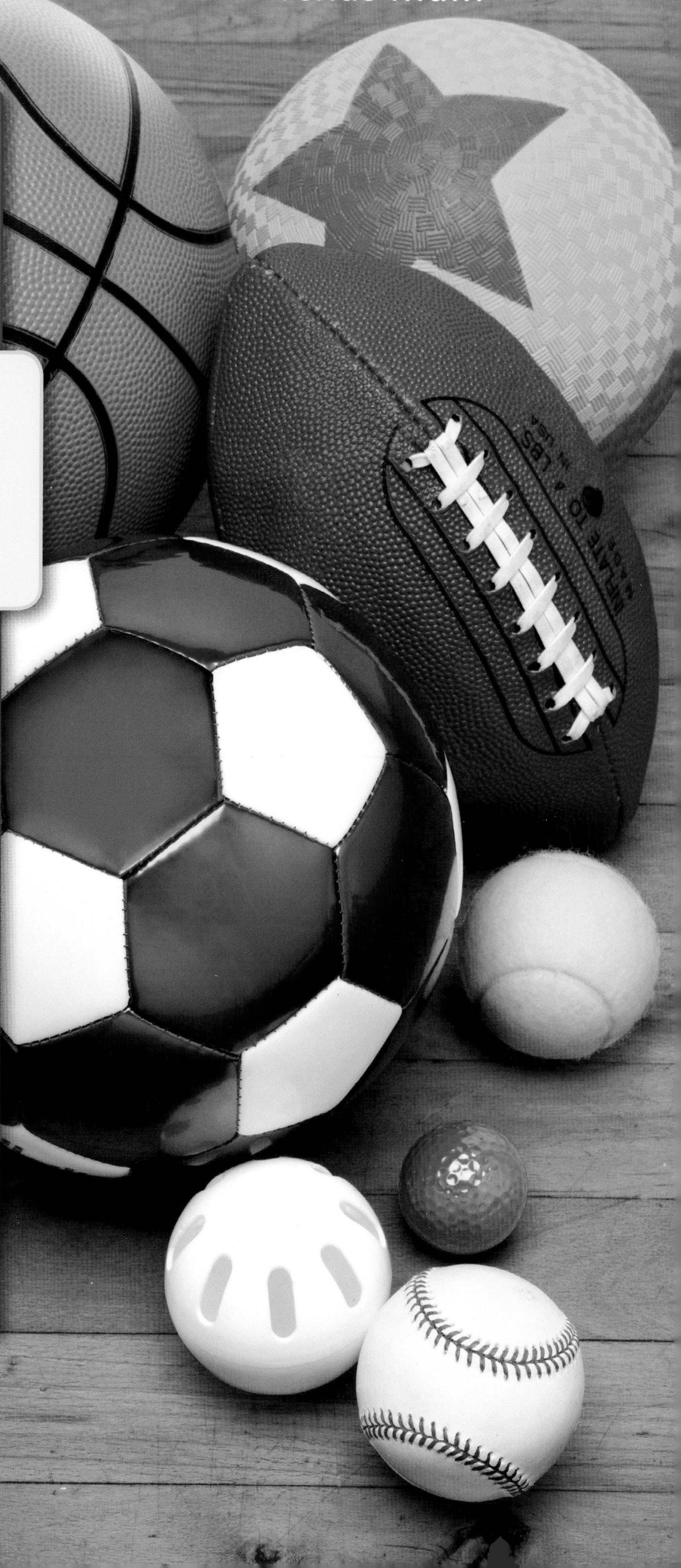

BIG IDEAS!

- You can collect and sort data.
- You can use graphs and tallies to record and organize data.
- You can use data to answer questions and make predictions.

Songs and Games

Math Music Track 5
What Will We Do?

eGames
www.eduplace.com/txmap/

Literature

Literature Big Book

- Five Creatures

Math Readers

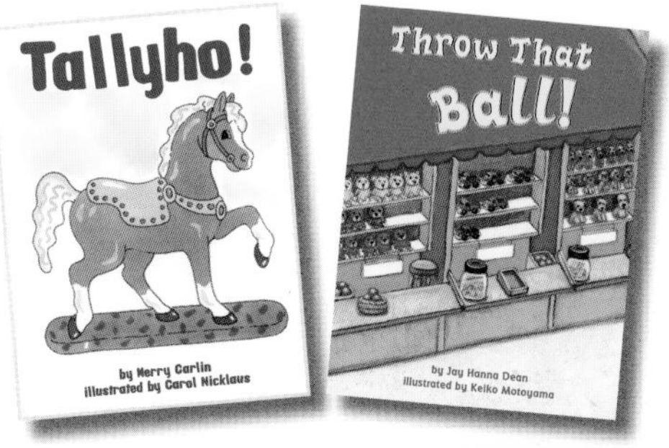

ISBN-13: 978-0-618-95274-8
ISBN-10: 0-618-95274-8
89- WC - 16 15 14 13 12

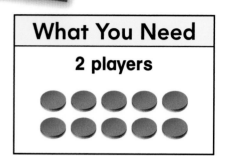

Get Ready Game

Shake and Spill

What You Need
2 players
10 counters

1. Choose ● or ○.
2. In turn, shake the 10 counters and spill them onto the board.
3. Sort. Compare ● and ○.
4. The player who chose the color with more gets 1 point.
5. Play until each player has 5 turns.

TAKS Objective 5
TEKS 1.9A Collect and sort data.
TEKS 1.9B Use organized data to construct real-object graphs, picture graphs, and bar-type graphs.

TEKS 1.10A Draw conclusions and answer questions using information organized in real-object graphs, picture graphs, and bar-type graphs.

Education Place
For eGames and Brain Teasers, visit **www.eduplace.com/txmap/**

Math at Home

Dear Family,

My class is starting Unit 5, **Data**. I will learn how to make and read graphs and tally charts. I will also learn to identify events as certain or impossible. You can help me learn these vocabulary words, and we can do the Math Activity together.

From,

____

Vocabulary

tally A mark used to count things.

𝍸 ||

These **tally** marks show 7.

picture graph Uses pictures to show information.

Children Playing

This **picture graph** shows 2 children are playing on the swings.

Education Place

Visit **www.eduplace.com/txmaf/** for

- eGames and Brain Teasers
- Math at Home in other languages

Family Math Activity

Give your child some buttons in two or three different colors. Have your child sort the buttons and then make a real-object graph. Ask questions such as, *Are there more black buttons or white buttons? How do you know?*

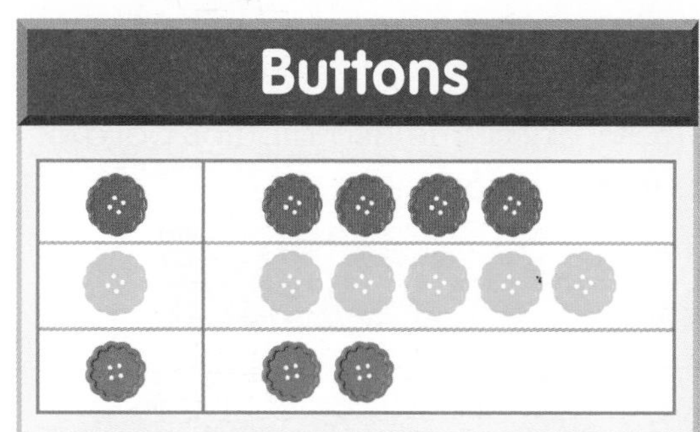

Literature

These books link to the math in this unit. Look for them at the library.

- **Apple Farmer Annie** by Monica Wellington *(Dutton Children's Books, 2001)*
- **The Best Vacation Ever** by Stuart J. Murphy
- **Dave's Down-to-Earth Rock Shop** by Stuart J. Murphy

Matemáticas en casa

Estimada familia:

Mi clase está comenzando la Unidad 5, **Datos**. Aprenderé cómo hacer y leer gráficas y tableros de conteo. También aprenderé a identificar eventos seguros o imposibles. Me pueden ayudar a aprender estas palabras de vocabulario y podemos hacer juntos la Actividad de matemáticas para la familia.

De:

____

Vocabulario

marca de conteo Marca que se usa para contar cosas.

Estas **marcas de conteo** muestran 7.

pictografía Gráfica que usa dibujos para mostrar la información.

Esta **pictografía** muestra que 2 niños están jugando en los columpios.

Education Place

Visite **www.eduplace.com/txmaf/** para
- Juegos en línea y acertijos
- Matemáticas en casa, en otros idiomas

Actividad de matemáticas para la familia

Dé a su niño algunos botones de dos o tres colores diferentes. Pida a su niño que clasifique los botones y haga una gráfica de objetos reales. Haga preguntas como *¿Hay más botones negros o más botones blancos? ¿Cómo lo sabes?*

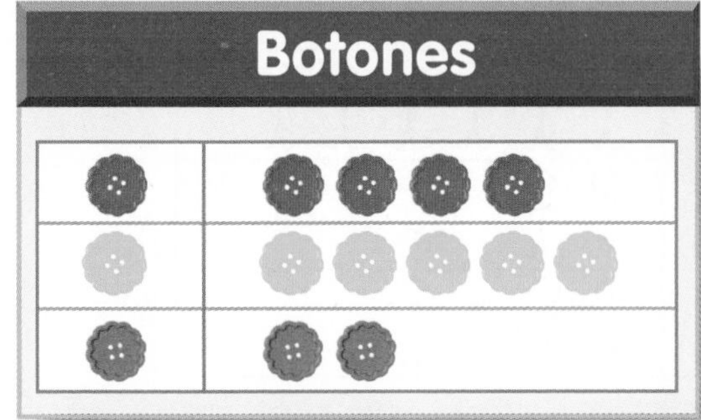

Literatura

Estos libros hablan sobre las matemáticas de esta unidad. Podemos buscarlos en la biblioteca.

- **Hagamos una gráfica** por Lisa Trumbauer *(Capstone Press, 2005)*
- **Come una y cuenta veinte** por Greg Tang

I saw acorns, birds, pinecones,
and pebbles on my walks.

Which do you like best?
Draw your favorite.

TAKS Objectives 4, 6
TEKS 1.1A, 1.10A, 1.11A

UNIT 5

My Nature Walks

written by Elvira Tippin

This Take-Home Book belongs to

____

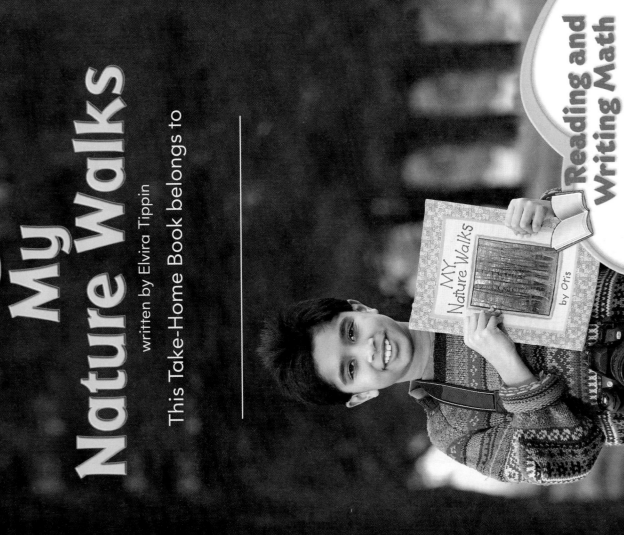

Reading and Writing Math

This take-home book will help you review counting and comparing sets.

My name is Otis.
My dad and I like to walk.
It's quiet. We listen.
We look for nature.

Pebbles are many shades
of brown, gray, and white.

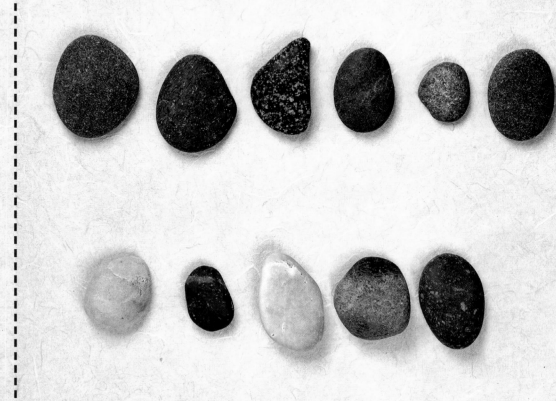

How many pebbles are there?

_____ pebbles

I find pebbles in a stream.
They are shiny.

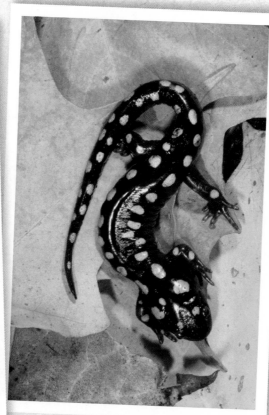

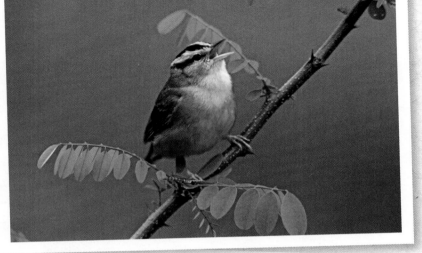

I take lots of pictures.
I put my pictures into
a scrapbook.

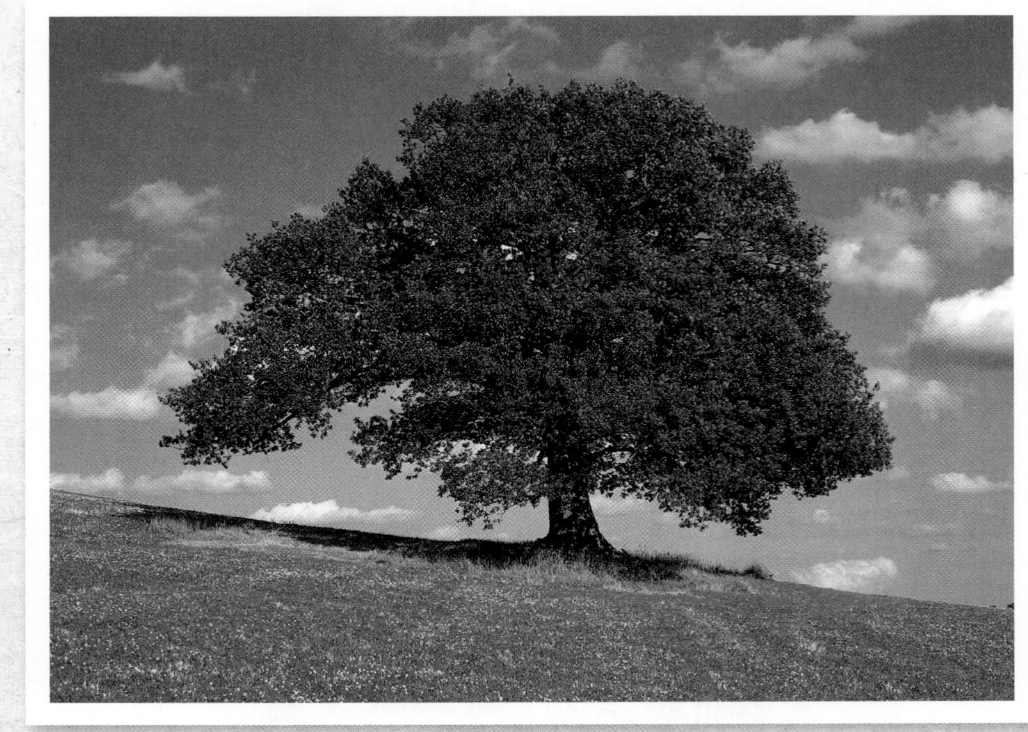

The oak tree is so big!
I find many acorns.

I find some pinecones
under the pine trees.
I line up the pinecones
to help me compare.

Are there fewer big pinecones or small pinecones?

____

I see pine trees,
some tall, some short.

How many trees are tall? _____ trees

How many trees are short? _____ trees

Here are acorns,
big ones and small,
All from the oak tree,
so wide and so tall.

How many acorns are there?

_____ acorns

Tell about them.

I see an indigo bunting.
It is so beautiful!
Dad and I see wild turkeys, too!

I keep a picture graph
of all the birds I see.

Did Otis see more indigo buntings
or wild turkeys? ______________

Graphs and Tables

TAKS Vocabulary

Here are some vocabulary words you will learn in the chapter.

real-object graph A graph that uses real objects to show information
This real-object graph shows there are more red crayons than blue crayons.

tally A mark used to show what you count.

|	||	|||	||||	~~||||~~
1	2	3	4	5

picture graph A graph that uses pictures to show information
This picture graph shows that most children like red bicycles.

See English-Spanish glossary pages 505–516.

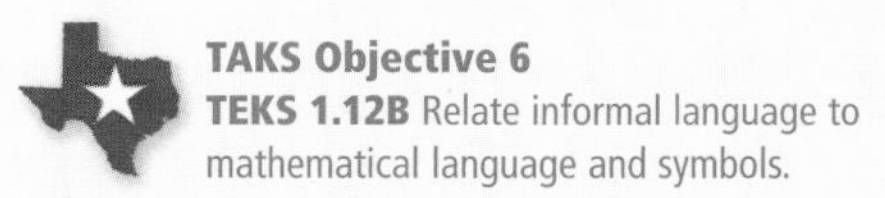

TAKS Objective 6
TEKS 1.12B Relate informal language to mathematical language and symbols.

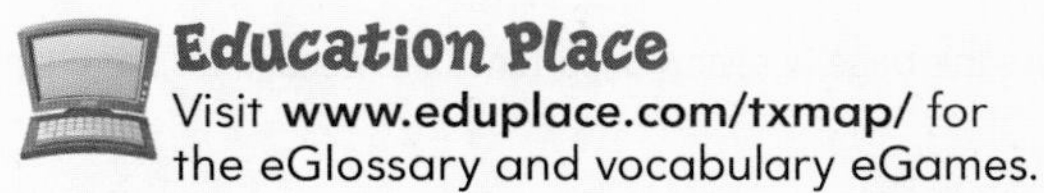

Education Place
Visit **www.eduplace.com/txmap/** for the eGlossary and vocabulary eGames.

Name ______________________

Circle the figure that goes with the group.

1.

2. Circle the set with more.

3. Circle the set with fewer.

4. Circle the sets with the same number.

Use this page to review important skills needed for this chapter.

Name ____________________

Chapter 11 Lesson 1

Make a Real-Object Graph

In a **real-object graph,** you place real objects on the graph.

TEKS Objective
Sort data and then use blocks to make real-object graphs.

TAKS Vocabulary
real-object graph

★ Explore

Find the pattern blocks in the picture. Place each block on the graph.

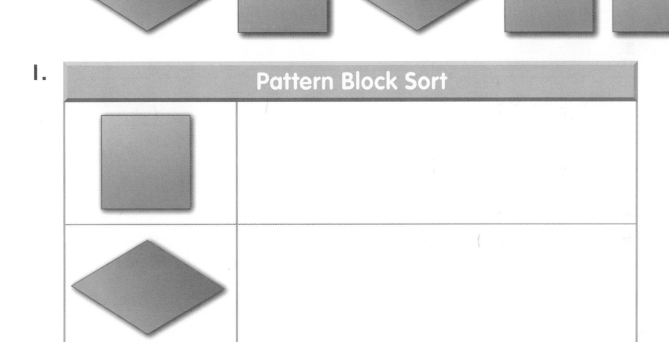

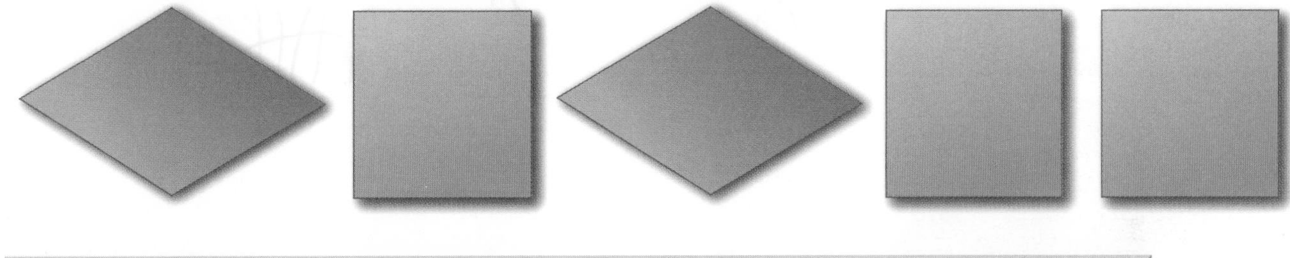

1.

Pattern Block Sort	
(square block)	
(rhombus block)	

Use the real-object graph to solve.

2. How many orange blocks are on the graph? _____

3. How many blue blocks are on the graph? _____

4. **Math Talk** How does the graph help show how many more orange blocks than blue blocks you have?

TAKS Objective 5
TEKS 1.9B Use organized data to construct real-object graphs, picture graphs, and bar-type graphs.

TEKS 1.10A Draw conclusions and answer questions using information organized in real-object graphs, picture graphs, and bar-type graphs.

★ Extend

Remember!
Count each block on your graph to solve.

Find the pattern blocks in the picture.
Place each block on the graph.

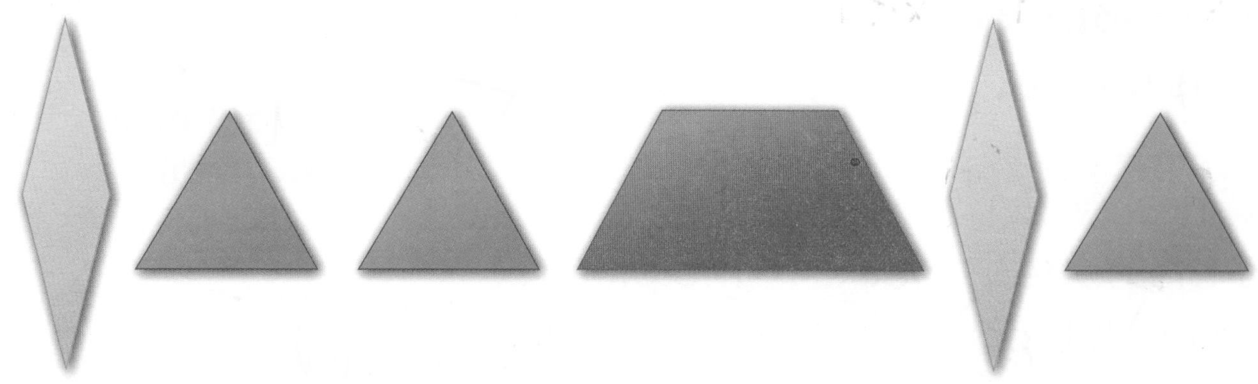

5.

Pattern Block Sort	

Use the real-object graph to solve.

6. How many green blocks are on the graph? _____

7. How many tan blocks are on the graph? _____

8. How many fewer tan than green blocks are there? _____

At Home Use small objects such as nickels and dimes and have your child make a real-object graph.

En casa Use objetos pequeños, como monedas de 5 centavos y de 10 centavos, y pida a su niño que los use para hacer una gráfica de objetos reales.

Name samir

Chapter 11 Lesson 2

Make a Tally Chart

Hands On

TEKS Objective
Collect, sort, and display data using tally marks.

TAKS Vocabulary
tally

Make 1 **tally** for each dot.

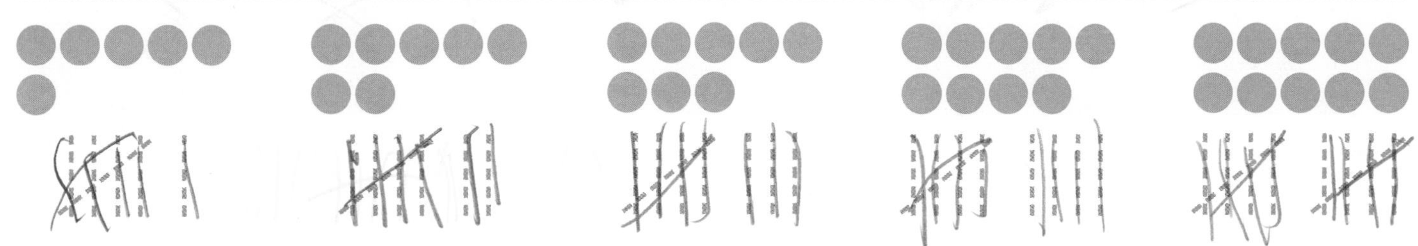

★ Explore

Ask 10 friends which of these activities they like best. Make 1 tally for each answer. Complete the tally chart.

1.

Activities	
	|||
	|
	卌

Use the tally chart. Write how many children choose each activity.

2.

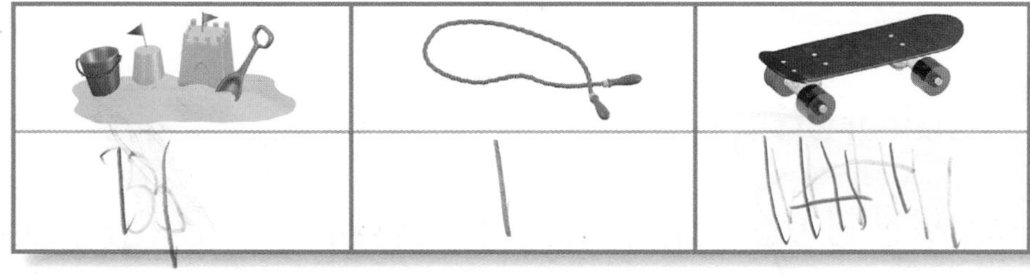

3. Use the picture. Complete the tally chart.

Remember!
Cross out 1 child.
Then make 1 tally.

Use the tally chart to solve.

4. How many  are there?

5. How many  are there?

6. Which has the most? Circle.

7. Which has the fewest? Circle.

8. How many  and are there?

_____ children

9. How many children are there in all?

_____ children

10. **Math Talk** How did you find the answer for Exercise 9?

At Home Pick three foods. Help your child survey family members or friends to find their favorite.

En casa Escoja tres alimentos. Ayude a su niño a hacer una encuesta a miembros de la familia o amigos para hallar su alimento favorito.

Name ____________________

Chapter 11 Lesson 3

Make a Picture Graph

TEKS Objective
Construct a picture graph and use it to answer questions.

TAKS Vocabulary
picture graph

A **picture graph** uses pictures to show information.

Cross out one truck.
Draw one wheel.

Toys	
truck	wheel wheel wheel

Guided Practice

Use the picture.
Make a picture graph.

Think!
I can draw 1 wheel for each police car.

1.

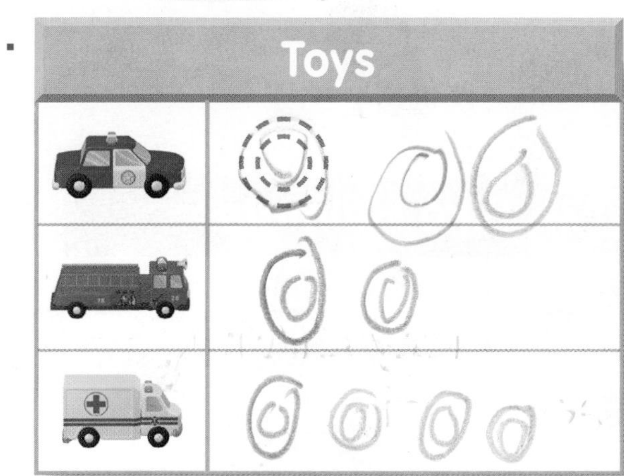

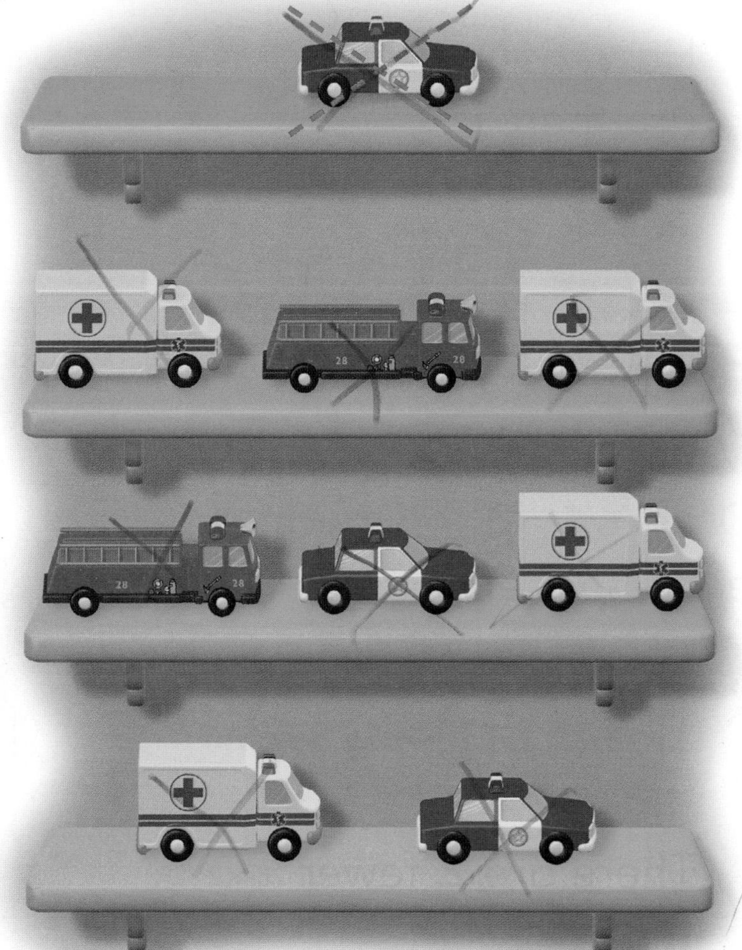

2. **Math Talk** Which toy is shown the most? Tell how you know.

★ Practice

Remember!
Cross out I car, bus, or truck. Draw I wheel on the graph.

Use the picture.
Make a picture graph.

3. 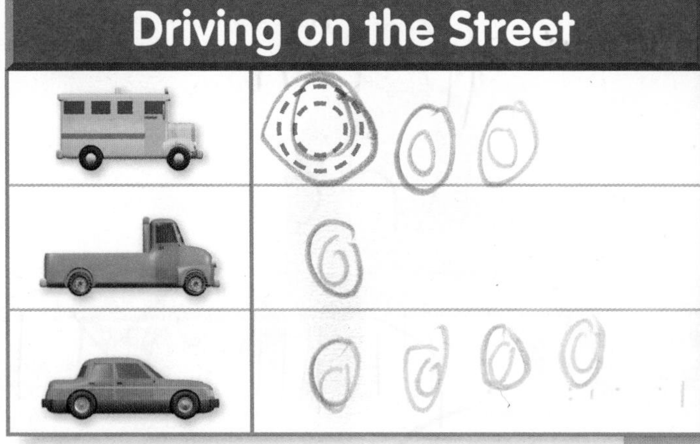

Use the picture graph to solve.

4. How many and are there?

______

5. How many more than are there?

______ more

Problem Solving: Logical Reasoning

Make a picture graph.
Draw a ◯ to stand for each helmet.

6. There are 3 .
There is I more than .
There are 2 fewer than .

At Home Help your child make a picture graph that tells about 3 food items in the house.

En casa Ayude a su niño a hacer una pictografía acerca de 3 alimentos que haya en la casa.

Name Samir

Chapter 11 Lesson 4

Read a Picture Graph

TEKS Objective
Answer questions using information organized in picture graphs.

★ Learn

You can read a picture graph to solve problems. Each 🯅 stands for 1 child.

Children Playing

3 children are playing with the ●.

★ Guided Practice

Children Playing

Think!
Count the 🯅 in the row.

Use the picture graph to solve.
Each 🯅 stands for 1 child.

1. How many children played on the ?

6 children

2. Which item do more children choose? Circle.

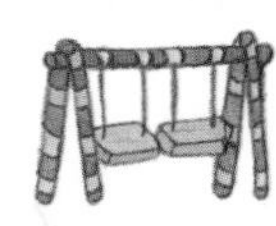

3. **Math Talk** How can you use the graph to tell if fewer children are on or ?

★ Practice

Remember!
Count the 웃 to find the answer.

Use the picture graph to solve.
Each 웃 stands for 1 child.

4. How many children drink  ?

5 children

5. How many children drink   and ?

6 children

6. Which do most children drink? Circle.

7. Which two drinks do the same number of children choose? Circle.

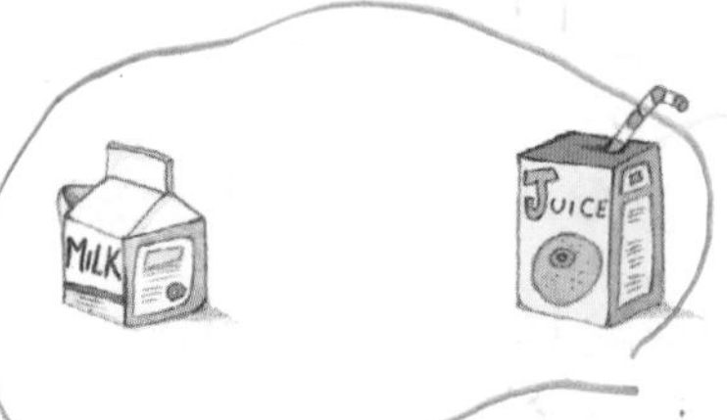 

Algebra Readiness: Number Sentences

Write a number sentence to find the answer.

8. Mr. Lo has 8 MILK. The children drink 3 MILK. How many MILK are left?

8 − 3 = 5

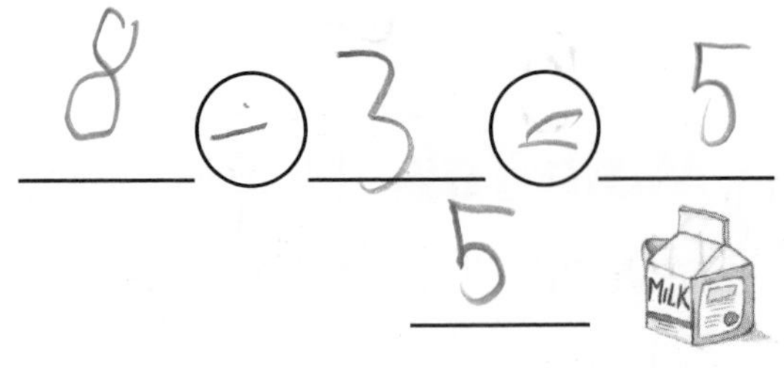
5

At Home Use the picture graph above. Have your child tell you what he or she knows about the graph.

En casa Use la pictografía de arriba. Pida a su niño que le diga lo que sabe de la pictografía.

Name ______________________

Chapter 11 Lesson 5

Use a Picture Graph

TEKS Objective
Use picture graphs to solve problems; create and solve data problems.

Learn

This graph shows how many boats are at one dock.

Boats at the Dock

Sailboat	🚣 🚣 🚣
Motorboat	🚣 🚣 🚣 🚣 🚣 🚣
Rowboat	🚣 🚣 🚣 🚣

Use the graph, then add to solve the problem.
How many sailboats and rowboats in all?

Think!
I can count the boats. Then I add to find the sum.

3 sailboats
+ 4 rowboats
7 in all

Use the graph, then subtract to solve the problem.
How many more motorboats are there than rowboats?

Think!
I can count the boats. Then I subtract to find the difference.

☐ motorboats
− ☐ rowboats
☐ more motorboats

★ Guided Problem Solving

Boats at Pier 6	
Tanker	
Fishing	
Ferry	

1. How many more tankers are there than ferry boats?

   Find the number of each kind of boat.

   Add or subtract to solve.

   _____ more tankers

2. **Math Talk** How did you find your answer?

★ Problem Solving Practice

Use the picture graph to solve.

3. How many tankers and fishing boats are there?

   _____ boats

4. How many more ferry boats are there than fishing boats?

   _____ more ferry boat

At Home Ask questions that your child can answer by using the graph.

En casa Haga preguntas que su niño pueda responder usando la gráfica.

Name Samir

Create and Solve

Susan is taking a survey. She asks 10 children about the shoes they wear. 5 children wear sneakers. 2 wear boots. 3 wear sandals.

Use the data from Susan's survey to complete the picture graph.

1.

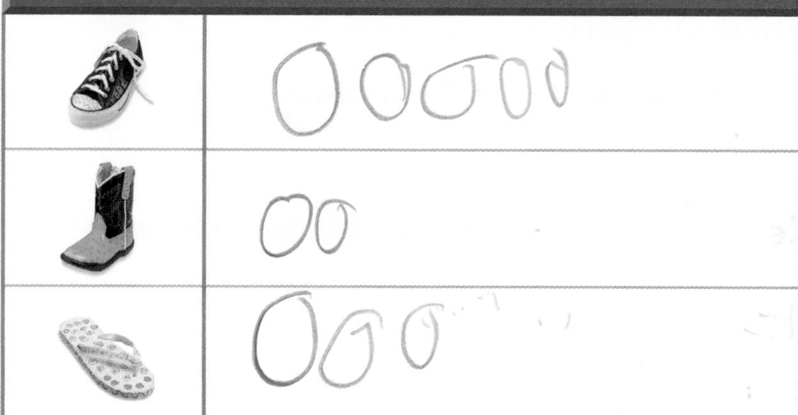

What Kind of Shoes Do You Wear?	
(sneaker)	O O O O O
(boot)	O O
(sandal)	O O O

2. How many more children wear sneakers than sandals? Write the number sentence.

5 – 3 = 2

3. How many children wear boots and sneakers? Write the number sentence.

5 + 2 = 7

TAKS Objectives 5, 6
TEKS 1.9A Collect and sort data.
TEKS 1.9B Use organized data to construct real-object graphs, picture graphs, and bar-type graphs.
TEKS 1.12A Explain and record observations using objects, words, pictures, numbers, and technology.

You are going to take a survey about the clothes 10 classmates are wearing.
Write a question for your survey.

4. What color is your shirt?

Now, take the survey.
Make a picture graph.

5.

clorch shits	
blue	0000000000
purple	0
red	000

Write one thing you learned from the picture graph.

6. Crarker pr

Name ______________________________

Use a Picture Graph

A [calculator] can help you compare numbers in a picture graph.

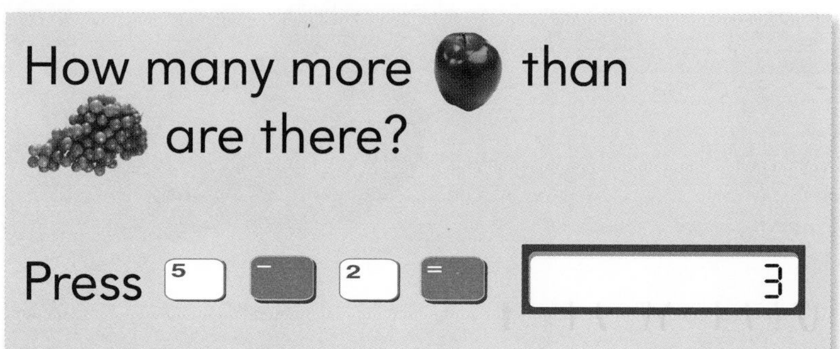

How many more than are there?
Press 5 − 2 =
3

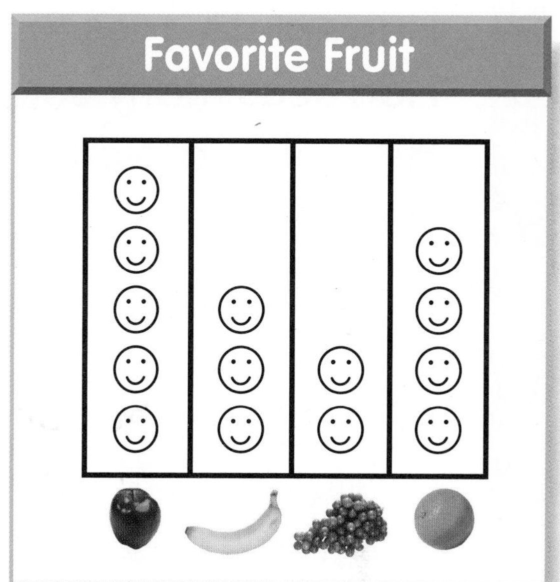

Use [calculator] and the picture graph.

1. How many [banana] and [orange] are there?

   _____ in all

2. How many fewer [grapes] than [banana] are there?

   _____ fewer

3. How many [grapes] and [orange] are there in all?

   _____ in all

4. Circle the one that has 2 fewer than [orange].

5. How many pieces of fruit are there altogether? _____

Sea Animals

Han's class goes to the aquarium.
Han sees many sea animals.
He makes a picture graph.

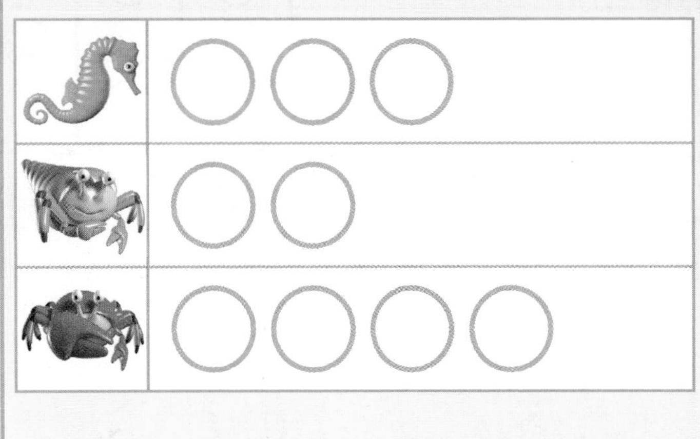

Use the picture graph to solve.

1. How many [seahorse] does he see?

   ______

2. How many [seahorse] and [hermit crab] does he see?

   ______

3. How many more [crab] than [seahorse] does he see?

   ______

TAKS Objective 5
TEKS 1.10A Draw conclusions and answer questions using information organized in real-object graphs, picture graphs, and bar-type graphs.

TEKS Science 2A, 2E

Name ______________________________

Concepts and Skills

Use the picture.
Complete the tally chart. TEKS 1.9A

1.

Our Pets	
dogs	
cats	
birds	

Use the tally chart.
Make a picture graph.
Draw a ☺ for each pet. TEKS 1.9B

2.

Our Pets	
dogs	
cats	
birds	

Use the picture graph to solve.
Each ☺ stands for 1 pet. TEKS 1.10A

3. How many birds are there?

_____

4. Which has the fewest?
Circle. TEKS 1.10A

dogs cats birds

Problem Solving TEKS 1.10A, 1.11A

Use the picture graph to solve.

5. How many children choose juice and pretzel?

_____ children

TAKS Prep and Spiral Review

Choose the answer for problems 1–4.

1. Which figure shows a cylinder?

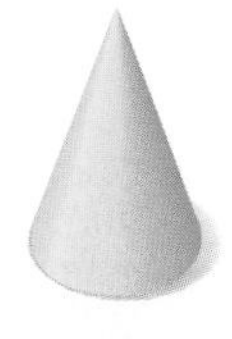
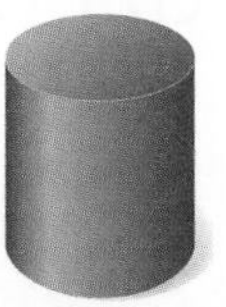

○ ○ ○ ○

TEKS 1.6B (page 167)

2. Which object matches the figure?

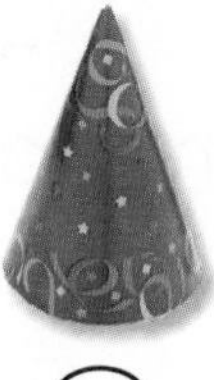

○ ○ ○ ○

TEKS 1.6B (page 167)

3. Lisa picks 2 red flowers. Then she picks 3 yellow flowers. How many flowers does she pick in all?

2	3	4	5
○	○	○	○

TEKS 1.3B (page 111)

4. Jim has 8 fish. He gives 1 fish away. How many are left?

9	7	6	5
○	○	○	○

TEKS 1.3B (page 123)

Education Place
Visit **www.eduplace.com/txmap/** for Test-Taking Tips and Extra Practice.

Graphing and Probability

TAKS Vocabulary

Here are some vocabulary words you will learn in the chapter.

bar-type graph Shaded boxes that look like bars show information

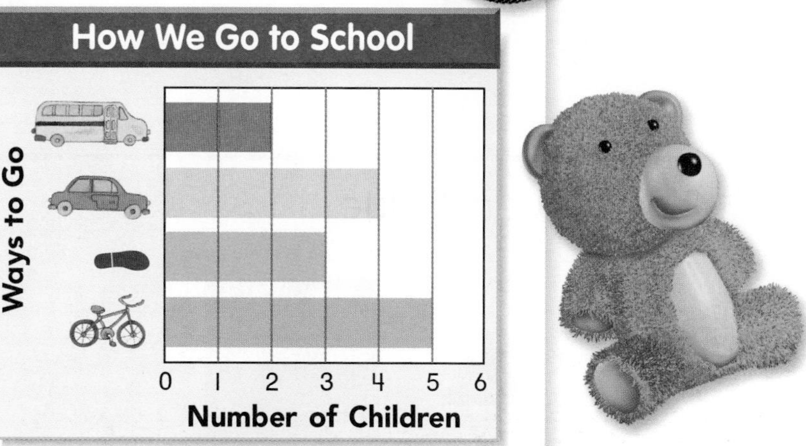

certain Sure to happen
It is certain you will spin blue on this spinner.

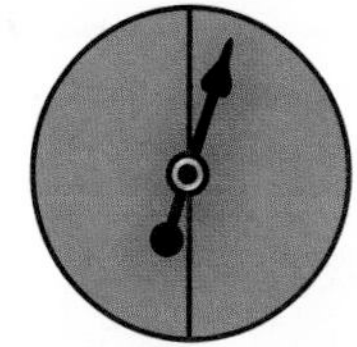

impossible Not able to happen
It is impossible to spin blue on this spinner.

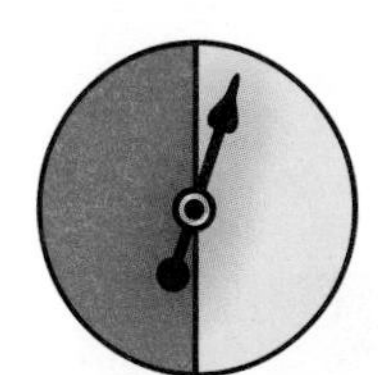

predict Use what you know to tell what you think will happen
I predict that the ice will melt.

See English-Spanish glossary pages 505–516.

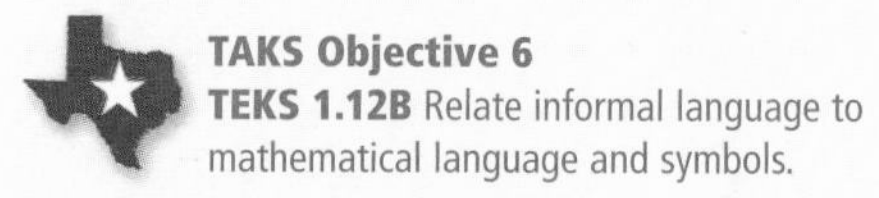

TAKS Objective 6
TEKS 1.12B Relate informal language to mathematical language and symbols.

Education Place
Visit www.eduplace.com/txmap/ for the eGlossary and vocabulary eGames.

Name ______________________

Check What You Know

Read the sorting rule.
Circle the figures that follow the rule.

1. 4 corners

2. Small and blue

     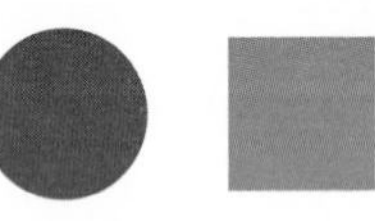

Use the picture to answer the question.

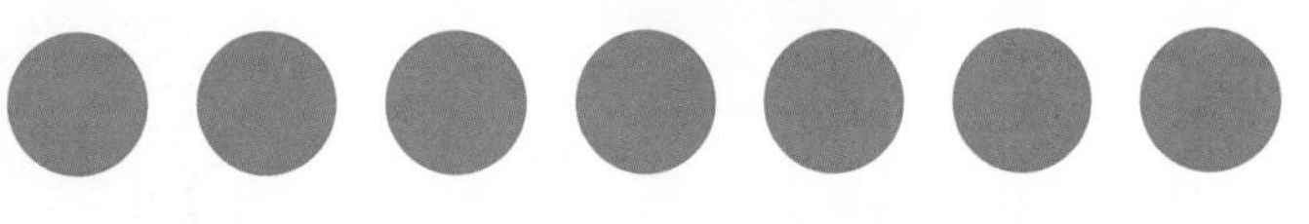

3. How many more than ? ____

4. How many fewer than ? ____

Name ______________________________

Chapter 12 Lesson 1

Make a Bar-Type Graph

★ Explore

Make a **tally chart.** Ask 8 children their favorite color bike.
Make 1 tally for each answer.

1.

Favorite Bike Color	
(bike)	
(bike)	
(bike)	
(bike)	

Hands On

TEKS Objective
Collect and sort data; use a tally chart to make a bar-type graph.

TAKS Vocabulary
tally chart
bar-type graph

Think!
How many choose red? I make that many tally marks.

Use the tally chart to make a **bar-type graph.** Color 1 box for each tally.

2.

3. Math Talk Ask a question about the bar-type graph.

TAKS Objective 5
TEKS 1.9A Collect and sort data.
TEKS 1.9B Use organized data to construct real-object graphs, picture graphs, and bar-type graphs.
TEKS 1.10A Draw conclusions and answer questions using information organized in real-object graphs, picture graphs, and bar-type graphs.

★ Extend

Use the picture.
Make a bar-type graph.

4.

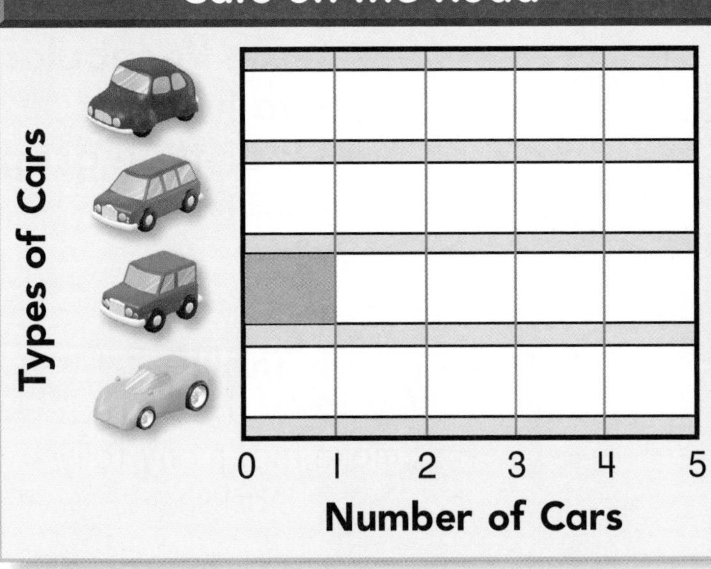

Use the bar-type graph to solve.

5. How many kinds of cars are there?
 4 kinds

6. How many are there?
 ____

7. Circle the one that has 1 more than .

8. How many more than are there?
 ____ more

9. Are there fewer or ? Circle.

10. How many and are there?

11. Circle which has the greatest number of cars.

12. Circle which has the least number of cars.

At Home Give your child various coins. Help him or her make a bar-type graph showing each type of coin.

En casa Dé un puñado de monedas variadas a su niño. Ayúdelo a hacer una gráfica de barras que muestre cada tipo de moneda.

Name ____________________

Chapter 12 Lesson 2

Read a Bar-Type Graph

TEKS Objective
Answer questions using information organized in bar-type graphs.

★ Learn

This bar-type graph tells how many children choose each snack.

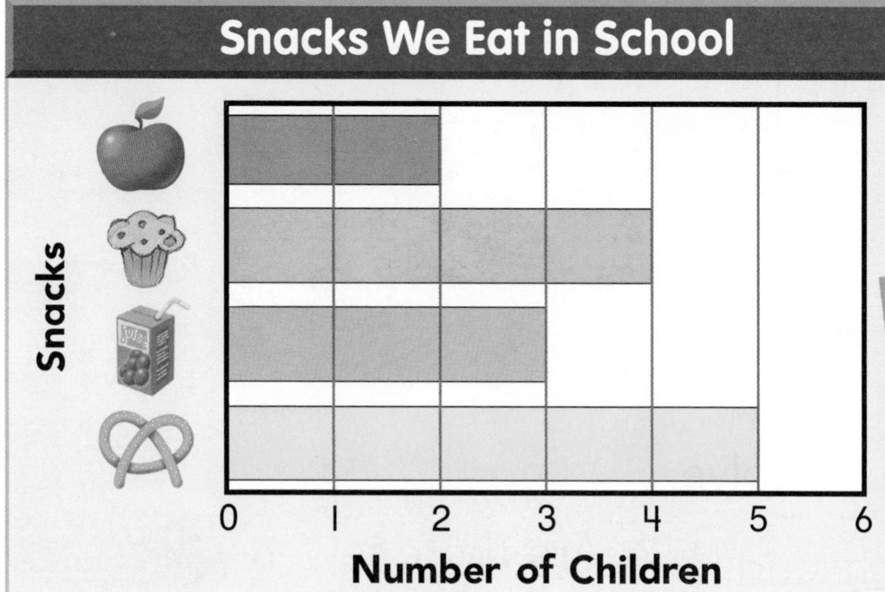

Think!
I look where the bar ends in the apple row.

★ Guided Practice

Use the bar-type graph to solve.

1. How many children choose ?

   _____ children

2. How many children choose ?

   _____ children

3. Circle the snack more children choose.

4. Circle the snack fewer children choose.

5. **Math Talk** If you choose a snack, how will the bar-type graph change?

TAKS Objective 5
TEKS 1.10A Draw conclusions and answer questions using information organized in real-object graphs, picture graphs, and bar-type graphs.

★ Practice

The bar-type graph shows the boats Nara sees.

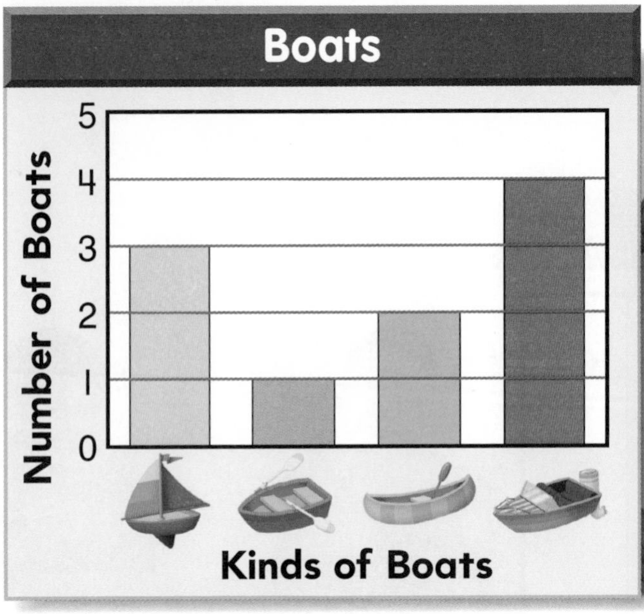
Boats
Number of Boats
0
1
2
3
4
5
Kinds of Boats

Remember!
Look at the number where the bar ends to know how many.

Use the bar-type graph to solve.

6. There are 4 of which kind of boat? Circle.

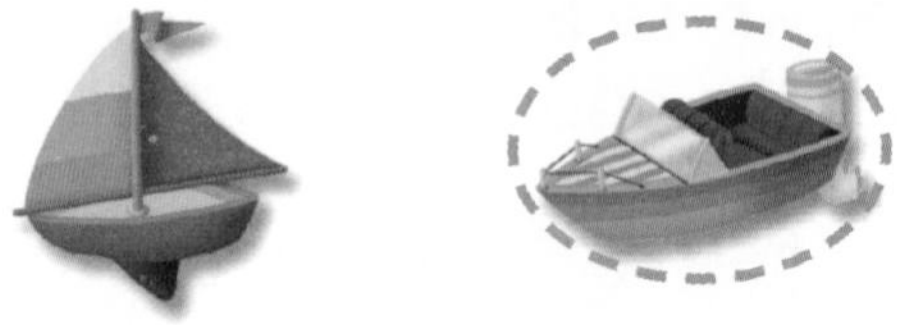

7. Are there fewer  or  ? Circle.

8. How many  and  are there?

_____

9. How many more  than  are there?

_____ more

Reading Math: Vocabulary

Show the tally marks for each number.

10. _______________ eleven

11. _______________ thirteen

12. _______________ eight

At Home Ask your child questions about the graph above.

En casa Haga preguntas a su niño sobre la gráfica de arriba.

Name ____________________

Chapter 12 Lesson 3

Certain or Impossible

TEKS **Objective**
Identify events as certain or impossible.

TAKS **Vocabulary**
certain
impossible

It is **certain** that the sun will set.

It is **impossible** for sheep to fly.

Guided Practice

Circle the sentence if it is certain.
Cross it out if it is impossible.

Think!
I know rain makes everything wet.

1. 
You get wet in the rain without an umbrella.

2. 
A ball rolls down a hill.

3. 
A real dinosaur comes into the classroom.

4. 
A crayon makes a mark on the paper.

5. **Math Talk** How do you know that something is certain?

TAKS Objective 5
TEKS 1.10B Identify events as certain or impossible such as drawing a red crayon from a bag of green crayons.

 Practice

Circle the sentence if it is certain.
Cross it out if it is impossible.

6. 

A strawberry grows to be as tall as you.

7. 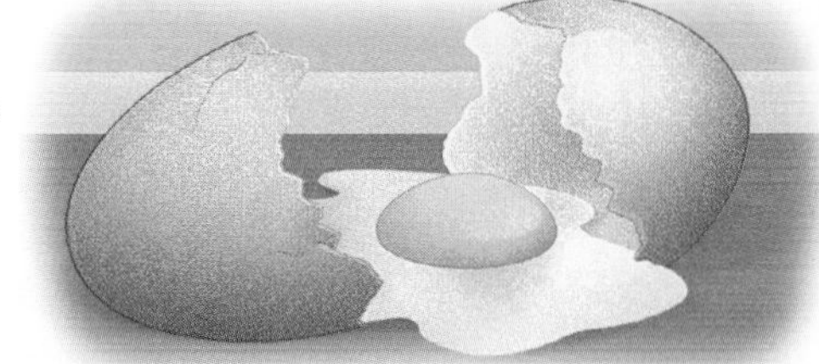

You drop an egg. It breaks.

8. 

A cat will jump rope.

9. 

A fish walks down the street.

10. 

Ice cream melts on a hot day.

11. 

You stand in the sun and you see your shadow.

Problem Solving: Reasoning

12. Draw something that is impossible.

At Home Think of some familiar events. Ask your child to identify each as certain or impossible.

En casa Piense en algunos eventos comunes. Pida a su niño que identifique cada uno como seguro o imposible.

Name ______________________________

Chapter 12 Lesson 4

Probability

TEKS Objective
Collect and sort data to make predictions.

TAKS Vocabulary
predict

Predict what will happen when you spin a spinner. Then check your predictions.

Step 1 **Predict**

What do you think will happen when you spin each spinner?

- **Spinner A**

1. It is certain that it will point to ___blue___.

Spinner A

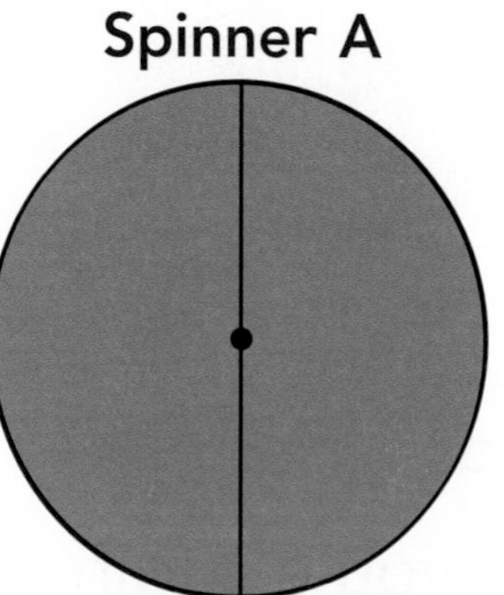

- **Spinner B**

2. It is impossible that it will point to ___blue___.

Spinner B

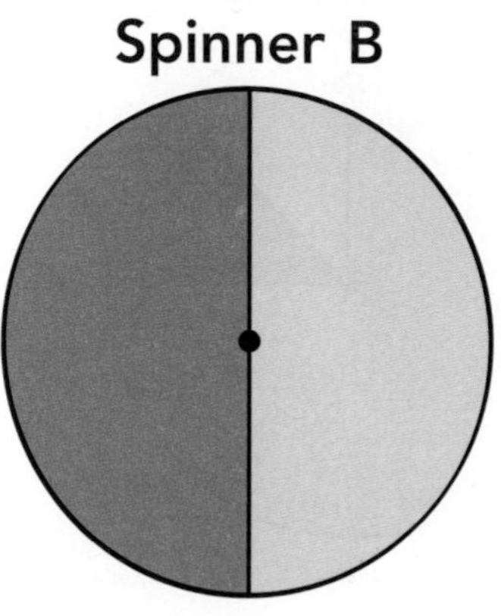

Step 2 **Spin**

Use Spinner C. Spin 10 times.
Record your spins in the tally chart.

3.

Spins	

Spinner C

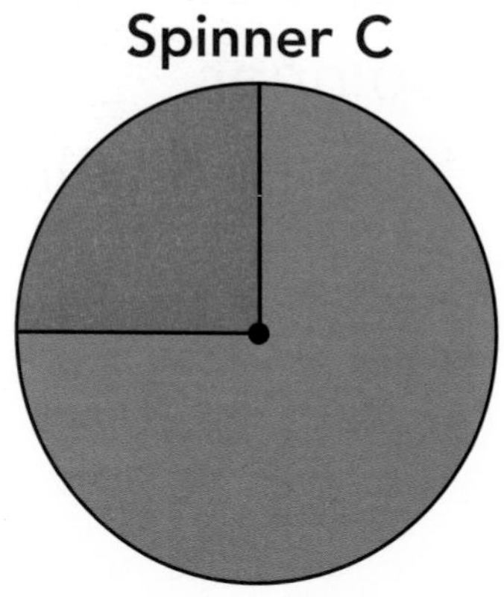

4. **Math Talk** Which color did you land on more often? Why?

★ Extend

Remember!
Record each spin as a tally.

Look at Spinner B. Predict.

5. Are you certain to spin red?

Spinner B ________________

6. Use a paper clip and a pencil. Spin 10 times. Record your spins in the tally chart.

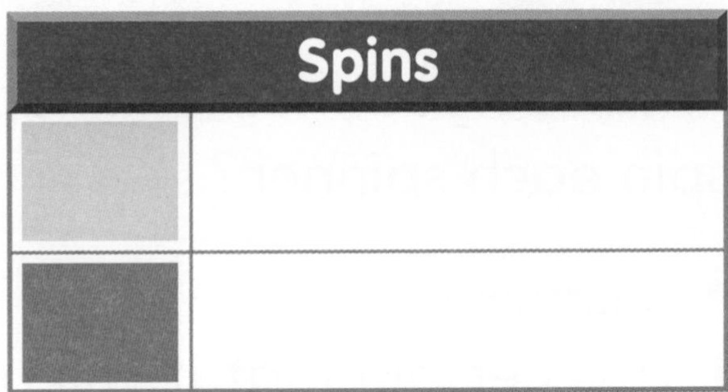

Look at Spinner D. Predict.

7. Are you certain to spin red?

Spinner D ________________

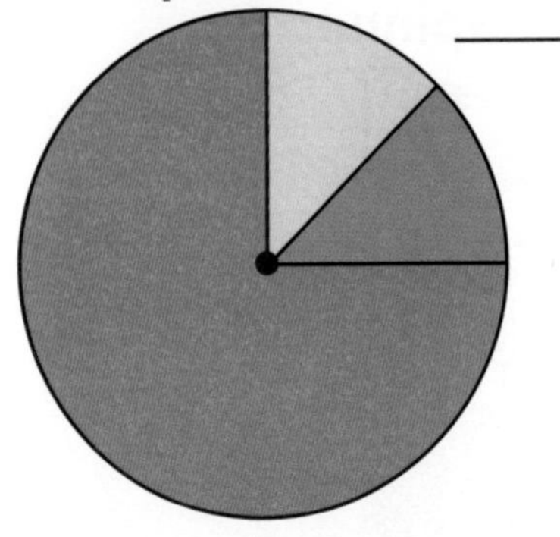

8. Spin 10 times. Record your spins in the tally chart.

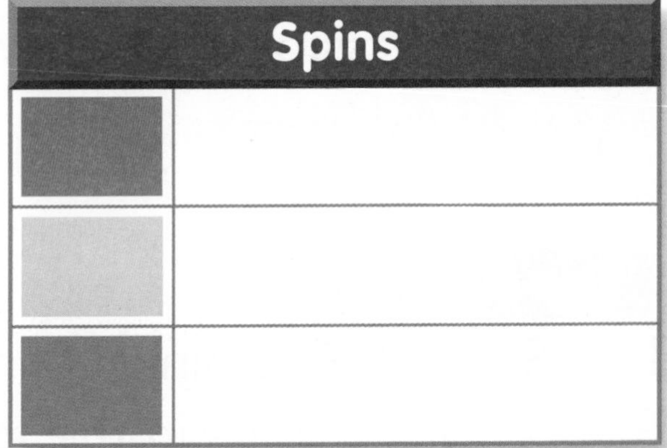

9. Draw and color your own spinner. Use blue and yellow.

Look at your spinner. Predict.

10. Are you certain to spin blue? ________________

11. Is it impossible to spin yellow? ________________

At Home Make and color a spinner. Use a paper clip and a pencil. Take turns making predictions and spinning.

En casa Haga una rueda giratoria. Use un sujetapapeles y un lápiz. Túrnense para hacer predicciones y girar la rueda.

Name ______________________

Chapter 12 Lesson 5

Guess and Check

Problem Solving Strategy

TEKS Objective
Solve problems by guessing and checking.

Learn

Manny has a bag of cubes. Hannah picks a cube from the bag. Is Hannah more likely to pick a red cube or a blue cube?

Understand

What do you know?

- There are 7 red cubes.
- There are 4 blue cubes.

Think!
There are more red cubes than blue cubes.

Plan

Make a prediction. Circle the one you think Hannah will be more likely to pick.

Solve

Try it. Pick a cube from the bag. Replace it and pick again. Pick a cube 10 times. Record what you pick in the tally chart.

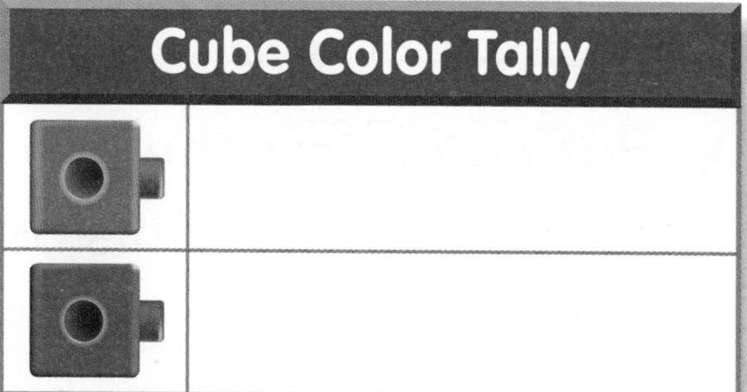

Cube Color Tally	
(red cube)	
(blue cube)	

Look Back

What color did you pick from the bag more often? Was your prediction correct?

TAKS Objectives 5, 6
TEKS 1.9A Collect and sort data.
TEKS 1.11B Solve problems with guidance that incorporates the processes of understanding the problem, making a plan, carrying out the plan, and evaluating the solution for reasonableness.
Also **TEKS 1.10B, 1.11C, 1.11D**

★ Guided Problem Solving

Think!
I count 8 green and 3 orange.

1. Gina picks a marble from the bag. Which color marble is she more likely to pick?

   Use the picture.

   Make a prediction.

   ____

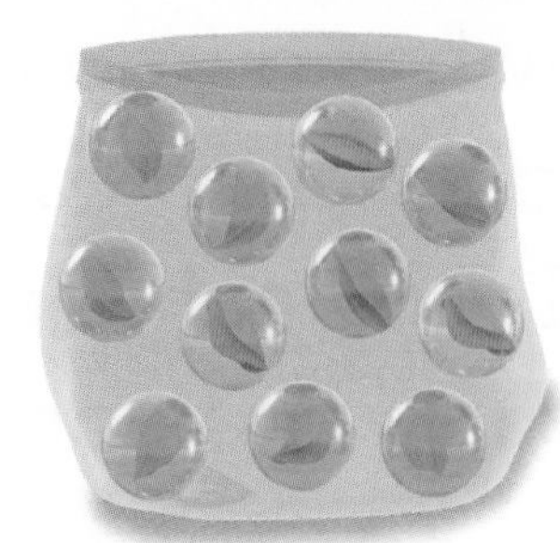

2. Math Talk How do you know which color is more likely to be picked?

★ Problem Solving Practice

Use the picture to solve.

3. Sam asks Jamal to pick a button from his bag. Which color button is he certain to pick?

   ____

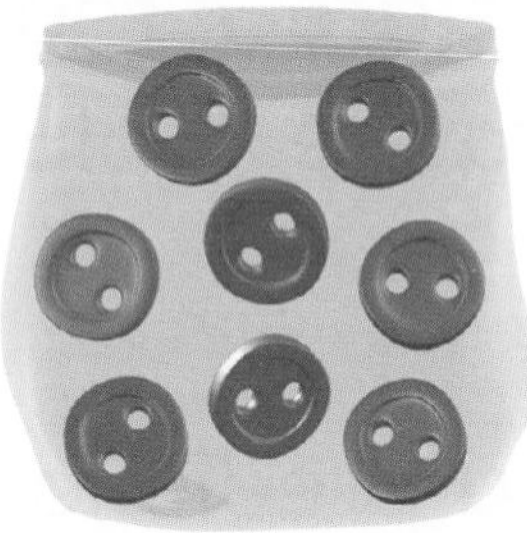

---

4. Pat compares the gold and green buttons in his bag. How many more gold than green buttons does he have?

   _____ more gold buttons

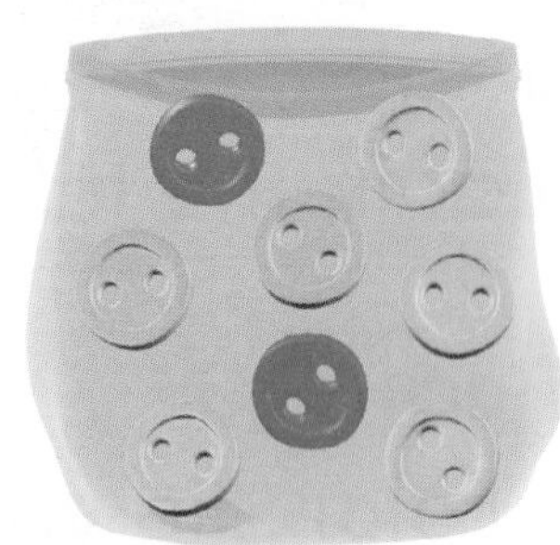

At Home Have your child try Exercise 1. Ask about the results.

En casa Pida a su niño que intente resolver el ejercicio 1. Pídale que le comente acerca del resultado.

Name ______________________________

Science

Expressions Exhibit

Texas Field Trip

Children's Museum of Houston

The Children's Museum of Houston has many things to see and do. You can explore how things work, create your own artwork, or learn about the market.

Solve. Show your work.

1. Lynn asks Carlos to pick a building block. Which color block is he more likely to pick?

   ____

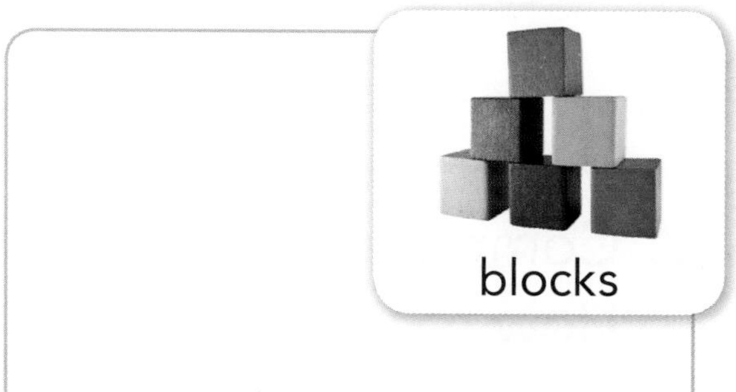

blocks

2. Nita paints this pattern at the easel. Circle the color that comes next in the pattern.

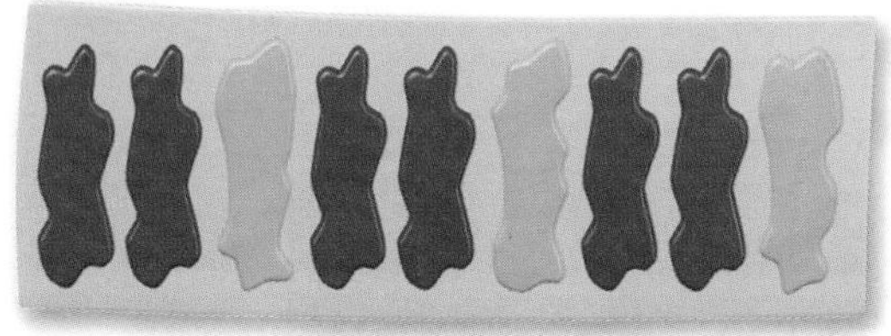

red

yellow

blue

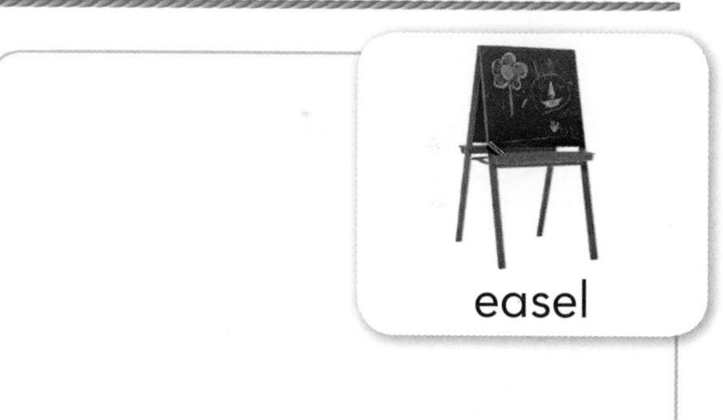

easel

3. Marta weighs 2 lemons and 2 limes in the market exhibit. She takes 1 lemon off the scale. How many fruits are being weighed now?

   _____ fruits

scale

TAKS Objective 6
TEKS 1.11A Identify mathematics in everyday situations.
TEKS 1.11C Select or develop an appropriate problem-solving plan or strategy including drawing a picture, looking for a pattern, systematic guessing and checking, or acting it out in order to solve a problem. **TEKS Science 2C**

TAKS Problem Solving
Listening Skills

Listen to your teacher read the problem. Choose the correct answer.

Select a Strategy
Guess and Check
Act It Out

1. Which color are you more likely to pick from this bag?

white ○ gray ○ black ○ blue ○

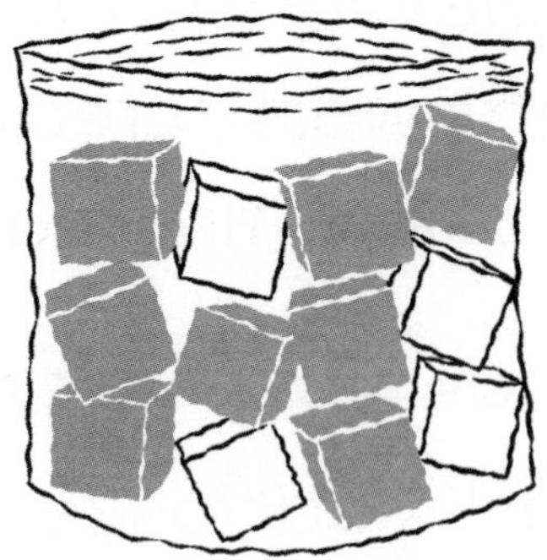

TEKS 1.11C

2. Compare the cubes in the bag. How many more gray cubes than white cubes are in there?

2 ○ 3 ○ 4 ○ 5 ○

TEKS 1.3A

3. red ○ blue ○ yellow ○ green ○

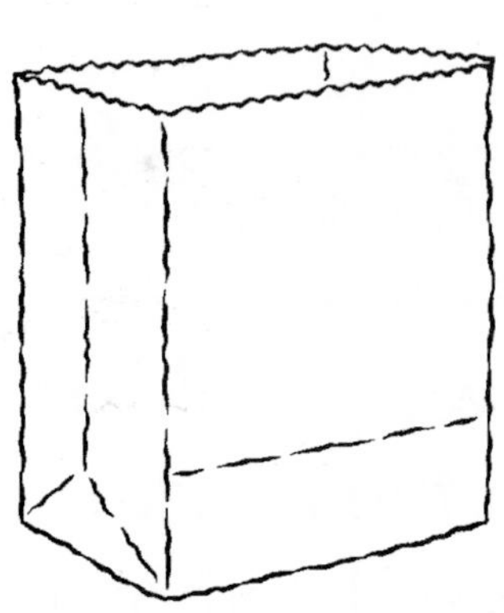

TEKS 1.10B

4. red ○ blue ○ yellow ○ green ○

TEKS 1.10B

Education Place
Visit www.eduplace.com/txmap/ for Test-Taking Tips and more TAKS Practice.

Name ______________________

Favorite Fruit Graph

Ask 10 friends which of these fruits they like best. Make 1 tally for each answer. Complete the tally chart.

Use the tally chart to make a bar-type graph.

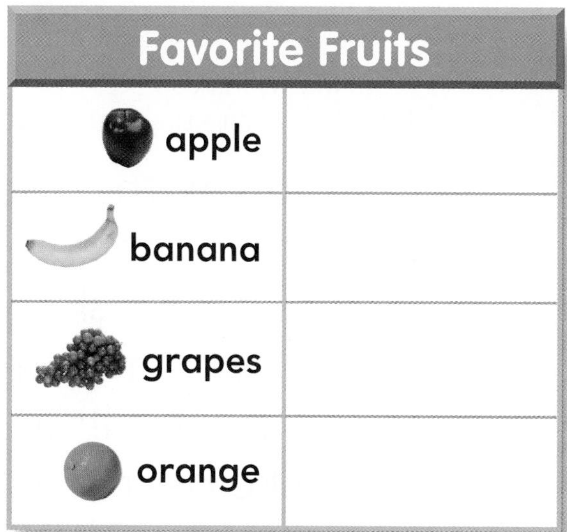

Favorite Fruits	
apple	
banana	
grapes	
orange	

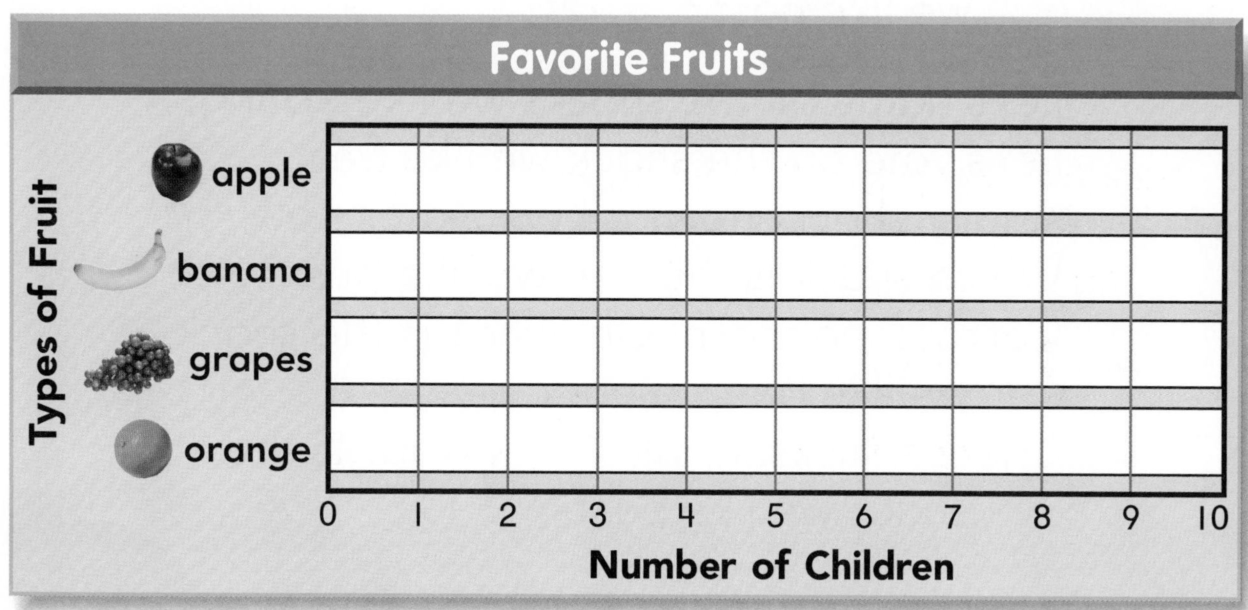

Use the graph to answer the questions.

1. Which fruit do most children choose? ______________

2. How many children choose grapes and apples? _____ children

3. How many children choose bananas and oranges? _____ children

Math Music

What Will We Do?

Math Music, Track 5
Tune: "My Bonnie Lies Over the Ocean"

Let's name all the sports we like playing.
Let's vote on the sport we like best.
A picture graph shows all our votes now.
Which sport is the one we like best?
Softball, kickball! Oh, what is the sport
we like best to play?
Soccer, tennis! Oh, what is the sport
we like best?

Let's name all the snacks we like eating.
Let's vote on the snack we like best.
A tally chart shows all our votes now.
Which snack is the one we like best?
Carrots, popcorn! Oh, what is the snack
we like best to eat?
Cheese sticks, apples! Oh, what is the
snack we like best?

TAKS Objective 5
TEKS 1.9B Use organized data to construct real-object graphs, picture graphs, and bar-type graphs.

Name ______________________________

Concepts and Skills

1. Use the picture.
   Make a bar-type graph. TEKS 1.9A, 1.9B

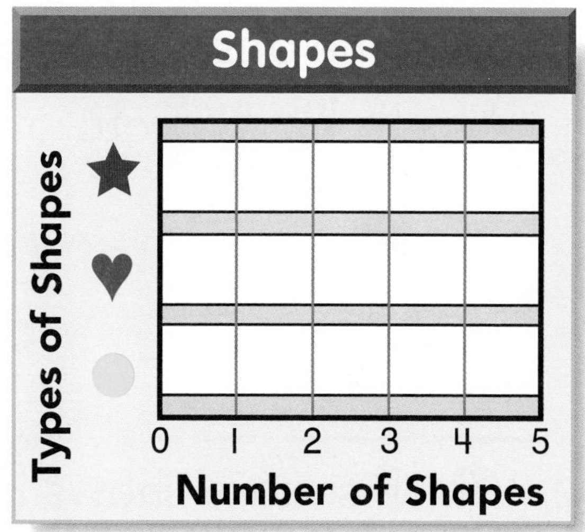

Use the bar-type graph to solve. TEKS 1.10A

2. There are 5 of which kind of shape? Circle.

3. Are there fewer  or ? Circle.

Look at the spinners.
Predict. TEKS 1.9A, 1.10B

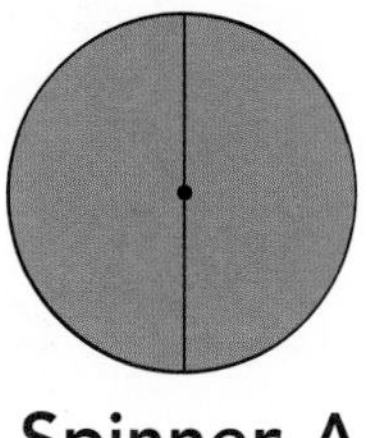
Spinner A

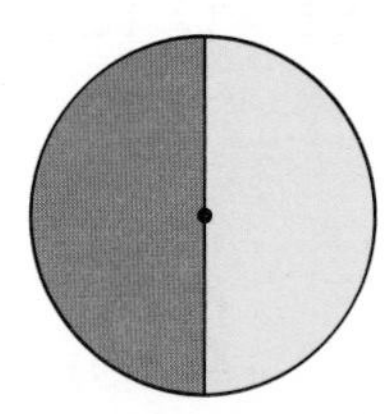
Spinner B

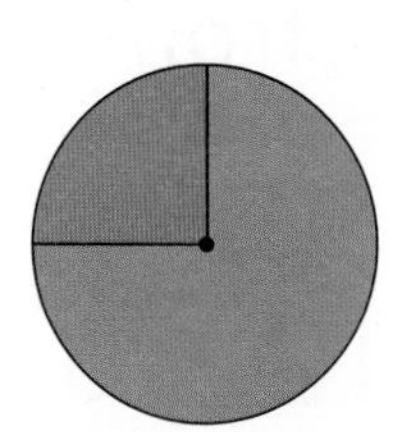
Spinner C

4. On which spinner is it impossible to spin blue? ______________

Problem Solving

Use the picture to solve. TEKS 1.9A, 1.10B, 1.11C

5. Chung picks a cube from the bag.
   Which color is he certain to pick?

   _____ cube

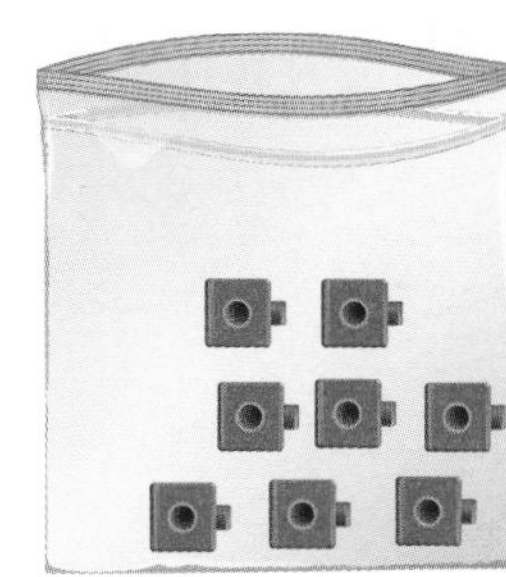

TAKS Prep and Spiral Review

Choose the answer for problems 1–4.

1. Which shows 1 out of 3 equal parts colored red?

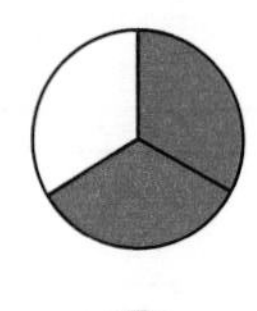 ○ 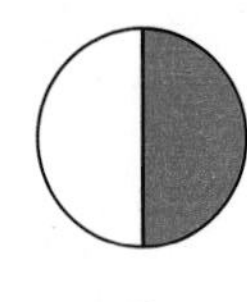 ○ 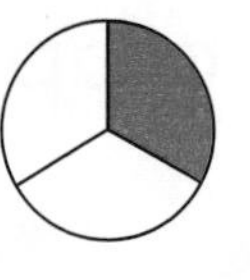 ○ 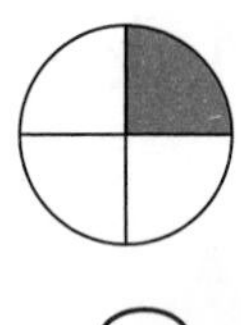 ○

TEKS 1.2A (page 185)

2. Which square shows 2 out of 4 equal parts colored yellow?

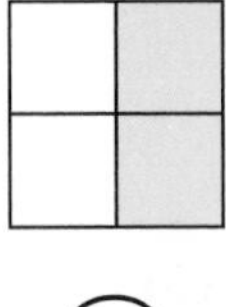 ○ 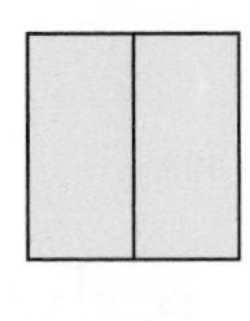 ○ 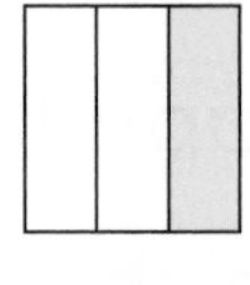 ○ 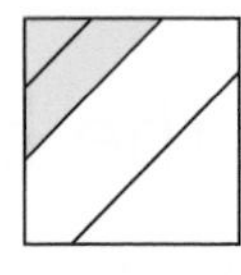 ○

TEKS 1.2A (page 185)

3. Which shows the number of marbles in order from greatest to least?

20  12 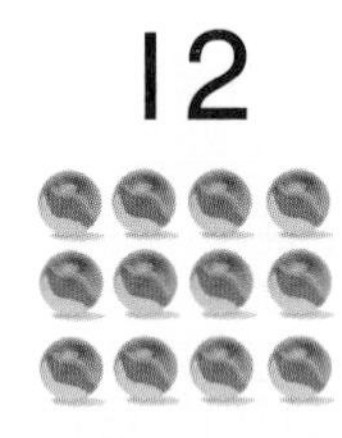 15 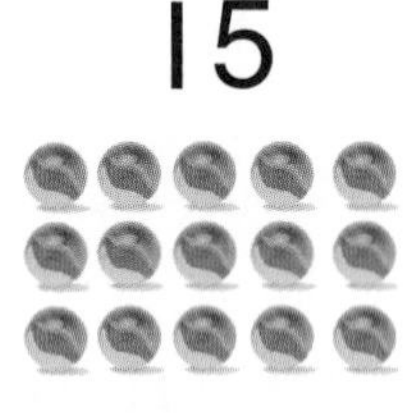

12, 15, 20 ○ 20, 15, 12 ○ 20, 12, 15 ○ 15, 12, 20 ○

TEKS 1.1A (page 45)

4. Amy reads 6 books in one week. The number of books Jake reads is less than the number of books Amy reads. Which shows the number of books Jake reads?

 9 ○   7 ○  6 ○  4 ○

TEKS 1.1A (page 25)

Education Place
Visit **www.eduplace.com/txmap/** for Test-Taking Tips and Extra Practice.

Name ______________________

Greg Tang's **Go Fast, Go Far**

Unit 5 **Mental Math Strategies**

Add 3

Adding 3 is fast and fun. First add 2 and then add 1.

I start with 4. I add 2 to get 6. Then I add 1 to get 7.

1. 4 + 3 = [7]
   [2] + [1]

2. 2 + 3 = [ ]
   [ ] + [1]

3. 5 + 3 = [ ]
   [ ] + [ ]

4. 6 + 3 = [ ]
   [ ] + [ ]

Keep It Up!

Take It Further: Now try doing everything in your head!

5. 5 + 3 = [ ]
6. 1 + 3 = [ ]
7. 4 + 3 = [ ]
8. 2 + 3 = [ ]
9. 7 + 3 = [ ]
10. 3 + 3 = [ ]

Name ______________________________

Reading and Writing Math

Aaron asked 10 classmates to choose a favorite pet. This tally chart shows their answers.

Favorite Pets	
dog	卌
cat	||||
bird	|

1. Use the tally chart to complete a bar-type graph.

2. **Writing Math** If there are 5 dog stickers, 4 cat stickers, and 1 bird sticker in a bag, are you certain to pick a dog sticker? Explain.

____

____

____

TEKS 1.12A Explain and record observations using objects, words, pictures, numbers, and technology.

TEKS 1.12B Relate informal language to mathematical language and symbols.

Name ______________________________

Concepts and Skills

Use the tally chart to make a bar-type graph. Color 1 box for each tally. TEKS 1.9A, 1.9B, 1.10A

1.

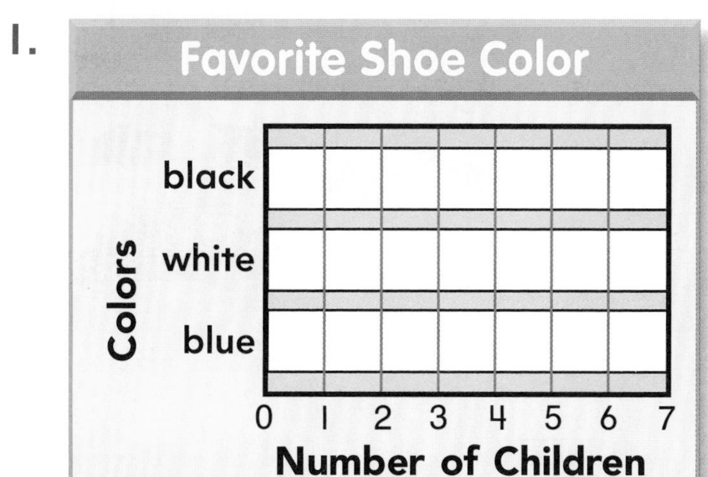

Favorite Shoe Color	
black	卌 |
white	|||
blue	卌

Use the bar-type graph to solve. TEKS 1.10A

2. How many children choose white shoes?

_____ children

3. Do more children choose black or blue shoes? Circle.

black blue

Circle the sentence if it is certain. Cross out if it is impossible. TEKS 1.10B

4.

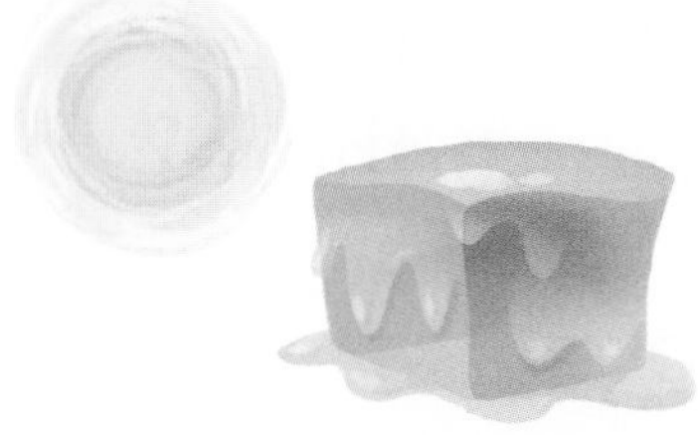

An ice cube will melt in the sun.

5.

A cow can jump over the moon.

6. Use the picture.
Complete the tally chart.
Cross out I toy. Then make I tally. TEKS 1.9A

Toys	

7. Use the tally chart.
Make a picture graph.
Draw I to stand for each toy. TEKS 1.9B, 1.10A

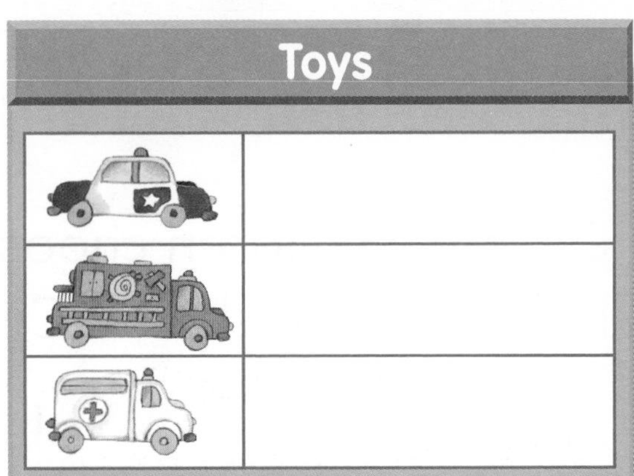

Problem Solving

Use the picture graph to solve. TEKS 1.10A, 1.11A

8. How many fewer than are there?

_____ fewer

9. How many more than are there?

_____ more

10. How many and are there? _____

Numbers Through 99

BIG IDEAS!

- You can model and name numbers through 99 in more than one way.
- You can count on, count back, or skip count to make a number pattern.
- You can use pairs of numbers to compare and order numbers.

Songs and Games

Math Music Track 6
The Skip-Counting Game!
eGames
www.eduplace.com/txmap/

Literature

Literature Big Book

- Round Up A Texas Number Book

Math Readers

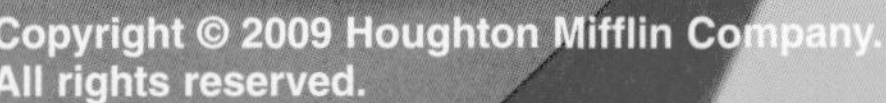

ISBN-13: 978-0-618-95275-5
ISBN-10: 0-618-95275-6
89- WC - 16 15 14 13 12

Get Ready **Game**

Trade Them!

What You Need
2 players

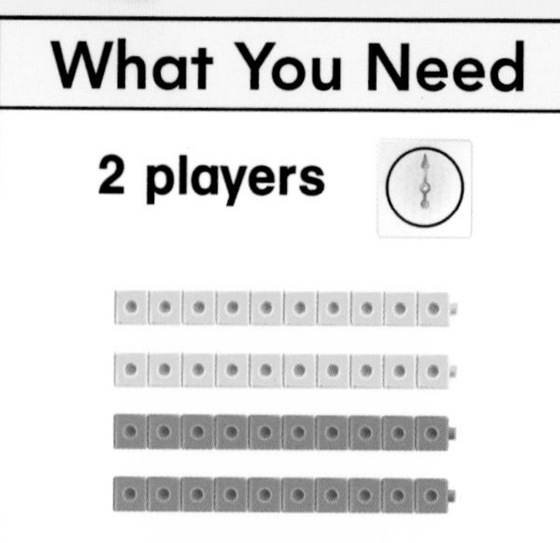

1. Take turns. Spin the spinner.
2. Take the same number of cubes as the number shown on the spinner.
3. Connect the cubes until your cube train is 10 cubes long.
4. Play until both players make 2 ten-cube trains.

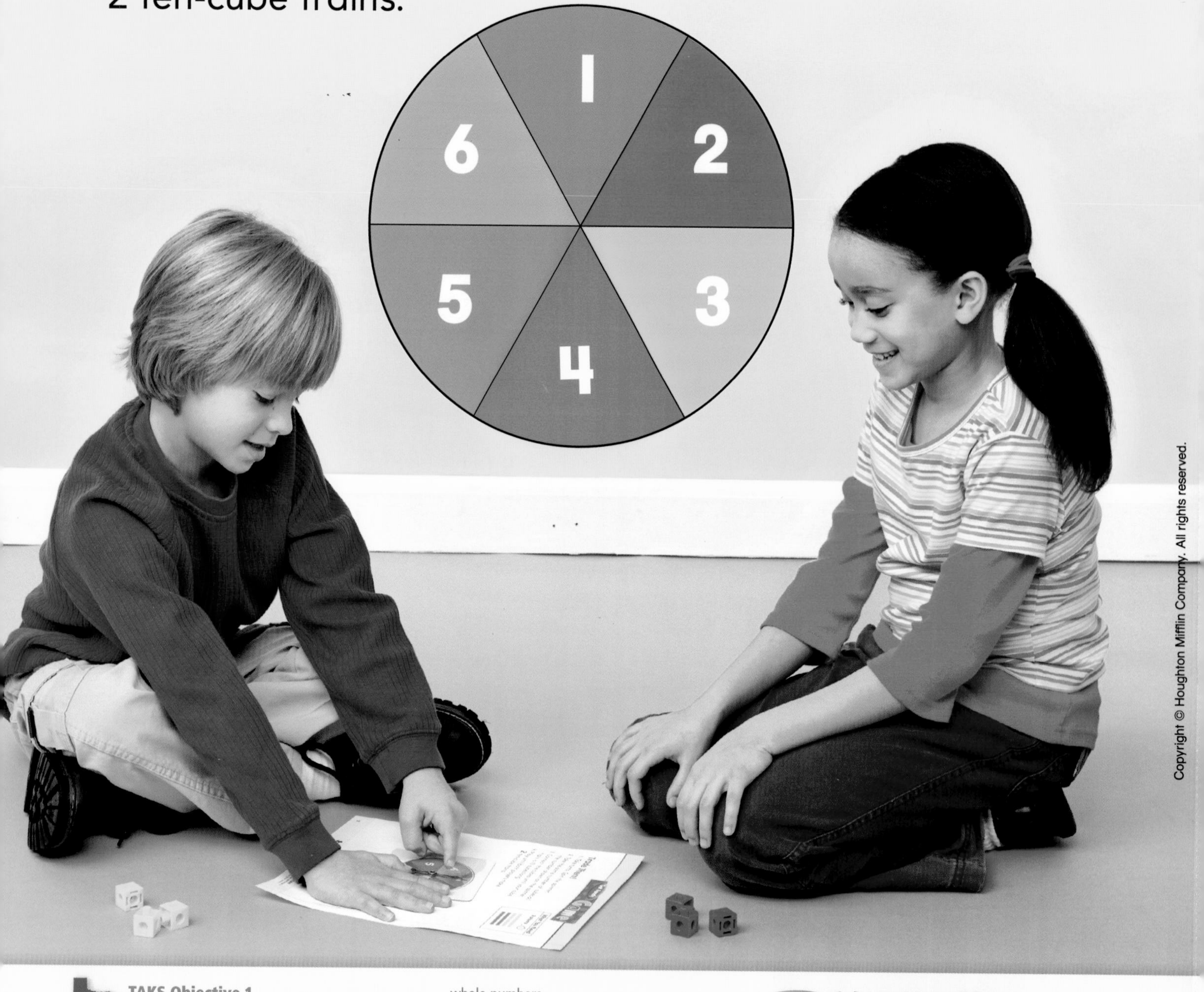

TAKS Objective 1
TEKS 1.1B Create sets of tens and ones using concrete objects to describe, compare, and order whole numbers.
TEKS 1.1D Read and write numbers to 99 to describe sets of concrete objects.

Education Place
For eGames and Brain Teasers, visit **www.eduplace.com/txmap/**

Math at Home

Dear Family,

My class is starting Unit 6, **Numbers Through 99**. I will learn about place value and number patterns. You can help me learn these vocabulary words, and we can do the Math Activity together.

From,

____

Vocabulary

ones Single objects.

These are 5 **ones**.

tens Groups of ten objects.

These are 2 **tens**.

In the number 25, the 2 stands for 2 **tens**, and the 5 stands for 5 **ones**.

skip count Start with a number and keep adding on the same number.

2, 4, 6, 8, 10, 12...

This shows a way to **skip count** by twos.

Education Place

Visit **www.eduplace.com/txmaf/** for

- eGames and Brain Teasers
- Math at Home in other languages

Family Math Activity

Give your child a bag of 46 small objects. Together make groups of ten. Ask, *How many tens? How many ones are left over?* Have your child write the number. Repeat with other numbers to 99.

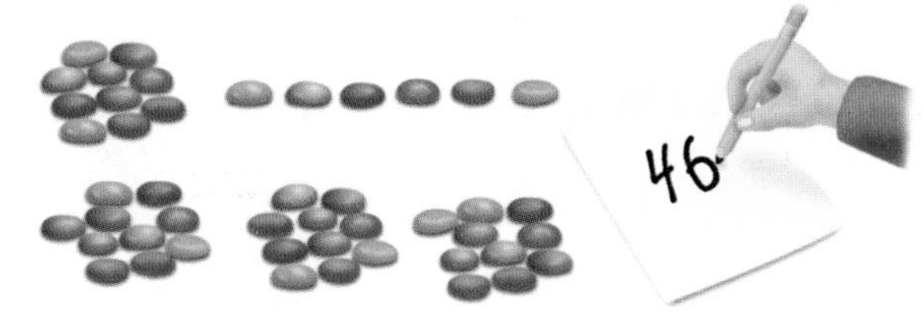

Literature

These books link to the math in this unit. Look for them at the library.

- **Ten Times Better**
  by Richard Michelson
  (Marshall Cavendish, 2003)
- **Each Orange Had 8 Slices: A Counting Book**
  By Paul Giganti, Jr.
- **One Watermelon Seed**
  by Cecilia Barker Lottridge

Matemáticas en casa

Estimada familia:

Mi clase está comenzando la Unidad 6, **Los números hasta el 99**. Voy a aprender sobre el valor de posición y los patrones numéricos. Me pueden ayudar a aprender estas palabras de vocabulario y podemos hacer juntos la Actividad de matemáticas para la familia.

De:

____

Vocabulario

unidades Objetos individuales.

Éstas son 5 **unidades.**

decenas Grupos de diez objetos.

Éstas son 2 **decenas.**

En el número 25, el 2 representa 2 **decenas,** y el 5 representa 5 **unidades.**

contar salteado Comenzar con un número y contar sumando siempre el mismo número.

2, 4, 6, 8, 10, 12...

Esto muestra una forma de **contar salteado** de dos en dos.

Education Place

Visite **www.eduplace.com/txmaf/** para

- Juegos en línea y acertijos
- Matemáticas en casa, en otros idiomas

Actividad de matemáticas para la familia

Dé a su niño una bolsa con 46 objetos pequeños. Juntos formen grupos de diez. Pregunte: *¿Cuántas decenas se forman? ¿Cuántas unidades quedan?* Pida a su niño que escriba el número. Repita con otros números hasta el 99.

Literatura

Estos libros hablan sobre las matemáticas de esta unidad. Podemos buscarlos en la biblioteca.

- **Los números (El osito estudiante)** por Arianna Candel *(Barron's Educational Series, Incorporated, 2004)*
- **Los 100 primeros días de escuela de Emilia** por Rosemary Wells, Liwaiwai Alonso

2, 4, 6, 8!
What kind of project would YOU make?
Draw your project idea here.

TAKS Objectives 2, 6
TEKS 1.5A, 1.11A, 1.11C

UNIT 6

What Did I Make?

written by Mike Mason

This Take-Home Book belongs to

____

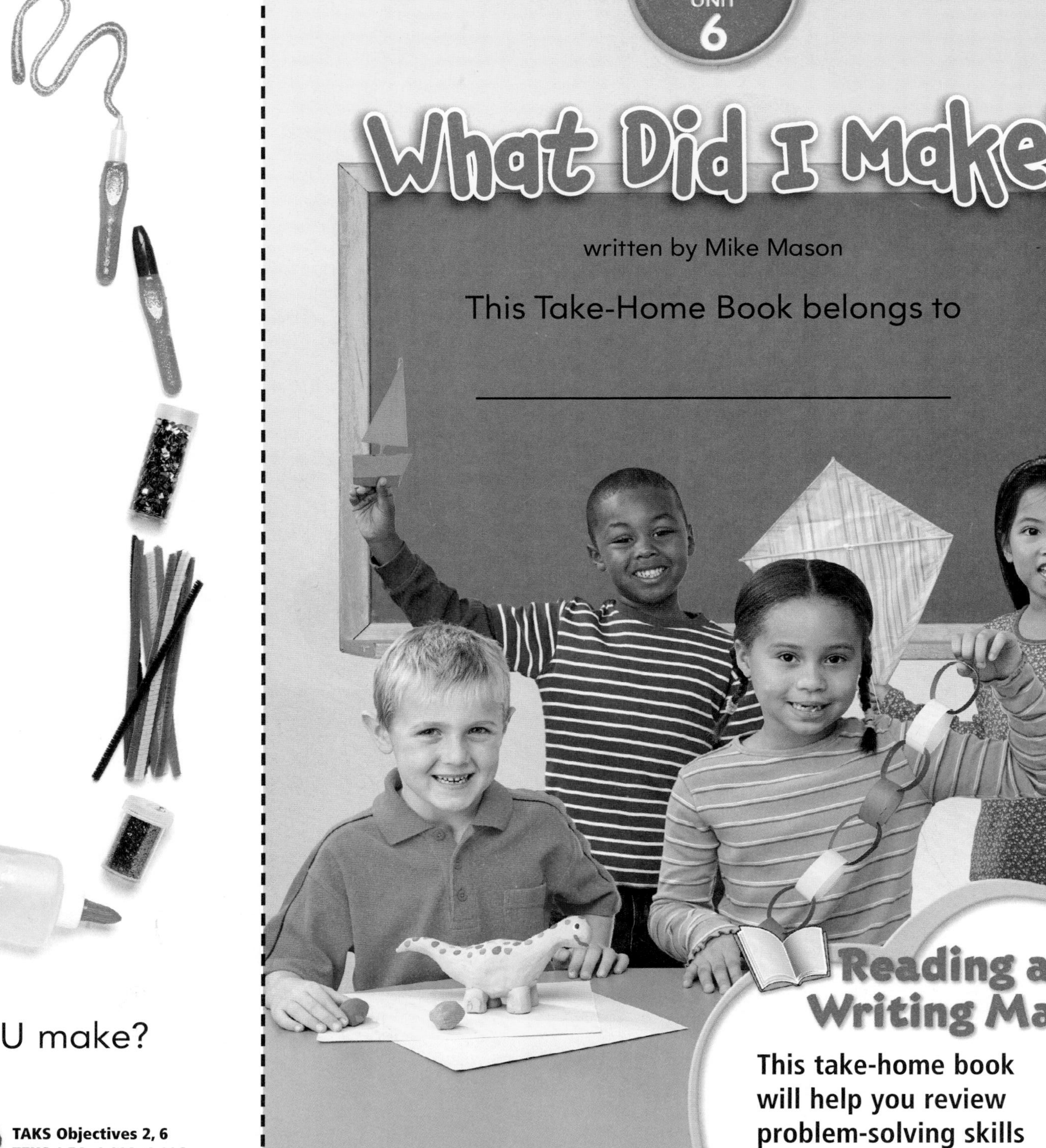

Reading and Writing Math

This take-home book will help you review problem-solving skills and counting by twos.

1, 2 . . . 3, 4 . . . 5, 6!
I used three sets of toothpicks.
I also used paper and glue.

Circle the projects that you think would be fun to make.

1, 2 . . . 3, 4 . . . 5, 6 . . . 7, 8!
Making things is really great!

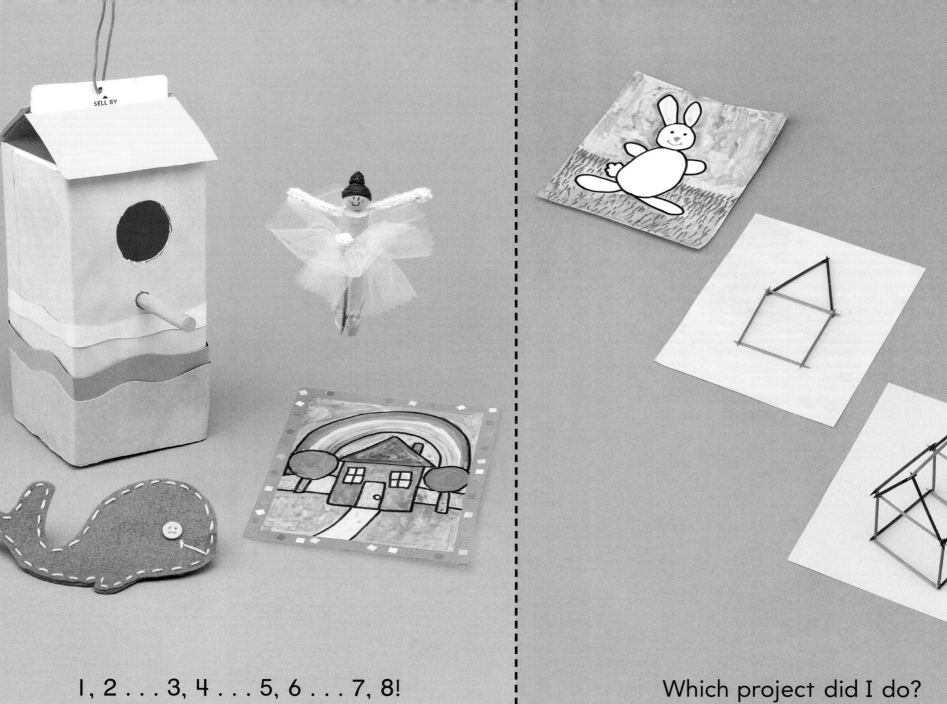

Which project did I do?
Circle my project.

2, 4, 6, 8!
I cut 8 strips and laid them straight.
I curled all 8 and stapled, too.

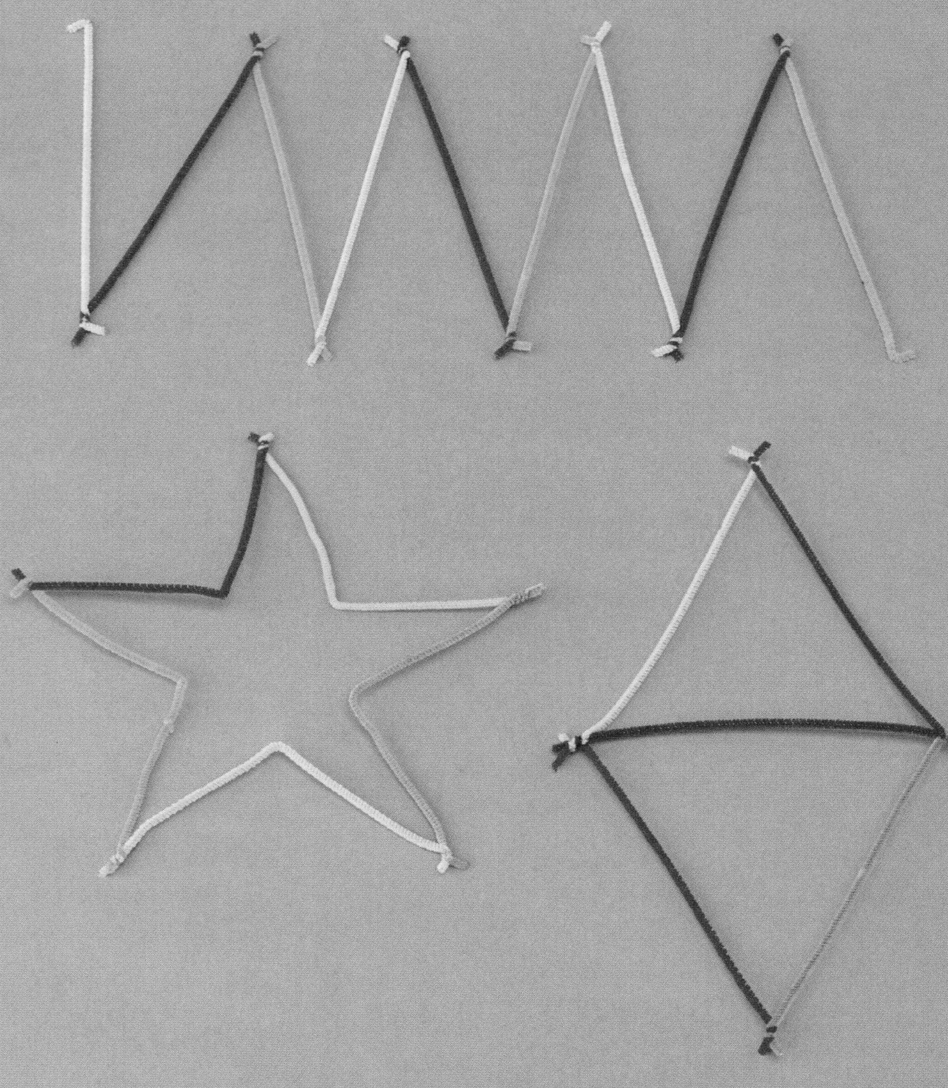

Which pipe cleaner project
could be mine?
Circle it.

1, 2, 3 . . . 4, 5, 6 . . . 7, 8, 9!
3 sets of pipe cleaners I did find.
I sat right down to use all 9,
And soon I had a great design.

Which project did I do?
Circle my project.

2, 4, 6, 8, 10!
I made this with my friend Ben.

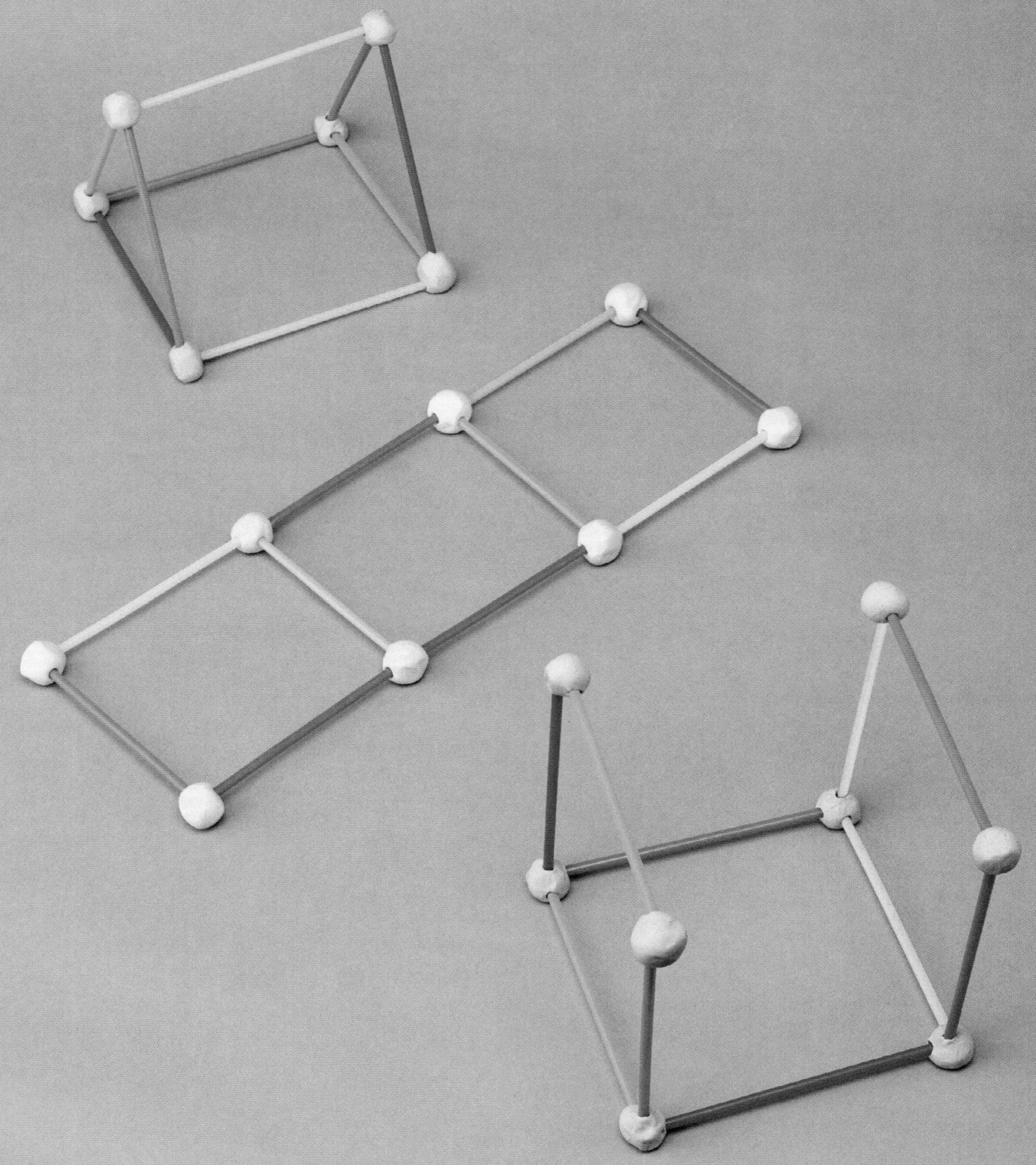

We used 10 straws, 8 balls of clay.
Which project did we do today?

Place Value Through 50

TAKS Vocabulary

Here are some vocabulary words you will learn in the chapter.

ones Single objects

4 ones

tens Groups of ten objects

2 tens

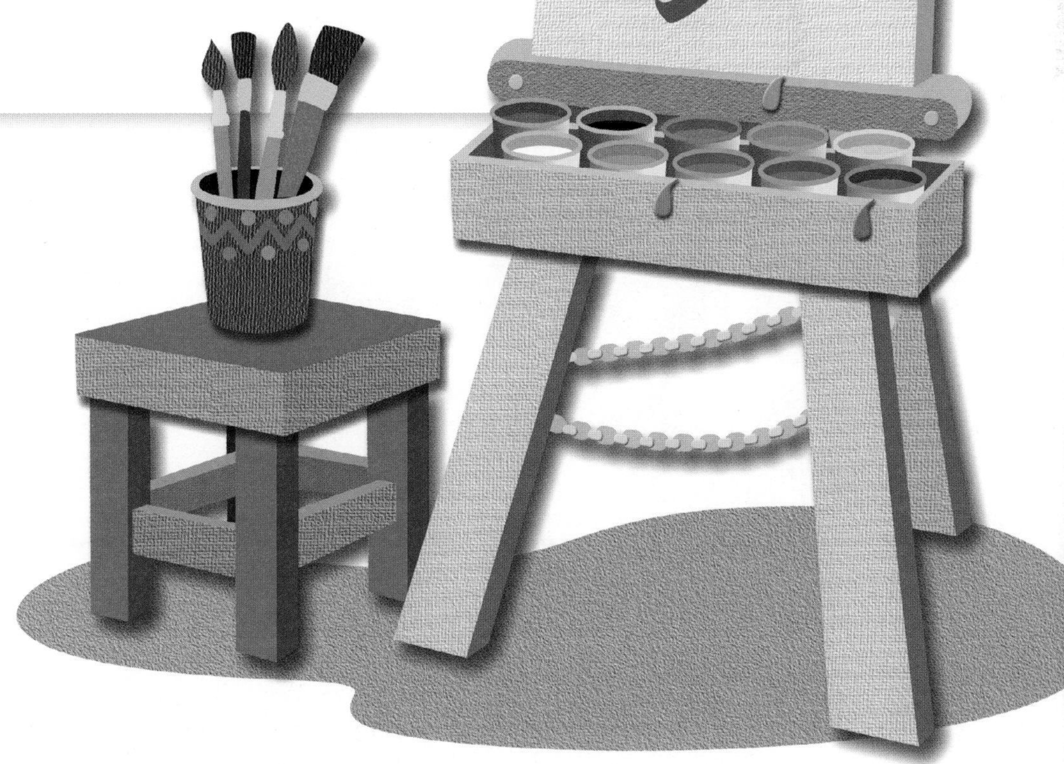

See English-Spanish glossary pages 505–516.

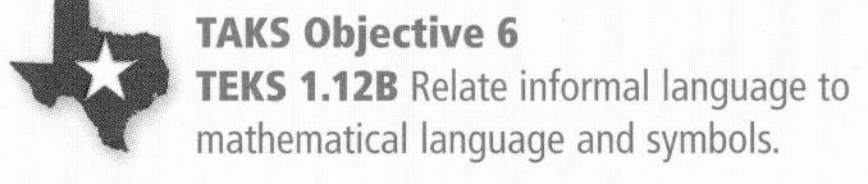

TAKS Objective 6
TEKS 1.12B Relate informal language to mathematical language and symbols.

Education Place
Visit **www.eduplace.com/txmap/** for the eGlossary and vocabulary eGames.

Name ________________________________

Check What You Know

Count how many.
Write the number.

1. ______

2. ______

3. Circle the set with 5.

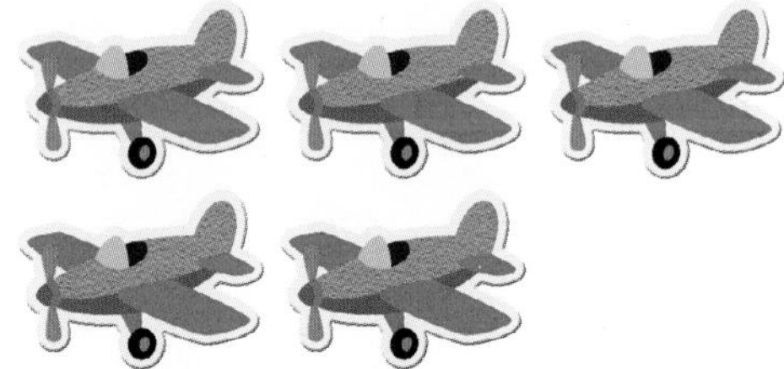

4. Circle the set with 7.

Write the missing numbers.

5. 1, 2, 3, ______, 5, 6, ______, ______, 9, ______

Use this page to review important skills needed for this chapter.

Name ___________________________

Chapter 13 Lesson 1

Count Tens

★ Learn

These cubes can be counted by **ones.**

You can also make groups of ten.
Then count the **tens.**

10 ones equal 1 ten. There are 2 tens.

Hands On

TEKS Objective
Create sets of ten; count, read, and write tens through 50.

TAKS Vocabulary
ones
tens

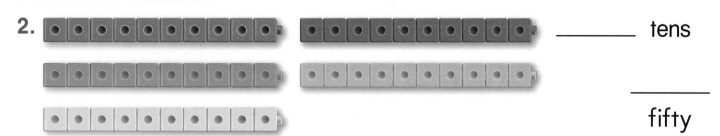

★ Guided Practice

Use ▪. Make groups of ten.
Draw the tens.
Say and write the number.

1. 3 tens

Think!
I need to show 3 tens.

_______ thirty

Write the number of tens shown.
Write the number.

2. _______ tens

_______ fifty

3. **Math Talk** How would you show the number forty with cubes?

TAKS Objective 1
TEKS 1.1B Create sets of tens and ones using concrete objects to describe, compare, and order whole numbers.

TEKS 1.1D Read and write numbers to 99 to describe sets of concrete objects.

★ Practice

Use [cube]. Make groups of ten.
Draw the tens.
Write the number.

Remember!
Count the groups of ten before you write the number.

4. 4 tens

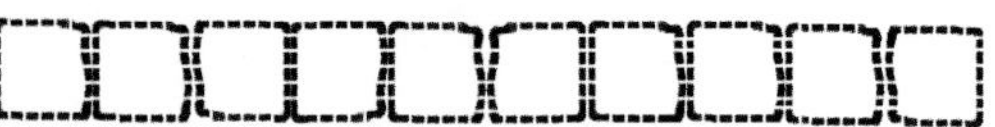

40
forty

Write the number of tens shown.
Write the number.

5. ______ tens

______
thirty

6. ______ tens

______
twenty

Problem Solving: Reasoning

This is one row of chairs.
How many chairs are in 4 rows?

7. ______ chairs

Draw or write to explain.

At Home Help your child make groups of 10 pennies. Then count the groups by tens to find the total.

En casa Ayude a su niño a hacer grupos de 10 monedas de 1 centavo. Luego cuente los grupos de diez en diez para hallar el número total de monedas de 1 centavo.

Name ________________________________

Chapter 13 Lesson 2

Teen Numbers

Hands On

TEKS Objective
Create sets of tens and ones; count, read, and write teen numbers.

Learn

Making groups of ten helps you count.

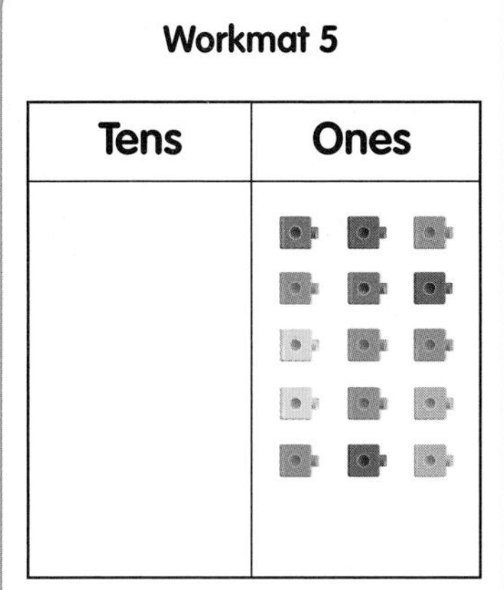

Make the 10 ones into 1 ten.

Workmat 5

Tens | Ones

15 ones is 1 ten and 5 ones.

15 ones

__1__ ten __5__ ones

Guided Practice

Think!
10 ones make 1 ten.
I have 1 one left.

Use Workmat 5 and [cube].

	Show.	Make 1 ten. Write the tens and the ones.	Write the number.
1.	11 ones	______ ten ______ one	______
2.	14 ones	______ ten ______ ones	______
3.	17 ones	______ ten ______ ones	______
4.	19 ones	______ ten ______ ones	______
5.	16 ones	______ ten ______ ones	______

6. **Math Talk** What does each digit stand for in 16?

TAKS Objective 1
TEKS 1.1B Create sets of tens and ones using concrete objects to describe, compare, and order whole numbers.

TEKS 1.1D Read and write numbers to 99 to describe sets of concrete objects.

★ Practice

Remember!
Count 10 cubes to make 1 ten.

Use Workmat 5 and ■.

	Show.	Make 1 ten. Write the tens and the ones.	Write the number.
7.	18 ones	1 ten 8 ones	18
8.	13 ones	____ ten ____ ones	____
9.	12 ones	____ ten ____ ones	____
10.	15 ones	____ ten ____ ones	____

Reading Math: Vocabulary

11. Match the blocks to the number and word.

	19	sixteen
	16	twelve
	12	nineteen
	13	thirteen

At Home Ask your child to show numbers from this lesson as tens and ones using small objects.

En casa Pida a su niño que muestre números de esta lección como decenas y unidades, usando objetos pequeños.

Name ___________________________

Chapter 13 Lesson 3

Tens and Ones

Hands On

TEKS Objective
Create sets of tens and ones; count, read, and write the number.

Learn

Remember to make groups of ten.

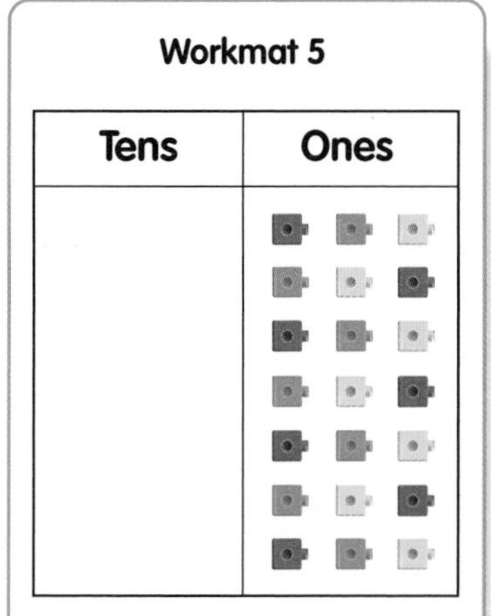

Make 10 ones into 1 ten.

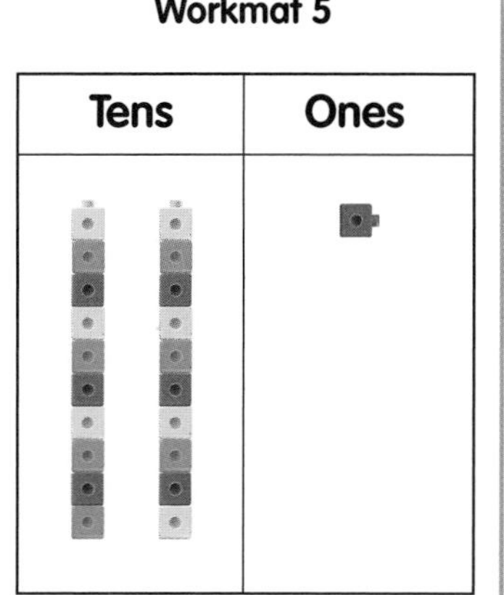

21 ones is 2 tens and 1 one.

21 ones

__2__ tens __1__ one

Guided Practice

Use Workmat 5 and ■.

	Show.	Make tens. Write the tens and the ones.	Write the number.
1.	47 ones	_____ tens _____ ones	_____
2.	31 ones	_____ tens _____ one	_____
3.	20 ones	_____ tens _____ ones	_____
4.	36 ones	_____ tens _____ ones	_____
5.	18 ones	_____ ten _____ ones	_____

6. **Math Talk** Why does it help to make 10 ones into 1 ten?

TAKS Objective 1
TEKS 1.1B Create sets of tens and ones using concrete objects to describe, compare, and order whole numbers.

TEKS 1.1D Read and write numbers to 99 to describe sets of concrete objects.

★ Practice

Use Workmat 5 and [cube].

Remember!
Make 10 ones
into 1 ten.

	Show.	Make tens. Write the tens and the ones.	Write the number.
7.	24 ones	2 tens 4 ones	24
8.	13 ones	____ ten ____ ones	____
9.	19 ones	____ ten ____ ones	____
10.	37 ones	____ tens ____ ones	____
11.	30 ones	____ tens ____ ones	____
12.	25 ones	____ tens ____ ones	____
13.	40 ones	____ tens ____ ones	____

Reading Math: Vocabulary

14. Circle the name for the missing number.
thirteen, ________, fifteen   twelve   sixteen   fourteen

15. Circle the word that is the same as five tens.   fifty   sixty   sixteen

16. Circle the word that is the same as 1 ten and 6 ones.   eighteen   thirteen   sixteen

At Home Have your child show numbers such as 25 and 14 by making tens and ones with small objects.

En casa Pida a su niño que muestre números, como 25 y 14, formando decenas y unidades con objetos pequeños.

Name ______________________________

Chapter 13 Lesson 4

Build Numbers Through 50

Hands On

TEKS Objective
Create sets of tens and ones to model, read, and write numbers through 50.

★ Learn

You can show a number as tens and ones.

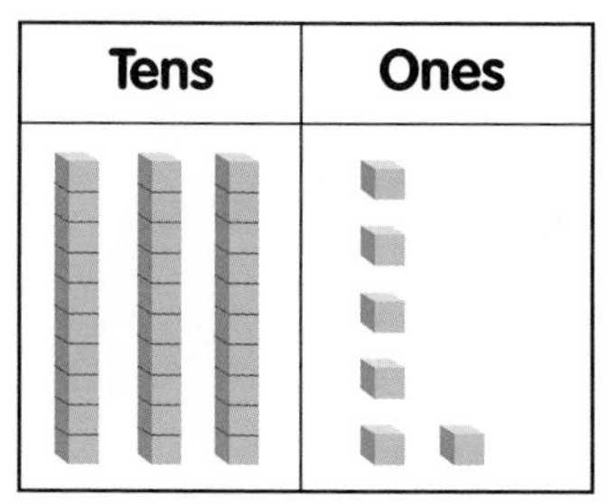

__3__ tens __6__ ones

__36__

thirty-six

★ Guided Practice

Use Workmat 5, [ten rod], and [one cube].
Show, say, and write the number.

1.

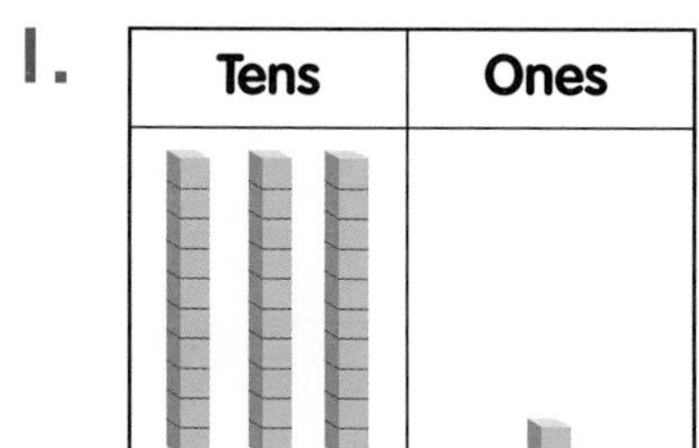

Think!
I count 3 tens and I one.

_____ tens _____ one _______
thirty-one

2.

Tens	Ones

_____ tens _____ ones _______
thirty-eight

3.

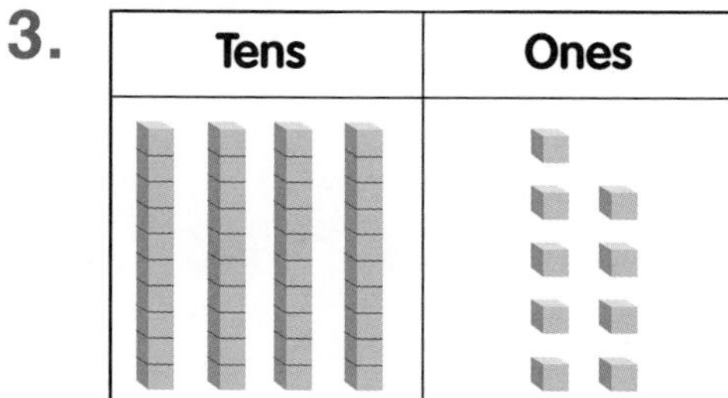

_____ tens _____ ones _______
forty-nine

4.

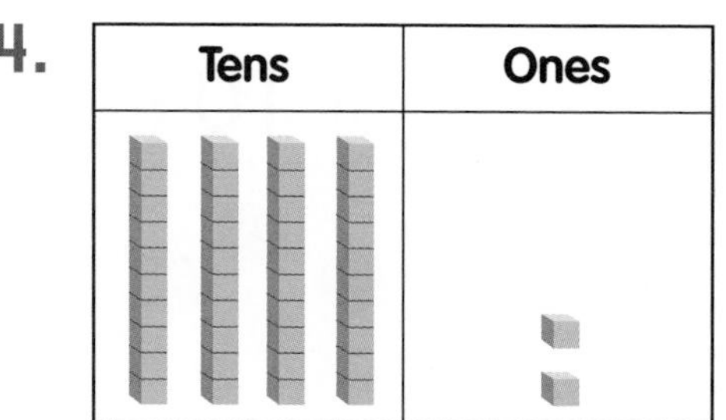

_____ tens _____ ones _______
forty-two

5. **Math Talk** How are 42 and 24 different?

TAKS Objective 1
TEKS 1.1B Create sets of tens and ones using concrete objects to describe, compare, and order whole numbers.

TEKS 1.1D Read and write numbers to 99 to describe sets of concrete objects.

★ Practice

Use Workmat 5, [ten rod], and [unit cube].
Show the number.
Write the number.

Remember!
Write the tens in the tens place.
Write the ones in the ones place.

6.

Tens	Ones
4 tens rods	4 ones cubes

4 tens 4 ones 44
forty-four

7.

Tens	Ones
3 tens rods	5 ones cubes

_____ tens _____ ones _____
thirty-five

8.

Tens	Ones
3 tens rods	7 ones cubes

_____ tens _____ ones _____
thirty-seven

9.

Tens	Ones
5 tens rods	

_____ tens _____ ones _____
fifty

Problem Solving: Number Sense

10. Circle groups of 10 buttons.

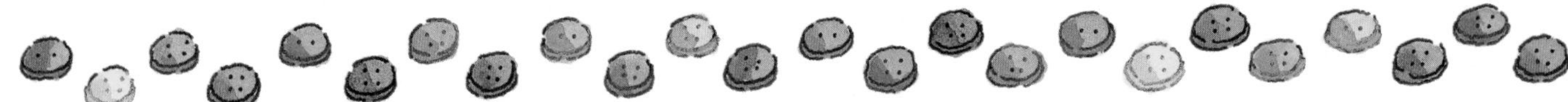

11. How many tens? _____ tens

12. How many ones? _____ ones

13. How many buttons altogether? _____

At Home Find a book with at least 50 pages. Open to different pages and ask your child to read the page number.

En casa Busque un libro que tenga al menos 50 páginas. Ábralo en diferentes páginas y pida a su niño que lea el número de página.

Name ______________________________

Chapter 13 Lesson 5

Find a Pattern

Problem Solving Strategy

TEKS Objective Identify, describe, and extend repeating and additive patterns to solve a problem.

★ Learn

Hana is making a number pattern.
What comes next in the pattern?

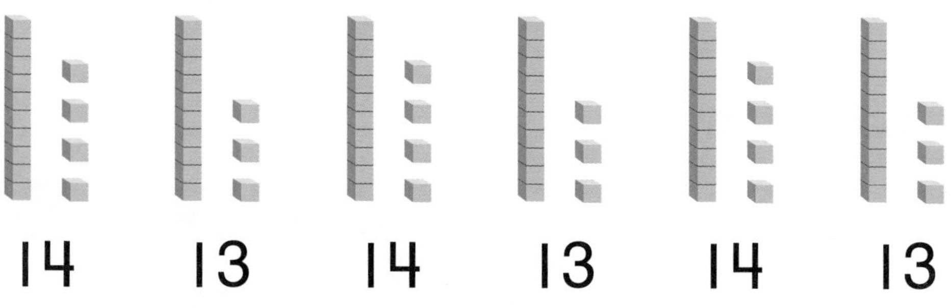

Understand

What do you know?

- The pattern is made with 2 numbers.
- 2 numbers repeat.

Plan

What part repeats?

- You can say it.

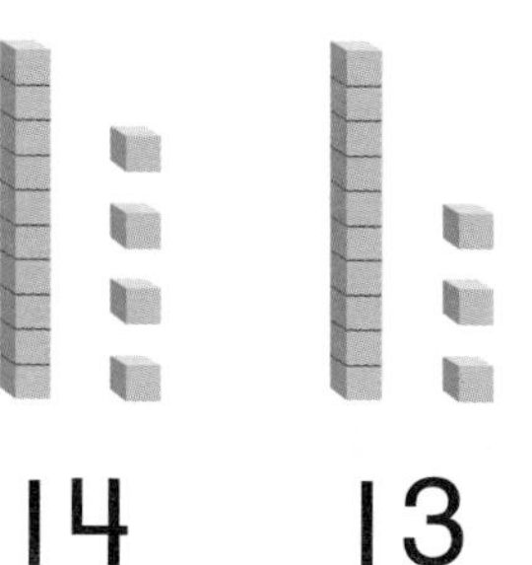

Solve

Draw and write what comes next.

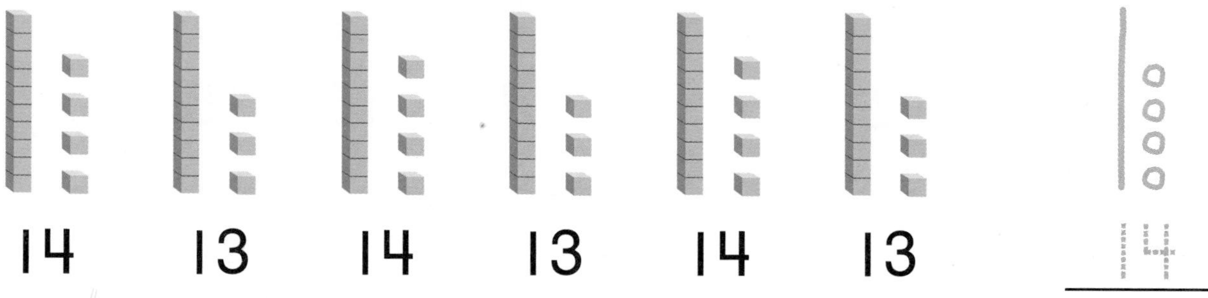

Look Back

Say the pattern. Does the number you picked fit the pattern?

TAKS Objectives 2, 6
TEKS 1.4 Identify, describe, and extend concrete and pictorial patterns in order to make predictions and solve problems.

TEKS 1.11C Select or develop an appropriate problem-solving plan or strategy including drawing a picture, looking for a pattern, systematic guessing and checking, or acting it out in order to solve a problem.

★ Guided Problem Solving

Think!
The part that repeats is 18, 16.

1. 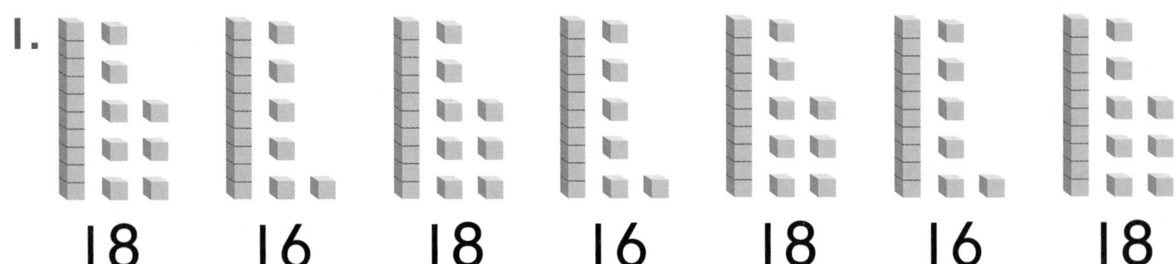

18 16 18 16 18 16 18 ______

Draw a line under the part that repeats.

Think about what comes next.

Draw and write to solve.

2. **Math Talk** How do you decide what comes next?

★ Problem Solving Practice

Find the pattern.
Draw and write what comes next.

3. 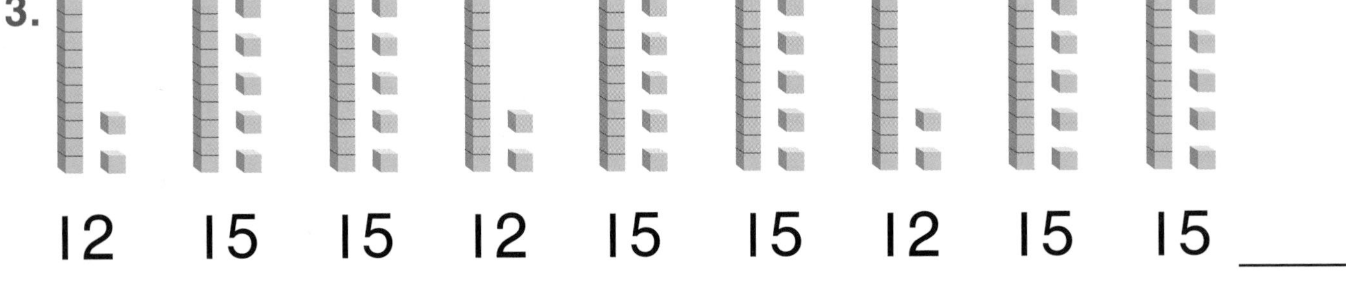

12 15 15 12 15 15 12 15 15 ______

4. 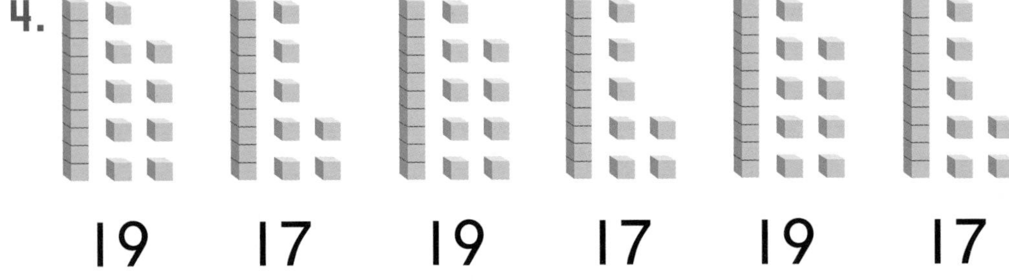

19 17 19 17 19 17 ______

At Home Ask your child to say the patterns on this page and tell how he or she decided what came next.

En casa Pida a su niño que diga en voz alta los patrones de esta página y que diga cómo decidió qué venía después en cada problema.

Name ___________________________

Create and Solve

Finding a pattern can help you solve problems.

Count and write the number of blocks. Draw and write what comes next.

Think! I know the pattern is plus 5.

1. 25 30 35 40

2. ______ ______ ______ ______

3. ______ ______ ______ ______

TAKS Objective 2
TEKS 1.4 Identify, describe, and extend concrete and pictorial patterns in order to make predictions and solve problems.

Count and write the number of blocks.
Draw and write what comes next.

4. _____ _____ _____ _____

5. _____ _____ _____ _____

Make your own pattern.
Draw the number of blocks.
Write the number.

6. _____ _____ _____ _____

Technology eManipulatives

Name ____________________

Build and Order Numbers

Use the base-ten blocks found at **www.eduplace.com/txmap/** to build and order numbers to 50.

1. Put your pointer over [icon].
   - Choose Place Value.

2. Put your pointer over the **stamp** tool.
   - Click the **ten block** 2 times.
   - Click the **one block** 4 times.
   - Click [1 2 3].

   This shows 24.

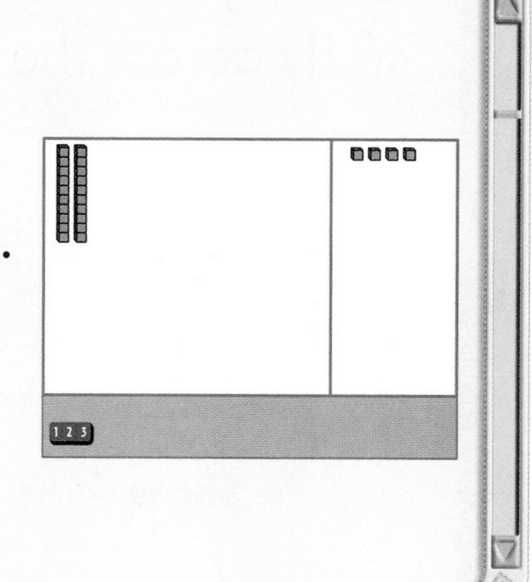

Use base-ten blocks. Write the number.

	Click the ten block.	Click the one block.	Write the number.
1.	3 times	7 times	____
2.	5 times	0 times	____
3.	2 times	2 times	____

4. Order the numbers from least to greatest.

____ ____ ____

5. **Math Talk** How does using the computer help you learn about numbers to 50?

Education Place
Visit www.eduplace.com/txmap/ for more activities.

Social Studies Link

Travel Time

Ways to travel have changed. It took weeks or months for early pioneers to cross the country by horse or train. Today it can take about 5 days to drive across the country. It takes about 5 hours to fly across the country.

Use Workmat 5 and [cube].
Find a pattern with 5.

1.

Show.	Write the number of tens.	Write the number of ones.	Write the number.
fifteen	_____ ten	_____ ones	_____
fifty	_____ tens	_____ ones	_____
five	_____ tens	_____ ones	_____
twenty-five	_____ tens	_____ ones	_____

2. Order the numbers in the chart from least to greatest.

_____ _____ _____ _____

TAKS Objective 2
TEKS 1.5A Use patterns to skip count by twos, fives, and tens.
TEKS 1.5C Compare and order whole numbers using place value.
TEKS Social Studies 16B

Name ______________________________

Concepts and Skills

Write the number of tens shown.
Write the number. TEKS 1.1D

1. ______ tens

______
fifty

Use Workmat 5 and . TEKS 1.1B, 1.1D

	Show.	Make tens. Write the tens and the ones.	Write the number.
2.	17 ones	______ ten ______ ones	______
3.	36 ones	______ tens ______ ones	______

Use Workmat 5, and .
Show the number. Write the number. TEKS 1.1B, 1.1D

4.

Tens	Ones

______ tens ______ ones ______
forty-three

Problem Solving

5. Find the pattern.
Draw and write what comes next. TEKS 1.4, 1.11B

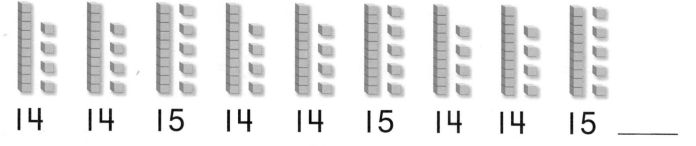

14 14 15 14 14 15 14 14 15 ______

TAKS Prep and Spiral Review

Choose the answer for problems 1–4.

1. Which figure has 3 sides and 3 corners?

 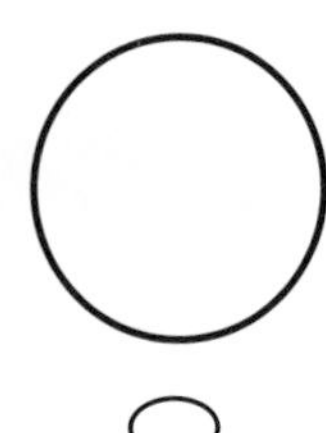 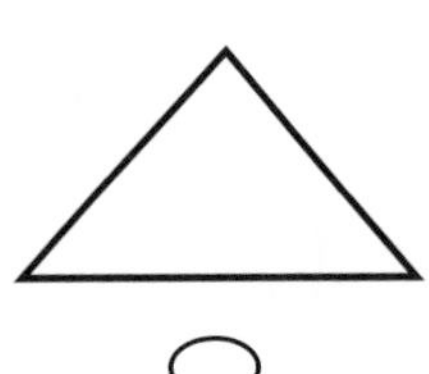  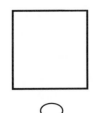

○ ○ ○ ○

TEKS 1.6C (page 147)

2. Which figure has a curved surface and a flat surface?

○ ○ ○ ○

TEKS 1.6C (page 165)

3. Mrs. Marc sewed 5 blue shirts.
She also sewed 4 red shirts.
How many shirts did she sew in all?

1	5	8	9
○	○	○	○

TEKS 1.3B (page 105)

4. Which number sentence can NOT be used to solve this problem?

$2 + 4 = 6$	$6 - 2 = 4$	$2 + 6 = 8$	$4 + 2 = 6$
○	○	○	○

TEKS 1.3B (page 131)

Education Place
Visit **www.eduplace.com/txmap/** for Test-Taking Tips and Extra Practice.

Place Value Through 99

TAKS Vocabulary

You learned these vocabulary words in Chapter 13.
You will use them again in this chapter.

ones Single objects

6 ones

tens Groups of ten objects

3 tens

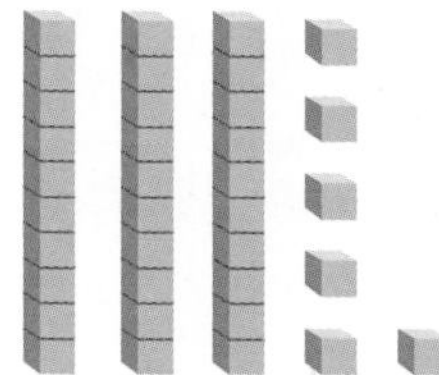

3 tens → 36 ← 6 ones

The number 36 is 3 tens and 6 ones.

See English-Spanish glossary pages 505–516.

Name ______________________________

Check What You Know

Count how many. Write the number.

1. 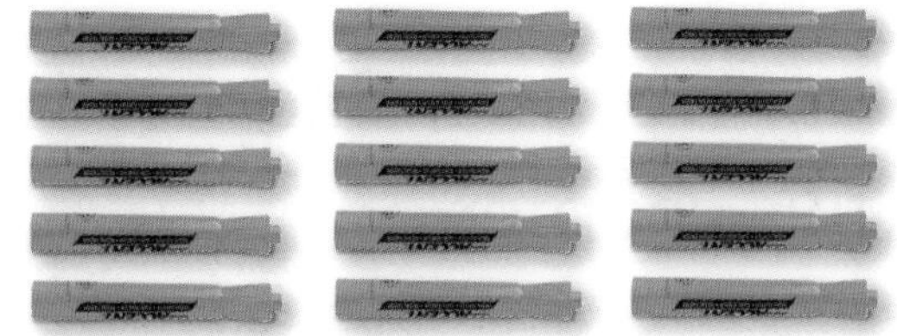

______

2. 

______

Circle a set of ten.
Write the number of tens and ones.
Write the number.

3. 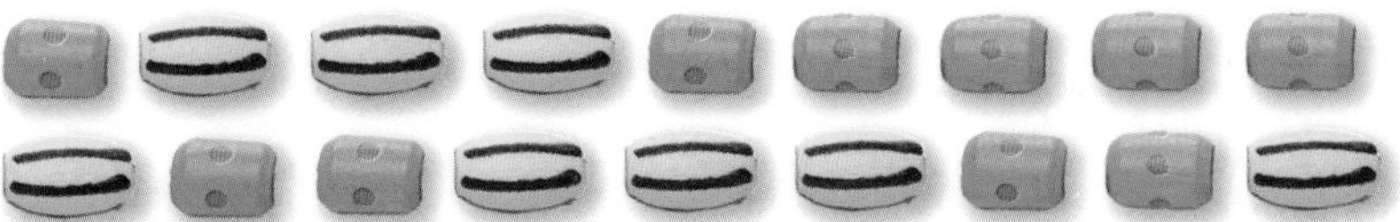

______ ten ______ ones ______

4. 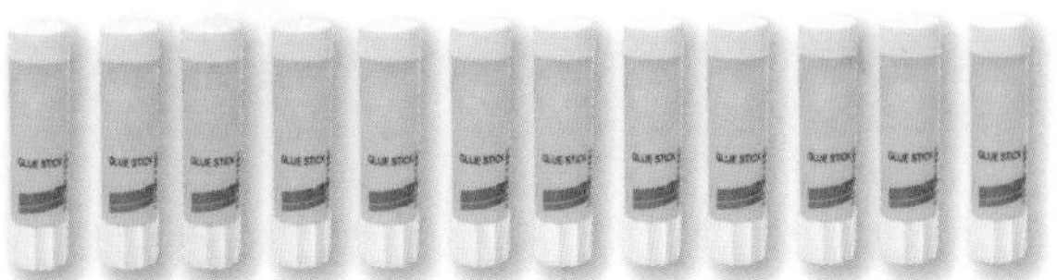

______ ten ______ ones ______

Use this page to review important skills needed for this chapter.

Name ______________________

Chapter 14 Lesson 1

Count Tens Through 90

Hands On

TEKS Objective
Create sets of ten; count, read, and write tens through 90.

★ Learn

These blocks can be counted by tens.

There are 4 tens.

4 tens equal 40.

40
forty

★ Guided Practice

Use [ten-block].
Make groups of ten. Draw the tens.
Say and write the number.

1. 5 tens

Think!
I need to show 5 tens.

______
fifty

Write the number of tens shown.
Write the number.

2. 

______ tens

______
sixty

3. **Math Talk** How would you show the number ninety?

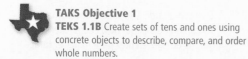

TAKS Objective 1
TEKS 1.1B Create sets of tens and ones using concrete objects to describe, compare, and order whole numbers.

TEKS 1.1D Read and write numbers to 99 to describe sets of concrete objects.

★ Practice

Use [ten rod].
Make groups of ten. Draw the tens.
Write the number.

Remember!
Count the groups of ten before you write the number.

4. 8 tens

80
eighty

Write the number of tens shown.
Write the number.

5. ______ tens

______
seventy

6. ______ tens

______
ninety

Problem Solving: Reasoning

7. Nora counts her stickers. She puts them in 6 groups of ten. How many stickers does Nora have?

______ stickers

Draw or write to explain.

At Home Help your child make groups of 10 small objects. Count the groups by tens to find the total.

En casa Ayude a su niño a hacer grupos de 10 con objetos pequeños. Luego cuenten los grupos de diez en diez para hallar el total.

Name ______________________

Chapter 14 Lesson 2

Place Value Through 99

TEKS Objective
Identify the place value of numbers through 99.

Show the number 98.

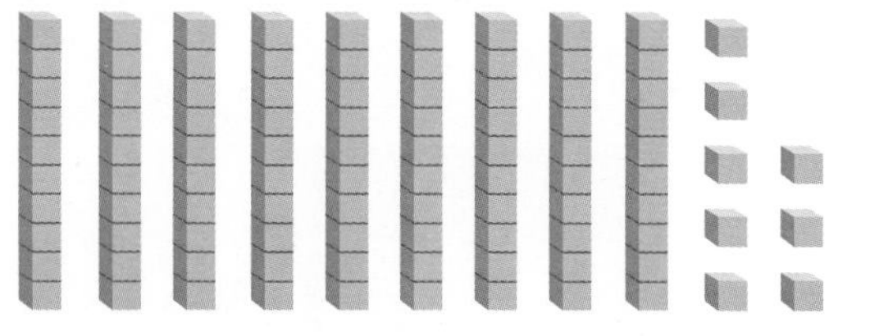

Tens	Ones
9	8

98

9 is in the tens place. 8 is in the ones place.

Guided Practice

Use [tens rod] and [ones cube].
Count the tens and the ones.
Write the tens and the ones.
Write the number.

1.

Think! I count 4 tens and 5 ones.

Tens	Ones

______

2.

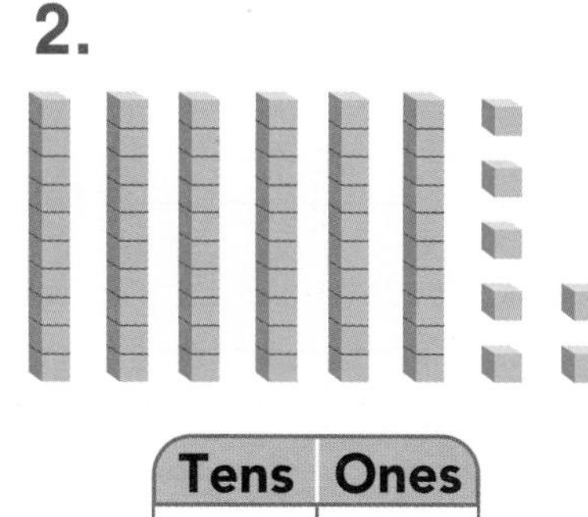

Tens	Ones

______

3.

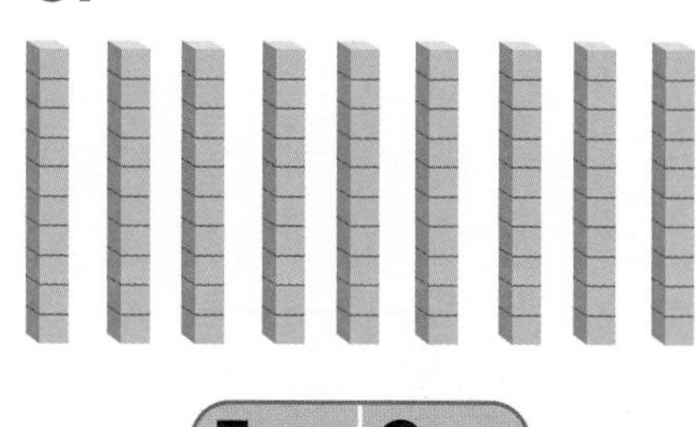

Tens	Ones

______

4. **Math Talk** The number 50 has 5 tens. How many ones are in the ones place?

TAKS Objective 1
TEKS 1.1B Create sets of tens and ones using concrete objects to describe, compare, and order whole numbers.

TEKS 1.1D Read and write numbers to 99 to describe sets of concrete objects.

★ Practice

Use [tens block] and [ones block].
Count the tens and the ones.
Write the tens and the ones.
Write the number.

Remember!
Write 0 in the ones place when there are 0 ones.

5.

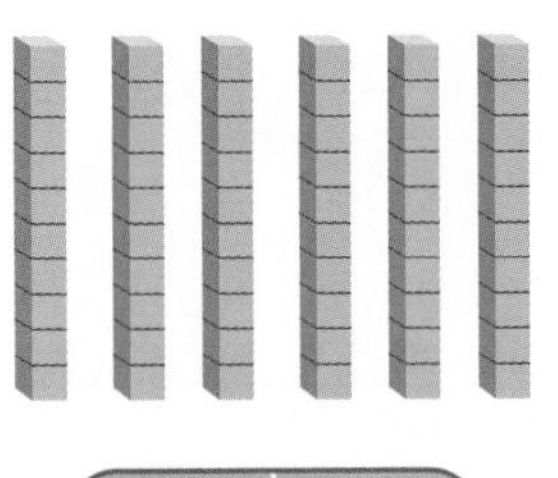

Tens	Ones
6	0

60

6.

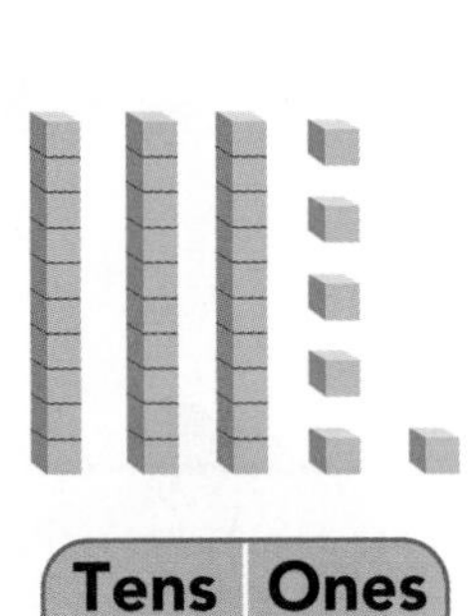

Tens	Ones

______

7.

Tens	Ones

______

8.

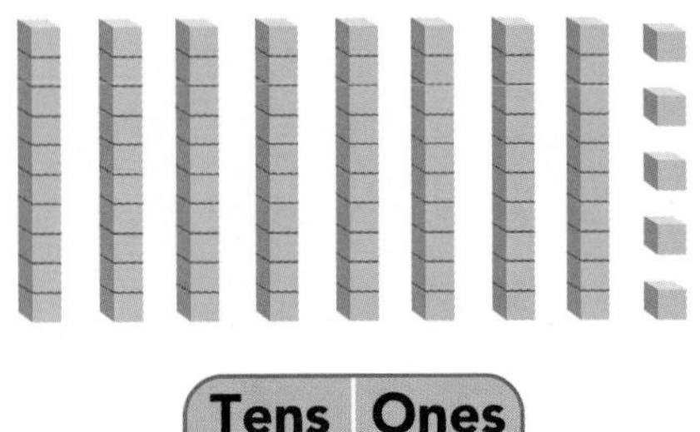

Tens	Ones

______

9.

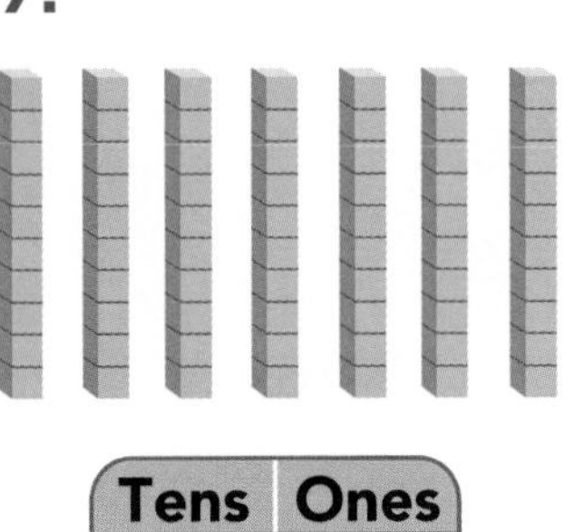

Tens	Ones

______

10.

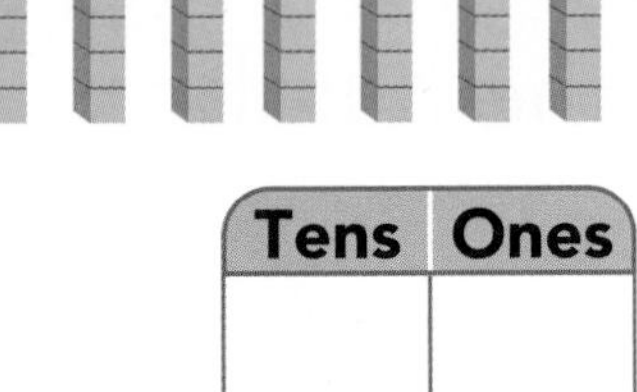

Tens	Ones

______

Problem Solving: Number Sense

11. How many tens are in the number? ______

12. Write the number for 8 tens. ______

13. How many ones are in the number? ______

At Home Ask your child to explain how the number 85 is different from numbers such as 80 or 90.

En casa Pida a su niño que explique en qué se diferencia el número 85 de números como 80 ó 90.

TEKS Objective
Describe, read, and write two-digit numbers in different ways.

Name ______________________

Chapter 14 Lesson 3

Different Ways to Show Numbers

You can write a number in different ways.

3 tens and 4 ones is the same as 30 + 4.

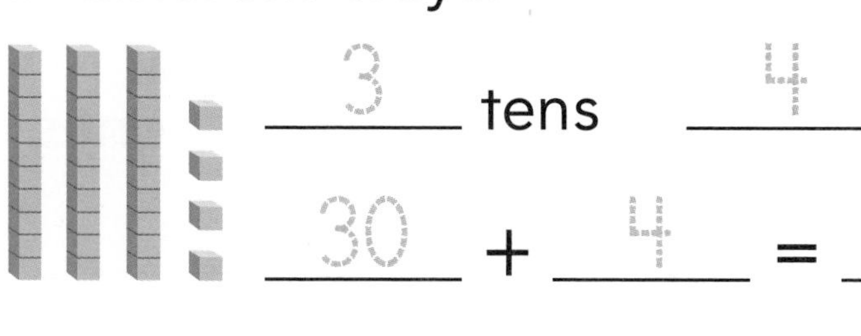

__3__ tens __4__ ones

__30__ + __4__ = __34__

Guided Practice

Use [tens rod] and [ones cube].
Write the number in different ways.

1.

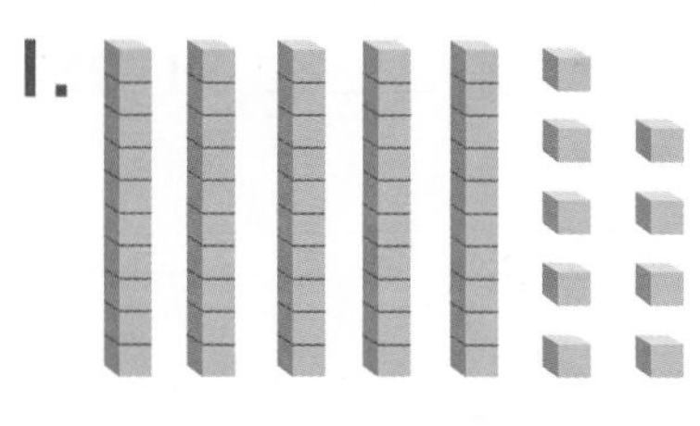

Think!
5 tens and 9 ones is the same as 50 + 9.

______ tens ______ ones

______ + ______ = ______

2.

______ tens ______ ones

______ + ______ = ______

3.

______ tens ______ ones

______ + ______ = ______

4.

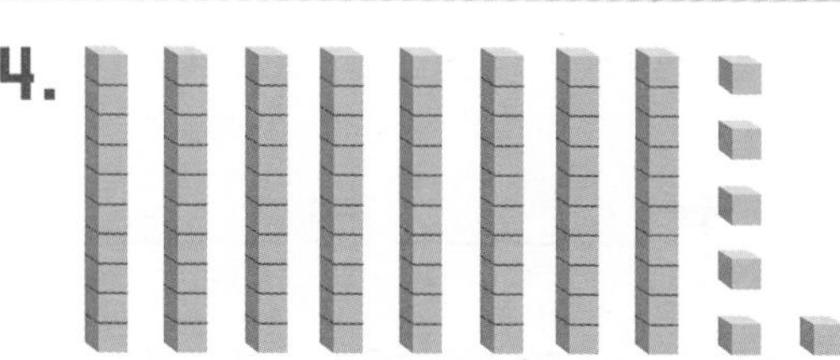

______ tens ______ ones

______ + ______ = ______

5. **Math Talk** In the number 45, does the number 4 mean 40 or 4? How do you know?

TAKS Objective 1
TEKS 1.1B Create sets of tens and ones using concrete objects to describe, compare, and order whole numbers.

TEKS 1.1D Read and write numbers to 99 to describe sets of concrete objects.

★ Practice

Use [tens block] and [ones block].
Write the number in different ways.

6. 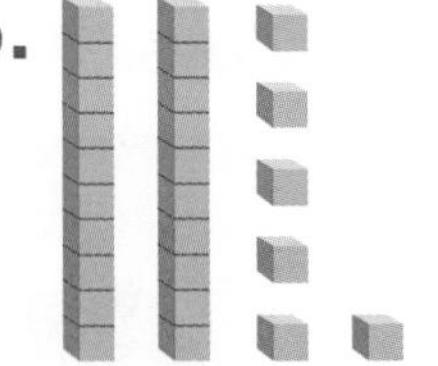

2 tens 6 ones

20 + 6 = 26

7. 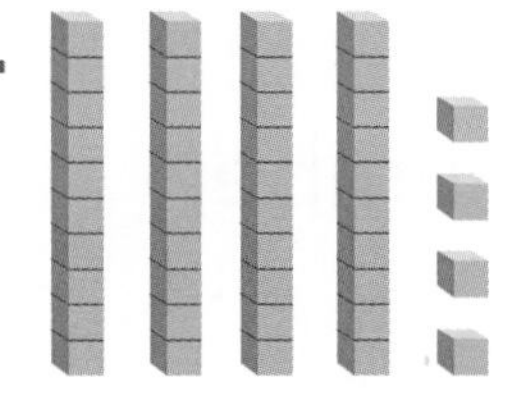

_____ tens _____ ones

_____ + _____ = _____

8. 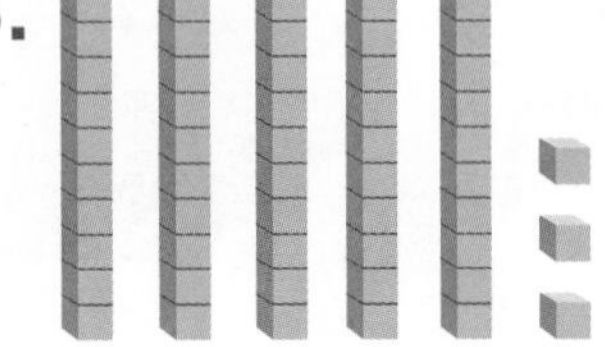

_____ tens _____ ones

_____ + _____ = _____

9. 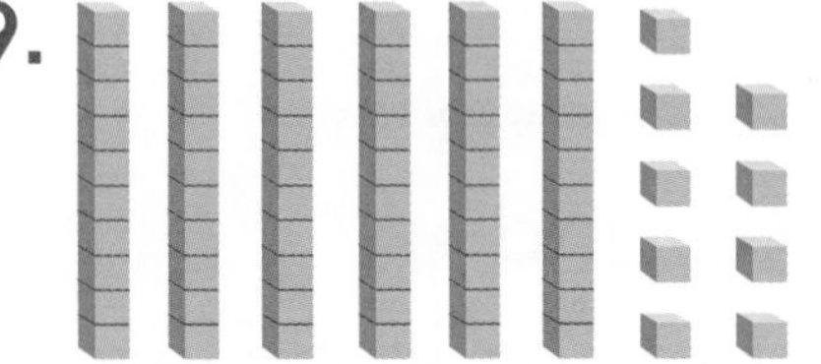

_____ tens _____ ones

_____ + _____ = _____

10. 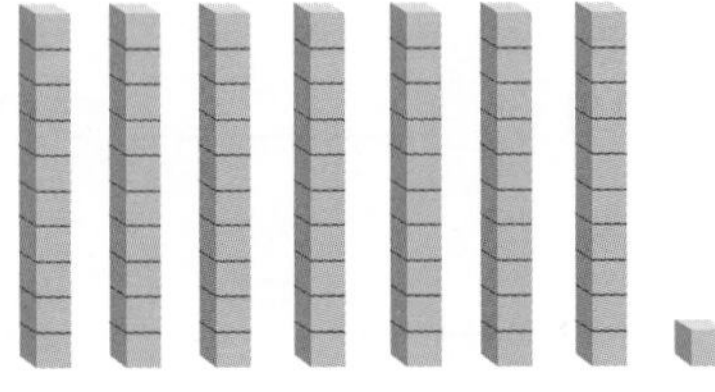

_____ tens _____ one

_____ + _____ = _____

11. 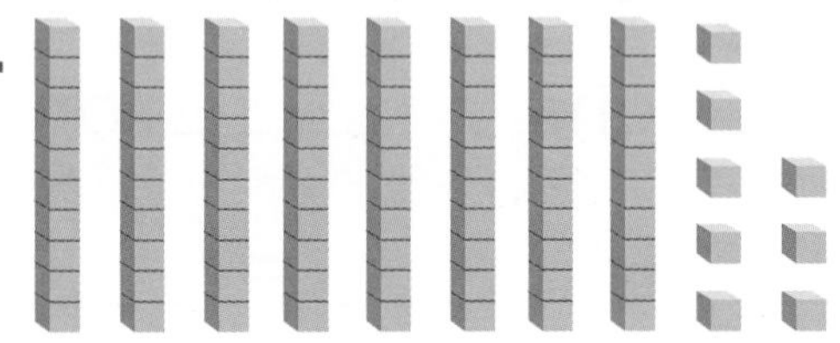

_____ tens _____ ones

_____ + _____ = _____

Problem Solving: Number Sense

12. Circle the ways that show 65.

6 tens 5 ones 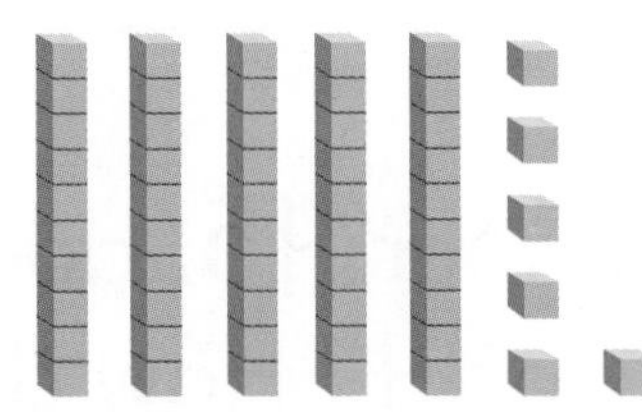 60 + 5

At Home Point out two-digit numbers in everyday places. Ask your child how many tens and ones are in each number.

En casa Señale números de dos dígitos en lugares comunes. Pregunte a su niño cuántas decenas y cuántas unidades hay en cada número.

Name ______________________________

Chapter 14 Lesson 4

More Place Value

When you count by 1s,
the number after 99 is 100.

Count by 10s.

10 tens = 100

10 tens 0 ones

100

one hundred

Hands On

TEKS Objective
Identify numbers through 100.

TAKS Vocabulary
one hundred

Guided Practice

Use [tens] and [ones].
Write the tens and the ones.
Write the number.

1. ______ tens ______ ones

______

eighty-five

Think!
I count 8 tens and 5 ones.

2. 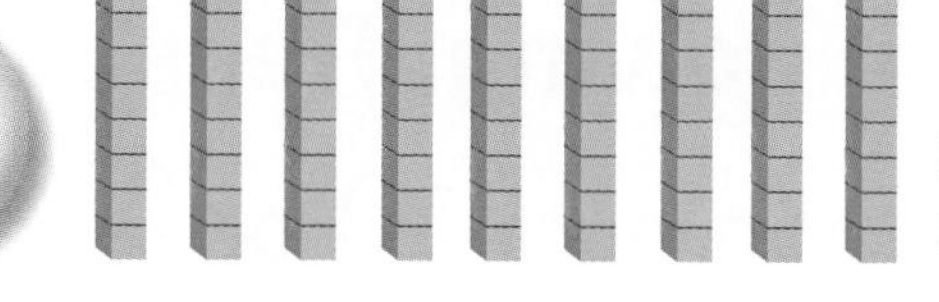

______ tens ______ ones

______

ninety-two

3. **Math Talk** How is 100 different from numbers like 80 and 90?

TAKS Objective 1
TEKS 1.1B Create sets of tens and ones using concrete objects to describe, compare, and order whole numbers.

TEKS 1.1D Read and write numbers to 99 to describe sets of concrete objects.

★ Practice

Use [tens block] and [ones block] .
Write the tens and the ones.
Write the number.

Remember!
Count the tens
and the ones.

4\. 1 tens 6 ones

16
sixteen

5\. 

____ tens ____ ones

____
eighty

6\. 

____ tens ____ ones

____
sixty-three

7\. 

____ tens ____ ones

____
seventy-eight

Problem Solving: Reasoning

8\. Mr. Simon puts 10 boxes into his truck. Each box has 10 cans in it. How many cans are in Mr. Simon's truck?

____ cans

Draw or write to explain.

At Home Have your child count by 10s to numbers through 100.

En casa Pida a su niño que cuente de 10 en 10 hasta 100.

Name ____________________

Chapter 14 Lesson 5

Act It Out

Problem Solving Strategy

TEKS Objective Use models and place value to solve problems.

★ Learn

Jesse puts 47 stickers in rows. 10 stickers fit in each row. How many rows does he make?

Understand

What do you know?

- There are 47 stickers.
- 10 stickers fit in each row.

Plan

You can use  and ▪ to act out the problem.

How many rows of 10 does he make? 4 rows

How many stickers does he put in the last row? 7 stickers

Solve

Use ▬ and ▪.
Show the rows he needs for 47 stickers.

He makes 5 rows.

4 tens make 4 rows.
7 ones are in the last row.
That makes 5 rows altogether.

Look Back

Does your answer make sense?
Did you answer the question?

TAKS Objective 6
TEKS 1.11C Select or develop an appropriate problem-solving plan or strategy including drawing a picture, looking for a pattern, systematic guessing and checking, or acting it out in order to solve a problem. **TEKS 1.11D** Use tools such as real objects, manipulatives, and technology to solve problems. Also **TEKS 1.11A, 1.11B**

★ Guided Problem Solving

Think!
3 strings have 10 beads and 1 more string has 2 beads.

1. Rosa puts 32 beads on strings. 10 beads fit on each string. How many strings does she use?

   Use [ten rod] and [unit cube] to show the number of beads.

   Draw a model and solve.

   _____ strings

2. Math Talk How did using the blocks help you solve the problem?

★ Problem Solving Practice

Use [ten rod] and [unit cube] to solve.

Draw or write to explain.

3. Keb puts 78 tubes of paint in cases. Each case can hold 10 tubes. How many cases does he need?

   _____ cases

4. Cindy puts 69 stickers in a book. Each page in the book can hold 10 stickers. How many pages does she need?

   _____ pages

At Home Change the number of beads in the first problem to 46 and have your child solve the problem.

En casa Cambie a 46 el número de cuentas en el primer problema y pida a su niño que resuelva el problema.

Name ______________________

Problem Solving

Texas Field Trip

Austin Museum of Art

Visitors learn about art at the Austin Museum of Art. There are many works of art to see. Children can make their own artwork, too.

FamilyLab

Solve. Show your work.

1. Ella has 10 feathers. She gives away 6 feathers. How many feathers does she have left?

   _____ feathers

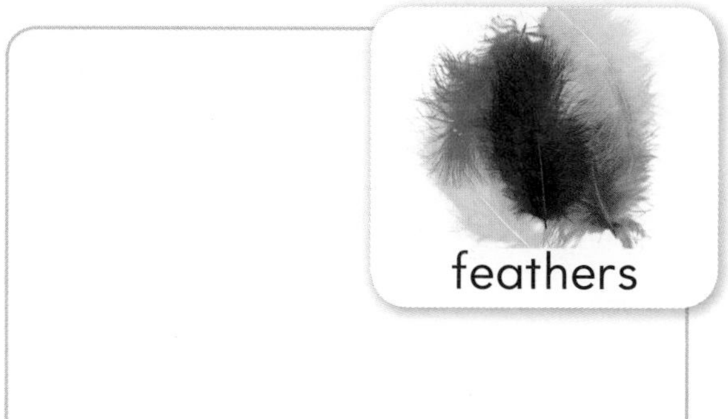

feathers

2. Gale puts 76 sequins in rows on a card. 10 sequins can fit in each row. How many rows does she need to make?

   _____ rows

sequins

3. Kele makes tissue paper masks. He makes 5 small masks and 3 large masks. How many masks does he make?

   _____ masks

tissue paper

TAKS Objective 6
TEKS 1.11A Identify mathematics in everyday situations.
TEKS 1.11C Select or develop an appropriate problem-solving plan or strategy including drawing a picture, looking for a pattern, systematic guessing and checking, or acting it out in order to solve a problem. Also **TEKS Social Studies 18B**

Texas Field Trip

Solve. Show your work.

4. Pedro puts 38 tubes of glitter glue in boxes. Each box can hold 10 tubes. How many boxes does he need?

_____ boxes

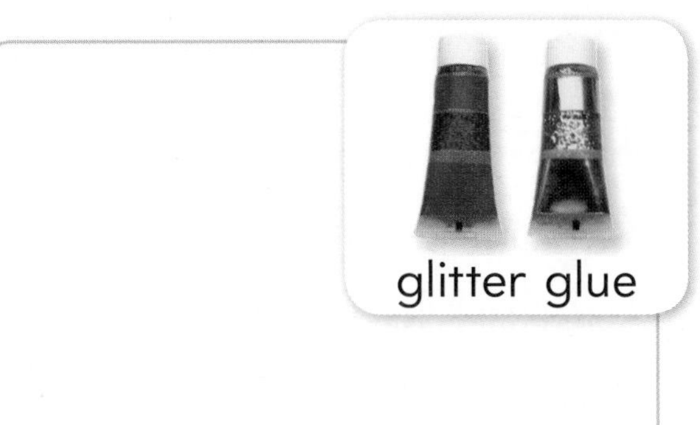
glitter glue

5. Dan makes 3 blue origami birds. Rose makes 7 red origami birds. How many birds do they make in all?

_____ birds

origami bird

6. Leon makes 8 sculptures. He gives away 2 sculptures. How many sculptures does he have left?

_____ sculptures

sculptures

7. Ana puts 90 mosaic tiles in rows. 10 tiles fit in each row. How many rows does she make?

_____ rows

mosaic tiles

Name ______________________

What's the Order?

Use [tens rod] and [ones cube].

1. Write the numbers in order from least to greatest.

_____ _____ _____

2. Write the numbers in order from greatest to least.

36

_____ _____ _____

3. Write the numbers in order from greatest to least.

59

80

_____ _____ _____

4. Match the blocks to the number.

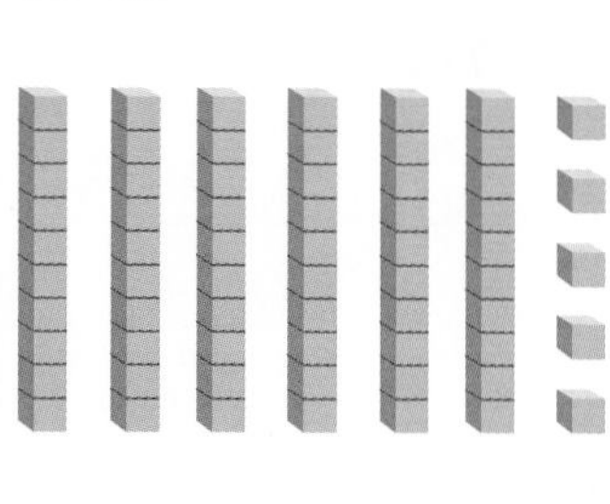

13

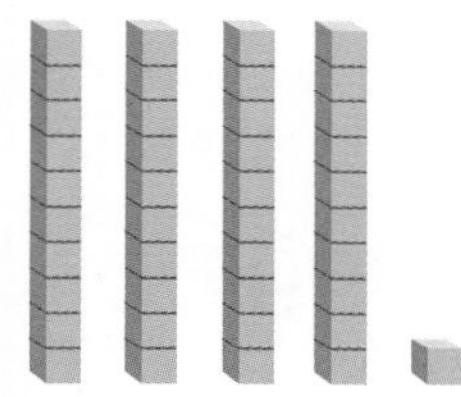

41

5. Write the numbers in order from least to greatest.

_____ _____ _____

Butterflies

Monarch butterflies fly south in the winter. Scientists study their travels. Children help by putting tags on butterflies.

Use and .
Write the number in different ways.

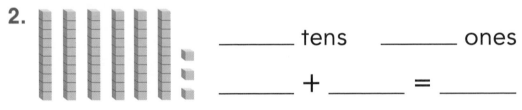

1. 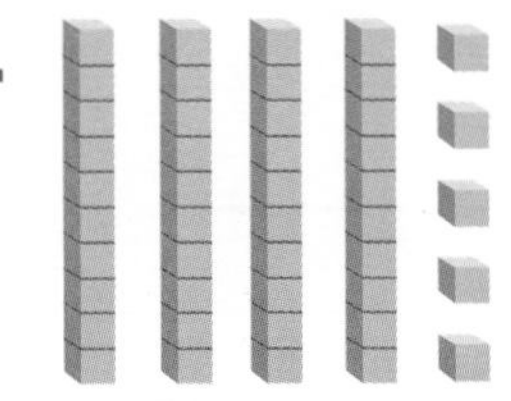

_____ tens _____ ones

_____ + _____ = _____

45 butterflies have tags.

2. 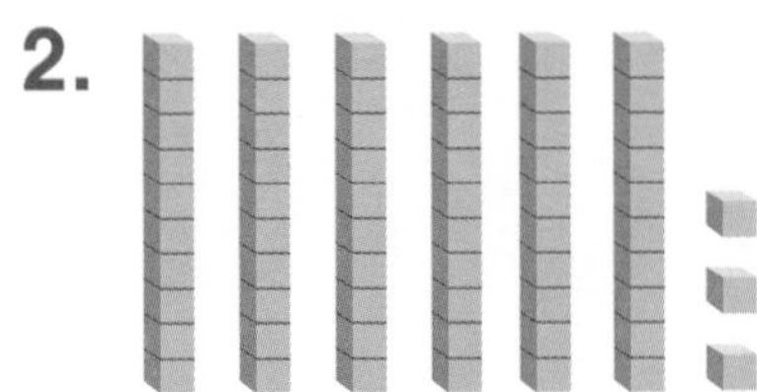

_____ tens _____ ones

_____ + _____ = _____

63 butterflies have no tags.

3. Circle which number is greater. 45 63

Use and to solve.

4. Mr. Yee gives 10 tags to each group of children. He gives tags to 8 groups.

How many tags does he give? _____ tags

TAKS Objectives 2, 6
TEKS 1.5A Use patterns to skip count by twos, fives, and tens.
TEKS 1.5C Compare and order whole numbers using place value.
Also **TEKS 1.11C**
TEKS Science 2A, 2E

Name ____________________

Concepts and Skills

Use and .
Write the number
of tens shown.
Write the number. TEKS 1.1B, 1.1D

1. ____ tens

____

eighty

Count the tens and the ones.
Write the tens and the ones.
Write the number. TEKS 1.1B, 1.1D

2.

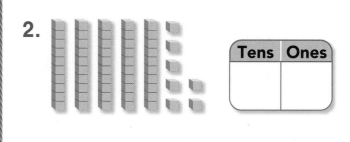

Tens	Ones

____

Write the number in different ways. TEKS 1.1B, 1.1D

3.

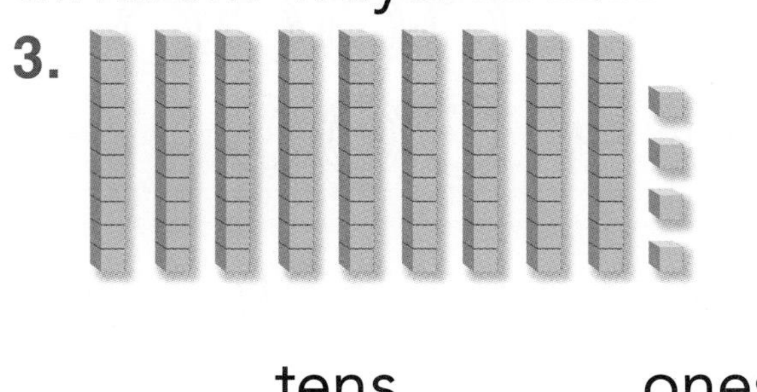

____ tens ____ ones

____ + ____ = ____

Write the tens and the ones.
Write the number. TEKS 1.1B, 1.1D

4.

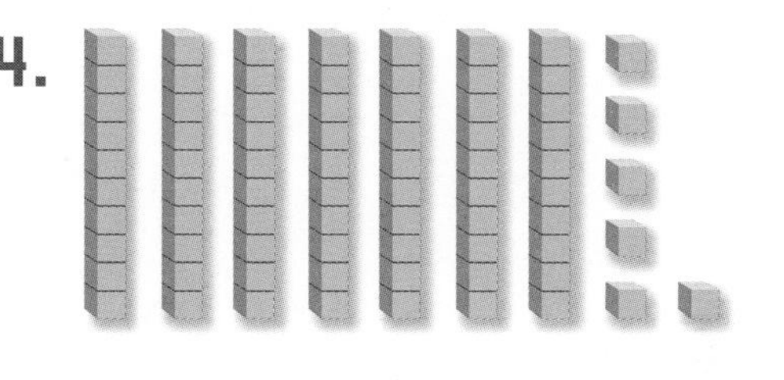

____ tens ____ ones

____

seventy-six

Problem Solving TEKS 1.11A, 1.11B, 1.11C, 1.11D

Use and to solve.

5. Awan puts 82 stickers in a book.
Each page holds 10 stickers.
How many pages does he need?

____ pages

Draw or write to explain.

TAKS Prep and Spiral Review

Choose the answer for problems 1–4.

1. Which group shows 4 out of 7 markers that are red?

 ○ 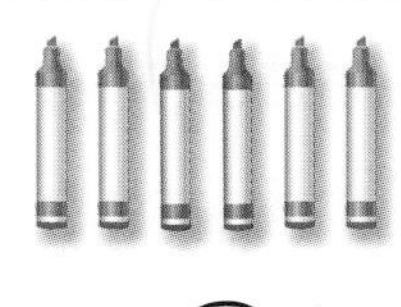 ○  ○  ○

TEKS 1.2B (page 187)

2. Which group shows 3 out of 6 pushpins that are green?

 ○ 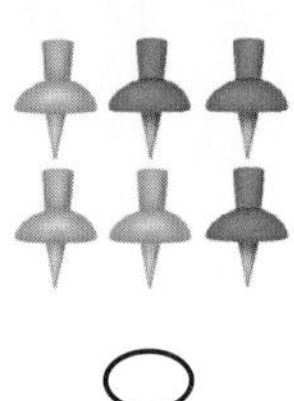 ○  ○ 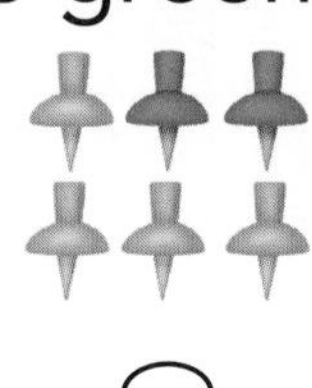 ○

TEKS 1.2B (page 187)

3. How many blue cars does Juan have? Each ◎ stands for 1 car.

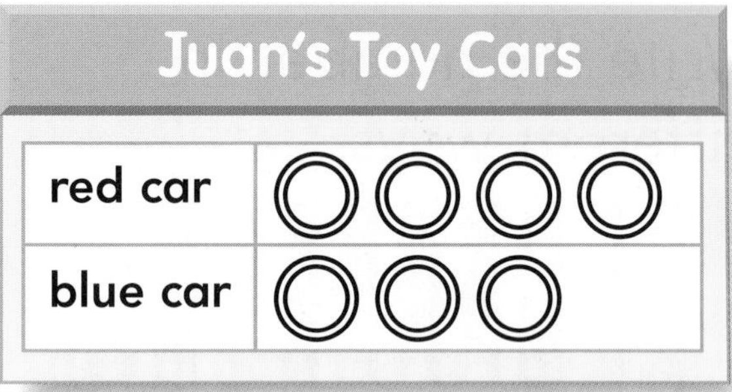

1 ○ 2 ○ 3 ○ 4 ○

TEKS 1.10A (page 209)

4. Which fruit do most children choose?

 ○ 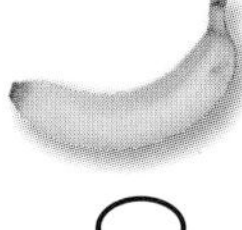 ○ 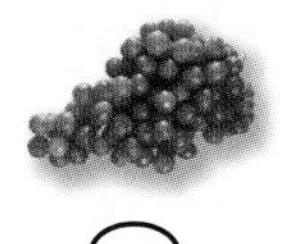 ○  ○

TEKS 1.10A (page 223)

Visit **www.eduplace.com/txmap/** for Test-Taking Tips and Extra Practice.

Compare and Order Numbers

TAKS Vocabulary

You learned these vocabulary words in Chapter 2. Now you will use them with greater numbers.

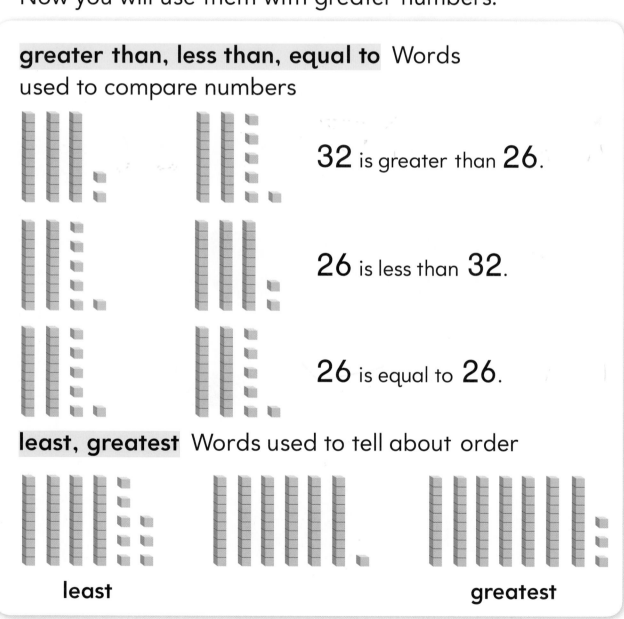

greater than, less than, equal to Words used to compare numbers

32 is greater than 26.

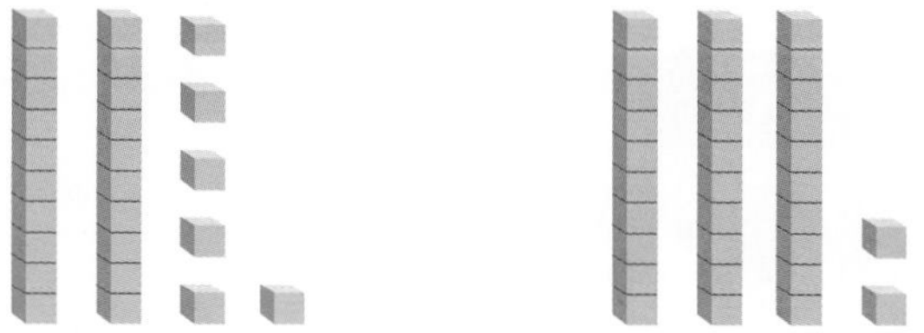

26 is less than 32.

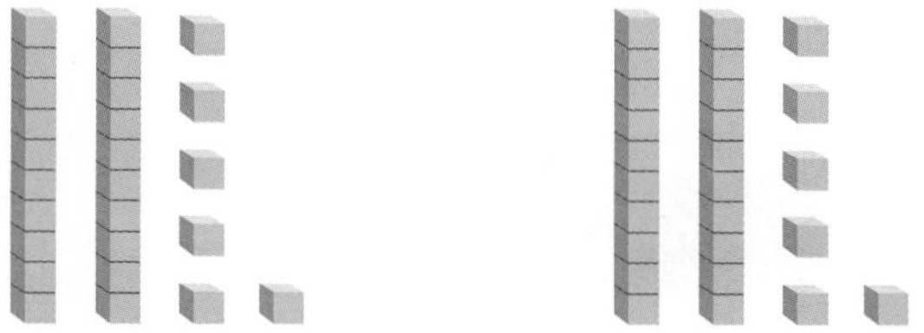

26 is equal to 26.

least, greatest Words used to tell about order

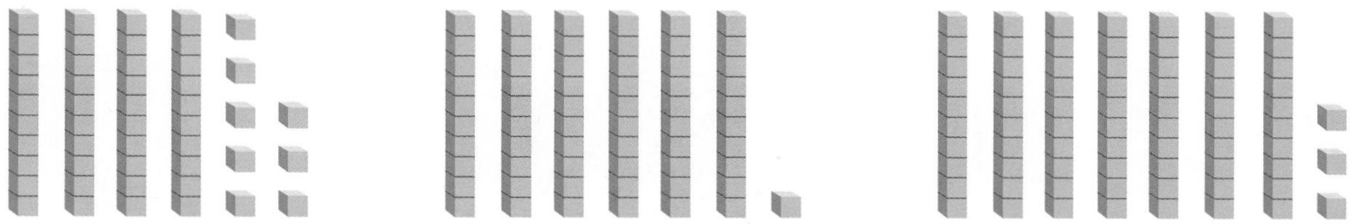

least greatest

See English-Spanish glossary pages 505–516.

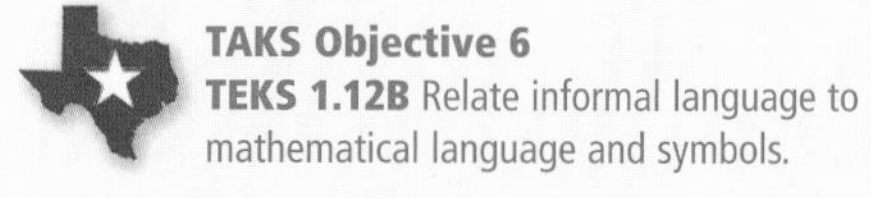
TAKS Objective 6
TEKS 1.12B Relate informal language to mathematical language and symbols.

Education Place
Visit **www.eduplace.com/txmap/** for the eGlossary and vocabulary eGames.

Name ______________________________

Draw a line from the number to the blocks.

1. 11

2. 16

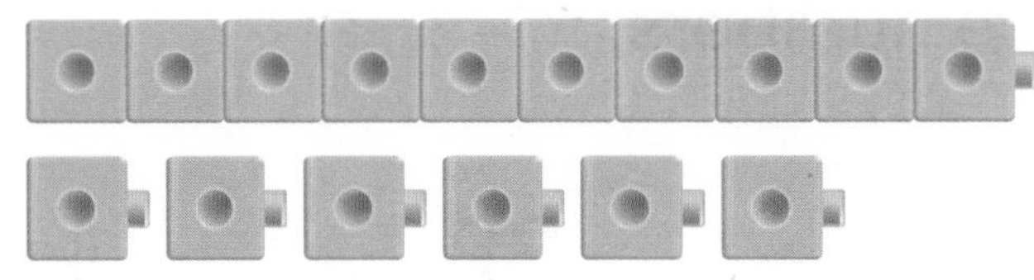

3. 20

4. 13

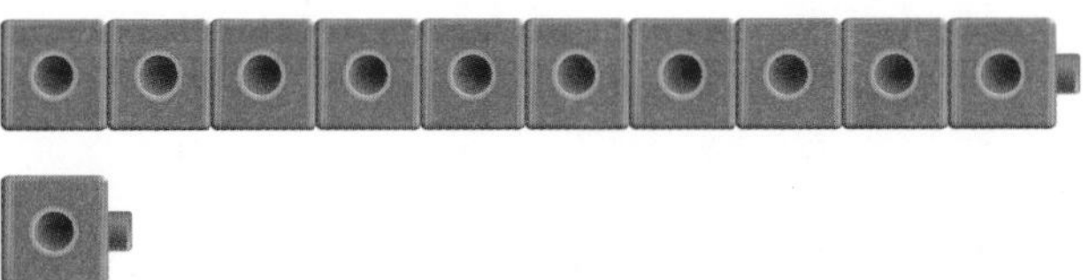

5. 19

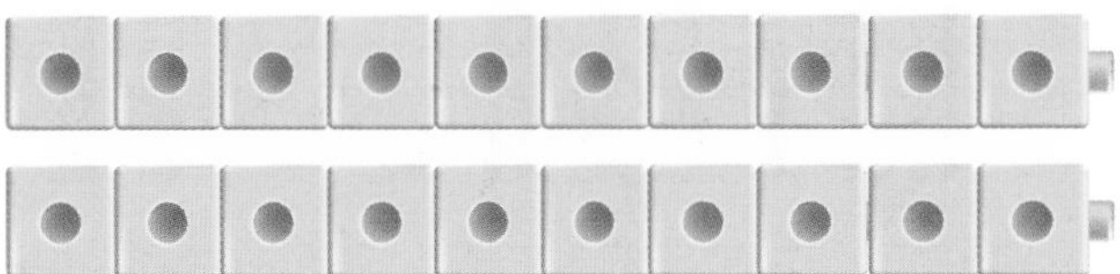

Use this page to review important skills needed for this chapter.

TEKS Objective Compare two numbers using greater than, less than, and equal to.

Name ______________________

Chapter 15 Lesson 1

Compare Numbers 20 Through 50

★ Learn

You can compare numbers using greater than, less than, and equal to.

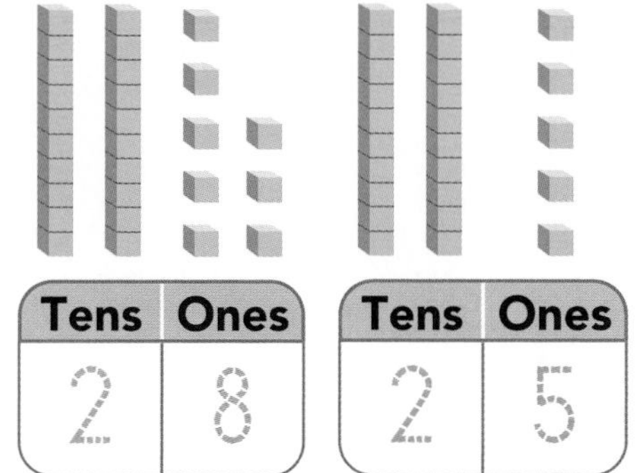

28 is greater than 25

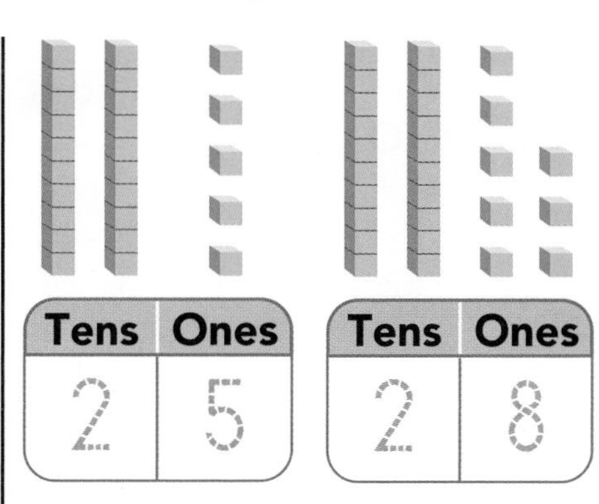

25 is less than 28

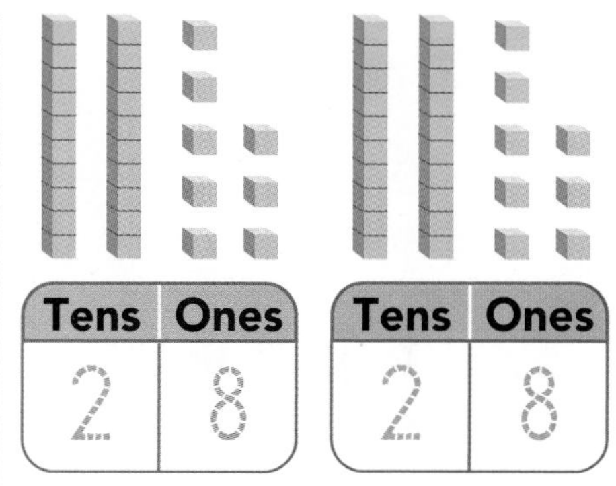

28 is equal to 28

★ Guided Practice

Use and . Write the numbers. Compare. Circle.

Think! Compare the tens. If the tens are the same, compare the ones.

1. | Tens | Ones |
|---|---|
| | |

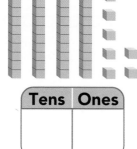

greater than

less than

equal to

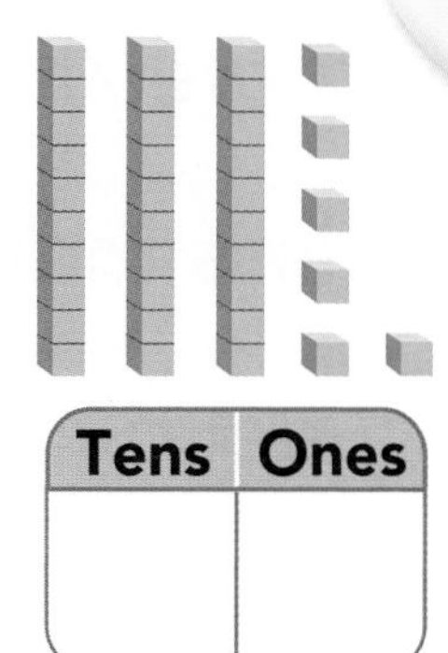

Tens	Ones

2. | Tens | Ones |
|---|---|
| | |

greater than

less than

equal to

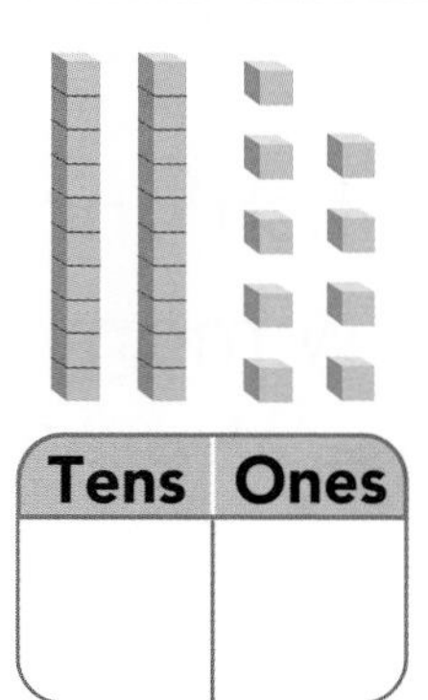

Tens	Ones

3. **Math Talk** Why is 46 greater than 36?

TAKS Objectives 1, 2, 6
TEKS 1.1B Create sets of tens and ones using concrete objects to describe, compare, and order whole numbers.
TEKS 1.5C Compare and order whole numbers using place value.
TEKS 1.12B Relate informal language to mathematical language and symbols. Also **TEKS 1.1A**

★ Practice

Remember! Compare the tens first.

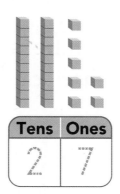

Use [tens] and [ones]. Write the numbers. Compare. Circle.

4. 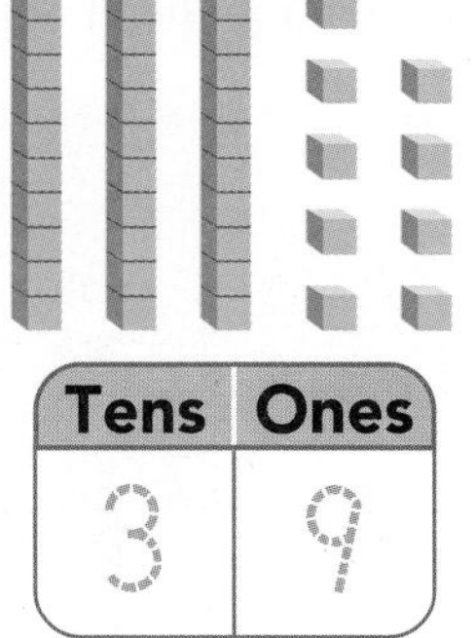

Tens	Ones
3	9

(greater than) less than equal to

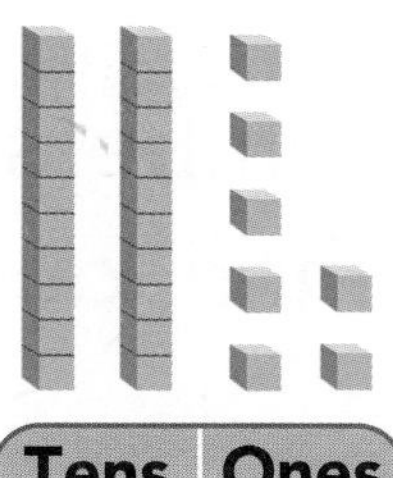

Tens	Ones
2	7

5. 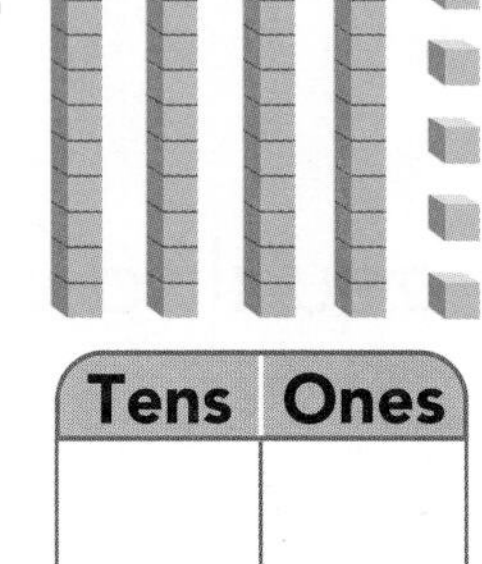

Tens	Ones

greater than less than equal to

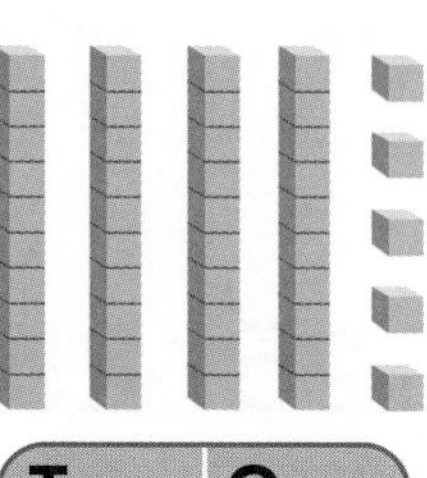

Tens	Ones

6. 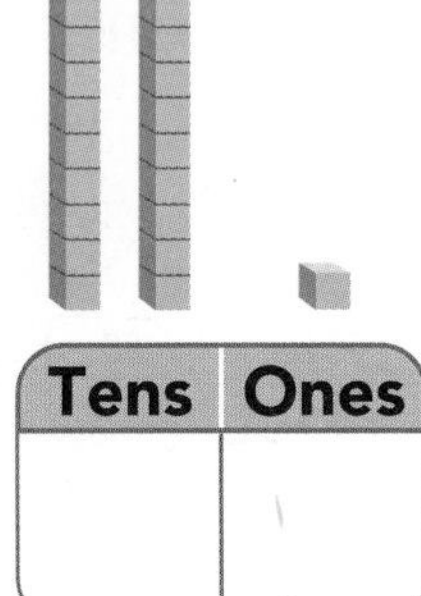

Tens	Ones

greater than less than equal to

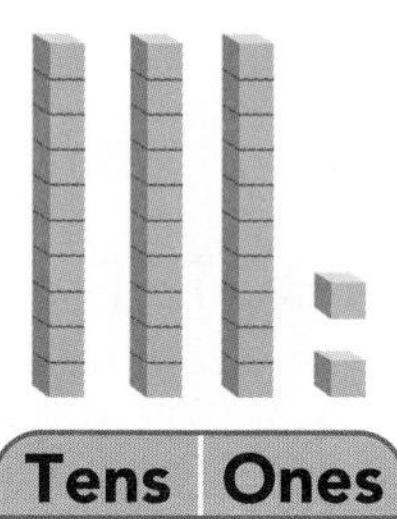

Tens	Ones

Problem Solving: Reasoning

7. There are 3 red fish and 6 green fish. How many fewer red fish are there?

_____ fewer red fish

Draw or write to explain.

At Home Write pairs of numbers between 20 and 50. Have your child compare the numbers.

En casa Escriba pares de números entre 20 y 50. Pida a su niño que compare los números.

Name ______________________

Chapter 15 Lesson 3

Order Numbers Through 99

Hands On

TEKS Objective
Order numbers through 99.

TAKS Vocabulary
greatest
least

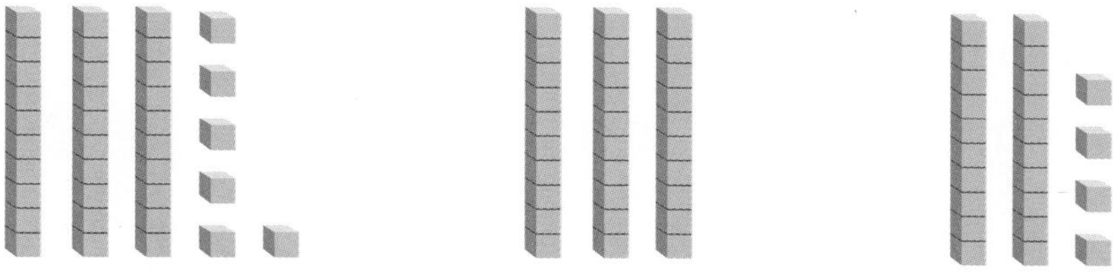

36 is the **greatest.** 30 24 is the **least.**

★ Explore

Use Workmat 5,  and . Show and write the number. Write the numbers from greatest to least.

1. ______ ______ ______

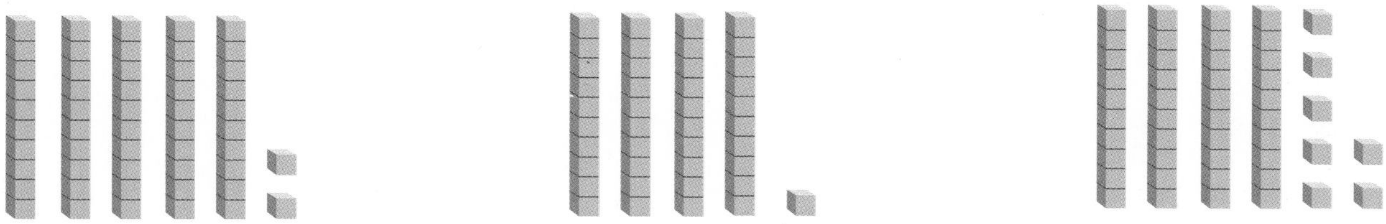

52 ______ 47 ______ 41 ______
greatest least

2. ______ ______ ______

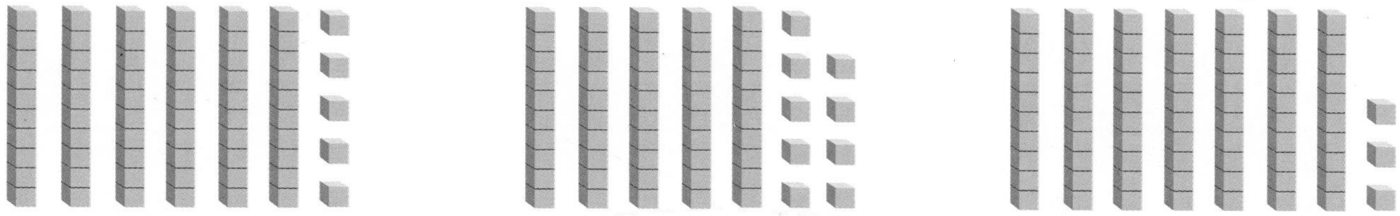

______ ______ ______
greatest least

3. **Math Talk** Read the answer to Exercise 2. How did you know which number was greatest?

TAKS Objectives 1, 2, 6
TEKS 1.1B Create sets of tens and ones using concrete objects to describe, compare, and order whole numbers.
TEKS 1.5C Compare and order whole numbers using place value.
TEKS 1.12B Relate informal language to mathematical language and symbols. Also **TEKS 1.1A**

★ Extend

Remember!
Look at the
tens first.

Use Workmat 5, [ten rod] and [unit cube].
Show and write the number.
Write the numbers from greatest to least.

4. 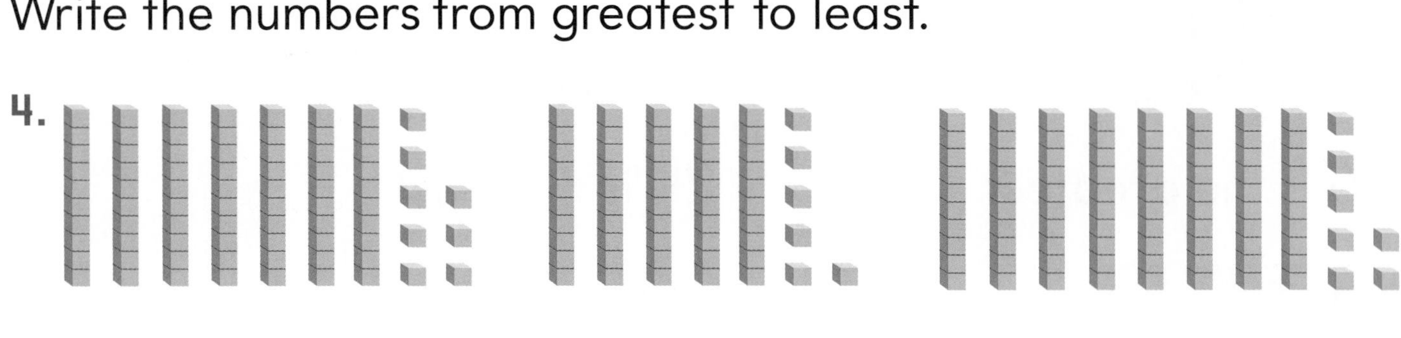

______ ______ ______

______ ______ ______
greatest least

5. 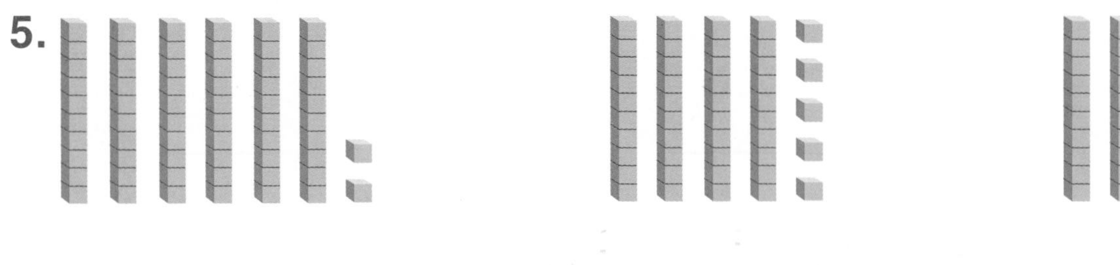

______ ______ ______

______ ______ ______
greatest least

6. 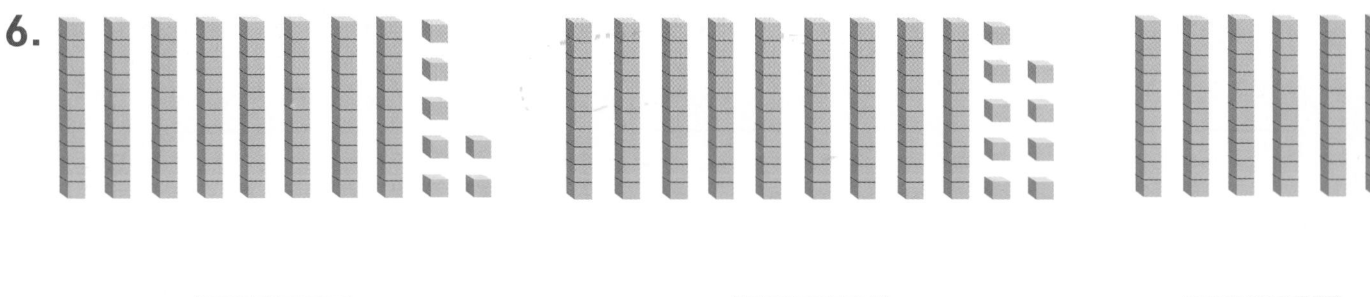

______ ______ ______

______ ______ ______
greatest least

At Home Write three numbers between 20 and 99. Have your child write them in order from greatest to least.

En casa Escriba tres números entre 20 y 99. Pida a su niño que los escriba en orden de mayor a menor.

Name ______________________

Chapter 15 Lesson 4

More Than, Less Than

Hands On

TEKS Objective
Use place value to identify 1 more, 1 less, 10 more, 10 less than a given number.

TAKS Vocabulary
more than
less than

★ Explore

You can use the words **more than** and **less than** to tell about number patterns.

11	12	13	14	15	16	17	18	19	20
21	22	23	24	25	26	27	28	29	30
31	32	33	34	35	36	37	38	39	40
41	42	43	44	45	46	47	48	49	50
51	52	53	54	55	56	57	58	59	60
61	62	63	64	65	66	67	68	69	70
71	72	73	74	75	76	77	78	79	80

20 is 10 less than 30.

40 is 10 more than 30.

74 is 1 less than 75.

76 is 1 more than 75.

Look for patterns on the hundred chart.

Use [tens rod] and [ones cube]. Show the number.

Show and write the number that is 1 more.

1. | 18 | |
2. | 26 | |
3. | 13 | |
4. | 31 | |

Show and write the number that is 1 less.

5. | | 16 |
6. | | 25 |
7. | | 48 |
8. | | 62 |

Show and write the number that is 10 more.

9. 15 / ___
10. 40 / ___

Show and write the number that is 10 less.

11. ___ / 56
12. ___ / 74

13. **Math Talk** How do you find 10 less than 26?

TAKS Objectives 1, 2, 6
TEKS 1.1B Create sets of tens and ones using concrete objects to describe, compare, and order whole numbers.

TEKS 1.5C Compare and order whole numbers using place value.
Also **TEKS 1.12B**

★ Extend

Write the number that is 1 more.

14. | 66 | 67 |

15. | 19 | |

16. | 72 | |

17. | 99 | |

1	2	3	4	5	6	7	8	9	10
11	12	13	14	15	16	17	18	19	20
21	22	23	24	25	26	27	28	29	30
31	32	33	34	35	36	37	38	39	40
41	42	43	44	45	46	47	48	49	50
51	52	53	54	55	56	57	58	59	60
61	62	63	64	65	66	67	68	69	70
71	72	73	74	75	76	77	78	79	80
81	82	83	84	85	86	87	88	89	90
91	92	93	94	95	96	97	98	99	100

Write the number that is 1 less.

18. | | 8 |

19. | | 40 |

20. | | 29 |

21. | | 84 |

Write the number that is 10 more.

22. 35

23. 22

24.  53

25.  71

26. 90

Write the number that is 10 less.

27.  15

28. 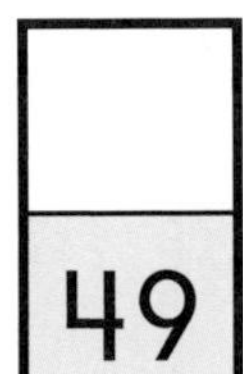 49

29. 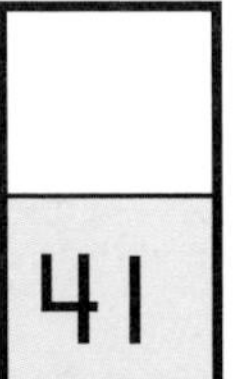 41

30. 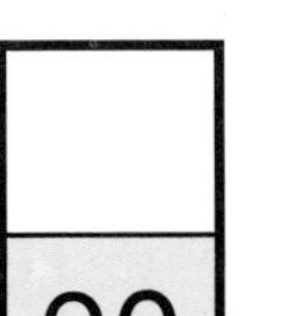 90

31. 96

32. **Math Talk** Tell how you use the hundred chart to find 10 more than 90.

At Home Open to a page in a book. Have your child find the page with a number that is 10 more or 10 less.

En casa Abra una página de un libro. Pida a su niño que busque la página con un número que sea 10 más o 10 menos.

Name ____________________

Chapter 15 Lesson 5

Reasonable Answers

Problem Solving
Plan

TEKS Objective
Find reasonable answers to problems.

Learn

Choose the answer that makes sense.

The children in Mr. Reed's class play a game. Each child takes one handful of ▪.

About how many ▪ can you pick up in one hand?

about 10 ▪

about 100 ▪

THINK	DECIDE
Do I need an exact answer?	No. The question asks about how many.
What should I use to solve the problem?	I can use what I know. I know how big a ▪ is. I know how big my hand is.
Which answer makes more sense?	I can hold about 10 ▪ in my hand. 100 ▪ is too many to hold.

I can pick up about 10 ▪ in one hand.

TAKS Objective 6
TEKS 1.11D Use tools such as real objects, manipulatives, and technology to solve problems.

TEKS 1.13 Justify thinking using objects, words, pictures, numbers, and technology.

★ Guided Problem Solving

1. Laura takes one handful of pennies. About how many can she hold in one hand?

Think!
A penny is
this big.

Look at the size of the penny.

Which answer makes sense?

about 20 pennies

about 100 pennies

2. **Math Talk** How did you choose your answer?

★ Problem Solving Practice

Estimate. Circle the answer that makes sense.

Draw or write to explain.

3. Ellis goes to bed after dinner. About how many hours does he sleep at night?

about 8 hours

about 42 hours

4. Carla's dad drives her friends to school. About how many people can fit in his van?

about 10 people

about 85 people

At Home Fill a bowl with small items. Ask your child to estimate about how many he or she can pick up with one hand.

En casa Llene un recipiente con objetos pequeños. Pida a su niño que estime aproximadamente cuántos puede recoger con una mano.

Name ___________________________

Social Studies

Texas Field Trip

The Alamo

The Alamo is in San Antonio.
It is a symbol of courage.
It stands for the people who fought for freedom in Texas.

The Alamo

Solve. Show your work.

1. 64 children visit the Alamo on Monday. 76 children visit on Tuesday. 72 children visit on Wednesday. When do the greatest number of children visit?

   ____

The Alamo

---

2. 8 children make dioramas. 6 children draw pictures. How many more children make dioramas than draw pictures?

   _____ children

diorama

---

3. Chris takes 7 photographs. Rosa takes 5. They make a book together. How many photographs are in the book?

   _____ photographs

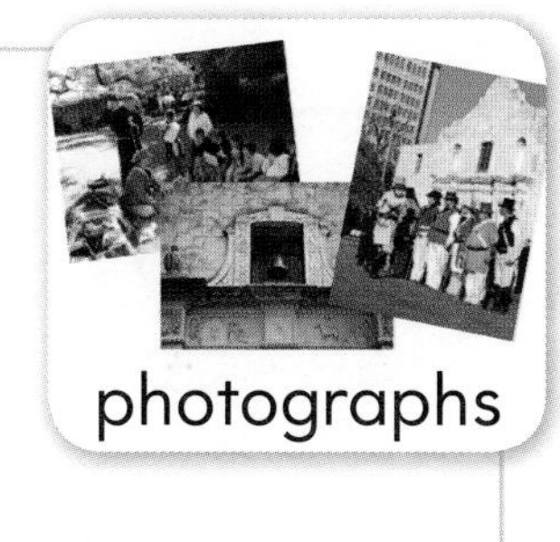

photographs

TAKS Objective 6
TEKS 1.11A Identify mathematics in everyday situations.
TEKS 1.11C Select or develop an appropriate problem-solving plan or strategy including drawing a picture, looking for a pattern, systematic guessing and checking, or acting it out in order to solve a problem.
TEKS Social Studies 13A

TAKS Problem Solving
Listening Skills

Select a Strategy
Draw a Picture
Guess and Check

Listen to your teacher read the problem.
Choose the correct answer.

1. Tam makes a necklace with 37 beads.
   Deb makes a necklace with 10 more beads.
   How many beads are in Deb's necklace?

   27 ○ 37 ○ 47 ○ 57 ○

   TEKS 1.5C

2. Pat has 18 markers.
   Lisa has 15 markers.
   Bob has 20 markers.
   Who has the least number of markers?

   Lisa ○ Pat ○ Bob ○ Ann ○

   TEKS 1.5C

3. 73 ○ 82 ○ 84 ○ 85 ○

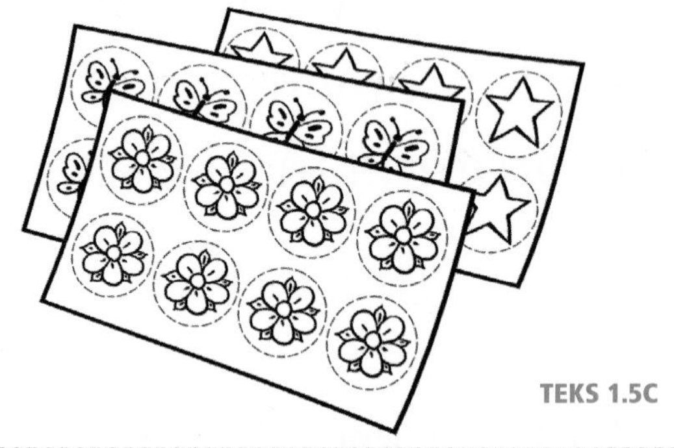

   TEKS 1.5C

4. 18, 34, 52 ○ 63, 61, 49 ○ 99, 76, 82 ○ 44, 54, 34 ○

   TEKS 1.5C

Education Place
Visit **www.eduplace.com/txmap/** for Test-Taking Tips and more TAKS Practice.

Math Works

Name ______________________________

Artist

Wade is an artist. He paints pictures of people. His tools are pencils and paintbrushes. He uses special paint and paper.

Use Workmat 5, [tens rod], and [ones cube] to solve.

1. Wade buys pads of paper.
   One pad has 32 sheets.
   One pad has 28 sheets.
   Is 28 greater than
   or less than 32? ______________

2. Wade paints pictures of 81 children.
   He paints pictures of 71 adults.
   Compare 81 to 71.
   How many more is 81? ______ more

3. Wade paints a picture of a baseball player. He makes copies. He puts a number on each copy. Some copies get out of order. Order them from least to greatest:
   99, 39, 48.

   ______, ______, ______

4. **Math Talk** How are the numbers 39 and 99 alike?

TAKS Objectives 1, 6
TEKS 1.1A Compare and order whole numbers up to 99 (less than, greater than, or equal to) using sets of concrete objects and pictorial models.
TEKS 1.11A Identify mathematics in everyday situations.

Social Studies Link

The Tortoise Race

People tell a story about the Texas tortoise and the jackrabbit who have a race. Who is faster? The tortoise is slow and steady. The jackrabbit starts and stops. Who will win?

Use the hundred chart.

1	2	3	4	5	6	7	8	9	10
11	12	13	14	15	16	17	18	19	20
21	22	23	24	25	26	27	28	29	30
31	32	33	34	35	36	37	38	39	40
41	42	43	44	45	46	47	48	49	50

1. The Texas tortoise takes 35 steps in the first hour. Write the number that comes just before.

   ______

2. The jackrabbit takes 40 hops in the first minute. Write the missing numbers.

   40, ______, ______, 43

3. The jackrabbit stops to nap for 23 minutes. He stops to eat for 33 minutes. Is 33 more than or less than 23?

   ____

TAKS Objective 1
TEKS 1.1A Compare and order whole numbers up to 99 (less than, greater than, or equal to) using sets of concrete objects and pictorial models.

TEKS Social Studies 15B

Name ____________________

Concepts and Skills

Use [tens rod] and [unit cube]. Write the numbers.
Compare. Circle. TEKS 1.1A, 1.1B, 1.5C

1. 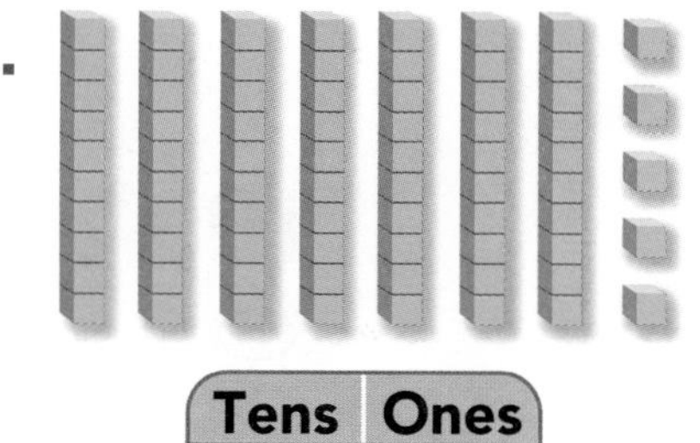

Tens	Ones

greater than

less than

equal to

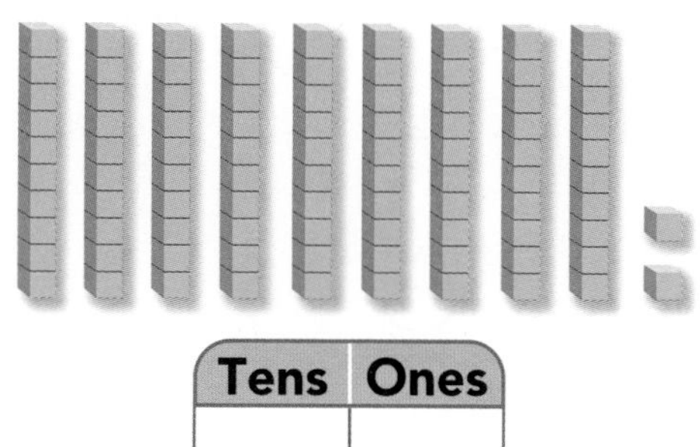

Tens	Ones

Use Workmat 5, [tens rod] and [unit cube].
Show and write the number.
Write the numbers from least to greatest. TEKS 1.1A, 1.1B, 1.5C

2. 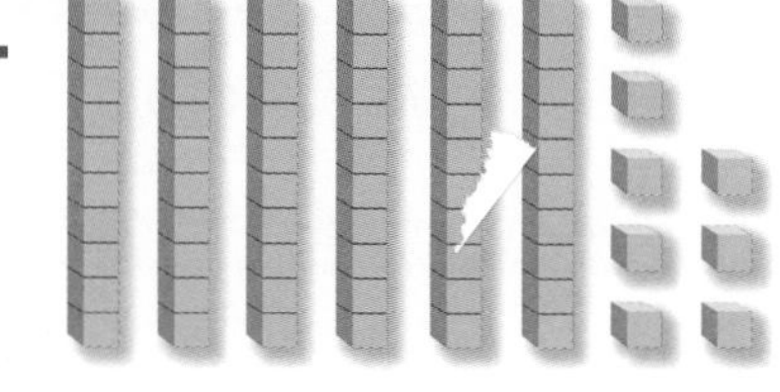 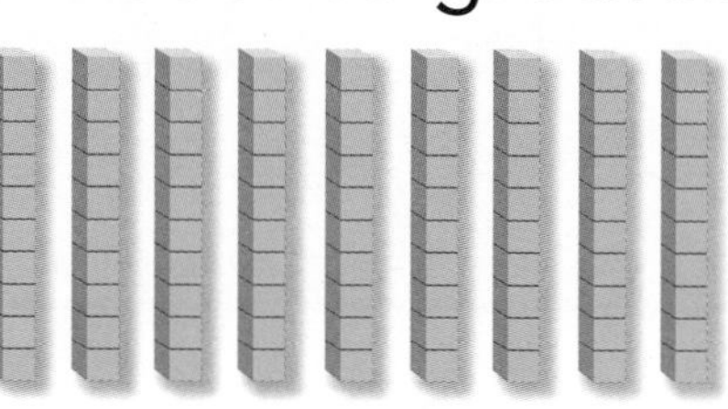 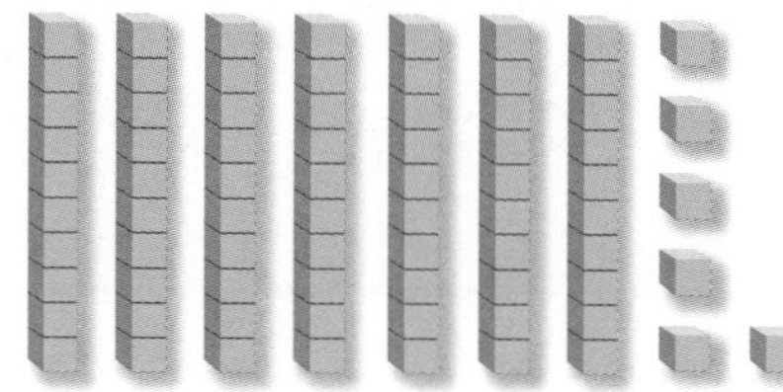

_____ _____ _____

_____ _____ _____

least greatest

Write the number that is 1 more. TEKS 1.1B, 1.5C

3. 

27	

Write the number that is 1 less. TEKS 1.1B, 1.5C

4.

	89

Problem Solving TEKS 1.11B, 1.11D, 1.13

5. About how many buttons can you hold in one hand?

about 20 buttons

about 50 buttons

TAKS Prep and Spiral Review

Choose the answer for problems 1–4.

1. Which number describes the set of tens and ones?

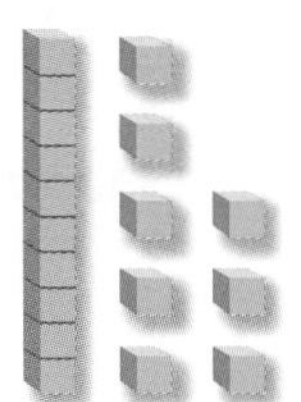

16 ○ 17 ○ 18 ○ 19 ○

TEKS 1.1D (page 247)

2. Which set of blocks shows 65?

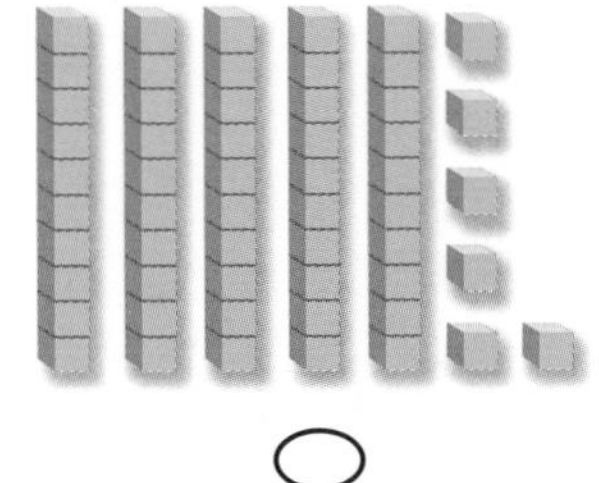 ○

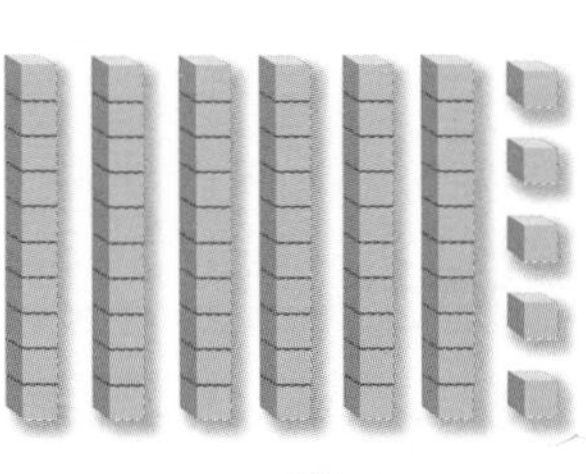 ○

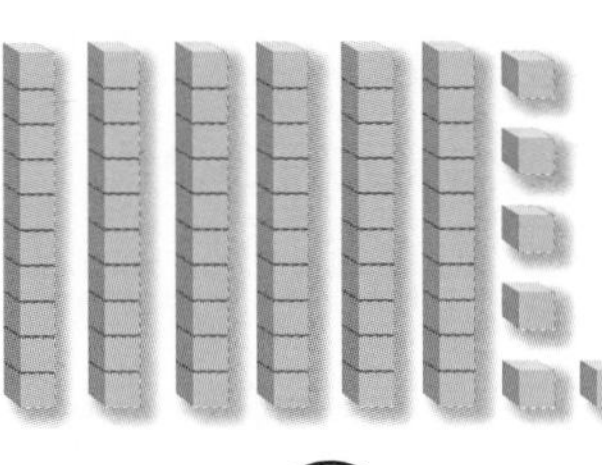 ○

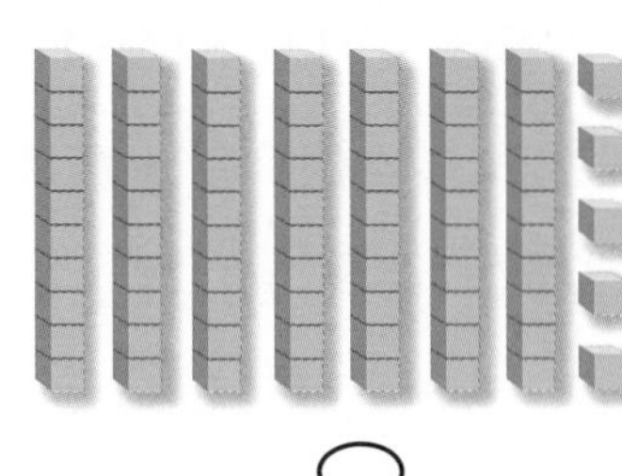 ○

TEKS 1.1D (page 265)

3. Which number shows how many dots come next in this pattern?

3 ○ 4 ○ 5 ○ 6 ○

TEKS 1.4 (page 9)

4. Liz puts this sticker pattern on her notebook. What comes next in the pattern?

 ○

 ○

 ○

 ○

TEKS 1.4 (page 13)

Education Place
Visit **www.eduplace.com/txmap/** for Test-Taking Tips and Extra Practice.

Number Patterns

TAKS Vocabulary

Here are some vocabulary words you will learn in the chapter.

skip count Start with a number and keep adding on the same number

2, 4, 6, 8, 10, 12...
You can skip count by twos.

5, 10, 15, 20, 25, 30...
You can skip count by fives.

even A number that can be grouped in twos with none left over

6 is an even number.

odd A number that, when it is grouped in twos, always has one left over

5 is an odd number.

See English-Spanish glossary pages 505–516.

TAKS Objective 6
TEKS 1.12B Relate informal language to mathematical language and symbols.

Education Place
Visit **www.eduplace.com/txmap/** for the eGlossary and vocabulary eGames.

Name ____________________

Check What You Know

Count how many.
Write the number.

1. 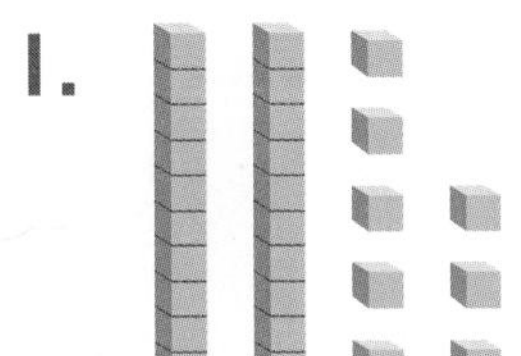

____

2. 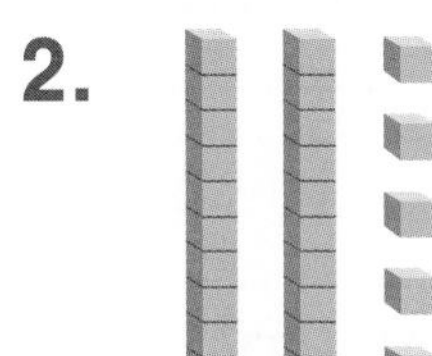

____

3.

____

4. 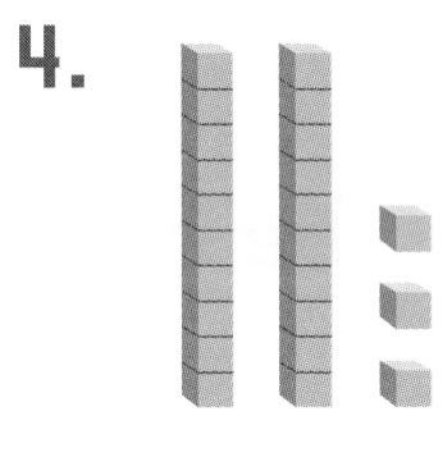

____

5. Draw the number 22 using [ten-rod] and [unit cube].

Use this page to review important skills needed for this chapter.

Name ____________________________

Chapter 16 Lesson 1

Count by Twos

Hands On

TEKS Objective
Use patterns to skip count by twos.

TAKS Vocabulary
skip count

★ Learn

To **skip count** by 2s, count two at a time.

2, 4, 6, 8, 10 — 10 cubes

★ Guided Practice

Find how many in all. Skip count by 2s.

1.     

____, ____, ____, ____, ____,

____, ____, ____, ____, ____ ____ sneakers

Think!
I write every other number when I skip count by 2s.

2.       

____, ____, ____, ____, ____, ____, ____,

____, ____, ____, ____, ____, ____ ____ socks

3. **Math Talk** What pattern do you see when you skip count by twos?

TAKS Objective 2
TEKS 1.5A Use patterns to skip count by twos, fives, and tens.

★ Practice

Write the missing numbers.
Skip count by 2s.

Remember!
Find the first number on the chart. Skip count.

4. 8, __10__, __12__, 14

5. 22, ______, ______, 28

6. 54, 56, ______, ______, 62

1	2	3	4	5	6	7	8	9	10
11	12	13	14	15	16	17	18	19	20
21	22	23	24	25	26	27	28	29	30
31	32	33	34	35	36	37	38	39	40
41	42	43	44	45	46	47	48	49	50
51	52	53	54	55	56	57	58	59	60
61	62	63	64	65	66	67	68	69	70
71	72	73	74	75	76	77	78	79	80
81	82	83	84	85	86	87	88	89	90
91	92	93	94	95	96	97	98	99	100

7. 76, ______, ______, 82, ______, ______

Count back by 2s.

8. 26, ______, ______, ______, ______, 16

9. ______, ______, 56, 54, ______, ______, ______

Algebra Readiness: Patterns

Write the missing numbers.
Skip count by twos.
Start with 2.

10.

At Home Have your child skip count by 2s to find the number of spoons in the kitchen.

En casa Pida a su niño que cuente de 2 en 2 para hallar el número de cucharas que hay en la cocina.

Name ____________________

Chapter 16 Lesson 2

Even and Odd Numbers

Hands On

TEKS Objective
Find a pattern in even and odd numbers.

TAKS Vocabulary
even
odd

Learn

Numbers are **even** or **odd.**

6

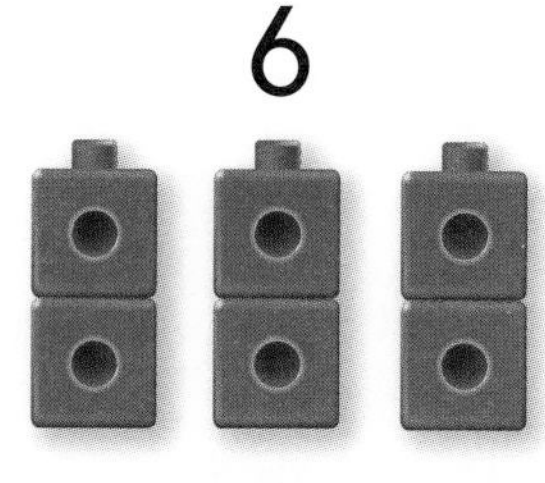

even

7

odd

You can make pairs with an even number of objects.

There is always one left with an odd number of objects.

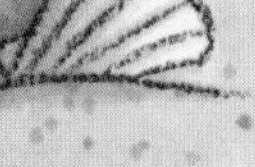

Guided Practice

Use [cube]. Circle even or odd.

1. 5  even odd

Think! The 5 cubes do not make even pairs.

2. 4   even odd

3. 7  even odd

4. 8  even odd

5. 9  even odd

6. 10  even odd

7. **Math Talk** What pattern do you see in the exercises above?

TAKS Objective 2
TEKS 1.5B Find patterns in numbers, including odd and even.

★ Practice

Use .
Circle even or odd.

8. 11

even

odd

9. 15

even

odd

10. 12

even

odd

11. 16

even

odd

12. 13

even

odd

13. 14

even

odd

Algebra Readiness: Patterns

14. Color even numbers ▭.

Color odd numbers ▭.

11	12	13	14	15	16	17	18	19	20
21	22	23	24	25	26	27	28	29	30
31	32	33	34	35	36	37	38	39	40

15. **Math Talk** What pattern do the numbers in the ones place make? Do you think 41 is even or odd? Why?

At Home Take turns with your child saying a number to 20 and identifying it as even or odd.

En casa Túrnese con su niño para decir un número hasta 20 e identificarlo como par o impar.

Name ______________________

Chapter 16 Lesson 3

Count by Fives

TEKS Objective
Use patterns to skip count by fives.

★ Learn

To skip count by 5s, count five at a time.

    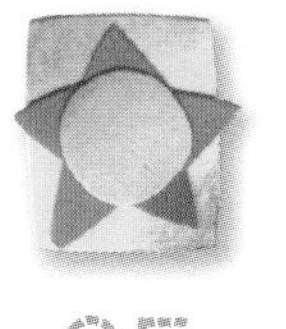

5, 10, 15, 20, 25 — 25 points

Count by 5s to count the points on the badges.

★ Guided Practice

Find how many points in all. Skip count by 5s.

1.  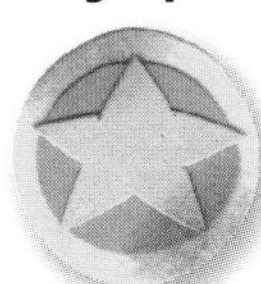   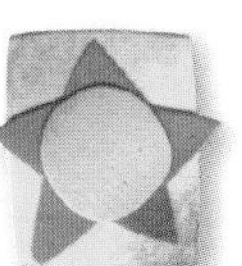

_____, _____, _____, _____, _____,

  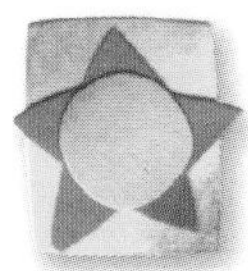  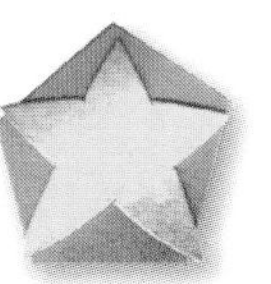

_____, _____, _____, _____, _____ — _____ points

2.  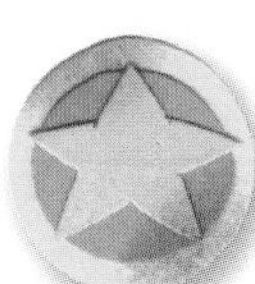   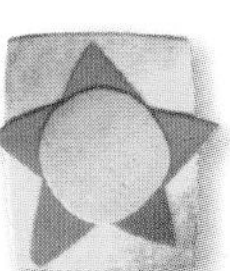 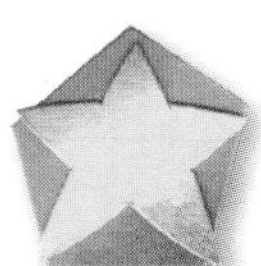 

_____, _____, _____, _____, _____, _____, _____,

  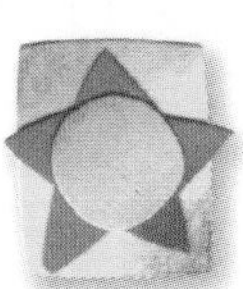  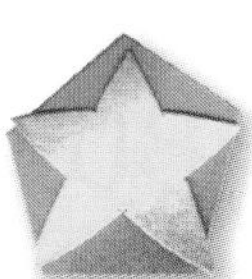 

_____, _____, _____, _____, _____, _____ — _____ points

3. **Math Talk** Why is it faster to skip count than to count by 1s?

TAKS Objective 2
TEKS 1.5A Use patterns to skip count by twos, fives, and tens.

★ Practice

Remember!
Find the first number on the chart.
Skip count.

1	2	3	4	5	6	7	8	9	10
11	12	13	14	15	16	17	18	19	20
21	22	23	24	25	26	27	28	29	30
31	32	33	34	35	36	37	38	39	40
41	42	43	44	45	46	47	48	49	50
51	52	53	54	55	56	57	58	59	60
61	62	63	64	65	66	67	68	69	70
71	72	73	74	75	76	77	78	79	80
81	82	83	84	85	86	87	88	89	90
91	92	93	94	95	96	97	98	99	100

Write the missing numbers.
Skip count by 5s.

4. 10, 15, 20, 25

5. 25, 30, ______, ______

6. 60, ______, ______, 75

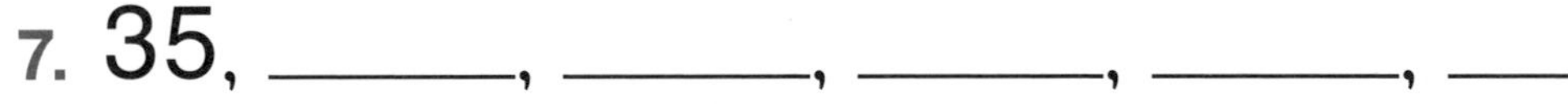

7. 35, ______, ______, ______, ______, ______

8. 75, ______, ______, 90, ______, ______

Count back by 5s.

9. 25, 20, ______, ______, ______, 0

10. ______, ______, 40, 35, ______, ______, ______

Problem Solving: Logical Reasoning

Write the mystery number.

11. It is greater than 80.
It is less than 90.
You say it when counting by 5s.
What number is it?

______

Draw or write to explain.

At Home Make groups of 5 pennies. Have your child skip count by 5s to find the number of pennies in all.

En casa Haga grupos de 5 monedas de 1 centavo. Pida a su niño que cuente de 5 en 5 para hallar el número total de monedas de 1 centavo.

Name ______________________

Chapter 16 Lesson 4

Count by Tens

TEKS **Objective**
Use patterns to skip count by tens.

★ Learn

To skip count by 10s, count ten at a time.

Count by 10s to count the pencils in each bundle.

10, 20, 30, 40, 50

50 pencils

★ Guided Practice

Find how many in all. Skip count by 10s.

Think! I add 10 when I skip count by tens.

1.  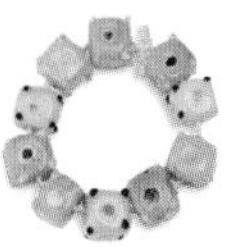  

_____, _____, _____, _____,

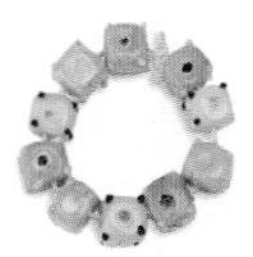   

_____, _____, _____, _____ _____ beads

2.     

_____, _____, _____, _____, _____,

_____, _____, _____, _____ _____ pieces of chalk

3. **Math Talk** What pattern do you see?

TAKS Objective 2
TEKS 1.5A Use patterns to skip count by twos, fives, and tens.

★ Practice

Write the missing numbers.
Skip count by 10s.

1	2	3	4	5	6	7	8	9	10
11	12	13	14	15	16	17	18	19	20
21	22	23	24	25	26	27	28	29	30
31	32	33	34	35	36	37	38	39	40
41	42	43	44	45	46	47	48	49	50
51	52	53	54	55	56	57	58	59	60
61	62	63	64	65	66	67	68	69	70
71	72	73	74	75	76	77	78	79	80
81	82	83	84	85	86	87	88	89	90
91	92	93	94	95	96	97	98	99	100

4. 30, 40, ___50___, ___60___

5. 60, 70, ______, ______

6. 30, ______, ______, 60

7. 10, ______, ______, 40, ______

8. 50, ______, ______, ______, ______, ______

Remember!
Find the first
number on the chart.
Skip count.

Count back by 10s.

9. 80, 70, ______, ______, ______, 30

10. ______, 90, 80, ______, ______, ______, ______

Problem Solving: Logical Reasoning

Write the mystery number.

11. It is greater than 60.
It is less than 80. You say it
when counting by 10s.
What number is it?

______

Draw or write to explain.

At Home Have your child skip count by 10s to find the number of toes and fingers in your family.

En casa Pida a su niño que cuente de 10 en 10 para hallar el número de dedos de las manos y de los pies que hay en su familia.

Name ______________________

Chapter 16 Lesson 5

Find a Pattern

Problem Solving Strategy

TEKS Objective
Create and solve problems with number patterns.

 Learn

Tina paints 10 boards on the fence on Monday. She paints 5 more boards each day. How many boards will she paint by Friday?

Understand

What do you know?

- Tina paints 10 boards on Monday.
- She paints 5 more boards each day.

Plan

You can use a pattern to solve.
How can you find the pattern?
Circle the way you could find the pattern.

draw a picture

make a table

use models

Solve

Find the pattern. Start with 10 on Monday.
Skip count by 5s until you reach Friday.

Monday	Tuesday	Wednesday	Thursday	Friday
10	15	20	25	30

Tina paints 30 boards by Friday.

Look Back

Did you answer the question?
Does your answer make sense?

TAKS Objectives 2, 6
TEKS 1.5A Use patterns to skip count by twos, fives, and tens.
TEKS 1.11B Solve problems with guidance that incorporates the processes of understanding the problem, making a plan, carrying out the plan, and evaluating the solution for reasonableness.
Also **TEKS 1.11C**

★ Guided Problem Solving

Think!
I need to start at 25 and skip count by 10.

1. Ryan has 25 stamps. He gets 10 more stamps each month. How many stamps will he have by the end of 4 months?

Start	1 month	2 months	3 months	4 months
25				

What number do you start with? ______ stamps

What skip counting pattern do you use?

2. **Math Talk** How does finding a pattern help you solve the problem?

★ Problem Solving Practice

Find the pattern. Solve.

Think!
Saturday and Sunday are weekend days.

3. On Friday Jenna makes 12 cards for her friends. She makes 2 more each day of the weekend. How many cards will she have on Sunday?

Friday	Saturday	Sunday
12		

______ cards

4. Pedro colors 5 pages in his coloring book each day. How many pages will Pedro color by the end of 5 days?

1 day	2 days	3 days	4 days	5 days
5				

______ pages

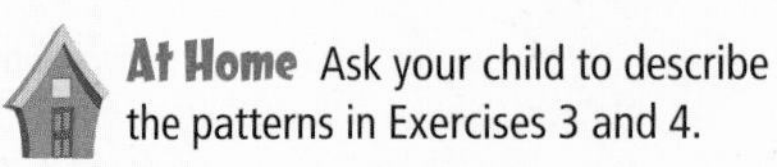

At Home Ask your child to describe the patterns in Exercises 3 and 4.
En casa Pida a su niño que describa los patrones de los Ejercicios 3 y 4.

Create and Solve

Read the problem about the masks.

There are 5 masks. Each mask has 2 eyes. How many eyes are there in all?

Use the table.
Use the pattern to find the total number of eyes.

1.

I mask	2 masks	3 masks	4 masks	5 masks
2	4	6	8	10

10 eyes

Write a problem about the whiskers on the masks.

2. ______________________________

____

____

Use the table.
Use the pattern to find the total number of whiskers.

3.

I cat	2 cats	3 cats	4 cats	5 cats

_____ whiskers

TAKS Objectives 2, 6
TEKS 1.5A Use patterns to skip count by twos, fives, and tens.
TEKS 1.11A Identify mathematics in everyday situations.

Write a problem about the ducks.

4. ____

____

____

Use the table.
Use the pattern to find the total number of feet.

5.

1 duck	2 ducks	3 ducks	4 ducks	5 ducks	6 ducks	7 ducks

______ feet

Write another problem about the ducks.

6. ____

____

____

Challenge Algebra

Name ______________________

Number Patterns

Complete the tables.

1.

Add 1.	
1	
2	
3	
4	

2.

Add 2.	
1	
2	
3	
4	

3. Think about adding odd and even numbers. What patterns do you see?

4.

Subtract 1.	
10	
9	
8	
7	

5.

Subtract 2.	
10	
9	
8	
7	

6. Think about subtracting odd and even numbers. What patterns do you see?

TAKS Objectives 2, 6
TEKS 1.5B Find patterns in numbers, including odd and even.
Also **TEKS 1.12A**

Education Place
Visit **www.eduplace.com/txmap/** for Brain Teasers.

Math Music

The Skip-Counting Game!

Math Music, Track 6

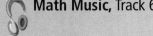

Listen to the numbers that I can name.
Listen for the patterns in the skip-counting game!

2, 4, 6, 8, 10, 12, yes!
14, 16, 18, 20, what success!
I counted by twos in the skip-counting game.
Listen for more numbers that I can name.

5, 10, 15, 20, keep on going!
25, 30, 35, 40, the numbers keep growing!
I counted by fives in the skip-counting game.
Listen for more numbers that I can name.

10, 20, 30, 40, 50, 60, wow!
70, 80, 90, 100, stop right now!
I counted by tens in the skip-counting game.
Think of more numbers that you can name!

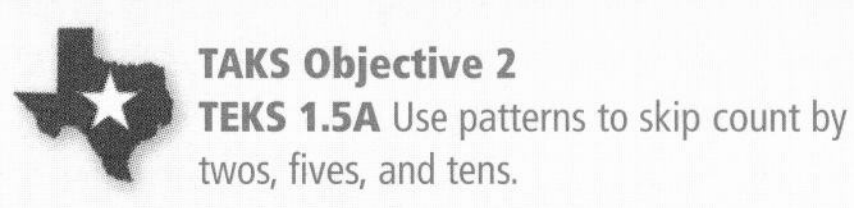

TAKS Objective 2
TEKS 1.5A Use patterns to skip count by twos, fives, and tens.

Name ______________________

Concepts and Skills

Write the missing numbers.
Skip count by 2s. TEKS 1.5A

1. 40, 42, ____, ____, 48, ____, ____, ____

Write the missing numbers.
Skip count by 5s. TEKS 1.5A

2. 70, ____, ____, ____, ____, ____, ____

Write the missing numbers.
Skip count by 10s. TEKS 1.5A

3. 40, 50, ____, ____, ____, ____, ____

Use ■. Circle even or odd. TEKS 1.5B

4. 13

even odd

Problem Solving

Find the pattern.
Solve. TEKS 1.5A, 1.11B, 1.11C

1 week	2 weeks	3 weeks	4 weeks	5 weeks
2				

5. Katie writes 2 stories a week. How many stories will she write by the end of 5 weeks?

____ stories

TAKS Prep and Spiral Review

Choose the answer for problems 1–4.

1. Which number sentence is missing from the fact family below?

$3 + 5 = 8$ $5 + 3 = 8$ $8 - 3 = 5$

$8 - 4 = 4$ ○ $8 - 1 = 7$  $8 - 5 = 3$ ○ $5 - 3 = 2$ ○

TEKS 1.5E (page 129)

2. Which number sentence is NOT in the same fact family as $5 + 4 = 9$?

$9 - 5 = 4$ ○ $7 + 2 = 9$ ○ $9 - 4 = 5$ ○ $4 + 5 = 9$ ○

TEKS 1.5E (page 129)

3. Which model shows 62?

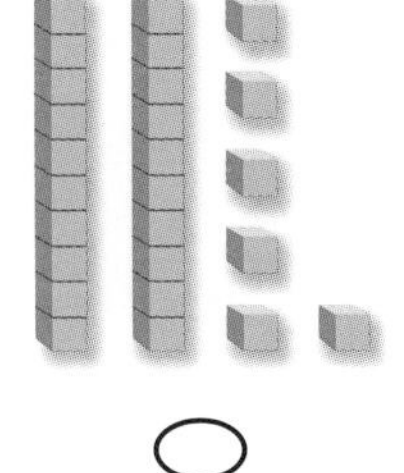 ○ 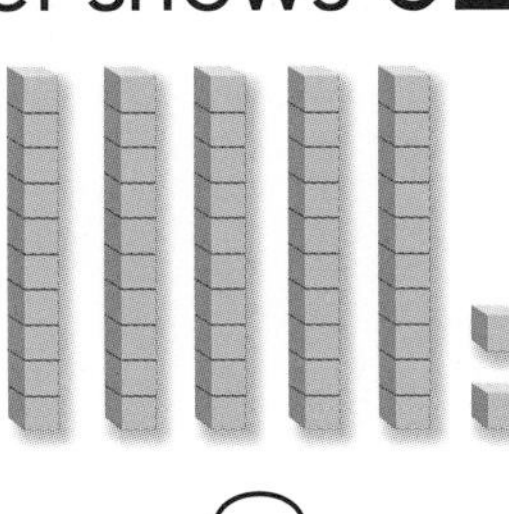 ○ 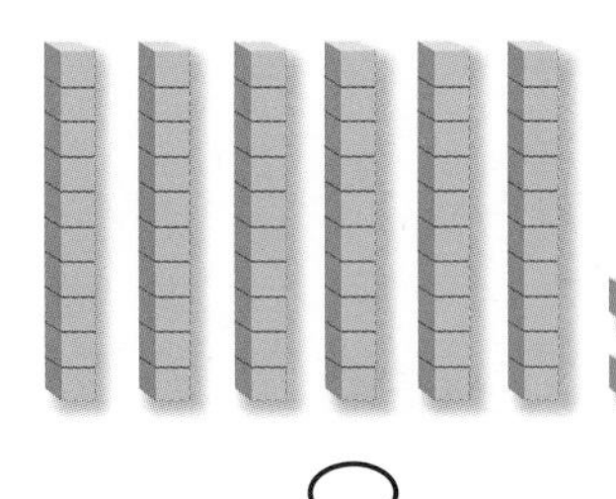 ○ 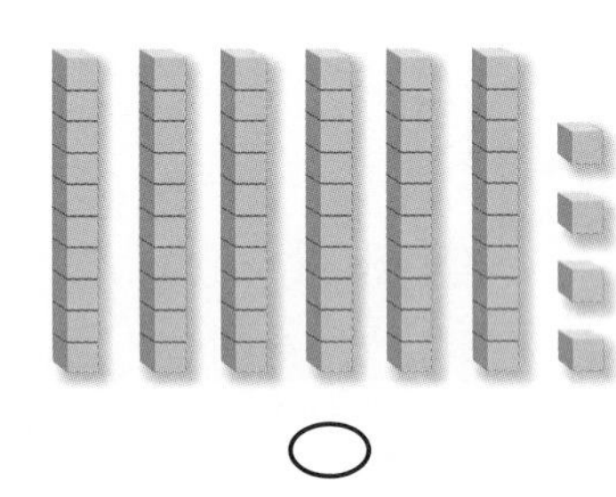 ○

TEKS 1.1B (page 267)

4. Each model shows the number of children riding on a school bus. Which model shows a number greater than 43?

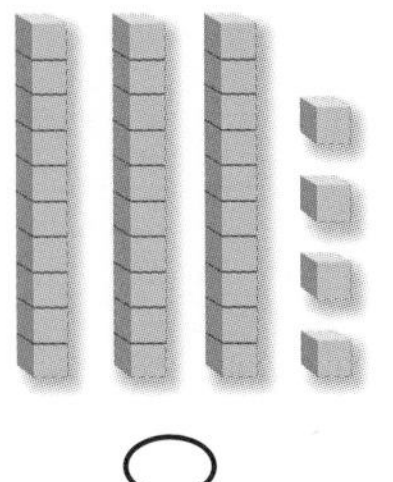 ○ ○ 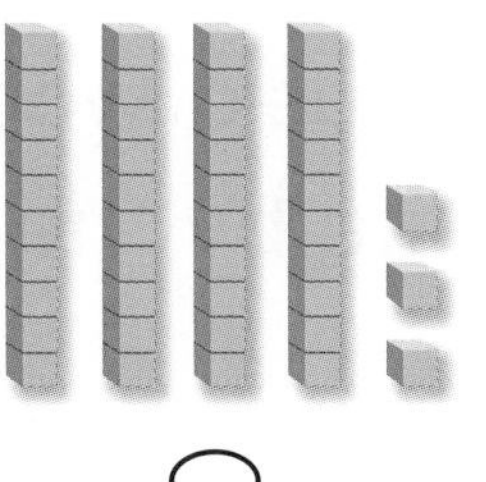 ○ ○

TEKS 1.1B (page 281)

Education Place
Visit **www.eduplace.com/txmap/** for Test-Taking Tips and Extra Practice.

Name ______________________________

Greg Tang's **Go Fast, Go Far**

Unit 6 **Mental Math Strategies**

Add 4

It is so easy to add 4.
Just add 2, and then 2 more.

I start with 5. I add 2 and get 7. Then I add 2 to get 9.

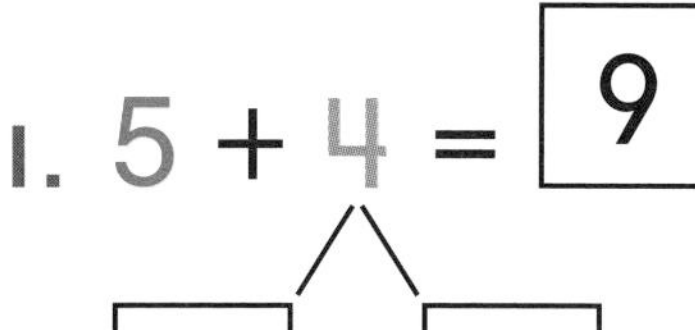

1. 5 + 4 = [9]
   [2] + [2]

2. 2 + 4 = [ ]
   [ ] + [2]

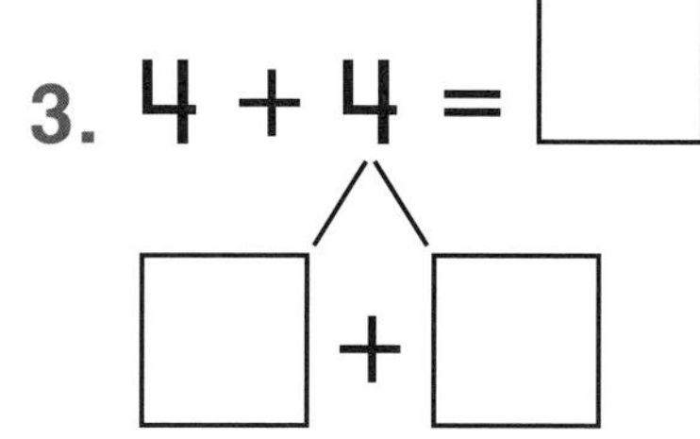

3. 4 + 4 = [ ]
   [ ] + [ ]

4. 3 + 4 = [ ]
   [ ] + [ ]

Take It Further: Now try doing everything in your head!

5. 4 + 4 = [ ]
6. 6 + 4 = [ ]
7. 5 + 4 = [ ]
8. 1 + 4 = [ ]
9. 3 + 4 = [ ]
10. 2 + 4 = [ ]

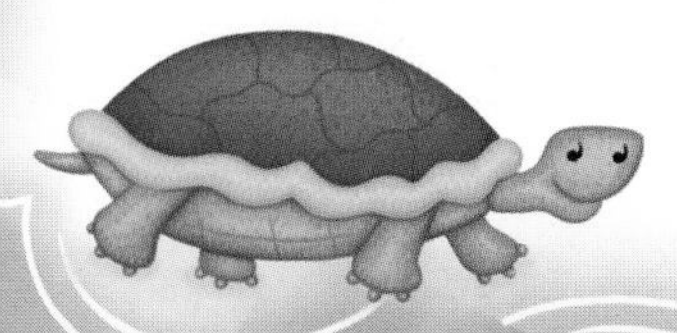

Name ______________________________

Reading and Writing Math

There are 28 days in the month of February.
Show 28 in different ways.

1. Draw a picture to show 28.

2. Write the number using tens and ones.

_____ tens _____ ones

3. Write the number for the word.

_____
twenty-eight

4. **Writing Math** Is 28 an odd number or an even number? How can you tell?

____

____

TEKS 1.12A Explain and record observations using objects, words, pictures, numbers, and technology. **TEKS 1.12B** Relate informal language to mathematical language and symbols.

Name ______________________________

Concepts and Skills

Use Workmat 5 and ▪. TEKS 1.1B, 1.1D

	Show.	Make tens. Write the tens and the ones.	Write the number.
1.	14 ones	_____ ten _____ ones	_____
2.	34 ones	_____ tens _____ ones	_____

Use ▭ and ▪.
Write the tens and the ones.
Write the number. TEKS 1.1B, 1.1D

3. 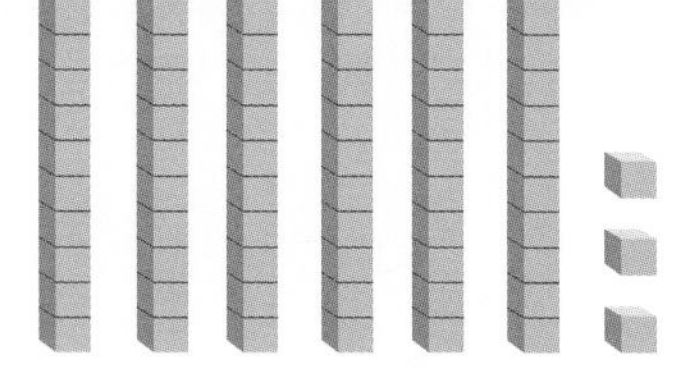

_____ tens _____ ones

_____ sixty-three

4. 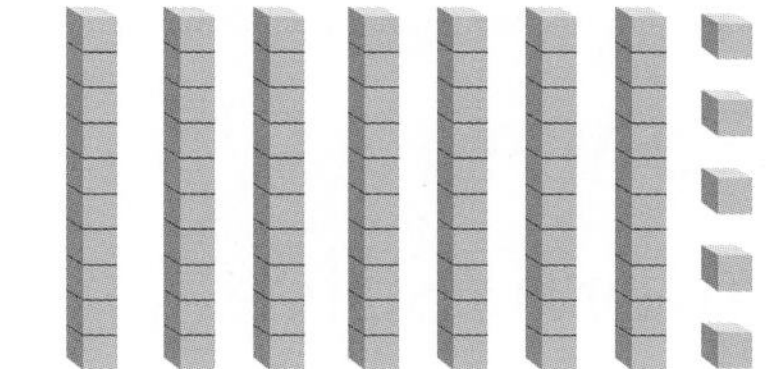

_____ tens _____ ones

_____ seventy-five

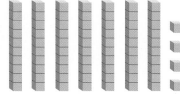

Use Workmat 5, ▭ and ▪.
Show and write the number.
Write the numbers from greatest to least. TEKS 1.1A, 1.1B, 1.5C

5. 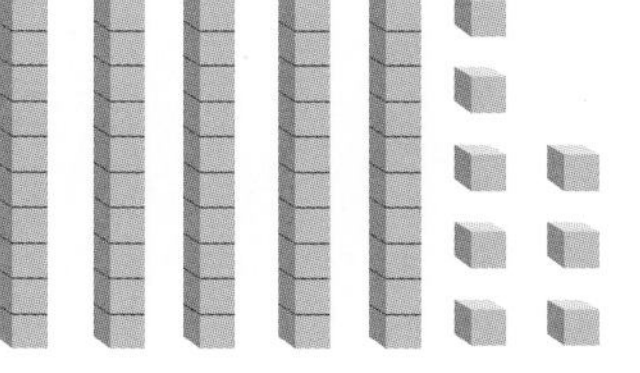

_____ _____ _____

_____ _____ _____
greatest least

Circle even or odd. TEKS 1.5B

6. 17

even

odd

7. 14

even

odd

8. 12

even

odd

9. 19

even

odd

Problem Solving

Find the pattern. Solve. TEKS 1.5A, 1.11B, 1.11C

Start	1 month	2 months	3 months	4 months
25				

10. Kyle has 25 birdhouses.
He makes 5 more birdhouses a month.
How many birdhouses will he have by the end of 4 months?

_____ birdhouses

Unit 7

Addition and Subtraction Facts Through 12

BIG IDEAS!

- It doesn't matter in what order you add numbers. The sum is still the same.
- You can relate addition and subtraction number sentences (fact families).
- Making a 10 can help you add greater numbers.

Songs and Games

Math Music Track 7
Let's Go Camping

eGames
www.eduplace.com/txmap/

Literature

Literature Big Book
- Ten Flashing Fireflies

Math Readers

ISBN-13: 978-0-618-95276-2
ISBN-10: 0-618-95276-4
89- WC - 16 15 14 13 12

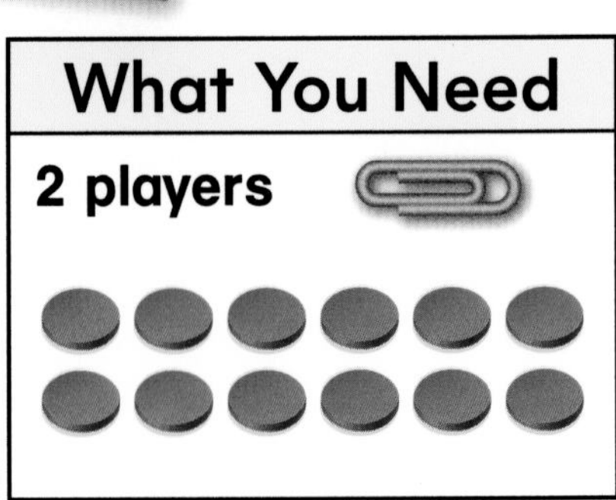

Domino Fun

1. Take turns tossing a paper clip onto a domino.
2. Add or subtract the dots. Put a counter on the answer.
3. If that number is already covered, it's your partner's turn.
4. Play until both players' number strips are covered.

Math at Home

Dear Family,

My class is starting Unit 7, **Addition and Subtraction Facts Through 12**. I will learn new strategies to help me add and subtract facts through 12. You can help me learn these vocabulary words, and we can do the Math Activity together.

From,

____

Vocabulary

order The way numbers follow one another.

$$4 + 7 = 11$$
$$7 + 4 = 11$$

You can add numbers in any **order** and get the same sum.

ten frame A chart to show groups of ten.

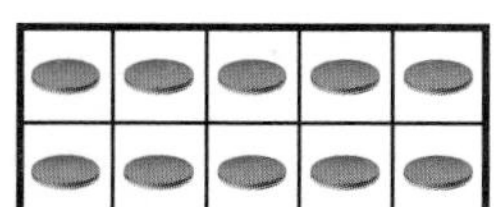 

This **ten frame** shows $10 + 3 = 13$.

addend A number that is added to another number.

6 + 5 = 11
↑ addend ↑ addend

Education Place
Visit **www.eduplace.com/txmaf/** for
- eGames and Brain Teasers
- Math at Home in other languages

Family Math Activity

Write down the numbers 6–12. Point to a number and have your child count on 1, 2, or 3 to add. Ask, *What is the sum?* Next, have your child select a number and count back 1, 2, or 3 to subtract.

0 1 2 3 4 5
6 7 8 9 10 11 12

Literature

These books link to the math in this unit. Look for them at the library.

- **Domino Addition** by Lynette Long, Ph.D. *(Charlesbridge Publishing, 1996)*
- **12 Ways to Get to 11** by Eve Merriam
- **Springtime Addition** by Jill Fuller

Matemáticas en casa

Estimada familia:

Mi clase está comenzando la Unidad 7, **Operaciones de suma y resta hasta 12**. Voy a aprender nuevas estrategias para resolver operaciones de suma y resta hasta el 12. Me pueden ayudar a aprender estas palabras de vocabulario y podemos hacer juntos la Actividad de matemáticas para la familia.

De:

____

Vocabulario

orden Forma en que los números siguen uno después de otro.

4 + 7 = 11
7 + 4 = 11

Se puede sumar números en cualquier **orden** y obtener la misma suma.

marco de diez Cuadro para mostrar grupos de diez.

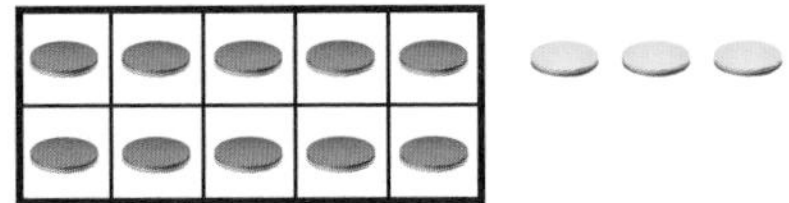

Este **marco de diez** muestra que 10 + 3 = 13.

sumando Número que se suma a otro número.

6 + 5 = 11

↑ sumando ↑ sumando

Education Place

Visite **www.eduplace.com/txmaf/** para

- Juegos en línea y acertijos
- Matemáticas en casa, en otros idiomas

Actividad de matemáticas para la familia

Escriba los números del 6 al 12. Señale un número y pida a su niño que cuente hacia adelante 1, 2 ó 3 para sumar. Pregunte: *¿Cuál es la suma?* Luego, pida a su niño que escoja un número y cuente hacia atrás 1, 2 ó 3 para restar.

0 1 2 3 4 5
6 7 8 9 10 11 12

Literatura

Estos libros hablan sobre las matemáticas de esta unidad. Podemos buscarlos en la biblioteca.

- **Cuenta con el béisbol** por Barbara Barbieri McGrath *(Charlesbridge Publishing, 2005)*
- **¿Cuántos son?** por Maribel Suarez

Now it's your turn to write or draw.
Think of summer and what you'd do,
If you could plan what's best for you!

TAKS Objectives 1, 6
TEKS 1.3B, 1.11A

UNIT 7

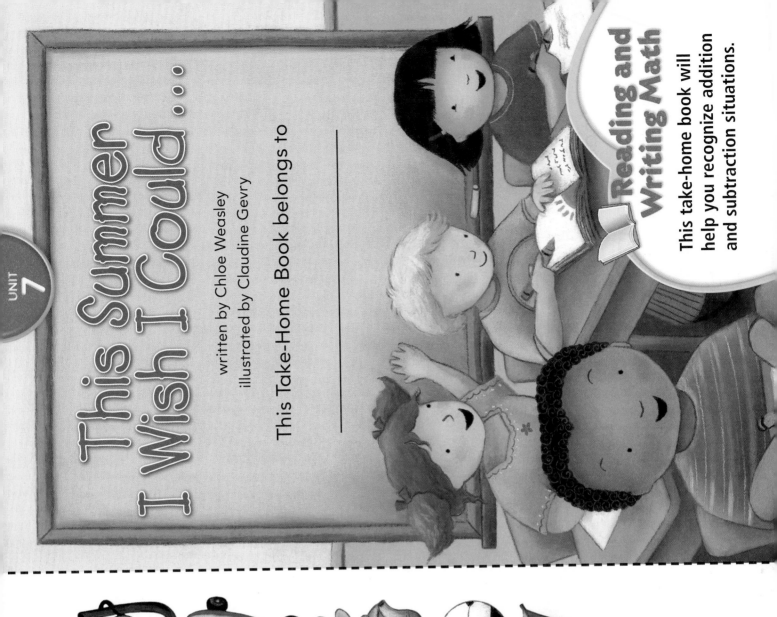

This Summer I Wish I Could . . .

written by Chloe Weasley
illustrated by Claudine Gevry

This Take-Home Book belongs to

____

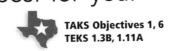

Reading and Writing Math

This take-home book will help you recognize addition and subtraction situations.

To my surprise and great delight
Our teacher asked us to draw or write
About something we would think so cool
To do this summer when out of school.
So many ideas swirled in my head!
"There are lots of things I'd do," I said.

But really and truly the most fun
Is when in summer I play and run,
Or read a book beneath a tree
And simply watch a bumble bee.

Or perhaps this summer time,
My goat and I would take a climb.
Then build a house up in a tree.
A farm and far off city we could see.
How many cows? How many horses?
How many fewer horses than cows?

_____ – _____ = _____ fewer horses

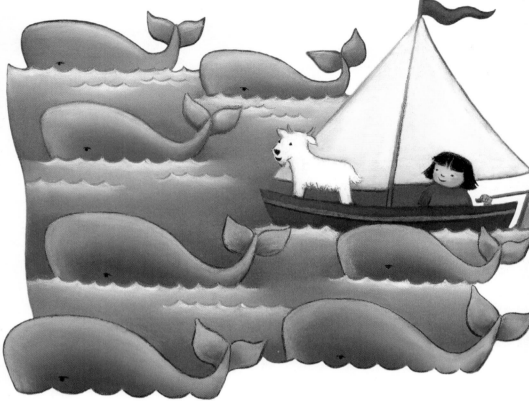

I'd sail the ocean in a boat.
My first mate would be a goat.
From the starboard side we'd see
A pod of whales. There would be 3.
Then I'd spy 4 whales more!
Oh, such a summer I'd adore.

How many whales do they see in all?

_____ + _____ = _____ whales

I'd take a rocket to where it's starry.
Oh, what fun, an outer space safari!
The first of many stops would be
Our moon, where moon mountains
I would see.

How many moon mountains are tall?
How many are short?
How many moon mountains are there in all?

____ + ____ = ____ moon mountains

Addition Facts Through 12

TAKS Vocabulary

Here are some vocabulary words you will learn in the chapter.

order The way numbers follow one another

$$5 + 6 = 11$$

$$6 + 5 = 11$$

You can add numbers in any order and get the same sum.

count on A way to add 1, 2, or 3

Start with 7.
Count on 2 by saying 8, 9.

$$7 + 2 = 9$$

ten frame A chart to show groups of ten

See English-Spanish glossary pages 505–516.

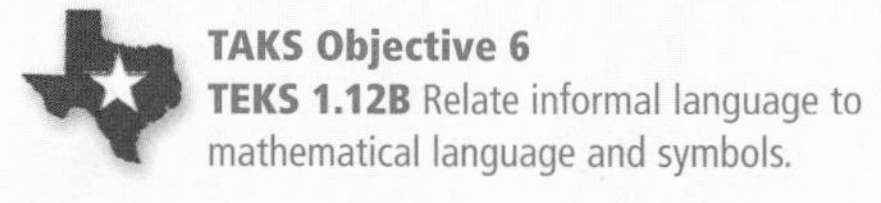

TAKS Objective 6
TEKS 1.12B Relate informal language to mathematical language and symbols.

Education Place
Visit **www.eduplace.com/txmap/** for the eGlossary and vocabulary eGames.

Name ______________________________

Solve.

1.  

$4 + 3 =$ ____

2.  

$7 + 2 =$ ____

3.  

$6 + 1 =$ ____

4.  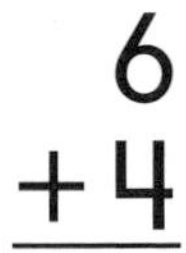

$$\begin{array}{r} 6 \\ +4 \\ \hline \end{array}$$

5. 

$$\begin{array}{r} 5 \\ +3 \\ \hline \end{array}$$

Use this page to review important skills needed for this chapter.

Name ______________________

Chapter 17 Lesson 1

Add in Any Order

TEKS Objective
Use order patterns in facts to find sums through 12.

TAKS Vocabulary
order

★ Learn

You can change the **order** of the addends and get the same sum.

Make a cube train.

8 + 4 = 12

Turn it around.

4 + 8 = 12

★ Guided Practice

Use cubes. Make the train.
Color and write to show.

Think!
I know 4 + 7 = 11, so I also know 7 + 4.

1. Make an 11 train.

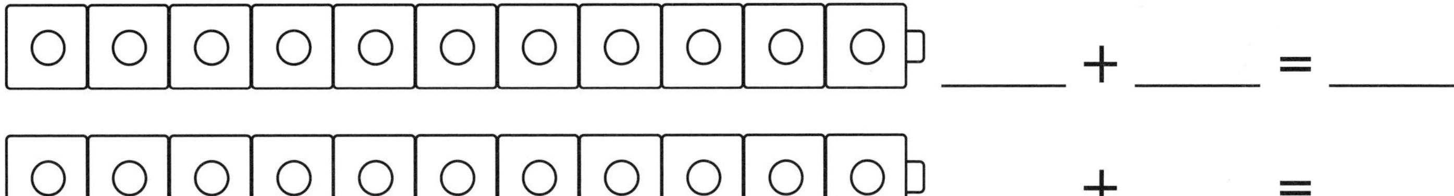

___ + ___ = ___

___ + ___ = ___

2. Make a 10 train.

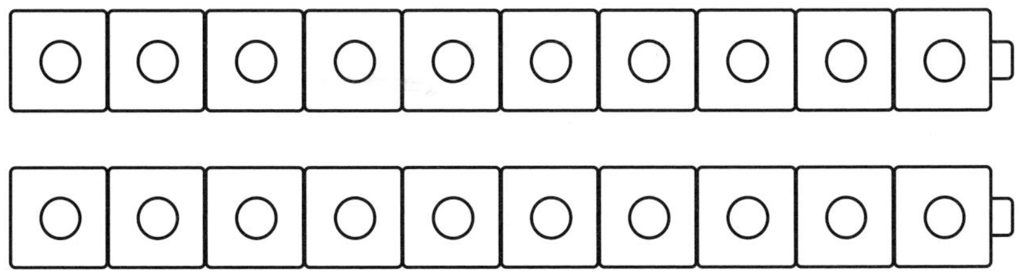

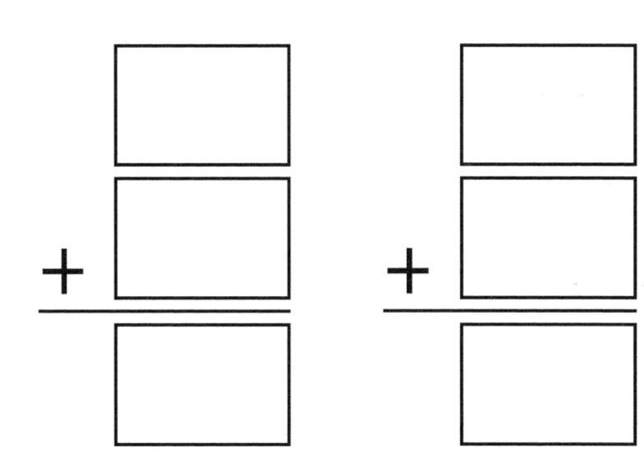

3. **Math Talk** Why is the sum of 5 + 7 the same as 7 + 5? What patterns do you see?

TAKS Objectives 1, 2
TEKS 1.3B Use concrete and pictorial models to apply basic addition and subtraction facts (up to 9 + 9 = 18 and 18 – 9 = 9).

TEKS 1.5D Use patterns to develop strategies to solve basic addition and basic subtraction problems.

★ Practice

Use cubes. Make the train.
Color and write to show.

Remember!
Turn your
train around.

4. Make a 9 train.

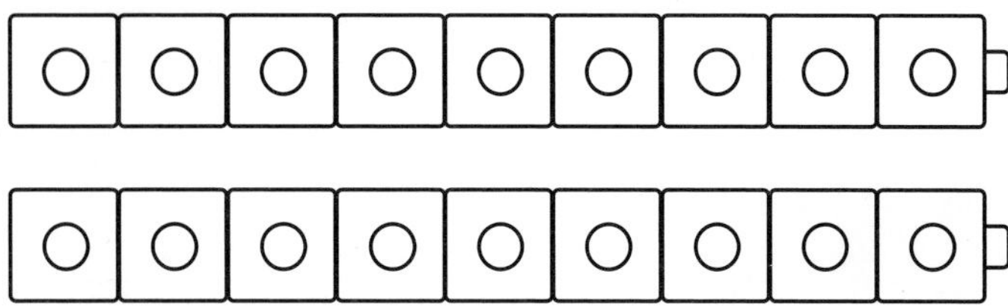

4 + 5 = 9

___ + ___ = ___

5. Make an 8 train.

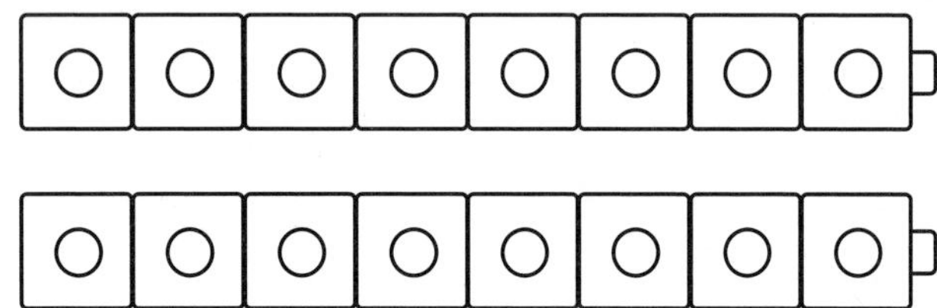

___ + ___ = ___

___ + ___ = ___

6. Make an 11 train.

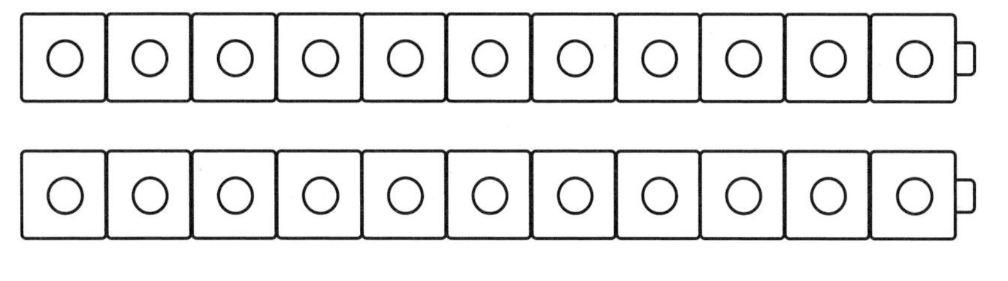

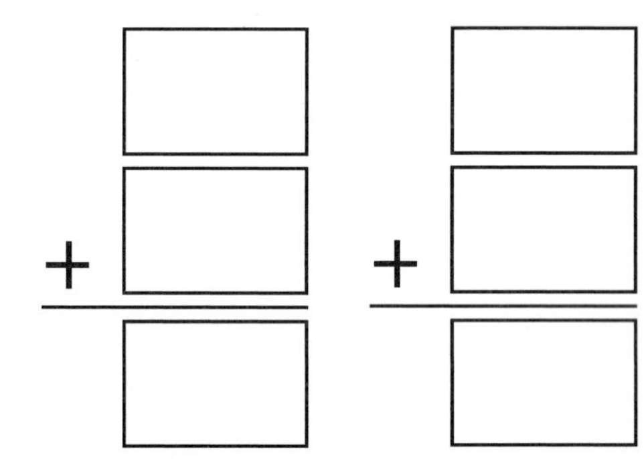

Problem Solving: Number Sense

Write a number sentence to solve.

7. 6 children play in the sand.
5 children join them.
How many children in all?

___ + ___ = ___

8. 5 children play ball.
6 children join them.
How many children in all?

___ + ___ = ___

At Home Ask your child to solve 8 + 4 and 4 + 8 and tell how he or she found the sum.

En casa Pida a su niño que resuelva 8 + 4 y 4 + 8, y que diga cómo halló la suma.

Name ________________________________

Chapter 17 Lesson 2

Count On to Add

TEKS Objective
Use the counting on 1, 2, or 3 strategy to find sums through 12.

TAKS Vocabulary
count on

★ Learn

Remember, you can **count on** to add.

How many balls are there?

$8 + 3 =$ ____

★ Guided Practice

Count on to add.
Use cubes if you wish.

Think!
I start with 9.
I count on 2.

1. 

____, ____

$9 + 2 =$ ____

2.  

____, ____, ____

$9 + 3 =$ ____

3. 

____

$$\begin{array}{r} 7 \\ +\ 1 \\ \hline \end{array}$$

4. 

____

$$\begin{array}{r} 9 \\ +\ 1 \\ \hline \end{array}$$

5. **Math Talk** What patterns help you find the sum?

TAKS Objectives 1, 2
TEKS 1.3B Use concrete and pictorial models to apply basic addition and subtraction facts (up to 9 + 9 = 18 and 18 – 9 = 9).

TEKS 1.5D Use patterns to develop strategies to solve basic addition and basic subtraction problems.

★ Practice

Count on to add.
Use cubes if you wish.

6.   

5, 6, 7

4 + 3 = 7

7. 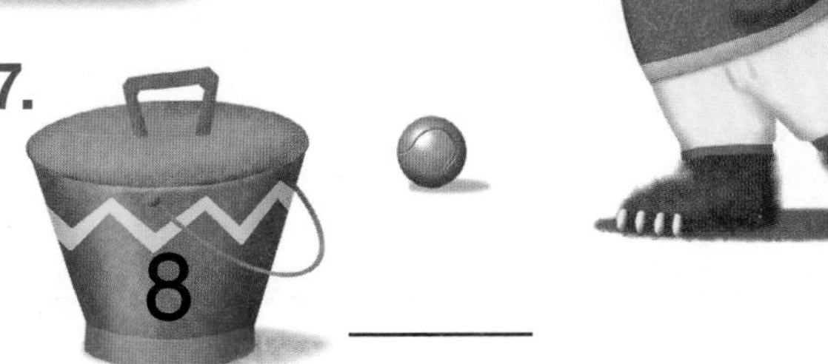

____

8 + 1 = ____

8.   

____, ____, ____

5 + 3 = ____

9.  

____, ____

8 + 2 = ____

10. 

____, ____

$$\begin{array}{r} 7 \\ +2 \\ \hline \end{array}$$

11. 

____, ____

$$\begin{array}{r} 10 \\ +\ 2 \\ \hline \end{array}$$

Problem Solving: Reasoning

12. Sam and Amy see 8 gloves. They see 3 bats. How many gloves and bats do they see in all?

Draw or write to explain.

____ gloves and bats

At Home Ask your child to count on to add 1, 2, or 3 to any number less than 10.

En casa Pida a su niño que cuente hacia adelante para sumar 1, 2 ó 3 a cualquier número menor que 10.

Name ______________________________

Chapter 17 Lesson 3

Sums of 10

Hands On

TEKS Objective
Use counters and a ten frame to make sums of 10.

TAKS Vocabulary
ten frame

Learn

There are different ways to make the sum of 10 on a **ten frame.**

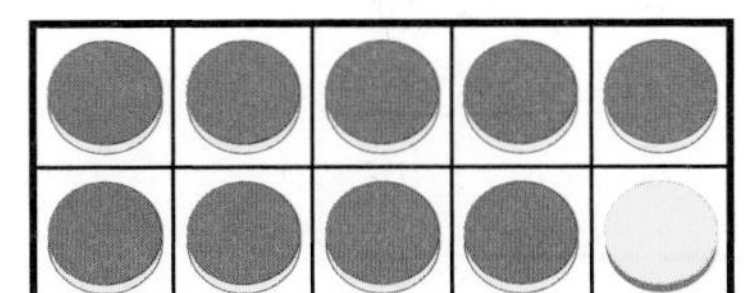

9 + ____ = 10

Guided Practice

Use Workmat 1 and ◯ to make 10.

Draw counters. Complete.

Think!
There are 8 counters.
I put in 2 more counters to make 10.

1. 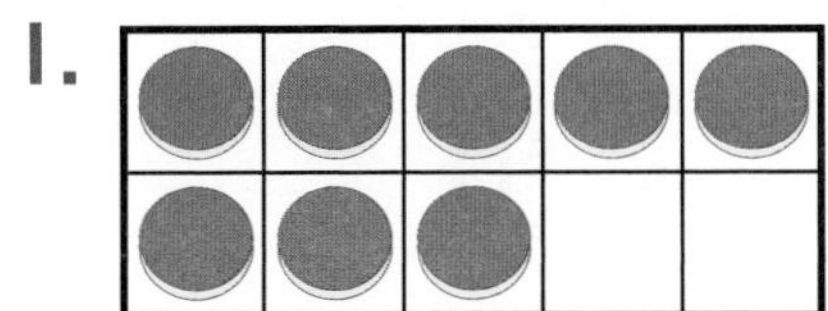

8 + ____ = 10

2. 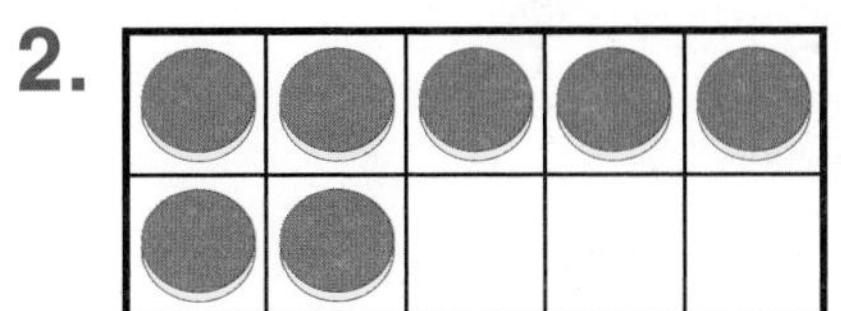

7 + ____ = 10

3. 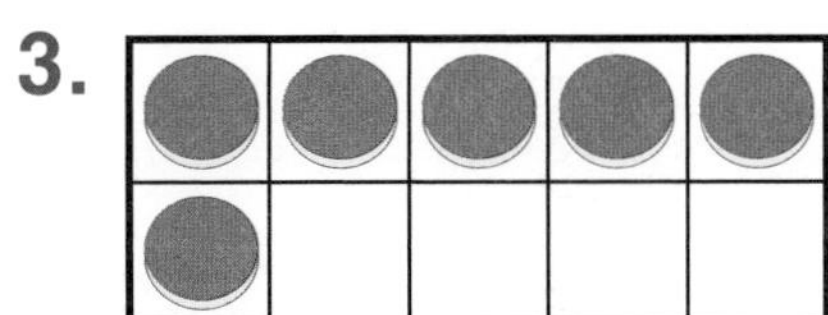

6 + ____ = 10

4. 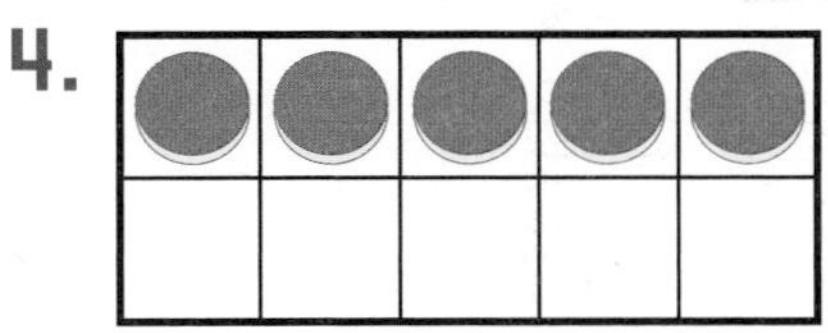

5 + ____ = 10

5. **Math Talk** How do the counters and workmat help you see how to make 10 on a ten frame?

TAKS Objective 1
TEKS 1.3B Use concrete and pictorial models to apply basic addition and subtraction facts (up to 9 + 9 = 18 and 18 – 9 = 9).

★ Practice

Use Workmat 1 and ◯ to make 10. Draw counters. Complete the addition sentence.

Remember! Fill the ten frame to make 10.

6. 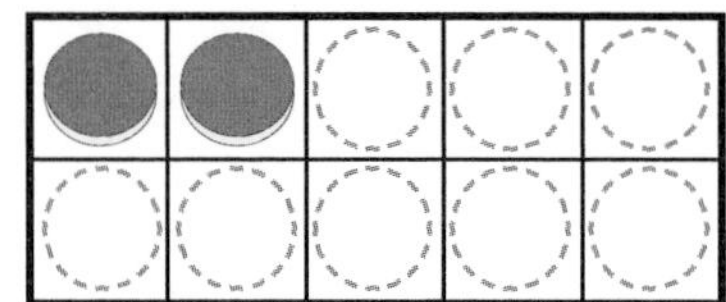

2 + 8 = 10

7. 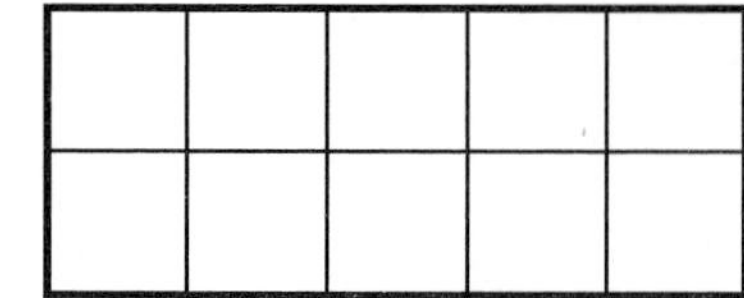

0 + ____ = 10

8. 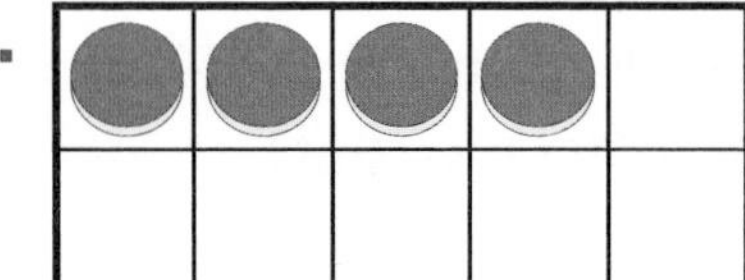

4 + ____ = 10

9. 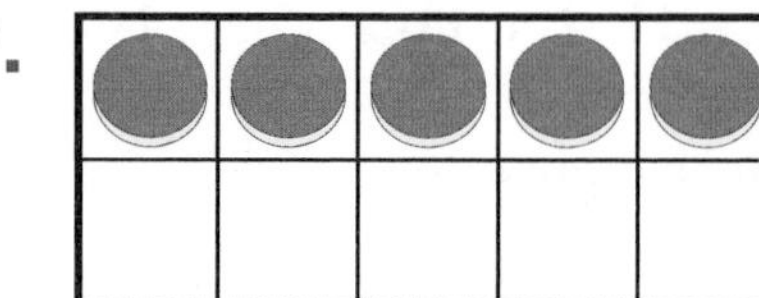

5 + ____ = 10

10. 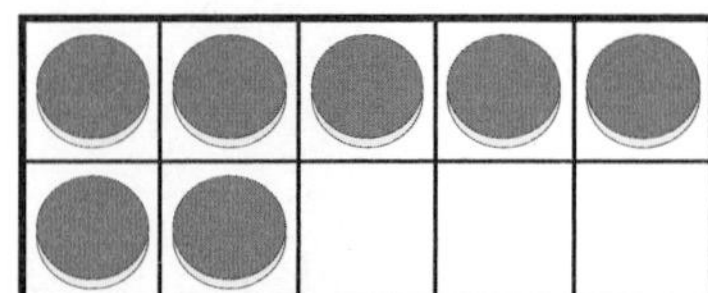

7 + ____ = 10

11. 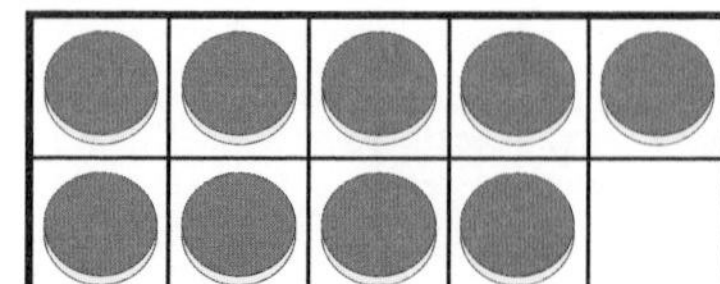

9 + ____ = 10

Algebra Readiness: Missing Addends

12. Ellen has 10 players on her team. 5 are playing. How many are not playing?

____ players

Draw or write to explain.

At Home Have your child tell you how to make 10.

En casa Pida a su niño que le diga cómo hacer 10.

Name ______________________________

Chapter 17 Lesson 4

Make 10 to Add

Hands On

TEKS Objective
Use making 10 to find sums greater than 10.

Making 10 can help you find other sums.

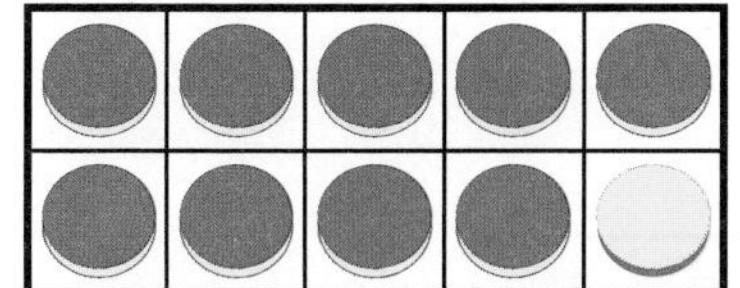
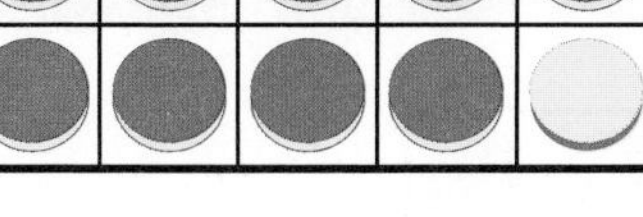

9 + 1 = 10   9 + 2 = 11

I know 9 + 1 = 10, so 9 + 2 must be one more than 10.

Guided Practice

Use Workmat 1 and ◯.
Use making 10 to help you find the sum.

Think!
I know 5 + 5 = 10, so 5 + 7 will be 2 more than 10.

Draw counters.

1. 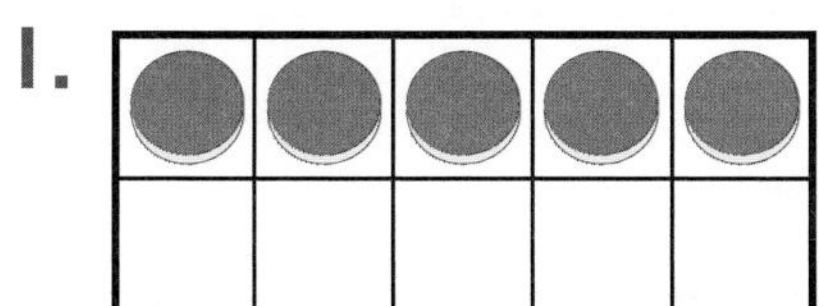

5 + 7 = ____

2. 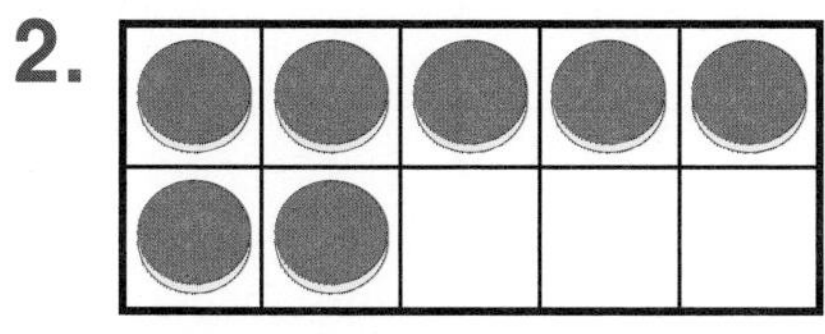

7 + 4 = ____

3. 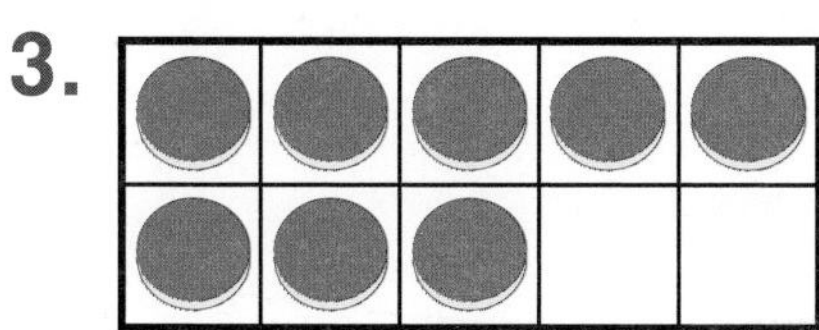

8 + 4 = ____

4. 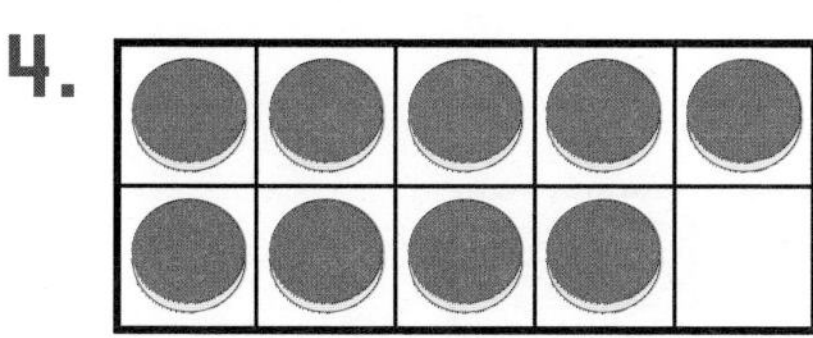

9 + 3 = ____

5. **Math Talk** What other strategy could help you find 9 + 3?

TAKS Objective 1
TEKS 1.3B Use concrete and pictorial models to apply basic addition and subtraction facts (up to 9 + 9 = 18 and 18 – 9 = 9).

★ Practice

Use Workmat 1 and ◯.
Use making 10 to help you find the sum.

Remember!
Two counters are outside the filled ten frame when you make 12.

6. 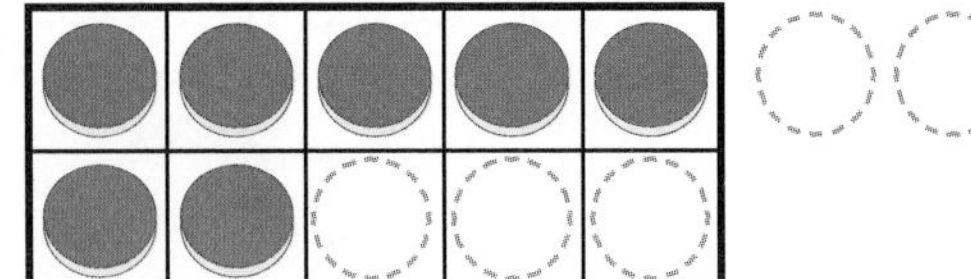

$7 + 5 =$ ____

7. 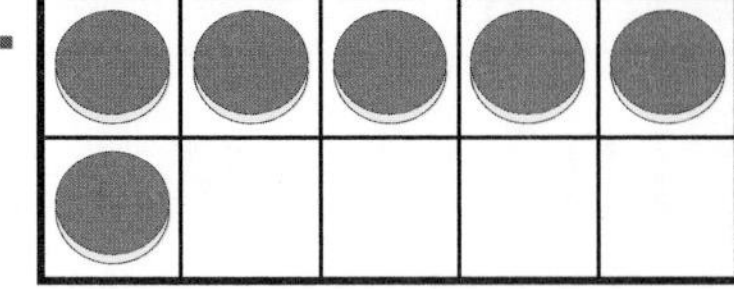

$6 + 5 =$ ____

8. 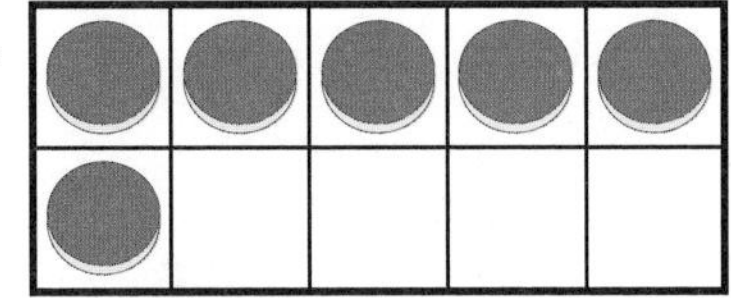

$6 + 6 =$ ____

9. 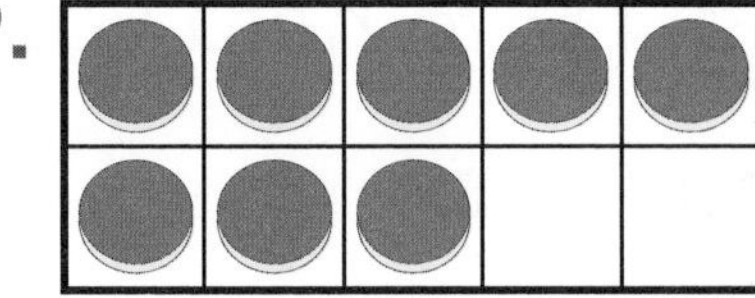

$8 + 3 =$ ____

10. 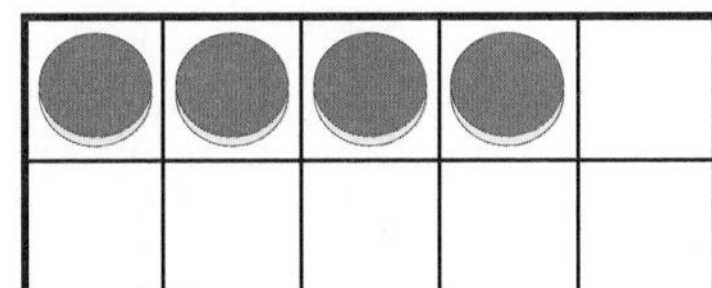

$4 + 8 =$ ____

11. 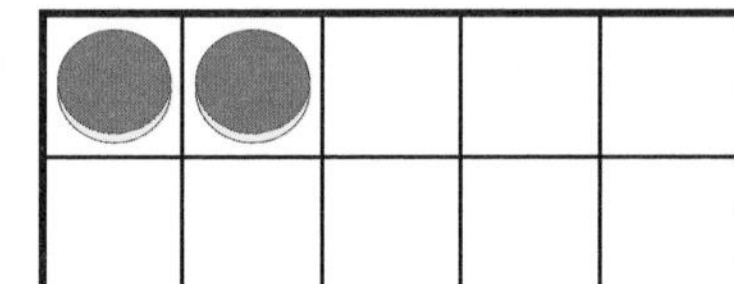

$2 + 9 =$ ____

Algebra Readiness: Number Sentences

Write the sum.

12. 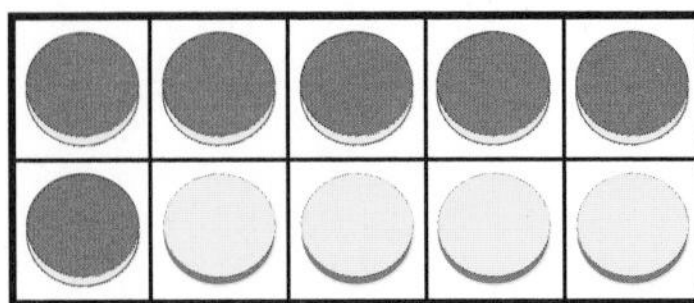

____ $= 6 + 4$

13. 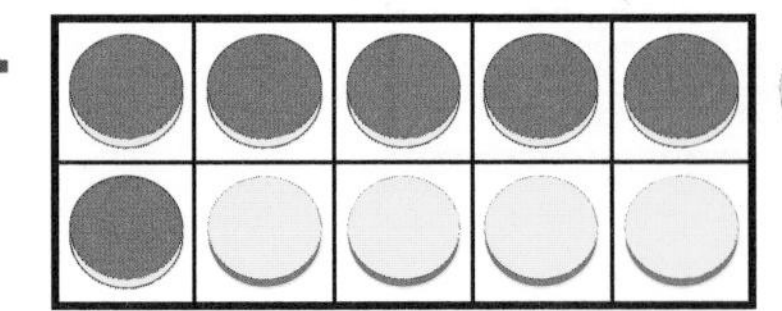

____ $= 6 + 5$

At Home Ask your child to tell several pairs of numbers that have a sum of 11.

En casa Pida a su niño que le diga varios pares de números que sumen 11.

Name ______________________

Chapter 17 Lesson 5

Draw a Picture

Problem Solving
Strategy
TEKS Objective
Draw pictures to solve problems.

Julio is first in line.
5 children are behind him.
How many children are in line?

Understand

What do you know?

- Julio is first in line.
- 5 more children are behind him.
- I need to find the number of children in all.

Plan

You can draw a picture.
Start with Julio.
Then draw 5 other children.

Solve

Draw a picture.
Draw to show Julio.

Draw 5 more children to show the children behind him.

How many children are in line? 6 children

Look Back

Did you answer the question?
Does your answer make sense?

TAKS Objectives 1, 6
TEKS 1.3B Use concrete and pictorial models to apply basic addition and subtraction facts (up to 9 + 9 = 18 and 18 – 9 = 9).

TEKS 1.11B Solve problems with guidance that incorporates the processes of understanding the problem, making a plan, carrying out the plan, and evaluating the solution for reasonableness. Also **TEKS 1.11C**

★ Guided Problem Solving

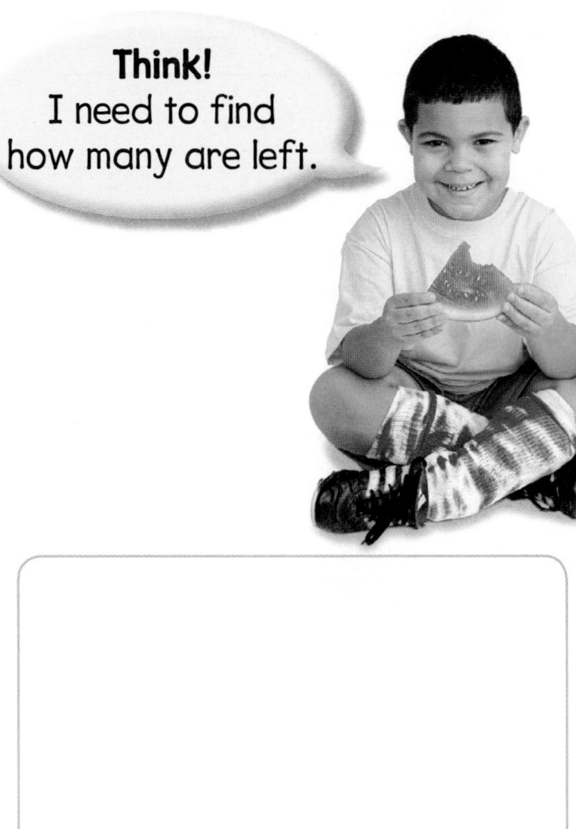

Think!
I need to find how many are left.

1. There are 8 watermelons on the table. 4 watermelons are eaten. How many watermelons are left?

   Draw a line under what you need to find out.

   Draw a model.

   Solve the problem.

   _____ watermelons

2. Math Talk How did drawing a picture help you to solve the problem?

★ Problem Solving Practice

Draw a picture to solve.

3. There are 5 burgers on the grill. There are 9 burgers on a tray. Are there more on the grill or on the tray?

   ____

4. Lee puts 8 sandwiches in a picnic basket. Then he puts in 3 more. How many sandwiches are in the basket now?

   _____ sandwiches

At Home Change the numbers in one or more of the problems on this page. Ask your child to draw a picture to solve.

En casa Cambie los números en uno o en más de uno de los problemas de esta página. Pida a su niño que haga un dibujo para resolver.

Name ______________________

Add It Up!

Use the cubes found at **www.eduplace.com/txmap/** to add.

Sam has 8 stamps. He finds 4 more. How many stamps does Sam have in all?

1. Put your pointer over the **stamp** tool.
   - Click the red cube 8 times.
2. Put your pointer over the **stamp** tool.
   - Click the blue cube 4 times.
3. Click [1 2 3].

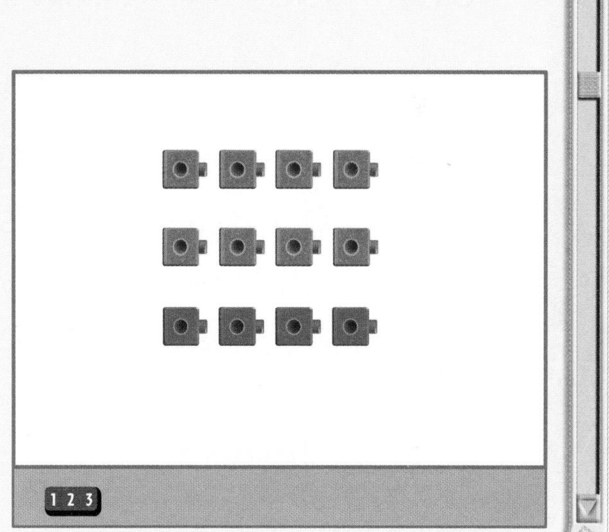

Use the cubes. Write each sum.

1. 6 + 5 = ____

2. 7 + 3 = ____

3. There are 7 girls and 5 boys in line. How many children are in line?

____ children

4. Lee draws 9 circles and 3 squares. How many figures does Lee draw?

____ ◯ ____ ◯ ____

____ figures

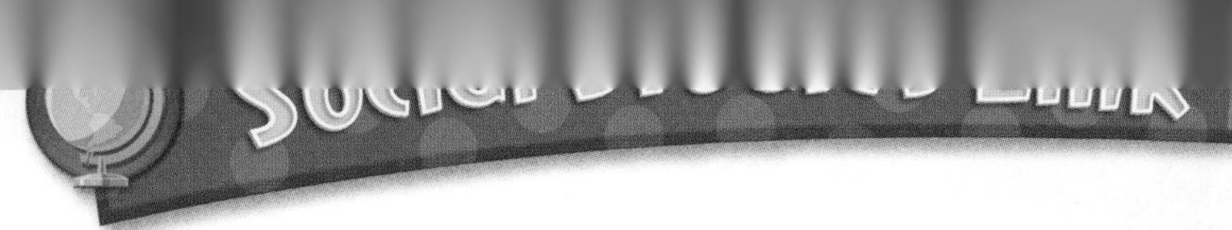

Fourth of July

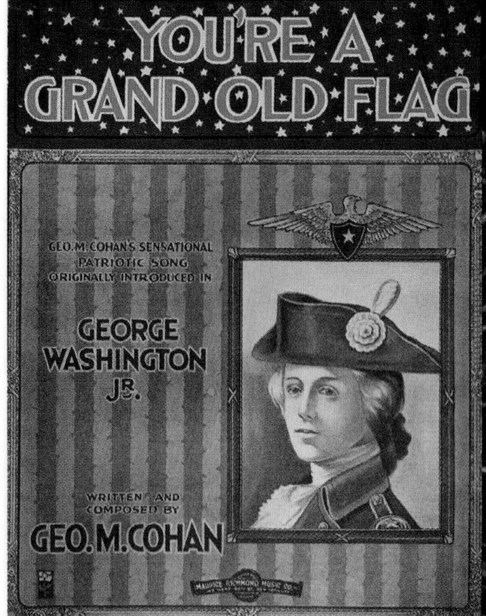

On July 4 we celebrate our independence and freedom as a country. We have barbeques, parades, and fireworks. 150 years ago, life was simpler. Food was cooked on wood fires. Parades had only horses, not cars and trucks. Towns had only a few fireworks.

Draw a picture to solve.

1. Abby makes lemonade. She uses 8 large lemons and 3 small lemons. How many lemons does she use in all?

   _____ lemons

2. There are 9 red balloons and 12 blue balloons. How many fewer red balloons are there?

   _____ fewer red balloons

3. **Math Talk** How did you solve each problem?

TAKS Objectives 1, 6
TEKS 1.3B Use concrete and pictorial models to apply basic addition and subtraction facts (up to 9 + 9 = 18 and 18 − 9 = 9).

TEKS 1.13 Justify thinking using objects, words, pictures, numbers, and technology.
TEKS Social Studies 2B, 13D

Name ______________________________

Concepts and Skills

Use cubes. Make the train.
Color and write to show. TEKS 1.3B, 1.5D

1. Make a 12 train.

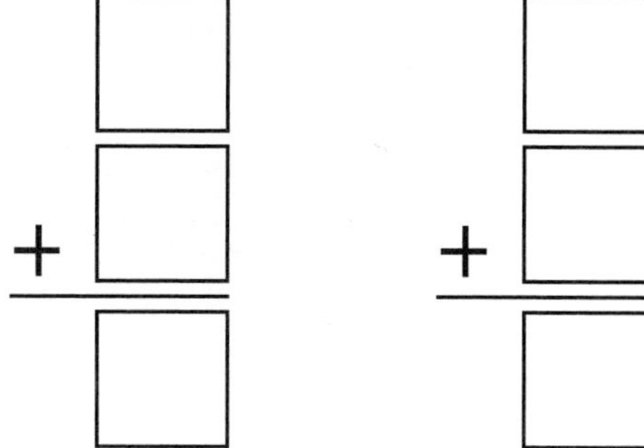

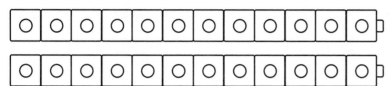

Count on to add.
Use cubes if you wish. TEKS 1.3B, 1.5D

2.   

_____, _____

9 + 2 = _____

Use Workmat 1 and  .
Draw counters.
Complete the addition sentence. TEKS 1.3B

3. 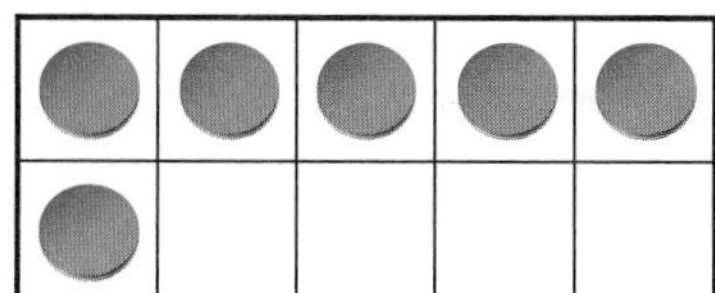

6 + _____ = 10

Problem Solving TEKS 1.3B, 1.11B, 1.11C

Draw a picture to solve.

4. Ann picked 9 peaches.
Then she picked 3 more.
How many peaches did she pick?

_____ peaches

TAKS Prep and Spiral Review

Choose the answer for problems 1–4.

1. Which shows the number of blocks in each model in order from least to greatest?

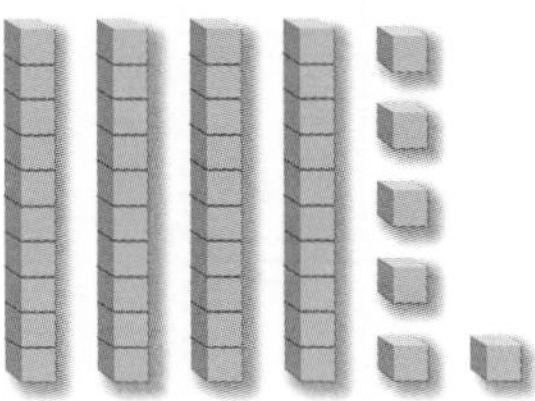
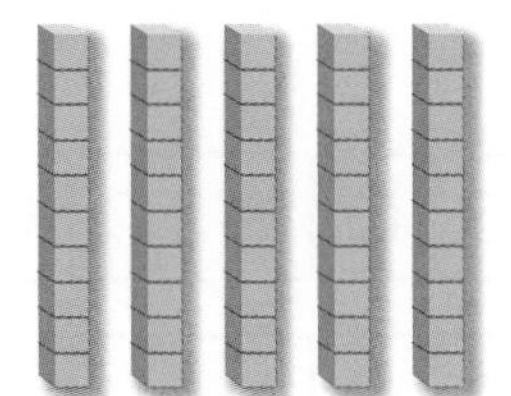
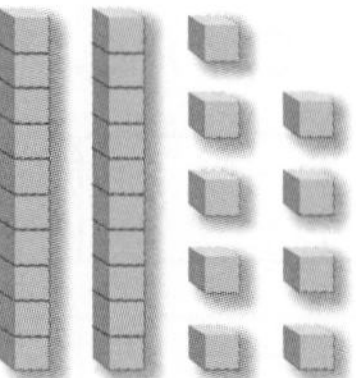

50, 46, 29	29, 50, 46	29, 46, 50	46, 50, 29
○	○	○	○

TEKS 1.5C (page 285)

2. The number of beads Ann used to make a necklace is greater than 33. It is less than 35. Which number shows how many beads Ann used?

30	32	34	35
○	○	○	○

TEKS 1.5C (page 281)

3. In which group would you put a circle?

0 sides, 0 corners	3 sides, 3 corners	4 sides, 4 corners	4 sides all the same
○	○	○	○

TEKS 1.6A, 1.6C (page 147)

4. Lee sorts figures by the number of corners. Which belongs in a group of figures with 4 corners?

○ ○ ○ ○

TEKS 1.6A, 1.6C (page 147)

Visit www.eduplace.com/txmap/ for Test-Taking Tips and Extra Practice.

Subtraction Facts Through 12

TAKS Vocabulary

Here are some vocabulary words you will learn in the chapter.

whole All of the parts

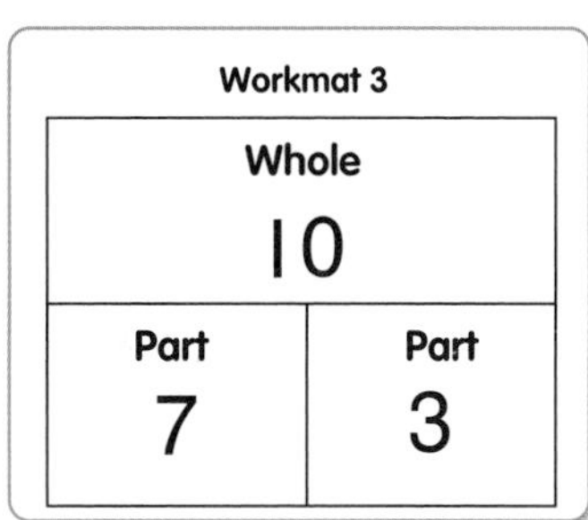

Whole	
10	
Part	Part
7	3

Workmat 3

count back A way to subtract 1, 2, or 3

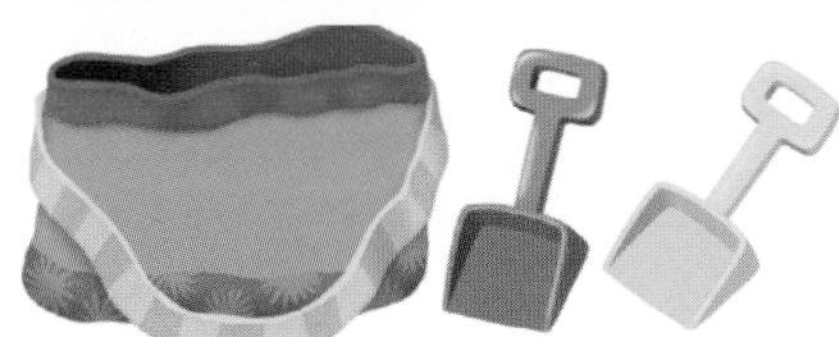

Start with 11. Count back 2 by saying 10, 9.

$$11 - 2 = 9$$

addend A number that is added to another number

$$8 + ? = 12 \leftarrow \text{sum}$$

↑ addend ↑ addend

If you know one addend and the sum, you can find the missing addend.

See English-Spanish glossary pages 505–516.

TAKS Objective 6
TEKS 1.12B Relate informal language to mathematical language and symbols.

Education Place
Visit **www.eduplace.com/txmap/** for the eGlossary and vocabulary eGames.

Name ______________________________

Check What You Know

Circle and cross out to subtract.
Write the difference both ways.

1.

$9 - 4 =$ ____

2.

$$\begin{array}{r} 9 \\ -\ 4 \\ \hline \end{array}$$

3.

$10 - 8 =$ ____

4.

$$\begin{array}{r} 10 \\ -\ 8 \\ \hline \end{array}$$

Match. Then subtract.

5. How many more bicycles than skateboards are there?

$10 - 3 =$ ____

Use this page to review important skills needed for this chapter.

Name ______________________

Chapter 18 Lesson 1

Model Subtraction Facts

Hands On

TEKS Objective
Model subtraction facts using parts and wholes.

TAKS Vocabulary
whole
part

★ Learn

If you know the **whole** and one **part**, you can subtract to find the other part.

There are 7 counters in all. 3 are in one part. How many are in the other part?

Whole	
7	
Part	Part
3	4

There are 4 counters in the other part.

★ Guided Practice

Use Workmat 3 and ◯.
Show the whole. Move counters to one part. Find the other part.

1.

Whole	
9	
Part	Part
2	____

Think!
There are 9 counters in all. One part has 2 counters.

2.

Whole	
6	
Part	Part
2	____

3.

Whole	
8	
Part	Part
1	____

4.

Whole	
11	
Part	Part
2	____

5.

Whole	
10	
Part	Part
4	____

6. **Math Talk** If you have 7 in all and 6 is in one part, can you have more than 1 in the other part? Why?

TAKS Objective 1
TEKS 1.3B Use concrete and pictorial models to apply basic addition and subtraction facts (up to 9 + 9 = 18 and 18 − 9 = 9).

★ Practice

Use Workmat 3 and ◯.
Show the whole. Move counters to one part. Find the other part.

Remember!
The parts make the whole.

7.

Whole	
8	
Part	Part
3	5

8.

Whole	
10	
Part	Part
2	____

9.

Whole	
9	
Part	Part
3	____

10.

Whole	
11	
Part	Part
3	____

11.

Whole	
12	
Part	Part
4	____

12.

Whole	
6	
Part	Part
1	____

Algebra Readiness: Number Sentences

Compare. Write the difference.

13.       

____ = 5 − 2

14. 

____ = 6 − 3

At Home Use 10 objects. Move some to show one part. Ask your child how many are in the other part.

En casa Use 10 objetos. Mueva algunos para mostrar una parte. Pregunte a su niño cuántos hay en la otra parte.

Name ________________________

Chapter 18 Lesson 2

Count Back to Subtract

TEKS **Objective**
Use the counting back 1, 2, or 3 strategy to apply subtraction facts.

TAKS **Vocabulary**
count back

★ Learn

You can **count back** to subtract.

Start with 11.
Count back 2.

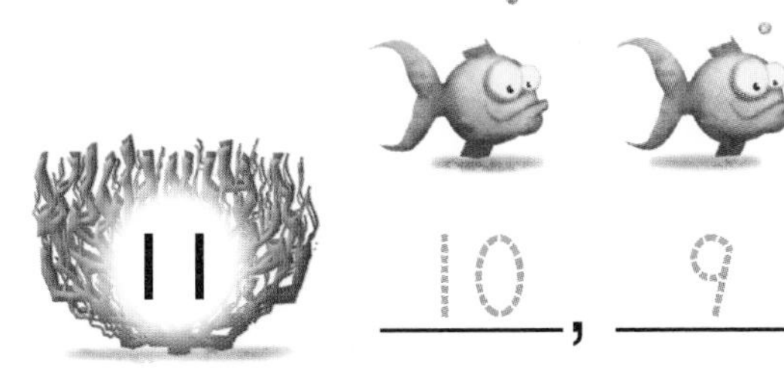

10, 9

11 − 2 = 9

Start with 12.
Count back 3.

11, 10, 9

12 − 3 = 9

★ Guided Practice

Count back to subtract.

Think!
I start with 10.
I count back 3.

1.

____, ____, ____

10 − 3 = ____

2.

10

____, ____

10 − 2 = ____

3.

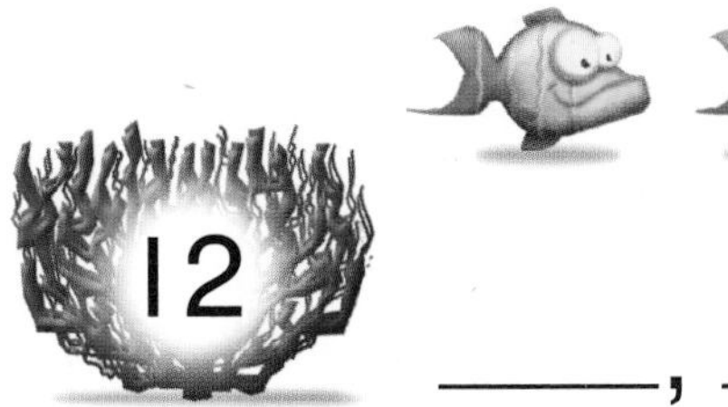

____, ____

$$\begin{array}{r} 12 \\ -\ 2 \\ \hline \end{array}$$

4.

____

$$\begin{array}{r} 10 \\ -\ 1 \\ \hline \end{array}$$

5. **Math Talk** What pattern helps you find the difference?

★ Practice

Count back to subtract.

6. 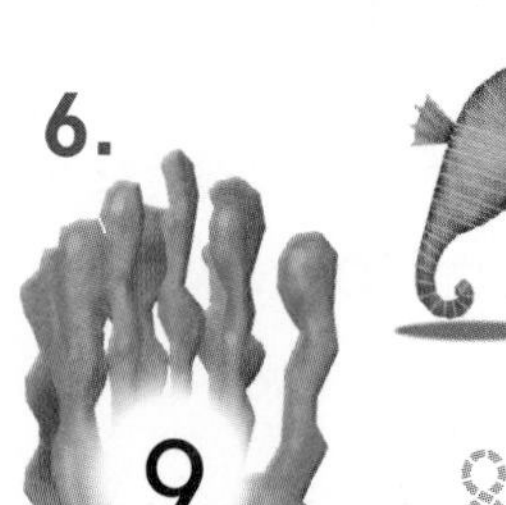    

8, 7, 6

9 − 3 = 6

7.  

7 ____, ____

7 − 2 = ____

8. 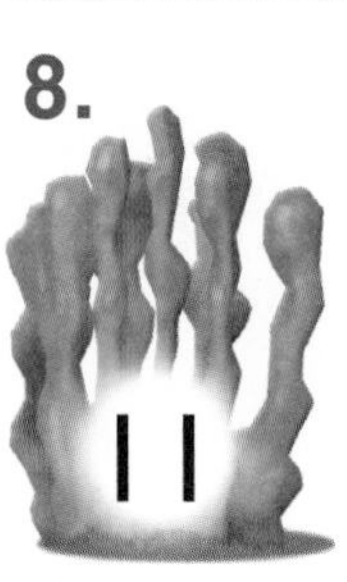  

11 ____

11 − 1 = ____

9. 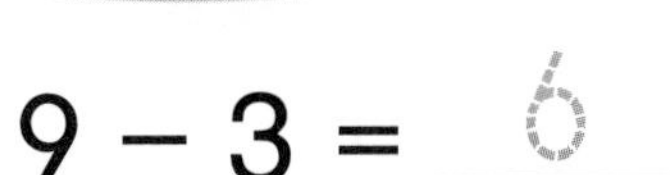 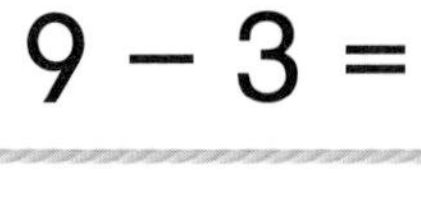

8 ____, ____

8 − 2 = ____

10. 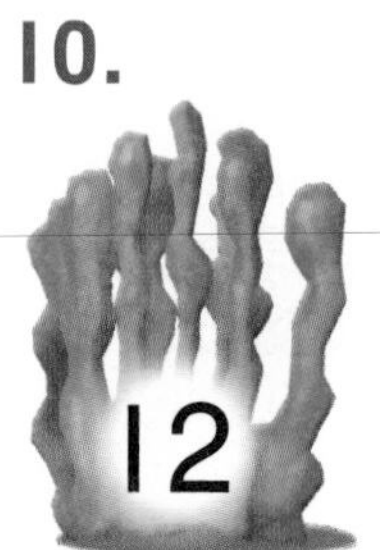 

12 ____

$$\begin{array}{r} 12 \\ -\ 1 \\ \hline \end{array}$$

11.  

13 ____, ____

$$\begin{array}{r} 13 \\ -\ 2 \\ \hline \end{array}$$

Problem Solving: Data Sense

12. Say a subtraction question that you can answer by using this graph. Have a friend answer.

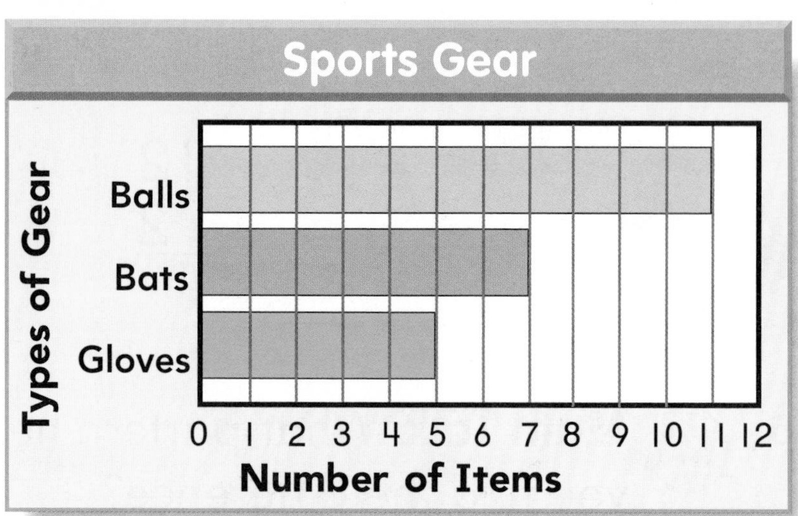

At Home Have your child count back 1, 2, and 3 from 12 and then from 11.

En casa Pida a su niño que cuente hacia atrás 1, 2 y 3 a partir de 12 y luego a partir de 11.

Name ______________________________

Chapter 18 Lesson 3

Parts and Wholes

Hands On

TEKS Objective
Use parts and wholes to model subtraction through 12.

★ Learn

If you know the whole and one of the parts, you can find the other part.

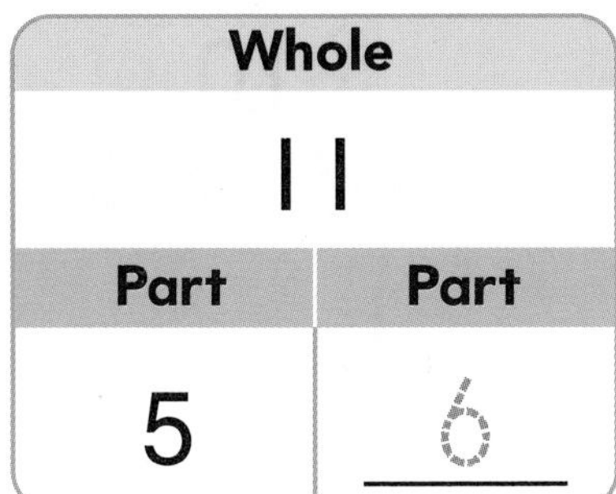

Whole	
11	
Part	Part
5	6

Whole	
12	
Part	Part
4	8

Write the missing part. Solve.

11 − 5 = 6

11 − 6 = 5

12 − 4 = 8

12 − 8 = 4

★ Guided Practice

Use Workmat 3 and ◯.
Write the missing part.
Write the difference.

Think!
I say 2 and what other part make 11?

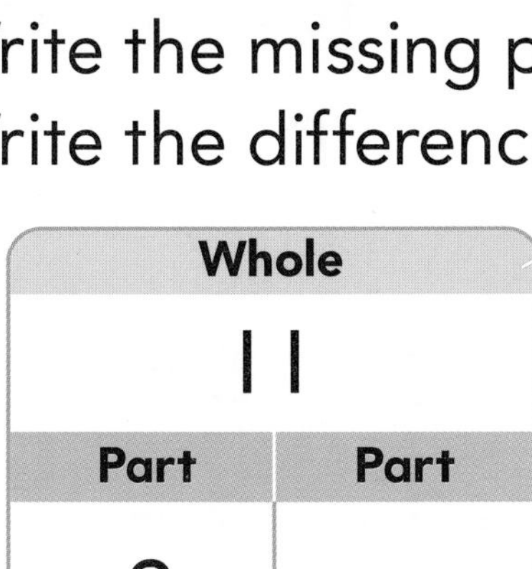

Whole	
11	
Part	Part
2	____

Whole	
12	
Part	Part
3	____

Whole	
10	
Part	Part
7	____

1. 11 − 2 = ____
   11 − 9 = ____

2. 12 − 3 = ____
   12 − 9 = ____

3. 10 − 7 = ____
   10 − 3 = ____

4. **Math Talk** How does 11 − 7 = 4 help you find the difference for 11 − 4?

TAKS Objective 1
TEKS 1.3B Use concrete and pictorial models to apply basic addition and subtraction facts (up to 9 + 9 = 18 and 18 − 9 = 9).

★ Practice

Use Workmat 3 and ◯.
Write the missing part.
Write the difference.

Remember!
One fact can help you find the other fact.

Whole	
11	
Part	Part
8	3

Whole	
12	
Part	Part
5	___

Whole	
10	
Part	Part
4	___

5. 11 − 8 = 3
   11 − 3 = 8

6. 12 − 5 = ___
   12 − 7 = ___

7. 10 − 4 = ___
   10 − 6 = ___

Whole	
11	
Part	Part
4	___

Whole	
12	
Part	Part
10	___

Whole	
12	
Part	Part
0	___

8. 11 − 4 = ___
   11 − 7 = ___

9. 12 − 10 = ___
   12 − 2 = ___

10. 12 − 0 = ___
    12 − 12 = ___

Reading Math: Vocabulary

11. What number would you subtract from eleven to get a difference of seven?

___

12. Write two addends that have a sum of eleven.

___ and ___

At Home Ask your child to tell you the differences for the following facts: 11 − 6, 11 − 5, 11 − 7, and 11 − 4.

En casa Pida a su niño que le diga las diferencias de las siguientes operaciones: 11 − 6, 11 − 5, 11 − 7 y 11 − 4.

Name ______________________________

Chapter 18 Lesson 4

Missing Addends

TEKS Objective
Model missing addends to apply addition facts.

TAKS Vocabulary
addend

★ Learn

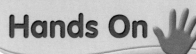

Sometimes you know one **addend** and the sum. Find the missing addend.

One addend is 5.
The sum is 8.
What is the missing addend?

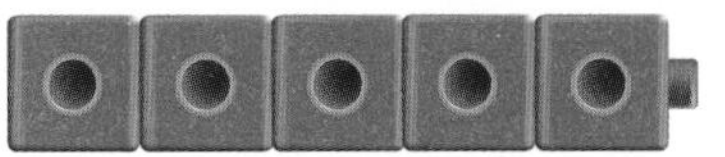 

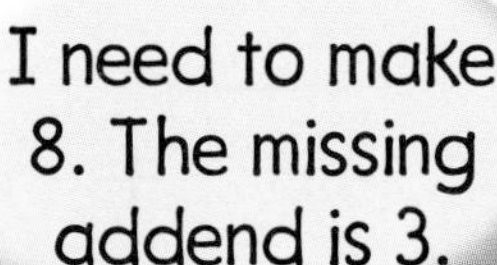

I need to make
8. The missing
addend is 3.

$5 + \boxed{3} = 8$

★ Guided Practice

Use cubes.
Find the missing addend.

Think!
I know one addend is 6.
The sum is 12.

1. 

$6 + \boxed{} = 12$

2. 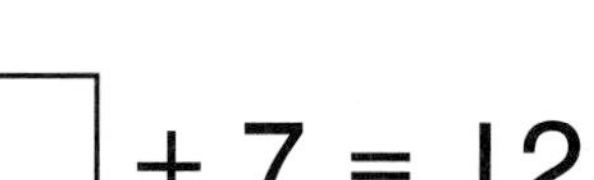

$\boxed{} + 7 = 12$

3. $\begin{array}{r} 6 \\ + \boxed{} \\ \hline 9 \end{array}$

4. $\begin{array}{r} \boxed{} \\ + 5 \\ \hline 7 \end{array}$

5. **Math Talk** How can you use counting on to find the sum in Exercise 3?

TAKS Objective 1
TEKS 1.3B Use concrete and pictorial models to apply basic addition and subtraction facts (up to 9 + 9 = 18 and 18 − 9 = 9).

★ Practice

Use cubes.
Find the missing addend.

Remember!
Addition strategies like counting on help you find the missing addend.

6. 

[4] + 5 = 9

7. 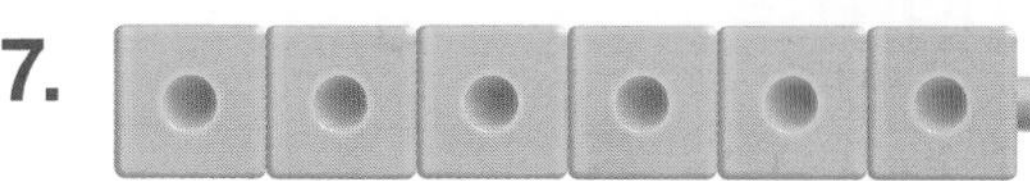

6 + [ ] = 10

8.

2 + [ ] = 8

9.

5 + [ ] = 11

10.

$$\begin{array}{r} 3 \\ + \square \\ \hline 12 \end{array}$$

11. 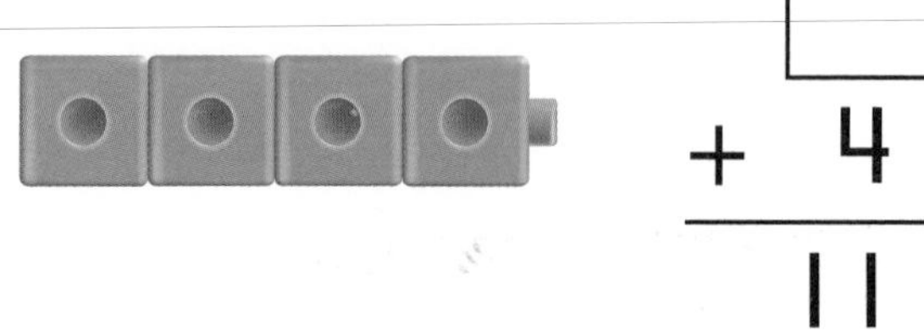

$$\begin{array}{r} \square \\ + 4 \\ \hline 11 \end{array}$$

Algebra Readiness: Missing Addends

12. Mia has 6 people in her family. The table is set for 10 people. How many friends are coming to the picnic?

_____ friends

Draw or write to explain.

At Home Ask your child questions such as, "What number plus six equals twelve?"

En casa Haga preguntas a su niño, como "¿Qué número más seis es igual a doce?"

Name ______________________

Chapter 18 Lesson 5

Create and Solve

Problem Solving
Plan

TEKS Objective
Create and solve addition and subtraction problems.

1. Write a story about the fish.

____

____

2. Tell a friend your story.
   Do you add or subtract?
   Write the number sentence.

   ____ ◯ ____ ◯ ____

3. Tell a different story about the fish.
   Model, then draw to show your story.

TAKS Objective 1
TEKS 1.3A Model and create addition and subtraction problem situations with concrete objects and write corresponding number sentences.

Also **TAKS Objective 6; TEKS 1.11D**

4. Write an addition story about the sea horses.

____

____

5. Write the addition sentence.

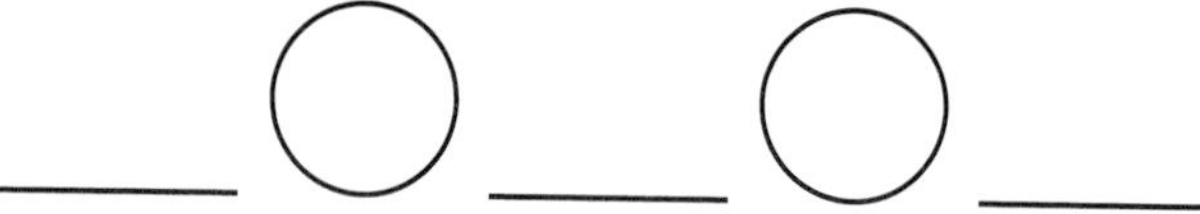

6. Tell a story for $8 + 3 = 11$.
Draw a picture to show your story.

At Home Display 4 little spoons and 6 big spoons. Ask your child to tell a story about the spoons.

En casa Muestre 4 cucharas pequeñas y 6 grandes. Pida a su niño que cuente un cuento sobre las cucharas.

Name ______________________________

Subtract 1, 2, or 3

Subtract. Look for a pattern.

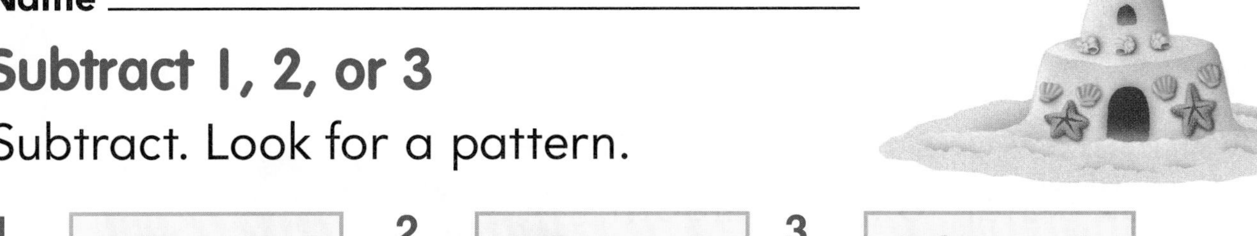

1.

Subtract 1.	
12	
11	
10	
9	
8	
7	
6	
5	
4	
3	
2	
1	

2.

Subtract 2.	
12	
11	
10	
9	
8	
7	
6	
5	
4	
3	
2	

3.

Subtract 3.	
12	
11	
10	
9	
8	
7	
6	
5	
4	
3	

4. What patterns do you see?

____

____

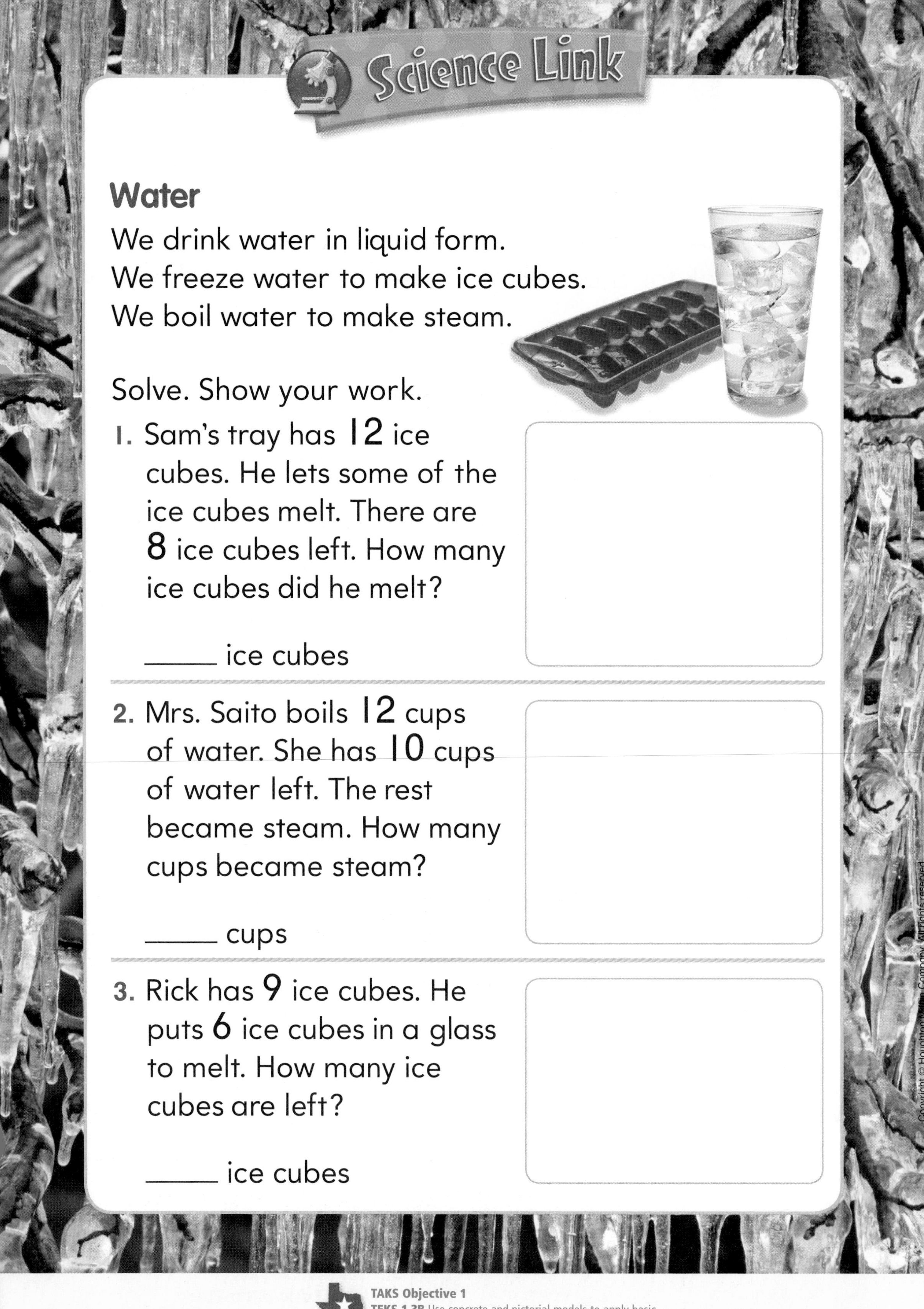

Water

We drink water in liquid form.
We freeze water to make ice cubes.
We boil water to make steam.

Solve. Show your work.

1. Sam's tray has 12 ice cubes. He lets some of the ice cubes melt. There are 8 ice cubes left. How many ice cubes did he melt?

   _____ ice cubes

2. Mrs. Saito boils 12 cups of water. She has 10 cups of water left. The rest became steam. How many cups became steam?

   _____ cups

3. Rick has 9 ice cubes. He puts 6 ice cubes in a glass to melt. How many ice cubes are left?

   _____ ice cubes

TAKS Objective 1
TEKS 1.3B Use concrete and pictorial models to apply basic addition and subtraction facts (up to 9 + 9 = 18 and 18 – 9 = 9).
TEKS Science 7A, 7B

Name ______________________

Concepts and Skills

Count back to subtract.
TEKS 1.3B, 1.5D

1. 

12 _____ , _____

12 − 2 = _____

Use cubes.
Find the missing addend.
TEKS 1.3B

2. 

2 + ☐ = 9

Use Workmat 3 and ◯. Write the missing part. Write the difference. TEKS 1.3B

3.

Whole	
10	
Part	**Part**
7	

10 − 7 = _____

10 − 3 = _____

4.

Whole	
12	
Part	**Part**
4	

12 − 4 = _____

12 − 8 = _____

Problem Solving TEKS 1.3A

5. Write an addition story about the fish. Write the addition sentence.

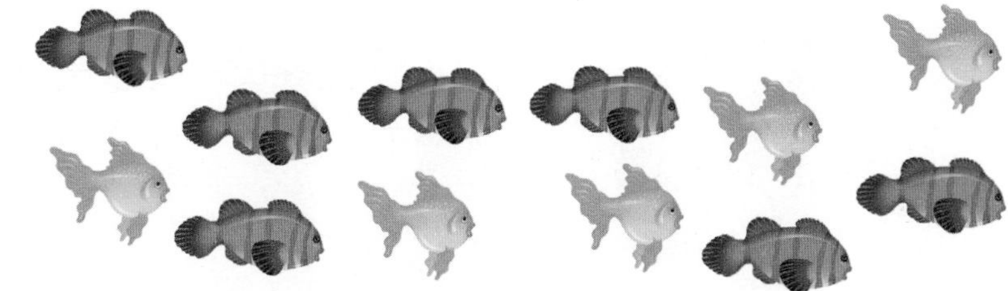

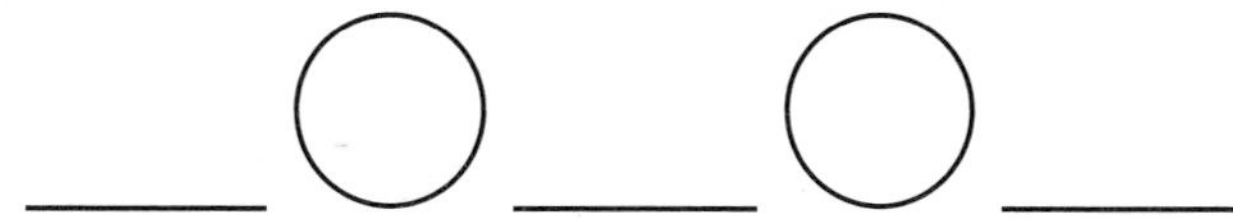

TAKS Prep and Spiral Review

Choose the answer for problems 1–4.

1. Which shows an odd number of cubes?

○ ○ ○ ○

TEKS 1.5B (page 301)

2. Which shows all even numbers?

16, 18, 20, 22, 24, 26 ○

16, 18, 21, 22, 24, 26 ○

16, 18, 20, 23, 24, 27 ○

16, 18, 21, 24, 26, 28 ○

TEKS 1.5B (page 301)

3. Chen pulls cubes from a bag. What color cube is Chen certain to pull from the bag?

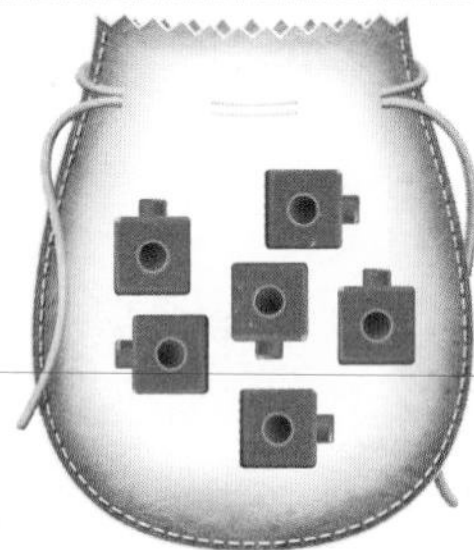

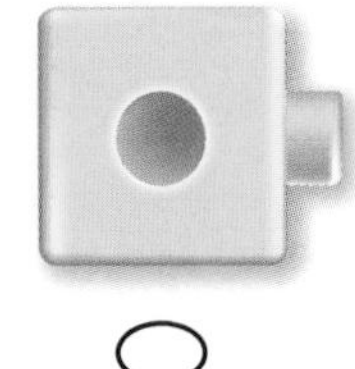   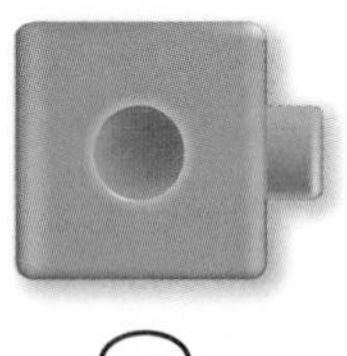

○ ○ ○ ○

TEKS 1.10B (page 225)

4. Rosa wants to spin a 2 on a spinner. On which spinner will it be impossible for Rosa to spin a 2?

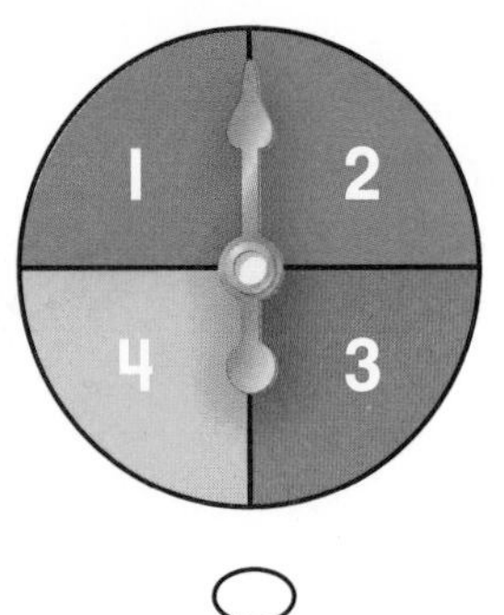

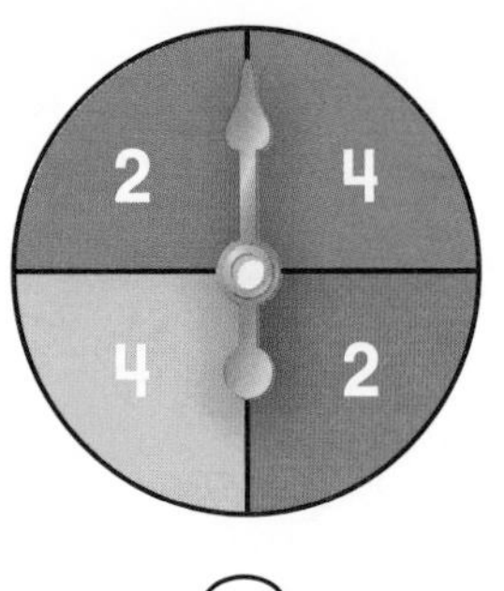

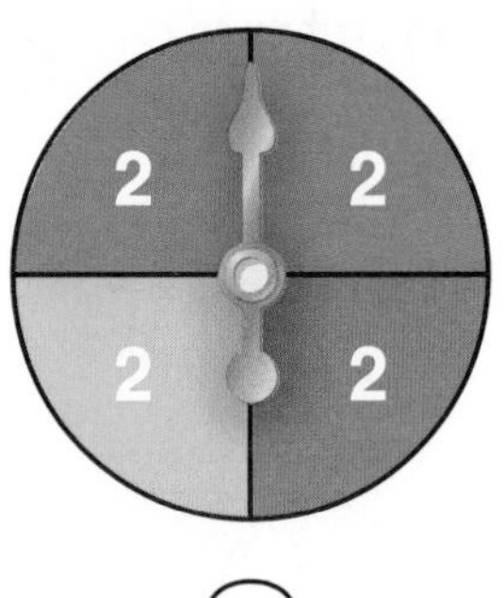

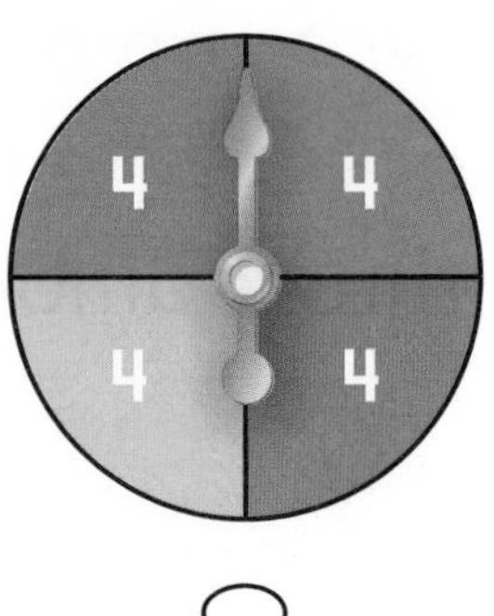

○ ○ ○ ○

TEKS 1.10B (page 227)

Relate Addition and Subtraction

TAKS Vocabulary

You learned these vocabulary words in Chapter 7. Now you will use them with greater numbers.

related facts Addition and subtraction facts that have the same parts and wholes

Whole	
14	
Part	Part
9	5

9 + 5 = 14 and 14 − 9 = 5 are related facts.

fact family All the addition and subtraction facts that use the same numbers

9 + 5 = 14   14 − 9 = 5
5 + 9 = 14   14 − 5 = 9

This fact family uses the numbers 9, 5, and 14.

See English-Spanish glossary pages 505–516.

TAKS Objective 6
TEKS 1.12B Relate informal language to mathematical language and symbols.

Education Place
Visit **www.eduplace.com/txmap/** for the eGlossary and vocabulary eGames.

Name ______________________________

Check What You Know

Use the picture.
Solve.

1. How many fish are there? _____ fish

2. If 2 fish join them, how many will there be altogether? _____ + _____ = _____

Use the picture. Solve.

3. How many sea horses are there? _____ sea horses

4. If 1 sea horse joins them, how many sea horses will there be?

   _____ + _____ = _____

5. If all the sea horses swim away, how many are left?

   _____ − _____ = _____

Use this page to review important skills needed for this chapter.

Name ________________________

Chapter 19 Lesson 1

Relate Addition and Subtraction

Hands On

TEKS Objective
Identify patterns in related addition and subtraction sentences.

TAKS Vocabulary
related facts

★ Learn

Knowing **related facts** can help you add and subtract.

4 red cubes and 6 blue cubes. How many in all?

10 cubes. 6 are blue. How many red?

Workmat 3	
Whole	
Part	Part

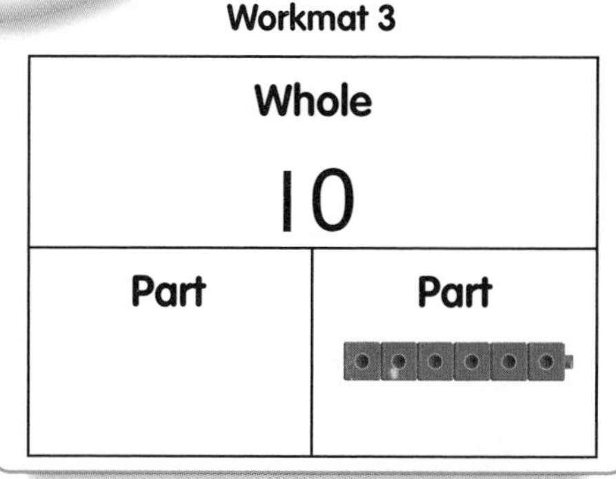

4 + 6 = 10　　10 − 6 = 4

★ Guided Practice

Use cubes, cubes, and Workmat 3.
Show the parts. Complete the related facts.

Think!
3 and 9 are the parts. I need to find the whole.

1. 3 and 9	___ + ___ = ___	___ − ___ = ___
2. 8 and 3	___ + ___ = ___	___ − ___ = ___
3. 5 and 6	___ + ___ = ___	___ − ___ = ___

4. **Math Talk** What patterns do you see?

TAKS Objectives 1, 2
TEKS 1.3B Use concrete and pictorial models to apply basic addition and subtraction facts (up to 9 + 9 = 18 and 18 − 9 = 9).

TEKS 1.5E Identify patterns in related addition and subtraction sentences (fact families for sums to 18) such as 2 + 3 = 5, 3 + 2 = 5, 5 − 2 = 3, and 5 − 3 = 2.

★ Practice

Use [cube], [cube], and Workmat 3.
Show the parts. Complete the related facts.

Remember!
Related facts have the same parts and wholes.

5.

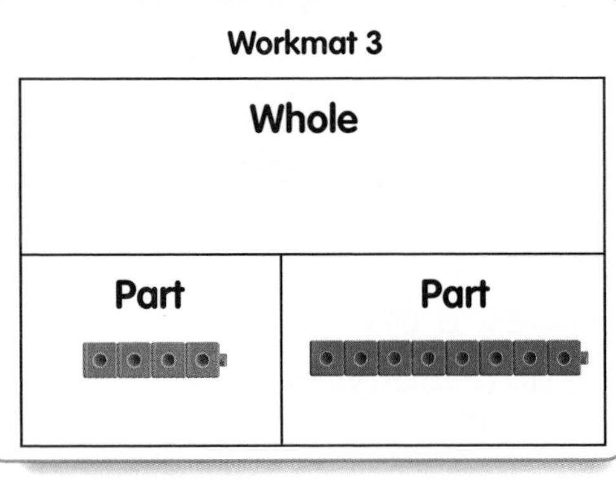

$4 + 8 =$ 12

$12 - 8 =$ 4

6.

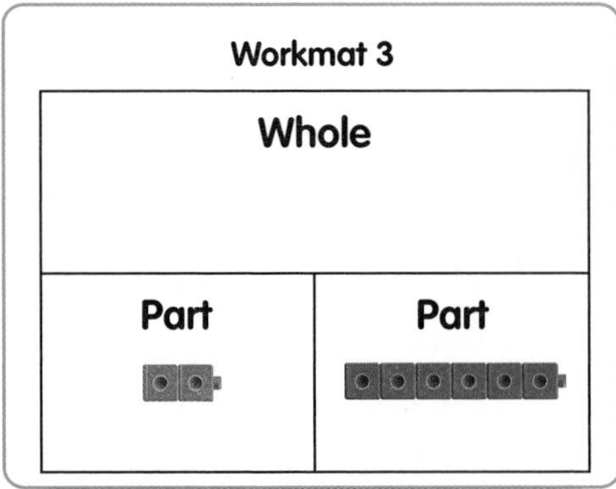

$2 + 6 =$ ____

$8 - 6 =$ ____

7. 8 and 2	____ + ____ = ____	____ − ____ = ____
8. 7 and 5	____ + ____ = ____	____ − ____ = ____
9. 3 and 7	____ + ____ = ____	____ − ____ = ____

Problem Solving: Reasoning

Choose three of the numbers.
Write two related facts.

10.

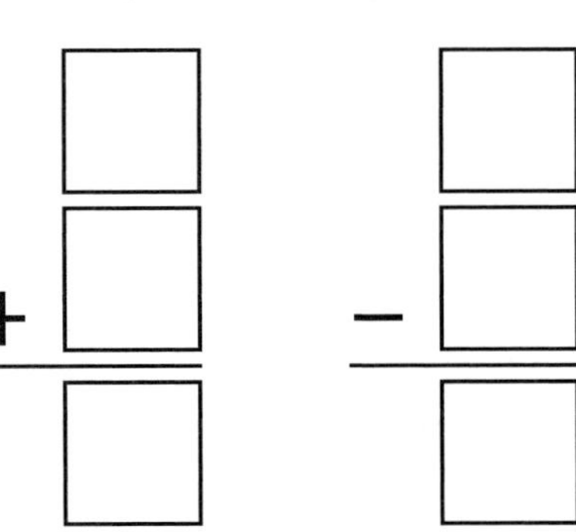

At Home Say an addition fact such as $8 + 3 = 11$. Ask your child to name a related subtraction fact.

En casa Diga una operación de suma como $8 + 3 = 11$. Pida a su niño que nombre una operación relacionada de resta.

Name ____________________

Chapter 19 Lesson 2

Fact Families for 11

Hands On

TEKS Objective
Identify fact families for sums through 11.

TAKS Vocabulary
fact family

★ Learn

A **fact family** has the same numbers.

This fact family has the numbers 11, 4, and 7.

11 is the whole.
4 and 7 are the parts.

Whole	
11	
Part	Part
4	7

4 + 7 = 11 11 − 4 = 7

7 + 4 = 11 11 − 7 = 4

★ Guided Practice

Use cubes and Workmat 3.
Complete the fact family.

Think!
I use 8 + 3 = 11 to complete the other 3 facts.

1.

11	
8	3

8 + 3 = ____ 11 − 3 = ____

3 + 8 = ____ 11 − 8 = ____

2.

11	
9	2

9 + 2 = ____ 11 − 2 = ____

2 + 9 = ____ 11 − 9 = ____

3.

11	
6	5

6 + 5 = ____ 11 − 6 = ____

5 + 6 = ____ 11 − 5 = ____

4. **Math Talk** Are 6 − 4 and 6 + 4 in the same fact family? Why?

TAKS Objectives 1, 2
TEKS 1.3B Use concrete and pictorial models to apply basic addition and subtraction facts (up to 9 + 9 = 18 and 18 − 9 = 9).

TEKS 1.5E Identify patterns in related addition and subtraction sentences (fact families for sums to 18) such as 2 + 3 = 5, 3 + 2 = 5, 5 − 2 = 3, and 5 − 3 = 2.

★ Practice

Use cubes and Workmat 3.
Complete the fact family.

5.

11	
7	4

7 + 4 = 11 11 − 7 = 4

4 + 7 = ____ 11 − 4 = ____

6.

9	
5	4

5 + 4 = ____ 9 − 5 = ____

4 + ____ = ____ 9 − 4 = ____

7.

10	
6	4

6 + 4 = ____ 10 − ____ = ____

4 + 6 = ____ 10 − 4 = ____

8.

11	
2	9

2 + 9 = ____ 11 − 9 = ____

9 + 2 = ____ ____ − 2 = ____

Problem Solving: Reasoning

9. Brad says he can use these balls to make two groups of 6 balls. Is he right? Explain.

At Home Ask your child to write a fact family using the numbers 8, 3, and 11.

En casa Pida a su niño que escriba una familia de operaciones usando los números 8, 3 y 11.

Name ______________________________

Chapter 19 Lesson 3

Fact Families for 12

Hands On

TEKS Objective
Identify fact families for sums through 12.

★ Learn

The facts in a fact family are related.

The numbers 12, 8, and 4 make a fact family.

Fact families always use the same numbers.

Whole	
12	
Part	Part
8	4

8 + 4 = 12   12 − 8 = 4

4 + 8 = 12   12 − 4 = 8

★ Guided Practice

Use cubes and Workmat 3.
Complete the fact family.

Think!
I use 12, 5, and 7 to write the missing fact.

1.

12	
5	7

5 + 7 = ____   12 − 5 = ____

12 − 7 = ____   ____ ◯ ____ ◯ ____

2.

12	
9	3

9 + 3 = ____   12 − 3 = ____

3 + 9 = ____   ____ ◯ ____ ◯ ____

3.

12	
6	6

6 + 6 = ____   ____ ◯ ____ ◯ ____

4. **Math Talk** When are there only two facts in a fact family?

★ Practice

Use cubes and Workmat 3.
Complete the fact family.

Remember!
Related facts have the same numbers.

12	
7	5

5. $7 + 5 =$ 12 $\quad 12 - 7 =$ 5

$12 - 5 =$ ____ $\quad$ ____ ◯ ____ ◯ ____

12	
4	8

6. $4 + 8 =$ ____ $\quad 12 - 8 =$ ____

$8 + 4 =$ ____ $\quad$ ____ ◯ ____ ◯ ____

11	
7	4

7. $11 - 7 =$ ____ $\quad 11 - 4 =$ ____

$7 + 4 =$ ____ $\quad$ ____ ◯ ____ ◯ ____

Algebra Readiness: Number Sentences

Write a fact family using the numbers **9**, **3**, and **12**.

8. ____ ◯ ____ ◯ ____

  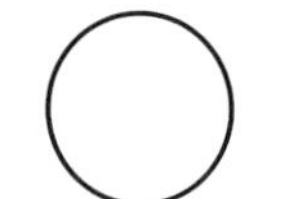

____ ◯ ____ ◯ ____

____ ◯ ____ ◯ ____

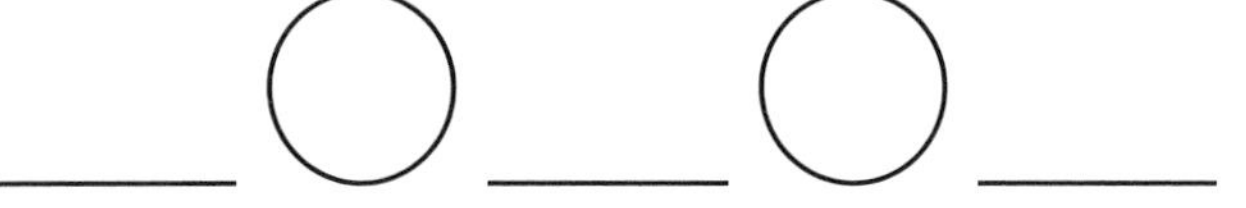

____ ◯ ____ ◯ ____

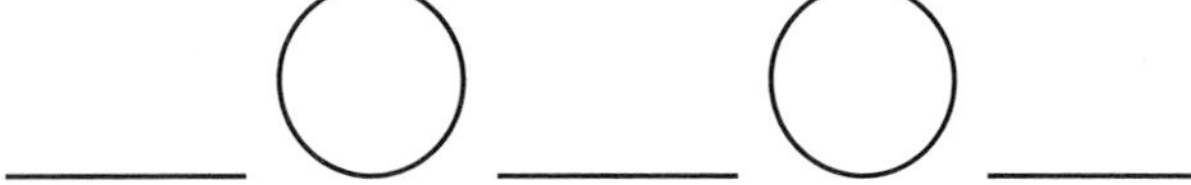

At Home Ask your child to write a fact family using the numbers 5, 7, and 12.

En casa Pida a su niño que escriba una familia de operaciones usando los números 5, 7 y 12.

TEKS Objective
Find different names for the same number.

Name ______________________

Chapter 19 Lesson 4

Names for Numbers

A number can have many different names. Use counters. Circle the names for 9.

4 + 5 and 12 − 3 are names for 9.

9	4 + 5	7 − 2	5 + 6	12 − 3
	9	5	11	9

Guided Practice

Use counters.
Write the sums and differences.
Circle the names for the number.

Think! 3 + 7 and 10 − 0 are both names for 10.

1.  10   9 − 1 ____   3 + 7 ____   10 − 0 ____

2.  8   7 + 1 ____   8 − 2 ____   11 − 3 ____

3.  12   9 + 3 ____   7 + 4 ____   4 + 8 ____

4. **Math Talk** Look at Exercise 1. Tell two more names for 10.

TAKS Objectives 1, 2
TEKS 1.3B Use concrete and pictorial models to apply basic addition and subtraction facts (up to 9 + 9 = 18 and 18 − 9 = 9).

TEKS 1.5E Identify patterns in related addition and subtraction sentences (fact families for sums to 18) such as 2 + 3 = 5, 3 + 2 = 5, 5 − 2 = 3, and 5 − 3 = 2.

Remember!
Check that you wrote the correct sum or difference.

Use counters.
Write the sums and differences.
Circle the names for the number.

5.  5

(3 + 2)	5 + 2	11 − 6	9 − 4
5	____	____	____

6.  11

11 − 0	6 + 4	8 + 3	9 + 2
____	____	____	____

7.  9

6 + 3	12 − 3	11 − 2	9 − 1
____	____	____	____

8.  8

12 − 5	5 + 3	8 − 3	11 − 3
____	____	____	____

9. 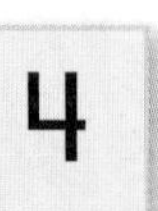 4

11 − 7	3 + 1	9 − 5	2 + 5
____	____	____	____

Algebra Readiness: Patterns

Write the sums. Look for a pattern.
Write the facts likely to come next.

10. $\begin{array}{r} 0 \\ +7 \\ \hline \end{array}$ $\begin{array}{r} 1 \\ +6 \\ \hline \end{array}$ $\begin{array}{r} 2 \\ +5 \\ \hline \end{array}$ $\begin{array}{r} 3 \\ +4 \\ \hline \end{array}$ $\begin{array}{r} \square \\ +\square \\ \hline \end{array}$ $\begin{array}{r} \square \\ +\square \\ \hline \end{array}$

At Home Say a number such as 8. Have your child tell you three or four names for 8, such as 6 + 2, 10 − 2, 3 + 5.

En casa Diga un número como 8. Pida a su niño que le diga tres o cuatro nombres para 8, como 6 + 2, 10 − 2, 3 + 5.

Name ______________________________

Chapter 19 Lesson 5

Choose the Operation

TEKS Objective
Choose addition or subtraction to solve problems.

You can use addition to solve a problem.
One team plays 3 games.
Another team plays 4 games.
How many games do both teams play?

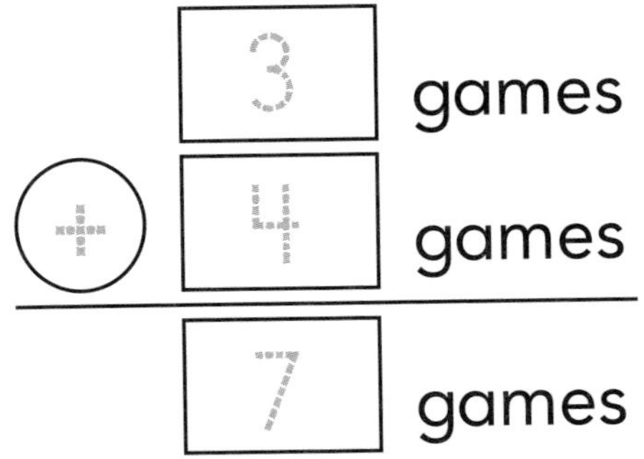

Think!

Whole	
?	
Part	**Part**
3	4

You can use subtraction to solve a problem.
There are 12 children on the team.
9 children are playing.
How many children are not playing?

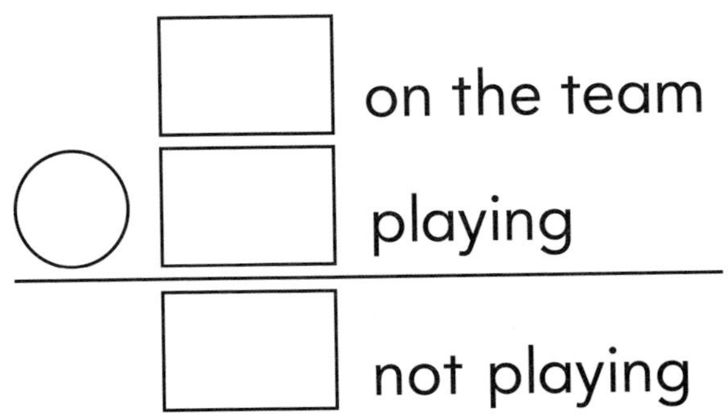

Think!

Whole	
12	
Part	**Part**
9	?

★ Guided Problem Solving

Think!
Do I add or subtract?

1. One team scores 4 goals. The other team scores 6 goals. How many goals do both teams score?

   Find the numbers in the problem.

   Draw to solve.

   _____ goals

2. Math Talk How do you know whether to add or subtract to solve a problem?

★ Problem Solving Practice

Draw a model.
Add or subtract to solve.

3. There are 6 children running in a race. 2 of them finish the race. How many children are still running?

   _____ children

4. Michael wins 4 ribbons at the fair on Monday. He wins 5 ribbons on Tuesday. How many ribbons does Michael win on both days?

1ST PLACE

   _____ ribbons

At Home Create a story problem about a sport. Ask your child to add or subtract to solve.

En casa Cree un problema sobre un deporte. Pida a su niño que sume o reste para resolver.

Name ______________________________

Science

Texas Field Trip

Big Bend National Park

There are tall mountains in this big park. There is a desert, too. There are many trails to hike. Hikers can see many plants and animals.

Rocks Along Lost Mine Trail

Solve. Show your work.

1. There are 8 hikers at the start of a trail. 2 more hikers join them. How many hikers are on the trail now?

   _____ hikers

hikers

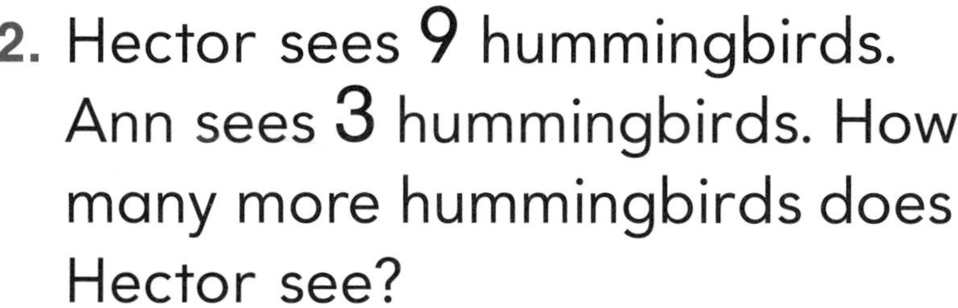

2. Hector sees 9 hummingbirds. Ann sees 3 hummingbirds. How many more hummingbirds does Hector see?

   _____ hummingbirds

hummingbird

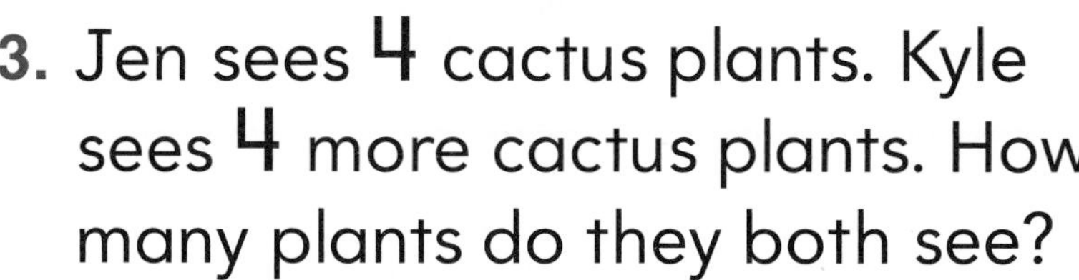

3. Jen sees 4 cactus plants. Kyle sees 4 more cactus plants. How many plants do they both see?

   _____ cactus plants

cactus plant

TAKS Objectives 1, 6
TEKS 1.3B Use concrete and pictorial models to apply basic addition and subtraction facts (up to 9 + 9 = 18 and 18 – 9 = 9).

Also **TEKS 1.11C**
TEKS Science 8B

TAKS Problem Solving
Listening Skills

Select a Strategy
Draw a Picture
Act It Out

Listen to your teacher read the problem.
Choose the correct answer.

1. The hikers see 9 lizards.
Then they see 3 more lizards.
How many lizards do they see in all?

9	10	11	12
○	○	○	○

TEKS 1.3B

2. There are 8 children looking at fossil bones. Then, 5 children go away. How many children are still looking at fossil bones?

5	4	3	2
○	○	○	○

TEKS 1.3B

3.

8	9	10	11
○	○	○	○

TEKS 1.3B

4.

4	5	6	7
○	○	○	○

TEKS 1.3B

Education Place
Visit **www.eduplace.com/txmap/** for Test-Taking Tips and Extra Practice.

Math Works

Name ______________________________

Mechanic

Kyle is a mechanic. He owns a garage with Frank. They fix cars and trucks. They know how engines work. People need their help every day.

Draw a model. Add or subtract to solve.

1. One day Kyle and Frank have 12 vehicles to fix. 5 are trucks. How many are cars?

   _____ cars

2. One day Kyle and Frank have 3 trucks and 9 cars to fix. How many vehicles are there in all?

   _____ vehicles

3. Another day the mechanics have 11 vehicles to fix. Write a name for 11. Tell how many are cars and how many are trucks.

   _____ cars + _____ trucks = 11

TAKS Objectives 1, 6
TEKS 1.3B Use concrete and pictorial models to apply basic addition and subtraction facts (up to $9 + 9 = 18$ and $18 - 9 = 9$).
TEKS 1.11A Identify mathematics in everyday situations.

Math Music

Let's Go Camping

Math Music, Track 7
Tune: "Skip to My Lou"

Let's go camping by the sea.
Bring some friends for company.
Put your tent beside a tree.
Camping is fun for you and me!

We will count on. Start with 4.
You can do it. Add 3 more.
5, 6, 7! It's no chore!
Count on with numbers. Add some more!

We will count back. Start with 8.
Count back 2. We just can't wait.
7, 6! Subtracting is great.
Count back with numbers. Don't be late!

It's your turn to count on now.
Count back, too. Please show me how.
When you're done, please take a bow.
Count on, then count back.
Start right now!

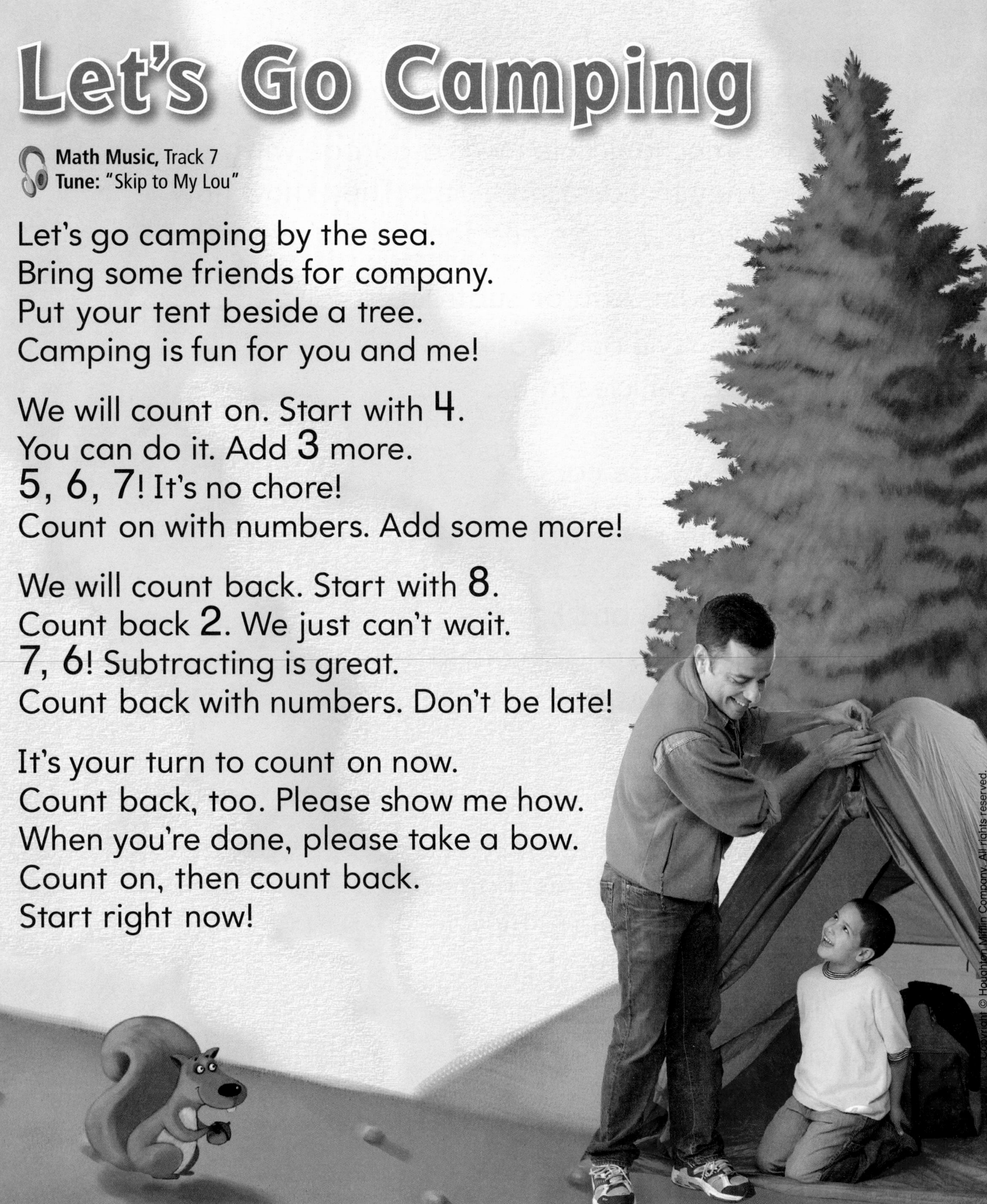

TAKS Objective 2
TEKS 1.5D Use patterns to develop strategies to solve basic addition and basic subtraction problems.

Name ______________________________

Concepts and Skills

Use ▪, ▪, and Workmat 3.

Show the parts. Complete the related facts. TEKS 1.3B, 1.5E

1. 8 and 3 ____ + ____ = ____ ____ − ____ = ____

Use cubes and Workmat 3.

Complete the fact family. TEKS 1.3B, 1.5E

2.

Whole	
12	
Part	Part
9	3

9 + 3 = ____ 12 − 3 = ____

3 + ____ = ____ 12 − 9 = ____

Use cubes. Write the sums and differences.

Circle the names for the number. TEKS 1.3B, 1.5E

3. **10** 11 − 1 ____ 5 + 6 ____ 7 + 3 ____ 8 + 2 ____ 6 + 4 ____ 8 + 4 ____

Problem Solving

Draw a model.

Add or subtract to solve. TEKS 1.3B

4. The team has 11 players.
Some go home. 4 players are left.
How many players go home?

____ players

TAKS Prep and Spiral Review

Choose the answer for problems 1–4.

1. Which number is missing?

25	30	35	?	45	50

36 ◯ 40 ◯ 44 ◯ 45 ◯

TEKS 1.5A (page 303)

2. Which row of numbers shows counting by 2s?

20, 30, 40 ◯ 20, 25, 30 ◯ 20, 22, 24 ◯ 20, 21, 22 ◯

TEKS 1.5A (page 299)

3. The picture graph shows the animals children saw at the zoo. Which animal did 9 children see?
Each 🯅 stands for 1 child.

Animals at the Zoo

 ◯

 ◯

 ◯

 ◯

TEKS 1.10A (page 209)

4. The bar-type graph shows the number of books children read. Who read the least number of books?

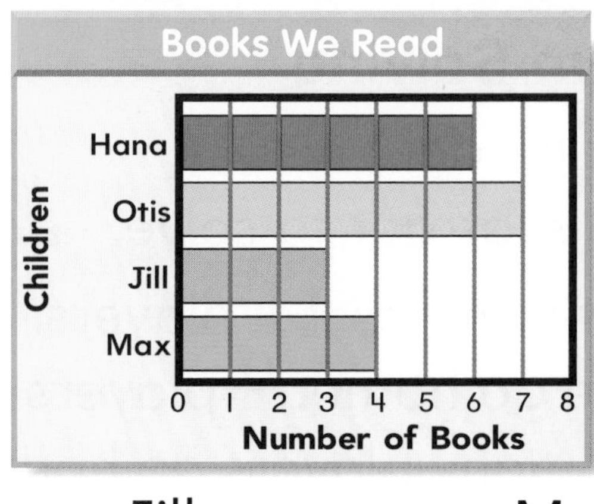

Hana ◯ Otis ◯ Jill ◯ Max ◯

TEKS 1.10A (page 223)

Education Place
Visit www.eduplace.com/txmap/ for Test-Taking Tips and Extra Practice.

Name ____________________

Go Fast, Go Far

Unit 7 Mental Math Strategies

Doubles

Adding won't be any trouble, when you master every double.

1. (2) (4)

2 + 2 = 4

I can double 2. So 2 + 2 is 4.

2. (4) (8)

4 + 4 = □

3. (3) (6)

3 + 3 = □

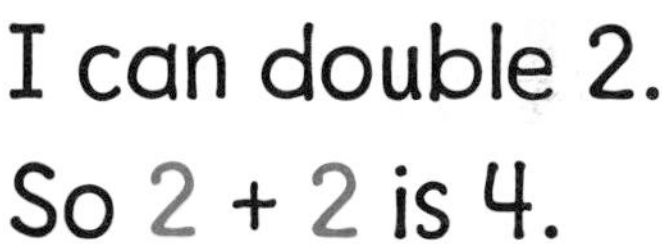

4. (5) (10)

5 + 5 = □

Take It Further: Try adding doubles in your head!

5. 3 + 3 = □

6. 6 + 6 = □

Name ______________________

Reading and Writing Math

Write *yes* if the sentence is true.
Write *no* if the sentence is not true.

1. You can count back to add. ____________

2. In the subtraction sentence $9 - 3 = 6$, the whole is 9. ____________

3. The sum of $4 + 6$ is the same as $6 + 4$. ____________

4. $1 + 4 = 5$ and $2 + 3 = 5$ are related facts. ____________

5. The facts in a fact family are related. ____________

6. **Writing Math** Use the ten frame. Draw counters to show how to add $7 + 5$.

TEKS 1.12A Explain and record observations using objects, words, pictures, numbers, and technology.

TEKS 1.12B Relate informal language to mathematical language and symbols.

Name ______________________

Concepts and Skills

Use cubes. Make the train.
Color and write to show. TEKS 1.3B, 1.5D

1. Make an 11 train.

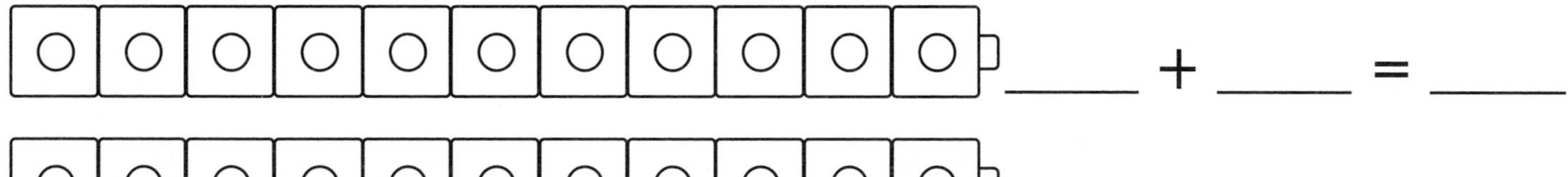

____ + ____ = ____

____ + ____ = ____

Count on to add.
Use cubes if you wish. TEKS 1.3B, 1.5D

2.

____, ____, ____

8 + 3 = ____

3.

____, ____

7 + 2 = ____

Use Workmat 1 and ◯.
Use making 10 to help you find the sum. TEKS 1.3B

4.

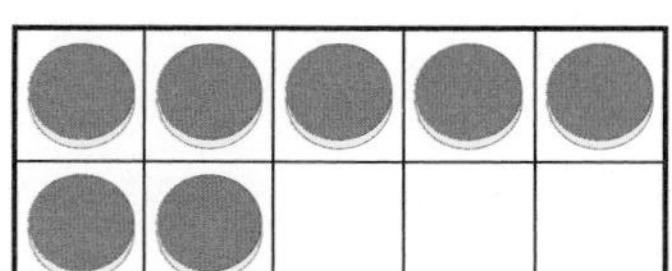

7 + 5 = ____

Count back to subtract. TEKS 1.3B, 1.5D

5.

____

10 − 1 = ____

6.

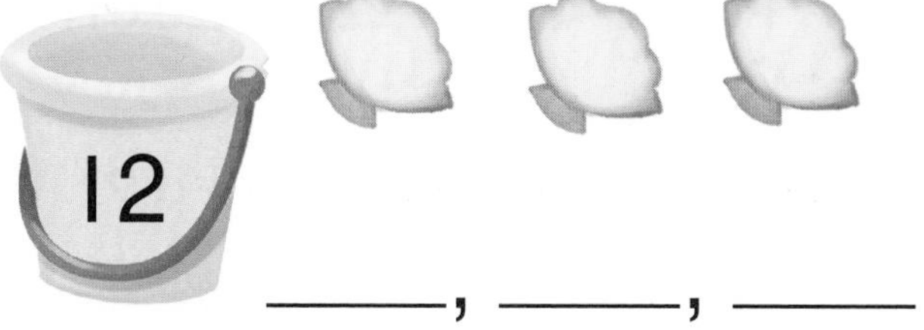

____, ____, ____

12 − 3 = ____

Use cubes.
Find the missing addend. TEKS 1.3B

7. 

$4 + \square = 11$

Use cubes and Workmat 3.
Complete the fact family. TEKS 1.3B, 1.5E

8. 

12	
5	7

7 + 5 = ____   12 − ____ = 5

____ + 7 = 12   ____ − 5 = 7

Use counters.
Write the sums and differences.
Circle the names for the number. TEKS 1.3B, 1.5E

9. 11

12 − 1   5 + 6   8 + 3

____   ____   ____

7 + 3   7 + 4   8 + 4

____   ____   ____

Problem Solving

Draw a model.
Add or subtract to solve. TEKS 1.3B

10. There are 12 children playing tag.
8 are boys.
How many are girls?

____ girls

Houghton Mifflin Texas Math

Unit 8

Money and Time

BIG IDEAS!

- Each coin has a different value. You can count to find the value of a group of coins.
- You can use a clock to tell time.
- You can use time to compare and order events.

Songs and Games

Math Music Track 8
Oh, Yes!

eGames
www.eduplace.com/txmap/

Literature

Literature Big Book

- Bunny Day

Math Readers

ISBN-13: 978-0-618-95277-9
ISBN-10: 0-618-95277-2
89- WC - 16 15 14 13 12

Get Ready Game

Five in a Row

What You Need
2 players   

1. Take turns spinning the spinner.
2. Skip count by 5s or 10s.
3. Stop when you get to a number that is on the board.
4. Put your counter on that number.
5. Play until all the numbers on the board are covered.

5	10
10	5

5	10	15	20	25
30	35	40	45	50
55	60	65	70	75
80	85	90	95	100

Math at Home

Dear Family,

My class is starting Unit 8, **Money and Time**. I will learn the value of a penny, nickel, dime, and quarter. I will also learn to tell time to the hour and half hour. You can help me learn these vocabulary words, and we can do the Math Activity together.

From,

____

Vocabulary

hour hand The shorter hand on a clock.

minute hand The longer hand on a clock.

digital A kind of clock without a minute hand or an hour hand.

This **digital** clock says twelve thirty.

penny, nickel, dime, quarter Names for coins.

penny	**nickel**	**dime**	**quarter**
one cent	five cents	ten cents	twenty-five cents
1¢	5¢	10¢	25¢

Education Place

Visit **www.eduplace.com/txmaf/** for

- eGames and Brain Teasers
- Math at Home in other languages

Family Math Activity

Display a collection of coins and have your child separate the nickels. Then have your child count the nickels to tell how much money in all. Similarly, have your child separate and count the pennies, the dimes, and the quarters.

5, 10, 15, 20, 25 cents

Literature

These books link to the math in this unit. Look for them at the library.

- **Jelly Beans for Sale** by Bruce McMillan *(Scholastic, 1996)*
- **Math Counts: Time** by Henry Pluckrose
- **Slugger's Car Wash** by Stuart J. Murphy

Matemáticas en casa

Estimada familia:

Mi clase está comenzando la Unidad 8, **El dinero y la hora**. Aprenderé el valor de monedas de 1 centavo, 5 centavos, 10 centavos y 25 centavos. También aprenderé a decir la hora en punto y la media hora. Me pueden ayudar a aprender estas palabras de vocabulario y podemos hacer juntos la Actividad de matemáticas para la familia.

De:

____

Vocabulario

manecilla de la hora La manecilla más corta de un reloj.

minutero La manecilla más larga de un reloj.

minutero — manecilla de la hora

digital Tipo de reloj sin minutero ni manecilla de la hora.

Este reloj **digital** dice doce y treinta.

monedas de 1 centavo, 5 centavos, 10 centavos, 25 centavos Nombres de las monedas.

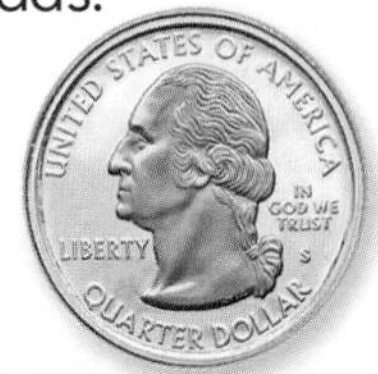

moneda de 1 centavo	moneda de 5 centavos	moneda de 10 centavos	moneda de 25 centavos
1¢	5¢	10¢	25¢

Education Place

Visite **www.eduplace.com/txmaf/** para
- Juegos en línea y acertijos
- Matemáticas en casa, en otros idiomas

Actividad de matemáticas para la familia

Muestre una colección de monedas y pida a su niño que separe las de 5 centavos y que las cuente para decir cuánto dinero hay en total. De forma similar, pida a su niño que separe y cuente las monedas de 1 centavo, las de 10 centavos y las de 25 centavos.

5, 10, 15, 20, 25 centavos

Literatura

Estos libros hablan sobre las matemáticas de esta unidad. Podemos buscarlos en la biblioteca.

- **Dime qué hora es** por Shirley Willis *(Franklin Watts, 2000)*
- **El baúl de mis amigos, un libro sobre el tiempo**

If you ran a bakery, what would you sell? How much would you charge for your bakery items? Draw pictures to show your ideas.

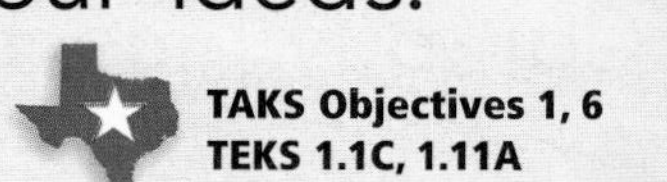
TAKS Objectives 1, 6
TEKS 1.1C, 1.11A

UNIT 8

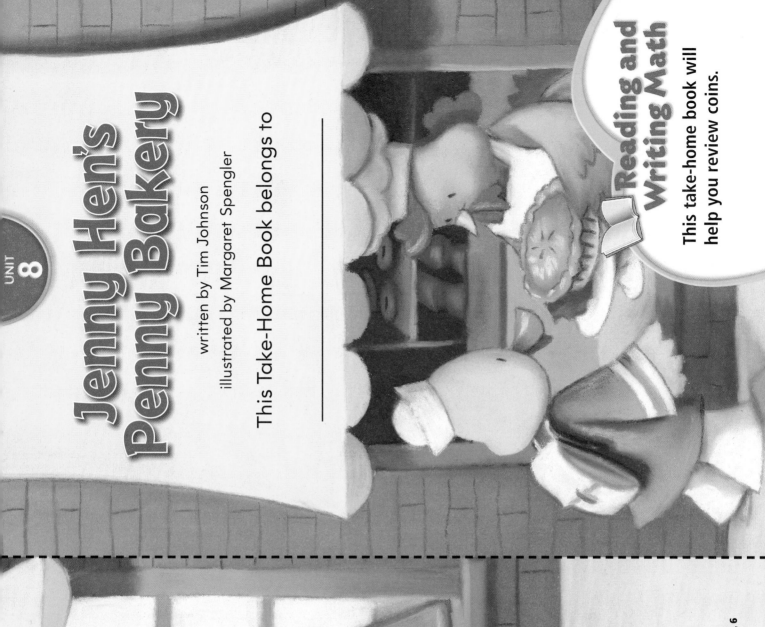

Jenny Hen's Penny Bakery

written by Tim Johnson

illustrated by Margaret Spengler

This Take-Home Book belongs to

____

Reading and Writing Math

This take-home book will help you review coins.

Jenny Hen, also known as Little Red,
Runs a bakery and sells bread.
She also sells some cakes and pies,
And pizzas too, in every size!

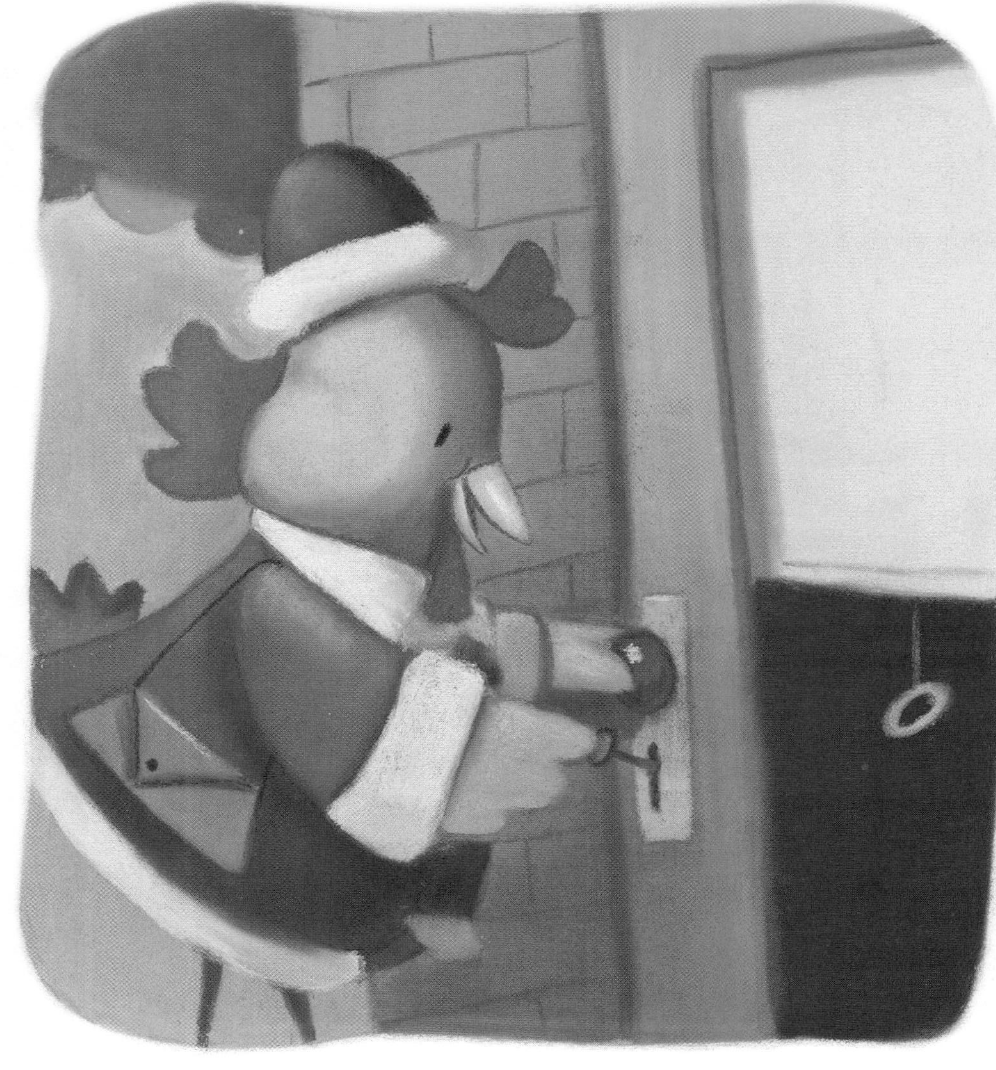

Such kind service is unsurpassed,
Jenny helps customers first to last.
All discover pennies, nickels, dimes
Can buy pies, bread, and happy times.

And so ends another day
With coins to count and bills to pay.
With so many things all day to do
Jenny's tired, but happy, too.

Duck comes in. He's first to buy.
He's come to get an apple pie.
"Five pennies for the pie," says Jenny.
"Oh, dear Hen, I haven't any."

"Oh me, oh my, this is a pickle.
I have no pennies, just a nickel!"
Jenny smiled, "Then you're in luck.
A nickel's worth five pennies, Duck!"

"I've got my bread, and that is that.
Thank you, Jenny," purred the cat.
"I hope you have a happy night,"
Said Jenny turning off the light.

Said Ted, "Oh woe is me, and
what a crime. I haven't pennies,
just this dime." Jenny smiled,
and said, "Oh, please don't fret!
A dime's worth ten pennies!
So you're all set!"

Happy he could buy his pie,
Duck let out a great big sigh.
He left the store and in came Ted,
A tabby cat, to buy some bread.

Said Ted, "I think it would be nice,
If I could buy some bread that's sliced."

"Wheat or white?" inquired Jenny.
"Either one will cost ten pennies."

Money

Vocabulary

Here are some vocabulary words you will learn in the chapter.

penny A coin that is worth one cent or 1¢

nickel A coin that is worth five cents or 5¢

dime A coin that is worth ten cents or 10¢

quarter A coin that is worth twenty-five cents or 25¢

See English-Spanish glossary pages 505–516.

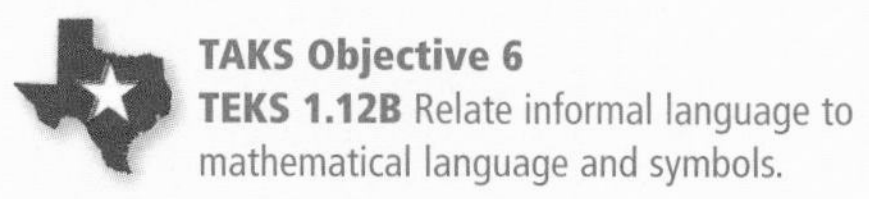

TAKS Objective 6
TEKS 1.12B Relate informal language to mathematical language and symbols.

Education Place
Visit **www.eduplace.com/txmap/** for the eGlossary and vocabulary eGames.

Name ______________________________

Check What You Know

Skip count by 2s, 5s, or 10s.
Write the numbers.

1.     

_____, _____, _____, _____, _____

2.     

_____, _____, _____, _____, _____

3.     

_____, _____, _____, _____, _____

Write the missing numbers.

4. 5, 10, 15, _____, 25, 30, _____, _____, 45, _____

Use this page to review important skills needed for this chapter.

Name ____________________

Chapter 20 Lesson 1

Penny

Learn

penny
1 cent
1¢

Hands On

TEKS Objective
Identify a penny; find the value of a group of pennies.

TAKS Vocabulary
penny
cent

Guided Practice

Use coins.
Count on by ones to find the value of the pennies.

Think!
The number I say last is the number of cents.

1.

____¢ ____¢ ____¢ ____¢ ____¢

____¢

2.

____¢ ____¢ ____¢ ____¢ ____¢ ____¢

____¢

3.

____¢ ____¢

____¢

4. **Math Talk** How many pennies do you need to show 10¢? How do you know?

★ Practice

Remember! Count on by ones for pennies.

Use coins.
Find the value of the coins.

5. 1 ¢ 2 ¢ 3 ¢ ____¢ ____¢ ____¢ ____¢ ____¢

6. ____¢ ____¢ ____¢ ____¢

7. ____¢ ____¢ ____¢ ____¢ ____¢ ____¢

8. ____¢ ____¢ ____¢ ____¢ ____¢

Problem Solving: Reasoning

9. Rosa has 8 pennies. Jon has 2 more pennies than Rosa. What is the value of Jon's coins?

____¢

10. May has 9 pennies. Lee has 2 fewer pennies than May. What is the value of Lee's coins?

____¢

At Home Place several coins on a table. Have your child identify the pennies and count to tell their value.

En casa Coloque varias monedas sobre una mesa. Pida a su niño que identifique las monedas de 1 centavo y que las cuente para decir su valor.

Name ________________________________

Chapter 20 Lesson 2

Nickel

Hands On

TEKS Objective
Identify a nickel; skip count by fives to find the value of a group of nickels.

TAKS Vocabulary
nickel

★ Learn

nickel
5 cents
5¢

1 nickel = 5¢

5 pennies = 5¢

★ Guided Practice

Think!
I skip count by 5s for nickels.

Use coins.
Find the value of the nickels.

1.    

_____¢ _____¢ _____¢ _____¢ _____¢

_____¢

2. 

_____¢ _____¢

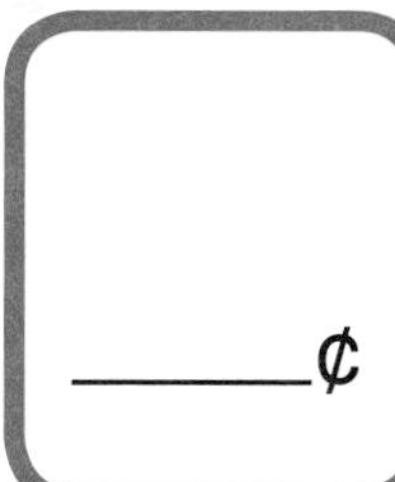

_____¢

3. 

_____¢ _____¢ _____¢

_____¢

4. **Math Talk** Would you rather have 1 nickel or 4 pennies? Why?

TAKS Objectives 1, 2
TEKS 1.1C Identify individual coins by name and value and describe relationships among them.
TEKS 1.5A Use patterns to skip count by twos, fives, and tens.

★ Practice

Use coins.
Find the value of the nickels.

Remember!
Skip count by fives for nickels.

5. 

5 ¢ 10 ¢ ____¢ ____¢

____¢

---

6. 

____¢ ____¢ ____¢

____¢

---

7. 

____¢ ____¢ ____¢ ____¢ ____¢ ____¢

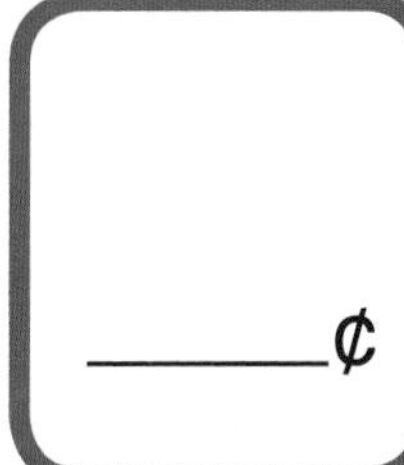

____¢

---

8. 

____¢ ____¢ ____¢ ____¢ ____¢

____¢

Problem Solving: Reasoning

9. Circle the set of coins with the greater value.

At Home Use nickels to make a set of coins with a value of 40¢. Have your child tell their value.

En casa Use monedas de cinco centavos para formar un conjunto de monedas con un valor de 40¢. Pida a su niño que diga su valor.

Name ______________________________

Chapter 20 Lesson 3

Dime

Hands On

TEKS Objective
Identify a dime; skip count by tens to find the value of a group of dimes.

TAKS Vocabulary
dime

★ Learn

dime
10 cents
10¢

1 dime = 10¢

2 nickels = 10¢

10 pennies = 10¢

★ Guided Practice

Think!
I skip count by 10s for dimes.

Use coins.
Find the value of the dimes.

1.   

_____¢ _____¢ _____¢

_____¢

2.      

_____¢ _____¢ _____¢ _____¢ _____¢ _____¢

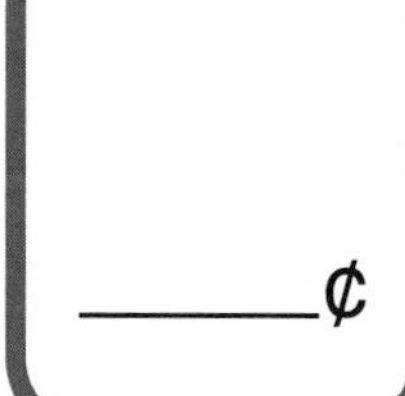

_____¢

3. **Math Talk** Name two ways to show 10¢.

TAKS Objectives 1, 2
TEKS 1.1C Identify individual coins by name and value and describe relationships among them.
TEKS 1.5A Use patterns to skip count by twos, fives, and tens.

★ Practice

Use coins.
Find the value of the dimes.

Remember!
Skip count by tens for dimes.

4. 10 ¢ 20 ¢ 30 ¢ ____¢ ____¢ ____¢ ____¢ | ____¢

5. ____¢ ____¢ | ____¢

6. ____¢ ____¢ ____¢ ____¢ ____¢ | ____¢

7. ____¢ ____¢ ____¢ ____¢ | ____¢

Problem Solving: Reasoning

8. Grace has 10 pennies.
What coins can she trade them for?

____ dime or ____ nickels

Draw or write to explain.

At Home Use pennies to make groups of coins totaling 40¢ or less. Have your child find the value.

En casa Use monedas de 1 centavo para hacer grupos que tengan un total de 40¢ o menos. Pida a su niño que halle el valor del grupo.

Name ______________________

Chapter 20 Lesson 4

Quarter

quarter
25 cents
25¢

25¢

Hands On

TEKS Objective
Identify a quarter; find the value of a group of quarters.

TAKS Vocabulary
quarter

★ Explore

Use coins. Find the value of the coins.

1.  

_____¢ _____¢

Think!
I know each quarter is 25¢.

_____¢

2.   

_____¢ _____¢ _____¢

_____¢

3.    

_____¢ _____¢ _____¢ _____¢

_____¢

4. **Math Talk** Can you make 25¢ with only dimes? Why?

TAKS Objectives 1, 2
TEKS 1.1C Identify individual coins by name and value and describe relationships among them.
TEKS 1.5A Use patterns to skip count by twos, fives, and tens.

★ Extend

Circle the coin set that equals the amount.

Remember!
You can skip count by fives for nickels and by tens for dimes.

5. 10¢

6. 5¢

7. 25¢

8. 5¢

At Home Use coins. Have your child show 25¢ in different ways using only one kind of coin at a time.

En casa Use monedas. Pida a su niño que muestre 25¢ de diferentes maneras, usando sólo un tipo de moneda cada vez.

Name ______________________

Chapter 20 Lesson 5

Act It Out

TEKS Objective
Use coins to act out and solve problems; create and solve problems with money.

★ Learn

Jack has 6 pennies.
The pencil costs 4¢.
Does Jack have enough money to buy the pencil?

Understand

What do you know?

- Jack has 6 pennies.
- The pencil costs 4¢.

Plan

You can act out the problem with pennies.

Solve

Try it. Count out 6 pennies.
Take the 4 you need.
There are 2 pennies left.
Jack can buy the pencil.

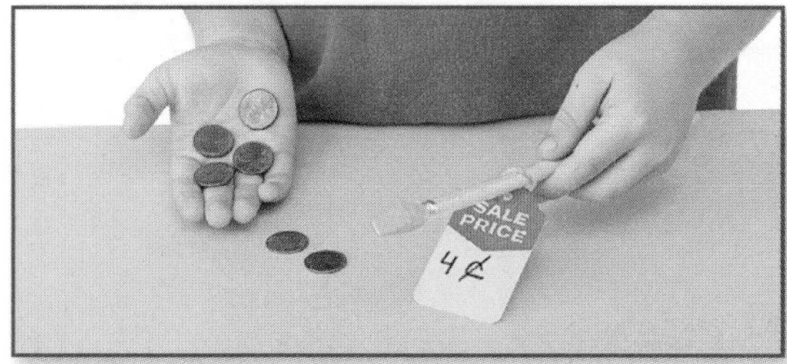

Look Back

Does your answer make sense?
Did you answer the question?

TAKS Objectives 1, 6
TEKS 1.1C Identify individual coins by name and value and describe relationships among them.
TEKS 1.11B Solve problems with guidance that incorporates the processes of understanding the problem, making a plan, carrying out the plan, and evaluating the solution for reasonableness.
Also **TEKS 1.11C** and **1.11D**

★ Guided Problem Solving

I. 

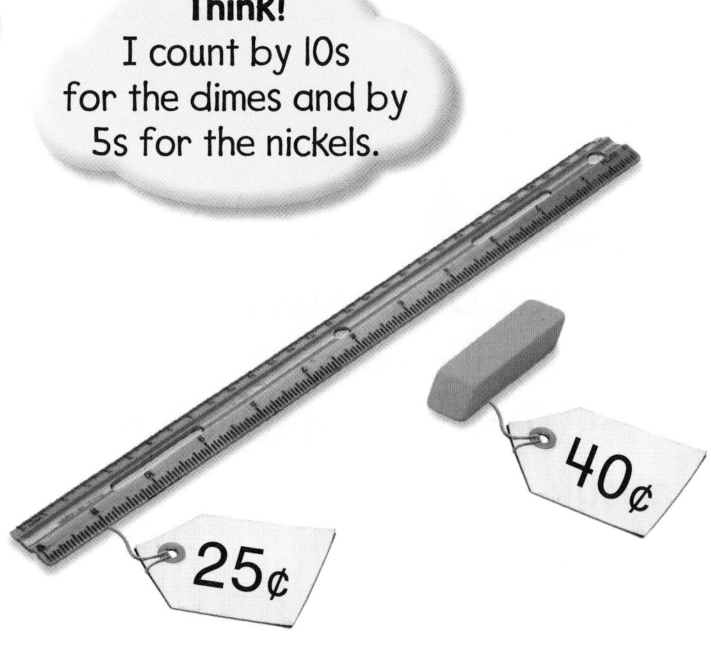
Think!
I count by 10s
for the dimes and by
5s for the nickels.
40¢
25¢

Which item can you buy?

Circle it.

Circle the coins you need.

2. **Math Talk** What coins could you use to buy something that costs 30¢?

★ Problem Solving Practice

Use coins. Circle the item you can buy.
Circle the coins you spend.

3.   

50¢
notes
33¢

4.  

11¢
25¢

At Home Find items under 50¢ in an advertisement. Have your child tell which coins to use to buy each item.

En casa En un aviso, busque artículos que cuesten menos de 50¢. Pida a su niño que le diga qué monedas podría usar para comprar cada artículo.

Name ____________________

Create and Solve

1. Kevin wants to buy the yo-yo. Which set of coins matches the price? Use coins. Circle the set of coins Kevin needs.

47¢

TAKS Objective 1
TEKS 1.1C Identify individual coins by name and value and describe relationships among them.

2. Draw a picture of something you can buy.

3. How much does it cost?
Write a price up to 50¢.

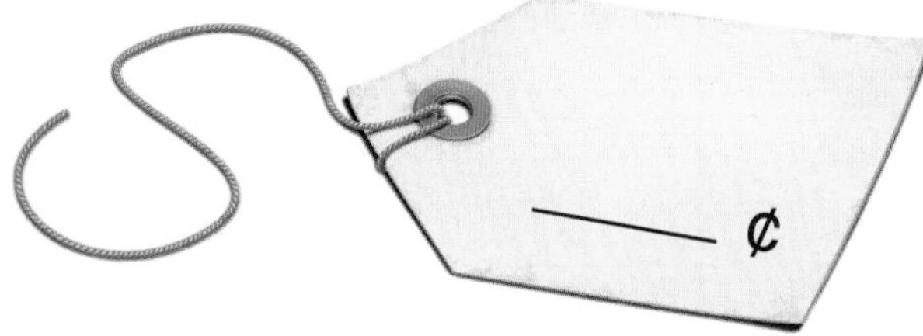

4. Draw the coins you will use to buy it.

Name ______________________

Fun with Coins

Use the coins found at
www.eduplace.com/txmap/

1. Put your pointer over the **stamp** tool.
   • Click the quarter.
2. Put your pointer over the **stamp** tool.
   • Click the penny 4 times.
3. Click [1 2 3].
   This shows 29¢.

Use the coins. Show the amount using the fewest coins.

1.

2.

Social Studies Link

Yard Sale

Ben and Jill go to a yard sale. They find coloring books for sale.

Use coins to solve.
Show your work.

1. Ben has 2 nickels. The reptile coloring book is 9¢. The trucks coloring book is 12¢. Which book can Ben buy?

   __________ coloring book

2. Jill has 1 quarter. The horses coloring book is 15¢. The fairy tales coloring book is 30¢. Which book can Jill buy?

   __________ coloring book

3. Ben has 1 penny left. Jill has 1 dime left. The trucks coloring book is 12¢. Can they buy it?

____

TAKS Objectives 1, 6
TEKS 1.1C Identify individual coins by name and value and describe relationships among them.
TEKS 1.11C Select or develop an appropriate problem-solving plan or strategy including drawing a picture, looking for a pattern, systematic guessing and checking, or acting it out in order to solve a problem.
TEKS Social Studies 8B, 8C

Name ______________________

Concepts and Skills

Use coins. Find the value of the coins. TEKS 1.1C, 1.5A

1.      

_____¢ _____¢ _____¢ _____¢ _____¢ _____¢

_____¢

2.     

 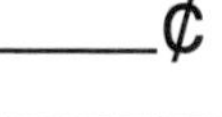 

_____¢ _____¢ _____¢ _____¢ _____¢

_____¢

3.       

_____¢ _____¢ _____¢ _____¢ _____¢ _____¢ _____¢

_____¢

4.   

_____¢ _____¢ _____¢

_____¢

Problem Solving TEKS 1.1C, 1.11B, 1.11C, 1.11D

Use coins. Circle the item you can buy.
Circle the coins you spend.

5. 

TAKS Prep and Spiral Review

Choose the answer for problems 1–4.

1. Which figure shows 1 out of 2 equal parts colored blue?

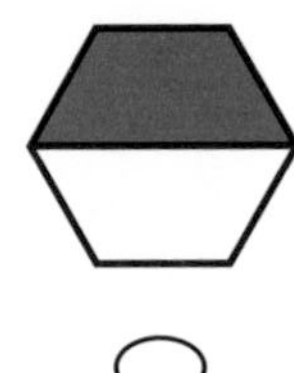 ○ 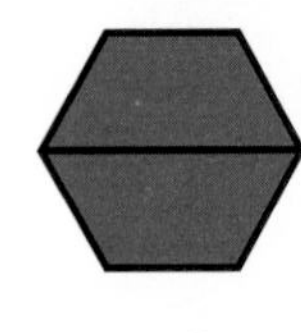 ○ 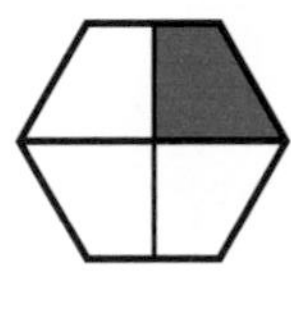 ○ 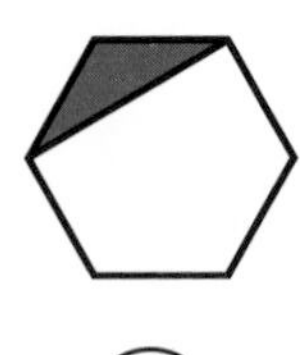 ○

TEKS 1.2A (page 183)

2. Chris made a snack. He cut a slice of bread into 4 equal parts. He put jam on 3 parts. Which shows the snack Chris made?

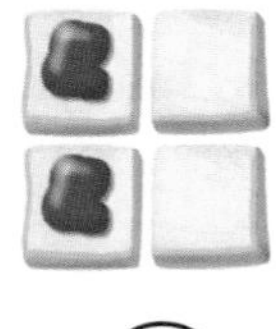 ○ 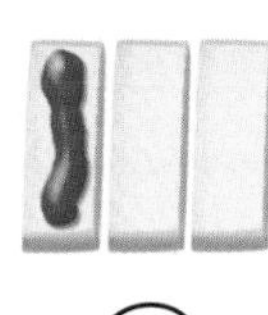 ○ 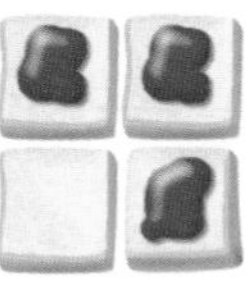 ○ 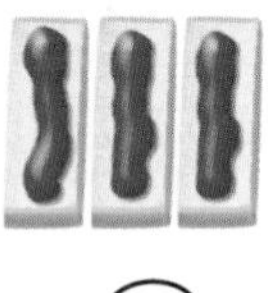 ○

TEKS 1.2A (page 185)

3. Which group has figures with only flat surfaces?

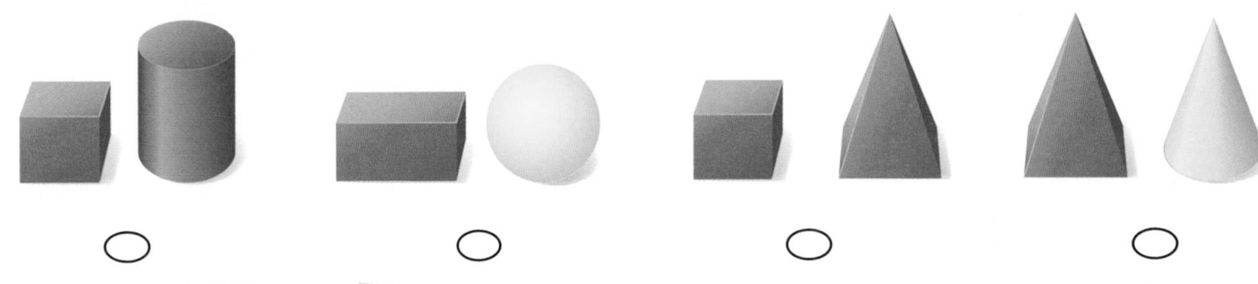

○ ○ ○ ○

TEKS 1.6B, 1.6C (page 165)

4. Sue Jung sorts figures. In which group should she put the cylinder?

all flat surfaces	curved surfaces and flat surfaces	all curved surfaces	no curved surfaces
○	○	○	○

TEKS 1.6B, 1.6C (page 165)

Education Place
Visit **www.eduplace.com/txmap/** for Test-Taking Tips and Extra Practice.

Time

TAKS Vocabulary

Here are some vocabulary words you will learn in the chapter.

hour hand The shorter hand on a clock

minute hand The longer hand on a clock

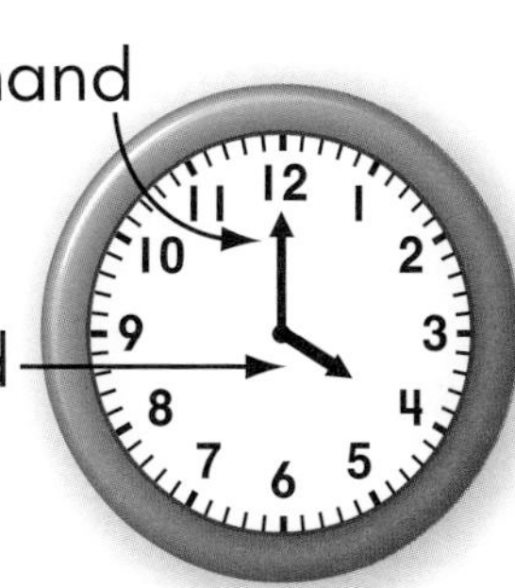

hour An amount of time equal to 60 minutes

half-hour An amount of time equal to 30 minutes

See English-Spanish glossary pages 505–516.

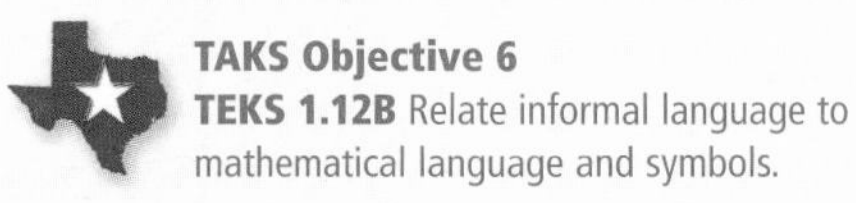

TAKS Objective 6
TEKS 1.12B Relate informal language to mathematical language and symbols.

Education Place
Visit **www.eduplace.com/txmap/** for the eGlossary and vocabulary eGames.

Name ______________________________

 Check What You Know

Soccer practice starts at 3:00.
Circle the one you would use.

1.

MAY						
Sunday	Monday	Tuesday	Wednesday	Thursday	Friday	Saturday
		1	2	3	4	5
6	7	8	9	10	11	12
13	14	15	16	17	18	19
20	21	22	23	24	25	26
27	28	29	30	31		

Circle the activity that takes more time.

2.

3.

Circle the activity that takes less time.

4.

5.

Use this page to review important skills needed for this chapter.

Name ________________________

Chapter 21 Lesson 1

Estimate Time

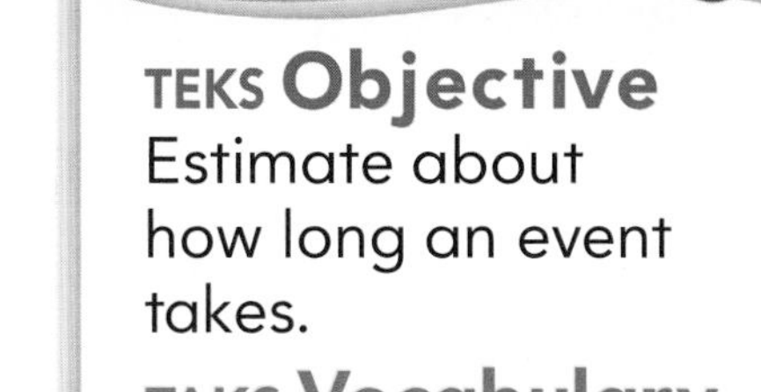

TEKS Objective
Estimate about how long an event takes.

TAKS Vocabulary
about 1 minute
about 1 hour
about 1 day

★ Learn

You can estimate the amount of time an activity takes. It can take **about 1 minute, about 1 hour**, or **about 1 day.**

about 1 minute
about 1 hour
about 1 day

about 1 minute
about 1 hour
about 1 day

★ Guided Practice

Estimate the amount of time the activity will take. Circle.

Think!
I know that brushing my teeth does not take too long.

1. 

about 1 minute
about 1 hour
about 1 day

2. 

about 1 minute
about 1 hour
about 1 day

3. **Math Talk** Tell something you do in the morning that takes about 1 minute.

TAKS Objective 4
TEKS 1.8A Order three or more events according to duration.

★ Practice

Estimate the amount of time the activity will take. Circle.

Remember!
Think about how much time the activity takes.

4.

about 1 minute
about 1 hour
about 1 day

5.

about 1 minute
about 1 hour
about 1 day

6.

about 1 minute
about 1 hour
about 1 day

7.

about 1 minute
about 1 hour
about 1 day

Problem Solving: Visual Thinking

8. Draw something that takes about 1 hour for you to do.

At Home Help your child identify activities that take about 1 minute and about 1 hour.

En casa Ayude a su niño a identificar actividades que toman aproximadamente 1 minuto y aproximadamente 1 hora.

Name ______________________

Chapter 21 Lesson 2

Order Events

TEKS **Objective**
Order events by the amount of time each one takes.

TAKS **Vocabulary**
least
greatest

★ Learn

You can order activities. The shortest activity takes the **least** amount of time. The longest activity takes the **greatest** amount of time.

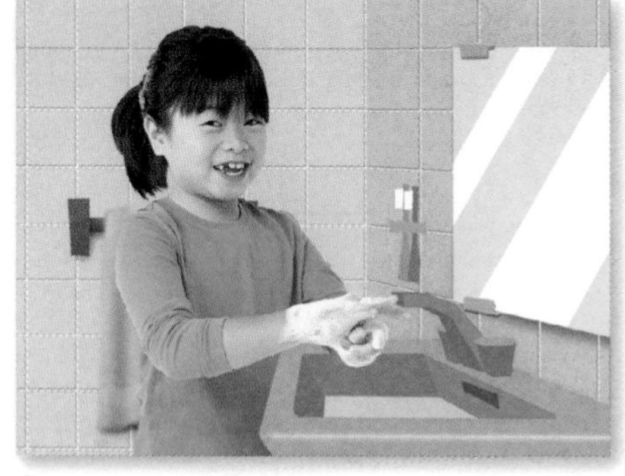

1

3

2

Think!
I know 1 means the least amount of time.

★ Guided Practice

Write 1, 2, and 3 to show the correct order.

1.

____

____

____

2. **Math Talk** How can you order Exercise 1 from greatest to least?

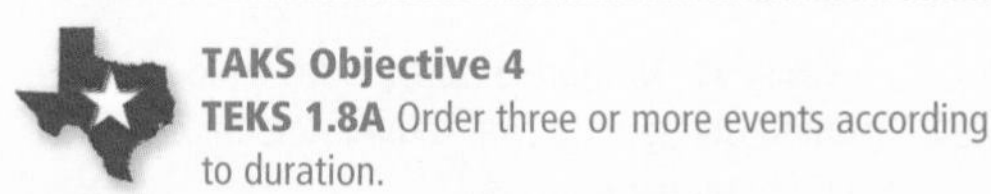

TAKS Objective 4
TEKS 1.8A Order three or more events according to duration.

★ Practice

Remember!
1 means the least amount of time.

Write 1, 2, and 3 to show the correct order.

3.

1

2

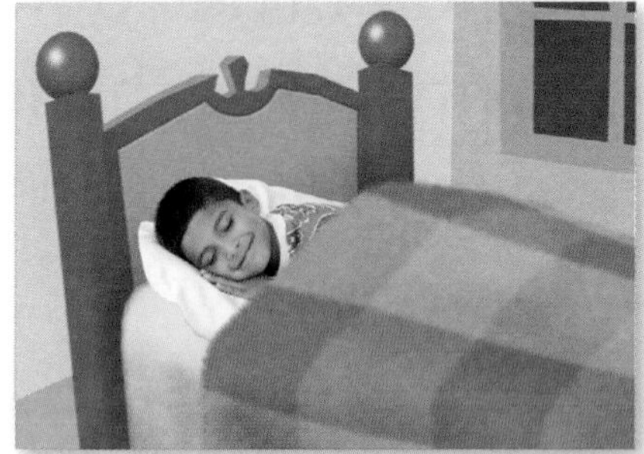

3

4.

____

____

____

Problem Solving: Visual Thinking

Look at the projects.

A

B

C

5. What project takes the greatest amount of time to make? ____

6. What project takes the least amount of time to make? ____

At Home Name 3 activities and ask your child to tell which takes the least amount of time and why.

En casa Nombre 3 actividades y pida a su niño que le diga cuál toma la menor cantidad de tiempo y por qué.

Name ____________________

Chapter 21 Lesson 3

Hour

★ Learn

The **hour hand** and the **minute hand** show the time on some clocks.

Digital clocks show the time using only numbers.

TEKS Objective
Read time to the hour using analog and digital clocks.

TAKS Vocabulary
hour hand
minute hand
digital
o'clock
hour

I play for 1 hour.
The minute hand is at the 12.
The hour hand is at the 4.

The game starts at 4 **o'clock.**

1 **hour** later is 5 o'clock.

★ Guided Practice

Read the clock. Write the time two ways.

Think!
The shorter hand is the hour hand.

1.

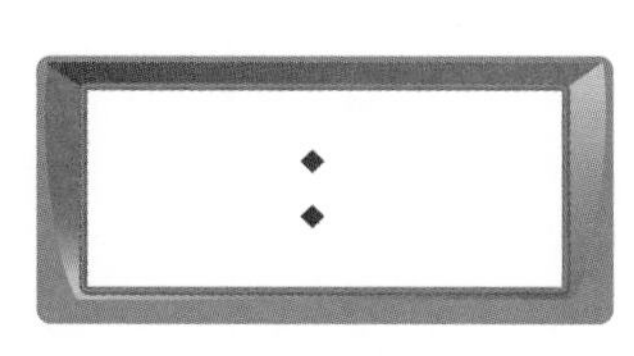

_____ o'clock

2.

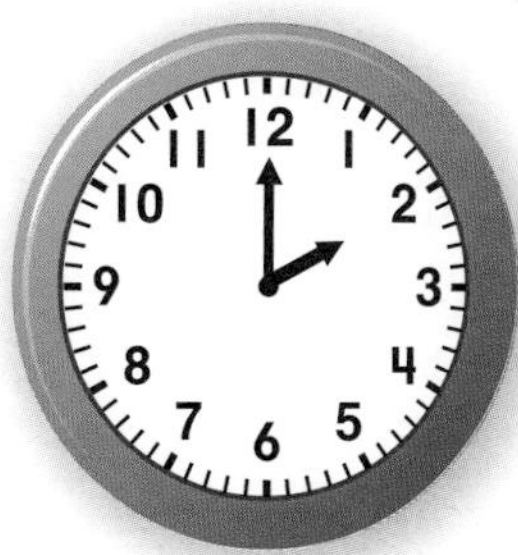

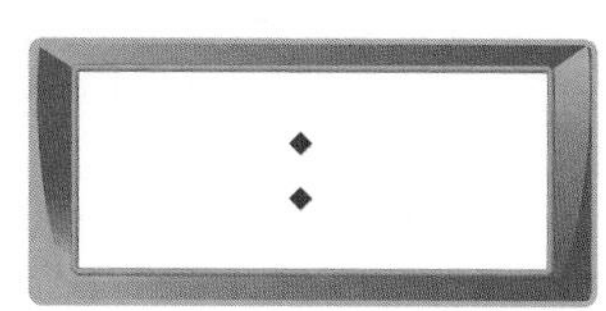

_____ o'clock

3. **Math Talk** Where do the hands point on a clock showing 7 o'clock?

TAKS Objective 4
TEKS 1.8B Read time to the hour and half-hour using analog and digital clocks.

★ Practice

Read the clock.
Write the time two ways.

Remember!
The shorter hand is the hour hand.

4.
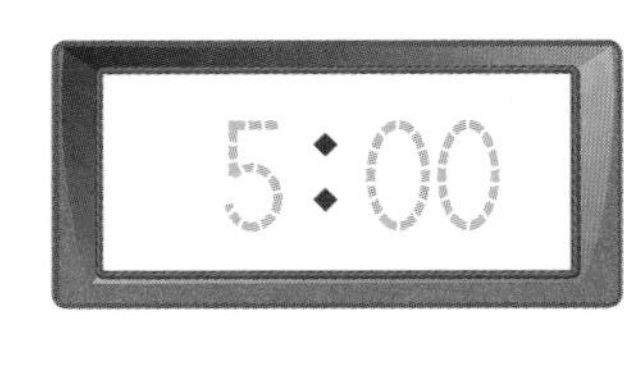

5 o'clock

5.

_____ o'clock

6.

_____ o'clock

7.

_____ o'clock

8.

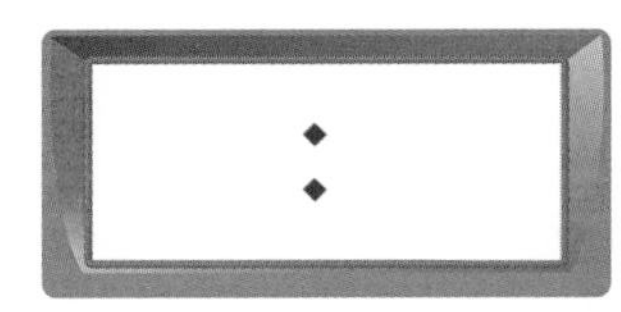

_____ o'clock

9.

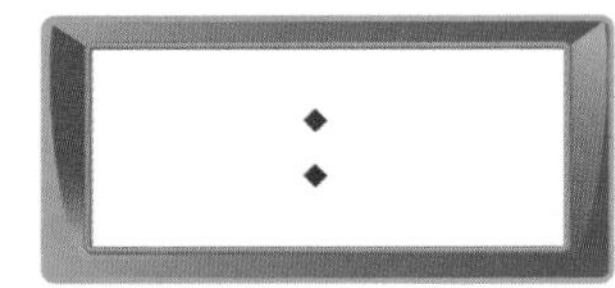

_____ o'clock

Problem Solving: Data Sense

Mia eats dinner at 6:00.

10. Ken eats dinner later than Mia. What time does he eat?

_____

11. How many children eat earlier than Mia?

_____ children

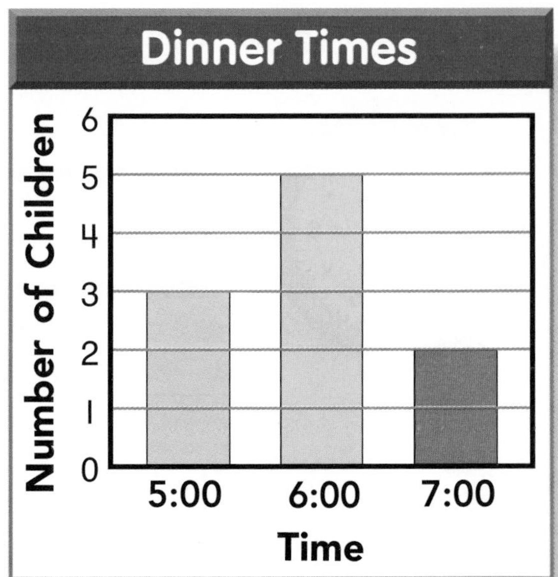

At Home Have your child practice telling time to the hour. Use a variety of clocks.

En casa Pida a su niño que practique cómo decir la hora en punto. Use una variedad de relojes.

Name ______________________________

Chapter 21 Lesson 4

Half-Hour

TEKS **Objective**
Read time to the half-hour.

TAKS **Vocabulary**
half-hour

★ Learn

An hour has **60** minutes.
A **half-hour** has **30** minutes.

The hour hand is halfway between the 8 and the 9.

The minute hand has gone halfway around the clock. It is at the 6.

8 o'clock

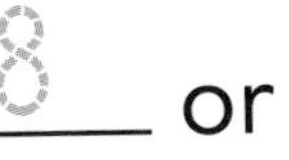

30 minutes after 8 or half past 8

★ Guided Practice

Say and write the time.

Think!
I know when the minute hand is on the 6, it is half past the hour.

1.

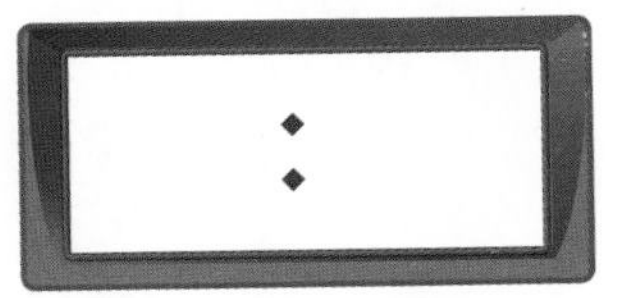

_____ o'clock half past _____

2.

half past _____ _____ o'clock

3. 123 **Math Talk** Tell the time **4:30** another way.

★ Practice

Remember!
When it is 30 minutes after the hour, the minute hand is at the 6.

Say and write the time.

4.

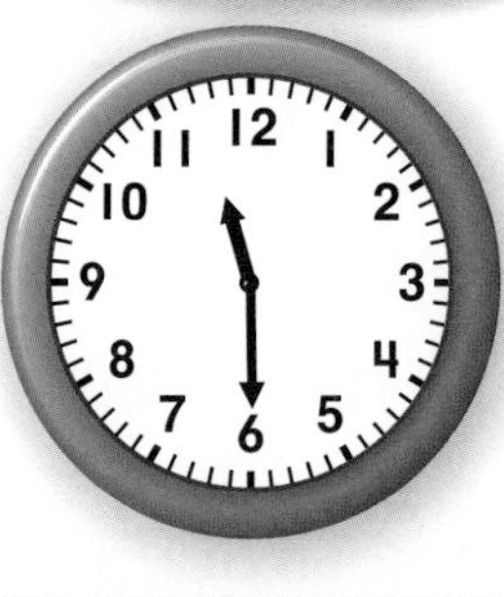

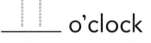

11 o'clock half past 11

5.

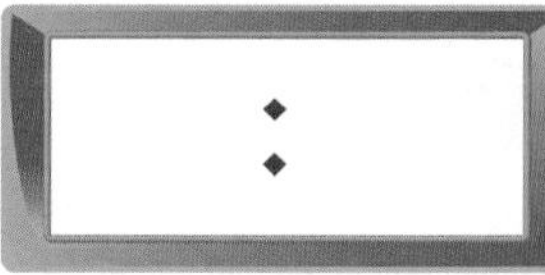

half past ____ ____ o'clock

Algebra Readiness: Patterns

Write the time the clock shows.

6.

____:____ ____:____ ____:____ ____:____

7. **Math Talk** Explain the pattern you see above.

At Home Talk with your child about daily activities that take about a half-hour.

En casa Hable con su niño sobre actividades diarias que toman aproximadamente media hora.

Name ___________________________

Chapter 21 Lesson 5

Act It Out

Problem
Solving
Strategy

TEKS Objective
Use clocks to solve problems.

★ Learn

This clock shows when Mary begins.

__2__ o'clock

My violin lesson lasts for 1 hour.

What does the clock look like when Mary's lesson ends?

Understand

- It is 2 o'clock.
- Mary's violin lesson is 1 hour long.

Plan

Write the time the lesson starts.

__2__ o'clock

What time will it be 1 hour later?

__3__ o'clock

Solve

Draw what the clock looks like when the lesson ends.

Think!
The minute hand is at the 12 again 1 hour later.

Look Back

Did you answer the question?
Does your answer make sense?

TAKS Objectives 4, 6
TEKS 1.8B Read time to the hour and half-hour using analog and digital clocks.
TEKS 1.11C Select or develop an appropriate problem-solving plan or strategy including drawing a picture, looking for a pattern, systematic guessing and checking, or acting it out in order to solve a problem.
Also **TEKS 1.11B**

★ Guided Problem Solving

1\.

_____ o'clock

We played at the beach for 3 hours.

_____ o'clock

Write the time on the first clock.

How long are they at the beach?

Draw and write to solve.

2\. **Math Talk** How did you solve the problem?

★ Problem Solving Practice

Write the time that the activity begins.
Draw and write the time it ends.

3\.

_____ o'clock

Mia played soccer for 1 hour.

_____ o'clock

4\.

_____ o'clock

Sue danced for 2 hours.

_____ o'clock

At Home Discuss when daily activities start and end. Help your child find out how long each activity takes.

En casa Comente con su niño en qué momento comienzan y terminan las actividades diarias. Ayude a su niño a calcular cuánto tiempo toma cada actividad.

Name ____________________

Texas Field Trip

Space Center Houston

When you visit Space Center Houston, you can see and feel what life in space is like. You can also see how Mission Control works.

Science

Astronaut Gallery

Solve. Show your work.

1. The clock shows 8:00. The space shuttle launches in 2 hours. What time will the shuttle launch?

   _____ o'clock

space shuttle

2. Dora measures how much she weighs on other planets. She weighs 60 pounds on Earth and 67 pounds on Neptune. On which planet does she weigh more?

   ____

Earth

3. Maria counts pictures of astronauts. They are in rows of 10. She counts 8 rows. How many pictures does she count?

   _____ pictures

astronaut

TAKS Objective 6
TEKS 1.11A Identify mathematics in everyday situations.
TEKS 1.11C Select or develop an appropriate problem-solving plan or strategy including drawing a picture, looking for a pattern, systematic guessing and checking, or acting it out in order to solve a problem. **TEKS Science 2A**

TAKS Problem Solving
Listening Skills

Listen to your teacher read the problem.
Choose the correct answer.

Select a Strategy
Guess and Check
Act It Out

1. Bala's violin lesson starts at 4:30. It lasts for 1 hour. What time does the lesson end?

3:30 ○ 4:30 ○ 5:00 ○ 5:30 ○

TEKS 1.8B

2. Will washes his hands, makes a snack, pours a drink, and watches a movie. Which activity takes the greatest amount of time?

washes hands ○ makes snack ○ pours drink ○ watches movie ○

TEKS 1.8A

3. 2:00 ○ 3:00 ○ 4:00 ○ 5:00 ○

TEKS 1.8B

4. 7:00 ○ 8:00 ○ 9:00 ○ 10:00 ○

TEKS 1.8B

Education Place
Visit **www.eduplace.com/txmap/** for Test-Taking Tips and more TAKS Practice.

Name ______________________________

What Time Is It?

Draw a line to the clock that answers the question.

1. Ann starts cleaning her room at 4:30. She spends 2 hours cleaning. What time does she finish?

2. Taro wakes up at 8:00. He gets to soccer practice 1 hour later. Soccer practice lasts for 2 hours. What time is soccer practice over?

3. Charley gets home from school at 3:30. He spends a half-hour having a snack. Then he spends 1 hour doing his homework. What time does he finish his homework?

4. Ella goes out to ride her bike at 11:00. She rides for 1 hour before her piano lesson. Her piano lesson lasts a half-hour. What time is her piano lesson over?

TAKS Objective 4
TEKS 1.8B Read time to the hour and half-hour using analog and digital clocks.

Education Place
Visit **www.eduplace.com/txmap/** for Brain Teasers.

Math Music

Oh, Yes!

Math Music, Track 8
Tune: "For He's a Jolly Good Fellow"

Oh, yes! One penny is 1 cent.
Oh, yes! One penny is 1 cent.
Oh, yes! One penny is 1 cent.
1 penny is 1 cent!

Oh, yes! One nickel is 5 cents.
Oh, yes! One nickel is 5 cents.
Oh, yes! One nickel is 5 cents.
5 pennies are 5 cents!

Oh, yes! One dime is 10 cents.
Oh, yes! One dime is 10 cents.
Oh, yes! One dime is 10 cents.
10 pennies are 10 cents!

TAKS Objective 1
TEKS 1.1C Identify individual coins by name and value and describe relationships among them.

Name ______________________________

Concepts and Skills

Estimate the amount of time the activity will take. Circle. TEKS 1.8A

1. 

about 1 minute

about 1 hour

about 1 day

Write 1, 2, and 3 to show the correct order.
1 means the least amount of time.
3 means the greatest amount of time. TEKS 1.8A

2.  _____ _____ _____

Read the clock. Write the time two ways. TEKS 1.8B

3. 

[:]

_____ o'clock

4. 

[:]

half past _____

Problem Solving

Write the time that the activity begins.
Draw and write the time it ends. TEKS 1.8B, 1.11C

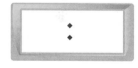

I played soccer for 2 hours.

5. 

_____ o'clock

_____ o'clock

TAKS Prep and Spiral Review

Choose the answer for problems 1–4.

1. If the 2 squares are joined, what figure is made?

 ○
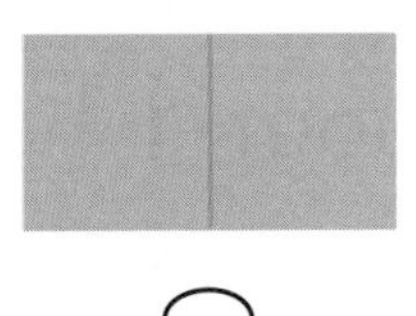 ○
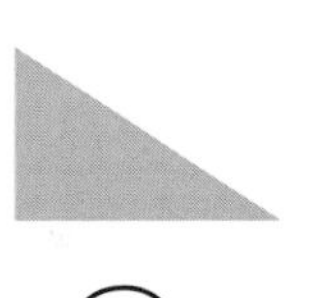 ○
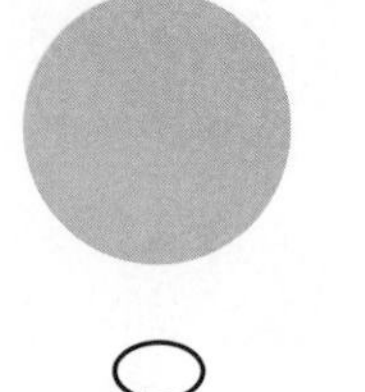 ○

TEKS 1.6D (page 153)

2. Tanya uses 3 triangles to make a new figure. Which figure does she make?

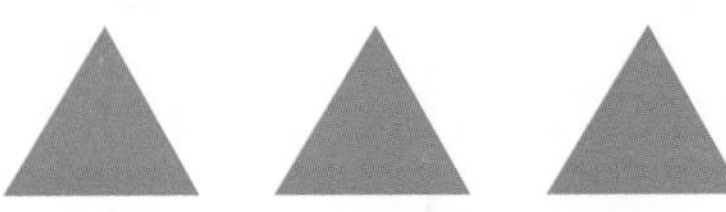

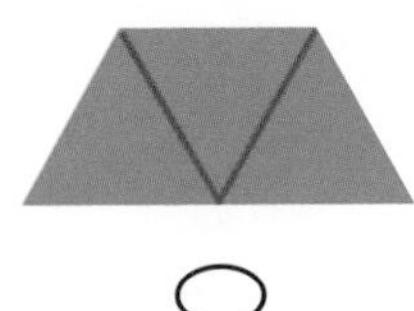 ○
 ○
 ○
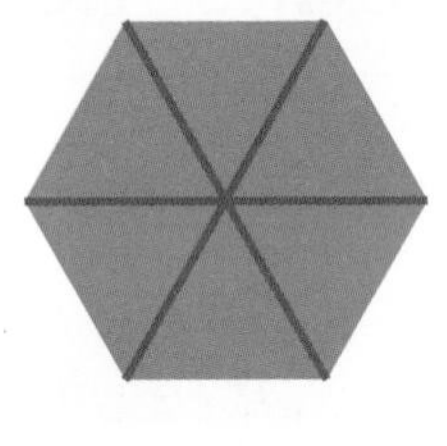 ○

TEKS 1.6D (page 153)

3. The number of children in first grade is greater than 71. It is less than 73. Which number shows how many children are in first grade?

70 ○ 71 ○ 72 ○ 73 ○

TEKS 1.5C (page 283)

4. Awan counted 49 math books, 33 science books, and 62 story books in the closet. Which shows these numbers in order from greatest to least?

33, 49, 62 ○ 62, 49, 33  49, 33, 62  62, 33, 49 

TEKS 1.5C (page 285)

Education Place
Visit www.eduplace.com/txmap/ for Test-Taking Tips and Extra Practice.

Name ______________________________

Unit 8 **Mental Math Strategies**

Doubles Plus 1

Adding can be quickly done.
Double first and then add 1!

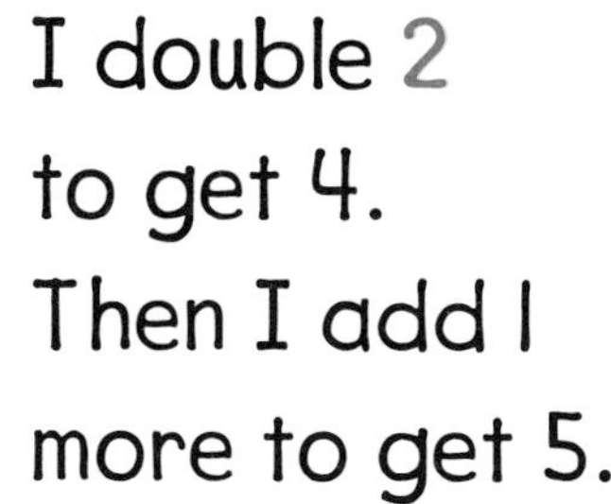

I double 2
to get 4.
Then I add 1
more to get 5.

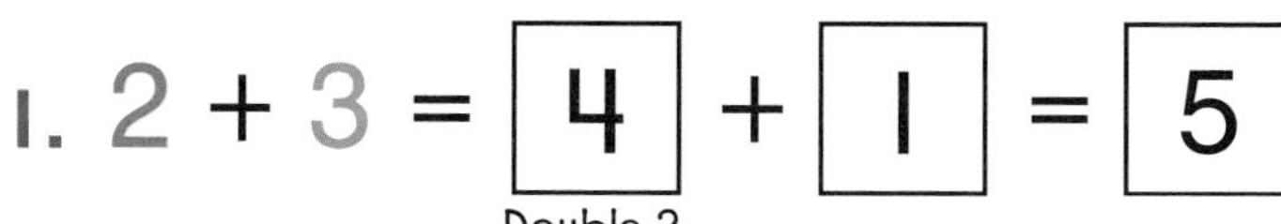

1. 2 + 3 = [4] + [1] = [5]
   Double 2.
2. 3 + 4 = [ ] + [1] = [ ]
   Double 3.
3. 4 + 5 = [ ] + [ ] = [ ]
   Double 4.
4. 5 + 6 = [ ] + [ ] = [ ]
   Double 5.

Doing Great!

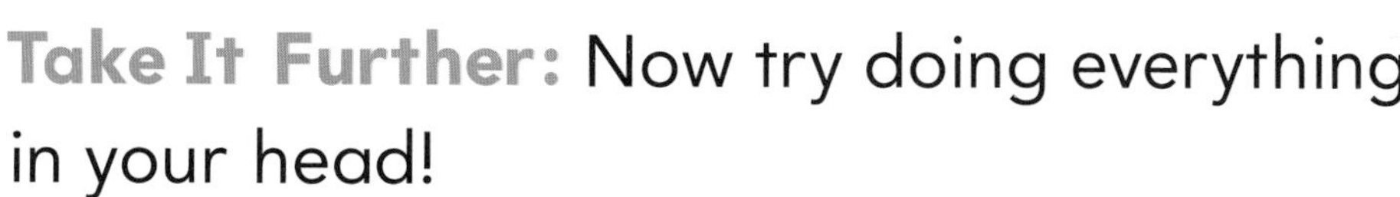

Take It Further: Now try doing everything in your head!

5. 3 + 4 = [ ]
6. 5 + 6 = [ ]
7. 2 + 3 = [ ]
8. 4 + 5 = [ ]
9. 6 + 7 = [ ]
10. 3 + 4 = [ ]

Name ______________________________

Reading and Writing Math

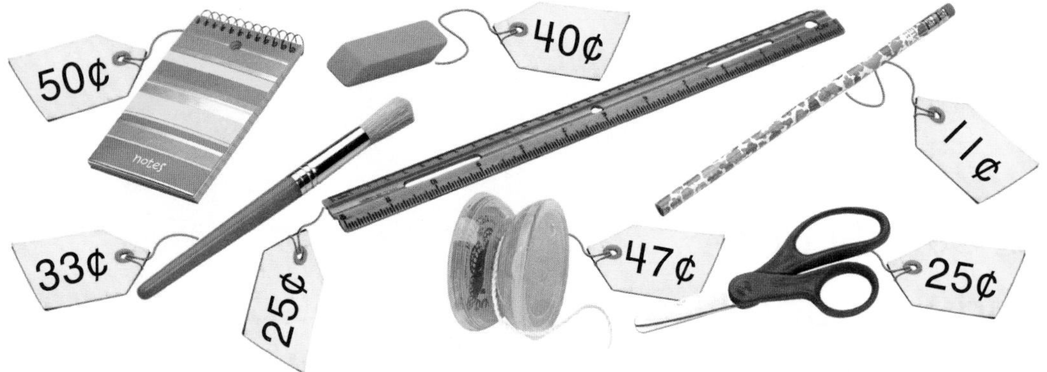

1. Pick an item you would like to buy. Write the price. ____

2. Use coins to show the price. Draw the coins.

3. How many quarters did you use? ____

4. How many dimes did you use? ____

5. How many nickels did you use? ____

6. How many pennies did you use? ____

7. **Writing Math** About how long does it take you to make your bed? Explain your answer.

____

____

TEKS 1.12A Explain and record observations using objects, words, pictures, numbers, and technology.

TEKS 1.12B Relate informal language to mathematical language and symbols.

Name ______________________________

Concepts and Skills

Find the value of the coins.

1.     

_____¢ _____¢ _____¢ _____¢ _____¢ _____¢ TEKS 1.1C

_____¢

2.    

_____¢ _____¢ _____¢ _____¢ TEKS 1.1C, 1.5A

_____¢

3.     

_____¢ _____¢ _____¢ _____¢ _____¢ TEKS 1.1C, 1.5A

_____¢

Estimate the time the activity will take. Circle. TEKS 1.8A

4. 

about 1 minute
about 1 hour
about 1 day

Write 1, 2, and 3 to show the correct order.
1 means the least amount of time.
3 means the greatest amount of time. TEKS 1.8A

5.   

_____ _____ _____

Read the clock. Write the time two ways. TEKS 1.8B

6. 

:

_____ o'clock

7. 

:

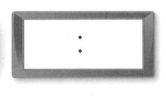

_____ o'clock

8. 

:

half past _____

9. 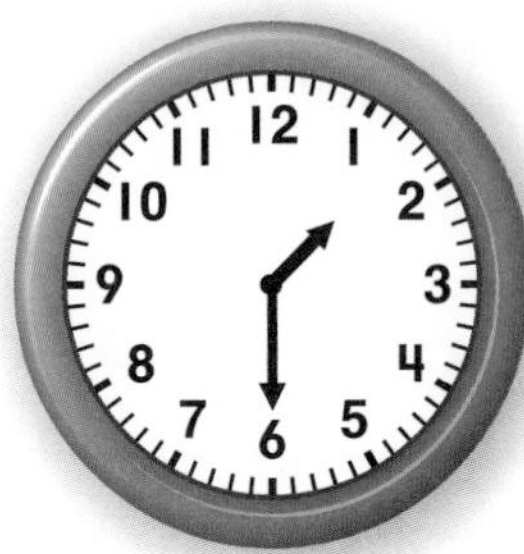

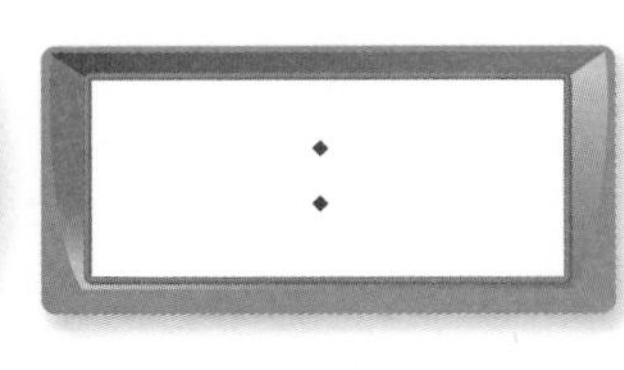

:

half past _____

Problem Solving

Write the time that the activity begins.
Draw and write the time it ends. TEKS 1.8B

10. 

_____ o'clock

Tyler read for 1 hour.

_____ o'clock

Houghton Mifflin Texas Math

Measurement

BIG IDEAS!

- You can compare and order length, area, weight, capacity, and temperature.
- You can use units to measure the length of an object.
- The smaller the unit, the greater the measure.

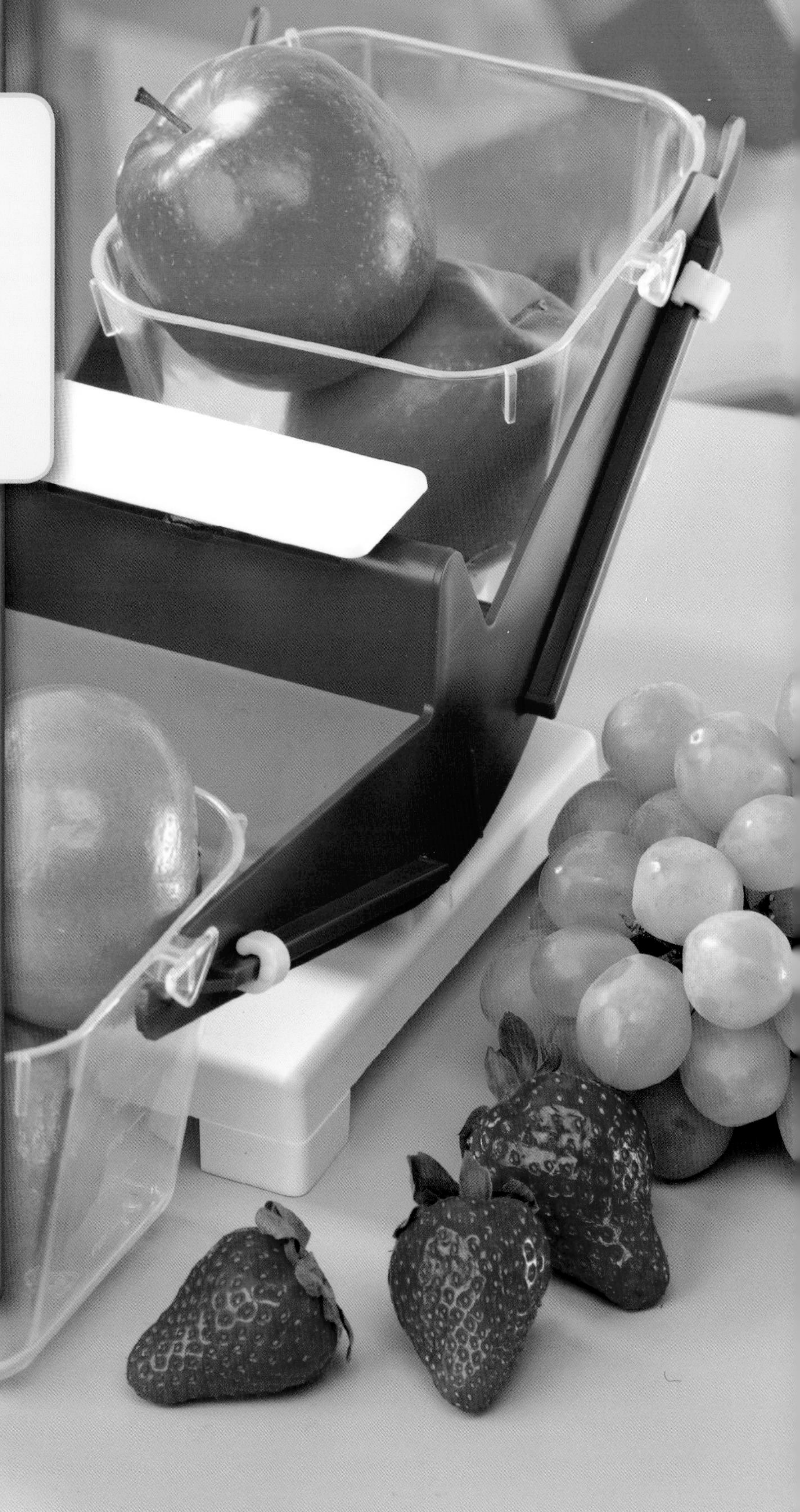

Songs and Games

Math Music Track 9
Let's Pretend

eGames
www.eduplace.com/txmap/

Literature

Literature Big Book

- Who's the Greatest?

Math Readers

ISBN-13: 978-0-618-95280-9
ISBN-10: 0-618-95280-2
89- WC - 16 15 14 13 12

Measure Up!

What You Need
2 players number cards 1–20

1. Mix the cards and place them face down in a pile.
2. Each player turns over a card.
3. Count out the same number of cubes as the number on the card.
4. Build, then compare trains. Tell which is longer or which is shorter.
5. The player with the longer train scores 1 point.
6. Play until each player has 5 points.

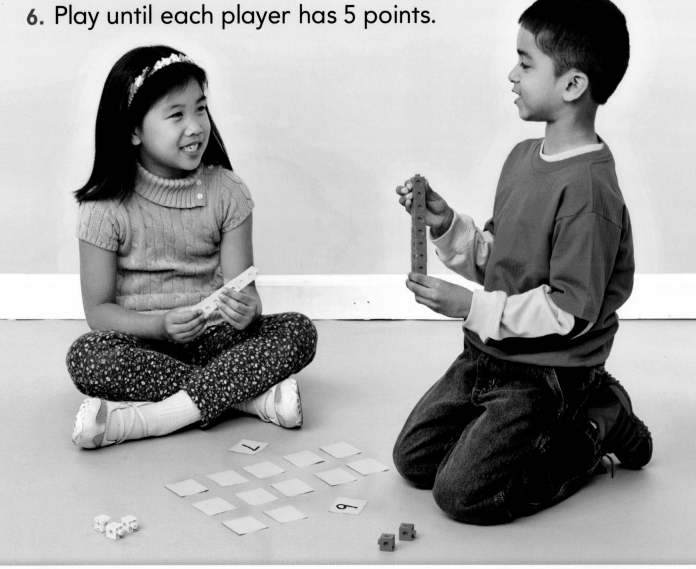

TAKS Objective 4
TEKS 1.7B Compare and order two or more concrete objects according to length (from longest to shortest).

Education Place
For eGames and Brain Teasers, visit **www.eduplace.com/txmap/**

Math at Home

Dear Family,

My class is starting Unit 9, **Measurement**. I will learn about length, area, weight, capacity, and temperature. You can help me learn these vocabulary words, and we can do the Math Activity together.

From,

____

Vocabulary

measure To find length, height, area, weight, capacity, and temperature.

unit What is used to measure something.

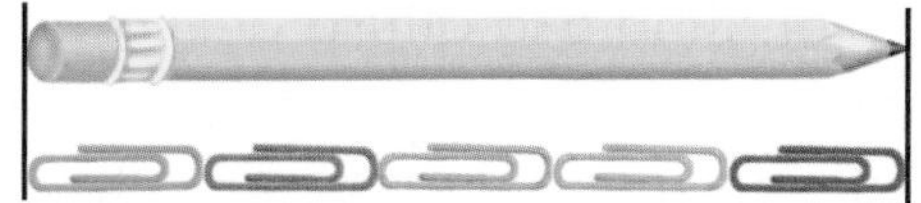

You can **measure** length using nonstandard **units**, such as paper clips.

heavier, **lighter** Words used to compare objects.

The apple is **heavier** than the strawberry. The strawberry is **lighter** than the apple.

Education Place

Visit **www.eduplace.com/txmaf/** for

- eGames and Brain Teasers
- Math at Home in other languages

Family Math Activity

Cut a piece of string several inches long. Have your child compare the length or height of the string to different things. Together find things that are longer, shorter, and taller than the string.

Literature

These books link to the math in this unit. Look for them at the library.

- **Equal Shmequal**
  by Virginia Kroll
  (Charlesbridge, 2005)
- **How Long?**
  by Elizabeth Dale
- **A Chair for My Mother**
  by Vera B. Williams

Matemáticas en casa

Estimada familia:

Mi clase está comenzando la Unidad 9, **La medición**. Voy a aprender sobre longitud, área, peso, capacidad y temperatura. Me pueden ayudar a aprender estas palabras de vocabulario y podemos hacer juntos la Actividad de matemáticas para la familia.

De:

____

Vocabulario

medir Hallar la longitud, la altura, el área, el peso, la capacidad y la temperatura.

unidad Lo que se usa para medir algo.

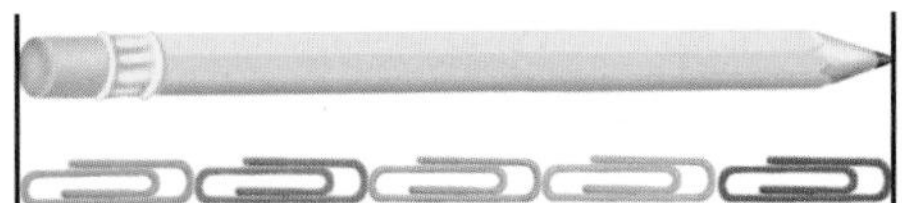

Se puede **medir** la longitud usando **unidades** no estándares, como sujetapapeles.

más pesado, más ligero Palabras que se usan para comparar el peso.

La manzana es **más pesada** que la fresa. La fresa es **más ligera** que la manzana.

Education Place

Visite **www.eduplace.com/txmaf/** para

- Juegos en línea y acertijos
- Matemáticas en casa, en otros idiomas

Actividad de matemáticas para la familia

Corte un pedazo de cordel de varias pulgadas de longitud. Pida a su niño que compare la longitud o la altura del cordel con diferentes cosas. Juntos hallen cosas que sean más largas, más cortas y más altas que el cordel.

Literatura

Estos libros hablan sobre las matemáticas de esta unidad. Podemos buscarlos en la biblioteca.

- **El problema de 100 libras** por Jennifer Dussling *(Kane Press, 2005)*
- **Pulgada a pulgada** por Leo Lionni

The world's full of similar things and different things, too.
Looking for each is a fun thing to do.

Compare the pictures. Circle 5 things that are different in the pictures.

TAKS Objectives 4, 6
TEKS 1.7B, 1.7G, 1.11A

UNIT 9

Our Classroom

written by Mary Gobles
illustrated by Julia Gorton

This Take-Home Book belongs to

____

Reading and Writing Math

This take-home book will help you review comparison and measurement concepts.

Look around and you will see,
Things are as different as can be.
Some things are short, while others tall.
Some things are big, while others small.

Look at the picture. Count 5 big things and 5 small things.

Sometimes it's dark, and other times it's sunny.
Some things are serious, while others are quite funny.

Some things are dull, others are shiny.
Some things are enormous, while
others are tiny.

Find something enormous and
something tiny.

Some things are short, others long.
Some things are right, while others wrong.

Look at the picture. Count 3 long things
and 3 short things.

Some things are square,
others are not.
Some things are cold,
and others are hot.

Find 2 cold things and 2 hot things.
Find 2 things shaped like a square.

Chapter 22 Length and Area

TAKS Vocabulary

Here are some vocabulary words you will learn in the chapter.

length How far from one end to the other

You can compare the length of two or more things.

longer

shorter

height How far from bottom to top

area The number of **square units** that will cover a shape

square unit

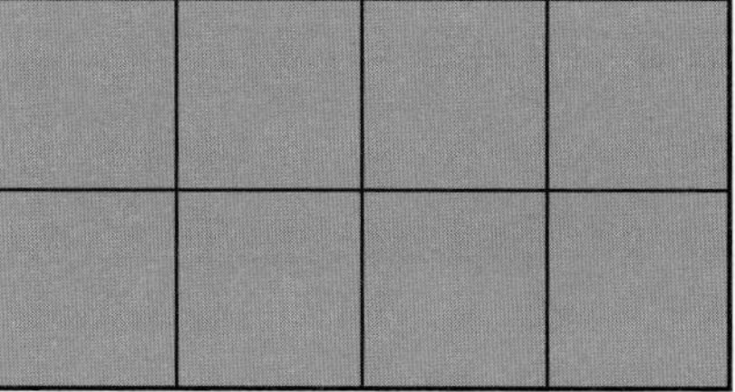

The area is 8 square units.

See English-Spanish glossary pages 505–516.

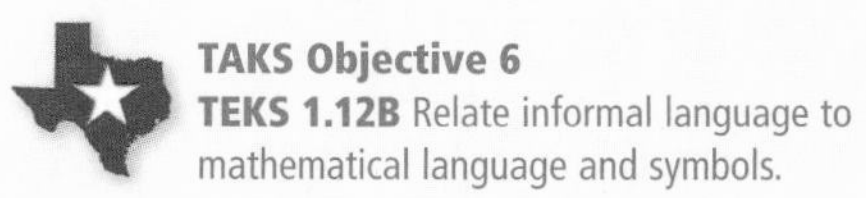

TAKS Objective 6
TEKS 1.12B Relate informal language to mathematical language and symbols.

Education Place
Visit www.eduplace.com/txmap/ for the eGlossary and vocabulary eGames.

Name ______________________________

Circle the object that is longer.

1. 

Circle the object that is shorter.

2. 

Circle the objects that are longer than the crayon.

3. 

Count the squares.
Circle the figure that covers more area.

4. 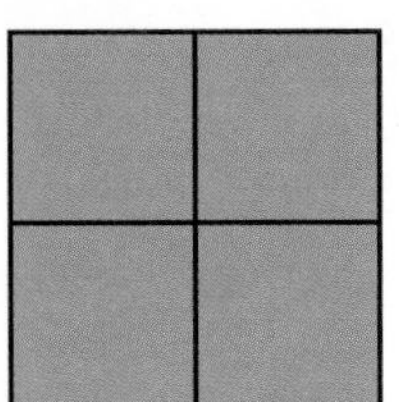 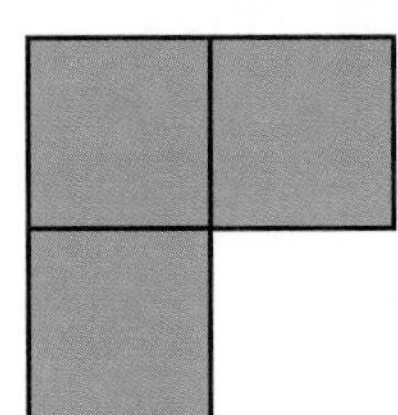

Use this page to review important skills needed for this chapter.

Name ______________________________

Chapter 22 Lesson 1

Compare and Order Length

Hands On

TEKS Objective
Compare and order objects by length and height.

TAKS Vocabulary
length
height
longer
taller
shorter

Compare **length** and **height.**
Use **longer, taller, shorter.**

The chair is shorter than you.

Step 1

Find the object.
Stand next to it.

Step 2

Your partner tells if the object is shorter or taller than you.

Use **tall**, **taller**, **tallest** to compare three things.

tall taller tallest

★ Explore

Is the object taller or shorter than you? Circle.

1. 

taller

shorter

2. 

taller

shorter

3. 

taller

shorter

4.  **Math Talk** Which object above is the tallest? Which is the shortest?

TAKS Objectives 4, 6
TEKS 1.7B Compare and order two or more concrete objects according to length (from longest to shortest).

TEKS 1.12B Relate informal language to mathematical language and symbols.

★ Extend

The book is longer than my hand.

Find the object.
Is the object longer or shorter than your hand?
Circle.

5. 

longer

shorter

6. 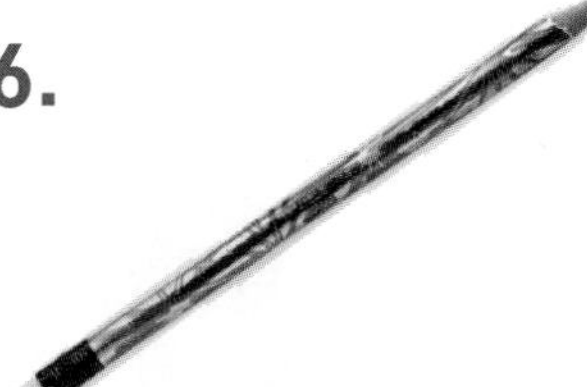

longer

shorter

7. 

longer

shorter

8. 

longer

shorter

Order your objects from shortest to longest.
Number the pictures.

The shortest object is 1. The longest object is 4.

9.  ____ ____  ____ ____

Color the longest pencil red.
Color the shortest pencil blue.
Draw a pencil that is longer than the red pencil.

10. 

11. **Math Talk** Is the red pencil still the longest? Why?

At Home Have your child choose three kitchen objects, and then place them in order by length.

En casa Pida a su niño que escoja tres objetos de la cocina y que los coloque en orden según su longitud.

Name ______________________________

Chapter 22 Lesson 2

Nonstandard Units

Hands On

TEKS Objective
Estimate and measure length using nonstandard units.

TAKS Vocabulary
measure
units

★ Learn

You can **measure** length with different **units.**

About how many [paper clips] long is the pencil?

about 4 [paper clips] long

Line up the units. Make sure they touch end to end.

About how many [cubes] long is the pencil?

about 7 [cubes] long

★ Guided Practice

Think! I need to line up the units end to end.

Complete the chart.

	Find the object.	Measure with [paper clip].	Measure with [cube].
1.	[paintbrush]	about ____ [paper clips]	about ____ [cubes]
2.	[book]	about ____ [paper clips]	about ____ [cubes]
3.	[crayon]	about ____ [paper clips]	about ____ [cubes]

4. **Math Talk** Can you mix cubes and paper clips when measuring an object? Why?

TAKS Objective 4
TEKS 1.7A Estimate and measure length using nonstandard units such as paper clips or sides of color tiles.

TEKS 1.7C Describe the relationship between the size of the unit and the number of units needed to measure the length of an object.

★ Practice

Remember!
Line up the unit with the end of the object.

Choose a unit to measure the length.

	Find the object.	Record the measure.	Circle the unit.
5.		about ____	
6.		about ____	
7.		about ____	
8.		about ____	

Problem Solving: Measurement Sense

Measure the length of an eraser with and with .

9. Did you use more paper clips or cubes? Circle your answer.

10. **Math Talk** Why did you need more of one unit than the other?

At Home Have your child use pennies as a unit to measure the length of objects at home.

En casa Pida a su niño que use monedas de 1 centavo como unidad para medir la longitud de objetos de su casa.

Name ___

Chapter 22 Lesson 3

Explore Area

Hands On

TEKS Objective
Find the area of a surface using models.

TAKS Vocabulary
area
square units

★ Learn

You can find the **area** of a figure by using **square units.**

About how many square units will cover the green figure?

square unit

Estimate: about ___ square units

Measure: about 3 square units

★ Guided Practice

Use the square unit. Estimate the area.
Find the area.

1.

Think!
I can put 1 square unit in the corner to help me estimate.

Estimate: about ___ square units

Measure: about ___ square units

2.

Estimate: about ___ square units

Measure: about ___ square units

3. **Math Talk** How did you estimate the area?

TAKS Objective 4
TEKS 1.7D Compare and order the area of two or more two-dimensional surfaces (from covers the most to covers the least).

★ Practice

Remember!
Use the square unit.

Estimate the area of each figure.
Find the area.

4.

Estimate: about _____ square units

Measure: about __4__ square units

5.

Estimate: about _____ square units

Measure: about _____ square units

6. If two figures have the same area, are they always the same shape? Why?

Problem Solving: Visual Thinking

7. Use 4 square units to make a new figure. Draw or trace it.

At Home Cut out a piece of paper for your child to use as a square unit. Ask your child to make a figure.

En casa Recorte un pedazo de papel para que su niño lo use como una unidad cuadrada. Pida a su niño que haga una figura.

Name ______________________

Chapter 22 Lesson 4

Compare and Order Area

TEKS Objective
Compare and order the area of two or more surfaces.

★ Learn

You can count square units.
The number of squares is the area.

The area is __4__ square units.

Think!
I count 4 squares in one figure. I count 3 in the other figure.

★ Guided Practice

Count the squares. Record.
Circle the figure with more area.

1. ______ squares ______ squares

2. ______ squares ______ squares

Count the squares. Record.
Circle the figure with lesser area.

3. ______ squares ______ squares

4. ______ squares ______ squares

5. **Math Talk** In Exercise 2, how can you tell which figure has more area?

TAKS Objective 4
TEKS 1.7D Compare and order the area of two or more two-dimensional surfaces (from covers the most to covers the least.)

★ Practice

Order the figures from most to least area.

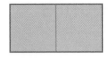

6. 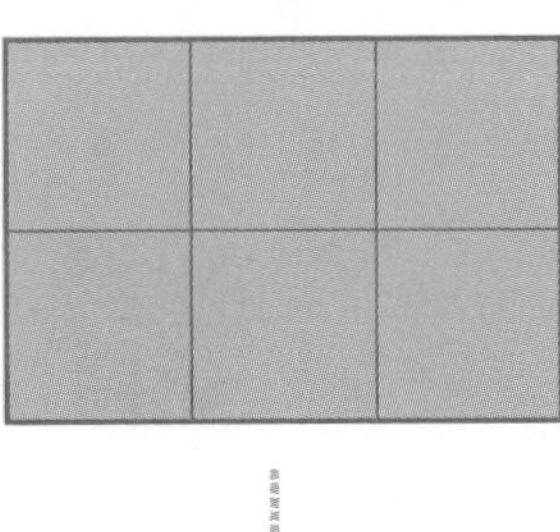 1 3 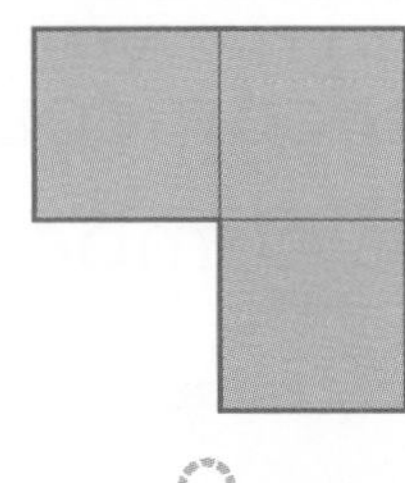 2

7.  ____  ____ 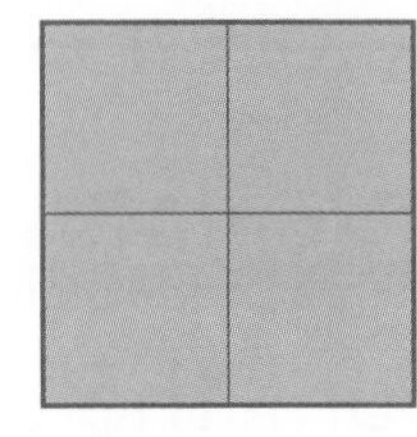 ____

8. 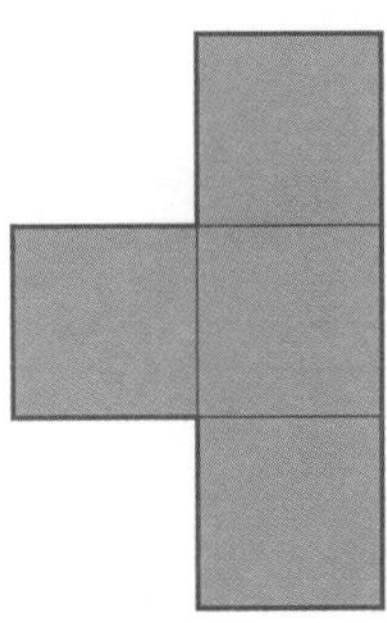 ____ 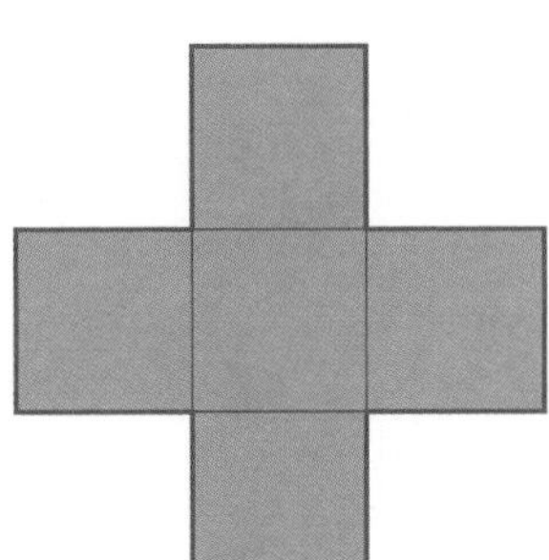 ____ 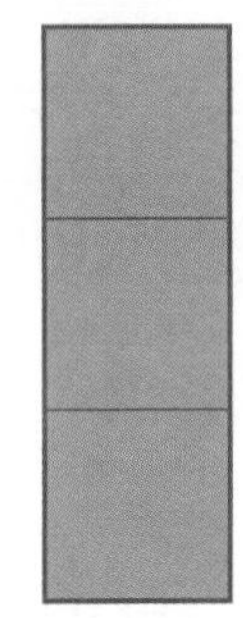 ____

Problem Solving: Measurement Sense

Order the figures from **least** to **most** area. The shape with the least squares will be 1.

9. 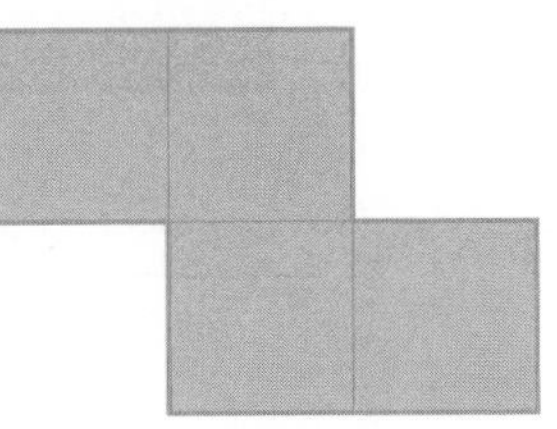 ____  ____  ____

At Home Cut out 3 different sized squares of paper and ask your child to order them from least to most area.

En casa Recorte 3 cuadrados de papel de diferentes tamaños y pida a su niño que los ordene de menor a mayor según el área.

Name ______________________

Chapter 22 Lesson 5

Guess and Check

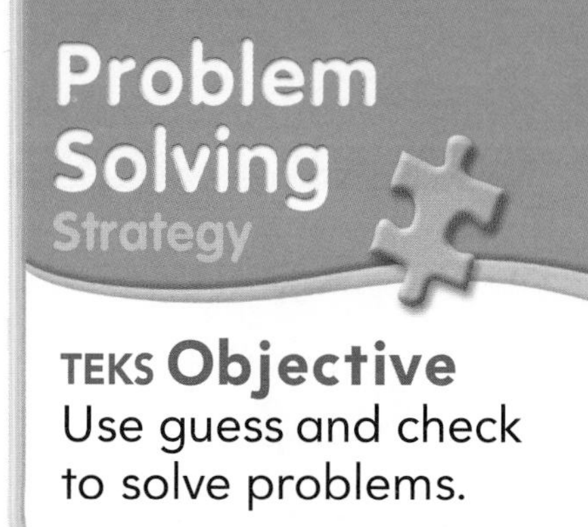

TEKS Objective
Use guess and check to solve problems.

Kim measures length two ways.

Kim measures with [cube].
Then she measures with [paper clip].
Did she use more paper clips or cubes?

Understand

What do you know?

- Kim measures with [cube].
- Kim measures with [paper clip].

Plan

Did Kim use more paper clips or cubes?
Circle.

Solve

Measure to check.

Measure with [cube]. about 9 [cube]
Measure with [paper clip]. about 5 [paper clip]

Did you use more paper clips or cubes?
Circle.

Look Back

Does your answer make sense?
Was your guess correct?

TAKS Objectives 4, 6
TEKS 1.7C Describe the relationship between the size of the unit and the number of units needed to measure the length of an object.

TEKS 1.13 Justify thinking using objects, words, pictures, numbers, and technology.
Also **TEKS 1.11B, 1.11C, 1.11D**

Guided Problem Solving

1. 
CRAYONS

Think!
Predict before you measure.
Crayons

Find the object.
Circle the one you think you will use more of.

Measure two ways. Record.

about _____ cube   about _____ paper clip

2. **Math Talk** Did you use more cubes or more paper clips? Why?

Problem Solving Practice

Will you use more paper clips or cubes?
Predict. Then measure to check.

	Find the object.	Predict. Circle.	Measure with cube.	Measure with paper clip.
3.	marker	cube / paper clip	about _____ cube	about _____ paper clip
4.	Math Book	cube / paper clip	about _____ cube	about _____ paper clip
5.	crayon	cube / paper clip	about _____ cube	about _____ paper clip

6. **Math Talk** Were your predictions correct?

At Home Have your child measure the length of objects around the house using two different tools.

En casa Pida a su niño que mida la longitud de objetos en la casa usando dos instrumentos diferentes.

Name ______________________________

Social Studies

Texas Field Trip

The Renner School

The Renner School is in Dallas.
It was built in 1888.
Today it is a museum.
You can visit the old schoolrooms.

Schoolroom desks

Solve. Show your work.

1. The desks in the Renner School are about 10 hands long. Measure your desk with your hand.

   about _____ hands

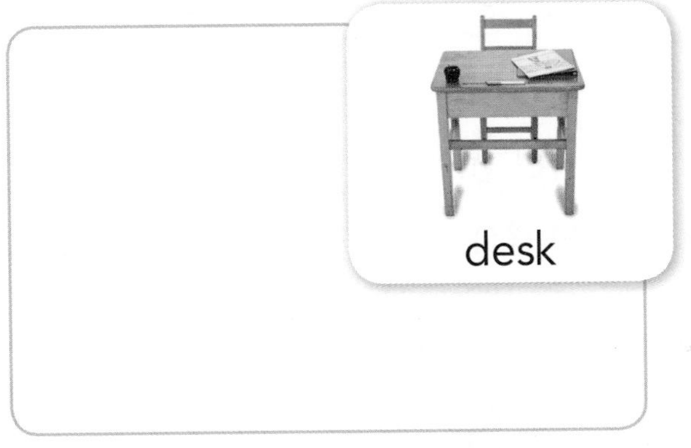

desk

2. Jamie has 12 colored pencils. He gives 5 to Marco. How many pencils does he have left?

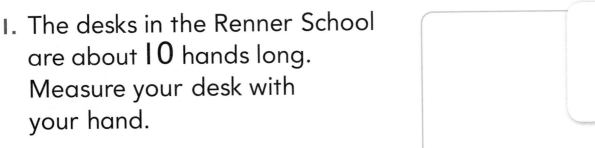

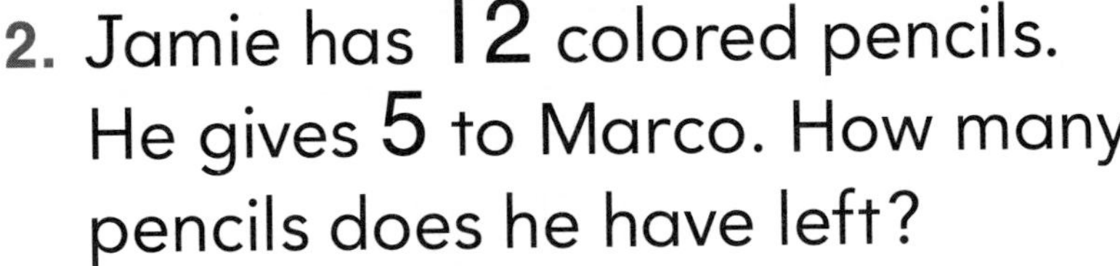

   _____ pencils

colored pencils

3. Kaya has 4 pockets inside her new backpack. There are 6 pockets on the outside. How many pockets are there?

   _____ pockets

backpack

TAKS Objectives 4, 6
TEKS 1.7A Estimate and measure length using nonstandard units such as paper clips or sides of color tiles.
TEKS 1.11A Identify mathematics in everyday situations.
Also **TEKS 1.11C**
TEKS Social Studies 3A

TAKS Problem Solving
Listening Skills

Select a Strategy
Guess and Check
Act It Out

Listen to your teacher read the problem. Choose the correct answer.

1. Milena is measuring this glue bottle with paper clips. How many paper clips long is the bottle?

6 ○ 5 ○ 4 ○ 1 ○

TEKS 1.7A

2. Paul is measuring these scissors with cubes. How many cubes long are the scissors?

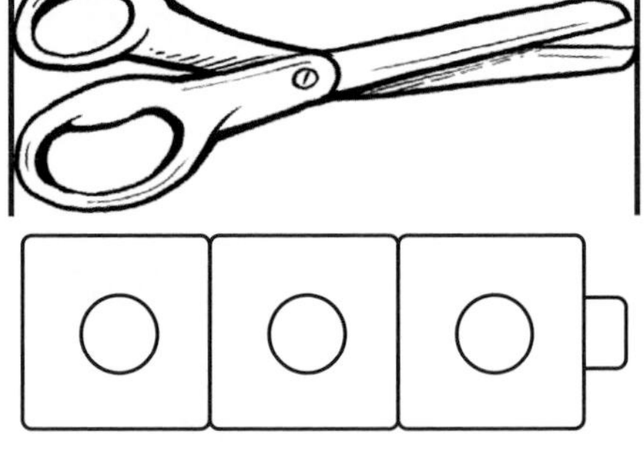

3 ○ 4 ○ 5 ○ 6 ○

TEKS 1.7A

3. Book 1 ○ Book 2 ○ Book 3 ○ Book 4 ○

TEKS 1.7B

4. Figure 1 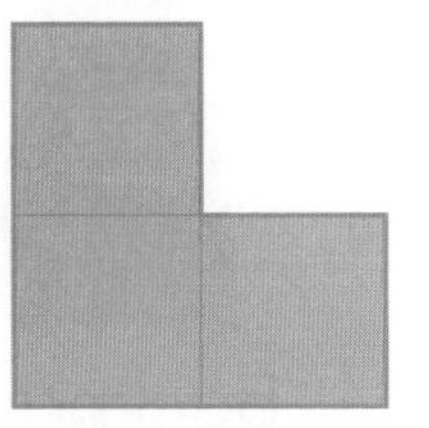 Figure 2  Figure 3 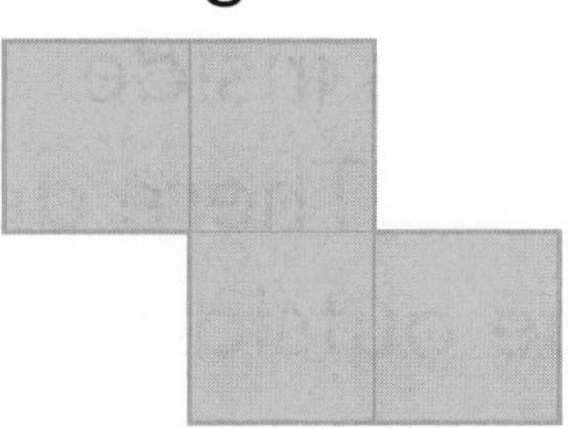 Figure 4 

Figure 1  Figure 2 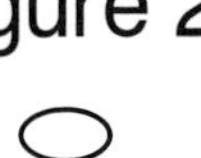 Figure 3  Figure 4 

TEKS 1.7D

Visit www.eduplace.com/txmap/ for Test-Taking Tips and more TAKS Practice.

Name ______________________

Measure This!

	Look at the line above.	Estimate.	Measure.
1.	blue part	about _____ cubes	about _____ cubes
2.	red part	about _____ cubes	about _____ cubes
3.	both parts	about _____ cubes	about _____ cubes

Draw your own line using two colors.
Measure.

4.

5. My first part is about _____ cubes.

6. My second part is about _____ cubes.

7. My whole line is about _____ cubes.

Nature Walk

On a nature walk you may see living things. Plants and animals are living things. You may also see nonliving things. Rocks and dirt are nonliving things.

1. Which is longer? Circle.

2. Which is shorter? Circle.

3. Use 1, 2, and 3 to order from longest to shortest.

_____ _____ _____

TAKS Objective 4

TEKS 1.7B Compare and order two or more concrete objects according to length (from longest to shortest).

TEKS Science 8B

Name ______________________________

Concepts and Skills

Find the object. Is the object longer or shorter than your hand? Circle. TEKS 1.7B

1.  longer shorter

Complete the chart. TEKS 1.7A

	Find the object.	Measure with paper clip.	Measure with cube.
2.		about ____ paper clips	about ____ cubes

Order the figures from most to least area. TEKS 1.7D

3. 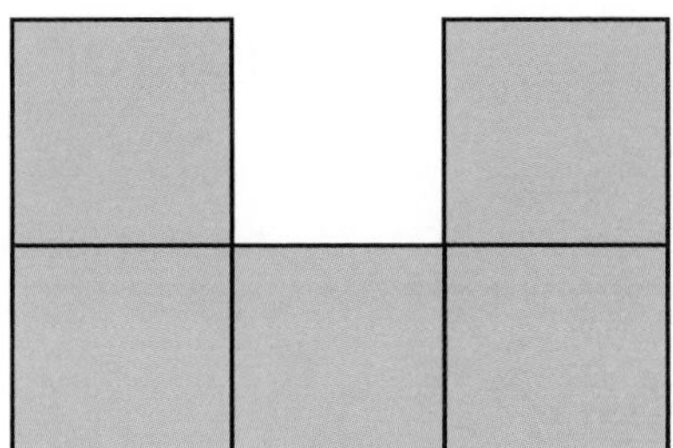

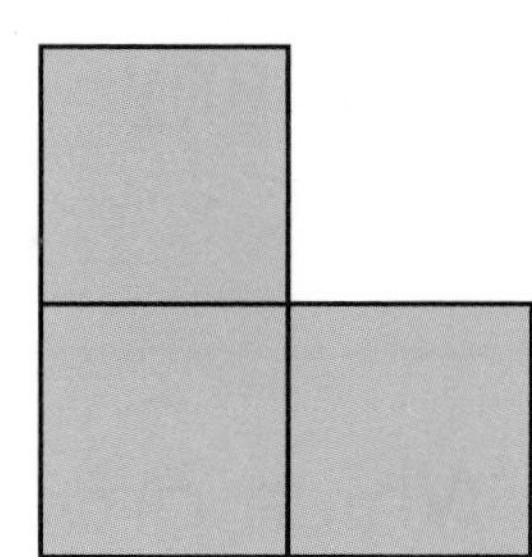

____ ____ ____

Problem Solving TEKS 1.7C, 1.11B, 1.11C

Will you use more paper clips or cubes? Predict. Then measure to check.

	Find the object.	Predict. Circle.	Measure with cube.	Measure with paper clip.
4.		cube / paper clip	about ____ cubes	about ____ paper clips

Prep and Spiral Review

Choose the answer for problems 1–4.

1. Which answer names the value of a nickel?

1 cent	5 cents	10 cents	25 cents
◯	◯	◯	◯

TEKS 1.1C (page 381)

2. Which coin has the same value as ten pennies?

penny	nickel	dime	quarter
◯	◯	◯	◯

TEKS 1.1C (page 383)

3. Which group shows 5 out of 8 blue folders?

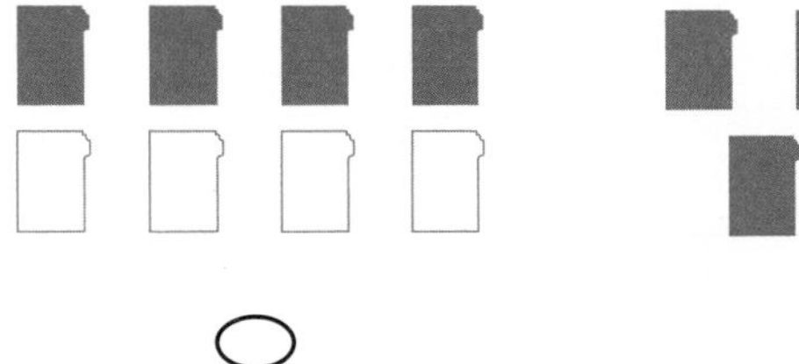

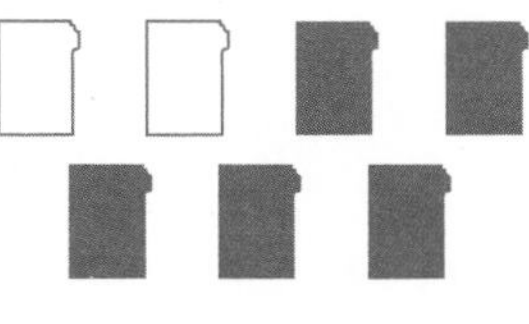

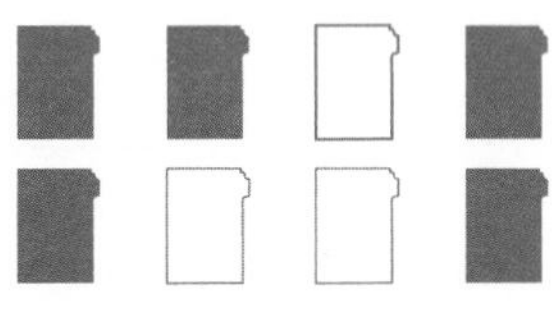

◯ ◯ ◯ ◯

TEKS 1.2B (page 187)

4. Mara has 5 apples on her lunch tray. 3 out of 5 apples are green. Which is Mara's tray?

◯	◯	◯	◯

TEKS 1.2B (page 187)

Education Place
Visit **www.eduplace.com/txmap/** for Test-Taking Tips and Extra Practice.

Weight, Capacity, and Temperature

TAKS Vocabulary

Here are some vocabulary words you will learn in the chapter.

heavier, lighter Words used to compare two objects

heavier **lighter**

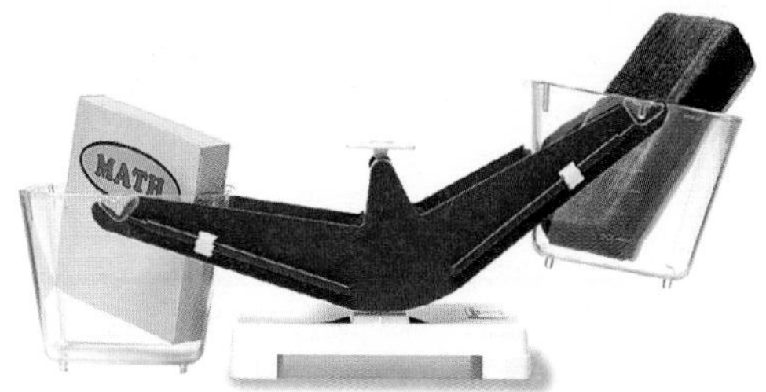

hotter, colder Words used to compare temperature

colder **hotter**

See English-Spanish glossary pages 505–516.

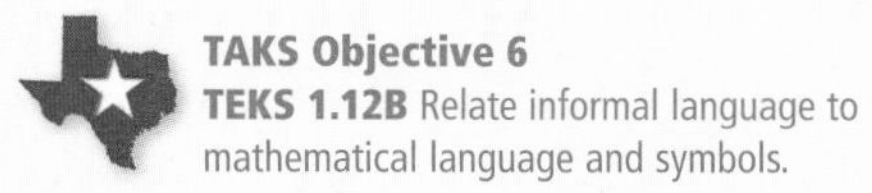

TAKS Objective 6
TEKS 1.12B Relate informal language to mathematical language and symbols.

Education Place
Visit **www.eduplace.com/txmap/** for the eGlossary and vocabulary eGames.

Name ______________________

Check What You Know

Circle the object that is heavier.

1.  

Circle the object that is lighter.

2. 

Circle the object that holds more.

3. 

Circle the object that holds less.

4.  

Circle the lunch that is colder.

5.  

Use this page to review important skills needed for this chapter.

Name ____________________

Chapter 23 Lesson 1

Compare Weight

Hands On

TEKS Objective
Compare two or more objects by weight.

TAKS Vocabulary
heavier
lighter

★ Learn

You can compare objects to find which is **heavier** and which is **lighter.**

Step 1

Find two objects. Estimate. Which feels heavier? Which feels lighter?

The book feels much heavier than the pencil.

Step 2

Put the objects on a balance scale. Compare.

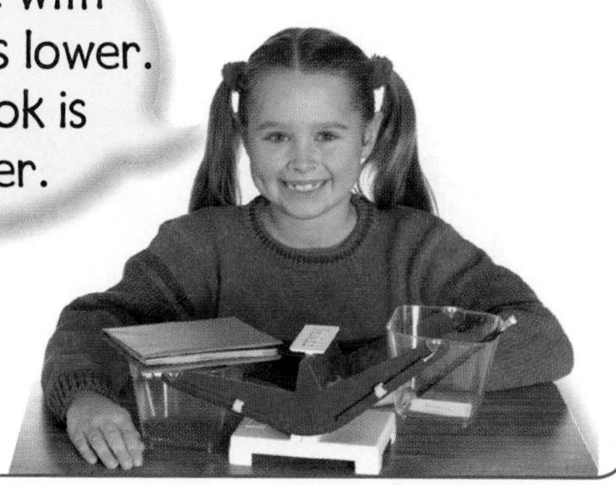

The side with the book is lower. The book is heavier.

★ Guided Practice

Find the object. Circle the heavier object.

Think!
I can feel that a backpack weighs more than a tissue box.

1. 

2.  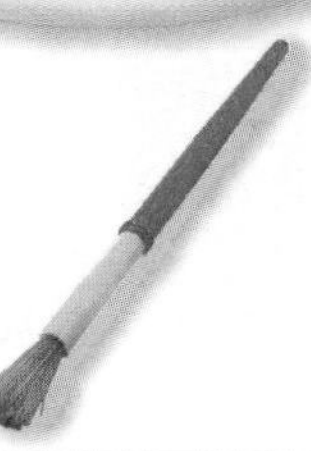

3.  

4.  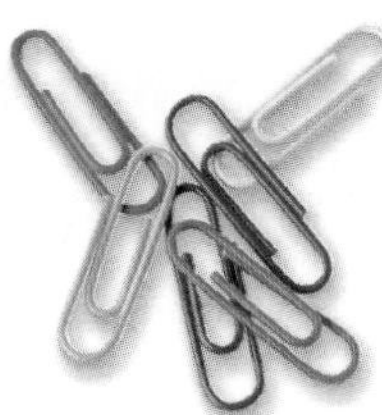

5. **Math Talk** How do you know which object is heavier?

TAKS Objective 4
TEKS 1.7F Compare and order two or more objects according to weight/mass (from heaviest to lightest).

★ Practice

Find the object. Circle the heavier object.

Remember!
Think about which object feels heavier.

6.  

7. 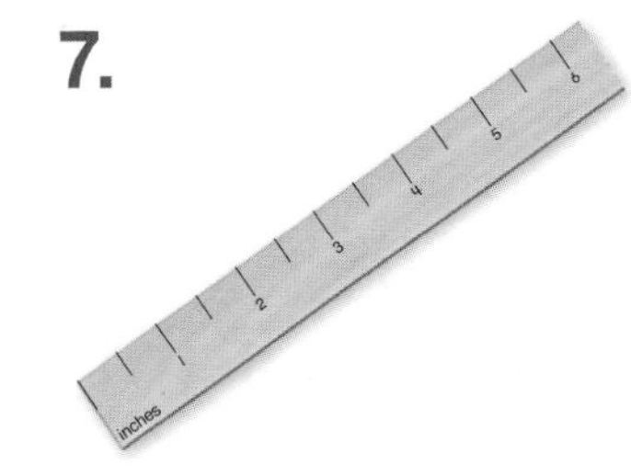

8. 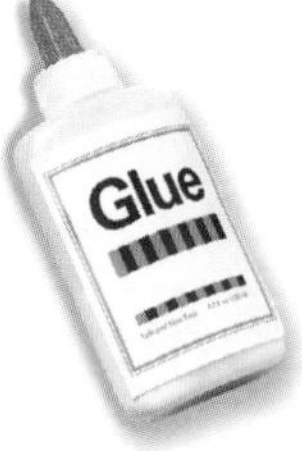

9.  

10.  

11.  

Problem Solving: Measurement Sense

Circle the object that weighs about the same as two boxes.

12. 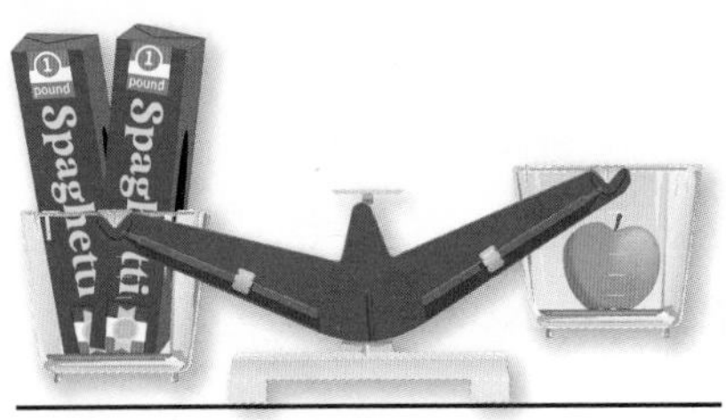

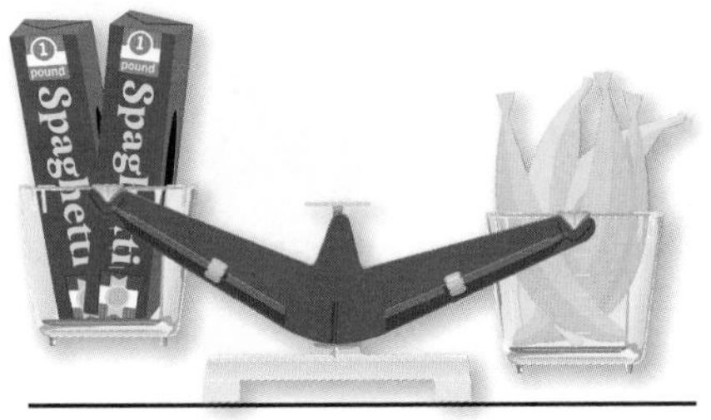

13. **Math Talk** How do you know the two objects weigh about the same?

____

____

At Home Have your child choose two household objects and estimate which is lighter and which is heavier.

En casa Pida a su niño que escoja dos objetos de la casa y que estime cuál es más liviano y cuál es más pesado.

Name ______________________________

Chapter 23 Lesson 2

Order Weight

TEKS Objective
Order two or more objects by weight.

TAKS Vocabulary
heaviest
lightest

★ Learn

Find 3 objects. Which is the **heaviest?** Which is the **lightest?** Compare.

Step 1

The glue is heavier than the ruler.

Step 2

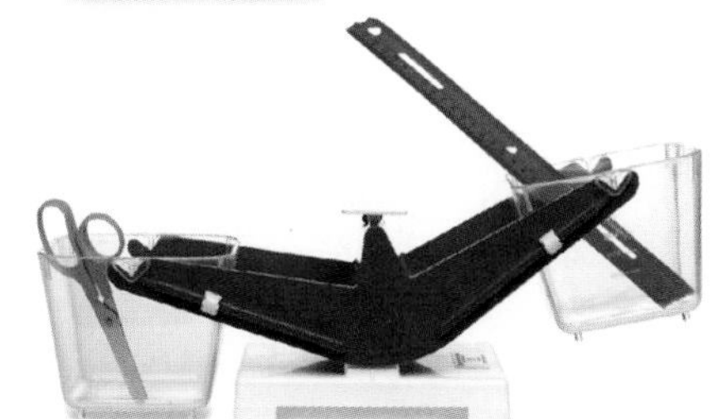

The scissors are heavier than the ruler.

Step 3

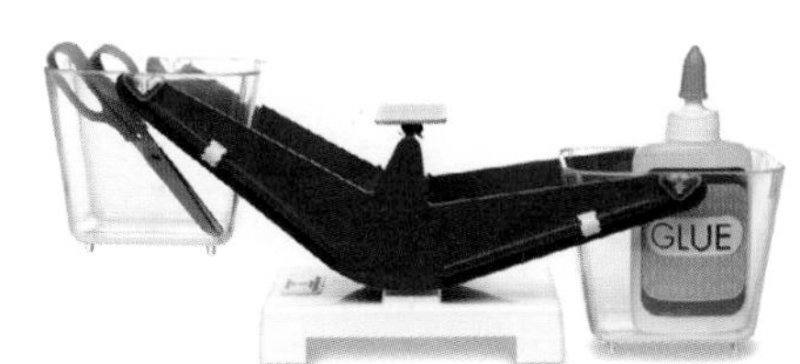

The glue is heavier than the scissors. The glue is the heaviest.

★ Guided Practice

Find the objects. Number them in order from heaviest to lightest.

Think!
I know the object that is the heaviest is 1.

1.

______

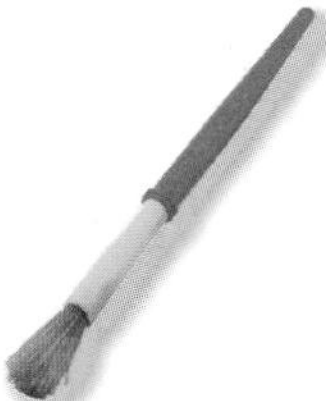
______

______

2. **Math Talk** How do you know which object is lighter?

TAKS Objective 4
TEKS 1.7F Compare and order two or more objects according to weight/mass (from heaviest to lightest).

★ Practice

Number the objects in order from heaviest to lightest.

Remember!
The object that is heaviest is 1.

3.

1 ____ 2 ____ 3 ____

4.

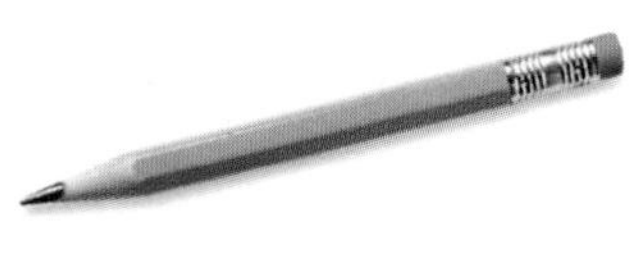

____ ____ ____

5.

____ ____ ____

6.

____ ____ ____

Problem Solving: Measurement Sense

7. Tom compares three different books. Use the picture. Which book is the heaviest? Explain.

At Home Choose three household objects. Ask your child to order them from heaviest to lightest.

En casa Escoja tres objetos de la casa. Pida a su niño que los ordene del más pesado al más liviano.

Name ______________________

Chapter 23 Lesson 3

Compare Capacity

Hands On

TEKS Objective
Compare two or more containers by capacity.

★ Learn

Compare the containers.
Find the container that can hold more.

Step 1

Use containers.
Fill one container.

Step 2

Pour it into the other container.

The pail is not full. So, the pail can hold more.

★ Guided Practice

Circle the container that can hold more.

1.  

Think! Pour from the bowl into the cup.

2.  

Circle the container that can hold less.

3.  

4.  

5. **Math Talk** How do you know which container holds less in Exercise 3?

TAKS Objective 4
TEKS 1.7E Compare and order two or more containers according to capacity (from holds the most to holds the least).

★ Practice

Circle the container that can hold more.

Remember!
Pour from the smaller container to the larger container.

6.

7.

Circle the container that can hold less.

8.

9.

Problem Solving: Measurement Sense

10. Write the name of something that holds more than the water bottle.

____

11. Write the name of something that holds less than the pail.

____

At Home Show your child two different bowls. Ask which bowl can hold more. Try it to check the answer.

En casa Muestre dos tazones diferentes a su niño. Pregúntele qué tazón puede contener más. Demuéstrelo para verificar la respuesta.

Name ______________________________

Chapter 23 Lesson 4

Order Capacity

TEKS Objective
Order two or more containers by capacity.

★ Learn

Look at the containers.
Which container can hold the most?

The smallest bowl holds the least.

The biggest bowl holds the most.

★ Guided Practice

Number the objects. 1 holds the most.
3 holds the least.

Think!
The biggest object holds the most.

1.

 ______

 ______

 ______

2.

 ______

 ______

 ______

3. **Math Talk** How does the size of the container help you decide which holds the most?

TAKS Objective 4
TEKS 1.7E Compare and order two or more containers according to capacity (from holds the most to holds the least).

★ Practice

Number the objects.
1 holds the most. 3 holds the least.

4.

1

3

2

5.

___

___

___

6.

___

___

___

7.

___

___

___

Problem Solving: Visual Thinking

8. Color the smallest box.
Color the largest box.

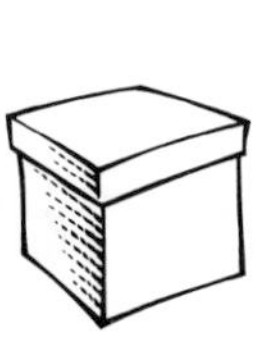

At Home Give your child three containers to order from holds the most to holds the least.

En casa Dé a su niño tres recipientes para que los ordene del que contiene más al que contiene menos.

Name ______________________________

Chapter 23 Lesson 5

Compare and Order Temperature

What looks **hotter?** What looks **colder?**

TEKS **Objective**
Compare and order two or more objects by temperature.

TAKS **Vocabulary**
hotter
colder
hottest
coldest

The soup looks hotter.

The lemonade is colder.

★ Guided Practice

Circle the one that is hotter.

Think!
I know popsicles have to stay cold or they will melt.

1.  

2.  

Circle the one that is colder.

3. 

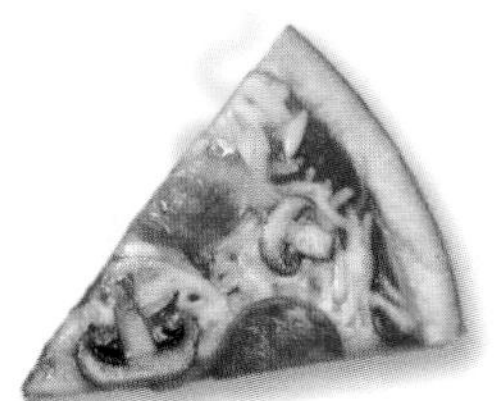

4.  

5. **Math Talk** How do you know if a drink is cold?

TAKS Objective 4
TEKS 1.7G Compare and order two or more objects according to relative temperature (from hottest to coldest).

★ Practice

Number the objects.
Write 1 for the **hottest.**
Write 3 for the **coldest.**

Remember!
Think about which food looks the hottest.

6.

1

2

3

7.

8.

9.

10.

Problem Solving: Logical Reasoning

11. Cup A is colder than Cup B.
    Cup C is colder than Cup A.
    Which cup is coldest? Explain.

At Home Ask your child to identify familiar foods as hot or cold.

En casa Pida a su niño que identifique, como calientes o fríos, alimentos que conozca.

Name ______________________________

Chapter 23 Lesson 6

Use Logical Reasoning

TEKS Objective
Use logical reasoning to solve problems about temperature; create and solve problems about temperature.

Min eats the hottest food first.
She eats the coldest food last.
In what order does she eat the foods?

1 2 3

DECIDE

THINK	DECIDE
Min eats the hottest food first.	Write a 1 under the hottest food.
She eats the coldest food last.	Write a 3 under the coldest food.
In what order does she eat the foods?	Write a 2 under the food that has not been numbered.

Min eats the soup first, then the sandwich, and the milk shake last.

TAKS Objectives 4, 6
TEKS 1.7G Compare and order two or more objects according to relative temperature (from hottest to coldest).

TEKS 1.13 Justify thinking using objects, words, pictures, numbers, and technology.

★ Guided Problem Solving

1. Ella goes to a shop. She buys the hottest food first and the coldest food last.

Think! I know the popsicle must be cold.

______

______

______

Look at the pictures. Use 1 for the hottest and 3 for the coldest. Order the food.

2. **Math Talk** How do you know what Ella buys first?

★ Problem Solving Practice

Order the food.

3. Jill eats the hottest food first. She eats the coldest food last.

______

______

______

4. Marco is eating breakfast. He eats the hottest food first and the coldest food last.

______

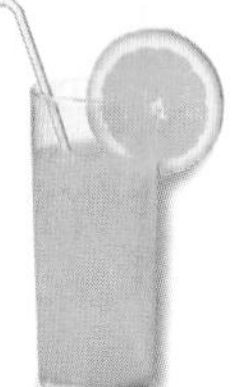
______

______

At Home Ask your child to explain how he or she ordered the food.

En casa Pida a su niño que explique cómo ordenó los alimentos.

Name ____________________

Create and Solve

This is Tim. Write a story about Tim and the temperature.

1. ____________________

____

____

It is a hot afternoon.

Draw what Tim should wear on a hot day.

2.

TAKS Objective 6
TEKS 1.11A Identify mathematics in everyday situations.

TEKS 1.13 Justify thinking using objects, words, pictures, numbers, and technology.

This is Lita. Lita is wearing clothes for warm weather.

Draw what Lita should wear on the coldest day of the year.

3.

Write a story about today's temperature. Draw a picture of your story.

4. ______________________________

____

____

5.

Name ______________________________

Measure It!

Complete the chart.

	Find the object.	Estimate.	Measure.
1.		about ____ about ____	about ____ about ____
2.	My Math	about ____ about ____	about ____ about ____
3.		about ____ about ____	about ____ about ____

4. Did you need more or to measure each object? Why?

5. Order the objects from shortest to longest.

____________ ____________ ____________

Math Music

 **Math Music,** Track 9

Pretend you're a bird.
Are you heavy or light?
You can fly through the air
In the day or night.

You are lighter than a cat.
You are lighter than a horse.
But you're heavier than a bee.
Yes, you are, of course!

Pretend you're a bus.
You can travel far.
You can hold more people
Than a van or car.

You can hold more people
Than a bike or horse.
But you hold less people
Than a train, of course!

TAKS Objective 4
TEKS 1.7E Compare and order two or more containers according to capacity (from holds the most to holds the least).

TEKS 1.7F Compare and order two or more objects according to weight/mass (from heaviest to lightest).

Name ______________________

Concepts and Skills

Circle the heavier object. TEKS 1.7F

1. 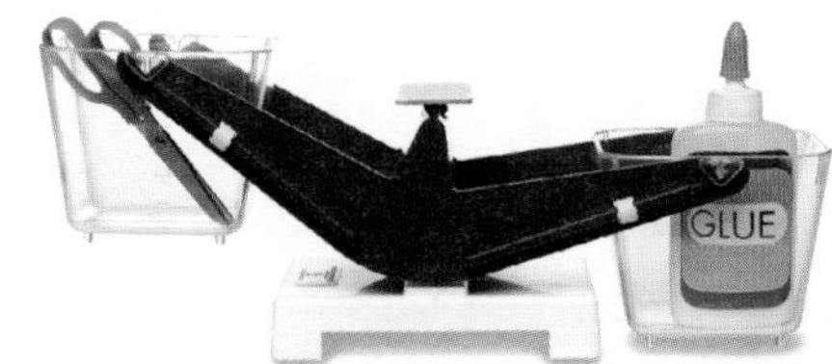

Number the objects in order from heaviest to lightest. TEKS 1.7F

2.   

____ ____ ____

Circle the container that can hold more. TEKS 1.7E

3.  

Number the objects. 1 holds the most. 3 holds the least. TEKS 1.7E

4.   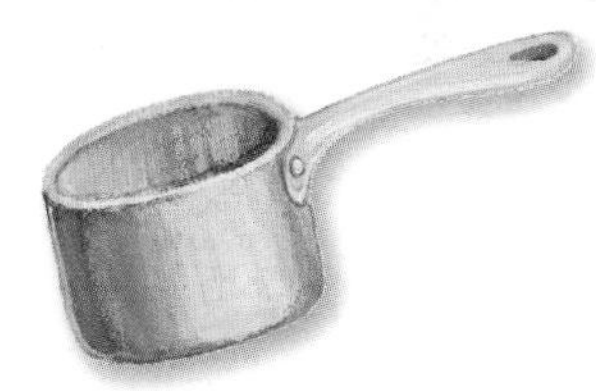

____ ____ ____

Problem Solving

Order the food. TEKS 1.7G

5. Chen eats the hottest food first.
He eats the coldest food last.

____ ____ ____

TAKS Prep and Spiral Review

Choose the answer for problems 1–4.

1. Which number sentence is missing from the fact family?

$6 + 4 = 10$	$10 - 4 = 6$	$10 - 6 = 4$

$8 + 2 = 10$ ○ $4 + 6 = 10$ ○ $10 - 3 = 7$ ○ $6 - 4 = 2$ ○

TEKS 1.5E (page 129)

2. Which number sentence is NOT in the same fact family as $5 + 6 = 11$?

$8 + 3 = 11$ ○ $11 - 6 = 5$  $6 + 5 = 11$ ○ $11 - 5 = 6$ ○

TEKS 1.5E (page 357)

3. Bess pulls stickers from a bag. Which sticker is impossible for Bess to pull from the bag?

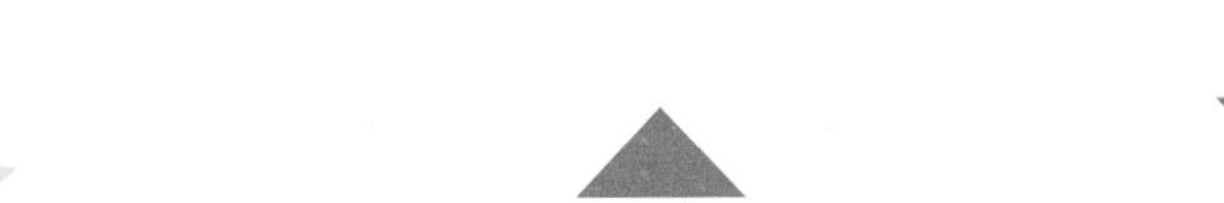

 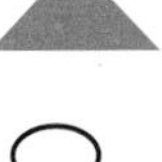   

TEKS 1.10B (page 225)

4. Chad wants to spin red on a spinner. On which spinner will it be certain for Chad to spin red?

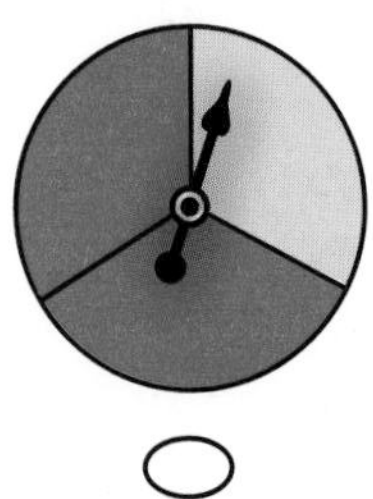 ○ 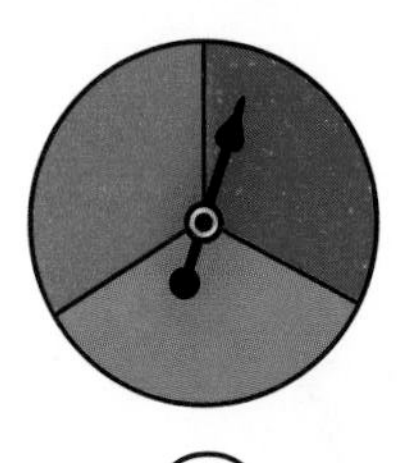 ○ 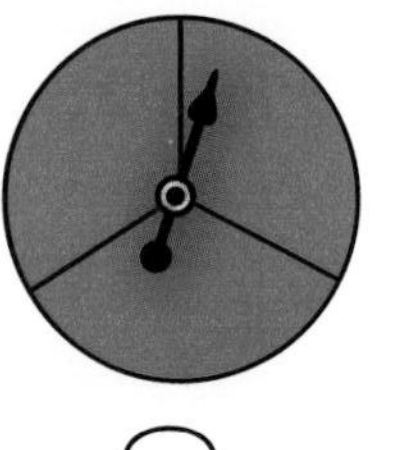 ○ 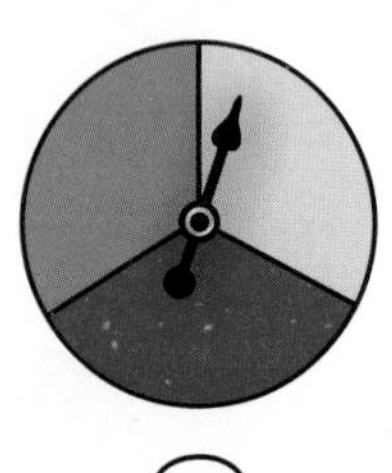 ○

TEKS 1.10B (page 227)

Education Place
Visit **www.eduplace.com/txmap/** for Test-Taking Tips and Extra Practice.

Name ____________________

Greg Tang's **Go Fast, Go Far**

Unit 9 **Mental Math Strategies**

Turn-Arounds

2 + 6 = ?
Now let's see.
6 + 2 = 8,
so 2 + 6 = 8.

For adding numbers 5 to 8,
"turn-arounds" will work just great!

1. 2 + 6 = [6] + [2] = [8]

2. 2 + 7 = [ ] + [ ] = [ ]

3. 1 + 8 = [ ] + [ ] = [ ]

4. 2 + 5 = [ ] + [ ] = [ ]

Take It Further: Now try doing everything in your head!

5. 3 + 6 = [ ]

6. 1 + 7 = [ ]

7. 4 + 7 = [ ]

8. 3 + 5 = [ ]

9. 2 + 8 = [ ]

10. 4 + 8 = [ ]

Name ______________________________

Reading and Writing Math

1. Circle the object that is heavier.

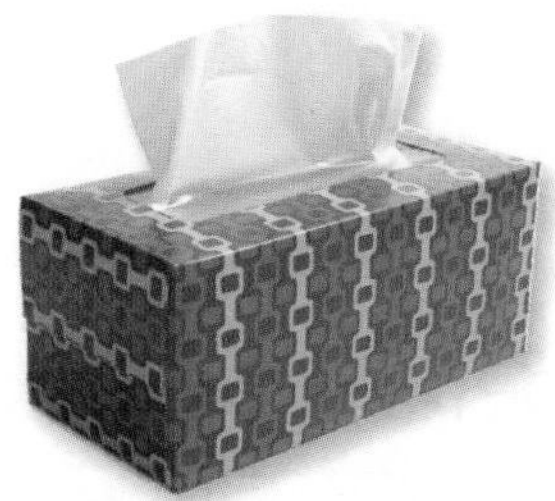

2. Circle the food that is hotter.

3. Circle the object that is longer.

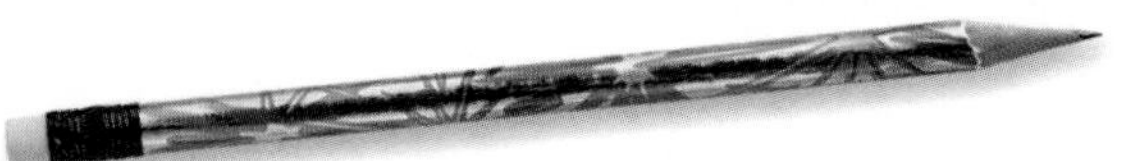

4. **Writing Math** Tell how you can measure the pencil.

____

____

TEKS 1.12A Explain and record observations using objects, words, pictures, numbers, and technology.

TEKS 1.12B Relate informal language to mathematical language and symbols.

Name ______________________

Concepts and Skills

Order the ribbons from shortest to longest.
Number the pictures. The shortest object is 1. TEKS 1.7B

1. ____

____

____

Measure the length with ▪. TEKS 1.7A

2. about ____ ▪

3. Use square units.
Estimate the area. Find the area. TEKS 1.7D

Estimate: about ____ square units

Measure: about ____ square units

Order the figures from most to least area.
The figure with the most squares will be 1. TEKS 1.7D

4. ____ ____ ____

Circle the heavier object. TEKS 1.7F

5.

Number the objects. 1 is the heaviest.
3 is the lightest. TEKS 1.7F

6.

 ____

 ____

 ____

Circle the container that can hold less. TEKS 1.7E

7.

Number the objects. 1 holds the most.
3 holds the least. TEKS 1.7E

8.

 ____

 ____

 ____

Problem Solving

Measure the length with paper clips and cubes. TEKS 1.7C

9. Did you use more paper clips or cubes?
Circle your answer.

10. Why did you need more of one unit than the other?

____

____

Unit 10

Addition and Subtraction Facts Through 18

BIG IDEAS!

- Sums of 10 can help you add greater numbers.
- You can relate addition and subtraction number sentences (fact families).
- You can model and name numbers using addition, subtraction, or both.

Songs and Games

Math Music Track 10
In This Garden

eGames
www.eduplace.com/txmap/

Literature

Literature Big Book

- Twenty Is Too Many

Math Readers

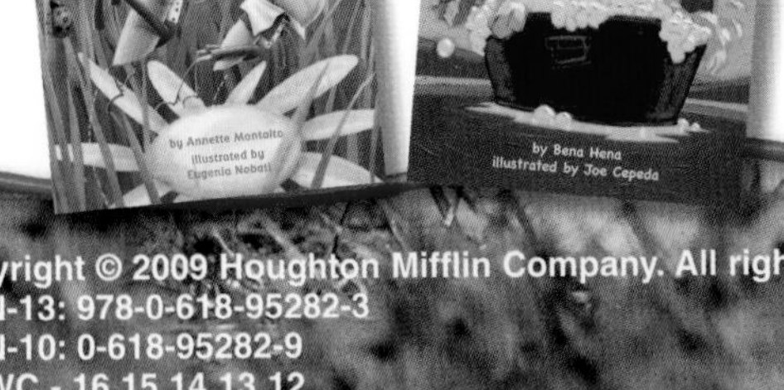

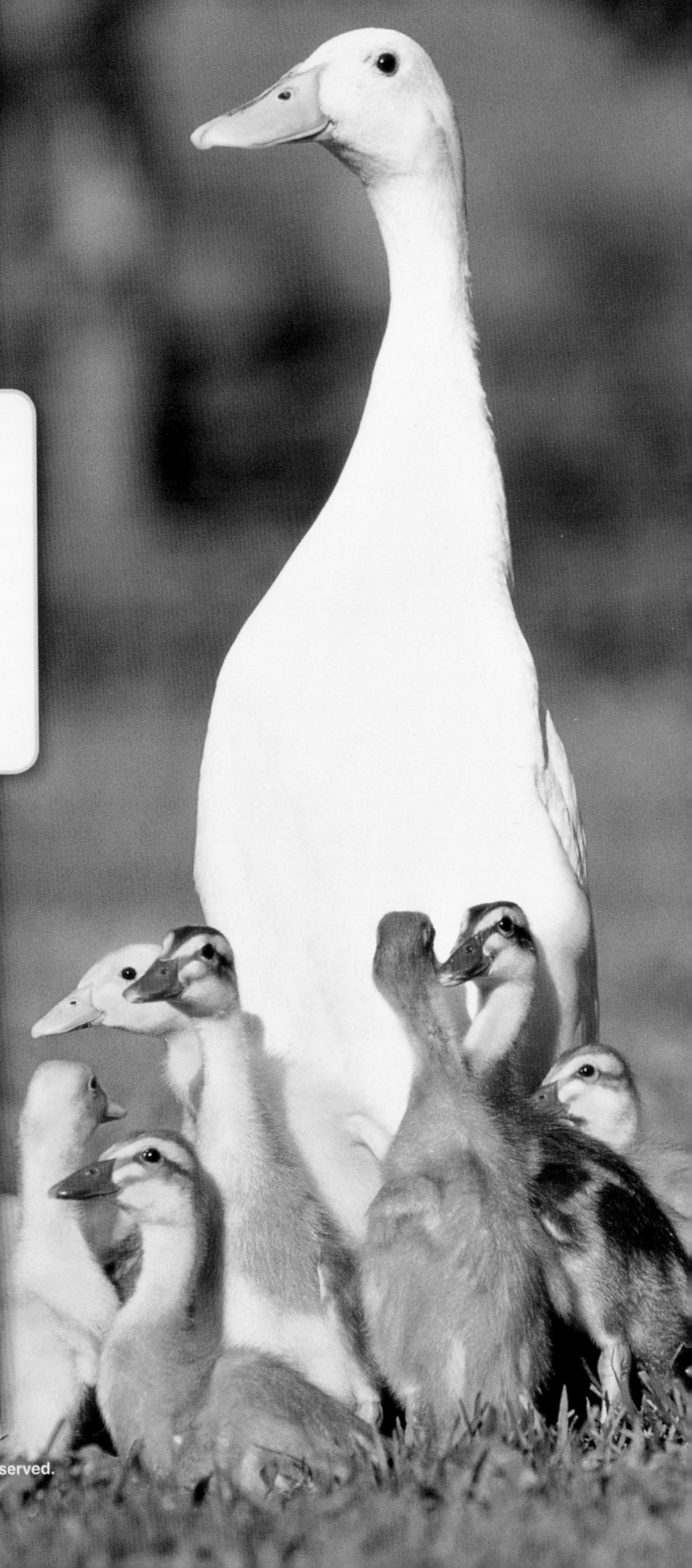

ISBN-13: 978-0-618-95282-3
ISBN-10: 0-618-95282-9
89- WC - 16 15 14 13 12

Get Ready **Game**

Rolling for Numbers

What You Need
2 players
number cube labeled 7–12 

1. Choose [crayon] or [crayon].
2. Toss the number cube to get an answer.
3. Find an addition or subtraction problem that equals the answer. Write the answer.
4. If you can't find a match, it's your partner's turn.
5. Play until all the answers are written.

12 − 3	11 − 4	8 + 2	7 + 4	12 − 5	9 + 2
6 + 6	7 + 3	11 − 2	11 − 3	8 + 4	12 − 4

TAKS Objective 1
TEKS 1.3B Use concrete and pictorial models to apply basic addition and subtraction facts (up to 9 + 9 = 18 and 18 − 9 = 9).

Math at Home

Dear Family,

My class is starting Unit 10, **Addition and Subtraction Facts Through 18**. I will learn about strategies to help me add and subtract facts through 18. You can help me learn these vocabulary words, and we can do the Math Activity together.

From,

____

Vocabulary

difference The answer to a subtraction problem.

$$\begin{array}{r} 17 \\ -\ 9 \\ \hline 8 \end{array}$$

In the subtraction problem above, 8 is the **difference**.

sum How many in all.

Education Place

Visit **www.eduplace.com/txmaf/** for

- eGames and Brain Teasers
- Math at Home in other languages

Family Math Activity

Use a ten-section egg carton to practice "making a ten." Display a group of 9 objects and a group of 6 objects. Have your child make a 10 to help add 9 + 6. Repeat with 8 and 4, 7 and 6.

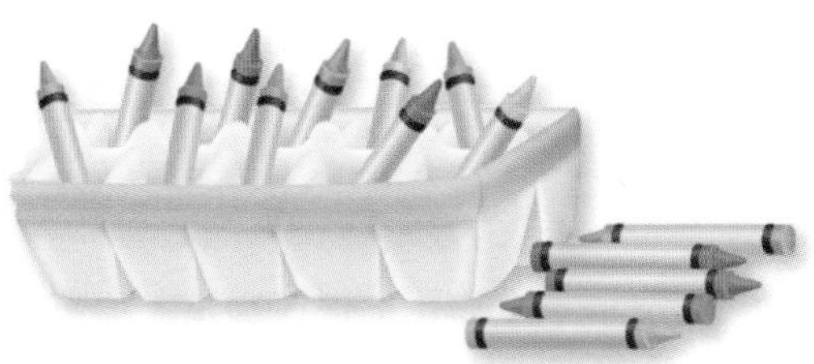

Literature

These books link to the math in this unit. Look for them at the library.

- **How Many Blue Birds Flew Away?** by Paul Giganti, Jr. *(Greenwillow, 2005)*
- **Sixteen Runaway Pumpkins** by Dianne Ochiltree and Anne-Sophie Lanquetin
- **Dinner at the Panda Palace** by Stephanie Calmenson

Matemáticas en casa

Estimada familia:

Mi clase está comenzando la Unidad 10, **Operaciones de suma y resta hasta 18**. Voy a aprender estrategias para resolver operaciones de suma y resta hasta 18. Me pueden ayudar a aprender estas palabras de vocabulario y podemos hacer juntos la Actividad de matemáticas para la familia.

De:

____

Vocabulario

diferencia Respuesta en un problema de resta.

$$\begin{array}{r} 17 \\ -\ 9 \\ \hline 8 \end{array}$$

En el problema de resta de arriba, 8 es la **diferencia.**

suma Cuántos hay en total.

Education Place

Visite **www.eduplace.com/txmaf/** para

- Juegos en línea y acertijos
- Matemáticas en casa, en otros idiomas

Actividad de matemáticas para la familia

Use un cartón de huevos de diez secciones para practicar cómo "hacer una decena". Muestre un grupo de 9 objetos y un grupo de 6 objetos. Pida a su niño que haga una decena como ayuda para sumar 9 + 6. Repita con 8 y 4, 7 y 6.

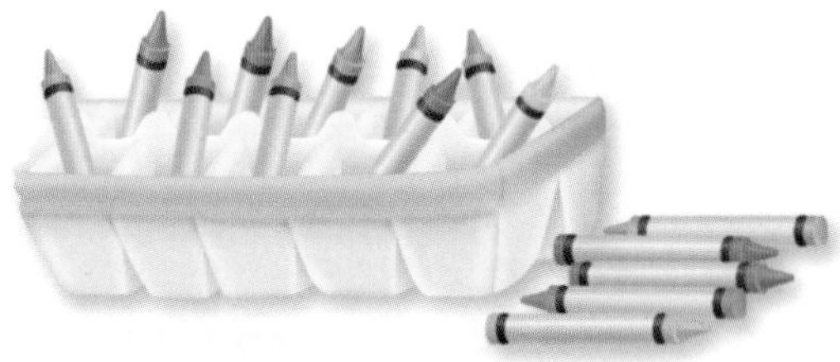

Literatura

Estos libros hablan sobre las matemáticas de esta unidad. Podemos buscarlos en la biblioteca.

- **Sumando animales del Ártico** por David Bauer *(Capstone Press, 2005)*
- **El centésimo día de escuela** por Angela Shelf Medearis

If you lived on a farm, what would you like to raise? Draw your ideas.

TAKS Objectives 1, 6
TEKS 1.3B, 1.11A

UNIT 10

My Farm

written by Tim Johnson
illustrated by Sophia Balzola

This Take-Home Book belongs to

____

Reading and Writing Math

This take-home book will help you review addition and subtraction facts.

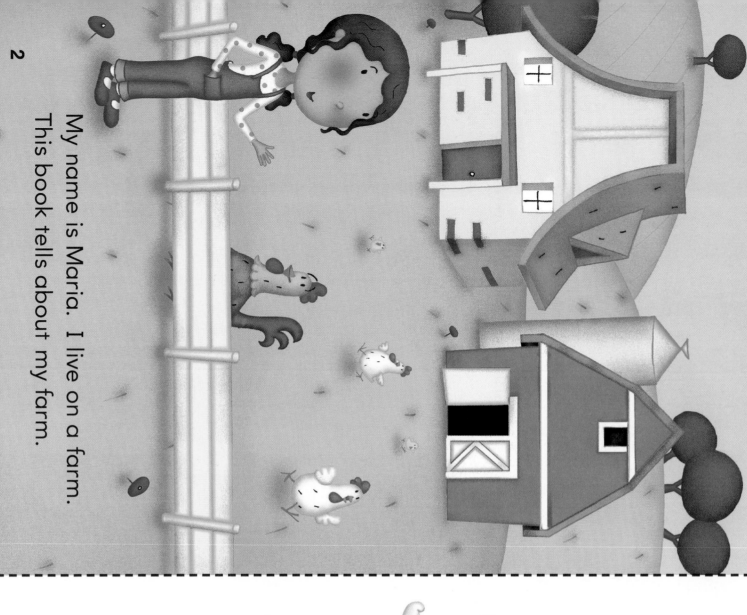

My name is Maria. I live on a farm.
This book tells about my farm.

We have a pond of ducks on our farm.
Some are white and some are brown.
How many fewer brown ducks are there?

____ − ____ = ____ brown ducks

We grow potatoes on our farm.
Some of the potatoes we keep,
and some we sell.
How many more bags do we take
to market than we leave behind?

_____ – _____ = _____ bags

On our farm we raise cows.
5 cows are big. The rest are small.
How many cows are there in all?

_____ + _____ = _____ cows

We have lots of chickens on our farm.
Here are two of our best hens.
Last week Dora laid 7 eggs.

Connie laid 5 eggs.
How many eggs are there in all?

____ + ____ = ____ eggs

Addition Facts Through 18

TAKS Vocabulary

Here are some vocabulary words you will learn in the chapter.

ten frame A chart to show groups of ten

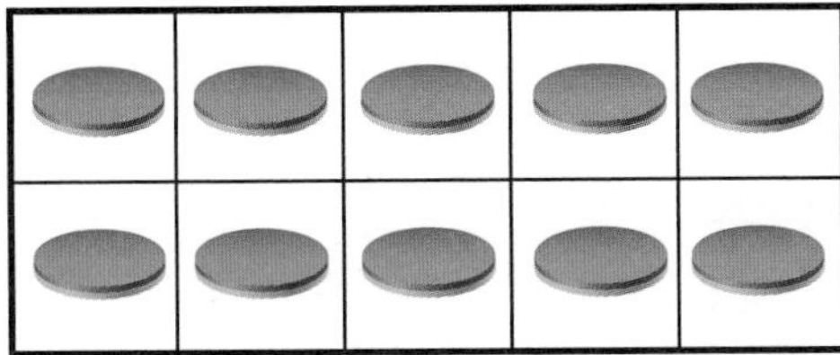

A ten frame can help you add.
10 and 4 more equals 14.
$10 + 4 = 14$

make a ten A way to help you add with 8 or 9

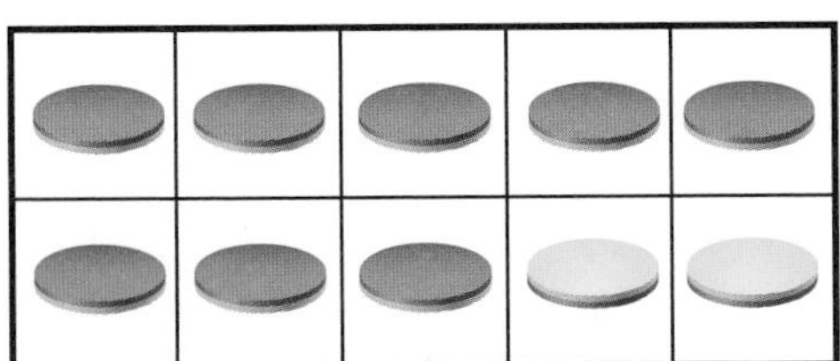

Start with 8.
Add 2 counters to make 10.
$8 + 5$ has the same sum as $10 + 3$.
$8 + 5 = 13$

See English-Spanish glossary pages 505–516.

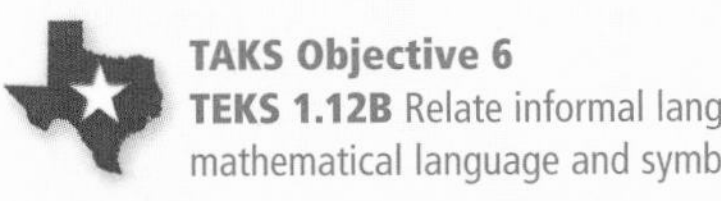

TAKS Objective 6
TEKS 1.12B Relate informal language to mathematical language and symbols.

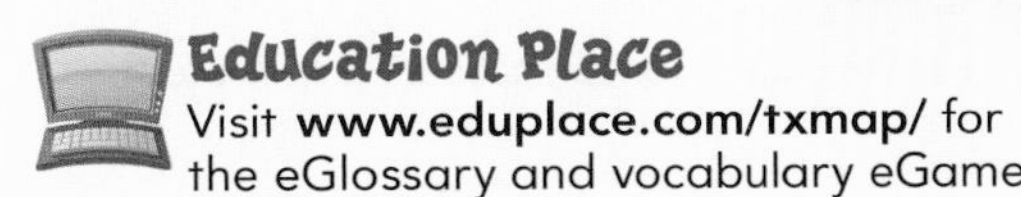

Education Place
Visit **www.eduplace.com/txmap/** for the eGlossary and vocabulary eGames.

Name ______________________________

Check What You Know

Use Workmat I and counters to make 10.
Write the addition sentences.

1. ____ + ____ = 10
2. ____ + ____ = 10
3. ____ + ____ = 10
4. ____ + ____ = 10

Write the sum.

5. 

$$\begin{array}{r} 6 \\ +5 \\ \hline \end{array}$$

6. 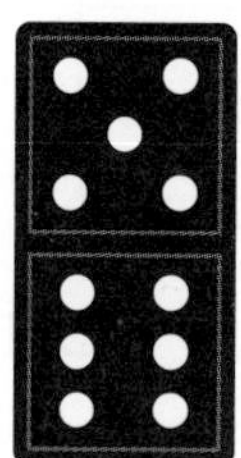

$$\begin{array}{r} 5 \\ +6 \\ \hline \end{array}$$

____, ____, ____

7. 8 + 3 = ____

____, ____

8. 7 + 2 = ____

Draw the counters. Solve.

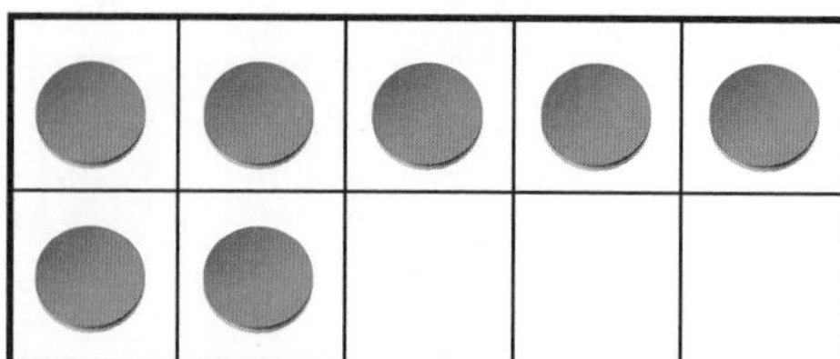

9. 7 + 5 = ____

10. 8 + 4 = ____

Use this page to review important skills needed for this chapter.

Name ____________________

Chapter 24 Lesson 1

Addition Stories

Hands On

TEKS Objective
Model addition situations through 18.

★ Explore

Listen to the story.
Show the story with ⚪.

1.

2. **Math Talk** How do you know if your answer is correct?

TAKS Objective 1
TEKS 1.3A Model and create addition and subtraction problem situations with concrete objects and write corresponding number sentences.

Remember!
Look for numbers in the story.

★ Extend

Read the story. Show the story with Workmat 2 and ●.
Write the addition sentence.

3. The hen lays 7 eggs in one week. She lays 9 eggs in the next week. How many eggs does the hen lay?

7 + ____ = ____

____ eggs

4. There are 8 cows in a field. Then 7 cows join them. How many cows are there in all?

____ + ____ = ____

____ cows

At Home Place a set of 6 objects and 9 objects on a table. Ask your child how many objects there are in all.

En casa Ponga sobre la mesa un conjunto de 6 objetos y otro de 9. Pregunte a su niño cuántos objetos hay en total.

Name ________________________

Chapter 24 Lesson 2

Add with Ten

Hands On

TEKS Objective
Use concrete models to add to the number 10.

★ Learn

Use ten frames to add a number to 10.
Find 10 + 4.

Show 10. Show 4 more.

Workmat 2

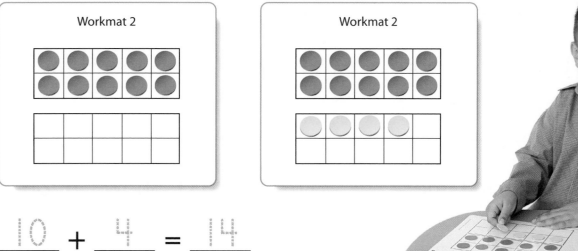

10 + 4 = 14

★ Guided Practice

Use Workmat 2 and ◯. Show the numbers.
Write the number sentence.

Think! Count on 2 more from 10.

1. Show 10. Show 2 more.

____ ◯ ____ ◯ ____

2. Show 10. Show 6 more.

____ ◯ ____ ◯ ____

3. Show 10. Show 8 more.

____ ◯ ____ ◯ ____

4. Show 10. Show 1 more.

____ ◯ ____ ◯ ____

5. **Math Talk** How is adding 10 + 5 like showing 15 with 1 ten and 5 ones?

TAKS Objective 1
TEKS 1.3B Use concrete and pictorial models to apply basic addition and subtraction facts (up to 9 + 9 = 18 and 18 – 9 = 9).

★ Practice

Use Workmat 2 and ◯.
Show the numbers.
Write the number sentence.

Remember!
Fill one ten
frame first.

6. Show 10. Show 7 more.

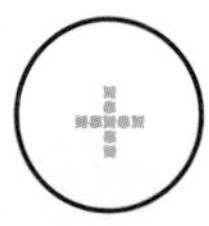   

7. Show 10. Show 3 more.

8. Show 10. Show 8 more.

9. Show 10. Show 4 more.

10. Show 10. Show 1 more.

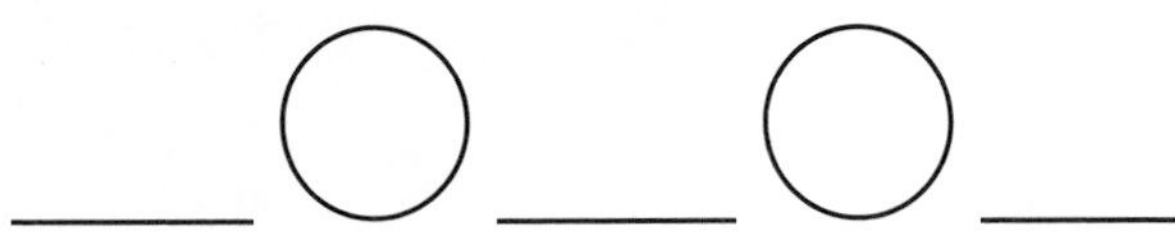

11. Show 10. Show 5 more.

12. Show 10. Show 2 more.

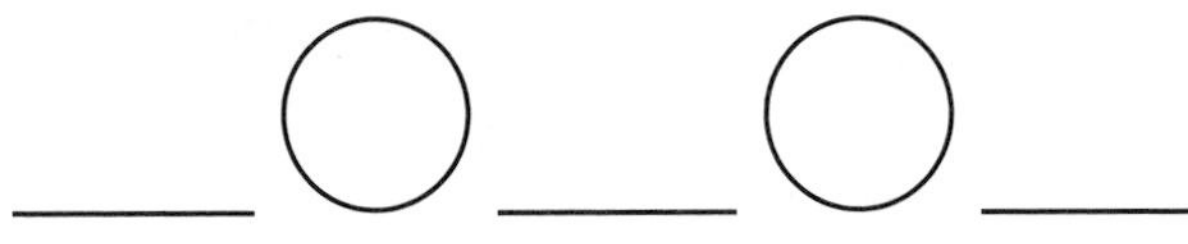

13. Show 10. Show 0 more.

Algebra Readiness: Number Sentences

Write a related subtraction fact for the addition fact.

14. $\begin{array}{r} 5 \\ +6 \\ \hline 11 \end{array}$

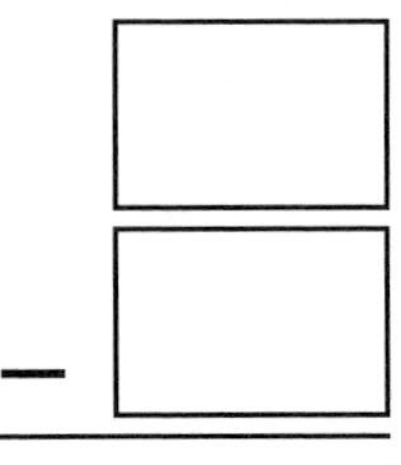

15. $\begin{array}{r} 7 \\ +5 \\ \hline 12 \end{array}$

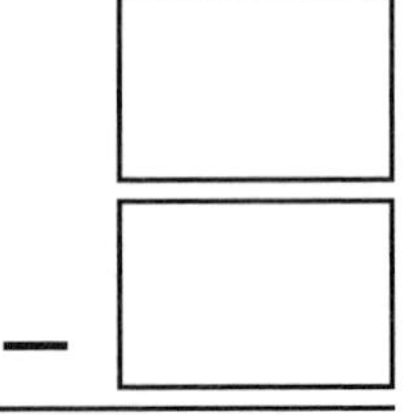

At Home Say a number between 1 and 8. Ask your child to add it to 10 to find the sum. Repeat.

En casa Diga un número entre 1 y 8. Pida a su niño que se lo sume a 10 para hallar la suma. Repita con otros números.

Name ______________________

Chapter 24 Lesson 3

Make a Ten to Add

Hands On

TEKS Objective
Model the make a ten strategy to apply addition facts.

Learn

Make a 10 to help you add with 8 or 9.
Find 8 + 4.
Show 8 and 4 more. Move 2 counters to make 10.

Think about 8 + 2 = 10.

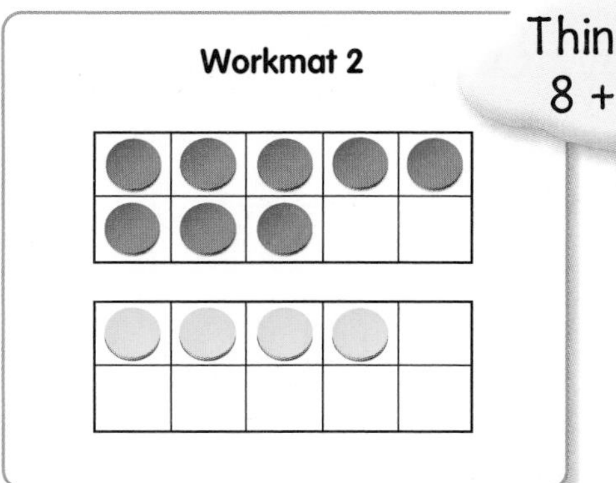
Workmat 2

8 + 4

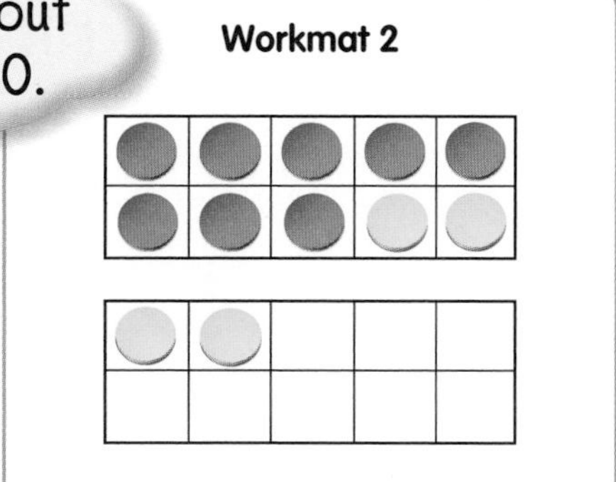
Workmat 2

10 + 2

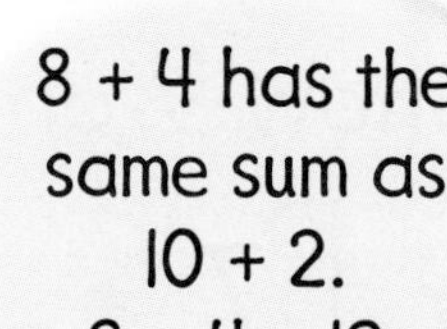
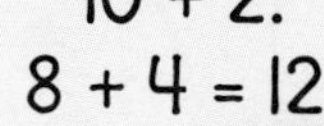
8 + 4 has the same sum as 10 + 2.
8 + 4 = 12.

Guided Practice

Use Workmat 2 and counters.
Make a ten. Find the sum.

Think!
Move 1 counter to make a 10. 9 + 6 has the same sum as 10 + 5.

1. Show 9 and 6 more.

   9 + 6 = ______

2. Show 8 and 5 more.

   8 + 5 = ______

3. Show 9 and 4 more.

   9 + 4 = ______

4. Show 9 and 5 more.

   9 + 5 = ______

5. Show 8 and 3 more.

   8 + 3 = ______

6. **Math Talk** How does making a 10 help you add 8 + 3?

TAKS Objectives 1, 2
TEKS 1.3B Use concrete and pictorial models to apply basic addition and subtraction facts (up to 9 + 9 = 18 and 18 – 9 = 9).

TEKS 1.5D Use patterns to develop strategies to solve basic addition and subtraction problems.

★ Practice

Remember!
Make a 10 first.

Use Workmat 2 and ⬤.
Make a ten. Find the sum.

7. Show 8 and 6 more.
   $8 + 6 = $ 14

8. Show 9 and 8 more.
   $9 + 8 = $ ______

9. Show 9 and 7 more.
   $9 + 7 = $ ______

10. Show 8 and 7 more.
    $8 + 7 = $ ______

11. Show 9 and 3 more.
    $9 + 3 = $ ______

12. Show 8 and 4 more.
    $8 + 4 = $ ______

13. Show 8 and 8 more.
    $8 + 8 = $ ______

14. Show 8 and 5 more.
    $8 + 5 = $ ______

15. Show 9 and 4 more.
    $9 + 4 = $ ______

16. Show 9 and 9 more.
    $9 + 9 = $ ______

Algebra Readiness: Patterns

Write the sums. Look for a pattern.
Write the addition fact you think will come next.

17. $12 + 2 = $ □ $13 + 2 = $ □ $14 + 2 = $ □ $15 + 2 = $ □   □ + □ = □

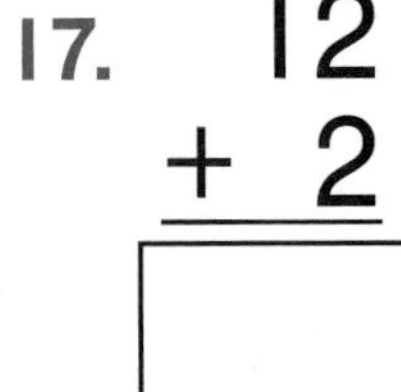

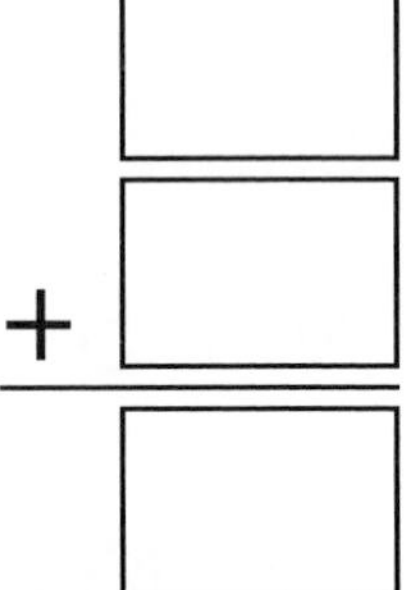

At Home Ask your child how he or she could make a 10 to help add 7 + 6.

En casa Pregunte a su niño cómo podría hacer una decena como ayuda para sumar 7 + 6.

Name ______________________

Chapter 24 Lesson 4

Names for Numbers

TEKS Objective
Model different names for the same number.

There are different ways to make the same sum. Use the counters to find different names for 14.

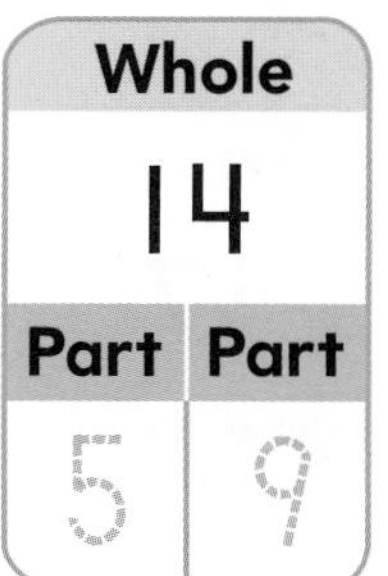

Whole	
14	
Part	Part
9	5

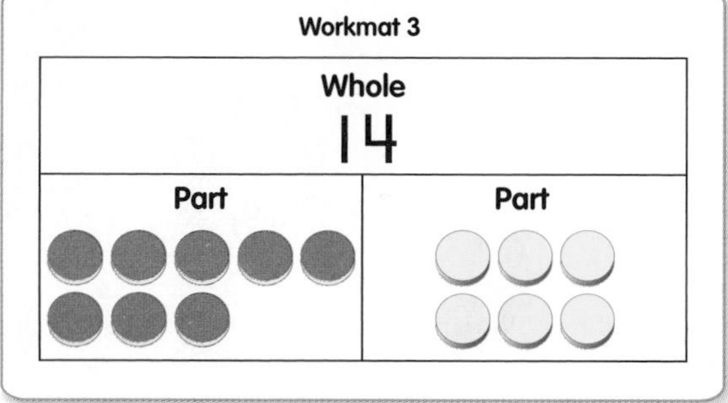

Whole	
14	
Part	Part
8	6

Whole	
14	
Part	Part
6	8

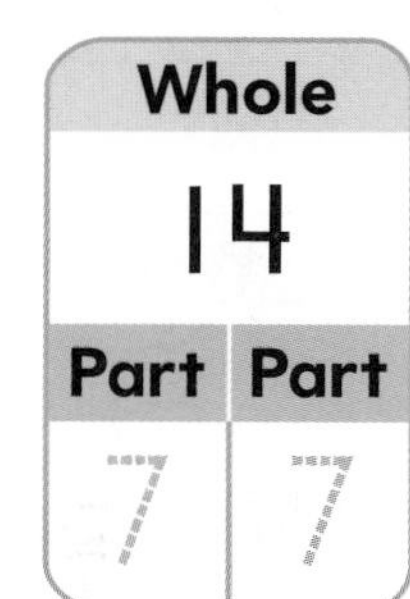

Guided Practice

Use Workmat 3 and ◯.
Find different names for the number.

Think!
What is the doubles fact for 16?

1.

Whole	
16	
Part	Part

Whole	
16	
Part	Part

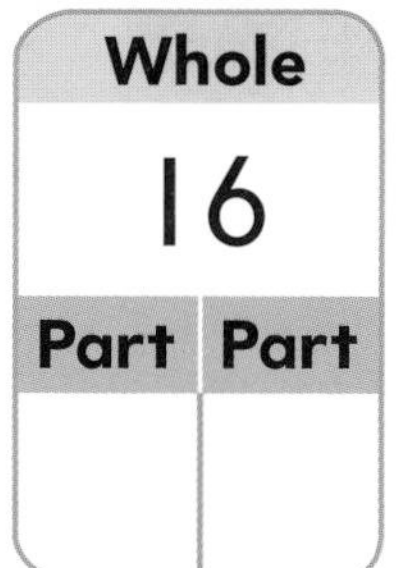

2.

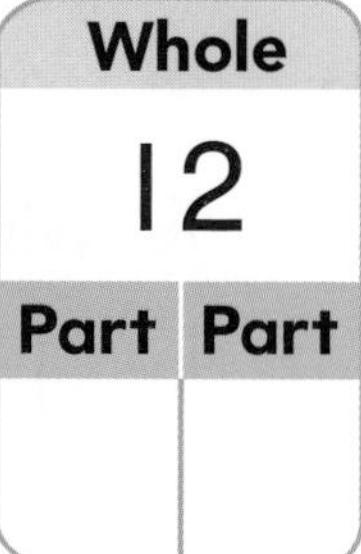

Whole	
12	
Part	Part

Whole	
12	
Part	Part

Whole	
12	
Part	Part

Whole	
12	
Part	Part

3. **Math Talk** Tell why 9 + 3 is not a name for 14.

TAKS Objective 1
TEKS 1.3B Use concrete and pictorial models to apply basic addition and subtraction facts (up to 9 + 9 = 18 and 18 − 9 = 9).

★ Practice

Remember!
Check that the parts equal the whole.

Use Workmat 3 and ◯.
Find different names for the number.

4.

Whole	
17	
Part	Part
9	8

Whole	
17	
Part	Part
8	9

5.

Whole	
15	
Part	Part

Whole	
15	
Part	Part

Whole	
15	
Part	Part

Whole	
15	
Part	Part

6.

Whole	
13	
Part	Part

Whole	
13	
Part	Part

Whole	
13	
Part	Part

Whole	
13	
Part	Part

Whole	
13	
Part	Part

Whole	
13	
Part	Part

Algebra Readiness: Missing Addends

Find the missing part.

7.

Whole	
17	
Part	Part
9	

8.

Whole	
18	
Part	Part
	9

9.

Whole	
14	
Part	Part
5	

At Home Help your child find different names for the numbers 10 and 11.

En casa Ayude a su niño a hallar diferentes nombres para los números 10 y 11.

Name ____________________

Chapter 24 Lesson 5

Write a Number Sentence

Problem Solving
Plan

TEKS Objective
Write a number sentence to solve addition situations.

Sue and Lee plant a garden.
They each plant 9 watermelon seeds.
How many watermelon seeds do they plant altogether?

Understand

What do you know?

- Sue plants 9 watermelon seeds.
- Lee plants 9 watermelon seeds.

Plan

How can you find how many in all?
You can use counters to show the parts.
You can add to find the whole.

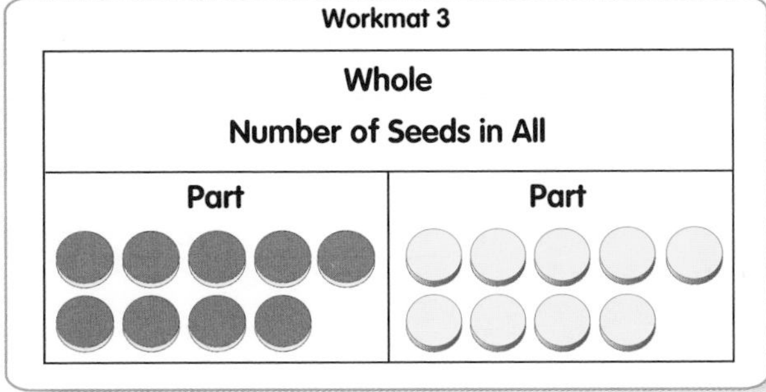

Whole	
18	
Part	**Part**
9	9

Solve

Write a number sentence.

 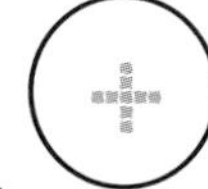  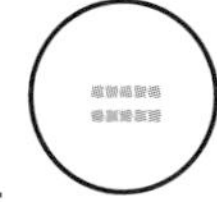  18 seeds

9 + 9 = 18 ______ 18 seeds

Look Back

Does your addition sentence show the two parts?
Does the sum show how many there are altogether?

TAKS Objectives 1, 6
TEKS 1.3A Model and create addition and subtraction problem situations with concrete objects and write corresponding number sentences.

Also, **TEKS 1.11B, 1.11D**

★ Guided Problem Solving

Think!
I add to find how many melons altogether.

1. The Clarks sell 9 melons. The Hales sell 8 melons. How many melons do they sell altogether?

   Draw a line under what you need to find out.

   ___ ◯ ___ ◯ ___

   Solve the problem.

   ___ melons

2.  **Math Talk** How did you find your answer?

★ Problem Solving Practice

Use Workmat 3 and ◯.
Write the number sentence to solve.

3. Luke picks 6 peppers. Donna picks 8 peppers. How many peppers do they pick in all?

   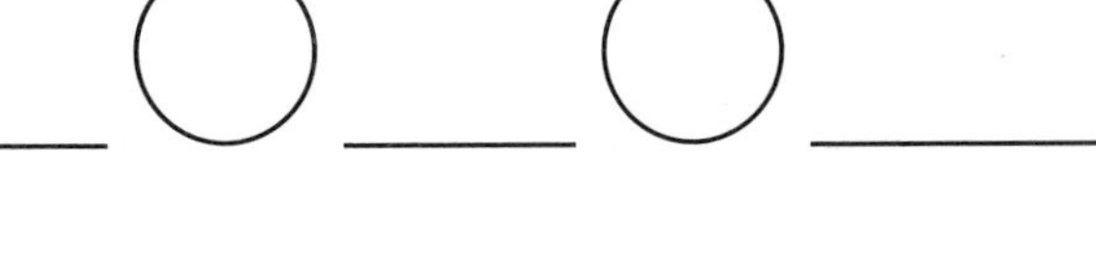

   ___ ◯ ___ ◯ ___

   ___ peppers

4. Kasey plants 1 row of pumpkin seeds. Then she plants 1 row of squash seeds. Each row has 8 seeds. How many seeds does she plant?

   ___ ◯ ___ ◯ ___

   ___ seeds

At Home Substitute different numbers in the problems above and have your child solve them.

En casa Sustituya diferentes números en los problemas de arriba y pida a su niño que los resuelva.

Name ____________________

Science

Texas Field Trip

Moore Farms

Moore Farms is in East Texas. You can visit a pumpkin patch and take a hayride. You can learn about growing corn and explore a corn maze.

Pumpkin Field at Moore Farms

Solve. Show your work.

1. There are 11 bales of hay on the wagon. The farmer takes 6 bales off the wagon. How many bales of hay are left?

   _____ bales of hay

bales of hay

2. Mrs. Tang's class carves 12 pumpkins. Mr. Cooper's class carves 9. How many more pumpkins does Mrs. Tang's class carve?

   _____ pumpkins

pumpkin

3. 9 children enter the corn maze. Then 9 more children go in the maze. How many children are in the corn maze?

   _____ children

corn maze

TAKS Objective 6
TEKS 1.11A Identify mathematics in everyday situations.
TEKS 1.11C Select or develop an appropriate problem-solving plan or strategy including drawing a picture, looking for a pattern, systematic guessing and checking, or acting it out in order to solve a problem.
TEKS Science 2A, 6B

TAKS Problem Solving
Listening Skills

Listen to your teacher read the problem. Choose the correct answer.

Select a Strategy
Draw a Picture
Find a Pattern

1. 7 children water the garden in the morning. 6 children water the garden in the afternoon. How many children water the garden that day?

   12 ○ 13 ○ 14 ○ 15 ○

   TEKS 1.3B

2. Ari puts 12 beans in a basket. Benny takes 4 beans. How many beans are in the basket now?

   8 ○ 9 ○ 10 ○ 11 ○

   TEKS 1.3B

3. 12 ○ 13 ○ 14 ○ 15 ○

TEKS 1.5A

4. 15 ○ 14 ○ 13 ○ 12 ○

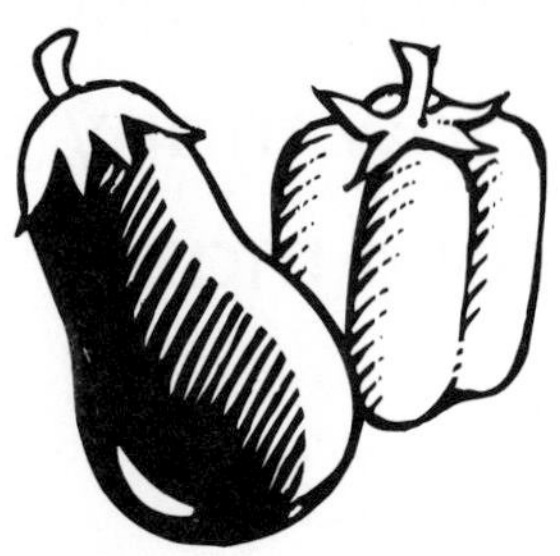

TEKS 1.3B

Education Place
Visit **www.eduplace.com/txmap/** for Test-Taking Tips and more TAKS Practice.

Name ______________________

Amazing!

Help the cow find her way home.

1. Use a calculator to check each number sentence.
2. Circle the number sentences that are incorrect.
3. Follow the path in which all the number sentences are correct.
4. Color the correct path.

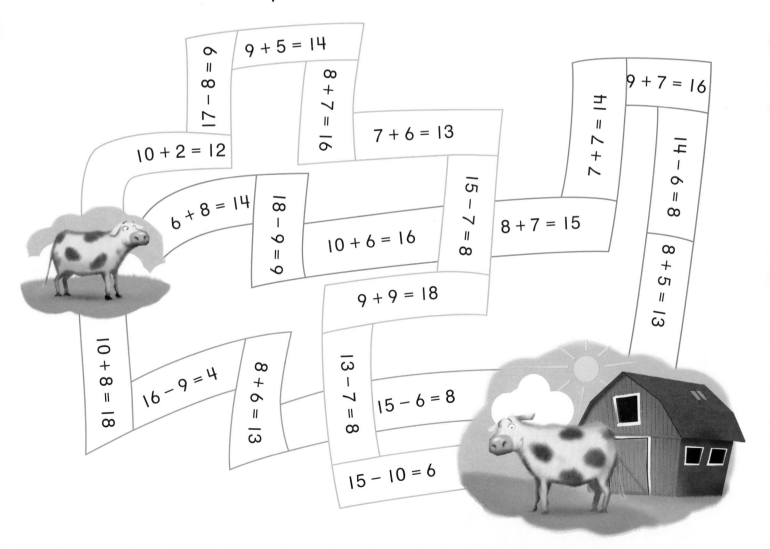

17 − 8 = 9

9 + 5 = 14

8 + 7 = 16

7 + 6 = 13

10 + 2 = 12

6 + 8 = 14

18 − 9 = 9

10 + 6 = 16

15 − 7 = 8

8 + 7 = 15

7 + 7 = 14

9 + 7 = 16

14 − 6 = 8

8 + 5 = 13

9 + 9 = 18

10 + 8 = 18

16 − 9 = 4

8 + 6 = 13

13 − 7 = 8

15 − 6 = 8

15 − 10 = 6

Prairie Dogs

Prairie dogs are burrowing rodents. They feed on grasses and insects and sleep in their underground burrows at night.

Use Workmat 3 and ◯.

Write the number sentence to solve.

1. 9 prairie dogs run in the desert. 8 sleep in the burrow. How many prairie dogs are there in all?

____ ◯ ____ ◯ ____

____ prairie dogs

2. 11 prairie dogs run down a hill. Then 4 more prairie dogs join them. How many prairie dogs are there now?

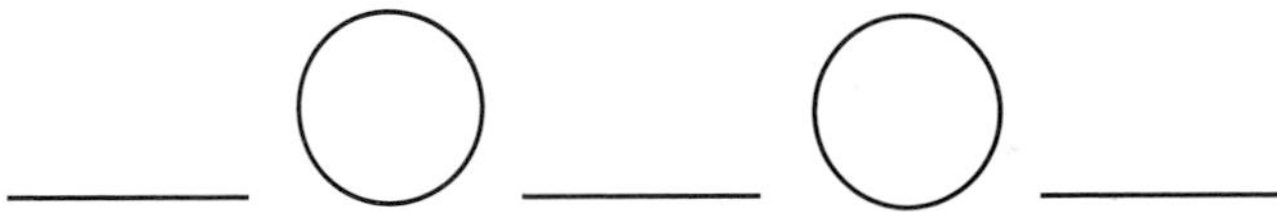

____ prairie dogs

TAKS Objectives 1, 6
TEKS 1.3A Model and create addition and subtraction problem situations with concrete objects and write corresponding number sentences.
TEKS 1.11A Identify mathematics in everyday situations.
TEKS Science 9A

Name ______________________________

Concepts and Skills

Use Workmat 2 and .
Write the addition sentence. TEKS 1.3A

1. There are 8 horses in the barn.
There are 9 horses outside the barn.
How many horses are there in all?

____ + ____ = ____

____ horses

Use Workmat 2 and .
Show the numbers.
Write the number sentence.
TEKS 1.3B

2. Show 10. Show 6 more.

____ ◯ ____ ◯ ____

Use Workmat 2 and .
Make a ten. Find the sum.
TEKS 1.3B, 1.5D

3. Show 9 and 4 more.

9 + 4 = ____

Use Workmat 3 and .
Find different names for the number. TEKS 1.3B

4.

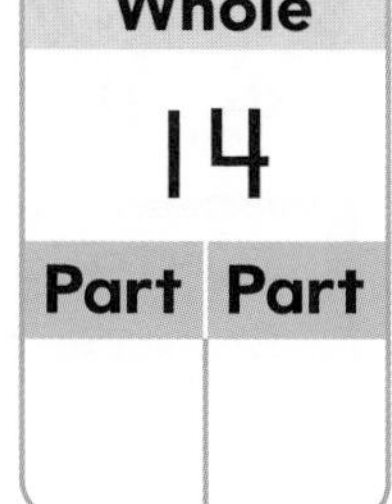

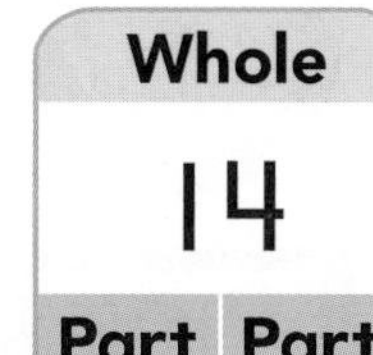

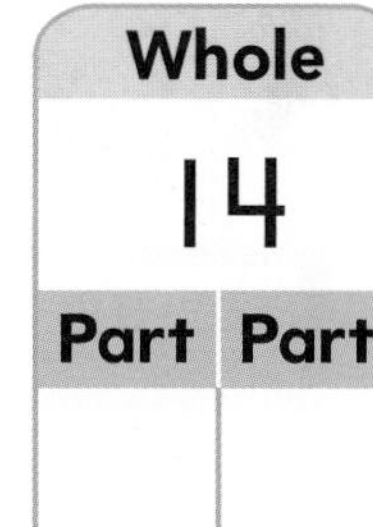

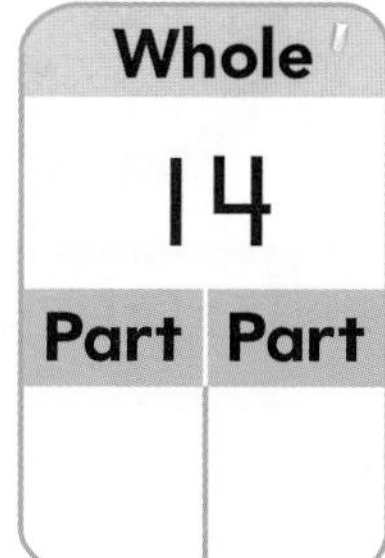

Problem Solving

Use Workmat 3 and .
Write the number sentence to solve. TEKS 1.3A, 1.11B

5. Ann picks 9 ears of corn. Then she picks 6 more. How many ears of corn does she pick in all?

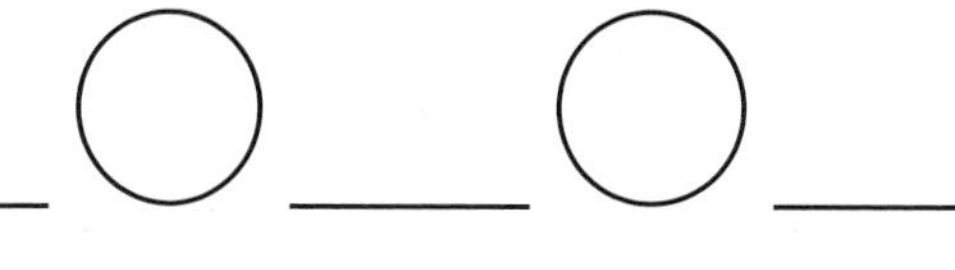

____ ears of corn

TAKS Prep and Spiral Review

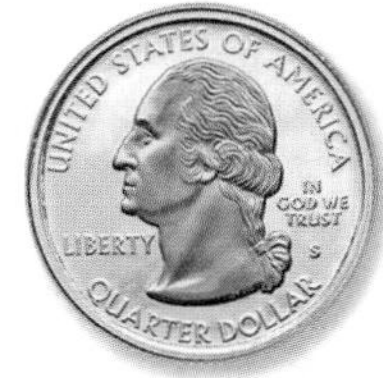

Choose the answer for problems 1–4.

1. Which answer names the value of a quarter?

1 cent	5 cents	10 cents	25 cents
◯	◯	◯	◯

TEKS 1.1C (page 385)

2. Which coin has the same value as two nickels?

penny	nickel	dime	quarter
◯	◯	◯	◯

TEKS 1.1C (page 383)

3. Which set of clocks shows 4 o'clock?

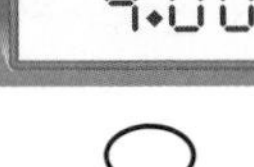

4:00	4:30	4:00	4:00
◯	◯	◯	◯

TEKS 1.8B (page 401)

4. Kelly woke up at eight-thirty this morning. Which clock shows eight-thirty?

◯ ◯ ◯ ◯

TEKS 1.8B (page 403)

Education Place
Visit **www.eduplace.com/txmap/** for Test-Taking Tips and Extra Practice.

Subtraction Facts Through 18

TAKS Vocabulary

Here are some vocabulary words you will learn in the chapter.

difference If you know the whole and one part, you can find the other part. The missing part is the difference.

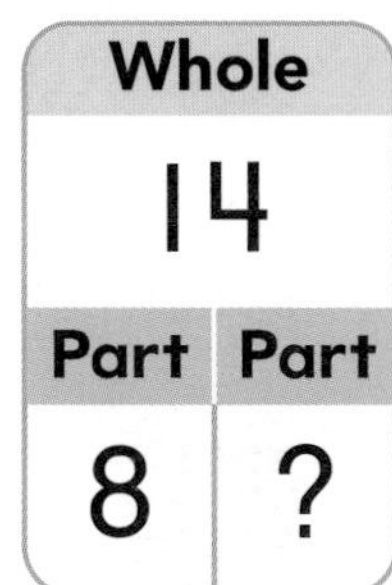

$$\begin{array}{r} 14 \\ -\ 8 \\ \hline 6 \end{array} \leftarrow \text{difference}$$

related facts Addition and subtraction facts that have the same parts and wholes

Related addition facts can help you subtract.

$$\begin{array}{r} 7 \\ +\ 5 \\ \hline 12 \end{array}$$

Whole	
Part	Part
●●●●●●●	○○○○○

$$\begin{array}{r} 12 \\ -\ 7 \\ \hline 5 \end{array} \qquad \begin{array}{r} 12 \\ -\ 5 \\ \hline 7 \end{array}$$

See English-Spanish glossary pages 505–516.

TAKS Objective 6
TEKS 1.12B Relate informal language to mathematical language and symbols.

Education Place
Visit **www.eduplace.com/txmap/** for the eGlossary and vocabulary eGames.

Name ____________________

Write the missing part.

1.

Whole	
9	
Part	Part
4	

2.

Whole	
12	
Part	Part
3	

Match. Then subtract.

3. How many more  than are there?

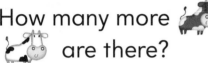

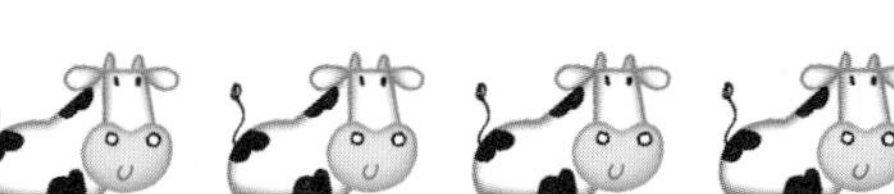

8 – 4 = ____

Write the missing part.
Complete the related facts.

4.

Whole	
12	
Part	Part
4	

12 – 4 = ____

12 – 8 = ____

5.

Whole	
11	
Part	Part
5	

11 – 5 = ____

11 – 6 = ____

Use this page to review important skills needed for this chapter.

Name ____________________

Chapter 25 Lesson 1

Model Subtraction

Hands On

TEKS Objective
Model subtraction using parts and wholes.

★ Learn

If you know the whole and one of the parts, you can subtract to find the other part.

There are 14 counters in all.
9 counters are in one part.
How many are in the other part?

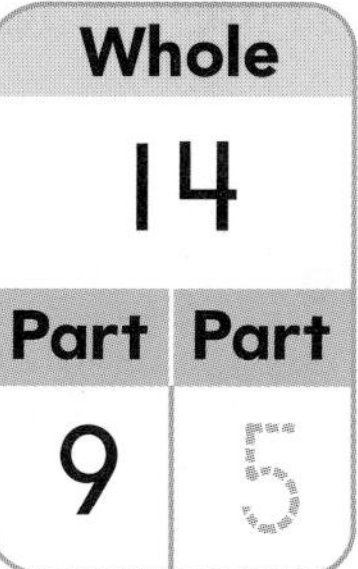

Whole	
14	
Part	Part
9	5

There are 5 counters in the other part.

★ Guided Practice

Use Workmat 3 and ◯.
Show the whole. Move counters to one part. Find the other part.

1.

Whole	
13	
Part	Part
6	

Think!
There are 13 counters in all. One part has 6 counters.

2.

Whole	
17	
Part	Part
8	

3.

Whole	
16	
Part	Part
8	

4.

Whole	
12	
Part	Part
7	

5.

Whole	
15	
Part	Part
9	

6. **Math Talk** If you have 15 in all and 9 is in one part, can you have more than 6 in the other part? Why?

TAKS Objective 1
TEKS 1.3B Use concrete and pictorial models to apply basic addition and subtraction facts (up to 9 + 9 = 18 and 18 − 9 = 9).

★ Practice

Use Workmat 3 and ⬤.
Show the whole.
Move counters to one part.
Find the other part.

Remember!
The parts make the whole.

7.

Whole	
11	
Part	Part
2	9

8.

Whole	
18	
Part	Part
9	

9.

Whole	
14	
Part	Part
6	

10.

Whole	
15	
Part	Part
8	

11.

Whole	
13	
Part	Part
4	

12.

Whole	
17	
Part	Part
9	

Problem Solving: Number Sense

Draw a set with one fewer.

13.     

14. 

At Home Start with 18 objects. Move some to show one part. Have your child tell the other part.

En casa Comience con un conjunto de 18 objetos. Mueva algunos para mostrar una parte. Pida a su niño que diga cuántos hay en la otra parte.

Name ________________________________

Chapter 25 Lesson 2

Parts and Wholes

Hands On

TEKS Objective
Use parts and wholes to model subtraction facts through 18.

TAKS Vocabulary
difference

★ Learn

If you know one of these facts, you can find the **difference** for the related fact.

Whole	
13	
Part	Part
5	8

$$\begin{array}{r} 13 \\ -\ 5 \\ \hline 8 \end{array} \qquad \begin{array}{r} 13 \\ -\ 8 \\ \hline 5 \end{array}$$

★ Guided Practice

Use Workmat 3 and ◯.
Write the missing part.
Write the difference.

1.

Whole	
14	
Part	Part
6	

Think! 6 and what other part make 14?

$$\begin{array}{r} 14 \\ -\ 6 \\ \hline \end{array} \qquad \begin{array}{r} 14 \\ -\ 8 \\ \hline \end{array}$$

2.

Whole	
18	
Part	Part
9	

$$\begin{array}{r} 18 \\ -\ 9 \\ \hline \end{array}$$

3.

Whole	
12	
Part	Part
7	

$$\begin{array}{r} 12 \\ -\ 7 \\ \hline \end{array} \qquad \begin{array}{r} 12 \\ -\ 5 \\ \hline \end{array}$$

4. **Math Talk** How does 12 − 7 help you find the difference for 12 − 5?

TAKS Objective 1
TEKS 1.3B Use concrete and pictorial models to apply basic addition and subtraction facts (up to 9 + 9 = 18 and 18 − 9 = 9).

★ Practice

Use Workmat 3 and ◯.
Write the missing part.
Write the difference.

Remember!
One fact can help you find another fact.

5.

Whole	
13	
Part	Part
10	3

$\begin{array}{r} 13 \\ -10 \\ \hline 3 \end{array}$ $\begin{array}{r} 13 \\ -3 \\ \hline 10 \end{array}$

6.

Whole	
17	
Part	Part
8	

$\begin{array}{r} 17 \\ -8 \\ \hline \end{array}$ $\begin{array}{r} 17 \\ -9 \\ \hline \end{array}$

7.

Whole	
11	
Part	Part
5	

$\begin{array}{r} 11 \\ -5 \\ \hline \end{array}$ $\begin{array}{r} 11 \\ -6 \\ \hline \end{array}$

8.

Whole	
15	
Part	Part
7	

$\begin{array}{r} 15 \\ -7 \\ \hline \end{array}$ $\begin{array}{r} 15 \\ -8 \\ \hline \end{array}$

9.

Whole	
18	
Part	Part
10	

$\begin{array}{r} 18 \\ -10 \\ \hline \end{array}$ $\begin{array}{r} 18 \\ -8 \\ \hline \end{array}$

10.

Whole	
14	
Part	Part
4	

$\begin{array}{r} 14 \\ -4 \\ \hline \end{array}$ $\begin{array}{r} 14 \\ -10 \\ \hline \end{array}$

Algebra Readiness: Number Sentences

Use the two parts to write subtraction sentences.

11. ______ − ______ = ______  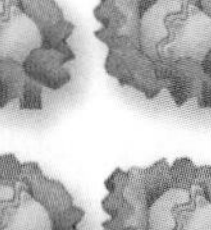 

12. ______ − ______ = ______  

At Home Ask your child to subtract 5 and 6 from 13 and 14.

En casa Pida a su niño que reste 5 y 6 de 13 y 14.

TEKS Objective
Identify patterns in related facts to subtract from 15 through 18.

Name ______________________

Chapter 25 Lesson 3

Relate Addition and Subtraction Facts

Use an addition fact to help you subtract.

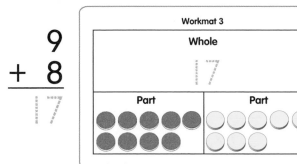

$$\begin{array}{r} 9 \\ +\ 8 \\ \hline 17 \end{array}$$

Workmat 3

Whole	
17	
Part	Part
●●●●● ●●●●	○○○○○ ○○○

$$\begin{array}{r} 17 \\ -\ 9 \\ \hline 8 \end{array} \qquad \begin{array}{r} 17 \\ -\ 8 \\ \hline 9 \end{array}$$

Guided Practice

Use Workmat 3 and ◯.
Add. Then subtract.

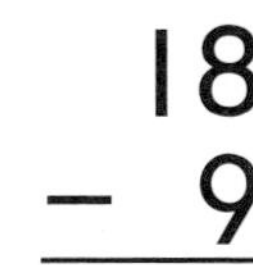

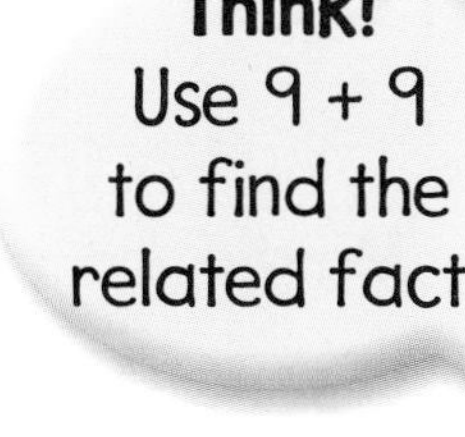

Think!
Use 9 + 9
to find the
related fact.

1. $\begin{array}{r} 9 \\ +\ 9 \\ \hline \end{array}$

Whole	
Part	Part
9	9

$\begin{array}{r} 18 \\ -\ 9 \\ \hline \end{array}$

2. $\begin{array}{r} 7 \\ +\ 9 \\ \hline \end{array}$

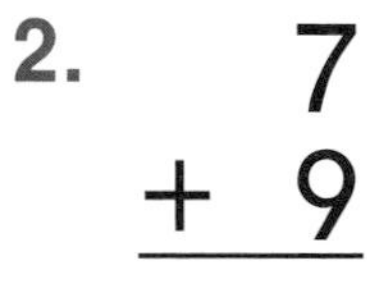

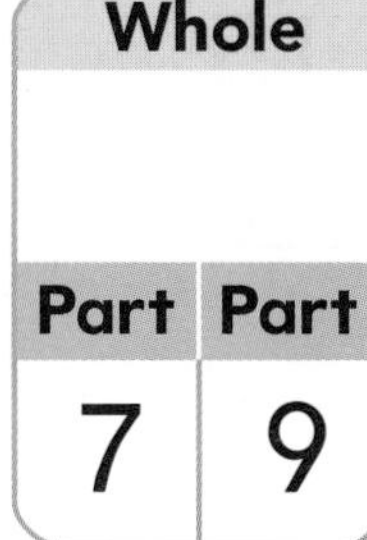

Whole	
Part	Part
7	9

$\begin{array}{r} 16 \\ -\ 7 \\ \hline \end{array} \qquad \begin{array}{r} 16 \\ -\ 9 \\ \hline \end{array}$

3. $\begin{array}{r} 9 \\ +\ 6 \\ \hline \end{array}$

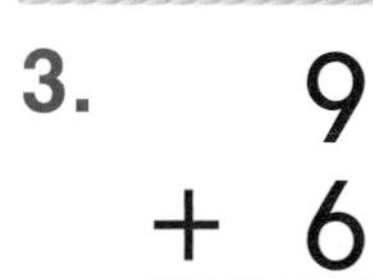

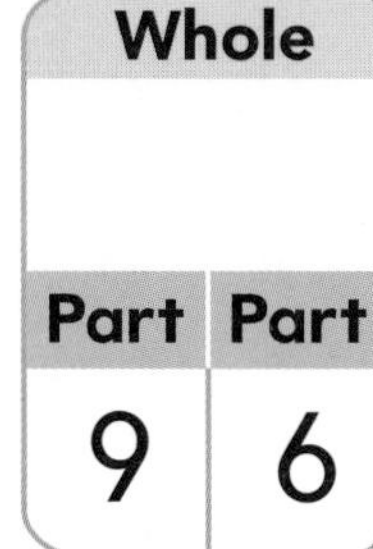

Whole	
Part	Part
9	6

$\begin{array}{r} 15 \\ -\ 9 \\ \hline \end{array} \qquad \begin{array}{r} 15 \\ -\ 6 \\ \hline \end{array}$

4.  **Math Talk** What patterns do you see?

TAKS Objectives 1, 2
TEKS 1.3B Use concrete and pictorial models to apply basic addition and subtraction facts (up to 9 + 9 = 18 and 18 − 9 = 9).

TEKS 1.5E Identify patterns in related addition and subtraction sentences (fact families for sums to 18) such as 2 + 3 = 5, 3 + 2 = 5, 5 − 2 = 3, and 5 − 3 = 2.

★ Practice

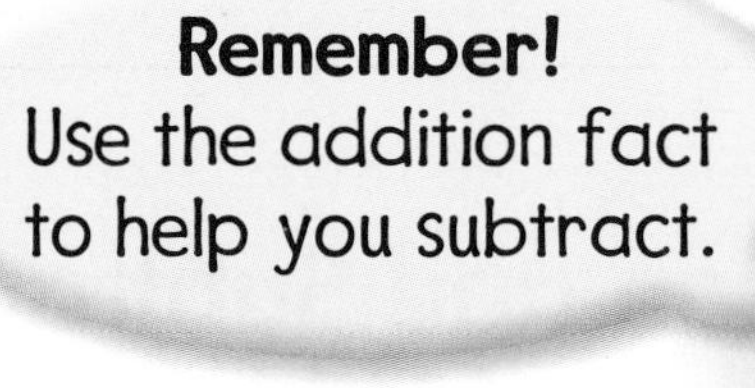

Remember!
Use the addition fact
to help you subtract.

Use Workmat 3 and ◯.
Add. Then subtract.

5.

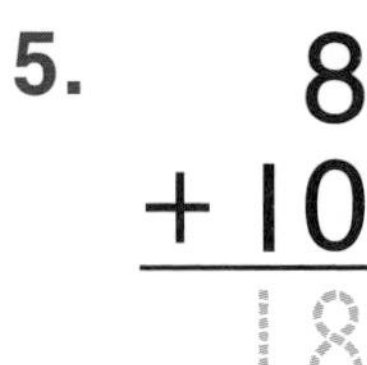

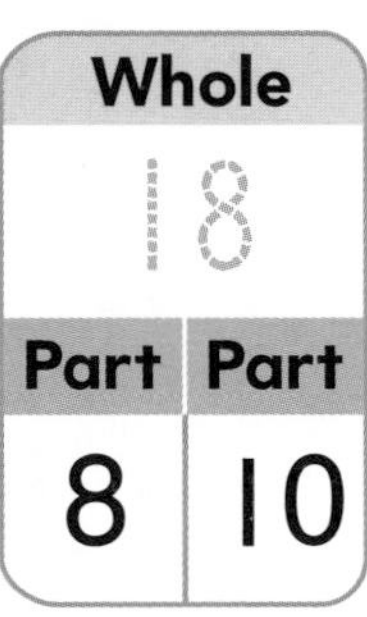

$$\begin{array}{r} 18 \\ -\ 8 \\ \hline \end{array} \qquad \begin{array}{r} 18 \\ -10 \\ \hline \end{array}$$

6.

$$\begin{array}{r} 10 \\ +\ 6 \\ \hline \end{array}$$

Whole	
Part	**Part**
10	6

$$\begin{array}{r} 16 \\ -10 \\ \hline \end{array} \qquad \begin{array}{r} 16 \\ -\ 6 \\ \hline \end{array}$$

7.

$$\begin{array}{r} 7 \\ +10 \\ \hline \end{array}$$

Whole	
Part	**Part**
7	10

$$\begin{array}{r} 17 \\ -\ 7 \\ \hline \end{array} \qquad \begin{array}{r} 17 \\ -10 \\ \hline \end{array}$$

8.

$$\begin{array}{r} 8 \\ +\ 7 \\ \hline \end{array}$$

Whole	
Part	**Part**
8	7

$$\begin{array}{r} 15 \\ -\ 8 \\ \hline \end{array} \qquad \begin{array}{r} 15 \\ -\ 7 \\ \hline \end{array}$$

Algebra Readiness: Missing Addends

Write the missing number.

9. 17 − _____ = 8

10. 18 − _____ = 9

At Home Read exercises from this page and have your child find the differences.

En casa Lea los ejercicios de esta página y pida a su niño que halle las diferencias.

Name ______________________________

Chapter 25 Lesson 4

Fact Families

Hands On

TEKS Objective
Identify patterns in fact families for sums through 18.

★ Learn

Use related facts to make a fact family.

These 4 facts make a fact family.

Whole	
15	
Part	Part
8	7

$8 + 7 = 15$

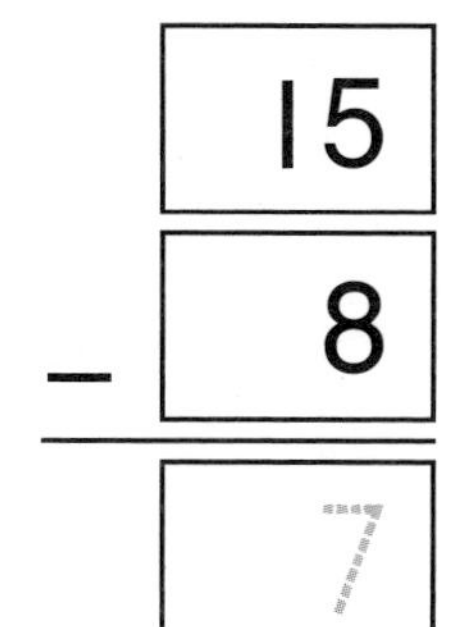

$15 - 8 = 7$

★ Guided Practice

Use Workmat 3 and 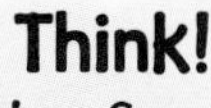.
Complete the fact family.

Think!
All the facts in this family use the numbers 13, 7, and 6.

1.

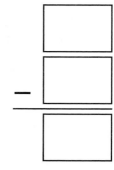

Whole	
13	
Part	Part
7	6

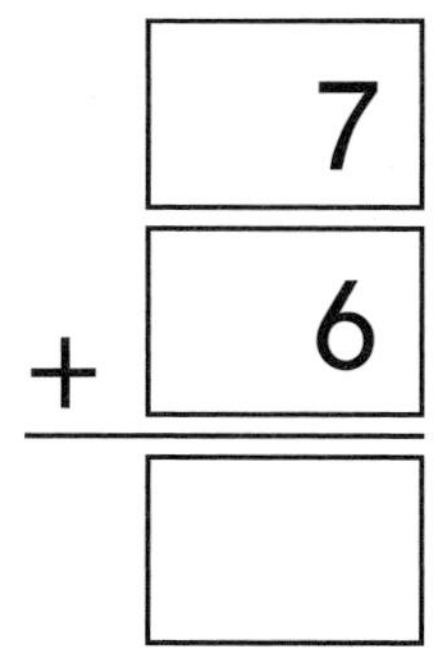

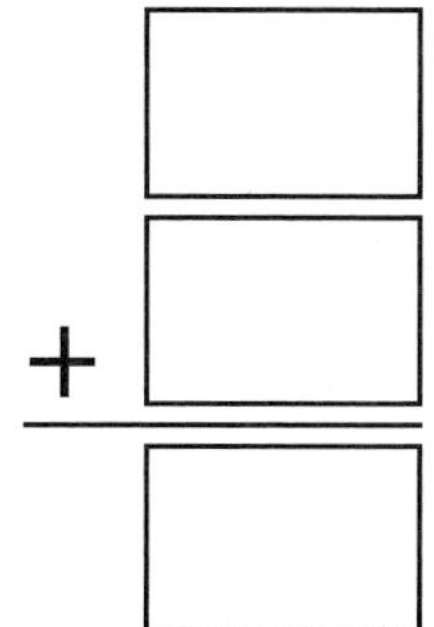

13
− 7
___

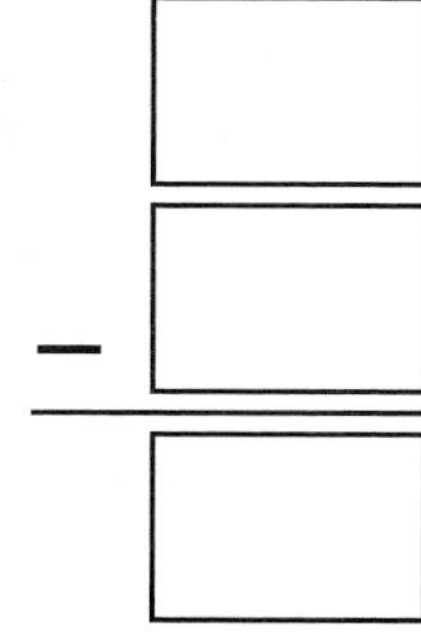

2.

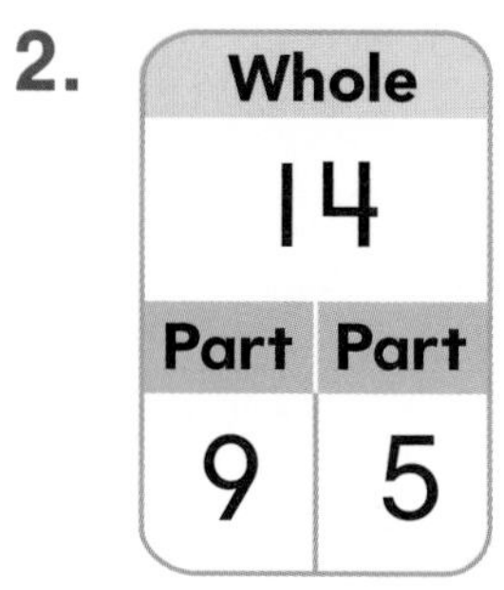

9
+ 5
___

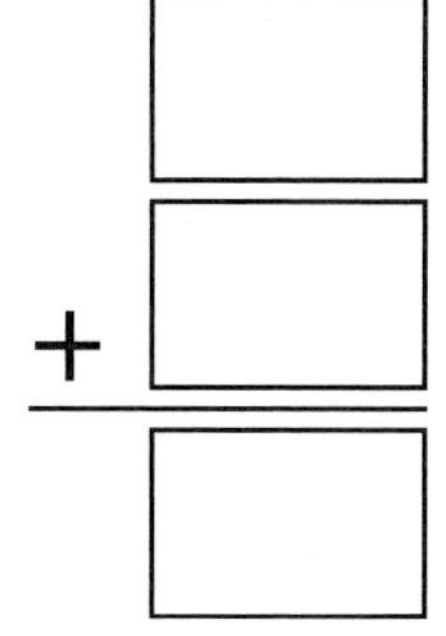

14
− 9
___

−
___

3. **Math Talk** Are 9 + 5 and 9 − 5 in the same fact family?

TAKS Objectives 1, 2
TEKS 1.3B Use concrete and pictorial models to apply basic addition and subtraction facts (up to 9 + 9 = 18 and 18 − 9 = 9).

TEKS 1.5E Identify patterns in related addition and subtraction sentences (fact families for sums to 18) such as 2 + 3 = 5, 3 + 2 = 5, 5 − 2 = 3, and 5 − 3 = 2.

★ Practice

Remember!
Each fact family has the same numbers.

Use Workmat 3 and ◯.
Complete the fact family.

4. Whole 18; Part 9, Part 9

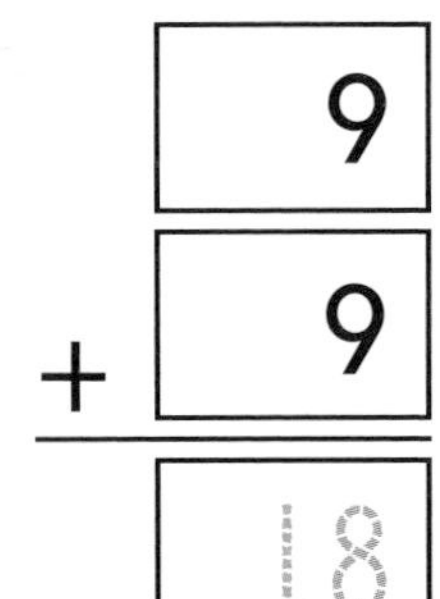

$9 + 9 = 18$

$18 - 9 = 9$

5. 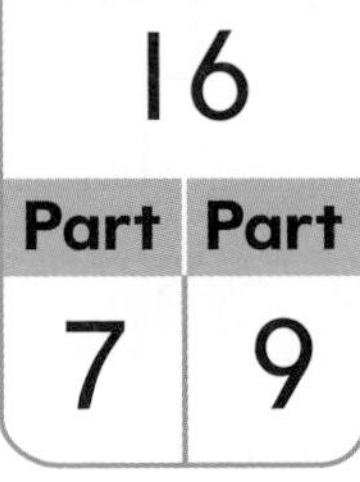

Whole 16; Part 7, Part 9

$7 + 9 = \square$

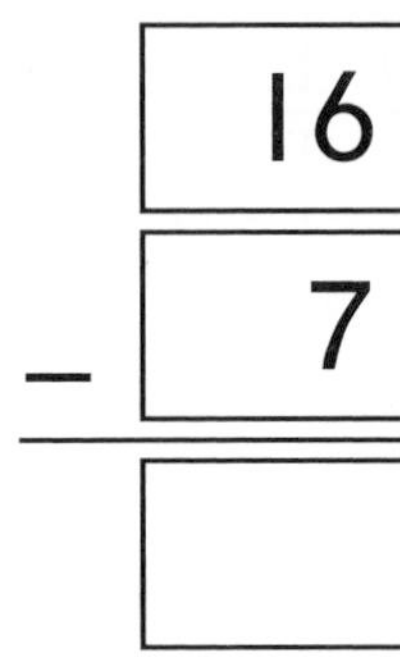

$\square + \square = \square$

$16 - 7 = \square$

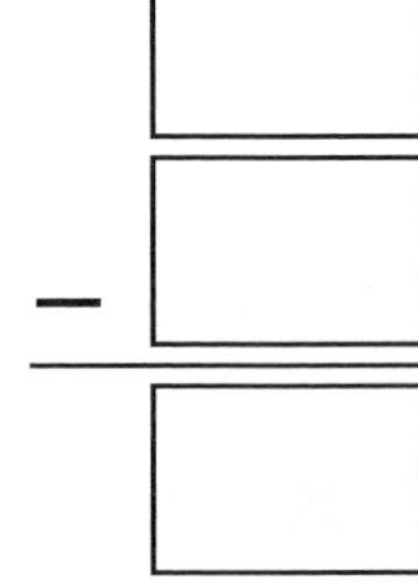

$\square - \square = \square$

6. Whole 17; Part 9, Part 8

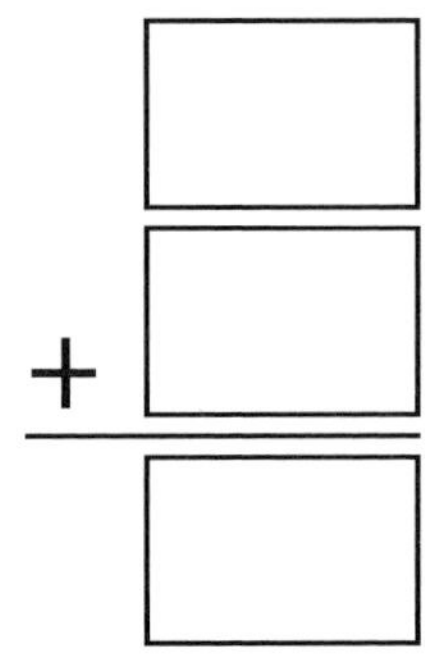

$9 + 8 = \square$

$\square + \square = \square$

$17 - 9 = \square$

$\square - \square = \square$

Problem Solving: Visual Thinking

7. Find the numbers that are outside the circle but inside the square. Use them to write a fact family.

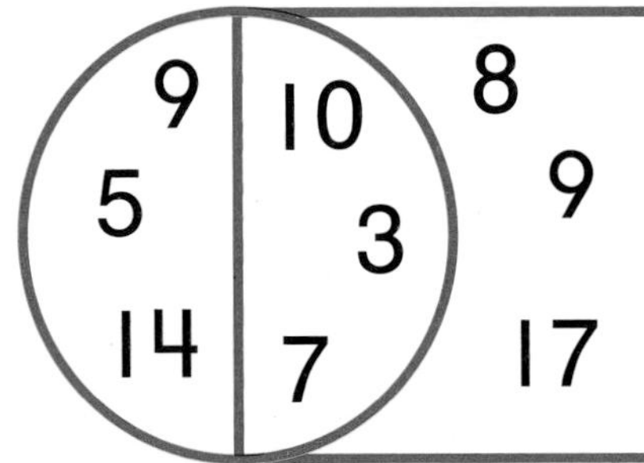

____ + ____ = ____

____ + ____ = ____

____ − ____ = ____

____ − ____ = ____

At Home Ask your child to write a fact family using the numbers 13, 9, and 4.

En casa Pida a su niño que escriba una familia de operaciones usando los números 13, 9 y 4.

Name ______________________

Chapter 25 Lesson 5

Too Much Information

TEKS Objective
Solve problems with too much information; model and create number sentences.

Some problems have more information than you need.

17 chickens are in the henhouse.
9 roosters are in the henhouse.
8 chickens are brown.
How many more chickens than roosters are there?

Decide what information you need.

THINK	DECIDE
Do I need to know that there are 17 chickens?	Yes. I need to compare the number of chickens to the number of roosters.
Do I need to know that there are 9 roosters?	Yes. I need to know the number of roosters.
Do I need to know that 8 of the chickens are brown?	No. I need to know the number, not the color.

17 chickens are in the henhouse.
9 roosters are in the henhouse.
~~8 chickens are brown.~~

Cross out the extra information.

How many more chickens than roosters are there? Subtract to compare the numbers.

__17__ − __9__ = __8__ __8__ more chickens

★ Guided Problem Solving

Think!
Do I need to know how many goats have horns?

1. 16 goats are in the yard.
   10 of the goats have horns.
   8 goats walk away.
   How many goats are in the yard now?

   Think about the information you need.

   Cross out what you do not need. Solve.

   _____ goats

2. **Math Talk** How do you decide what you need to solve the problem?

★ Problem Solving Practice

Cross out the information you do not need. Solve.

Draw or write to explain.

3. There are 15 ducks in the pond.
   Ducks have 2 feet.
   6 ducks fly away.
   How many ducks are left?

   _____ ducks

4. There are 13 cows in the barn.
   There are 9 cows on the hill.
   2 cows are brown.
   How many more cows are in the barn than on the hill?

   _____ cows

At Home Create a subtraction story problem. Include extra information. Ask your child to solve the problem.

En casa Cree un problema de resta. Incluya información adicional. Pida a su niño que resuelva el problema.

Name ______________________________

Create and Solve

Draw 15 tomatoes in a garden.
Color some .
Color the rest .

I. My Garden

Write two addition and two subtraction sentences that you can solve with your picture.

2. _____ ◯ _____ ◯ _____

3. _____ ◯ _____ ◯ _____

4. _____ ◯ _____ ◯ _____

5. _____ ◯ _____ ◯ _____

TAKS Objectives 1, 2
TEKS 1.3A Model and create addition and subtraction problem situations with concrete objects and write corresponding number sentences.

TEKS 1.5E Identify patterns in related addition and subtraction sentences (fact families for sums to 18) such as 2 + 3 = 5, 3 + 2 = 5, 5 – 2 = 3, and 5 – 3 = 2.

Draw 13 apples in a tree.
Color some.
Color the rest.

6.

Write two addition and two subtraction sentences that you can solve with your picture.

7. _____ ◯ _____ ◯ _____

8. _____ ◯ _____ ◯ _____

9. _____ ◯ _____ ◯ _____

10. _____ ◯ _____ ◯ _____

Name ______________________________

Hot and Cold Food

Four children are each eating something different.

- Matt's food is colder than Anil's.
- Anil's food is the hottest.
- Rosa's food is colder than Matt's.
- Haley's food is the coldest.

What is each child eating?
Write each child's name under the food he or she is eating.

1.  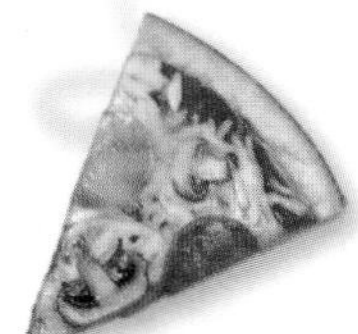  

__________ __________ __________ __________

2. Write 1, 2, 3, and 4 to order the food from coldest to hottest.

 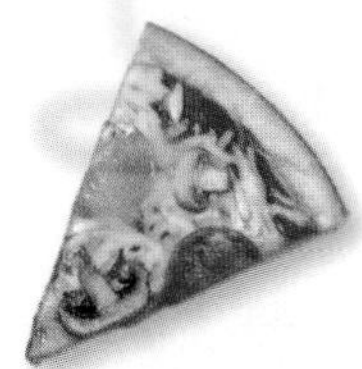  

_____ _____ _____ _____

TAKS Objective 4
TEKS 1.7G Compare and order two or more objects according to relative temperature (from hottest to coldest).

Education Place
Visit www.eduplace.com/txmap/ for Brain Teasers.

Math Music

In This Garden

Math Music, Track 10
Tune: "Twinkle, Twinkle, Little Star"

In this garden, add each bean.
5 plus 9 will make 14.
Switch around the 5 and 9.
Add again. You'll do just fine!
Either way you get 14.
Check your work and count each bean!

In this garden, let's subtract
5 from 14, what is that?
There are 9 beans left, you see.
Try another fact with me.
9 from 14, what is that?
5 beans left and that's a fact!

TAKS Objective 1
TEKS 1.3B Use concrete and pictorial models to apply basic addition and subtraction facts (up to $9 + 9 = 18$ and $18 - 9 = 9$).

Name ______________________________

Concepts and Skills

Use Workmat 3 and ◯.
Write the missing part.
Write the difference. TEKS 1.3B

1\.

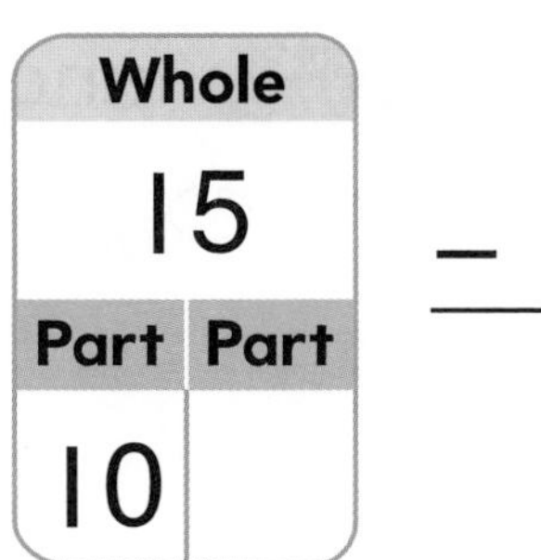

Whole	
15	
Part	Part
10	

$$\begin{array}{r} 15 \\ -\ 10 \\ \hline \end{array} \qquad \begin{array}{r} 15 \\ -\ 5 \\ \hline \end{array}$$

Use Workmat 3 and ◯.
Add. Then subtract. TEKS 1.5E

2\.

$$\begin{array}{r} 9 \\ +\ 8 \\ \hline \end{array}$$

Whole	
Part	Part
9	8

$$\begin{array}{r} 17 \\ -\ 9 \\ \hline \end{array} \qquad \begin{array}{r} 17 \\ -\ 8 \\ \hline \end{array}$$

Use Workmat 3 and ◯. Complete the fact family. TEKS 1.5E

3\.

Whole	
15	
Part	Part
9	6

$$\begin{array}{r} \square \\ +\ \square \\ \hline \square \end{array}$$

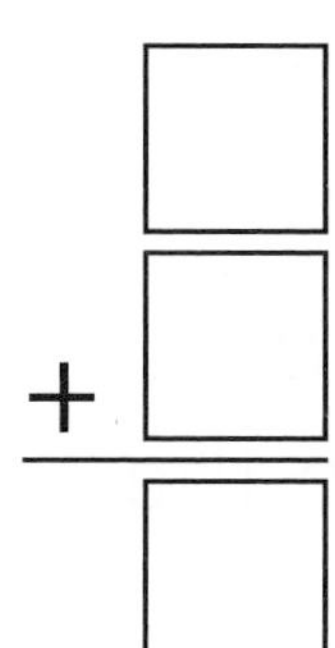

$$\begin{array}{r} \square \\ +\ \square \\ \hline \square \end{array}$$

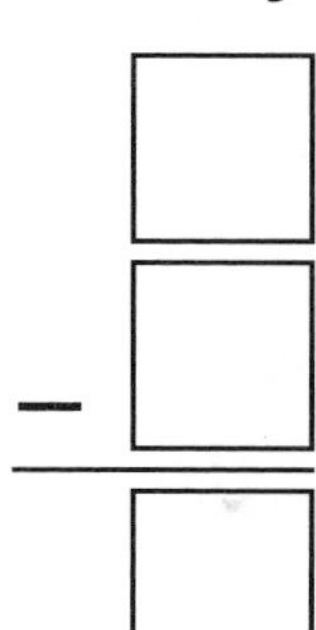

$$\begin{array}{r} \square \\ -\ \square \\ \hline \square \end{array} \qquad \begin{array}{r} \square \\ -\ \square \\ \hline \square \end{array}$$

Problem Solving

Cross out the information you do not need. Solve. TEKS 1.11A

4\. 17 cows are in the yard.
6 cows are brown.
10 cows walk away.
How many cows are in the yard now?

_____ cows

Draw or write to explain.

TAKS Prep and Spiral Review

Choose the answer for problems 1–4.

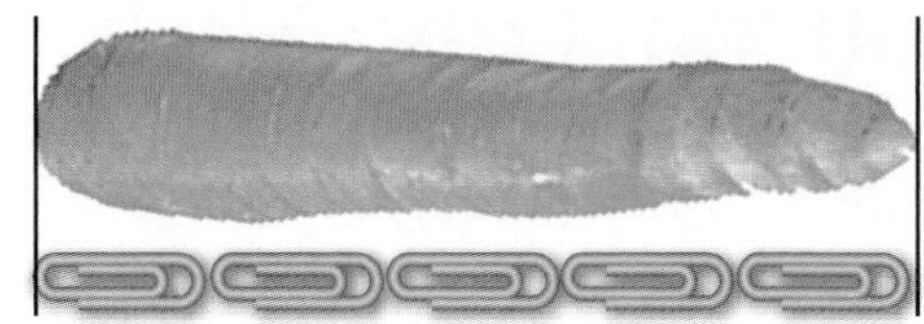

1. About how many paper clips long is the carrot?

about 4 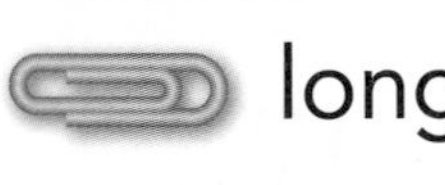 long	about 5  long	about 6 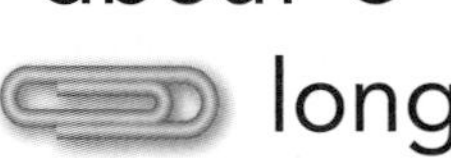 long	about 7 long
○	○	○	○

TEKS 1.7A (page 423)

2. Which would take the most to equal the length of a car?

	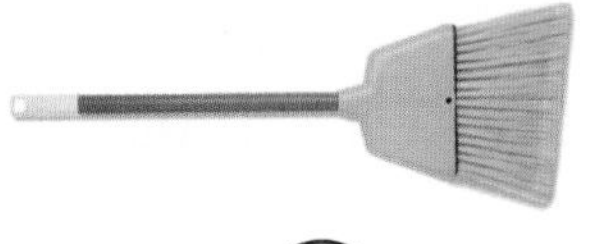		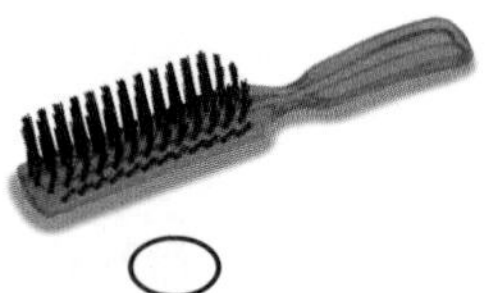
○	○	○	○

TEKS 1.7C (page 423)

3. Which shows the containers in order from the one that holds the least to the one that holds the most?

○	○	○	○

TEKS 1.7E (page 445)

4. Jim goes to the snack table at the fair. He buys the coldest snack. Which snack does Jim buy?

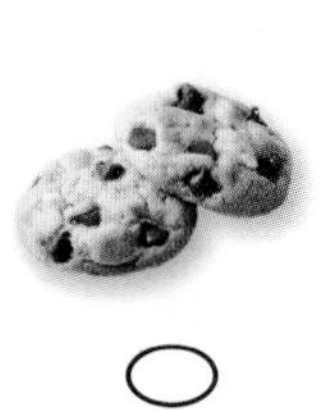			
○	○	○	○

TEKS 1.7G (page 447)

Education Place
Visit **www.eduplace.com/txmap/** for Test-Taking Tips and Extra Practice.

Name ______________________________

Unit 10 Mental Math Strategies

Make a 10

A clever strategy works best.
First make 10, then add the rest.

1. 8 + 6 = [14]
   [2] + [4]
   Make 10. 8 + 2 | Add the rest.

2. 6 + 7 = [ ]
   [4] + [ ]
   Make 10. 6 + 4 | Add the rest.

3. 9 + 8 = [ ]
   [ ] + [ ]
   Make 10. 9 + 1 | Add the rest.

4. 6 + 5 = [ ]
   [ ] + [ ]
   Make 10. 6 + 4 | Add the rest.

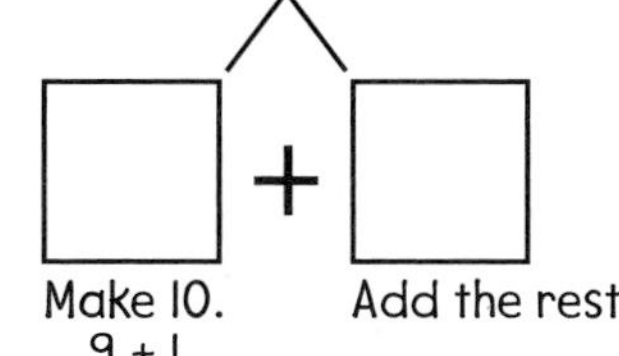

I think of 6 as 2 + 4. First I add 2 to 8 to get 10. Then I add the rest. Add 4 to 10 to get 14.

Take It Further: Now try doing everything in your head!

Keep It Up!

5. 5 + 8 = [ ]
6. 8 + 7 = [ ]
7. 6 + 5 = [ ]
8. 7 + 6 = [ ]
9. 3 + 9 = [ ]
10. 9 + 5 = [ ]

Name ______________________________

Reading and Writing Math

Word Bank
difference
sum

Use Workmat 2 and ●.
Make a ten to solve.
Draw the counters.

1. Eve picks 9 kiwis. Bea picks 8 kiwis. How many kiwis do they pick in all?

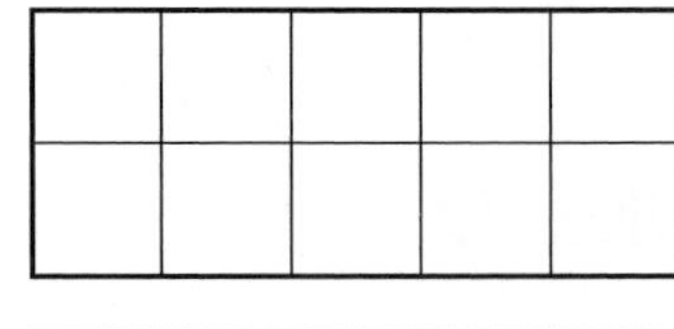

2. Write the number sentence.

____ ◯ ____ ◯ ____

____ kiwis

3. 17 is the ____________.

Use Workmat 3 and ●.

4. Together Eve and Bea pick 15 kiwis. Bea picks 8 of them. How many kiwis does Eve pick?

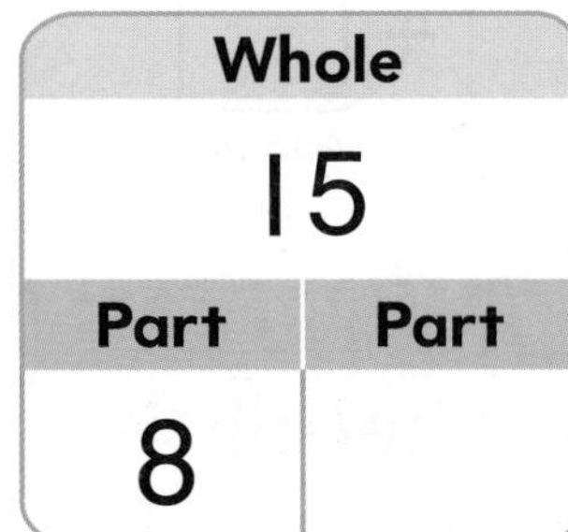

5. Write the number sentence.

____ ◯ ____ ◯ ____

6. 7 is the ____________.

7. **Writing Math** How can you solve Exercises 1 and 2 another way? ______________________________

____

TEKS 1.12A Explain and record observations using objects, words, pictures, numbers, and technology.

TEKS 1.12B Relate informal language to mathematical language and symbols.

Name ______________________________

Concepts and Skills

Use Workmat 2 and ◯. Show the numbers.
Write the number sentence. TEKS 1.3B

1. Show 10. Show 4 more.

Use Workmat 2 and ◯.
Make a ten. Find the sum. TEKS 1.3B, 1.5D

2. Show 9 and 6 more. 9 + 6 = ____

Use Workmat 3 and ◯.
Find different names for the number. TEKS 1.3B

3.

Whole	
13	
Part	Part

Whole	
13	
Part	Part

Whole	
13	
Part	Part

Use Workmat 3 and ◯.
Show the whole. Move counters to one part.
Find the other part. TEKS 1.3B

4.

Whole	
17	
Part	Part
9	

5.

Whole	
18	
Part	Part
10	

Use Workmat 3 and .

Write the missing part. Write the difference. TEKS 1.3B

6.

Whole	
16	
Part	Part
10	

$$\begin{array}{r} 16 \\ -\ 10 \\ \hline \end{array} \qquad \begin{array}{r} 16 \\ -\ 6 \\ \hline \end{array}$$

7.

Whole	
14	
Part	Part
8	

$$\begin{array}{r} 14 \\ -\ 8 \\ \hline \end{array} \qquad \begin{array}{r} 14 \\ -\ 6 \\ \hline \end{array}$$

Use Workmat 3 and .

Add. Then subtract. TEKS 1.5E

8.

$$\begin{array}{r} 9 \\ +7 \\ \hline \end{array}$$

Whole	
Part	Part
9	7

$$\begin{array}{r} 16 \\ -\ 9 \\ \hline \end{array} \qquad \begin{array}{r} 16 \\ -\ 7 \\ \hline \end{array}$$

Complete the fact family. TEKS 1.5E

9.

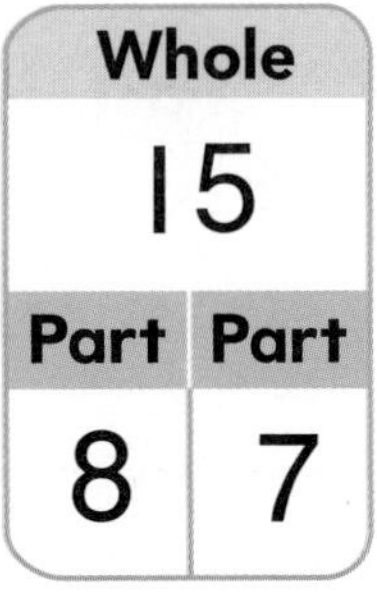

$$\begin{array}{r} \boxed{8} \\ +\ \boxed{7} \\ \hline \boxed{} \end{array} \qquad \begin{array}{r} \boxed{} \\ +\ \boxed{} \\ \hline \boxed{} \end{array}$$

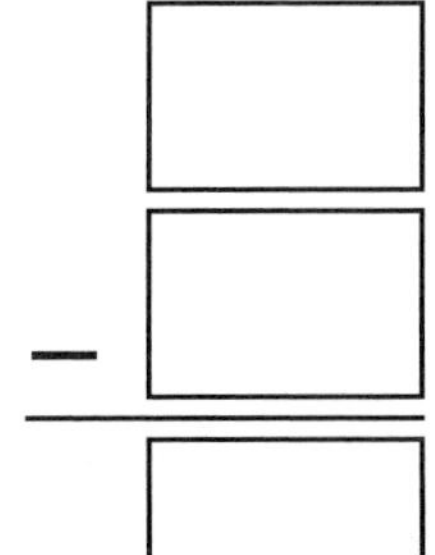

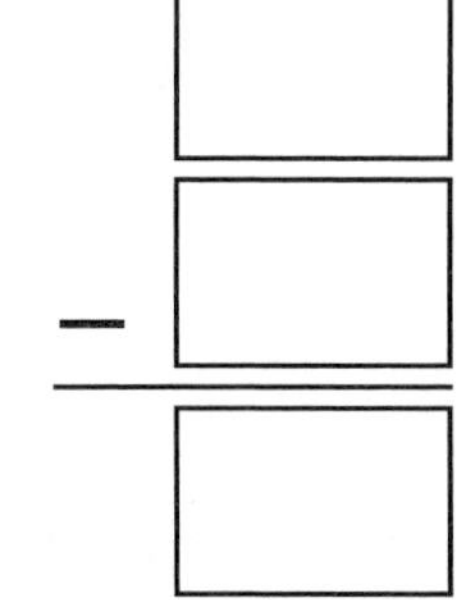

Problem Solving

Use Workmat 3 and .

Write the number sentence to solve. TEKS 1.3A, 1.11B

10. Ken plants 7 rows of beans. He plants 6 rows of tomatoes. How many rows does he plant in all?

_____ rows

Looking Ahead

Name ______________________________

THIS YEAR
I learned to . . .

NUMBER SENSE

skip count

2, 4, 6, 8, __10__, ______, ______, ______ TEKS 1.5A

add and subtract.

2 + 3 = ______

5 − 3 = ______

TEKS 1.3B

DATA AND GRAPHING

read graphs

How many green boats are there?

______ green boats

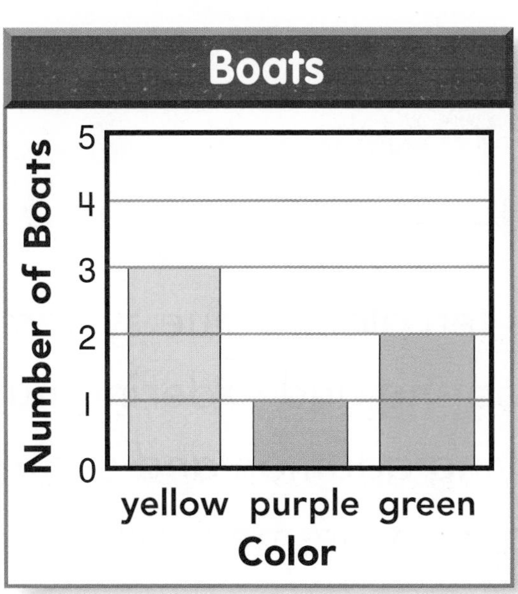

TEKS 1.10A

THIS YEAR
I learned to . . .

GEOMETRY

name two-dimensional figures

triangle square circle

name three-dimensional figures

cone cylinder cube

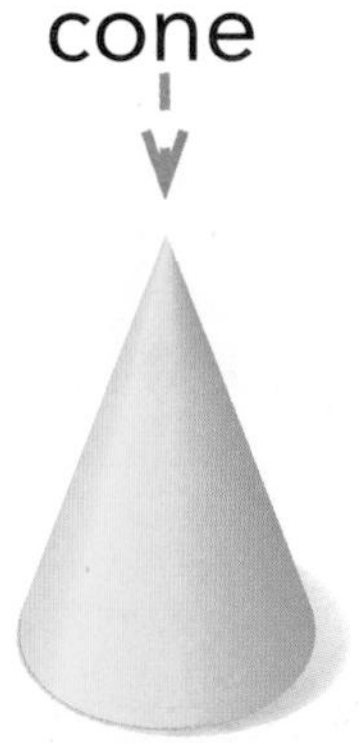

NEXT YEAR
I will learn more about . . .

- base-ten place value system.
- comparing and ordering numbers.
- applying addition and subtraction.
- using measurement processes.

I can use the Looking Ahead Activities to get ready for next year.

Texas English-Spanish

Glossary

A

add

2 + 1 = 3

sumar

addend

5 + 5 = 10

addends

sumandos

sumando

addition sentence

4 + 2 = 6

oración de suma

area

The area is 3 square units.

El área es de unas 3 unidades cuadradas.

área

B

bar-type graph

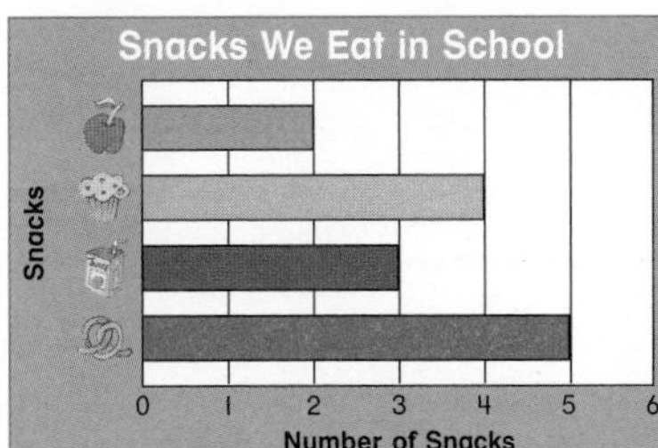

gráfica de barras

Glossary

certain

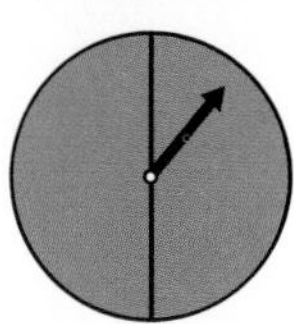

It is certain the spinner will point to blue.

Es seguro que la flecha giratoria señalará el azul.

seguro

---

circle

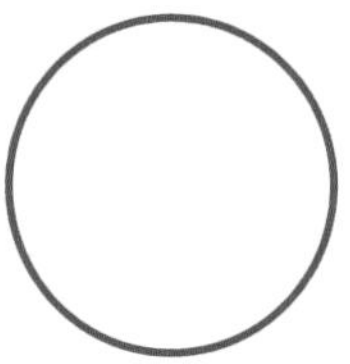

círculo

---

colder

colder

más frío

más frío

cone

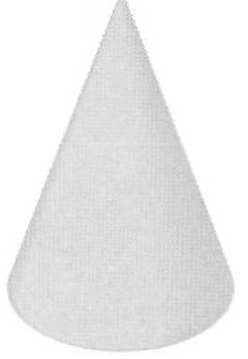

cono

---

corner

A corner is where the sides meet.

Un vértice es donde se encuentran los lados.

vértice

---

count back

8, 7, 6

9 − 3 = 6

contar hacia atrás

---

count on

8, 9

7 + 2 = 9

contar hacia adelante

cube

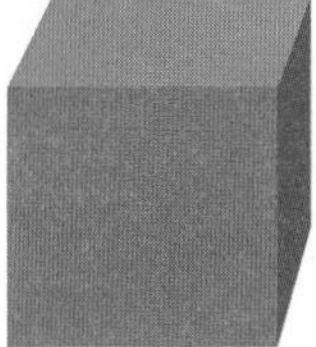

cubo

---

curved surface

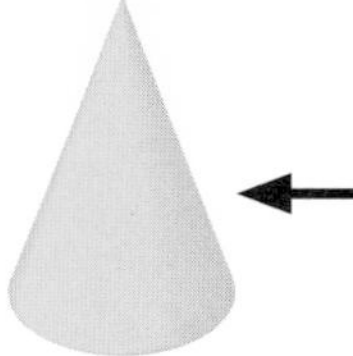

superficie curva

---

cylinder

cilindro

difference

7 − 2 = 5

difference

diferencia

$$\begin{array}{r} 7 \\ -\ 2 \\ \hline 5 \end{array}$$

diferencia

---

digital clock

reloj digital

---

dime 10 cents or 10¢

moneda de diez centavos

10 centavos ó 10¢

equal parts

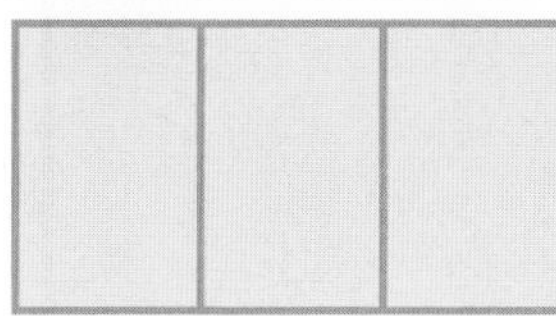

3 equal parts

3 partes iguales

partes iguales

---

equal sign

2 + 3 = 5

equal sign

signo de igual

signo de igual

equal to

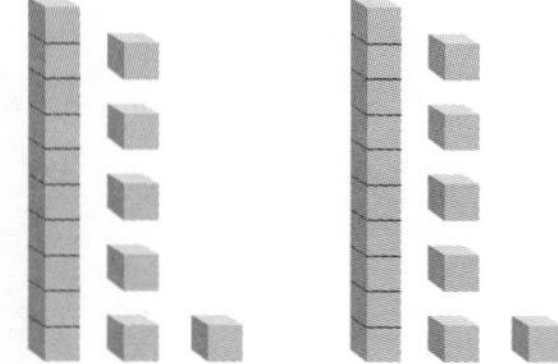

16 = 16

16 is equal to 16.

16 es igual que 16.

igual que

---

even

You can make pairs with an even number of objects and have none left.

4 is an even number.

4 es un número par.

par

Puedes formar pares con un número par de objetos sin que te sobre ninguno.

face The flat surface on a solid figure.

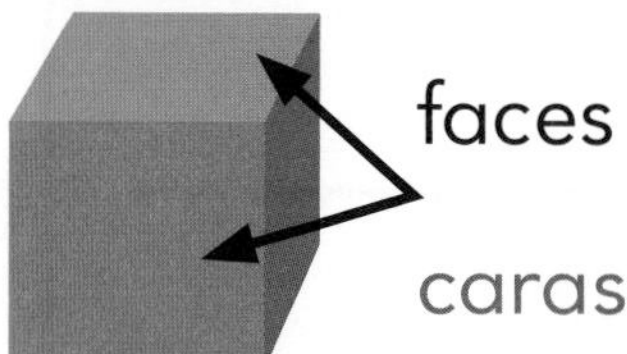

cara

La superficie plana de un cuerpo geométrico.

---

fact family Related facts make a fact family.

6 + 4 = 10   10 − 4 = 6

4 + 6 = 10   10 − 6 = 4

familia de operaciones

Las operaciones relacionadas forman una familia de operaciones.

---

flat surfaces

superficies planas

greater than

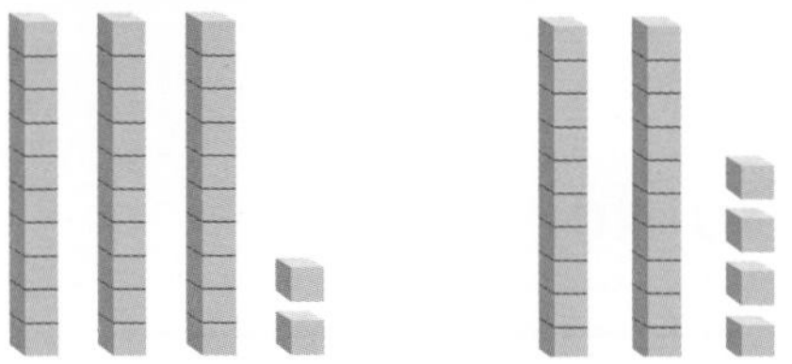

32 is greater than 24.

32 es mayor que 24.

mayor que

---

greatest

2, 6, 10

2 6 10

10 is the greatest number.

10 es el número mayor.

mayor

half-hour 30 minutes is one half-hour.

media hora

30 minutos son media hora.

---

heavier

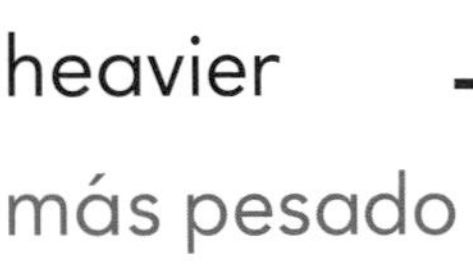

heavier

más pesado

más pesado

---

heaviest

heaviest

el más pesado

el más pesado

height How tall someone is

altura cuán alto es alguien

---

hotter

hotter

más caliente

más caliente

---

hour

about 1 hour

cerca de 1 hora

hora

hour hand

hour hand

manecilla de la hora

manecilla de la hora

I

impossible

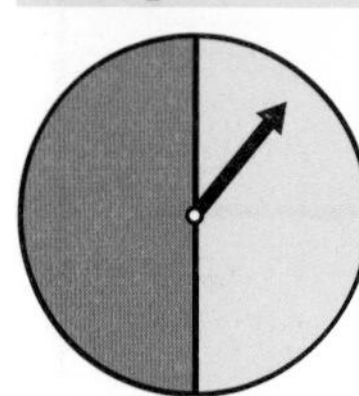

It is impossible that the spinner will point to blue.

Es imposible que la flecha giratoria señale el azul.

imposible

L

least

5, 8, 12

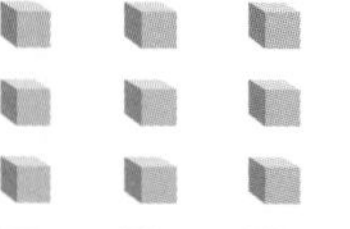

5 is the least.

5 es el menor.

menor

length How long something is

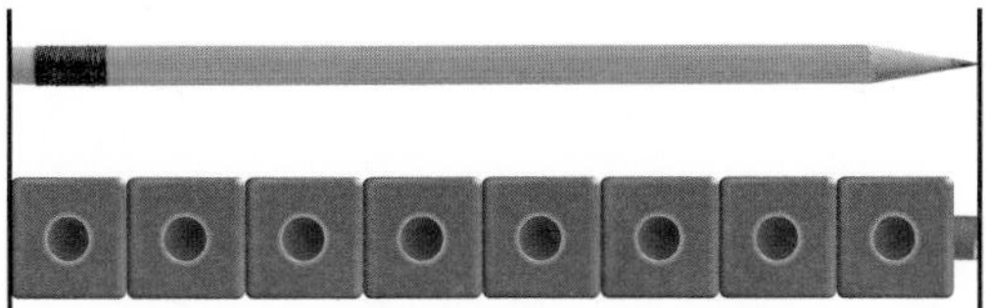

longitud cuán largo es algo

less than

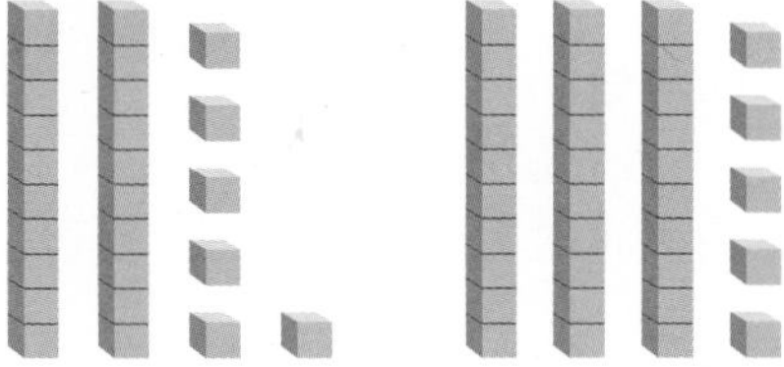

26 is less than 35.

26 es menor que 35.

menor que

lighter

lighter

más liviano

más liviano

lightest

lightest

el más liviano

el más liviano

longer

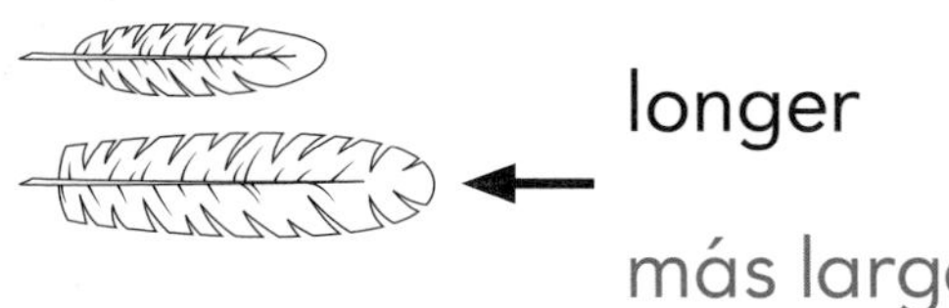

longer

más larga

más largo

minus sign

6 − 3 = 3

minus sign

signo de menos

signo de menos

minute

about 1 minute

cerca de 1 minuto

minuto

minute hand

minute hand

minutero

minutero

Glossary

more than

more ★ than ▲

más ★ que ▲

más que

nickel 5 cents or 5¢

moneda de cinco centavos

5 centavos ó 5¢

number words one, two, three, four, five, six, seven, eight, nine, ten, eleven, twelve, thirteen, fourteen, fifteen, sixteen, seventeen, eighteen, nineteen, twenty

números en palabras uno, dos, tres, cuatro, cinco, seis, siete, ocho, nueve, diez, once, doce, trece, catorce, quince, dieciséis, diecisiete, dieciocho, diecinueve, veinte

o'clock

5 o'clock

5 en punto

en punto

odd When you make pairs with an odd number of objects you always have one left.

7 is an odd number.

7 es un número impar.

impar Cuando formas pares con un número impar de objetos, siempre te sobra uno.

ones

3 ones

unidades

order Add numbers in any order and the sum will be the same.

2 + 4 = 6

4 + 2 = 6

orden Puedes sumar números en cualquier orden y la suma será la misma.

part

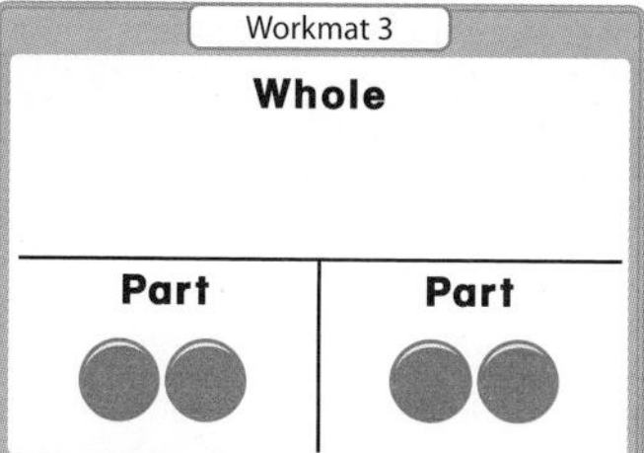

parte

---

pattern

patrón

---

penny 1 cent or 1¢

moneda de un centavo

1 centavo ó 1¢

picture graph

pictografía

---

plus sign

2 + 2 = 4

↑

plus sign

signo de más

signo de más

---

predict to tell what you think will happen

predecir decir lo que crees que sucederá

---

pyramid

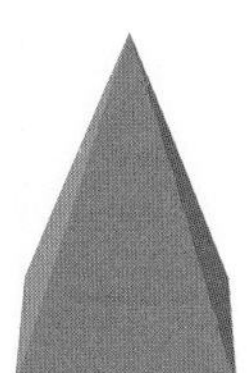

pirámide

Glossary

Glossary

quarter 25 cents or 25¢

moneda de veinticinco centavos 25 centavos ó 25¢

real-object graph

gráfica de objetos reales

---

rectangle

rectángulo

---

rectangular prism

prisma rectangular

---

related facts Related facts have the same parts and wholes.

$6 + 3 = 9$

$9 - 3 = 6$

operaciones relacionadas

Las operaciones relacionadas tienen las mismas partes y los mismos enteros.

shorter

más corto

---

sides

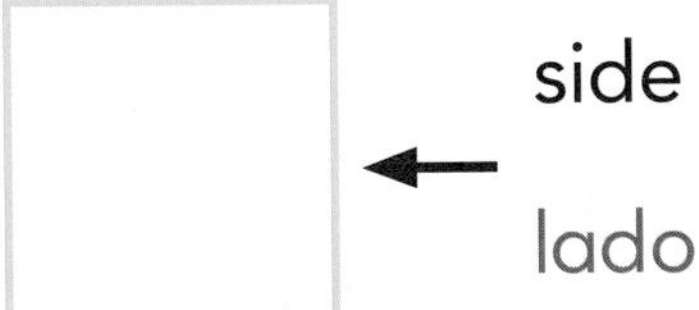

lados

---

skip count

contar salteado

sphere

esfera

---

square

cuadrado

---

square units

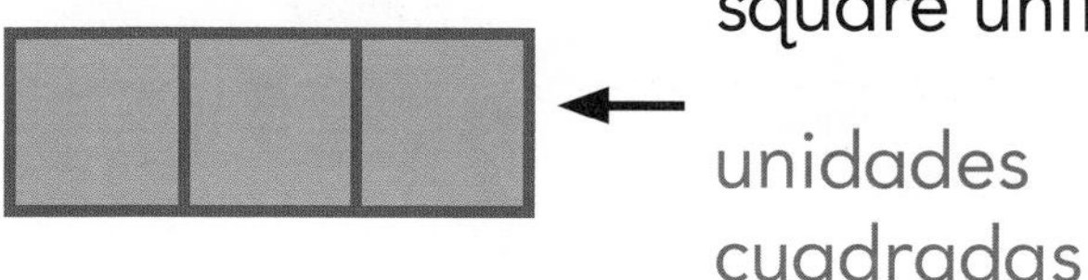

The area is 3 square units.

El área es de unas 3 unidades cuadradas.

unidades cuadradas

---

subtract

5 − 2 = 3

restar

---

subtraction sentence

6 − 4 = 2

oración de resta

---

sum

4 + 1 = 5 ← sum

	4
+	1
→	5

sum

suma

suma

taller

más alto

---

tally

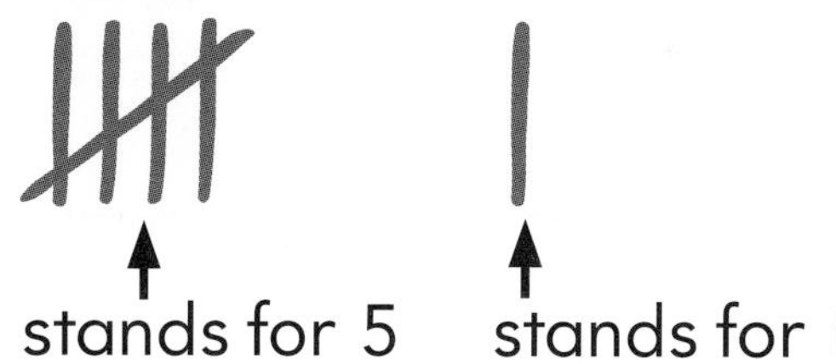

stands for 5   stands for 1

representa 5   representa 1

conteo

---

tally chart

Favorite Bike Color	
🚲	![tally 6] HH I
🚲	HH IIII
🚲	II
🚲	IIII

tablero de conteo

ten frame

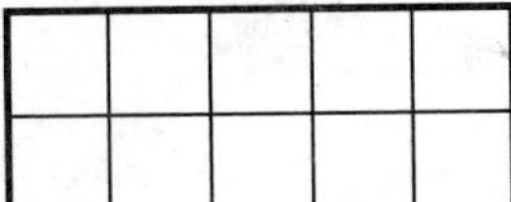

marco de diez

---

tens

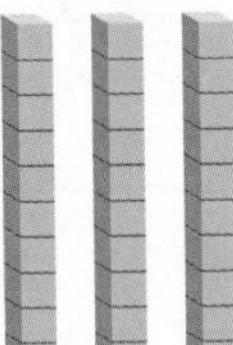

3 tens

3 decenas

decenas

---

triangle

triángulo

units what are used to measure the height, capacity, or heaviness of something

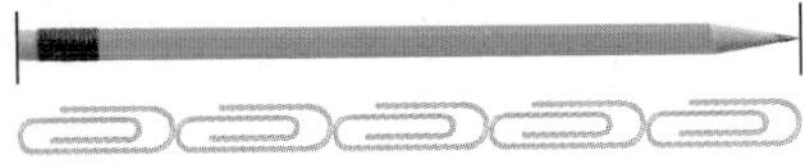

unidades lo que se usa para medir la altura, la capacidad o el peso de algo

weight

The weight of the book is more.

El peso del libro es mayor.

peso

---

whole

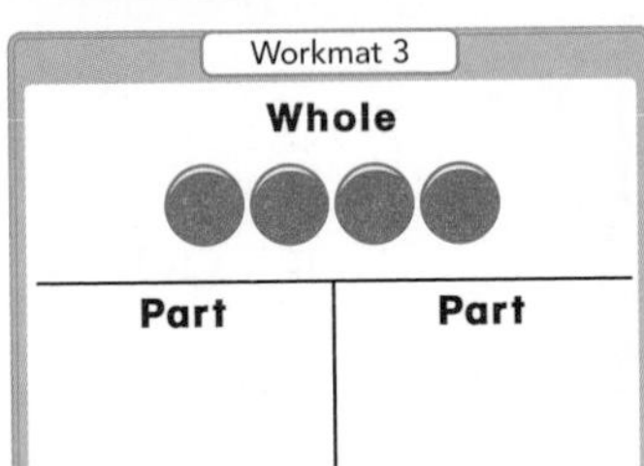

entero

zero

six tomatoes

seis tomates

zero tomatoes

cero tomates

cero